Guinness Film Facts and Feats

PATRICK ROBERTSON

GUINNESS
BOOKS

Editor: Anne Marshall
Design and layout: Jean Whitcombe

© Patrick Robertson and Guinness Superlatives
Limited, 1985

Published in Great Britain by
Guinness Superlatives Limited
2 Cecil Court, London Road, Enfield, Middlesex

Distributed by Sterling Publishing Co. Inc.
2 Park Avenue, New York, USA

Set in Palatino
Filmset by Fakenham Photosetting Ltd, Fakenham, Norfolk
Printed and bound in Great Britain by Butler and
Tanner Ltd, Frome, Somerset

British Library CIP Data
Robertson, Patrick
   Guinness film facts and feats.
   2nd ed.
   1. Moving-pictures—History
   I. Title
   791.43'09   PN1993.~~5.A1~~ 45 . R 58 1985

   ISBN 0–85112–278–7

Previous page
John Loder and Mary Brian in the first British talkie, *Black Waters* (GB 29). It was produced in Hollywood by Herbert Wilcox for a British production company.

Opposite page
This book is dedicated to the First Lady of the Silver Screen—Miss Lillian Gish.

Contents

Preface and Country Abbreviations   6

1   Fade In   7

2   The Industry   12

3   Box Office and Budgets   36

4   Story and Script   39

5   Character and Themes   46

6   Performers   76

7   Film Making and Film Makers   108

8   Colour, Sound and Scope   135

9   Music   150

10   Titles and Credits   154

11   Censorship   160

12   Audiences and Exhibitors   167

13   Press and Print   192

14   Awards and Festivals   200

15   Animation   206

16   Shorts and Documentaries   210

17   Television and the Movies   220

18   Amateur Films   225

Index   231

Acknowledgements   240

Preface

Most books on films are concerned about quality—the cinema as art. This book is unashamedly about *quantity*—together with 'firsts', records, oddities, remarkable achievements, historic landmarks and the wilder extravagances of the motion picture business during the 90 years of its colourful history. This is not the place to seek potted biographies of favourite stars or great directors, but it does offer a gamut of film facts, ranging from the significant to the absurd, many of which have never appeared in any film book before. For the historically minded there are old orthodoxies explored and often rejected—Who really 'invented' the close-up? What was the first western? Where did full-length feature films begin? Hollywood receives due attention, of course, as the centre of world film production, but many other countries—no less than 80 in all—have been approached for information. There is something about each of them, including a chart which records the number of features made each year by every film producing nation since the earliest days (pp. 18–21).

Devotees of Dracula will find a complete filmography; Shakespeare buffs a listing of all 40 versions of Hamlet, including the four in which the Prince was played by a woman; film fans may read about other film fans, including Queen Victoria, Stalin, Hitler and the last Emperor of China (who wore Harold Lloyd spectacles as a tribute to his favourite star). Records range from the largest and smallest cinema theatres, the longest career in movies, the biggest cast (300,000) and the most remakes to the heaviest actress, the last silent picture and the longest and shortest film titles. And the poor relations of cinema are not neglected either—did you know that both home movies and advertising films were already in existence in the 1890s?

This is the second edition of the *Guinness Film Facts & Feats*. It contains not only updated and revised material, but many new features. There is a comprehensive survey of the different types of films being made in the USA and Britain at each ten-year point from 1914 to 1984. From this it is possible to chart, for example, the rise and fall of the western, or note the curious fact that until recently a higher proportion of crime films were made in Britain than America. Another new feature is a chart showing which TV channel has the newest movies—and which the oldest—and the split between foreign and English language films.

Corrections, updates and suggestions for new features will always be welcome. Many of the names included on p. 240 are of those who wrote in after the first edition was published. Their contribution has helped to make this edition of the *Guinness Film Facts & Feats* more accurate and more comprehensive. With a little help from our readers, each edition will be better than the last.

COUNTRY ABBREVIATIONS

Afg	Afghanistan	Egy	Egypt	Jap	Japan	SA	South Africa
Alg	Algeria	Fin	Finland	Ken	Kenya	Sp	Spain
Arg	Argentina	Fr	France	Kor	Korea	Swe	Sweden
Aus	Australia	Ger	Germany	Lby	Libya	Swz	Switzerland
Aut	Austria	GDR	Germany, East	Mex	Mexico	Syr	Syria
Ban	Bangladesh	FRG	Germany, West	Mor	Morocco	Sen	Senegal
Bel	Belgium	Gha	Ghana	Moz	Mozambique	S. Kor	South Korea
Bra	Brazil	Gre	Greece	Mau	Mauritania	Tai	Taiwan
Bul	Bulgaria	Gab	Gabon	Neth	Netherlands	Tha	Thailand
Can	Canada	HK	Hong Kong	NZ	New Zealand	Tun	Tunisia
Chn	China	Hun	Hungary	Nor	Norway	Tur	Turkey
Col	Colombia	Ind	India	Phi	Philippines	USSR	USSR
Cz	Czechoslovakia	Ice	Iceland	Pol	Poland	US	United States
CayI	Cayman Islands	Ire	Ireland	Por	Portugal	Uru	Uruguay
Cur	Curacao	Isr	Israel	Rom	Romania	Ven	Venezuela
Den	Denmark	It	Italy	Rus	Russia	Yug	Yugoslavia
		IvC	Ivory Coast	Sin	Singapore		
		Jam	Jamaica				

1 Fade In

The first motion picture films were taken with a camera patented in Britain by French-born Louis Aimé Augustin Le Prince (1842–90?) in November 1888. Two fragments survive: one taken at a speed of 10–12 frames per second early in October 1888 in the garden of his father-in-law, Mr Joseph Whitley, at Roundhay, Leeds; the other taken at 20 frames per second later in the month and showing traffic crossing Leeds Bridge. According to Le Prince's mechanic, James Longley, the latter film was shown on a projector incorporating a Maltese cross for intermittent picture shift. He claimed that the image obtained was sufficiently clear for smoke to be visible rising from the pipe of a lounger on the bridge. Both films were made on sensitised paper rolls 2⅛ in wide and it was not until a year later that Le Prince was able to obtain Eastman celluloid roll film, which had just been introduced into Britain. This provided a far more suitable support material and it seems likely that the inventor was able to start the commercial development of his motion picture process by the beginning of 1890. A new projector was built so that a demonstration could be given before M. Mobisson, the Secretary of the Paris Opera. On 16 September 1890 Le Prince boarded a train at Dijon bound for Paris with his apparatus and films. He never arrived. No trace of his body or his equipment was ever found and after exhaustive enquiries the police were unable to offer any rational explanation of his disappearance. The mystery has never been solved.

The first commercially developed motion picture process was instigated by Thomas Alva Edison (1847–1931), American electrical engineer. His initial attempt to produce an illusion of movement, by means of an apparatus called the 'optical phonograph', resulted in failure, and in January 1889 Edison assigned William Kennedy Laurie Dickson (1860–1935), an assistant at his laboratories in West Orange, NJ, to work on the development of what was to become the Kinetoscope, a film-viewing machine designed for use in amusement arcades. Dickson, the French-born son of English parents, had early training as a photographer and was better suited to this kind of research than his mentor who knew little of optics. Abandoning the use of rectangular sheets of celluloid for camera work, he sub-

The Le Prince camera of 1888.

stituted 50 ft lengths of celluloid film produced by the firm of Merwin Hulbert. These long rolls were first purchased on 18 March 1891, which is the earliest date at which it seems likely that Dickson could have made successful films for viewing in the peep-show Kinetoscope apparatus.

The first public demonstration of motion pictures took place at the Edison Laboratories at West Orange, NJ, on 22 May 1891, when 147 representatives of the National Federation of Women's Clubs, having lunched with Mrs Edison at Glenmont, were taken over her husband's workshops and allowed to view the new Kinetoscope. The New York *Sun* reported: 'The surprised and pleased clubwomen saw a small pine box standing on the floor. There were some wheels and belts near the box, and a workman who had them in charge. In the top of the box was a hole perhaps an inch in diameter. As they looked through the hole they saw the picture of a man. It was a most marvellous picture. It bowed and smiled and waved its hands and took off its hat with the most perfect naturalness and grace. Every motion was perfect...'. The film used for this demonstration appears to have been taken with a

7

horizontal-feed camera without sprockets. This would have been an imperfect apparatus at best, and not until October 1892 is there evidence that William Dickson had built an effective vertical-feed camera using perforated film. In that month the *Phonogram* published an illustration showing sequences from four films evidently taken with such a device. These included pictures of Dickson himself, together with his helper, William Heise, and also shots of wrestling and fencing. By this date, then, it can be positively asserted that Dickson had overcome all the obstacles that had stood in the way of making films suitable for commercial exhibition. He was to receive little thanks for his work. After Dickson left West Orange in 1895, following a dispute with his employer, Edison stead-

fastly refused to concede that anyone but himself was responsible for bringing the invention to fruition. Most historians were content to accept Edison's own version of events until the appearance in 1961 of a painstaking work of scholarship titled *The Edison Motion Picture Myth*. The author, Gordon Hendricks, demonstrates by reference to hitherto unpublished papers in the Edison archives that all the experimental work on the Kinetoscope was conducted by Dickson, or under his direction, and that Edison himself can be credited with little more than instigating the research programme and providing facilities for carrying it out.

The practical development of motion pictures in Britain can be dated from a camera built in 1895 by

---

HOW THE CINEMA SPREAD ROUND THE WORLD

Few inventions have spread more rapidly than cinematography. By the end of 1896, a mere twelve months after the real start of commercial cinema in France, nearly all the major countries of the western world had witnessed their first demonstration of the new art. It is clear from the following chronology that the Lumière Brothers of Lyon were the most positive force in introducing motion pictures to the world. (The designation 'Lumière' below signifies that the programme was made up of Lumière films.) The presentations listed were public shows before a paying audience unless otherwise indicated.

1895
March 22 FRANCE *La Sortie des Ouvriers des l'Usine Lumière* (Fr 94), presented by Louis and Auguste Lumière before the Société d'Encouragement pour l'Industrie Nationale at 44 rue de Rennes, Paris (see p. 9).
May 20 UNITED STATES *Young Griffo* v. *Battling Charles Barnett* (US 95) presented before paying audience at 153 Broadway, New York (see p. 10).
November 1 GERMANY Eight short films (for subjects, see Production: firsts by countries, p. 10) presented by Max and Emil Skladanowski at Berlin Wintergarten.
November 10 BELGIUM Lumière programme before invited audience of scientists etc., in Brussels. First before paying audience at 7 de la Galerie du Roi, Brussels, 1 Mar 1896.

1896
January 14 UNITED KINGDOM Programme (subjects see p. 10) presented by Birt Acres before Royal Photographic Society, London. First before paying audience: Lumière programme by F. Trewey at Regent Street Polytechnic, London, 20 Feb 1896.
February ?? ITALY Lumière presented by Vittorio Calcina at the Ospedale di Carita, Turin.
March 19 AUSTRIA Lumière presented by E. J. Dupont at the Graphic Arts Teaching & Research Centre, Vienna.
April 6 NORWAY Skladanowski programme presented at Circus Variété, Oslo.
April 20 IRELAND Unidentified programme presented at Star of Erin Variety Theatre, Dublin.

May 4 RUSSIA Lumière presented by Francis Doublier at Aquarium Theatre, St Petersburg.
May 9 SOUTH AFRICA R. W. Paul's Theatrograph programme—*Highland Dancers* (GB 96), *Street Scenes in London* (GB 96), *Trilby Dance* (GB 96), *A Military Parade* (GB 96), *The Soldier's Courtship* (GB 96)—presented at Empire Theatre of Varieties, Johannesburg.
May 10 HUNGARY Lumière presented at Royal Hotel, Budapest. Included street scenes taken in front of Opera House and Chain Bridge, Budapest, and Hungarian Millenary Procession.
May 15 SPAIN Lumière presented by M. Promio at 34 Carrera de San Jeronimo, Madrid.
May 27 ROMANIA Lumière presented at Salon l'Independanta Romana, Bucharest.
June 7 YUGOSLAVIA (SERBIA) Lumière presented at Kod Zlatnog Krsta Café, Belgrade.
June 7 DENMARK Lumière presented by Vilhelm Pacht in Raadhuspladsen, Copenhagen.
June 9 NETHERLANDS Lumière presented at the Kurhaus, Scheveningen.
June 18 PORTUGAL Lumière (?) presented by Erwin Rousby at Real Coliseu, Rua da Palma, Lisbon.
June 28 SWEDEN Lumière presented by C. V. Roikjer at the Industrial Exhibition, Malmö.
June 28 FINLAND Lumière presented at the Societetshuset, Helsinki.
July 7 INDIA Lumière presented at Watson's Hotel, Bombay.
July 8 BRAZIL 'Omniographo' presented at 57 Rua do Ouvidor, Rio de Janiero.
July 15 CZECHOSLOVAKIA Lumière presented at the Lázeňský dům, Karoly Vary.
July 21 CANADA Edison Vitascope programme presented at West End Park, Ottawa.
July 28 ARGENTINA Lumière presented by Francisco Pastos and Eustaquio Pellier at Colón Theatre, Buenos Aires.
August 11 CHINA French programme (negative evidence suggests *not* Lumière) presented as act of variety show at Hsu Gardens, Shanghai.
August 15 MEXICO Lumière presented by engineering student Salvador Toscano Barragan at 17 Calle de Jesus, Mexico City.
August 22 AUSTRALIA R. W. Paul programme presented by conjurer Carl Hertz at Melbourne Opera House.

September 26 GUATEMALA Lumière presented by Arnold Tobler at 11 Passage Aycinena, Guatemala City.
October 13 NEW ZEALAND R. W. Paul (?) programme of English films presented by Profs Hausmann and Gow at Auckland Opera House.
October ?? POLAND Edison programme presented at Lvov.
Date unknown EGYPT unidentified programme at Zavani Café, Alexandria.

1897
January 24 CUBA Lumière presented by Gabriel Veyre at Teatro Tacón, Havana.
January 28 VENEZUELA Edison presented by Manuel Trujillo at Teatro Baralt, Maracaibo.
March 2 PERU Edison Vitascope presented on the Plaza de Armas, Lima.
June ?? JAPAN Lumière presented by Katsutaro Inahata at Osaka.
December 25 URUGUAY Lumière at Montevideo.
Date unknown TUNISIA Lumière at store show established by Albert Samama on rue Es-Sadika, Tunis.

1898
Spring GREECE Lumière at Place Kolokotronis, Athens.
Date unknown BULGARIA unidentified programme presented by Frencz Echer in Sofia.

1899
Date unknown TURKEY unidentified programme presented privately before Sultan by Spaniard Don Ramirez and then publicly at his Electric Circus, Constantinople.

1900
November 30 (?) INDONESIA Nederlandsche Bioscope Maatschappij presented at Batavia.
Date unknown KOREA free film show sponsored by Anglo-American Tobacco Co. of Shanghai. Admission in exchange for cigarette coupons.
Date unknown SENEGAL Lumière presented at Dakar.
Date unknown IRAN unidentified programme presented before Shah by Mirza Ebrahim Khan at Royal Palace, Teheran. First public show opened in Avenue Cheraq Gaz, Teheran, by Sahâf Bâshi in 1905.

Birt Acres (1854–1918) and R. W. Paul (1869–1943) at the latter's optical instrument works in Saffron Hill. Paul's interest in films had been aroused the previous October when he was approached by a Greek showman, George Trajedis, with a request to manufacture some Edison Kinetoscopes. This Paul agreed to do on learning that Edison had omitted to patent the machine in Britain. Since Edison's agents understandably refused to sell films for the pirated machines, Paul approached Acres with the suggestion that they should construct a camera together (later each claimed to have been the only begetter of the apparatus) so that they could make their own Kinetoscope subjects, Acres to be the cameraman. Using film obtained from the American Celluloid Co. of Newark, NJ, Acres tried out the camera for the first time with a scene of a cricketer (his assistant Henry Short) coming out of Acres' home in Barnet, Clovelly Cottage. This was followed by what Paul described as 'our first saleable film', *The Oxford and Cambridge University Boat Race*, which was premièred in a Kinetoscope at the India Exhibition, Earl's Court on 27 May 1896. This film, together with *The Derby* and *The Opening of the Kiel Canal* (see News Film, p. 213), formed the first programme presented on screen in Britain since Le Prince's experiments, when Acres gave a private show with his Kineopticon projector in a coach-house at Wrotham Cottage, Barnet in August 1895. Acres was also the first to give a public screening (see below), while Paul became the first manufacturer of projectors (q.v.) and Britain's pioneer film producer.

The first commercial presentation of motion pictures took place at Holland Bros' Kinetoscope Parlor, 1155 Broadway, New York, which opened for business on 14 April 1894. The Kinetoscopes were arranged in two rows of five, and for 25c viewers were allowed to watch five films—to see the whole programme they had to pay double entrance money. The first day's take of $120 suggests that this first 'cinema audience' totalled nearly 500. The films, made in the Edison 'Black Maria' (see Film Studio, p. 130) at West Orange, were titled: *Sandow*, *Bertholdi (mouth support)*, *Horse Shoeing*, *Bertholdi (table contortion)*, *Barber Shop*, *Blacksmiths*, *Cock Fight*, *Highland Dance*, *Wrestling*, *Trapeze*.

The first commercial presentation of films in Britain took place at the Kinetoscope parlour opened by the Continental Commerce Co. of New York at 70 Oxford Street, London, on 18 October 1894. The twelve machines offered such titillating delights as *Carmencita* (a buxom vaudeville artiste) and *Annabelle Serpentine Dance*, as well as more prosaic fare like *Blacksmith Shop*, *Wrestling Match* and *The Bar Room*.

The first film presented publicly on screen was *La Sortie des Ouvriers de l'Usine Lumière* (Fr 94) which was shown before members of the Société d'Encouragement pour l'Industrie Nationale by Auguste and

The earliest known motion-picture film—*Traffic Crossing Leeds Bridge* (GB 88).

Louis Lumière at 44 rue de Rennes, Paris, on 22 March 1895. Believed to have been taken in August or September 1894, the film showed workers leaving the Lumière photographic factory at Lyons for their dinner-hour.

The first public screening in Britain was given by Birt Acres at the London headquarters of the Royal Photographic Society, 14 Hanover Square on 14 January 1896. The programme, comprised of films taken by Acres himself, consisted of *The Opening of the Kiel Canal*, *The Derby*, *Boxers*, *Three Skirt Dancers* and *Rough Seas at Dover*.

The first film to be screened before a paying audience was a four-minute boxing subject, *Young Griffo* v. *Battling Charles Barnett*, presented by Major Woodville Latham of the Lamda Co. at 153 Broadway, New York on 20 May 1895. The projector was a primitive and imperfect machine called the Eidoloscope, designed for the Lamda Co. (the first film company established as such) by former Edison employee Eugene Lauste. Although some authorities have cast doubt on the Eidoloscope's ability to create an illusion of movement on a screen, it must have achieved a sufficient level of technical acceptability, however jerky and inadequate the picture, for Latham to have attracted paying customers. Another commercial show was given by C. Francis Jenkins and Thomas Armat, using a projector they had designed themselves, at a purpose-built temporary cinema at the Cotton States Exposition at Atlanta, Ga., in September 1895. After making various improvements to the machine, Armat came to an arrangement with Thomas Edison, who had failed to produce a workable projector himself, by which the celebrated inventor would be allowed to exploit it as his own. As the Edison Vitascope, the improved machine was debuted at Koster and Bial's Music Hall on Broadway on 23 April 1896, an occasion which has often and erroneously been heralded as the first time that motion pictures were presented on a screen to a paying audience.

The first screening before a paying audience in Europe was given by Max and Emil Skladanowski with a projector of their own invention at the Berlin Wintergarten on 1 November 1895. The films were made up of endless loops and the action lasted only a few seconds before it was repeated. Taken at the rate of eight pictures a second, the films were flickering and jerky, but the fact that there was movement on the screen at all was sufficient for the Nazis to claim, some 40 years later, that Germany was the cradle of the cinema industry. In fact neither the work of Lauste and Latham in America, nor that of the Skladanowskis in Germany was destined to have any lasting effect on the development of the cinema. It is generally agreed that the première of the Lumière brothers' show, before a paying audience at the Grand Café, 14 Boulevard des Capucines, Paris,

THE FIRST A[

on 28 December 1895, marks the debut of the motion picture as a regular entertainment medium. Their projector was the first to advance beyond the experimental stage and the first to be offered for sale.

The first screening before a paying audience in Britain took place at the Regent Street Polytechnic on 20 February 1896, when the French magician Felicien Trewey exhibited the Lumière Cinématographe with

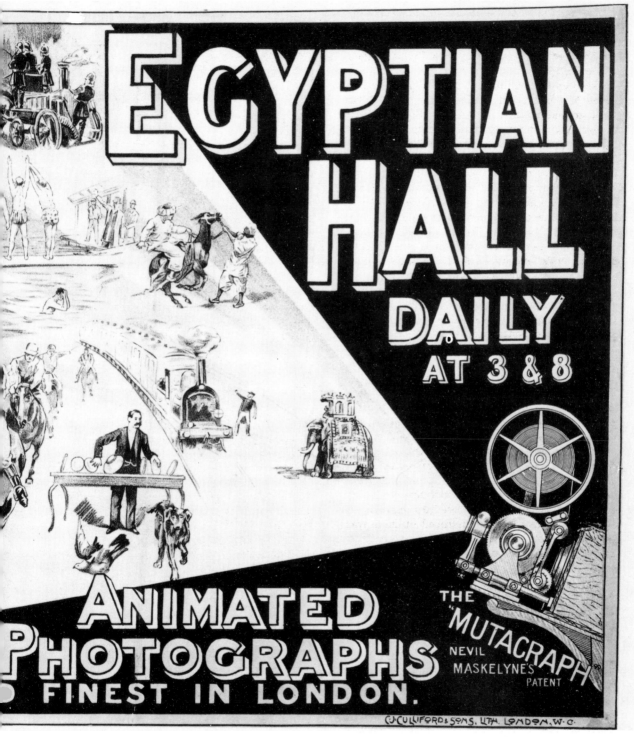

accompanying commentary by M. Francis Pochet. Admission was 1s and the engagement lasted three weeks, hours 2–4 p.m. The opening programme included the Lumière films *Arrival of a Train at a Station*, *The Baby and the Goldfish*, *The Family Tea Table* and *M. Trewey: Prestigidateur*. The first commercial show outside London was presented by Birt Acres at Cardiff Town Hall on 5 May 1896.

Possibly the earliest pictorial poster advertising a cinema show in Britain, believed to date from the latter part of 1897. The claim to have been 'the first' was advertising puffery. In fact the Egyptian Hall had been the second place of entertainment to show films in London.

2 The Industry

Feature Films

The first feature film, according with the Cinématheque Française definition of a feature being a commercially made film of over one hour duration, was Charles Tait's *The Story of the Kelly Gang* (Aus 06), which was 4000 ft (1219 m) long and had a running time of 60–70 min. A biopic of Victoria's notorious bushranger Ned Kelly (1855–80), the film was produced by the theatrical company J. & N. Tait of Melbourne, Victoria, and shot on location over a period of about six months at Whitehorse Road, Mitcham (Glenrowan Hotel scenes, including the last stand of the Kelly Gang); at Rosanna (railway scenes); and on Charles Tait's property at Heidelberg, Vic. (all other scenes). The actual armour which had belonged to Ned Kelly—a bullet-proof helmet and jerkin fashioned from ploughshares—was borrowed from the Victorian Museum and worn by the actor playing the role, an unidentified Canadian from the Bland Holt touring company who disappeared before the film was finished. It had to be completed with an extra standing in as Ned, all these scenes being taken in long shot. Elizabeth Veitch played Kate Kelly, and others in the cast included Ollie Wilson, Frank Mills, Bella Cole and Vera Linden.

Made on a budget of £450, *The Story of the Kelly Gang* was premièred at the Athenaeum Hall, Melbourne, on 24 December 1906 and recovered its cost within a week, eventually grossing some £25,000, including receipts from the English release. No complete print survives but stills from the film were issued as picture postcards and give the impression of a vigorous, all-action drama made with imaginative use of outdoor locations—a significant advance on the studio-bound one-reelers being turned out in Europe and America at this period. It was long believed that the film had been totally lost, but recently a 210 ft (64 m) long fragment was discovered in Melbourne. Other versions of the Ned Kelly story survive. There were remakes in 1910, 1917, 1920, 1923, 1934, 1951 and 1970, all of them Australian productions except the last, a British film with Mick Jagger in the title role.

Australia was the only country in the world to have established regular production of feature-length films prior to 1911. For figures on early output, see Production: World Output (pp. 18–21).

The first feature-length film made in Europe was Michel Carré's 90-minute long production *L'Enfant prodigue* (Fr 07), premièred at the Théâtre des Variétés in the Boulevard Montmartre, Paris, on 20 June 1907. This was a straightforward screen representation of a stage play, with little or no attempt at adaptation.

The first European feature film scripted for the screen was a four-reel version of *Les Misérables* (Fr 09), produced by Pathé from the novel by Victor Hugo.

The first feature film exhibited in the United Kingdom was Charles Tait's *The Story of the Kelly Gang* (Aus 06), which had its British première at the Assembly Rooms, Bath, in January 1908. The film was released by the Colonial Picture Combine.

The first feature film produced in the United Kingdom was Thomas Bentley's *Oliver Twist* (GB 12), a Hepworth production in four reels starring ex-beauty queen Ivy Millais as Oliver Twist, Alma Taylor as Nancy and John McMahon as Fagin. It was released in August 1912, two months after Vitagraph's version in America (see below).

The first feature film produced in the United States was Vitagraph's four-reel production of *Les Misérables* (US 09), released in separate one-reel parts between 18 September and 27 November 1909. Charles Kent's Vitagraph production of *The Life of Moses* (US 09), in five reels, was also released in separate parts (4 December 1909–19 February 1910) because the producers did not consider that the American public were prepared to sit through a film that lasted over an hour. The first feature film to be released in its entirety in the USA was *Dante's Inferno* (It 11) in August 1911. *Queen Elizabeth* (Fr 12), which is nearly always cited as the first feature film shown in America, was in fact the third, because in the meantime the first domestic feature-length production to be shown whole had been released. This was *Oliver*

THE FIRST 12 FEATURE FILMS PRODUCED IN THE USA
June 1912 *Oliver Twist* (5 reels) H. A. Spanuth
Dec 1912 *The Beloved Vagabond* (6 reels) Gold Rooster
Jan 1913 *Cleopatra* (6 reels) United States Film Co.
Jan 1913 *From the Manger to the Cross* (6 reels) Kalem
Aug 1913 *Moths* (5 reels) Thanhouser
Aug 1913 *Arizona* (6 reels) All Star Feature Corp.
Oct 1913 *In the Bishop's Carriage* (5 reels) Famous Players
Nov 1913 *The Count of Monte Cristo* (5 reels) Famous Players
Nov 1913 *Traffic in Souls* (6 reels) Imp
Dec 1913 *The Sea-Wolf* (7 reels) Bosworth
Dec 1913 *Ten Nights in a Bar-room* (5 reels) Photo Drama
Dec 1913 *Hoodman Blind* (5 reels) Pilot

It is worthy of note that neither Cecil B. DeMille's *The Squaw Man* (US 14) nor D. W. Griffith's *Judith of Bethulia* (US 14), each of which has been cited as the first feature produced in the US, appears above.

THE FIRST 12 FEATURE FILMS PRODUCED IN THE UK
Aug 1912 *Oliver Twist* (4 reels) Hepworth
Dec 1912 *Lorna Doone* (5 reels) Clarendon
May 1913 *East Lynne* (6 reels) Barker
July 1913 *The Battle of Waterloo* (5 reels) British & Colonial
July 1913 *Ivanhoe* (6 reels) Zenith Films
July 1913 *A Message from Mars* (4 reels) United Kingdom Films
Aug 1913 *David Copperfield* (8 reels) Hepworth
Sept 1913 *King Charles* (4 reels) Clarendon
Sept 1913 *A Cigarette-Maker's Romance* (4 reels) Hepworth
Sept 1913 *The House of Temperley* (5 reels) London Films
Oct 1913 *The Grip* (4 reels) Britannic Films
Oct 1913 *Hamlet* (6 reels) Hepworth

COUNTRIES PRODUCING FEATURE FILMS BY 1914
By the outbreak of World War I, the following countries had commenced feature-film production:
1906 Australia
1909 France
1911 Denmark, Germany, Italy, Poland, Russia, Spain, Yugoslavia (Serbia)
1912 Austria, Greece, Hungary, Japan, Norway, Romania, United Kingdom, United States
1913 Brazil, Finland, India, Sweden, Venezuela, Canada

FILM PRODUCING NATIONS
The following list chronicles, wherever known, the first motion picture production, the first dramatised (i.e. acted) production, the first feature film (over one hour duration) and the first talkie feature of each of the film-producing countries of the world, signified by the abbreviations Film, Drama, Feature, Talkie. The first feature film in natural colour is included for major film-producing nations. The first motion picture production means a film made by a native or permanent resident of the country, as opposed to a visiting cameraman or non-resident producer. Where a category has been omitted no information is available. Drama/Feature and Feature/Talkie signify respectively that the first feature-length film was also the first dramatic production of any length and that the first talkie was also the first feature-length production. Other abbreviations: doc. = documentary; f. = filmed; d. = directed; pr. = première; prod. = produced.

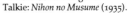

ALGERIA
Film: *La Prière du muezzin* (1906), d. Felix Mesguich.
Drama: *Ali Bouf a l'huile* (1907), d. Felix Mesguich.
Feature/Talkie: *Peuple en marche* (1963), d. Ahmed Rachedi and René Vautier.

ANGOLA
Film: *Monangambé* (1968), d. Sarah Maldoror.
Feature/Talkie: *Des fusils pour Banta* (1970), d. Sarah Maldoror.

ARGENTINA
Film: *La Bandera Argentina* (1897), d. Eugenio Py.
Drama: *El Fusilamiento de Dorrego* (1908), d. Mario Gallo and Salvador Rosich.
Feature: *Nobleza Gaucha* (1915), d. Humberto Cairo.
Talkie: *Muñequitas porteñas* (1931), with Maria Turguenova—Vitaphone system.

AUSTRALIA
Film: *The Melbourne Cup* (3 Nov 1896), d. Marius Sestier.
Drama: untitled 75 ft drama by Joseph Perry of the Salvation Army about man sent to gaol for stealing bread and helped by Army's 'prison-gate brigade' on release, c. 1897.
Feature: *The Story of the Kelly Gang* (pr. 26 Dec 1906), d. Charles Tait. (NB: **First feature film** (q.v.) **in world.**)
Talkie: *Fellers* (press shown 23 May 1930), d. Arthur Higgins and Austin Fay, prod. Artaus Films, starring Arthur Tauchert.

AUSTRIA
Drama: *Ein Walzertraum* (scene from opera) f. 2 Mar 1907.
Feature: *Zweierlei Blut* (1912), starring Luise Kohn and Jakob Fleck.

Talkie: *G'schichten aus der Steiermark* (pr. 23 Aug 1929), d. Hans Otto Löwenstein, prod. Eagle Film and Ottoton Film, starring Hilde Maria and Anny Burg.

BANGLADESH
Feature/Talkie: *Mukh O Mukhosh* (1956), d. Jabbar Khan.

BELGIUM
Film: *Le Marché aux poissons de Bruxelles* (1897) and other actualities, d. M. Alexandre.
Drama: *'chand d'habits* (1897), d. M. Alexandre.
Feature: *Belgique meurtrie* (1920), d. Paul Flon.
Talkie: *La Famille Klepkens* (1930), d. Gaston Schoukens and Paul Flon.

BOLIVIA
Film: actualities by Luis Castillo, 1913.
Feature: *La Profecia del Lago* (1923), d. José Maria Velasco Maidana (film banned).
Talkie: *La Guerra del Chaco* (1936), d. José Luis Bazoberry.

BRAZIL
Film: *View of Guanabara Bay* (f. 19 July 1898), d. Alfonso Segreto.
Drama: *Os Estranguladores* (1906)—crime film based on true story in police files, d. Isaac Sandenberg.
Feature: *O Crime dos Banhados* (1913), d. Francisco Santos, prod. Guarany Film.
Talkie: *Acabaram-se os Otarios* (1930), country comedy d. Luis de Barros, starring Genésio Arruda and Tom Bill.

BULGARIA
Film: actuality about Bulgarian army, 1910.
Drama: *Such is the War* (1914).
Feature: *The Bulgar is a Gentleman* (1915), satire about Sofia snobbery, d. Vassil Guendov, starring ditto and Mara Lipina.
Talkie: *A Song of the Balkan Mountains* (1934), d. Peter Stoychev.

BURMA
Feature: *Dana Pratap* (1925), prod. London Art Photo Co. of Rangoon.
Talkie: *Nihon no Musume* (1935).

CAMEROON
Film: *L'Aventure en France* (1962), d. Jean-Paul N'Gassa.
Feature/Talkie (doc.): *Une Nation est née* (1972).
Feature/Talkie (drama): *Pousse-pousse* (1975), d. Daniel Karawa.

CANADA
Film: actualities of life on the prairies made by James Freer of Brandon, Manitoba, 1897.
Drama: *The Great Unknown* (1913), d. Oscar Lund, starring Barbara Tennent and Fred Truesdell.
Feature: *Evangeline* (1913), d. E. P. Sullivan and W. H. Cavanaugh, prod. Canadian Bioscope Co., starring Laura Lyman and John F. Carleton.
Talkie (English): *North of '49* (1929), d. Neal Hart, prod. British Canadian Pictures.
Talkie (French): *A la croisée des chemins* (1943), d. and starring Paul Guévrement.
Colour: *Talbot of Canada* (1938), Kodachrome.

CHILE
Film: *Un Ejercicio General de Bomberos*, pr. 26 May 1902.
Feature: *La Baraja de la muerte* (1916), d. Salvador Giambastiane.
Talkie: *Norte y Sur* (1934), d. Jorge Délano.

CHINA
Film/Drama: *Tingchun Mountain* (1908), d. Lin Tenlun of the Feng Tai Photo Shop, Peking, starring Tan Hsin-pei.
Feature: *Yen Rei-sun* (1921), about embezzler who murders prostitute, d. Ren Pun-yen, prod. China Film Research Society, starring Chun Tso-Tze and Wang Tsai-yun.
Talkie: *Singsong Girl Red Peony* (1930), d. Chang Shih-chuan, prod. Star Film Co., starring Butterfly Wu.

COLOMBIA
Film/Drama: *The Life of General Rafael Uribe* (1914), d. brothers Di Domenico.
Feature: *La Maria* (1922), d. Alfredo Del Diestro.
Talkie: *Flowers of the Valley* (1939), d. Pedro Moreno Garzón.

CONGO
Film: *Kayako* (c. 1967), d. Sébastien Kamba.
Feature/Talkie: *La Rançon d'une alliance* (1973), d. Sébastien Kamba.

CUBA
El Brujo desapareciendo (1898), d. José E. Casasús.
Drama: *El Cabildo de ña Romualda* (1908), d. Enrique Diaz Quesada, prod. Metropolitan Films.
Feature: *El Rey de los campos de Cuba* (1913), d. Enrique Diaz Quesada, starring Gerardo Artecona and Evangelina Adams.
Talkie: *El Caballero de Max* (1930), d. Jaime San-Andrews, starring Nancy Norton and Wilfredo Genier—Vitaphone. (The Cuban government had made a sound-on-film documentary by the Phonofilm process in 1926.)

CYPRUS
Feature/Talkie: *Avrianos Polemistis/Tomorrow's Warrior* (1981), d. Michael Papas, prod. Cyprian (MP) Films, starring Christos Zannidea.

CZECHOSLOVAKIA
Film/Drama: *Výstavní Párkař a Lepič Plakátů* (1898), *Dostaveníčko Ve Mlýnici* (1898), *Pláč a Smích* (1898), etc., actualities and short comedies featuring Bohemian cabaret artiste Josef Šváb-Malostranský, d. Prague student Jan Kříženecký.
Feature: *Pražští Adamité* (1917), d. Antonín Fencl, prod. Lucernafilm, starring Josef Vošalik.
Talkie (Czech): *Tonka of the Gallows* (1930), d. Karel Anton. Talkie (Slovak): *The Singing Land* (1932), d. Karel Plicka.
Colour: *Jan Roháč of Duba* (1947), d. Vladamír Borský.

DAHOMEY (BENIN)
Film: *Ganvié, mon village* (1966), d. Pascal Abikanlou.
Feature/Talkie: *Sous le signe du Vaudoun* (1974), d. Pascal Abikanlou.

DENMARK
Film: *Kørsel med grønlandske Hunde* (1896), d. Peter Elfelt.
Drama: *Henrettelsen* (1903), d. Peter Elfelt, starring Francesca Nathansen and Victor Betzonich.
Feature: *Den sorte Drøm* (pr. 4 Sept 1911), circus drama, d. Urban Gad, starring Valdemar Psilander and Asta Nielsen.
Talkie: *Eskimo* (pr. 9 Oct 1930), d. G. Schneevogt, starring Mona Martenson and Paul Richter.
Colour: *Tricks* (pr. 7 May 1956), d. Erik Balling.

DOMINICAN REPUBLIC
Drama: *Las Emboscados de Cupido* (1924), d. Francisco Palau.
Feature/Talkie: *La Serpiente de la Luna de los Piratas* (1972), d. Jean-Louis Jorge.

ECUADOR
Feature/Talkie: *Se Conocieron en Guayaquil* (1949), d. Alberto Sanatana, prod. Ecuador Sono Films.

EGYPT
Film: *Dans les rues d'Alexandrie* (1912), d. M. de Lagarne.
Drama: *Sharaf el Badawi* (1918), prod. Italo-Egyptian Cinematographic Co.
Feature: *Koubla Fil Sahara'a* (1927), d. Ibrahim Lama, prod. Condor Film. (NB: Shooting on *Laila* (1927), generally credited as first Egyptian feature, started earlier, but the film was released later.)
Talkie: *Onchoudet el Fouad* (pr. 14 Apr 1932), d. Mario Volpi.

FINLAND
Film: *Pupils of Nikolai Street School during Break* (1904).
Drama: *Salaviinanpolttajat* (1907), d. Louis Sparre, starring Teuvo Puro and Jussi Snellman.
Feature: *Kun Onni Pettää* (pr. 23 Nov 1913), d. Konrad Tallroth, starring Axel Precht and Sigrid Precht.
Talkie: *The Log-Driver's Bride* (1931), d. Erkki Karu.

FRANCE
Film: *La Sortie des Usines* (1894), d. Louis Lumière.
Drama: *L'Arroseur arrosé* (1895), d. Louis Lumière, starring Lumière's gardener M. Clerc and apprentice boy Duval.
Feature: *L'Enfant prodigue* (pr. 20 June 1907), d. Michel Carré.
Talkie: *Les Trois masques* (1929), d. André Hugon, prod. Pathé-Natan, starring Renée Heribel and Marcel Vibert.
Colour: *L'Eternal amour* (1921), d. Gaston Colombani in Héraute Colour.

GABON
Film: *M'Bolo Gabon* (1967).
Feature/Talkie: *Où vas-tu Koumba* (1971), d. Alain Ferrari and Simon Auré.

GERMANY
Films: *Italian Dance*, *Kangaroo Boxer*, *Juggler*, *Acrobats*, *Russian Dance*, *Serpentine Dance*, *Lutte*, *Apothéose* (all pr. 1 Nov 1895), d. Max and Emil Skladanowski.
Feature: *In dem grossen Augenblick* (pr. 11 Aug 1911), d. Urban Gad, prod. Deutsche Bioscop GmbH, starring Asta Nielsen and Hugo Hink.
Talkie: *Melodie der Welt* (pr. 12 Mar 1929), d. Walter Ruttman, starring J. Kowal Samborsky and Renée Stobrawa.

GHANA
Drama: *Amenu's Child* (1949), d. Sean Graham.
Feature/Talkie: *Boy Kumasenu* (1951), d. Sean Graham.

GREECE
Film: Olympic Games actuality (1906).
Drama: *Quo Vadis Spiridion* (1911), comedy, d. Spiros Dimitracopoulos, prod. Athina Films.
Feature: *Golfo* (1912), d. Costas Bahatoris from Spiros Peressiadis' folk-story play.
Talkie: *Les Apaches d'Athenes* (1930), musical, d. D. Gaziadis, prod. Dag Films, starring Mary Sayannou and Petros Epitropakis.

GUATEMALA
Drama: *Agent No 13* (1912), d. Alberto de la Riva.
Feature/Talkie: *El Sombreron* (1950).

GUINEA
Film: *Mouramani Mamadou Touré* (1953).
Feature/Talkie: *Sergeant Bakary Woolén* (1966), d. Lamine Akin.

GUYANA
Feature/Talkie: *Aggro Seizeman* (1975), d. James Mannas and Brian Stuart-Young, starring Gordon Case and Martha Gonsalves.

HONG KONG
Dramas: *The Widowed Empress*, *The Unfilial Son*, *Revealed by the Pot*, *Stealing the Cooked Ducks* (all 1909), d. Benjamin Polaski, prod. Asia Film Co.

HUNGARY
Film: *The Emperor Franz Josef opening the Millenial Exhibition* (1896), d. Arnold Sziklay.
Drama: *Siófoki kaland* (pr. 29 Apr 1898)—shown as sequence in stage production *Mozgáfényképek/Moving Pictures*.
Feature: *Ma és holnap* (1912), d. Mihály Kertész (Michael Curtiz).
Talkie: *A Kék Bálvány* (pr. 25 Sept 1931), d. Lajos Lázár, starring Pál Jávor.
Colour: *Ludas Matyi* (1949), d. K. Nádasdy.

ICELAND
Film: various short subjects shot 1904.
Drama: *Aevintýri Jóns og Gvendar/The Adventures of Jön and Gvendur* (1923), d. Loftur Gudmundsson.
Feature/Talkie: *Milli fjalls og fjöru/Between Mountain and Shore* (1948), d. Loftur Gudmundsson.

INDIA
Film: *Cocoanut Fair* (1897), maker unknown, probably English. First by Indian: *The Wrestlers* (f. Nov 1899), d. Harishchandra S. Bhatvadekar of Bombay.

Drama: *Pundalik* (pr. 18 May 1912), d. R. G.
Torney.
Feature: *Raja Harishandra* (pr. 17 May 1913),
d. D. G. Phalke of Bombay.
Talkie (Hindi): *Alam Ara* (pr. 14 Mar 1931), d.
A. M. Irani, prod. Imperial Film Co.,
starring Master Vithal and Zubeida.
Talkie (Bengali): *Jamai Sasthi* (1931), prod.
Madan Theatres.
Colour: *Kisan Kanya* (1937), d. Moti B.
Gidwani, prod. Imperial Film
Co.—Cinecolor.

INDONESIA
Feature: *Loetoeng Kasaroeng* (1927), d. G.
Kruger at Bandung.
Talkie: *Njai Dasima* (1931), d. Lie Tek Soi and
Bakhtiar Effendi, prod. Tan's Film.

IRAN
Film: scenes of religious procession and of
Shah's private zoo, d. Mirza Ebrahim Khan
(Court Photographer to Shah
Mozaffareddin) 1900.
Drama/Feature: *Abi and Rabi* (1932), comedy,
d. Ohanian.
Talkie: *Dokhta Lor* (1934), d. Abdol Hoseyn
Sepenta.

IRAQ
Drama/Feature/Talkie: *Leila in Iraq* (1949).

IRELAND
Drama: *Fun at Finglas Fair* (1915), d. F. J.
McCormick. Never released, as all prints
destroyed in Easter Rising.
Feature: *Knocknagow* (1918), d. Fred
O'Donovan, prod. Film Co. of Ireland,
starring Fred O'Donovan and Kathleen
Murphy, featuring Master Cyril Cusack in
screen debut.
Talkie (English): *The Voice of Ireland* (1932), d.
Col Victor Haddick. Talkie (Irish): see
Languages: Irish Gaelic (p. 146).

ISRAEL
Film: documentary about Jewish settlement in
Palestine (1912), d. Akiva Arie Weiss.
Drama: *Yerahmiel the Shlemiel* and other short
comedies (1926), d. Nathan Axelrod.
Feature: *Oded Hanoded* (1933), d. Nathan
Axelrod.
Talkie: *Me'al Hekhoravot* (1936), d. Nathan
Axelrod.

ITALY
Film: *Arrivo del treno stazione di Milano* (1896),
d. Italo Pacchioni.
Drama: *La Presa di Roma* (1905), d. Filoteo
Albernini, starring Carlo Rosaspina.
Feature: *La Portatrice di pane* (1911), d. S. De
Montépin, prod. Vesuvio Films, Naples.
Talkie: *La Canzone dell' amore* (1930), d.
Genarro Righelli.
Colour: *Toto a colori* (1952)—Ferraniacolor.

IVORY COAST
Film: *Sur la dune de la solitude* (1964), d. Timité
Bassori.
Feature/Talkie: *Korogo* (1964), d. Georges
Keita.

JAMAICA
Feature/Talkie: *The Harder They Come* (1972),
d. Perry Henzell, starring Jimmy Cliff and
Janet Bartley.

JAPAN
Film: street scenes in Tokyo's Ginza and shots
of geisha from Shimbasi and Gion districts,
d. Tsunekichi Shibata of the Mitsukoshi
Department Store's photo dept., 1897.

Drama: *Momiji-gari* (1897), Noh drama, d.
Tsunekichi Shibata, starring Kikugoro V
and Danjuro IX.
Feature: *The Life Story of Tasuke Shiobara* (1912).
Talkie: *Taii no Musume* (1929), prod. Nikkatsu
Co.
Colour: *Karumen Kokyo ni Kaeru* (1951).

JORDAN
Feature/Talkie: *Watani Habibi* (1964).

KOREA
Drama: *The Righteous Revenge* (1919), d. Kim
Do-san.
Feature: *A Pledge in the Moonlight* (1923),
morality tale about importance of keeping
money in banks, d. Yun Paek-nam.
Talkie: *Chun Hyang-jon* (1939), d. Yi Pil-u and
Yi Myong-u.

KUWAIT
Feature/Talkie: *Bas Ya Bahar* (1972), d. Khaled
el Seddik, starring Mohamad Monsour and
Amal Baker.

LAOS
Feature/Talkie: *Gun Shots in the Valley of the
Jugs* (1983).

LEBANON
Drama/Feature: *The Adventures of Elias
Mabrouk* (1929), comedy about Lebanese
emigrant returning from USA, d. Jordano
Pidutti.
Talkie: *In the Ruins of Ba'albak* (1936), d.
George Costi, prod. Lumnar Film Co.

LIBYA
Feature/Talkie: *Lorsque le destin s'acharne*
(1972), d. A. Zarrouk.

MADAGASCAR
Film: Centenary celebrations of martyrdom of
Malagasy hero Rasalama, d. M. Raberono
1937.
Feature/Talkie: *Le Retour* (1973), d.
Randrasana Ignace Solo.

MALAYSIA (MALAYA)
Talkie: *Chandu* (1939), prod. Malayan Films
Inc.

MALI
Drama: *Bambo* (1968).
Feature/Talkie: *Les Wandyalankas* (1973), d.
Alkaly Kaba.

MALTA
Feature/Talkie: *Katarin* (1977), d. Cecil
Satariano, starring Anna Stafrace.

MAURITANIA
Feature/Talkie: *Soleil O* (1971), d. Med Hondo.

MEXICO
Drama: *Don Juan Tenorio* (1898), d. Salvador
Toxano Barragan.
Feature: *Fatal Orgullo* (1916), prod. México
Lux.
Talkie: *Más fuerte que el deber* (1930), d.
Raphael J. Sevilla.
Colour: *Novillero* (1936), d. Boris
Maicon—Cinecolor.

MOROCCO
Feature/Talkie: *Itto* (1934), d. Jean
Benoit-Levy.

NEPAL
Feature/Talkie: *Harischandra* (1951).

NETHERLANDS
Drama: *The Misadventures of a Small French
Gentleman without Trousers in Zandvoort*
(1902), d. Albert and Willy Mullens.

Talkie: *Vader des Vaderlands* (1933), d. G. J.
Teunissen.

NEW ZEALAND
Film: *Opening of the Auckland Exhibition* (f. 1
Dec 1898), d. A. E. Whitehouse.
Drama: *A Message from Mars* (1903), d. W. F.
Brown.
Feature: *The Test* (1916), d. and starring
Rawdon Blandford.
Talkie: *Down on the Farm* (1935), d. Lee Hill
and Stuart Pitt, prod. Sound Film
Productions Ltd.

NICARAGUA
Feature/Talkie: *Alsino y el Condor* (1982), d.
Miguel Littin.

NIGER
Film: *Aouré* (1962), d. Mustapha Allasane.
Feature/Talkie: *FVVA* (1971), d. Mustapha
Allasane.

NIGERIA
Drama: *My Father's Burden* (1961), d. Segun
Olusola.
Feature/Talkie: *Two Men and a Goat* (1966), d.
Edward Jones Horatio.

NORWAY
Film: reception of the newly-elected King
Haakon VII in Oslo, 1905.
Drama: *The Dangerous Life of a Fisherman*
(1907), prod. Norsk Kinematograf A/S,
starring Alma Lund.
Feature: *Anny—Story of a Prostitute* (1912), d.
Adam Eriksen, starring Julie Jansen.
Talkie: *The Great Christening* (pr. 26 Dec 1931),
d. Einar Sissener and Tancred Ibsen,
starring Einar Sissener.

OUTER MONGOLIA
Feature/Talkie: *At the Frontier* (1937).

PAKISTAN
Feature/Talkie: *Teri Yaad* (1948), prod. Dewan
Pictures, d. Dawood Chand, starring Asha
Posley and Nasir Khan. Urdu.

PARAGUAY
Feature/Talkie: *Cerro Cora* (1978), starring
Rosa Ros and Roberto de Felice, d. Ladislao
Gonzalez.

PERU
Film: *Peruvian Centaurs* (1908), actuality of
cavalry manoeuvres.
Drama: *Negocio al Agua* (1913), d. Frederico
Blume.
Feature: *Luis Pardo* (1927), biopic of brigand of
that name, d. and starred Enrique Cornejo
Villanueva.
Talkie: *Resaca* (1934), d. Alberto Santana.

PHILIPPINES
Film: *El Fusilamiento de Rizal*.
Feature: *Dalagang Bukid* (1919), d. Jose
Nepomuceno.
Talkie: *Punyal na Ginto* (1932).

POLAND
Film: actualities made by Kazimierz
Proszynski with a camera of his own
invention—the 'pleograph'—1894.
Drama: *His First Visit to Warsaw* (1908),
comedy starring Antoni Fertner.
Feature: *Dzieje Grzechu* (pr. 26 Aug 1911), d.
Antoni Bednarczyk, starring Maria Mirska
and Teodor Roland.
Talkie: *The Morals of Madame Dulska* (1930), d.
B. Newolyn.

PORTUGAL
Film: *Leaving the Factory* (1896), d. Aurelio Da
Paz Dos Reis.

Drama: *Rapto duma Actriz* (1907), d. Lino Ferreira, starring Carlos Leal and Luz Velozo.

Feature: *A Rosa do Adro* (1919).

Talkie: *A Severa* (pr 17 June 1931), d. Jose Leitao de Barros, prod. Super-Filmes, starring Dina Teresa and Conde Marialava.

ROMANIA

Film: actuality f. 10 May 1897 by Paul Menu.

Drama: *Amor fatal* (pr. 26 Sept 1911), d. Grigore Brezeanu, starring Lucia Sturdza and Tony Bulandra.

Feature: *Războiul Independentei* (pr. 1 Sept 1912), d. Grigore Brezeanu, starring C. Nottra and Ar. Demetriade.

Talkie: *Ciuleandra* (pr. 30 Oct 1930), d. Martin Berger, starring Jeana Popovici-Voinea.

SENEGAL

Film: *C'était il y a 4 ans* (1955), d. Paulin Vieyra.

Feature/Talkie: *La Noire de . . .* (1967), d. Ousmane Sembène.

SINGAPORE

Feature/Talkie: *White Golden Dragon* (1936).

SOMALIA

Film/Drama: *The Love that Knows no Barrier* (1961), d. Hossein Manrok.

Feature/Talkie: *Town and Village* (1968), d. El Hadji Mohamed Giumale.

SOUTH AFRICA

Film: scene taken from front of tram travelling down Commissioner Street, Johannesburg, d. Edgar Hyman, 1896.

Drama: *The Star of the South* (1911), about theft of diamond found on banks of Vaal by a Hottentot, prod. Springbok Film Co.

Feature: *De Voortrekkers* (pr. 16 Dec 1916), d. Harold Shaw, prod. African Film Productions Ltd, starring Dick Cruickshanks and Zulu actor Goba as Dingaan. Claimed (in S. Africa) that *The Covered Wagon* (US 23) was inspired by this film.

Talkie (Afrikaans): *Mocdertjie* (1931), d. Joseph Albrecht, starring Carl Ricjter and Joan du Toit.

Talkie (English): *They Built a Nation* (1938), d. Joseph Albrecht, prod. African Film Productions Ltd.

SPAIN

Film: *Salida de misa de doce en la Iglesia del Pilar en Zaragoza* (1896), d. Eduardo Jimeno.

Drama: *Riña en un Café* (1897), d. Fructuoso Gelabert.

Feature: *Lucha por la herencia* (1911), d. Otto Mulhauser, prod. Alhambra Films.

Talkie: *Yo quiero que me lleven a Hollywood* (pr. 20 June 1932), d. Edgar Neville.

Colour: *En un rincon de España* (1949), d. Jerónimo Mihura.

SRI LANKA

Feature/Talkie: *Banda Nagarayata Pemineema* (1953).

SUDAN

Feature/Talkie: *Hopes and Dreams* (1969), d. Al Rachid Mehdi.

SURINAM

Feature/Talkie: *Wan Pipel* (1976), d. Pim de la Parra, starring Borger Breeveld and Diana Gangaram.

SWEDEN

Film/Drama: *Slagsmål i Gamla Stockholm* (pr. 3 July 1897), two 17th-century cavaliers fighting over a girl, d. Ernest Florman, prod. Numa Handels & Fabriks AB.

Feature: *Blodets Röst* (pr. 20 Oct 1913), d. Victor Sjöström, prod. Svenska Biografteatern, starring Victor Sjöström and Ragna Wettergreen.

Talkie: *Konstgjorda Svensson* (pr. 14 Oct 1929), d. Gustaf Edgren, prod. Film AB Minerva, starring Fridolf Rhudin and Brita Apelgren.

SWITZERLAND

Films: *Zurcher Sechseläuten-Umzag* (c. 1901) and *Montreux Fête des Narcisses* (c. 1901), d. Georges Hipleh-Walt.

Feature: *Der Bergführer* (1917), d. Eduard Bienz, prod. La Société Bâloise EOS.

Talkie: *Bünzli's Grosstadtabenteuer* (1930), d. Robert Wohlmut, starring Freddy Scheim.

SYRIA

Drama/Feature: *Al Moutaham al Bari* (1928), gangster movie, d. and starring Ayoub Badri, prod. Hermon Film.

Talkie: *Leila Al-Amira* (1947), d. Niazi Mustafa.

TAIWAN

Drama: *The Orphan who Saved his Grandfather* (1922).

TANZANIA

Feature/Talkie: *Gumu* (1935).

THAILAND

Drama/Feature: *Miss Suwan* (1922), d. and prod. Henry McRay and the Wasuvati family. Performers were 'noble families and high-ranking government officials'.

TRINIDAD

Drama: *Callaloo* (1937), starring Ursula Johnson.

Feature/Talkie: *The Right and Wrong* (1970), d. Harbance Kumar, prod. De Luxe Films, starring Ralph Maharaj and Jesse Macdonald.

TUNISIA

Drama: *Ain el Ghezal* (1924), d. Haydée Samama-Chikly, starring Si Haj Hadi Djeheli.

Feature: *The Secret of Fatouma* (1928), d. Dedoncloit, starring Véra de Yourgaince.

Talkie: *Majnunal Kairouan* (1937), d. J. A. Creuzi, starring Fliza Chamia and Habib el Manaa.

TURKEY

Film: *Collapse of the Russian Monument in Ayestafanos* (1914), d. Fuat Uzkinay.

Drama: *The Wedding of Himmet Aga* (1916).

Feature: *Pençe* (1917), d. Sedat Simavi.

Talkie: *Istanbul Sokaklarinda* (1931), d. Muhsin Ertugrul, prod. Ipek Film.

UK

Film: *Traffic Crossing Leeds Bridge* (1888), d. Louis Aimé Augustin Le Prince.

Drama: *The Soldier's Courtship* (f. Apr 1896), d. Robert Paul, starring Fred Storey.

Feature: *Oliver Twist* (1912), d. Thomas Bentley, prod. Hepworth, starring Ivy Millais and Alma Taylor.

Colour Feature: *The World, the Flesh and the Devil* (1914), d. F. Martin Thornton, prod. Union Jack Photoplays and Natural Colour Kinematograph Co., starring Frank Esmond.

Talkie: *Blackmail* (pr. 21 June 1929), d. Alfred Hitchcock, prod. British International Pictures, starring Anny Ondra and John Longden.

UPPER VOLTA

Film: *A Minuit . . . l'Independence* (1960).

Feature/Talkie: *Le Sang des parias* (1973), d. Mamadou Djim Kolla.

URUGUAY

Film: *Una Carrera de Ciclismo en el Velodrome de Arroyo Seco* (1898), d. Felix Oliver.

Drama: *Oliver, Juncal 108* (1900), d. and starring Felix Oliver.

Feature: *Del Pingo al Volante* (1928), d. Roberto Kouri, prod. Bonne Garde.

Talkie: *Dos Destinos* (1936), d. Juan Etchebchere, prod. Estudios Ciclolux, starring Pepe Corbi.

USA

Film: actualities of fencers and wrestlers, etc., d. W. K. L. Dickson, prod. Edison Co., 1892.

Drama: *The Execution of Mary Queen of Scots* (f. 28 Aug 1895), d. Alfred Clark, prod. Raff & Gammon and Edison Co., starring Mr R. L. Thomas (as Mary!).

Feature: *Oliver Twist* (pr. 1 June 1912), prod. H. A. Spanuth, starring Nat C. Goodwin and Winnie Burns.

Colour Feature: *The Gulf Between* (pr. 21 Sept 1917), prod. Technicolor Motion Picture Corp., starring Grace Darmond and Niles Welch.

Talkie: *The Jazz Singer* (pr. 6 Oct 1927), d. Alan Crosland, prod. Warner Bros, starring Al Jolson.

USSR

Film: *Cossack Trick Riders* (f. 29 Sept 1896), d. amateur cinematographer A. P. Fedetsky at Kharkov.

Drama: *Boris Gudonov* (1907), d. A. O. Drankov, starring F. G. Martini and Z. Lopanskaya.

Feature: *Story of Sin* (pr. 15 Nov 1911), d. unknown, prod. S. Mintus of Riga, starring M. Mirskaya and S. Zheromsky.

Soviet Feature: *Signal* (1918), d. Alexander Arkatov, prod. Moscow Cinema Committee, starring Grabevetskaya.

Talkie: *The Earth Thirsts* (1930), d. Yuli Raizman.

Colour: *Nightingale, Little Nightingale* (1936), d. Nikolai Ekk.

VENEZUELA

Film: *Muchachas bañádose en el Lago* (1897) and *Un gran especialista sacando muelas en el Hotel Europa* (1897), d. Manuel Trujillo Durán at Maracaibo.

Drama: *Carnival in Caracas* (1909), d. Augusto Gonzalez Vidal and M. A. Gonham.

Feature: *The Lady of Cayenas* (1913), parody of *Camille*, d. E. Zimmerman.

Talkie: *El Rompimiento* (1938), d. Antonio Delgado Gomez, starring Rafael Guinard.

VIETNAM

Drama: *Vie du Detham* (1910), biopic of guerilla leader, d. Rene Batisson.

Talkie: *Canh dong ma* (1940).

YUGOSLAVIA

Film: *Odhod od mase v Ljutomeru* (1905), made in 17·5 mm by Ljutomer lawyer Karl Grossman.

Drama/Feature: *Zivot i Dela Besmrtnog Vožda Karadjordje* (pr. 17 Nov 1911), biopic of 'Immortal Leader Karadjordje', d. I. Stojadinović, starring M. Petrović.

Talkie: *Nevinost Bez Zastite* (1939), d. D. Aleksić.

ZAIRE

Feature/Talkie: *La Nièce captive* (1969), d. Luc Michez.

Twist (US 12), produced by H. A. Spanuth and starring Nat C. Goodwin and Winnie Burns, which was premièred on 1 June 1912, nearly six weeks before *Queen Elizabeth* (12 July 1912). However, the prejudice against long films was so insistent in America (at least amongst producers and distributors) that even in 1913 the major European success of that year, August Blom's feature *Atlantis* (Den 13), had to be compressed into a half-length version for US release. Domestic production was a modest two in 1912 and twelve in 1913, the real watershed being in 1914, when no less than 212 features were produced. The delay in going over to feature-film making suggests that the impact of *Queen Elizabeth*'s successful exploitation by Adolph Zukor in 1912 may not have been so influential as historians of the cinema have generally believed. Competition from the major European film-producing nations, most of whom had a two-year lead on America in feature production (see p. 13), may in fact have been the deciding factor.

Production Output

Total world output of feature films is nearly 4000 annually. Asian countries (including Australasia) account for approx. 50 per cent of output, European countries (including USSR) for approx. 33 per cent, the Middle East and Africa for approx. 5·5 per cent, North America for approx. 6 per cent, and Latin America for approx. 5·5 per cent.

The country with the largest production output in the world is India, with a total of 833 full-length feature releases in 1984 and an annual output that has exceeded 700 each year since 1979.

The twelve major film-producing countries of the past decade in terms of output are the following (average annual output in brackets): India (667); Japan (340); France (191); USA (190); Taiwan (*c.* 190); Turkey (*c.* 166); Philippines (*c.* 156); USSR (*c.* 148); Italy (139); Thailand (126); Hong Kong (124); Spain (96).

Germany's first full-length talkie, *Melodie der Welt* (Ger 29), had the unusual distinction of being commercially sponsored. Released as a major motion picture, it was nevertheless intended as an advertisement for the Hamburg–Amerika Line. (*Stiftung Deutsche Kinemathek*)

FEATURE-FILM PRODUCTION
The following countries have held the production record since the inception of feature films:

1906–11 Australia	**1922–32** Japan	**1940** Japan
1912 Hungary	**1933–35** USA	**1941–53** USA
1913 Germany	**1936–38** Japan	**1954–70** Japan
1914–22 USA	**1939** USA	**1971–** India

The smallest country with an established film industry is Iceland, whose population of 220,000 are among the most frequent filmgoers in the world with an average of 11·2 visits a year (about four times the Scandinavian average). Feature production began in 1948 with Loftur Gudmundsson's *Between Mountain and Shore* and continued sporadically through the next three decades with a dozen features made up to 1977. The breakthrough for the establishment of a permanent film industry came in 1978 with the setting up of the Icelandic Film Fund by Act of Parliament. The first grants from the fund were made the following year and three full-length features went into production immediately. The number of features released annually since then has fluctuated between three and five, and it is estimated that the more successful productions are seen by as many as a quarter of the population of the nation.

The best year for UK film production was 1936, with 192 features released. The most productive year of the silent era was 1920, with 155 features.

The worst year for UK film production (since 1914) was 1981 when only 32 features were released. The worst years of silent pictures were 1925 and 1926 with 33 releases. On two occasions in the past 60 years, production in Britain has come to a total halt. No films were made during November 1924 and for a three-week period in 1975.

The best year for US film production was 1921 with 854 feature releases.

The worst year for US film production (since 1913) was 1963 with 121 feature releases.

The highest output of any Hollywood studio was 101 features from Paramount in 1921; highest of the sound era was 68 by Paramount in 1936 and the same number from Warner's in 1937.

WORLDWIDE PRODUCTION OF
FEATURE FILMS 1906–84
The figures given in the chart on pp. 18–21 refer to feature films of an hour or more in length, including co-productions and feature-length documentaries. Television movies (TVM's) are excluded unless they have had a theatrical release. Production is attributed to the country in which the production company is registered. The figure quoted for any year represents the number of features completed and released.

In addition to the 55 countries listed in the chart, the following have a significant annual output but were excluded because of insufficient data: Burma (approx. 70 p.a.); Iran (post-revolution approx. 12 p.a.); Mongolia (approx. 10 p.a.); Taiwan (180–200 p.a.).

Worldwide Feature Film Production 1906–1945

	1906	1907	1908	1909	1910	1911	1912	1913	1914	1915	1916	1917	1918	1919	1920	1921	1922	1923
Albania	0	0	0	0	0	0	0	0	0	0	0	0	0	0	0	0	0	0
Algeria	0	0	0	0	0	0	0	0	0	0	0	0	0	0	0	0	0	0
Argentina	0	0	0	0	0	0	0	0	0	4	12	16	2	15	5	11	10	15
Australia	1	2	0	0	3	16	8	4	3	8	15	6	13	16	10	15	7	7
Austria	0	0	0	0	0	0	1	6	9	10	7	9	40	56	48	47	64	45
Bangladesh	0	0	0	0	0	0	0	0	0	0	0	0	0	0	0	0	0	0
Belgium	0	0	0	0	0	0	0	3	0	0	0	0	0	1	1	7	8	3
Brazil	0	0	0	0	0	0	0	2	–	3	6	4	2	6	6	2	4	6
Bulgaria	0	0	0	0	0	0	0	0	0	1	0	2	0	0	0	3	3	1
Canada[1]	0	0	0	0	0	0	0	1	0	1	2	2	1	2	2	0	8	2
China	0	0	0	0	0	0	0	0	0	0	0	0	0	0	0	–	–	–
Cuba	0	0	0	0	0	0	0	1	1	1	1	3	1	2	5	8	5	0
Czechoslovakia	0	0	0	0	0	0	0	0	0	0	0	1	13	23	17	25	30	18
Denmark	0	0	0	0	0	1	2	13	16	24	34	40	21	20	8	10	8	15
Egypt	0	0	0	0	0	0	0	0	0	0	0	0	0	0	0	0	0	0
Eire	0	0	0	0	0	0	0	0	0	0	0	1	0	0	3	0	3	0
Finland	0	0	0	0	0	0	0	1	1	0	1	0	0	0	1	2	3	3
France	0	1	0	1	–	–	–	–	–	–	–	–	–	–	–	–	–	–
Germany, Fed. Rep.	0	0	0	0	0	1	3	49	29	60	107	117	211	345	485	646	474	347
Germany, Dem. Rep.																		
Greece	0	0	0	0	0	0	1	0	0	0	1	0	1	0	0	0	3	2
Hong Kong[3]	–	–	–	–	–	–	–	–	–	–	–	–	–	–	–	–	–	–
Hungary	0	0	0	0	0	0	14	11	19	27	52	77	107	48	54	25	6	13
India	0	0	0	0	0	0	0	3	1	0	0	3	7	8	27	44	64	52
Indonesia[2]	0	0	0	0	0	0	0	0	0	0	0	0	0	0	0	0	0	0
Iraq	0	0	0	0	0	0	0	0	0	0	0	0	0	0	0	0	0	0
Israel	0	0	0	0	0	0	0	0	0	0	0	0	0	0	0	0	0	0
Italy	0	0	0	0	0	2	5	29	16	39	57	37	46	151	152	56	34	38
Japan	0	0	0	0	0	0	2	0	5	3	–	–	–	–	–	–	–	–
Korea, South	0	0	0	0	0	0	0	0	0	0	0	0	0	0	0	0	0	–
Malaysia	0	0	0	0	0	0	0	0	0	0	0	0	0	0	0	0	0	0
Mexico	0	0	0	0	0	0	0	0	0	0	1	11	6	13	7	8	4	3
Netherlands	0	0	0	0	0	0	–	–	–	–	–	–	–	1	–	–	–	–
New Zealand	0	0	0	0	0	0	0	0	0	0	1	0	0	0	0	0	2	0
Norway	0	0	0	0	0	0	1	0	0	0	2	3	3	2	2	3	3	1
Pakistan																		
Philippines	0	0	0	0	0	0	0	0	0	0	0	–	–	–	–	–	–	–
Poland	0	0	0	0	0	3	2	5	5	3	5	7	6	7	8	17	15	11
Portugal	0	0	0	0	0	0	0	0	0	0	0	0	0	4	2	3	2	7
Romania	0	0	0	0	0	0	1	10	0	0	0	0	0	0	2	1	0	1
Singapore	0	0	0	0	0	0	0	0	0	0	0	0	0	0	0	0	0	0
South Africa	0	0	0	0	0	0	0	0	0	0	14	7	5	6	4	2	3	1
Spain	0	0	0	0	0	–	–	–	–	–	–	–	–	17	12	8	4	8
Sri Lanka	0	0	0	0	0	0	0	0	0	0	0	0	0	0	0	0	0	0
Sweden[3]	0	0	0	0	0	0	0	4	5	2	4	7	6	11	20	7	11	23
Switzerland	0	0	0	0	0	0	0	0	0	0	0	–	–	–	–	–	–	–
Thailand	0	0	0	0	0	0	0	0	0	0	0	0	0	0	0	0	1	1
Tunisia	0	0	0	0	0	0	0	0	0	0	0	0	0	0	0	1	2	0
Turkey	0	0	0	0	0	0	0	0	0	0	0	2	1	3	0	3	2	3
UK	0	0	0	0	0	0	2	18	15	73	107	66	76	122	155	137	110	68
Uruguay	0	0	0	0	0	0	0	0	0	0	0	0	0	0	1	0	0	1
USA	0	0	0	0	0	0	2	12	212	419	677	687	841	646	797	854	748	576
USSR	0	0	0	0	0	1	9	31	17	44	74	57	27	12	8	5	9	12
Venezuela	0	0	0	0	0	0	0	1	0	1	0	0	0	0	0	0	0	0
Yugoslavia	0	0	0	0	0	1	–	–	–	–	–	–	6	–	–	–	–	–

– No data available   [1] Completions per year   [2] Starts per year   [3] Financial year April–March

1924	1925	1926	1927	1928	1929	1930	1931	1932	1933	1934	1935	1936	1937	1938	1939	1940	1941	1942	1943	1944	1945
0	0	0	0	0	0	0	0	0	0	0	0	0	0	0	0	0	0	0	0	0	0
0	0	0	0	0	0	0	0	0	0	0	0	0	0	0	0	0	0	0	0	0	0
13	15	7	6	6	4	5	4	2	6	6	13	15	28	41	50	49	47	56	36	24	23
10	9	16	4	13	3	3	6	4	7	9	3	6	5	7	4	3	3	1	0	1	1
30	24	17	18	19	22	17	9	11	18	17	32	25	18	11	11	10	5	6	10	8	1
0	0	0	0	0	0	0	0	0	0	0	0	0	0	0	0	0	0	0	0	0	0
4	10	2	2	1	4	3	3	5	1	6	5	3	7	5	3	2	3	5	1	1	9
4	12	12	10	10	13	14	4	8	6	2	2	3	0	3	2	7	1	1	1	7	5
0	1	0	2	2	7	3	2	0	2	2	0	1	1	1	1	2	4	1	3	1	2
0	0	0	2	3	0	1	0	0	1	2	3	5	6	0	1	0	0	0	0	1	0
–	–	80	75	50	40	–	–	60	–	69	80	–	75	86	58	–	–	–	–	–	–
0	1	3	2	1	3	2	0	0	0	0	0	0	1	2	8	2	1	1	3	1	2
8	17	31	24	16	35	23	23	24	44	34	34	31	49	41	41	31	21	11	10	9	3
9	8	7	6	4	3	5	4	6	10	8	11	6	13	10	9	12	16	18	18	18	10
0	0	0	2	3	2	2	4	6	6	7	12	13	17	10	15	12	12	22	15	23	42
0	2	0	0	0	0	0	1	0	0	1	1	0	2	0	0	0	0	0	0	0	0
4	2	2	6	3	7	2	7	3	5	4	5	9	12	20	21	22	15	18	22	16	20
68	73	55	74	94	52	98	157	156	152	119	128	145	124	122	94	40	41	74	81	27	50
271	228	195	241	226	194	180	199	150	129	142	111	128	108	113	118	89	71	64	83	75	72
1	2	2	2	2	4	13	6	6	2	1	0	0	1	3	1	0	1	0	3	2	5
–	–	–	–	–	–	–	–	–	–	–	–	–	150	55	100	–	–	–	–	–	–
9	3	3	8	2	5	3	3	8	9	12	18	28	36	35	27	39	41	48	53	22	3
54	86	94	90	109	140	194	228	148	144	171	233	217	179	172	165	170	167	173	161	127	99
0	0	1	1	2	5	7	5	5	1	3	3	2	3	4	4	13	31	1	0	6	0
0	0	0	0	0	0	0	0	0	0	0	0	0	0	0	0	0	0	0	0	0	0
0	0	0	0	0	0	0	0	0	1	–	–	–	–	–	–	–	–	–	–	–	–
35	16	10	15	22	10	6	12	20	34	35	21	37	32	68	79	85	89	119	70	19	28
875	–	–	648	798	850	–	–	498	450	413	470	558	583	554	437	497	232	87	61	46	38
–	–	–	–	–	–	–	–	–	–	–	–	–	5	–	–	–	–	–	–	–	–
0	0	0	0	0	0	0	0	0	0	0	0	0	0	0	0	6	0	1	0	0	0
0	7	4	2	2	2	1	1	6	21	23	22	25	38	57	37	29	37	47	70	73	82
–	–	–	–	–	0	0	1	0	7	–	9	3	2	–	–	–	–	–	–	–	2
1	1	0	2	1	0	0	0	0	0	0	1	3	0	0	0	1	1	0	0	0	0
1	2	5	5	3	2	2	1	5	3	2	1	1	2	5	4	4	4	5	4	3	4
–	–	3	4	–	–	–	16	20	–	–	–	15	32	55	–	–	–	–	–	–	–
8	5	8	12	12	16	12	10	14	11	14	14	24	28	21	18	0	0	0	0	0	0
3	0	1	1	1	1	5	2	0	0	3	1	1	3	4	1	3	2	4	4	3	4
1	6	4	3	4	5	3	3	1	0	2	0	0	1	0	3	0	0	1	2	0	1
0	0	0	0	0	0	0	0	0	0	0	0	1	–	–	–	0	0	0	0	0	0
1	1	0	0	0	0	0	2	0	0	0	0	1	0	1	1	3	0	0	0	1	0
10	38	39	25	12	21	8	2	9	17	23	44	19	10	4	20	40	33	49	53	34	33
0	0	0	0	0	0	0	0	0	0	0	0	0	0	0	0	0	0	0	0	0	0
16	18	18	11	6	6	13	24	22	22	19	20	28	22	27	30	36	34	34	43	43	44
–	–	–	–	–	–	–	–	–	6	–	–	3	1	1	9	11	13	5	–	–	–
1	2	3	3	8	–	–	–	–	–	–	–	–	–	10	12	–	–	–	–	–	–
1	0	0	2	2	1	1	0	0	0	0	2	0	1	1	0	0	0	0	0	0	0
1	0	0	0	1	1	0	1	1	7	3	0	0	1	1	4	4	1	4	2	2	3
49	33	33	48	80	81	75	93	110	115	145	165	192	176	134	84	50	46	39	47	35	39
0	0	0	1	1	1	0	1	0	0	0	0	1	0	3	0	0	0	0	0	0	0
579	579	740	678	641	562	509	501	489	507	480	525	522	538	455	483	477	492	488	397	401	350
41	76	77	106	125	103	123	88	67	35	59	34	49	45	41	52	50	50	26	27	21	20
1	0	1	0	3	1	0	1	1	3	0	0	0	1	0	2	1	1	2	0	0	4
–	–	–	–	0	–	–	–	4	2	0	0	0	0	0	1	0	0	0	0	0	0

Worldwide Feature Film Production 1946–1984

	1946	1947	1948	1949	1950	1951	1952	1953	1954	1955	1956	1957	1958	1959	1960	1961	1962
Albania	0	0	0	0	0	0	0	0	0	0	0	1	1	1	1	1	1
Algeria	0	0	0	0	0	0	0	0	0	0	0	0	0	0	0	0	0
Argentina	32	38	41	47	56	53	35	37	45	43	36	15	32	22	31	25	32
Australia	3	1	1	4	1	3	1	1	2	2	2	3	1	2	2	1	1
Austria	4	13	25	25	17	28	19	28	22	28	37	26	23	19	20	23	20
Bangladesh	0	0	0	0	0	0	0	0	0	0	1	0	0	3	2	5	5
Belgium	8	3	3	1	2	1	2	4	5	5	8	3	12	6	9	9	11
Brazil	11	9	14	18	30	22	31	31	25	24	21	36	41	30	29	36	28
Bulgaria	4	3	0	0	1	2	2	1	4	2	9	5	9	3	10	9	8
Canada[1]	3	0	2	5	3	3	1	2	2	0	2	3	3	4	2	5	4
China[4]	–	–	–	7	26	–	–	17	–	24	42	–	52	70	82	85	80
Cuba	1	2	2	4	10	5	5	4	11	7	5	3	6	5	2	2	2
Czechoslovakia	11	19	17	20	20	8	16	18	14	16	21	25	29	33	30	39	35
Denmark	13	13	10	8	14	18	12	12	13	13	13	16	16	14	19	22	23
Egypt	52	55	49	44	48	52	59	62	65	51	39	40	55	58	59	52	49
Eire	0	0	0	0	0	0	0	0	0	0	0	1	3	2	0	1	0
Finland	16	15	16	16	14	19	28	25	28	30	18	21	17	15	18	18	21
France	81	88	84	97	104	109	100	111	98	110	129	142	126	133	158	167	125
Germany, Fed. Rep.	1	6	21	56	61	69	73	103	109	128	122	107	115	106	94	80	61
Germany, Dem. Rep.	3	4	7	12	10	8	6	7	9	13	19	22	17	28	24	27	24
Greece	4	6	6	8	6	12	17	19	19	16	26	28	38	59	68	56	78
Hong Kong[3]	–	–	–	256	202	192	259	188	167	235	311	223	237	239	293	303	261
Hungary	2	4	5	7	4	9	5	6	8	10	10	15	13	18	14	19	17
India	200	281	263	291	241	221	233	260	278	289	295	294	294	304	318	298	315
Indonesia[2]	0	0	3	8	23	40	42	50	59	64	36	21	19	16	38	37	12
Iraq	0	2	0	3	0	0	0	0	0	1	1	3	5	1	2	0	7
Israel	–	–	–	–	–	–	–	–	–	–	–	–	–	–	–	3	4
Italy	66	69	49	95	74	113	142	170	145	133	114	155	137	160	129	200	197
Japan	57	97	123	156	215	212	258	302	370	423	514	443	516	500	555	537	378
Korea, South	–	–	–	–	–	–	–	–	–	26	40	44	80	109	85	91	115
Malaysia	0	2	3	3	8	11	18	16	11	9	9	16	23	28	13	19	18
Mexico	72	58	81	108	124	101	99	83	105	84	87	106	92	84	64	49	–
Netherlands	1	0	2	2	0	1	1	2	0	2	0	3	4	1	6	1	5
New Zealand	0	0	0	0	0	0	1	0	0	0	0	0	0	0	0	0	0
Norway	6	1	4	3	2	7	7	6	9	9	8	9	9	8	6	6	5
Pakistan		0	0	4	15	10	7	10	7	19	31	27	33	34	38	34	34
Philippines	10	24	–	–	–	–	–	–	–	–	–	–	97	92	112	108	152
Poland	1	2	2	3	4	2	4	3	10	8	6	16	16	16	21	23	23
Portugal	6	7	4	7	2	2	8	4	3	0	4	1	4	5	2	2	5
Romania	4	0	0	1	0	2	1	2	3	4	3	8	4	4	9	10	8
Singapore	–	–	–	–	–	15	14	21	13	20	12	13	19	17	12	19	27
South Africa	4	2	1	4	2	5	1	5	5	4	2	2	5	6	8	19	13
Spain	41	48	44	37	49	41	41	43	69	56	75	72	75	68	73	91	89
Sri Lanka	0	0	0	0	0	0	0	6	5	7	7	8	9	9	9	8	6
Sweden[3]	36	43	40	34	25	31	25	31	30	30	34	32	29	24	23	18	17
Switzerland	0	2	2	1	1	1	4	0	1	3	3	3	3	5	7	9	4
Thailand	–	–	–	10	–	–	–	–	–	–	–	–	–	50	43	35	96
Tunisia	0	0	1	0	0	1	0	0	1	0	0	0	1	1	0	1	0
Turkey	6	12	16	18	21	32	52	50	53	64	52	60	80	71	68	116	127
UK	41	58	74	101	81	75	101	102	110	95	91	115	111	99	110	109	126
Uruguay	1	1	1	2	2	1	2	0	0	0	0	1	2	1	0	0	0
USA	378	369	366	356	383	391	324	344	253	254	272	300	241	187	154	131	147
USSR	19	22	22	13	14	10	20	42	35	84	98	144	130	145	139	137	97
Venezuela	1	0	3	4	4	1	3	1	1	2	3	2	1	1	1	0	3
Yugoslavia	0	2	4	3	4	6	5	9	7	14	10	15	15	14	14	32	22

– No data available   [1] Completions per year   [2] Starts per year   [3] Financial year April–March   [4] 1949–66: 614   * estimated

1963	1964	1965	1966	1967	1968	1969	1970	1971	1972	1973	1974	1975	1976	1977	1978	1979	1980	1981	1982	1983	1984
1	1	1	2	3	4	–	4	3	4	5	5	7	10	–	12	–	–	–	–	–	–
1	0	3	1	2	4	2	8	1	9	6	10	3	4	1	5	2	–	–	–	–	–
27	37	30	34	27	32	29	28	38	32	39	38	33	21	21	22	33	34	24	17	17	24
0	0	0	3	2	1	6	14	10	7	12	11	24	16	17	10	18	14	9	21	19	15
15	19	16	18	12	7	3	7	5	9	6	8	6	5	8	3	9	8	11	13	11	14
4	17	12	24	22	34	30	41	6	28	31	30	34	44	31	42	52	44	39	42	45	50
4	2	5	3	31	10	15	12	16	20	27	16	21	11	30	20	10	21	–	–	–	–
21	23	26	30	41	47	46	70	69	81	58	82	90	78	73	101	93	102	80	86	84	–
9	10	8	12	15	6	14	25	18	22	18	19	25	20	21	21	22	21	–	17	22	–
5	14	15	10	11	13	25	46	32	32	43	41	39	30	39	39	55	54	33	27	34	27
–	–	47	4	2	4	–	1	1	5	6	5	9	13	–	–	12	82	–	105	114	–
4	6	4	2	3	4	1	0	4	2	3	2	2	5	3	3	5	1	–	–	8	–
36	38	40	31	40	36	25	38	37	35	36	38	39	46	42	46	46	45	44	44	41	34
21	19	16	18	20	19	23	28	33	17	12	14	17	20	20	16	11	12	12	7	12	13
48	45	43	39	33	40	44	48	46	41	43	44	49	47	50	51	39	–	55	41	–	–
0	0	0	0	0	1	0	0	0	1	0	0	0	0	1	2	0	–	–	1	2	3
14	6	9	7	3	12	9	13	9	6	8	3	5	9	7	10	9	11	16	19	17	20
141	148	142	130	120	117	154	138	127	169	200	234	222	214	142	227	234	189	231	164	131	161
66	77	69	60	96	107	121	113	99	85	98	80	81	61	60	64	66	49	76	70	77	77
20	16	14	16	20	16	13	–	12	17	16	15	16	17	15	17	17	15	16	16	16	–
66	94	96	106	76	95	88	86	83	63	63	38	47	38	21	18	–	26	25	46	48	37
260	235	204	171	169	156	158	138	127	133	201	147	109	112	116	135	145	132	127	126	114	125
21	18	20	20	22	21	20	20	20	21	18	19	19	17	19	23	25	21	24	27	26	–
302	310	322	311	329	349	379	398	432	411	448	432	470	507	555	612	714	742	737	763	741	800*
19	19	15	13	13	8	9	21	52	50	58	84	39	58	124	81	51	68	71	52	74	78
6	3	1	1	4	1	2	2	0	1	0	0	1	0	3	2	3	–	–	–	–	–
5	6	7	6	10	11	10	9	14	15	14	9	9	11	14	11	13	13	12	12	14	16
254	245	206	217	280	297	246	228	223	316	207	265	158	223	156	123	141	163	103	114	110	103
363	346	487	442	410	494	494	423	421	400	405	333	333	356	337	326	335	320	332	322	363	379
146	148	189	124	155	175	229	224	202	122	–	142	99	86	66	90	80	116	110	97	85	–
15	13	12	9	10	11	11	9	2	2	3	6	4	4	3	4	5	9	14	13	15	13
–	–	52	–	48	90	93	–	–	81	48	44	40	43	59	63	85	108	87	74	80	–
2	3	1	6	7	4	6	3	4	6	11	9	14	8	8	9	14	7	11	13	16	–
0	1	0	1	0	0	0	0	1	0	1	0	1	0	4	2	3	2	5	5	4	11
6	6	8	7	6	6	5	11	6	8	12	12	14	12	10	6	13	10	10	10	7	7
46	67	54	72	66	99	91	85	79	99	93	107	111	109	74	87	80	58	84	66	85	82
142	161	161	201	180	175	169	194	253	181	146	120	143	174	141	135	170	173	179	149	143	–
26	25	20	26	21	18	22	25	25	20	25	31	36	28	32	27	32	37	41	33	32	32
8	8	6	5	7	4	4	4	7	8	6	11	10	18	19	5	6	13	8	7	4	10*
10	11	14	15	14	7	12	8	13	16	16	18	23	22	20	23	28	32	31	30	32	26
21	19	11	12	10	5	5	4	3	3	4	1	4	2	2	0	0	0	0	0	0	0
7	8	6	10	9	12	12	17	17	24	22	32	26	18	18	14	11	9	6	3	5	6
113	123	133	152	138	117	123	105	107	104	112	115	102	90	97	79	73	110	92	146	99	75
11	15	15	20	21	20	20	17	14	20	18	41	31	30	75	35	29	75	56	65	33	34
18	24	19	25	27	34	24	20	19	14	18	24	20	16	22	17	18	26	25	18	23	–
4	4	10	5	4	7	–	7	–	–	18	15	15	10	–	10	–	–	16	13	17	17
48	44	44	54	51	52	64	73	74	70	81	83	90	130	98	148	150	142	138	117	109	141
0	0	1	2	7	3	5	4	2	4	2	2	3	1	2	3	2	4	3	3	3	–
125	178	214	238	206	177	229	225	266	298	208	188	124	164	225	123	195	–	–	–	–	–
107	75	80	69	89	73	85	103	97	90	80	81	80	64	43	49	38	41	32	37	33	42
0	0	0	0	0	0	0	0	0	0	0	0	0	0	0	0	1	1	1	–	–	–
121	141	153	156	178	180	177	231	223	224	201	179	161	188	157	162	167	200	181	187	231	262
96	108	127	131	136	121	141	130	133	127	150	140	148	149	143	141	151	151	145	158	148	–
4	9	3	3	2	5	1	4	4	1	5	3	5	13	29	12	9	5	4	7	9	–
18	17	20	21	31	36	29	23	23	21	16	11	19	18	15	16	24	26	24	32	28	34

Accidents

The largest number of fatalities incurred in the production of a film was 27 when the ship *Viking* blew up off Newfoundland on 15 March 1931 during the shooting of *The Viking* (Can 31), a drama about the seal fishing industry. The producer, Varick Frissell, was amongst those killed.

Reports of prodigious death rolls on Hollywood movies tend to be exaggerated. Neither version of *Ben Hur* (US 25 and US 59) resulted in any deaths, except of horses. **Hollywood's worst accident** took place during production of *Such Men Are Dangerous* (US 30), when two planes collided on the way to shoot a scene. Ten members of the film crew were killed.

Deaths in the course of production have a macabre tendency to come in threes. A helicopter crash during the making of *Twilight Zone* (US 82) resulted in three dead, two of them child actors; three stuntmen were killed shooting the Cooper River rapids for *The Trail of '98* (US 28); three extras were drowned in the *Noah's Ark* (US 28) flood scenes; three aerial stuntmen were killed on *Hell's Angels* (US 30), though only one of them while actually filming; three horsemen died in the cavalry charge in *They Died with Their Boots On* (US 41). One of the latter was Bill Mead, whose horse tripped as he rode by the side of Errol Flynn. He had the presence of mind to fling his sword forward to avoid falling with it, but by incredible mischance the hilt stuck in the ground and Mead fell on the tip of the blade, impaling himself.

It is rare for scenes of actual deaths during filming to be retained in the completed picture, but one known example is the anti-British propaganda drama *Mein Leben für Irland* (Ger 41). In the final battle scene several extras were killed when one stepped on a live land-mine and the footage was included in the release prints.

Archives

The first film archive was the Danish Statens Arkiv for historiske Film og Stemmer, which had its origins in the spring of 1910 when Anker Kirkeby of the Copenhagen newspaper *Politiken* approached Ole Olsen of Nordisk Films with the idea of preserving a selection of films likely to be of historic interest in the future. During the ensuing three years a collection of films was assembled, including a number, specially taken for the archive, which showed prominent Danish writers, scientists, politicians, etc., and shots of parts of old Copenhagen due for redevelopment. The archive was formally established at the Royal Library in Copenhagen on 9 April 1913.

By the outbreak of war in 1914, film collections had

This was the only known copy of an historic New Zealand film, *The Birth of New Zealand* (NZ 22). Archives all over the world are racing against time to transfer old nitrate prints to acetate film before they decompose like this one. (*New Zealand Film Archive*)

been formed at the Louvre in Paris, the National Records Office in Madrid, the New York Public Library, and in Brussels, Rome, Berlin, and the Indian state of Baroda. These pioneer efforts, and those that followed in the 1920s, were generally concerned with the preservation of films as a record of national or civic history.

The first National Film Archive formed as a record of the film industry, rather than as a retrospective of public events, was the Reichsfilmarchiv established in Germany at the instigation of Arnold Raether on 4 February 1935. The Svenska Filminstituter Archive claims an earlier date of foundation, but it originated with the Filmhistorika Samlingarna, a private collection formed in 1933 by Einar Lauritzen.

Two other major archives were founded in 1935. The British Film Institute (founded 1933) set up the National Film Archive under Ernest Lindgren in May, and in New York Iris Barry and John Abbott established the Museum of Modern Art Film Library. The following year, Henri Langlois formed the Cinémathèque Française from his own private film collection and this rapidly grew into a national institution, though the government support enjoyed since the end of World War II was withdrawn in 1969 when the French government established its own archive. The USSR's giant Gosfilmofond, which occupies a 150-acre site at Bielye Stolbi near Moscow and employs a staff of 600, was not founded until 1948.

The largest collection of films in the world is preserved by the Motion Picture, Broadcasting and Recorded Sound Division of the Library of Congress in Washington, DC, which has 80,000 titles spanning a period of some 90 years. **The oldest film in the collection**, which is also **the oldest American film in existence** anywhere in the world, is catalogued as *Indian Club Swinger*. Made by W. K. L. Dickson at the

Edison laboratory at West Orange, NJ, it shows a young man exercising with Indian clubs and was made either in 1892 or 1893.

The Library of Congress's Motion Picture Division is a copyright repository rather than a film archive in the conventional sense.

The world's largest service film archive is Britain's National Film Archive, with 70,000 films. The Cinémathèque Française and the archive of the Centre Nationale de la Cinématographie, both based in Paris, each claim to hold 60,000 films, while the Soviet Union's Gosfilmofond has about 50,000.

The smallest national archive is the Icelandic Film Archive, which contains some 200 films about or made in Iceland.

The biggest single loss of archive film occurred in March 1982 when 6506 films were destroyed by fire and explosions at the Cineteca Nacional in Mexico City. A commentator described the disaster as 'the most terrible cultural loss in modern Mexican history—the filmic memory of our country is erased'.

The largest collection of film stills in the world is the three million housed at the Department of Film of the Museum of Modern Art in New York.

The largest collection of film stills in Europe is the National Film Archive Stills Collection in London, which consists of two million black-and-white stills from 40,000 films, 200,000 colour transparencies and 9500 portraits of performers.

Co-productions

The first co-production was *Das Geheimnis der Lüfte* (Aut/Fr 13), a full-length feature thriller starring Julius Brandt. The Austrian production company was Wiener Autorenfilm; the French company is believed to have been Pathé.

The first Anglo-American co-production was James Whale's *Journey's End* (GB/US 30), from R. C. Sheriff's war drama of the same name, which was made in Hollywood by Gainsborough/Welsh-Pearson of Britain and Tiffany-Stahl of the US. The film had an all-male cast headed by Colin Clive as the alcoholic war hero.

The first Anglo-Soviet co-production was *Anna Pavlova* (USSR/GB 85), made by Mosfilm (Moscow) and Poseidon Films (London) and starring Galina Belayeva as Pavlova, Martin Scorcese and James Fox.

The most cosmopolitan co-productions are the seven-nation films *Soldaty svobody* (USSR/Bul/Hun/GDR/Pol/Rom/Cz 77) and *West Indies Story* (Tun/Mali/IvC/Mau/Alg/Sen/Fr 79). *Soldaty svobody* involved the most production companies, namely Mosfilm (USSR), Za Ugrakbu Film (Bul), Mafilm (Hun), Defa (GDR), PRF EF (Pol), Bukuresti (Rom), Barrandov (Cz) and Koliba (Cz).

Films co-produced by five different countries have included *The Behest of the Inca* (Bul/FRG/It/Sp/Peru 66); *Love at 20* (Fr/It/Jap/Pol/FRG 63); *Marco the Magnificent* (Afg/Egy/Fr/It/Yug 66); *The Call of the Wild* (GB/FRG/Sp/It/Fr 72).

> Walter Winchell on Hollywood: *A town that has to be seen to be disbelieved.*

Hollywood

The first European inhabitant of the area now known as Hollywood, then called Nopalera, was Mexican-born Don Tomas Urquidez, who built an adobe dwelling in 1853 at what is now the northwest corner of Franklin and Sycamore Avenues.

The name 'Hollywood' was conferred on her Cahuenga Valley ranch by Mrs Harvey Henderson Wilcox, wife of one of the district's earliest real-estate developers, in 1886. The name had nothing to do with holly-bushes imported from England, as some accounts have it. Mrs Wilcox had been travelling by train to her old home in the east when she met a lady with a summer home near Chicago called 'Hollywood'. She was so charmed by the name that she decided to borrow it for her own property. In 1903 the village of Hollywood and its environs were incorporated as a municipality, but in 1910 the citizens voted to become a district of Los Angeles in order to secure water supplies. At that date the population was 5000; by 1919 it was 35,000 and by 1925 it had grown to 130,000.

Orson Welles had every reason to look worried in *The Lady of Shanghai* (US 48). He had wangled a $50,000 loan out of Columbia president Harry Cohn by offering to film a novel he had not even read.

BEVERLY HILLS

The exodus of Hollywood's upper crust to Beverly Hills began when Douglas Fairbanks rented sports goods manufacturer Syl Spaulding's 36-room house on Summit Drive in 1919. At that time Beverly Hills was mainly agricultural land given over to the cultivation of beans and there was only one house between Fairbanks' rented property and the sea seven miles away. Early in 1920 he bought a hunting lodge adjacent to the Spaulding mansion and rebuilt it in a style befitting his new bride, Mary Pickford. Named *Pickfair* after the first syllables of their names, Doug's wedding gift to Mary was, and remained, Beverly Hills' most regal establishment, a magnet that drew the elite of the film colony to what was soon to become America's richest suburb. In 1980, following the death of Mary Pickford, the 45-room mansion was put up for sale at an asking price of $10 million.

The first dramatic film made in the Los Angeles area was Francis Boggs' *The Count of Monte Cristo* (US 08), a Selig production made partly in Colorado and partly in the Laguna and Venice districts of what is now Greater Los Angeles. The first made wholly in LA was Francis Boggs' *The Power of the Sultan* (US 09), starring Hobart Bosworth, a Broadway actor who had lost his voice through TB and was seeking recuperative sunshine. The movie was shot in three days, 8–10 May 1909, on a rented lot next to a Chinese laundry on Olive and Seventh Streets, Los Angeles. Boggs, who might have become prominent as California's pioneer director, was unfortunately cut down in his prime, murdered by a crazed Japanese studio gardener in 1911.

The first studio in the Los Angeles area was established by the Selig Co. at 1845 Allesandro Street, Edendale. Construction began in August 1909 and enlargements were made in 1910 and again in 1911, so that within two years of opening it was occupying a 230 × 220 ft (70 × 67 m) building.

The first film made in Hollywood was D. W. Griffith's *In Old California* (US 10), a Biograph melodrama about the liaison between a Spanish maiden (Marion Leonard) and a dashing hero, destined to become Governor of California (Frank Grandin), who have an illegitimate wastrel son (Arthur Johnson). It was shot in two days, 2–3 February 1910, and released on 10 March.

At the 1984 American Film Institute Life Achievement Award presentation to 90-year-old Lillian Gish, John Houseman recalled that many years ago Miss Gish and her sister Dorothy were offered the chance of buying the Sunset Strip in Hollywood for $300. The Gish sisters talked the matter over, weighing the pros and cons. They then went down to fashionable Bullock's and bought a dress each instead.

Originally the term 'movies' meant not films, but the people who made them. In early Hollywood before World War I, the local inhabitants, many of them retired Middle Westerners come to relax in the sunshine, spoke of the strange invading groups of Easterners in their back-to-front caps as 'those movies', generally with disdain.

The first studio in Hollywood was established there as the result of a toss of a coin. Al Christie, chief director of the Centaur Co., wanted to make westerns in California, since he was tired of having to simulate sagebrush country in New Jersey. Centaur's owner, David Horsley, thought that Florida would be better, but agreed to abide by a heads-or-tails decision. Christie tossed and won. After viewing various possible sites in Southern California, he found a derelict roadhouse on Sunset Boulevard which looked suitable and cost only $40 a month to rent. This building was converted into a studio in October 1911. It was called the Nestor Studio, after the name of the western branch of the company. Today the site is occupied by the West Coast headquarters of CBS. By the end of the following year there were 15 film companies operating in Hollywood. Uninterrupted sunshine and a comforting distance from the agents of the Patents Co. were not the only attractions of Southern California as a film-making base. The astonishing range and variety of its scenery enabled locations to be found that could reasonably represent any terrain from Cornwall to the Urals; westerns could be located in the real west rather than New Jersey, South Sea island pictures could be shot on Catalina and neighbouring islands, an oil field in Los Angeles itself served for Texan oilman dramas, Spanish missions set the scene for old Mexico, and there were even sufficient baronial mansions to cater for the needs of pictures playing in Hollywood's England. Only a jungle was missing, but studios like Selig and Universal established their own zoos and built their African locales on the backlot.

The first talking picture made in Hollywood was a Fox Movietone short *They're Coming to Get Me* (US 26), with comedian Chic Sale, released in May 1926.

THE CELEBRATED HOLLYWOOD SIGN

The sign was erected on Hollywood Hills in 1923 at a cost of $21,000. Originally the sign spelt out the word HOLLYWOODLAND, in letters 30 ft (9 m) wide and 50 ft (15 m) tall and built up from 3 × 9 ft (1 × 3 m) sheet metal panels attached to a scaffolding frame. Each letter was studded with 20-watt light bulbs at eight-inch intervals. A man called Albert Kothe, who lived on the job—in a hut behind one of the 'L's'—was employed full time to change the bulbs when they burned out. The sign has often been featured in movies as a means of establishing locale, most recently in *The Day of the Locust* (US 75) and *1941* (US 79). It has been put to more macabre use for frequent suicide attempts. First to take a death dive from the top of the sign was failed starlet Peg Entwhistle in 1932.

Declared an historic landmark in 1973, the original and much dilapidated sign was replaced five years later after a fund for this purpose had been established by Gene Autry, Alice Cooper and Playboy chief Hugh Hefner. The new sign cost $27,000 for each letter. The remains of the old one were sold to a Mr Hank Berger, who cut the scrap metal into one-inch squares and retailed them to the more obsessive nostalgia buffs at $29.95 a time.

Longest Films

The longest film ever made was the underground movie titled *The Longest Most Meaningless Movie in the World* (GB 70), produced by Anthony Scott in association with the Swiss Film Centre, London, directed by Vincent Patouillard and featuring Hermine Demoriane, Roger Dixon, Graham Stevens, Carla Liss and Martine Meringue. It was premièred in its original 48-hr version at the Cinémathèque de Paris in October 1970.

The longest commercially-made film was *The Burning of the Red Lotus Temple* (Chn 28–31), adapted by the Star Film Co. from a newspaper serial *Strange Tales of the Adventurer in the Wild Country* by Shang K'ai-jan. It was released in 18 feature-length parts over a period of three years. Although never shown publicly in its 27-hr entirety, some cinemas would put on all-day performances of half-a-dozen parts in sequence.

The longest commercially-made American movie to be released uncut was Erich von Stroheim's *Foolish Wives* (US 22), which was distributed to Latin American countries in its original 6 hr 24 min version. In the United States, however, it was seen only in a severely cut form, a 12-reel version for the road show and a 10-reel version for general release.

The 42-reel version of von Stroheim's masterpiece *Greed* (US 24)—**Hollywood's longest-ever film in its original form**—was shown only once at a 9-hr screening at MGM on 12 January 1924. Idwal Jones, drama critic of the *San Francisco Daily News*, who was present, commented that it had 'every comma of the book put in'. It was subsequently cut to 24 reels by an aggrieved von Stroheim, who had already spent four unpaid months editing the original footage down to 48 reels; then to 18 reels by Rex Ingram, and finally 10 reels by Joe Farnham. The 32 reels of cut negative were melted down by MGM to retrieve the minute quantity of silver nitrate they contained.

The longest commercially-made American movie shown in America was the ill-fated $43 million epic *Cleopatra* (US 63) at a seemingly endless 4 hr 3 min. The only other Hollywood productions longer than *Gone with the Wind* (US 39), which ran for 3 hr 40 min,

Dedication of the Hollywood sign 1923. Originally it marked a real-estate development. (*Bruce Torrence Historical Collection, c/o Pacific Federal Savings*)

were *The Greatest Story Ever Told* (US 65) at 3 hr 45 min and Bob Dylan's 3 hr 55 min *Renaldo and Clara* (US 77). Otto Preminger's *Exodus* (US 60) was exactly the same length as *Gone with the Wind*. Prior to *Gone with the Wind* the record for the longest Hollywood talkie was held by MGM's *The Great Ziegfeld* (US 36), which ran for 2 hr 59 min.

The longest commercially-made British film was A. E. Coleby's *The Prodigal Son* (GB 23), a Stoll Film Co. production from the novel by Hall Caine, shot on location in Iceland, and starring Stewart Rome. The 4 hr 40 min picture was released in two parts, one of eight and the other of nine reels. **The longest commercially-made talkie** was David Lean's 3 hr 42 min *Lawrence of Arabia* (GB 62), which was two minutes longer than *Gone with the Wind.*

The longest film to be shown commercially in its entirety was Rainer Werner Fassbinder's 15 hr 21 min opus *Berlin Alexanderplatz* (FRG 83) at the Vista cinema in Hollywood on 6–7 August 1983. Tickets cost $20 and there was a two-hour break for dinner. The slightly longer *Heimat* (FRG 84), at 15 hr 40 min, was shown in several German cities and at the London Film Festival during 1984, but these were weekend shows with a night in between the first half and the second.

Cinema Museums

The first cinema museum was the Čescoslovenskyé Filmové Museum, founded by Jindřrich Brichta at Prague in 1923.

The first cinema museum in America was the Crocker Museum which Charles Chaplin's assistant Harry Crocker, who had a mania for collecting movie memorabilia, established on Sunset Boulevard, Hollywood in 1928. The exhibits consisted of props and

---

FILMS RUNNING FOUR HOURS
The following are films shown in public in a version lasting four hours or longer. The list includes films issued in parts, but not serials. The duration of the silent films listed is calculated on the assumption that they were projected at 16 f.p.s.

4 hr
 Chusingura (Jap 55)
 Gosta Berlings Saga (Swe 24)
 Heaven's Gate (US 81)[1]
 Ludwig (It/Fr/FRG 73)[2]
4 hr 3 min
 Cleopatra (US 63)
4 hr 5 min
 The Keys of Happiness (Rus 13)
 Siberiade (USSR 79)
4 hr 12 min
 L'Amour Fou (Fr 68)
4 hr 15 min
 Parsifal (FRG/Fr 82)
 Paths of Life (GDR 81)
 Molière (Fr 78)
 Out 1: Spectre (Fr 72)
 Mera Naam Joker (Ind 70)
4 hr 16 min
 The Age of Cosimo de Medici (It 72)
 Gustaf Wasa (Swe 28)
4 hr 17 min
 Les Plouffe (Can 81)
4 hr 20 min
 Amor der Perdicao (Por 80)
 The Greatest Story Ever Told (US 62)[3]
 Rubens (Neth 78)
4 hr 25 min
 The Idiot (Jap 51)
4 hr 30 min
 Measure for Measure (Bul 81)
 Imagen de Caracas (Ven 68)
 The Great Citizen (USSR 38)
 Le Chagrin et la Pitié (Fr 70)
 La Hora de los Hornos (Arg 68)
4 hr 34 min
 Atvaltozas/Point of Departure (Hun 84)
4 hr 38 min
 The Memory of Justice (FRG 76)
4 hr 40 min
 Amerikanske Billeder (Den 81)
 The Prodigal Son (GB 23)
4 hr 45 min
 Rameau's Nephew by Diderot (Can 74)

4 hr 58 min
 Percal (Mex 50)
5 hr 2 min
 Winifred Wagner und die Geschichte des Hauses Wahnfried (FRG 75)
5 hr 5 min
 Les Misérables (Fr 27)
5 hr 6 min
 Petersburgskije truscoby (Rus 15)
5 hr 14 min
 Potop/The Deluge (Pol 74)
5 hr 16 min
 1900 (It 78)
5 hr 20 min
 Vindicta (Fr 23)
5 hr 32 min
 Les Misérables (Fr 33)
5 hr 50 min
 Fanny and Alexander (Swe 83)[4]
5 hr 54 min
 Soldati Svobodi (USSR/Bul/Hun/Cz/GDR/ Rom/Pol 77)
6 hr
 Idade de Terra (Bra 79)
 Khan Asparouch (Bul 82)
6 hr 10 min
 Die Nibelungen (Ger 24)
6 hr 24 min
 Foolish Wives (US 22)[5]
6 hr 30 min
 Sleep (US 63)
6 hr 40 min
 Hitler: a Film from Germany (FRG 77)
7 hr
 Der Hund von Baskerville (Ger 14–20)
7 hr 45 min
 Francais si vous savez (Fr 73)
7 hr 58 min
 Iskry Plamja (Rus 25)
8 hr
 Empire (US 64)
8 hr 27 min
 War and Peace (USSR 63–67)[6]
8 hr 32 min
 La Roue (Fr 21)[7]
9 hr
 Wagner (GB/Hun/Aut 83)[8]
 Napoleon (Fr 27)[9]
9 hr 29 min
 The Human Condition (Jap 58–60)

12 hr 40 min
 Out 1: Noli me Tangerey (Fr 71)[10]
12 hr 43 min
 Comment Yukong deplace les montagnes (Fr 76)
13 hr
 The Old Testament (It 22)
15 hr 21 min
 Berlin Alexanderplatz (FRG/It 80)[11]
15 hr 40 min
 Heimat (FRG 84)
24 hr
 * * * * (US 67)[12]
27 hr
 The Burning of the Red Lotus Temple (Chn 28–31)
48 hr
 The Longest Most Meaningless Movie in the World (GB 70)[13]

[1] Long version shown Venice Film Festival 1982 and elsewhere.
[2] General release print 3 hr; 4-hr version shown Rome 1980, Paris 1983.
[3] At première only. Release prints were 3 hr 58 min.
[4] Long version shown at Venice Film Festival 1983.
[5] Released at this length in South America only. US general release: 10 reels.
[6] Russian language version. English language version 6 hr 13 min.
[7] Released in 4-hr version, but VGIK in Moscow has print of 8½ hr original.
[8] Premièred in 9-hr entirety at Dominion, Tottenham Court Road, May 1983. Release version 5 hr.
[9] Abel Gance's 42-reel version définitive; trade and press shown at the Apollo, Paris in 1927 and believed to have been shown commercially in Nice and other provincial centres. The version shown at the Paris première was 3 hr 40 min. The 5 hr 13 min version reconstructed by Kevin Brownlow was first shown at Le Havre on 13 November 1983.
[10] Shown only once at this length, then re-edited as 4½-hr *Out 1: Spectre*.
[11] Long version: see **Longest film shown commercially** entry above.
[12] Shown only once, then re-edited as two features of conventional length.
[13] Premièred at this length, then cut to 1½ hr.

CINEMA MUSEUMS

The following museums are either wholly devoted to cinema or have substantial cinema collections. Film archives are only included if they also administer a museum.

ARGENTINA
Museo Municipal de Arte Moderno, Mendoza.
AUSTRALIA
Australian Film Institute Museum, Canberra.
Movie Museum, Buderim.
AUSTRIA
Osterreichisches Filmmuseum, Vienna.
BELGIUM
Musée du Cinéma, Brussels.
Musée de la Photographie et du Cinéma, Brussels.
Provinciaal Museum voor Kunstambachten het Sterckshof, Deurne.
BRAZIL
Embrafilme Cinema Museum, Rio de Janeiro.
The Cinema Museum, São Paulo.
CZECHOSLOVAKIA
Museum of Animated and Puppet Films, Kratochvile Castle, Bohemia.
DENMARK
Det Danske Filmmuseum, Copenhagen.

FRANCE
Film Museum, Palais de Chaillot, Paris.
Musée du Cinéma, Rue de Courcelles, Paris.
Musée du Cinéma, Lyons (Lumière collection).
GERMANY, DEM. REP. OF
Kreismuseum, Bitterfeld.
GERMANY, FED. REP. OF
Munich City Museum (Film and Photography Department).
Deutsches Film Museum, Frankfurt-am-Main.
GREAT BRITAIN
Barnes Museum of Cinematography, St Ives, Cornwall.
The National Museum of Photography, Film and Television, Bradford.
Laurel & Hardy Museum, Ulverston, Cumbria (birthplace of Stan Laurel).
Buckingham Movie Museum (home movies).
The Museum of the Moving Image, South Bank, London (due to open *c.* 1986).
ITALY
Museo Nazionale del Cinema, Turin.
MEXICO
Cinematica Luis Bunuel, Puebla.
Cinematica Mexicana, Mexico City.

NETHERLANDS
Stichting Nederlands Filmmuseum, Amsterdam.
NORWAY
Norsk Filminstitutt, Oslo.
SWEDEN
Asta Nielsen Filmmuseum, Lund.
SWITZERLAND
Museum des Films, Basel.
USA
Tom Mix Museum, Dewey, Oklahoma.
Will Rogers Memorial, Claremore, Oklahoma.
International Museum of Photography, George Eastman House, Rochester, NY.
Museum of Modern Art, New York.
Hollywood Stuntmen's Hall of Fame, Mojave, California.
The Hollywood Museum, 7051 Hollywood Boulevard (opened 1984).
USSR
Ukrainian State Museum of Theatrical, Musical and Cinema Art, Kiev.
Cinema History Museum, Odessa (history of cinema in Georgia).
The Eisenstein Museum, Moscow (housed in Eisenstein's widow's small apartment).
YUGOSLAVIA
Muzej Jugoslavenske Kinoteke, Belgrade.

costumes from silent movies, including Chaplin's original tramp costume, Harold Lloyd's glasses, William S. Hart's first leather chaps, Keaton's pancake boater, Gloria Swanson's 'Sadie Thompson' costume, the cabin that tottered on the brink from *The Gold Rush* (US 24), and the winning chariot from *Ben Hur* (US 26).

Publicity

The largest publicity budget was the $24 million spent by the Samuel Goldwyn Co. on the launch of *The Care Bears Movie* (US 85). It is not unknown for the publicity budget to exceed the production cost of a film. A notable example was the Brooke Shields starrer *The Blue Lagoon* (US 80), another Columbia release, which cost $4·5 million to make but $6·3 million to promote.

SLOGANS

Slogans extolling movies have tended towards hyperbole ever since impresario George Belmont announced his presentation of the 'Theatrograph' at Sadler's Wells in 1896 with the words: 'A mighty mirror of Promethean Photographs and a superb, brilliant, and electrifying entertainment specially adapted to cheer the toiling millions'.

A travelling bioscope showman encountered by a correspondent of *The Pelican* in a Kentish village in 1908 stretched credulity with a sign proclaiming: 'The most extraordinary invention of modern times, as presented before the Emperor Napoleon!'

Impressive figures have often engaged the attention of publicists. India's first feature film *Raja Harischandra* (Ind 12) was advertised as 'a performance with 57,000 photographs . . . a picture two miles in length . . . all for only three annas!' *After Rain, Clear Sky* (Chn 31), one of China's earliest all-talkies, was promoted with the information that 'on the 977 occasions for dialogue, 6935 sentences are spoken'. The quantitative attractions of Twentieth Century-Fox's *The Egyptian* (US 54) stimulated a slogan writer to even greater flights of figurative fancy with the claim that it had '10,965 pyramids, 5337 dancing girls, one million swaying bulrushes, 802 sacred bulls'.

Promoting a film to the wrong audience may be deliberate, in the case of a weak attraction, or perpetrated through sheer ignorance. In 1918 a Chicago theatre urged: 'Tomorrow—Ibsen's *Doll's House*— Bring the Kiddies!' Equally inappropriate was a Toronto cinema's slogan for David Lean's gentle evocation of middle-aged suburban romance *Brief Encounter* (GB 45): 'Girls who live dangerously'. A cinema on New York's 42nd Street, an area noted for vice, booked a nature film titled *The Love Life of a Gorilla* (US 37) and brought the crowds flocking in with a poster asking the searing question 'Do native women live with apes?' Anyone paying good money to see the film was rewarded with the answer—they don't.

Carl Laemmle knew that what audiences really want

What Hollywood publicists lack in finesse they make up for in originality. Patrons of *Blood Feast* (US 63) were supplied with paper bags to be sick into.

is escapist nonsense and signalled the fact loud and clear by billing his *Fighting American* (US 24) as the picture 'guaranteed not to make you think'.

Attempts to summarise the story in a phrase could involve criminal assault on the English language. *Bridal Suite* (US 39) was encapsulated: 'Howl Bent for Laugh Heaven, Four Zanies Tangle with Cock-Eyed Love'. Real extravagance of prose style, though, was reserved for the epics. Cecil B. De Mille's *King of Kings* (US 27) was advertised in New York as abounding in 'Dramatic Magnificence, Spectacular Splendor, Riotous Joy, Tigerish Rage, Undying Love, Terrifying Tempests, Appalling Earthquakes'. (Audiences might be forgiven for not recognising this as the story of the Gospels.)

In contrast, publicity could hardly be more downbeat than the announcement on the marquee of a drive-in in Cleveland County, NC in 1960: 'Two Features'. The manager explained that he never advertised the titles of the films because 'the people who patronise this drive-in don't care what's playing'.

Devastating honesty was seldom an attribute of movie publicists, but individual cinema managers would occasionally give a frank opinion of their offerings. In 1947 an exhibitor in Hastings, Neb. announced: 'Double Feature—One Good Show and One Stinker'.

Slogans could be used to take a side-swipe at another star. Fox's advertising to promote George O'Brien in *The Iron Horse* (US 24), which declared 'He's not a Sheik or a Caveman or a Lounge Lizard—He is a Man's Man and An Idol of Women', was clearly meant to draw a denigratory comparison with Latin lover Rudolph Valentino.

If the star was not the main attraction, someone else might be. When Oscar, the well-known Negro bootblack on the Paramount lot, played a bit part in *Gambling Ship* (US 33), a black cinema on Los Angeles' Central Avenue billed the film with the legend: 'Sensational star in *Gambling Ship*, Oscar supported by Cary Grant'. The pictures outside were entirely of Oscar.

There is nothing like a good scandal to hype an indifferent picture. Released at the time of the Profumo affair, *The Man who Couldn't Walk* (US/Can 64) was billed as 'the story behind the scandal that shocked London ... baring untold secrets of vice, intrigue and international party girls'. What was actually delivered on screen amounted to no more than a routine meller about safecrackers. There was no character remotely resembling the Defence Minister and none that bore any connection with Miss Keiler.

Another attempt at topicality was made by the British distributors of a florid Indian romance titled *Red Rose* (Ind 82). The original slogan ran 'Petals from a beautiful film flower named Red Rose', to which some enterprising publicist had added 'Adapted from "The Yorkshire Ripper"'.

Howard Hughes made immediate impact with the posters promoting his controversial picture *The Outlaw* (US 43) when it was briefly released in 1943 before being withdrawn again. The slogan—'Mean, Moody and Magnificent'—was spread below a picture of a rampant-breasted Jane Russell standing bare-legged bestride a haystack with a pistol in each fist. When released in 1946 a far more decorous though equally striking copy-line had taken its place, a quote from Judge Twain Michelsen, who had tried the film for indecency: 'We have seen Jane Russell. She is an attractive specimen of American womanhood. God made her what she is.'

Briefer, but equally apt, was the slogan promoting Tony Richardson's *The Loved One* (US 65): 'The Picture with Something to Offend Everyone'. Briefer still and perhaps even more effective was the slogan accompanying *Baby Doll* (US 56): 'Condemned by Cardinal Spellman'.

POSTERS

The most valuable movie poster to be sold at auction was for Disney's *Alice in the Jungle* (US 25), offered for sale by Collector's Showcase in Hollywood in October 1980. It was bought by a San Francisco Disneyana collector for $5400—nearly three times the total production cost of the movie itself, which was made for $1900.

BEST SELLING POSTERS
In 1981 a survey was made of the best selling repro movie posters in London ephemera shops. The top ten were:
  1 *Casablanca* (US 42)
  2 *Rebel without a Cause* (US 55)
  3 *Some Like It Hot* (US 59)
  4 *A Fistful of Dollars* (It/FRG/Sp 64)
  5 *Doctor No* (GB 62)
  6 *The Painted Veil* (US 34)
  7 *The Blue Angel* (Ger 30)
  8 *Duck Soup* (US 33)
  9 *The Mask of Fu Manchu* (US 32)
  10 *King Kong* (US 33)

PUBLICITY STUNTS

These began decorously enough in the early days of cinema and became progressively more outrageous during the days of Hollywood's greatest extravagances, the 1920s. Initially a little ingenuity was made to go a long way. One of the earliest stunts, reported by *Kinematograph Weekly* in 1907, was dreamed up by the proprietor of a Chicago nickelodeon who had letters printed in simulated handwriting purporting to be from a girl called Lizzie, on a visit to the city, writing to her friend Mary about an exciting excursion to the cinema. They were scattered in the streets and the advertiser relied on the baser human impulse to read other people's letters. Other gimmicks employed in the USA prior to World War I included making arrangements with grocers to give 13 eggs for every dozen ordered, the extra egg being paid for by the cinema and stamped with details of the next attraction; distributing oversized neckties of a garish hue and

In the twenties and thirties every big picture was ballyhooed with publicity stunts organised by local exhibitors. This not very hostile looking tank was helping to boost *The Big Parade* (US 25) into the biggest grossing silent picture of all time.

offering free seats to any man willing to wear one throughout the performance; and giving free admission to anyone slender enough to pass through a narrow wicket set up in the lobby or alternatively short enough to pass under a low bar.

The Vaudette Theater of West Point, Ga. announced that they would be giving away a free 'one-piece coat and garment hanger' to every patron on an advertised date in 1914. Those who attended were handed a very small envelope which contained a two-inch nail. The distributors of *Neptune's Daughter* (US 14), in which Annette Kellerman was clad in rather less than that customary for the period, sent out 36-inch tape measures which bore, at appropriate intervals, Miss Kellerman's vital statistics.

When Kalem reissued *The Colleen Bawn* (US 11), they had several tons of earth shipped from Killarney to New York and made up into four foot square sods for distribution to cinemas exhibiting the film. For the price of a theatre ticket, Irish immigrants could savour the pleasure of once again standing on Irish soil.

One of the most sure-fire stunts, repeated in small towns all over the USA from about 1912, was known as

'Giving Away a Baby'. The exhibitor announced that a baby would be given away on the stage on a certain day. He then arranged for someone to write to the local newspaper deploring this act of inhumanity, to which the cinema manager would reply in a hurt tone saying that the baby had made no objection and the mother was indifferent to its fate. This would provoke a shoal of letters, a lively public debate in the community, and threats of police prosecution. On the appointed night a packed house, usually including a contingent of police, would see the manager give away a baby pig.

The first of the great press agent hoaxes was perpetrated by the publicist for Thanhouser's serial *The Million Dollar Mystery* (US 14), who gave an anonymous tip-off to the police and newspapers that an heiress had disappeared. For seven days the police hunt continued, while Thanhouser's press agent fed them with information that paralleled the action of the forthcoming film. When the deception was exposed, the 'missing heiress' turned out to be the heroine of *The Million Dollar Mystery*.

Ace publicist Harry Reichenbach stimulated public interest in *The Virgin of Stamboul* (US 20) by conning the New York police into dragging a lake in Central Park for the body of the virgin. Meanwhile a Turkish Government Commission (recruited from loafers in Turkish coffee houses on the East Side) was installed at the Hotel Navarre to provide a focus for press attention.

> One good movie deserves another. Producer Bryan Foy claimed that he made ten other films with the same plot as his successful *Tiger Shark* (US 32) simply by changing the names, locale and title.

As a promotion for the serial *Bride 13* (US 20), the manager of the Lyric Theater at Easley, S. Carolina persuaded an engaged couple to be married in front of the screen immediately following the first episode. A capacity audience watched the event, which included an unscheduled moment of drama when the bride's mother, who was present but had no idea that her daughter was involved in the stunt, shouted 'Stop!' from the stalls. She was persuaded, in the interests of her daughter's happiness and the manager's profits, to let the show go on.

Hollywood's tsars were not above a little stunt work themselves. Carl Laemmle turned the expensive luxury of employing Erich von Stroheim as a director to good account by erecting a mammoth electric sign on Broadway flashing out the prodigious budget allocated for *Foolish Wives* (US 22), then in the course of its year-long shooting schedule. As von Stroheim's extravagances pushed the budget even higher, Laemmle arranged for the New York Fire Brigade to tear down Broadway every Wednesday to change the light bulbs to the latest spiralling figure. The 'S' in Stroheim was replaced on the billboard by a $ sign.

It was about this period that publicity stunts involving stars reached their apogee. During a dip in Valentino's popularity, Harry Reichenbach, arch-exponent of ballyhoo, persuaded the great lover to grow a beard, and then proceeded to orchestrate a chorus of protest from outraged legions of female fans and the proprietors of barber shops. A few months later he arranged a ceremonial debearding by experts nominated by the Master Barbers of America.

To promote Raoul Walsh's *The Honor System* (US 25), the producers arranged for a practical demonstration of the 'honor' system in action, with a prisoner being released for a single day on his honour to return. Alas, he was not seen again.

Another stunt that backfired was the misguided one perpetrated by Universal when *The Phantom of the Opera* (US 25) was brought to England. By some means the studio publicity department persuaded Lt. Col. W. H. Barrell, Commanding Officer of the 153rd Heavy Brigade of the Royal Artillery, to give the English release prints a military escort from Southampton docks to the station and from Waterloo to Wardour Street. For the ceremonial march through London, the prints were preceded not only by troops but also an armoured car and a full regimental band. Press and public were equally scandalised by the vulgarity of the operation and the 'outrage on British troops', as one newspaper put it. There was a full-scale War Office enquiry and questions were asked in the House. To make matters worse, Universal's English representative, James Bryson, confessed that the military had been escorting empty boxes, since the prints of *The Phantom of the Opera* had been left safely in his trunks on the *Berengaria*, the liner which had brought them from New York. The uproar was so great that the film was never released in Britain and when, some years later, there was a second and more discreet attempt to bring it over, permission was flatly refused.

When *The Man I Killed* (US 32) went on release, an American exhibitor engaged a man to be buried alive for 24 hours. Unfortunately a storm during the night obliterated the grave marker and long after the 24 hours were up a team of 30 rescuers were desperately digging to release the entombed man. His first demand on being brought to the surface was for overtime pay.

Publicist Pete Smith was inspired with the idea of getting Sam Goldwyn to say that there were only 13 real actors in Hollywood and to name them. Goldwyn liked the stunt, but for the fact that he felt that as a result he would only be on speaking terms with 13 actors. He found the solution himself, naming twelve of the actors and leaving Hollywood to guess the name of the 13th.

Mom and Dad aka *A Family Story* (US 47), an exploitation movie with a live childbirth scene, was shown to sexually segregated audiences. According to publicity, this was 'so as not to offend the delicate'. To improve the effect, promotional manager Joe Solomon arranged to have a nauseous chemical put into the ventilation system and then called the local press to take pictures of the women reeling and retching out of the cinema. This ensured a full house of men in the evening.

When *Psycho* (US 60) was released, producer–director Alfred Hitchcock had it written into every booking contract that no one was to be admitted after the film began. The master showman created a publicity gimmick that was actually enforceable in law.

Remakes

The longest interval between remakes with the same actor playing the same role was 34 years in the case of Tito Lusiardo's performances in *El Dia que me Quitas*/*The Day You Leave Me* (US 35 and Arg 69).

The story which has been remade the most times is Cinderella, of which there have been 69 productions since 1898, including cartoon, modern, ballet, operatic, pornographic and parody versions (see filmography).

Right
Jeanne d'Alcy played an earthy, peasant Cinderella in the earliest French version of the immortal story, *Cendrillon* (Fr 99).

CINDERELLA FILMOGRAPHY

In the following filmography the player performing the title role precedes the title (if known):

Laura Bayley *Cinderella and the Fairy Godmother* (GB 98)
Jeanne d'Alcy *Cendrillon* (Fr 99)
Cendrillon (Fr 02) talking version
Cinderella (GB 05) not in Gifford's *British Film Catalogue*; shown as *Askepot* in 10-part version at Kosmorama, Copenhagen 27 July 1905
Dolly Lupone *Cinderella* (GB 07)
Louise Legrange *Cendrillon* (Fr 07)
Cenerentola (It 08)
Cendrillon (Fr 09)
Florence LaBadie *Cinderella* (US 11)
Mabel Taliaferro *Cinderella* (US 11)
Louise Legrange *Cendrillon ou le pantouffle mysterieuse* (Fr 12)
Cinderella (GB 12) animated toys
Fernanda Negri Pouget *Cenerentola* (It 13)
Lillian Walker *Cinderella's Slipper* (US 13)
Gertie Potter *Cinderella* (GB 13)
Cinderella and the Boob (US 13)
Daisy Dormer *Potted Pantomimes* (GB 14)
Cinderella (US 14) Selig version
Mary Pickford *Cinderella* (US 14) Famous Players version
Cinderella and the Magic Slipper (US 18)
Agnes Ayres *Forbidden Fruit* (US 21) story told in flashback sequence
Viola Dana *Cinderella's Twin* (US 21) modern version

Aschenputtel (Ger 22) Lotte Reiniger silhouette film
Helga Thomas *Der verlorene Schuh* (Ger 23)
Cinderella (US 25) Dinkey Doodle cartoon
Betty Bronson *A Kiss for Cinderella* (US 25) story recalled in dream sequence
Cinderella (US 30) Krazy Kat cartoon
Cinderella (US 33) Terry-Toon cartoon
Poor Cinderella (US 34)
Joan Warner *Cendrillon* (Fr 37)
The Glass Slipper (US 38) Terry-Toon cartoon
Deanna Durbin *First Love* (US 39) modern version
Lubova Orlova *Bright Path* (USSR 40) Communist interpretation of story
Juanita Quigley *Cinderella's Fella* (US 40)
Cinderella Goes to a Party (US 42)
M. Shapiro *Cinderella* (USSR 47)
Billy Daniels *Sepia Cinderella* (US 47) black version
Lori Landi *Cenerentola* (It 49) opera
Erase una Vez (Sp 50) cartoon feature
Ilene Woods (voice) *Cinderella* (US 50) cartoon feature
Leslie Caron *The Glass Slipper* (US 54)
Rita-Maria Nowotny *Aschenputtel* (FRG 55)
Renee Stobrawa *Aschenputtel* (GDR 55)
Cinderella (US 58)
Jerry Lewis *Cinderfella* (US 60) male parody
Raissa Stroutckova *The Glass Slipper* (USSR 61) ballet film
Suzanne Sybele *SINderella and the Golden Bra* (US 64) soft porn

Lesley Ann Warren *Cinderella* (US 65) Rodgers & Hammerstein TVM musical
Princess Cinderella (US c. 67)
Cinderella (GB? 67) cartoon
Hey Cinderella (Can 68) Jim Henson puppet and live action combo
Marja Kok *Cinderella Comes Back* (Neth 69)
Rindercella (US 70) porno movie
Eva Reuber-Staier *Grimm's Fairy Stories for Adults* (FRG 71) soft porn
Sinderella (GB 72) porno cartoon
Libuša Saffanková *Three Nuts for Cinderella* (Cz 73)
Meena Rai *Rani aur Lalpuri* (Ind 73)
Cinderella (Sp 76) feature cartoon
Cheryl Smith *Cinderella*/GB title *The Other Cinderella* (US 76) soft porn
Gemma Craven *The Slipper and the Rose* (GB 76)
Catherine Erhardt *Cinderella 2000* (US 77) musical parody
Cinderella (Iran 77)
A Fairy Story (GB 78) updated version
Cinderella (GDR/Cz 79)
Cinderella (GB 79) puppet film
Cinderella (Yug 79) animated
Jane Laurie *The Last of Linda Cleer* (GB 81) modern version ('Linda Cleer' anagram of 'Cinderella')
Frederica von Stade *Cenerentola* (It 81) opera
Bonnie Bianco *Cinderella 80* (It 84) modern version billed as 'the first rock fairytale'.

Left
Mary Pickford starred in the first feature-length *Cinderella* in 1914. Many others were to follow, including rival West German and East German versions in 1955 and a succession of porno versions in the sixties and seventies.

Right
Helga Thomas (*above left*) played a traditionally frail and waiflike Cinderella in *Der verlorene Schuh* (Ger 23), in contrast to Lori Landi's buxom wench (*below*) in the operatic version *Cenerentola* (It 49).

Above right
The knowing look in Cheryl Smith's eyes is not there by accident. *Cinderella* (US 76) was one of a number of porno versions of the well-loved fairy tale.

The following works have had twelve or more movies based on them: *Carmen* (Merimée's story and Bizet's opera)—52 + 2 parody versions; Shakespeare's *Hamlet*—42 + 9 parody versions; *Faust* (Marlowe, Goethe and Gunod's opera)—47; R. L. Stevenson's *Dr Jekyll and Mr Hyde*—45 (including parodies and variants); Defoe's *Robinson Crusoe*—38 (inc. 2 porno); Dumas fils' *La Dame aux camelias*—36; Cervantes' *Don Quixote*—34; Dumas père's *The Three Musketeers*—30 + 10 variants featuring the character d'Artagnan; Shakespeare's *Romeo and Juliet*—28 + 5 modern + 8 parodies; Shakespeare's *Macbeth*—26 + 2 modern versions + 1 parody; Hugo's *Les Misérables*—28; the Hindu epic *Harischandra*—25 in 9 languages; Dumas père's *The Count of Monte Cristo*—21 + 13 variants featuring the character Edmund Dantes; Tolstoy's *Resurrection*—23; Dickens' *Oliver Twist*—21; Shakespeare's *A Midsummer Night's Dream*—19; Shakespeare's *Julius Caesar*—18 + 1 modern version; Dickens' *A Christmas Carol*—18; *William Tell* (Schiller and legend)—15; Dostoevsky's *Crime and Punishment*—15; Shakespeare's *Othello*—14; Harriet Beecher Stowe's *Uncle Tom's Cabin*—14; Tolstoy's *Anna Karenina*—13; Tolstoy's *The Living Corpse*—13; Dumas père's *The Corsican Brothers*—13; Mrs Henry Wood's *East Lynne*—13; Shakespeare's *King Lear*—12; Lewis Carroll's *Alice in Wonderland*—12.

DECLINE OF THE REMAKE

Remakes, at one time a staple of Hollywood product, appear to be in decline. In 1981 they accounted for some 3 per cent of N. American rentals, in 1982 for 4 per cent, but in 1983 only 1 per cent. In contrast, series films and sequels average about 12 per cent of market share.

Sequels

The longest interval between a sequel and its original was 34 years in the case of *The Maltese Falcon* (US 41) and *The Black Bird* (US 75) and a similar period between *National Velvet* (US 44) and *International Velvet* (GB 78). In *The Black Bird* George Segal played Sam Spade's son, who has inherited Effie (Lee Patrick), the elder Spade's secretary in *The Maltese Falcon*, along with his father's detective agency. Miss Patrick had also played Effie in the 1941 picture. The role of Velvet grown up in *International Velvet* was offered to Elizabeth Taylor, who had played the child

Lee Patrick looks as if she had a higher regard for the cigarette-smoking Humphrey Bogart in *The Maltese Falcon* (US 41) than she had for cigar-chomping George Segal in the sequel, *The Black Bird* (US 75) (*right*).

Velvet when she was 12 years old, but she turned it down and the role was played with mature dignity and charm by Nanette Newman. The star of the picture was Tatum O'Neal as Velvet's niece from America, who comes to live with her aunt in Britain, becomes a show-jumper, and wins an Olympic Gold Medal.

The first 'roman numeral' sequel was *Quatermass II* (GB 57), the follow-up to *The Quatermass Experiment* (GB 54).

The longest interval between a 'I' and 'II' picture was 23 years in the case of Alfred Hitchcock's *Psycho* (US 60) and Richard Franklin's *Psycho II* (US 83). Anthony Perkins returned in his role as the psychotic murderer Norman Bates, released after spending 22 years in a mental institution.

The sequel that wasn't. *Surf II* (US 82) was a cod—there had never been a *Surf I*.

'PREQUELS'

These are sequels that relate the story that *preceded* the original film. *Another Part of the Forest* (US 47) recounted the earlier lives of the Hubbard family portrayed in *The Little Foxes* (US 41); Steve McQueen's title role in *Nevada Smith* (US 66) centred on the earlier life

Left: Elizabeth Taylor as Velvet in *National Velvet* (US 44).
Above: Thirty-four years later Tatum O'Neal played Velvet's niece in the sequel, *International Velvet* (GB 78).

of the character played by Alan Ladd in *The Carpetbaggers* (US 64); Michael Winner's *The Night Comers* (GB 71) told the story of how the ghosts in *The Innocents* (GB 61)—the manservant Quint and the 'former governess'—lost their lives; *Rhapsody* (US 54), from Henry Handel Richardson's novel *Maurice Guest*, was followed 25 years later by the film of the preceding volume of the story, *The Getting of Wisdom* (Aus 79), Richard Lester's *Butch and Sundance—The Early Days* (US 79) recounts the story of how the outlaw pair (Tom Berenger and William Katt) met and teamed up together, while the earlier George Roy Hill picture *Butch Cassidy and the Sundance Kid* (US 69) related the events leading up to the death of Butch and Sundance (Paul Newman and Robert Redford) in a shoot-out with the Bolivian army. Zoltán Fábri brought Jósef Baláz's novel *Hungarians* (Hun 79) to the screen before embarking on the preceding story of the hero's father in his youth, told in *Bálint Fábián's Encounter with God* (Hun 80). Both Bálint Fábián and his son András were played by the same actor, Gábor Koncz. *Indiana Jones and the Temple of Doom* (US 84) was set in 1935, preceding by three years the action of the earlier Indiana Jones caper *Raiders of the Lost Ark* (US 81).

3 Box Office and Budgets

Box Office

The film seen by the most cinemagoers. There are no reliable figures to authenticate the most popular film of all time in terms of the highest number of paying patrons. However, *Mother India* (Ind 57), which has been on almost continuous release in various parts of India since 1957, is claimed by some authorities on Indian cinema to have been seen by more cinemagoers than *Gone With the Wind* (US 39).

The film with the highest earnings worldwide is *E.T. The Extra-Terrestial* (US 82), which has earned a gross $680 million in rentals by March 1985.

Previous box office champions were *Snow White and the Seven Dwarfs* (US 37), which was the first talkie to overtake the record for silent pictures set by *The Big Parade* (US 25) (see below); *Gone with the Wind* (US 39), which held the record from 1940 until overtaken by *The Sound of Music* (US 65) in August 1966 and again in 1971–2 as the result of a reissue; *The Godfather* (US 72), which set a new record the year of its release; and *Jaws* (US 75), also a record-breaker in its first year and box office champion until surpassed by *Star Wars* in 1977. The crown passed to *E.T. The Extra-Terrestrial* (US 82) in January 1983, 31 weeks after its release.

The top grossing silent film was King Vidor's *The Big Parade* (US 25), with worldwide rentals of $22 million. No exact figure is available for D. W. Griffith's *The Birth of a Nation* (US 15), which was long thought of as the top grossing silent, with estimates of up to $50 million receipts in the domestic market alone. This is now considered to be a wildly exaggerated figure, and *Variety* quotes $5 million as a reasonable 'guestimate'. Griffith himself stated in 1929 that the film had earned $10 million worldwide.

ANNUAL TOP MONEYMAKER USA
Prior to 1947 there are no consistent records. Since that date *Variety* has identified the following pictures as top moneymaker of the year in the domestic market (US and Canada). Where the top moneymaker is a non-American production, the top American grosser is listed second:
1947 *The Best Years of Our Lives*
1948 *The Road to Rio*
1949 *Jolson Sings Again*
1950 *Samson and Delilah*
1951 *David and Bathsheba*
1952 *The Greatest Show on Earth*
1953 *The Robe*
1954 *White Christmas*
1955 *Cinerama Holiday*
1956 *Guys and Dolls*
1957 *The Ten Commandments*
1958 *The Bridge on the River Kwai* (GB)
    Peyton Place (US)
1959 *Auntie Mame*
1960 *Ben Hur*
1961 *The Guns of Navarone* (GB)
    The Absent-Minded Professor (US)
1962 *Spartacus*
1963 *Cleopatra*
1964 *The Carpetbaggers*
1965 *Mary Poppins*
1966 *Thunderball* (GB)
    Doctor Zhivago (US)
1967 *The Dirty Dozen*
1968 *The Graduate*
1969 *The Love Bug*
1970 *Airport*
1971 *Love Story*
1972 *The Godfather*
1973 *The Poseidon Adventure*
1974 *The Sting*

1975 *Jaws*
1976 *One Flew Over the Cuckoo's Nest*
1977 *Star Wars*
1978 *Grease*
1979 *Superman* (GB)
    Every Which Way But Loose (US)
1980 *The Empire Strikes Back*
1981 *Raiders of the Lost Ark*
1982 *E.T. The Extra-Terrestrial*
1983 *Return of the Jedi*
1984 *Ghostbusters*
Of the 42 top grossers listed above, 9 were contemporary dramas, 8 were historical epics, 5 were comedies, 6 were musicals, 5 were science-fiction, 3 were war films, 2 were adventure films, one was a Bond movie and one a Cinerama travelogue. Only 2 took crime as a principal theme (*The Godfather* and *The Sting*).

ANNUAL TOP MONEYMAKER GB
The following have been the annual top moneymaking British films in the domestic market since 1936:
1936 *The Ghost Goes West*
1937 *Good Morning Boys*
1938 *A Yank at Oxford*
1939 *Pygmalion*
1940 *Convoy*
1941 *49th Parallel*
1942 *The First of the Few*
1943 *In Which We Serve*
1944 *This Happy Breed*
1945 *The Seventh Veil*
1946 *The Wicked Lady*
1947 *The Courtneys of Curzon Street*
1948 *Spring in Park Lane*
1949 *The Third Man*
1950 *The Blue Lamp*
1951 *Laughter in Paradise*

1952 *Where No Vultures Fly*
1953 *The Cruel Sea*
1954 *Doctor in the House*
1955 *The Dam Busters*
1956 *Reach for the Sky*
1957 *Doctor at Large*
1958 *The Bridge on the River Kwai*
1959 *Carry on Nurse*
1960 *Doctor in Love*
1961 *The Swiss Family Robinson*
1962 *The Young Ones*
1963 *From Russia with Love*
1964 *Goldfinger*
1965 *Help!*
1966 *Thunderball*
1967 *You Only Live Twice*
1968 *Up the Junction*
1969 *Oliver!*
1970 *Battle of Britain*
1971 *On the Buses*
1972 *Diamonds are Forever*
1973 *Live and Let Die*
1974 *Confessions of a Window Cleaner*
1975 *The Man with the Golden Gun*
1976 *The Return of the Pink Panther*
1977 *The Spy Who Loved Me*
1978 *The Revenge of the Pink Panther*
1979 *Moonraker*
1980 *Monty Python's Life of Brian*
1981 *Superman II*
1982 *Chariots of Fire*
1983 *Octopussy*
1984 *Never Say Never Again*
Of the 49 films listed, 16 were comedies, 9 were war films, 11 were Bond movies, 7 were contemporary dramas, 3 were historical, 2 were musicals, and one was science-fiction. Significantly only one straight crime drama (*The Blue Lamp*) is included.

THE TWENTY-FIVE TOP GROSSING FILMS
The list below was published by the American trade paper *Variety*
in 1985 and represents the North American (US and Canada)
rentals for the 25 top grossing films of all time. As a very
approximate guide, films which are successful in the North
American market can usually expect to earn about the same in
overseas rentals as they do in domestic rentals. Source: *Variety*

1	*E.T. The Extra-Terrestial* (US 82)	$209,976,989
2	*Star Wars* (US 77)	$193,500,000
3	*Return of the Jedi* (US 83)	$165,500,000
4	*The Empire Strikes Back* (US 80)	$141,600,000
5	*Jaws* (US 75)	$129,961,081
6	*Ghostbusters* (US 84)	$127,000,000
7	*Raiders of the Lost Ark* (US 81)	$115,598,000
8	*Indiana Jones and the Temple of Doom* (US 84)	$109,000,000
9	*Grease* (US 78)	$96,300,000
10	*Tootsie* (US 82)	$95,197,000
11	*The Exorcist* (US 73)	$89,000,000
12	*The Godfather* (US 72)	$86,275,000
13	*Superman* (GB 78)	$82,800,000
14	*Close Encounters of the Third Kind* (US 77)	$82,750,000
15	*The Sound of Music* (US 65)	$79,748,000
16	*Gremlins* (US 84)	$78,500,000
17	*The Sting* (US 73)	$78,198,000
18	*Gone With the Wind* (US 39)	$76,700,000
19	*Saturday Night Fever* (US 77)	$74,100,000
20	*National Lampoon's Animal House* (US 78)	$70,778,176
21	*Rocky III* (US 82)	$65,800,000
22	*Superman II* (GB 81)	$65,100,000
23	*On Golden Pond* (US 81)	$63,990,088
24	*Kramer Vs Kramer* (US 79)	$59,986,335
25	*Smokey and the Bandit* (US 77)	$59,859,515

'There will never be any real money in these galloping
tintypes...'—William De Mille (brother of Cecil) to
David Belasco, 1911.

Dirk Bogarde and anonymous co-star in the box-office hit of
1954 *Doctor in the House*.

The highest loss on any film was incurred by United
Artists on the ill-fated *Heaven's Gate* (US 80), which
earned $1,500,000 in North American rentals against
an estimated negative cost of $44 million and a total
cost, including distribution and studio overheads, of
$57 million. It brought in a better return (or lesser
loss) per dollar, however, than the $24 million *Honky
Tonk Freeway* (US 81), which earned only $500,000 in
North American rentals and in terms of budget/box
office ratio is Hollywood's biggest box office flop of
all time.

The lowest reported box office gross for any film in the
last decade was $1500 for *Contaminacion* (Col 82).

The country with the highest box office gross is the
USA whose 1190 million paid admissions in 1984
were worth $4036 million.

WHAT HOLLYWOOD EARNS
Worldwide theatrical rentals of feature films released
by the major US distributors totalled $2142 million in
1983, of which $1278 million was earned in the dom-
estic market and the balance overseas. Top foreign
market for Hollywood pictures is Japan, which
returned $114 million to the distributors in 1983.
Britain is in fifth place in the export league, notching
up $59 million in rentals.

The highest single day gross for any film was achieved by Paramount's *Indiana Jones and the Temple of Doom* (US 84), which took $9,324,760 at 1687 sites on Sunday 27 May 1984. The same picture also earned the **highest week's gross** at $45,709,328 in its opening week. **The highest opening day gross** was scored by *Return of the Jedi* (US 83) on Wednesday 25 May 1983 with a take of $6,219,629 at 1002 sites.

The most bankable star is Clint Eastwood, whose films have grossed $1400 million in the last decade (1974–84).

The most expensive film ever made is believed to be *Superman* (GB 78), of which the negative cost is estimated by *Variety* to have been $55 million. Higher estimates, some in excess of $60 million, have been made for *Superman II* (GB 80), but the same source quotes $54 million. Producer Alexander Salkind told *Variety* in June 1983 that *Superman I* had cost as much as $80 million, attributing this to the trial and error on the special effects and because 'the distributor wasn't a partner in that one and wasn't too worried about expenses'. It is likely that the higher figure includes additional costs such as interest charges, prints, etc. The film earned $82·8 million in North American rentals, which suggests that the film probably made a profit from worldwide rentals even when distributor's costs are taken into account.

The most expensive film from continental Europe was *The Neverending Story* (FRG 84) with a negative cost of $27 million.

The most expensive silent film was Fred Niblo's *Ben Hur* (US 25) at $3·9 million.

MOST EXPENSIVE PRODUCTIONS

Prior to *Superman*, the record for the most expensive production had been held successively by the films listed below. Figures quoted are those reported at the time the films were produced and in most cases are impossible to verify.

$30,000 *Napoleon* (US 08)	$2,000,000 *The Thief of Baghdad* (US 24)
$34,000 *For the Term of his Natural Life* (Aus 08)	$3,900,000 *Ben Hur* (US 25)
$47,500 *Queen Elizabeth* (Fr 12)	$3,950,000 *Hell's Angels* (US 30)
$50,000 *The Prisoner of Zenda* (US 13)	$4,250,000 *Gone with the Wind* (US 39)
$210,000 *Cabiria* (It 14)	$5,200,000 *Wilson* (US 44)
$575,000 *Intolerance* (US 16)	$6,000,000 *Duel in the Sun* (US 46)
$1,000,000 *A Daughter of the Gods* (US 16)	$8,250,000 *Quo Vadis* (US 51)
$1,100,000 *Foolish Wives* (US 22)	$13,500,000 *The Ten Commandments* (US 56)
$1,500,000 *When Knighthood was in Flower* (US 22)	$15,000,000 *Ben Hur* (US 59)
$1,800,000 *The Ten Commandments* (US 23)	$19,000,000 *Mutiny on the Bounty* (US 62)
	$44,000,000 *Cleopatra* (US 63)

The least expensive full-length feature film on record is Victorian Film Productions' part-colour *The Shattered Illusion* (Aus 27), which took twelve months to complete and included spectacular scenes of a ship being overwhelmed by a storm. Total cost of production was £300 ($1460).

The least expensive all-colour talkie was Pat Rocco's 80-minute psychological drama *Someone* (US 65), with Joe Adair and four other paid performers, which was made on an eight-day schedule for $1200 (£500).

> Victor Fleming, director of *Gone with the Wind* (US 39), to producer David O Selznick on being offered a percentage of the profits instead of salary: 'Don't be a damn fool, David. This picture is going to be one of the biggest white elephants of all time.'

Other low budget movies which have achieved box office and/or critical success include Marco Bellocchio's *I Pugni in Tasca* (It 66), which cost $78,000; Truffaut's *The Four Hundred Blows* (Fr 59), $65,000; *Never on Sunday* (Gre 59), $100,000; Nasser Gholam-Rezai's highly acclaimed *How Starry was My Night* (Iran 77), $28,000; Philippe Garrel's *La Concentration* (Fr 68), $14,000; Celestino Coronado's *Hamlet* (GB 77), $5000; Jon Jost's colour feature *Angel City* (US 77), $6000; Ingmar Bergman's *Prison* (Swe 48), $40,000; Ermano Olmi's *Il Posto* (It 61), $15,000; Akira Kurosawa's *Rashomon* (Jap 50), $40,000; Claude Lelouch's *Smic, Smac, Smoc* (Fr 71), $30,000; Wim Verstappen's award-winning *Joszef Katus* (Neth 67), $2400; Jon Jost's *Last Chants for a Slow Dance* (US 79), $2000; Josef Rodel's *Albert—Why* (FRG 78), winner of the 1979 German Critics' Film Prize, $5000. *The Night of the Living Dead* (US 68) was made for $114,000 and brought in $12 million in worldwide rentals; John Waters' *Pink Flamingos* (US 72), billed as 'An Exercise in Poor Taste' and described in one review as 'the sickest movie ever made', cost $12,000 to produce and grossed $1,250,000 in two years; while the notorious *Deep Throat* (US 71), made for $25,000, grossed $4·6 million over the same length of time.

The lowest budgeted British film to win an international release was Bill Forsyth's *That Sinking Feeling* (GB 79), made for £6000. Cost of dubbing new voices for the North American release in 1983—the original Glaswegian accents were impenetrable to US audiences—exceeded the budget of the picture.

The record budget/box office ratio was 1:285 in the case of the $350,000 Australian production *Mad Max* (Aus 80), which grossed $100 million in its first two years of international distribution.

AVERAGE HOLLYWOOD BUDGETS FOR FEATURE FILMS ($)

1915 21,800 (5 reels)	**1955** 900,000	**1978** 5,300,000
1919 60,000 (5 reels)	**1960** 1,000,000	**1979** 6,700,000
1924 300,000	**1965** 1,500,000	**1980** 7,500,000
1932 153,000	**1970** 1,750,000	**1981** 9,750,000
1935 209,000	**1972** 1,890,000	**1982** 10,900,000
1940 314,000	**1974** 2,500,000	**1983** 9,700,000
1941 400,000	**1976** 4,000,000	**1984** 11,300,000
1948 1,000,000		

Figures prior to 1972 are quoted from *Motion Picture Almanac*. The decrease in the average budget between 1924 and the early 1930s may be accounted for by the increase in the number of cheap 'B' pictures, economies forced on studios by the Depression, and a decline in the general index of prices. Early talkies also tended to have smaller casts and less elaborate sets than the silent features of the 1920s. The apparent stability between 1948 and 1960 is harder to explain, particularly as this period saw a vogue for expensive historical epics, a substantial increase in the use of colour, and the demise of the 'B' picture. The figures quoted for this decade should therefore be regarded with caution.

4 Story and Script

Authors

Producers began turning to literature for their plots soon after the turn of the century. In 1902 Ferdinand Zecca of Pathé succeeded in compressing Zola's *L'Assommoir* into five minutes of screen time as *Les Victimes de l'Alcolisme* (Fr 02), while Edwin S. Porter of the Edison Co. presented *Uncle Tom's Cabin* (US 02) in 14 'tableaux' lasting some 17 minutes. Probably the first novel to be adapted at sufficient length for an adequate presentation of the story was *Robbery Under Arms*, by Rolf Boldrewood, which was brought to the screen by the Australian producer C. McMahon in a five-reel version premièred at the Athenaeum Theatre, Melbourne, on 2 November 1907. The first in Europe was Viggo Larsen's three-reel version of Guy Boothby's *Dr. Nicola* (Den 09), starring August Blom. In America the same year Vitagraph produced a four-reel version of Dickens' *Oliver Twist* (US 09) and soon found they had set a trend, eight versions of the story appearing in various countries during the following three years. Among them was Britain's first essay at a 'full-length' screen adaptation, Thomas Bentley's *Oliver Twist* (GB 12), with Ivy Millais in the title role.

The payment of film rights was first put on an organised basis in France, where the Société Cinématographique des Auteurs et Gens de Lettres was established in 1908 to act as a performing rights society interceding between companies like Film d'Art—who based all their films on works of literature—and the members of the two leading literary associations, the Société des Auteurs and the Société des Gens de Lettres.

It was only the previous year that the matter of film rights to an author's work had arisen for the first time, when the Kalem Co. produced a one-reel version of *Ben Hur* (US 07). The publishers of Lew Wallace's novel, Harper's, and the producers of the very successful play based on the book, promptly sued. Kalem defended themselves on the grounds that neither publisher nor author had suffered damage and that the film was a good advertisement for the book and the play. The case lasted four years, Kalem finally conceding defeat and settling for $25,000.

The first copyright fee paid in the US for film rights had been negotiated in the meantime between Biograph and Little, Brown & Co., publishers of Helen Hunt Jackson's *Ramona*, a bestselling romance about an Indian maiden, originally published in 1884. The

Some books have been turned into movies for the unlikeliest of reasons. Orson Welles decided to make a movie of Sherwood King's novel *If I Die Before I Wake* without having read so much as a synopsis. In a desperate financial situation over a stage play he was producing in Boston, Welles called Harry Cohn of Columbia to ask him for a $50,000 loan. When Cohn sounded reluctant, Welles offered to direct a film for him and added that he had an excellent thriller in mind which could be produced very inexpensively. The director was momentarily nonplussed when Cohn asked the title, but glancing over his shoulder he noticed that the wardrobe mistress was reading a paperback and signalled to her to hold it up so that he could see the cover. He told Cohn the title was *If I Die Before I Wake* and was promised a loan in exchange for making the film. It was released as *The Lady from Shanghai* (US 48) with Welles himself playing opposite Rita Hayworth.

film of *Ramona* (US 10) was directed by D. W. Griffith with Mary Pickford in the title role. The fee was $100 and the authoress received the rare distinction of a credit following the main title.

Film rights were not to remain on this modest level for long. In Italy Gabriele D'Annunzio (1863–1938) signed an historic contract with Ambrosio-Films in May 1911 disposing of rights to six of his works at 40,000 lire each, equivalent to $7845 at the then rate of exchange. Ambrosio later bought eight more, but far from delighting in this good fortune D'Annunzio displayed only contempt for the medium which had so wholeheartedly embraced his work. He saw only one of the films, *La Leda senza cigno* (It 12), which he dismissed as 'childish and grotesque'. So far as the 40,000 lire fees were concerned, he declared that they were just a means of buying meat for his dogs.

The record fees noted below do not take account of *The Birth of a Nation* (US 15), for which the copyright fee was paid on a royalty basis. The film was based on a disagreeably racist novel called *The Clansman*, for which author Thomas Dixon had demanded an unprecedented (for the US) rights fee of $25,000. Producer–director D. W. Griffith was unable to raise such a sum and offered him a $2000 advance against a 25 per cent royalty instead. Dixon ultimately received some $750,000, **the highest sum made by the author of any silent film property**.

The highest sum made by any novelist in film history has almost certainly accrued to William Peter Blatty, author of *The Exorcist*. The amount of money involved is indeterminate, since Mr Blatty, as producer of the film, was on 40 per cent of the gross. *The Exorcist* (US 73) has grossed over $89 million in North American rentals alone.

The highest price ever paid for film rights is the $9,500,000 (£4,950,000) by Columbia for Charles Strouse's Broadway musical *Annie*. When the $35 million picture was eventually released in 1982, *Variety* remarked in a thumbs-down review that the price of the rights was 'about what the whole film should have cost'.

There is every likelihood that *Annie*'s record sum for rights will be overtaken by *A Chorus Line* (US 85). The original fee paid for rights to Michael Bennett's Broadway musical in 1975 was $5·5m, but the deal made by Embassy Pictures/Polygram Pictures, who acquired Universal's rights in 1980, includes an additional 20 per cent of gross rentals for Bennett and other royalty participants once the picture has returned $30m.

The highest sum paid for rights during the silent era was $600,000 (£170,000) by the Classical Cinematograph Corporation in 1921 for *Ben Hur*, the Lew Wallace novel made into a 1925 movie.

The first million dollar property was Garson Kanin's Broadway show *Born Yesterday*. Kanin had instructed his agent to refuse any offers from Columbia owing to a long-standing feud with production chief Harry Cohn. The unprecedented size of the offer undermined Kanin's resolve and Columbia made the picture (US 50) with Judy Holliday and Broderick Crawford.

The highest ratio of rights to budget was 78 per cent in the case of Pathé's *Les Misérables* (Fr 11). The film had a budget of 230,000 f, of which 180,000 f was paid to the Victor Hugo estate for the rights.

STARRING . . . THE AUTHOR

Novelists and playwrights have occasionally appeared in the screen version of their own works. The American black writer Richard Wright played the lead in *Native Son* (Arg 50), a film of his novel about a black youth afflicted by racism in the Chicago ghetto. A young Japanese student called Kunie Iwahashie, who won early renown as a novelist in the Françoise Sagan idiom, starred in the film of her novel *Nissholu no Natsu/Summer in Eclipse* (Jap 57). The film of Sir Compton Mackenzie's bestselling novel *Whisky Galore!* (GB 49)—US title *Tight Little Island*—featured the author in the role of the ship's captain. The role of private eye Mike Hammer was played by his creator Mickey Spillane in *The Girl Hunters* (US 63), and bestselling novelist Peter Benchley played a reporter in his own *Jaws* (US 75). Anne-Cath Vestly starred in *Mormor og de Atte Ungene I Byen* (Nor 76), based on her own short stories, while another Norwegian film, *Anette* (Nor 80), not only featured the author of the novel, Astri Nustad, but was directed by her son. Amos Kolek, son of the Mayor of Jerusalem, had the satisfaction of playing a character based on himself in the film of his autobiographical novel *Don't Ask Me Why I Love* (Isr 79). Another autobiographical novel brought to the screen was Vergilio Ferreira's *Manha Submersa* (Por 80), in which the author played the rector of a seminary to which a boy is sent against his will to train for the priesthood. The boy's experiences were based on Ferreira's own. The distinguished American author and playwright Gore Vidal appeared as a senator in the film of his play *The Best Man* (US 64). Among the rare instances in which the author of the original story played a leading role was Birgit Tengroth's performance in Ingmar Bergman's sombre rendering of *Törst/Thirst* (Swe 49).

The most filmed author is William Shakespeare (1564–1616), whose plays have been presented in 273 straight or relatively straight film versions, 31 'modern versions' (where the story line has been loosely based on Shakespeare, e.g. *West Side Story*) and innumerable parodies. Not surprisingly *Hamlet* has appealed most to film-makers, with 41 movie versions (see filmography and also Remakes, p. 31), followed by *Romeo and Juliet*, which has been filmed 29 times, and *Macbeth*, filmed 26 times.

It will be noted from the checklist below that on four occasions Hamlet has been played by a woman: Sarah Bernhardt in a French synchronised sound short of 1900 (see also Sound Film, First, p. 137); the great Danish star Asta Nielsen in a German version of 1920 where Hamlet is revealed at the very end to have been a girl raised as a boy; Caroline Johnson, who interchanged with male thespian Rick McKenna in the 1971 film version of Toronto's Theatre of God production; and, recently, Fatma Girik in the explicitly titled *Female Hamlet* (Tur 77).

Among the more bizarre film versions of Shakespeare's greatest play is one in which the Prince of Denmark has undergone a metamorphosis into a gunslinger in the Wild West — *Quella sporca storia del West* (It 68). Hamlet has yet to meet Frankenstein's

---

Sir Compton Mackenzie played Captain Buncher in the film of his own novel, *Whisky Galore!* (GB 49).

Monster, but one fears this is only a matter of time. Even the most well-intentioned treatment of Shakespeare's work can be subject to the grossest liberties. One of the most inexplicable is the translation of the sub-titles on the US/GB release prints of Grigori Kozintsev's *Hamlet* (USSR 64), intended as a word-for-word film version of the play. The title-writer has given a modern English rendering of Boris Pasternak's scrupulous Russian translation of Shakespeare's original text. Other debasements of the bard's work have been more deliberate. We may be thankful that there has been no follow-up to the soft-porn British film *The Secret Sex Life of Romeo and Juliet* (GB 70) and even more so that among the many projected Shakespeare films that have failed to go into production was Joseph Goebbels' viciously anti-semitic version of *The Merchant of Venice*.

The most filmed novelist is Edgar Wallace (1875–1932), whose books and short stories have been made into 132 British, American and German films. In addition there have been 19 films based on Edgar Wallace plays, making him the most filmed 20th-century writer. (The total of 151 films excludes those based on his characters only.) The first movie derived from one of Wallace's works was *The Man who Bought London* (GB 16), from his novel of the same name. Despite the royalties from his prodigious literary output, his film rights (37 of the films were made in his lifetime), and fees for scriptwriting, directing, and chairing the board of British Lion, Edgar Wallace died owing $315,000.

The most filmed American writer is the western novelist Zane Grey (1875–1939), with 103 films of his works, starting with *Riders of the Purple Sage* (US 18) and ending with *The Maverick Queen* (US 56). All but one were American movies (including a Spanish language western), the exception being *Rangle River* (Aus 37). Grey wrote over a hundred novels, not all of which have been filmed, though a number have been made four times. Zane Grey movies nearly always featured on the bottom half of the bill and the

HAMLET FILMOGRAPHY
Fr oo with Sarah Bernhardt
Fr 07 with Georges Méliès
It 08 (Cornerio)
It 08 (Milano)
It 08 (Cines)
Fr 09
It 10 with Dante Capelli
Fr 10 with Jacques Grétillat
Den 10 with Alwin Neuss
GB 12 with Charles Raymond
Fr 13 with Paul Mounet-Sully
GB 13 with Sir Johnston Forbes-Robertson
It 14 with Hamilton A. Revelle
US 14 with James Young
GB 14 with Eric Williams
US 14 with Alla Nazimova (there is some doubt whether this film was ever made, nor is it known whether Nazimova played Hamlet or Ophelia if it was)
It 17 with Ruggero Ruggeri

Ger 20 with Asta Nielsen
Ind 28
US 33 with John Barrymore (test reel of Act I Scene 5 and Act II Scene 2)
Ind 35 with Sohrab Modi
GB 48 with Sir Laurence Olivier
Ind 54 with Kishore Sahu
US 58 (Baylor Theater production)
US 59 (Encyclopaedia Britannica 16mm production)
Ger 60 with Maximilian Schell
Pol 60 (short directed by Jerzy Skolimowski)
US 64 with Innokenti Smoktunowski
USSR 64 with Innokenti Smoktunowski
Hamile aka *The Tongo Hamlet* Gha 65 with Kofi Middleton-Mends
Hun 65 (animated)
GB 69 with Nicol Williamson
US 70 with Richard Chamberlain (TVM)
Heranca aka *Hamlet* Bra 70 with David Cardaso
US 71 with David Suchet (16mm)

Can 71 (musical) with Rick McKenna and Caroline Johnson
Un Amleto di meno It 73 with Carmelo Bene
Dogg's Troupe Hamlet GB 77
Female Hamlet Tur 77 with Fatma Girik
GB 78 with Anthony and David Meyer
Dome to Elsinore USSR 78—made by workers of the Paris Commune Shoe Factory, Moscow.
MODERN VERSIONS
Der Rest ist Schweigen Ger 59 with Hardy Kruger
Ophelia Fr 61 with André Jocelyn
Ithele na yini vasilas/He Wanted to be King Gre 67 with Angelos Theodoropoulos
Quella sporca storia del West It 68 with Enio Girolami.
PARODIES

GB 15	It 16	Den 22	US 37
US 16	GB 19	Den 32	It 52
US 16	US 19		

(1809–49), whose works have directly contributed to 99 movies (a great number more have invoked his name in their publicity), and catching up is the great Russian playwright and short-story writer Anton Chekhov (1860–1904), with 82 films.

Script

The first scriptwriter was New York journalist Roy McCardell, who was hired in 1900 by Henry Marvin of the American Mutoscope & Biograph Co. to write ten scenarios a week at $15 each. Since most of the films made by the Biograph at that time were 50–100 ft in length (about 1½ minutes), McCardell found he was able to complete his first week's assignment in a single afternoon.

The first contract writer (i.e. full-time employee of a studio) was Louis Feuillade, who joined the Gaumont Studios in Paris in 1905.

Britain's first regular scriptwriter was Harold Brett, engaged by H. O. Martinek of the British & Colonial Kinematograph Co., whose earliest known scenario was for a spy picture called *A Soldier's Honour* (GB 11). Previously it had been the custom of British film producers to shoot without a script or write their own screenplays.

The first writer of literary distinction to be engaged to produce a scenario was the French playwright Henri Lavedan, whose *L'Assassination du Duc de Guise* (Fr 08) was made by Film d'Art.

In the USA the first eminent writer under contract was Emmett Campbell Hall, who was engaged by D. W. Griffith to script the Biograph pictures *His*

Left, Hamlet as played by the old tragedians—Sir Johnston Forbes-Robertson in the Hepworth production of 1913. *Below*, Hamlet sixties-style—Nicol Williamson as the Prince of Denmark, Marianne Faithful as Ophelia in Tony Richardson's 1969 production of the most-filmed Shakespeare play.

finish of Hollywood 'B' movie production in the mid-fifties brought an end to the filming of his works.

Since both the Edgar Wallace and Zane Grey literary lodes seem to have been fully worked (the last Wallace was made in 1971), it seems probable that their records will be overtaken within a few years by one of the runners-up, all of them writers of enduring quality. Sandwiched between Wallace and Grey are Alexandre Dumas (père) (1802–70), author of *The Count of Monte Cristo* and *The Three Musketeers*, whose works have been brought to the screen in 118 films, and Charles Dickens (1812–70) with 107 films to his credit, while Count Leo Tolstoy (1828–1910) exactly equals Zane Grey with a total of 103. Not far behind, and still eminently filmable, is Edgar Allan Poe

Trust (US 11) and *His Trust Fulfilled* (US 11), a two-part story of the American Civil War.

The first scriptwriter to 'have his name in lights'—in other words, to be credited on a cinema marquee—was H. H. Van Loon, author and adaptor of *The Virgin of Stamboul* (US 20), who was afforded this tribute by the Strand Theater, San Francisco, in November 1920.

The first scriptwriters to write dialogue for a sound feature film were Joseph Jackson and Edward T. Lowe Jr., who composed the four talking sequences of Warner Bros' crime melodrama *Tenderloin* (US 28). The dialogue was so ludicrous that two of the sequences were cut after the first week of the film's run. (The dialogue sequences in *The Jazz Singer* (US 27) had been ad libbed by Al Jolson in the title role.)

The shortest dialogue script since the introduction of talkies was written for Mel Brooks' *Silent Movie* (US 76), which had only one spoken word throughout. The dialogue sequence in the otherwise silent movie occurs when mime artiste Marcel Marceau, having been invited by telephone (silently) to appear in a silent movie, replies (audibly) 'Non!' The person making the call is asked (according to the inter-title) 'What did he say?' Response, also by inter-title: 'I don't know. I don't understand French.'

The only other film with but a single word of dialogue, Paul Fejos's *Marie, A Hungarian Legend* (Hun 32), used a longer word—the name 'Marie'.

The most co-writers credited for any film was 21 in the case of *Forever and a Day* (US 43). They included C. S. Forester, John van Druten, Christopher Isherwood, R. C. Sherriff, James Hilton and Frederick Lonsdale.

A Yank at Oxford (GB 38) credited only eight scriptwriters, but at least 31 are known to have been employed by MGM on the screenplay. Among those uncredited were Herman J. Mankiewicz, John Paddy Carstairs, Hugh Walpole and F. Scott Fitzgerald.

PROFANITIES, OBSCENITIES AND EXPLETIVES

It is Hollywood myth that Clark Gable's celebrated closing line in *Gone with the Wind* (US 39)—'Frankly, my dear, I don't give a damn'—was the first occasion on which the word 'damn' had been spoken on the screen. It was said by both Leslie Howard and Marie Lohr in *Pygmalion* (GB 38) and had featured in at least two earlier Hollywood pictures. Fred Stone said 'Damn you!' to the heroine's boss (who had wronged her) in *Alice Adams* (US 35) and three years before that Emma Dunn had exclaimed 'Well, I'll be damned' in

Blessed Event (US 32). Nothing stronger was allowed until the sixties, the obscenities voiced by Mickey Shaughnessy in *Don't Go Near the Water* (US 56) being bleeped out.

British censors had less reserve about the use of realistic language where it was appropriate. 'Bloody' was heard for the first time in *Pygmalion* (GB 38), 'fanny' in *Convoy* (GB 40), and 'arse' in *The Guinea Pig* (GB 49). The British also pioneered the on-screen use of 'bugger' in *Poor Cow* (GB 67) and the most over-used four-letter word in *I'll Never Forget Whatshisname* (GB 68), in which Marianne Faithful made a little piece of film history by breaking the ultimate 'word barrier'. (Critic Kenneth Tynan had, however, said it earlier on television.) The Americans were first, however, with 'shit', which was heard in *In Cold Blood* (US 67) a year earlier than its first appearance on a British soundtrack in *Boom!* (GB 68), while the permissive Danes led with the first on-screen use of a four-letter word in reference to female genitalia in *Quiet Days in Clichy* (Den 69). This was the era of the permissive society and the breakdown of old taboos, aptly summed up by Bob Hope in 1968: 'Last year Hollywood made the first pictures with dirty words. This year we made the pictures to go with them.'

Most of the above words had been used at one time or other by actors in silent films. When Edmund Lowe and Victor McLaglen indulged in a fine exchange of Billingsgate in *What Price Glory* (US 26), the studio received hundreds of letters of protest from outraged lip-readers. Likewise in *Sadie Thompson* (US 28), lip-readers would be the only ones to appreciate the full rich flavour of Gloria Swanson's language as Sadie—which made no concessions to the censors. The title cards only reproduced what she was *not* saying.

The most hackneyed line in movie scripts is 'Let's get outta here'. A survey of 150 American features of the period 1938–74 (revived on British television) showed that it was used at least once in 84 per cent of Hollywood productions and more than once in 17 per cent. Film critic David McGillivray disputes this finding with the assertion that no single phrase has been so overworked in movie scripts as 'Try to get some sleep now'.

The most improbable scenario ever to reach the screen must be a matter of opinion, but the editor would like to nominate George Dewhurst's plot for the Hepworth production *Mist in the Valley* (GB 23), in which

'If my books had been any worse I should not have been invited to Hollywood, and if they had been any better I should not have come'—Raymond Chandler.

Alma Taylor played an ex-nun who marries an amnesia victim and is framed for allegedly murdering a usurping uncle who was posing as her father.

The longest monologue in a dramatic film is a 20-minute speech by Edwige Feuillère in *L'Aigle à deux têtes/The Eagle has Two Heads* (Fr 48).

The longest monologue in a Hollywood movie is by Lionel Barrymore in *A Free Soul* (US 31). Six cameras were used to film the 14-minute speech in one take, since sound editing had yet to be perfected.

STATESMEN AS SCRIPTWRITERS

A number of statesmen have turned their hands to scriptwriting, including Sir Winston Churchill, who was under contract to London Films from 1934 until the war and worked on such films as *The Twenty Five Year Reign of King George V* (uncompleted) and *Conquest of the Air* (GB 38). He is also said to have contributed a speech to the script of *Lady Hamilton/US That Hamilton Woman* (GB 42). On the other side of the Atlantic, President Roosevelt wrote the original scenario for *The President's Mystery* (US 36), about a lawyer (Henry Wilcoxson) who fakes his own death so that he can right the wrongs he did in the name of big business. Carmine Gallone's vast and sprawling epic *Scipio Africanus* (It 37), a story of Roman victories in Africa intended to parallel Mussolini's contemporary victories in Abyssinia, was alleged to have been written by Il Duce himself. Another dictator with a screenplay to his credit was General Franco who wrote the scenario for *The Spirit of Race* (Sp 41) an adaptation of his own novel, under the pen-name Jaime de Andrade. In more recent times former Philippines Prime Minister Kurkrit Pramoj wrote *Fai Dang/The Red Bamboo* (Phi 79). Field Marshal Idi Amin Dada, before he was deposed as President-for-Life of Uganda, scripted an adulatory biopic of himself, but happily this was never made. India's former premier Moraji Desai is probably the only world leader to have scripted a film while in office. Having committed himself to producer J. G. Mohla before being gaoled under Mrs Gandhi's State of Emergency, and finding himself Prime Minister shortly after his release, he nevertheless felt under an obligation to fulfil his undertaking. Working in the early mornings he completed his English-language script of *Yogeshwar Krishna*, the story of Lord Krishna, a few months later.

The full ripe flavour of what US Marines Victor McLaglen and Edmund Lowe really said to each other when they quarrelled over the girl in *What Price Glory* (US 26) was known only to lip-readers.

5 Character and Themes

Screen Characters

The character most often portrayed on screen since the inception of the story film has been Sherlock Holmes, the master detective created by Sir Arthur Conan Doyle (1859–1930), who has been played by 67 actors, including one black (Sam Robinson), in 186 films produced between 1900 and 1984 (see filmography). The only actor to have played both Sherlock Holmes and Dr Watson was Reginald Owen, who was Watson in *Sherlock Holmes* (US 32) and Holmes in *A Study in Scarlet* (US 33).

The other fictitious or legendary characters most frequently represented on screen have been Count

SHERLOCK HOLMES FILMOGRAPHY
The filmography below includes feature-length TVMs, but excludes filmed television series. Where known the actor playing Sherlock Holmes is included.

Sherlock Holmes Baffled (US 00)
Maurice Costello *The Adventures of Sherlock Holmes* (US 03)
Sherlock Holmes Returns (US? 06?)
Bauman Károly *Sherlock Holmes* (Hun 08)
Viggo Larsen *Sherlock Holmes I Livsfare* (Den 08)
Viggo Larsen *Sherlock Holmes II* (Den 08)
Viggo Larsen *Sherlock Holmes III* (Den 08)
Sherlock Holmes in the Great Murder Mystery (US 09)
Viggo Larsen *Sangerindens Diamanter* (Den 09)
August Blom *Droske No 519* (Den 09)
Viggo Larsen *Den Graa Dame* (Den 09)
The Latest Triumph of Sherlock Holmes (Fr 09)
Sherlock Holmes (It 09?)
Viggo Larsen *Der Alte Sekretar* (Ger 10)
Viggo Larsen *Der Blaue Diamant* (Ger 10)
Viggo Larsen *Die Falschen Rembrandts* (Ger 10)
Viggo Larsen *Die Flucht* (Ger 10)
Otto Lagoni *Sherlock Holmes I Bondefangerklør* (Den 10)
Forrect Holger-Madsen (?) *Forklaedte Barnepige* (Den 11)
Holger Rasmussen *Medlem af den Sorte Hand* (Den 11)
Alwin Neuss *Millionobligation* (Den 11)
Hotel Mysterierne (Den 11)
Viggo Larsen *Arsène Lupins Ende* (Ger 11)
Viggo Larsen *Sherlock Holmes contra Professor Moryarty* (Ger 11)
Henri Gouget *Les Aventures de Sherlock Holmes* (Fr 11)
Schlau, Schlauer, am Schlauesten (Fr 12) French title unknown
Georges Treville *The Speckled Band* (GB 12)
Georges Treville *The Reigate Squires* (GB 12)
Georges Treville *The Beryl Coronet* (GB 12)

Georges Treville *The Adventure of the Copper Beeches* (GB 12)
Georges Treville *A Mystery of Boscombe Vale* (GB 12)
Georges Treville *The Stolen Papers* (GB 12)
Georges Treville *Silver Blaze* (GB 12)
Georges Treville *The Musgrave Ritual* (GB 13)
Verrater Zigarette (Ger 13)
Schwarze Kappe (Ger 13)
Gli artigli di griffard (It 13)
Forte di Sherlock Holmes (It 13)
Harry Benham *Sherlock Holmes Solves the Sign of Four* (US 13)
Ferdinand Bonn *Sherlock Holmes contra Dr Mors* (Ger 14)
En Raedsom Nat (Den 14)
Em Gregers (?) *Hvem er Hun?* (Den 14)
James Bragington *A Study in Scarlet* (GB 14)
Francis Ford *A Study in Scarlet* (US 14)
Alwin Neuss *Der Hund von Baskerville* (Ger 14)
Alwin Neuss *Der Hund von Baskerville II* (Ger 14)
Alwin Neuss *Der Hund von Baskerville III* (Ger 15)
Alwin Neuss *Der Hund von Baskerville IV* (Ger 15)
Eugen Burg *Der Hund von Baskerville V* (Ger 15)
Alwin Neuss *Ein Schrei in der Nacht* (Ger 15)
Bloomer Tricks Sherlock Holmes (It 15)
Alwin Neuss *William Voss* (Ger 15)
William Gillette *Sherlock Holmes* (US 16)
H. A. Saintsbury *The Valley of Fear* (GB 16)
Alwin Neuss *Sherlock Holmes auf Urlaub* (Ger 16)
Alwin Neuss *Sherlock Holmes Nächtliche Begegnung* (Ger 16)
Hugo Flink *Der Erstrommotor* (Ger 17)
Hugo Flink *Die Kasette* (Ger 17)
Hugo Flink *Der Schlangenring* (Ger 17)
Hugo Flink *Die Indische Spinne* (Ger 18)
Viggo Larsen *Rotterdam-Amsterdam* (Ger 18)
Ferdinand Bonn *Was er im Spiegel sar* (Ger 18)
Ferdinand Bonn *Die Giftplombe* (Ger 18)

Ferdinand Bonn *Das Schicksal der Renate Yongk* (Ger 18)
Ferdinand Bonn *Die Dose des Kardinals* (Ger 18)
Sam Robinson *Black Sherlock Holmes* (US 18) only time Holmes has been played by a black
Viggo Larsen *Drei Tage Tot* (Ger 19)
Kurt Brenkendorff *Der Mord im Splendid Hotel* (Ger 19)
Erich Kaiser-Titz (?) *Dr Macdonald's Sanitorium* (Ger 20)
Adolf D'Arnaz (?) *Harry Hill contra Sherlock Holmes* (Ger 20)
Lu Jurgens (?) *Das Haus ohne Fenster* (Ger 20)
Eille Norwood *The Dying Detective* (GB 21)
Eille Norwood *The Devil's Foot* (GB 21)
Eille Norwood *A Case of Identity* (GB 21)
Eille Norwood *The Yellow Face* (GB 21)
Eille Norwood *The Red-Headed League* (GB 21)
Eille Norwood *The Resident Patient* (GB 21)
Eille Norwood *A Scandal in Bohemia* (GB 21)
Eille Norwood *The Man with the Twisted Lip* (GB 21)
Eille Norwood *The Beryl Coronet* (GB 21)
Eille Norwood *The Noble Bachelor* (GB 21)
Eille Norwood *The Copper Beeches* (GB 21)
Eille Norwood *The Empty House* (GB 21)
Eille Norwood *The Tiger of San Pedro* (GB 21)
Eille Norwood *The Priory School* (GB 21)
Eille Norwood *The Solitary Cyclist* (GB 21)
Eille Norwood *The Hound of the Baskervilles* (GB 21)
Eille Norwood *Charles Augustus Milverton* (GB 22)
Eille Norwood *The Abbey Grange* (GB 22)
Eille Norwood *The Norwood Builder* (GB 22)
Eille Norwood *The Reigate Squires* (GB 22)
Eille Norwood *The Naval Treaty* (GB 22)
Eille Norwood *The Second Stain* (GB 22)
Eille Norwood *The Red Circle* (GB 22)
Eille Norwood *The Six Napoleons* (GB 22)
Eille Norwood *Black Peter* (GB 22)
Eille Norwood *The Bruce-Partington Plans* (GB 22)
Eille Norwood *The Stockbroker's Clerk* (GB 22)

Left

As long as there are Sherlock Holmes movies, argument will reign as to which portrayal is most faithful to the character as illustrated by Sidney Paget in *The Strand Magazine*. Some Holmesians plump for Arthur Wotner, seen here in *Silver Blaze* (GB 37).

Dracula—138 films (see p. 57); Frankenstein's monster—96; Tarzan—94 (see p. 48); Zorro—68; Hopalong Cassidy—66 (see p. 103); Robin Hood—55; Charlie Chan—49.

Ballet

The first ballet films were presented at the Phono-Cinéma-Théâtre at the Paris Exposition on 8 June 1900 and consisted of three single-scene subjects—Rosita Mauri dancing in *Korrigane* and Zambelli in *Le Cid* and *Sylvia*—and a longer film of *The Prodigal Son*, with Felicia Mallet dancing in three scenes from the ballet. All these films had a synchronised musical accompaniment on records.

The first complete ballet to be presented on film was Luigi Manzotti's *Excelsior* (It 14), produced by Comerio Film of Milan as an 'Azione ciné-fono-coreografica' ('Ciné-phono-choreographic Action') with Romualdo Marenco's music on synchronised discs.

The first feature film on a ballet theme was *Roman russkoj baleriny*/*The Romance of a Russian Ballerina* (Rus 13), a five-reel tear-jerker directed by Georg Jacobi and featuring the Imperial Ballet star Smirnova in the title role.

The first British feature on a ballet theme was *Dance Pretty Lady* (GB 32), from Compton Mackenzie's novel *Carnival* about a Cockney ballerina (Ann Casson), which featured the Ballet Rambert in the dance sequences.

The first original full-length film ballet was Sir Frederick Ashton's *The Tales of Beatrix Potter*/US: *Peter Rabbit and Tales of Beatrix Potter* (GB 71), with Sir Frederick himself dancing the role of Mrs Tiggie Winkle the hedgehog. *Don Quixote* (Aus 73), co-directed by Robert Helpmann and Rudolf Nureyev, was also an original ballet for the screen.

Eille Norwood *The Boscombe Valley Mystery* (GB 22)
Eille Norwood *The Musgrave Ritual* (GB 22)
Eille Norwood *The Golden Pinz-Nez* (GB 22)
Eille Norwood *The Greek Interpreter* (GB 22)
John Barrymore *Sherlock Holmes* (US 22)
Eman Fiala *The Abduction of Banker Fusee* (Cz 23)
Eille Norwood *Silver Blaze* (GB 23)
Eille Norwood *The Speckled Band* (GB 23)
Eille Norwood *The Gloria Scott* (GB 23)
Eille Norwood *The Blue Carbuncle* (GB 23)
Eille Norwood *The Engineer's Thumb* (GB 23)
Eille Norwood *His Last Bow* (GB 23)
Eille Norwood *The Cardboard Box* (GB 23)
Eille Norwood *Lady Frances Carfax* (GB 23)
Eille Norwood *The Three Students* (GB 23)
Eille Norwood *The Missing Three-Quarter* (GB 23)
Eille Norwood *Thor Bridge* (GB 23)
Eille Norwood *The Stone of Mazarin* (GB 23)
Eille Norwood *The Dancing Men* (GB 23)
Eille Norwood *The Crooked Man* (GB 23)
Eille Norwood *The Final Problem* (GB 23)
Eille Norwood *The Sign of Four* (GB 23)
Philip Beck *Kobenhavns Sherlock Holmes* (Den 25)
Carlyle Blackwell *Der Hund von Baskerville* (Ger 29)
Clive Brook *The Return of Sherlock Holmes* (US 29)
Clive Brook *Paramount on Parade* (US 30)
Arthur Wontner *The Sleeping Cardinal* (GB 31)
Raymond Massey *The Speckled Band* (GB 31)
Robert Rendel *The Hound of the Baskervilles* (GB 32)
Clive Brook *Sherlock Holmes* (US 32)
Arthur Wontner *The Sign of Four* (GB 32)
Arthur Wontner *The Missing Rembrandt* (GB 32)
Martin Fric *Lelicek ve Sluzbach Sherlocka Holmese* (Cz 32)
Richard Gordon *The Radio Murder Mystery* (US 33)
Reginald Owen *A Study in Scarlet* (US 33)

Arthur Wontner *The Triumph of Sherlock Holmes* (GB 35)
Arthur Wontner *Silver Blaze* (GB 37)
Bruno Güttner *Der Hund von Baskerville* (Ger 37)
Hermann Speelmans *Die Graue Dame* (Ger 37)
Hans Albers *Der Mann, der Sherlock Holmes War* (Ger 37)
Basil Rathbone *The Hound of the Baskervilles* (US 39)
Basil Rathbone *The Adventures of Sherlock Holmes* (US 39)
Basil Rathbone *Sherlock Holmes and the Voice of Terror* (US 42)
Basil Rathbone *Sherlock Holmes and the Secret Weapon* (US 42)
Basil Rathbone (cameo role) *Crazy House* (US 43)
Basil Rathbone *Sherlock Holmes in Washington* (US 43)
Basil Rathbone *Sherlock Holmes Faces Death* (US 43)
Basil Rathbone *Sherlock Holmes and the Spider Woman* (US 44)
Basil Rathbone *The Scarlet Claw* (US 44)
Basil Rathbone *The Pearl of Death* (US 44)
Basil Rathbone *The House of Fear* (US 45)
Basil Rathbone *The Woman in Green* (US 45)
Basil Rathbone *Pursuit to Algiers* (US 45)
Basil Rathbone *Terror by Night* (US 45)
Basil Rathbone *Dressed to Kill* (US 45)
John Longden *The Man with the Twisted Lip* (GB 51)
Peter Cushing *The Hound of the Baskervilles* (GB 59)
Christopher Lee *Sherlock Holmes und das Halsband des Todes* (FRG 62)
Jerome Raphel *The Double-Barrelled Detective Story* (US 65)
John Neville *A Study in Terror* (GB 65)
Nando Gazzolo *La Valle della paura* (It 68, TVM)
Nando Gazzolo *L'Ultimo dei Baskerville* (It 68)
Robert Stephens *The Private Life of Sherlock Holmes* (GB 70)

Radovan Lukavsky *Touha Sherlocka Holmese* (Cz 71)
George C. Scott *They Might Be Giants* (US 72)
The Case of the Metal-Sheathed Elements (GB 72) cartoon
Stewart Granger *The Hound of the Baskervilles* (US 72, TVM)
Keith McConnell *Murder in Northumberland* (GB 74)
Rolf Becker *Monsieur Sherlok Holmes* (Fr 74, TVM)
Harry Reems *Sherlock Holmes* (US 75) porno
Douglas Wilmer *The Adventure of Sherlock Holmes' Smarter Brother* (GB 75)
Roger Moore *Sherlock Holmes in New York* (US 76, TVM) released theatrically in Europe)
Keith McConnell *Murder by Death* (US 76) SH role cut in some release prints
Sherlock Holmes (Swz 76)
A Case of Royal Murder (GB 77)
The Case of the Exhumed Client (GB 77)
Nicol Williamson *The Seven-Per-Cent Solution* (GB 77)
Trevor Ainsley *The Case of the Mounting Fortune* (GB 78)
Peter Cook *The Hound of the Baskervilles* (GB 78)
Christopher Plummer *Murder by Decree* (GB/Can 79)
Jeremy Young *The Case of the Fantastical Passbook* (GB 79)
Aljgis Masjulis *The Blue Carbuncle* (USSR 80, TVM)
Peter O'Toole (voice) *Sherlock Holmes and the Baskerville Curse* (Aus 82)—animated
Ian Richardson *The Hound of the Baskervilles* (GB 83)
Ian Richardson *The Sign of Four* (GB 83)
Vassily Livanov *The Sign of Four* (USSR 83)
Vassily Livanov *Trouble in Bohemia* (USSR 83)
Guy Rolfe *The Case of Marcel Duchamp* (Fr 83)
Peter Cushing *The Masks of Death* (GB 84, TVM)
Nicholas Rowe *Young Sherlock Holmes* (UK i.p.)

TARZAN FILMOGRAPHY

Gordon Griffith (as a boy) and Elmo Lincoln *Tarzan of the Apes* (US 18)
Elmo Lincoln *The Romance of Tarzan* (US 18)
Gene Pollar *The Revenge of Tarzan* (US 20)
P. Dempsey Tabler *The Son of Tarzan* (US 20)
Elmo Lincoln *The Adventures of Tarzan* (US 21) serial
James Pierce *Tarzan and the Golden Lion* (US 27)
Frank Merrill *Tarzan the Mighty* (US 28) serial
Frank Merrill *Tarzan the Tiger* (US 29) serial
Charlie Chase *Nature in the Wrong* (US 32) parody
Johnny Weissmuller *Tarzan the Ape Man* (US 32)
Buster Crabbe *Tarzan the Fearless* (US 33)
Johnny Weissmuller *Tarzan and His Mate* (US 34)
Herman Brix *The New Adventures of Tarzan* (US 35) serial
Johnny Weissmuller *Tarzan Escapes* (US 36)
John Cavas *Toofani Tarzan* (Ind 37)
Herman Brix *Tarzan in Guatemala* (US 38) feature derived from first half of *The New Adventures of Tarzan* above
Herman Brix *Tarzan and the Green Goddess* (US 38) feature derived from last half of *The New Adventures of Tarzan* (above)
Glenn Morris *Tarzan's Revenge* (US 38)
Manek *Tarzan Ki Beta* (Ind 38)
Johnny Weissmuller *Tarzan Finds a Son!* (US 39)
Peng Fei *The Adventures of Chinese Tarzan Parts 1–3* (Sin 39–40)
Johnny Weissmuller *Tarzan's Secret Treasure* (US 41)
Johnny Weissmuller *Tarzan's New York Adventure* (US 42)
Johnny Weissmuller *Tarzan Triumphs!* (US 43)
Johnny Weissmuller *Tarzan's Desert Mystery* (US 43)
Johnny Weissmuller *Tarzan and the Amazons* (US 45)
Johnny Weissmuller *Tarzan and the Leopard Women* (US 46)
Johnny Weissmuller *Tarzan and the Huntress* (US 47)

Johnny Weissmuller *Tarzan and the Mermaids* (US 48)
Lex Barker *Tarzan's Magic Fountain* (US 49)
Lex Barker *Tarzan and the Slave Girl* (US 50)
Toto *Toto Tarzan* (It 50) parody
Lex Barker *Tarzan's Peril* (US 51)
Lex Barker *Tarzan and the She-Devil* (US 53)
Gordon Scott *Tarzan's Hidden Jungle* (US 55)
Tarzan and Boy (US c. 55) porno
Gordon Scott *Tarzan and the Lost Safari* (GB 57)
Gordon Scott *Tarzan's Fight for Life* (US 58)
Manchar *Thozhan* (Ind 59) Tamil
Gordon Scott *Tarzan's Greatest Adventure* (GB 59)
Denny Miller *Tarzan the Ape Man* (US 59)
Gordon Scott *Tarzan the Magnificent* (GB 60)
Azad *Toofani Tarzan* (Ind 62)
Jock Mahoney *Tarzan Goes to India* (GB 62)
Rudolph Hrušínský *Tazanova smot/The Death of Tarzan* (Cz 62)*
Azad *Tarzan aur Gorilla* (Ind 63)
Indrajeet *Rocket Tarzan* (Ind 63)
Jock Mahoney *Tarzan's Three Challenges* (US 63)
Azad *Tarzan aur Jadugar* (Ind 63)
Kit Morris *Tarzan chez les coupeurs de tête* (It 63)*
Joe Robinson *Tarzan roi de la force brutale* (It 63)*
Vladamir Korenev *Tarzan des mers* (USSR 63)*
Azad *Tarzan and Captain Kishore* (Ind 64)
Azad *Tarzan and Delilah* (Ind 64)
Azad *Tarzan aur Jalpari* (Ind 64)
Brick Bardo *Jungle Tales of Tarzan* (FRG 64)
Don Bragg *Tarzan and the Jewels of Opar* (Jam 64) uncompleted
Taylor Mead *Tarzan and Jane Regained Sort Of . . .* (US 64) Warhol
Dara Singh *Tarzan and King Kong* (Ind 65)
Dara Singh *Tarzan Comes to Delhi* (Ind 65)
Azad *Tarzan and Circus* (Ind 65)
Ralph Hudson *Tarzak Against the Leopardmen* (It 65)
Mike Henry *Tarzan and the Valley of Gold* (US 66)
Gordon Scott *Tarzan and the Trapper* (US 66)
Hercules *Tarzan and Hercules* (Ind 66)

Azad *Tarzan Ki Mehbooba* (Ind 66)
Azad *Tarzan aur Jadui Chirag* (Ind 66)
Mike Henry *Tarzan and the Great River* (US 67)
Tarzans Kampf mit dem Gorilla (FRG 68) short
Mike Henry *Tarzan and the Jungle Boy* (US 68)
Azad *Tarzan in Fairy Land* (Ind 68)
Steve Hawkes *Tarzan en la Gruta del Oro* (Sp/It 69)
Ron Ely *Tarzan's Jungle Rebellion* (US 70) theatrical release derived from TV series
Ron Ely *Tarzan's Deadly Silence* (US 70) theatrical release derived from TV series
Azad *Tarzan 303* (Ind 70)
Tarzan the Swinger (US 70) underground movie
Steve Hawkes *Tarzan y el Arco Iris* (Sp/It 72)
David Carpenter *Tarzan en las Minas de Rey Salomon* (Sp 73)
Richard Yesteran *Tarzan y el Misterio de la Selva* (Sp 73)
Richard Yesteran *Tarzan y el Tesoro Kawana* (Sp 74)
Silver Fox *Tarz and Jane and Boy and Cheeta* (US 75) porno
Johnny Weissmuller Jnr. (voice) *Tarzoon, Shame of the Jungle* (Bel 75) animated feature
Tarzan and the Valley of Lust (US? 76) porno
Tarzan of Bengal (Ban 76)
Tarzann . . . O Bonitão Sexy (Bra 77) porno
Karl Blomer *Jane is Jane Forever* (FRG 78)
La Infancia de Tarzan (Sp 79)
Andy Luotto *Tarzan Andy* (It 80) parody
Miles O'Keeffe *Tarzan the Apeman* (US 81)
Elle Voit des Nains Partout (Fr 82) parody
Christopher Lambert *Greystoke: The Legend of Tarzan, Lord of the Apes* (GB/US 84).

Azad has been listed in a French filmography as starring in *Tarzan's Beloved* (Ind 64) and *Tarzan and Cleopatra* (Ind 65), but the release of these titles in India cannot be traced. If the films were made, Azad has played the role 13 times to Johnny Weissmuller's 12. A Hindustani version of *Tarzan Goes to India* (GB 62) was released in 1974 as *Tarzan Mera Sathi*.

* Titles changed after threat of legal action from the Edgar Rice Burroughs Estate.

Biopics

The historical character who has been represented most often on screen is Napoléon Bonaparte (1769–1821), Emperor of the French. The role has been played in at least 172 films (see p. 50).

Other historical characters most often represented on screen include Jesus Christ, of whom there are 135 recorded film portrayals; Vladymir Ilich Lenin (1870–1924)—72; Adolf Hitler (1889–1945)—60; Cleopatra (69–30 BC)—37; Queen Victoria (1819–1901)—36; Henry VIII (1491–1547)—34; Queen Elizabeth I (1553–1603)—32; Grigori Rasputin (1871?–1916)—27; Josef Stalin (1879–1953)—26; St Joan of Arc (c. 1412–31)—23; Pancho Villa (1877–1923)—21; Sir Winston Churchill (1874–1965)—16. Chairman Mao Tse-Tung (1893–1976) was portrayed for the first time in *The Great Flowering River* (Chn 79) and Queen Elizabeth II (1926–) by Jeanette Charles in *Marcia* (GB 77). The first screen portrayal of Mrs Thatcher (1925–) was by Janet Brown in the James Bond movie *For Your Eyes Only* (GB 81). See also Western hero most often portrayed on screen (p. 75).

The first portrayal of a reigning British monarch was by Thomas R. Mills, who played King George V (1865–1936) in a fictionalised version of Sir Roger Casement's life *Whom the Gods Destroy* (US 16).

The US President most often portrayed on screen has been Abraham Lincoln in 120 films. See pp. 52–5.

Black Films

The first black film was *The Railroad Porter* (US 12), a chase comedy with an all-black cast directed by pioneer black film-maker Bill Foster.

The first black production company was the Lincoln Motion Picture Co., founded in Los Angeles in 1915 by black actors Clarence Brooks and Noble Johnson, a prosperous black druggist called James T. Smith and white cameraman Harry Grant. The company's first release was *The Realisation of a Negro's Ambition* (US 16), with Noble Johnson starring as an oil engineer who makes good.

The first black feature film was the Frederick Douglass Film Co.'s six-reel *The Coloured American Winning his Suit* (US 16), which was premièred at Jersey City on 14 July 1916. The all-black cast was largely amateur, made up of 'young men and women of the race from . . . the best families in New Jersey'.

The first black talkie was Christie Comedies' two-reel *Melancholy Dame* (US 28), featuring Roberta Hyson and Spencer Williams. The picture was about black 'high society' in Birmingham, Ala.

The first feature-length black talkie was MGM's *Hallelujah!* (US 29), directed by King Vidor and starring Daniel Haynes. **The first made by a black production company** was the Oscar Micheaux Corporation's *The Exile* (US 31), directed by Oscar Micheaux and starring Stanley Murrell.

The first feature-length film produced by blacks in Britain was Horace Ove's *Reggae* (GB 70), a 60-min documentary about the distinctive Jamaican music form. **The first dramatic feature** was Horace Ove's *Pressure*, made on location in the Ladbroke Grove area of London in 1974, but not released until February 1978. Originally commissioned by the BBC, but rejected as 'too heavy', the film told the story of a British-born younger son (Herbert Norville) of an immigrant family from Trinidad who finds himself adrift between two cultures. **The first dramatic feature released** in Britain was *Black Joy* (GB 77), a delightful comedy about an innocent and unsophisticated Guyanan immigrant (Trevor Thomas) exposed to the 'hustlin'' way of life of the Brixton ghetto.

BLACK FILMS MADE BY THE MAJOR STUDIOS

During the silent period the 'majors' showed little or no interest in black movies and even when black characters were required they were generally played by white actors in black-face. D. W. Griffith's *The Birth of a Nation* (US 15) had a large cast of black roles, since the controversial plot revolved round the black 'takeover' of the South following the Civil War, yet only one genuine black—the curiously named Madame Sul-Te-Wan—was employed on the film.

The coming of sound altered the picture, since the trend towards greater realism demanded that blacks be played by blacks, though their roles were generally confined to the menial or the comic (usually both combined). At the same time the major studios began to turn out the occasional all-black picture, most of them dependent upon the vocal talents of the black American and aimed principally at white audiences. Those made prior to the sudden explosion of 'superspade' black exploitation pictures in the late sixties were as follows: *Hallelujah!* (MGM 29) with Daniel Haynes; *Hearts in Dixie* (Fox 29) with Clarence Muse; *Green*

Left to right

Tarzan old and new: Elmo Lincoln, the first Tarzan, in *Tarzan of the Apes* (US 18). Note the chap in the monkey suit behind the tree. Sir Hugh Greene, who saw the film as a child, recalls that the apes wore sneakers. The noble savage up-to-date—Miles O'Keeffe in *Tarzan the Apeman* (US 81) and French actor Christopher Lambert in *Greystoke: The Legend of Tarzan, Lord of the Apes* (GB/US 84). The latter was claimed to be the first Tarzan film to stick to the original Edgar Rice Burroughs story, with Tarzan as the boy lost in the jungle who grows up to inherit the title of Lord Greystoke. To account for Christopher Lambert's Gallic accent, though, the scriptwriter had to introduce a Belgian explorer who teaches him the English language.

NAPOLEON FILMOGRAPHY

The following filmography records the actor playing Napoleon, where this is known:

Napoléon et la Sentinelle (Fr 97)
Entrevue de Napoléon et du Pape (Fr 98)
Napoleon Crossing the Alps (It 04)
L'Epopée Napoléonienne (Fr 04)
William Humphrey *Napoleon* (US 06)
Napoleone I (It 07)
Herbert Darnley *Napoleon and the English Sailor* (GB 08)
Napoleon—Man of Destiny (Fr 08)
Napoleon on Elba (It 08)
Napoleon (US 08)
Napoléon (Fr 09)
Decorated by the Emperor (Fr 09)
Napoleon and the Princess Hatfield (It 09)
Napoleon Bonaparte and the Empress Josephine of France (US 09)
Napoleon Outwitted by a Clergyman (Fr 09)
William Humphreys *Napoleon—The Man of Destiny* (US 09)
William Humphrey *Incidents in the Life of Napoleon and Josephine* (US 09)
Napoleon in Russia (Rus 09)
August Blom *Madame Sans-Gêne* (Den 09)
Napoleone (It 09)
Viggo Larsen *Budskab til Napoleon paa Elba* (Den 09)
Napoleone e la Principessa di Katzfeld (It 09)
Una Congiura sotto Napoleone (It 09)
V. Krivtsov *Napoleon in Russia* (Rus 10)
Napoléon (Fr 10)
Il Disertore (It 10)
Un Ammivatore di Bounaparte (It 10)
Il Granatiere Rolland (It 10)
Napoleon og Hans lille Trompetisr (Den 10)
Theo Bouwmeester *Checkmated—A Story of Napoleon* (GB 10)
Henri Etievant *Napoléon et la sentinelle* (Fr 10)
Annette's Rival or The Emperor Napoleon (Fr 11)
Arrigo Frusta *Il Granatiere Roland* (It 11)
Un Ammivatore di Bounaparte (It 11)
Napoleone a Sant' Elena (It 11)
Duquesne *Madame Sans-Gêne* (Fr 11)
Bonaparte (Bel 11)
La Bataille de Waterloo (Bel 11)
Napoleon in 1814 (Fr 11)
Napoleon and his Son (Fr 11)
The Emperor's Return (Fr 11)
Salustiano *Salustiano, Napoleon* (It 12)
The Two Grenadiers (Fr 12)
Johnny Butt *The Emperor's Messenger* (GB 12)
P. Knorr *The Year 1812* (Rus 12)
George Hernandez *The Count of Monte Cristo* (US 12)
Napoléon, Bébé et les Cosaques (Fr 12)
Mémorial de Saint-Hélène (Fr 12)
Charles Sutton *The Prisoner of War* (US 12)
Napoleon and the English Sailor (Fr 12)
Napoleon and the Sentinel (GB 12)
Josephine Empress and Queen (Fr 12)
A Bogus Napoleon (US 12)
Epopea Napoleonica (It 13)
Ernest G. Batley *The Battle of Waterloo* (GB 13)
Fred Evans *Adventures of Pimple—The Battle of Waterloo* (GB 13)

Episodes de Waterloo (Fr 13)
Napoleon (US 13) (Solax)
Napoleon (US 13) (Vitagraph)
Stephan Jaracz *Bog Wojny* (Pol 14)
Carlo Campogalli *Epopea Napoleonica* (It 14)
Albert A. Capozzi *Napoleone* (It 14)
Hector Mozzanti *I Cento giorni di Napoleone* (It 14)
Napoléon (Fr 14)
Charles Sutton *Man of Destiny* (US 14)
The Rise and Fall of Napoleon (US 14)
Hector Mozzanti *Germania* (It 14)
War and Peace (Rus 15)
Vladamir Gardin *War and Peace* (Rus 15) (rival version)
The Fortunes of Fifi (US 17)
Madame Récamier (Fr 20)
Rudolph Lettinger *Napoleon und die kleine Wäscherin* (Ger 20)
Camillo de Rossi (?) *Madame Sans-Gêne* (It 20)
Rainer Simons *Der Herzog von Reichstadt* (Aut 20)
Rudolph Lettinger *Grafin Walenska* (Ger 20)
Karel Faltys *Cikani* (Cz 21)
Emile Drain *L'Aiglonne* (Fr 21)
Karl Etlinger *Die Schauspieler des Kaisers* (Aut 21)
George Campbell *Monte Cristo* (US 22)
Rainer Simons *Napoleon in Schönbrunn* (Aut 22)
Otto Matieson *Vanity Fair* (US 23)
Gwylim Evans *A Royal Divorce* (GB 23)
Charles Barratt *Madame Récamier* (GB 23)
Charles Barratt *Empress Josephine* (GB 23)
Michael Xantho *Der junge Medardus* (Aut 23)
Slavko Vorkapitch *Scaramouche* (US 24)
Napoleon and Josephine (Fr 24)
Jean-Napoléon-Michel *Destinée* (Fr 25)
Emile Drain *Madame Sans-Gêne* (US 25)
Wladamir Roudenko (boy) and Albert Dieudonne (man)
Napoléon vu par Abel Gance (Fr 27)
Max Barwyn *Fighting Eagle* (US 27)
Otto Matieson *The Lady of Victories* (US 27)
Charles Vanel *Konigen Louise* (Ger 27)
Pasquale Amato *Glorious Betsy* (US 28)
Stephan Jaracz *Pan Tadeusz* (Pol 28)
Paul Muni *Seven Faces* (US 29)
Werner Krauss *Napoléon à Saint-Hélène* (Fr 29)
Otto Matieson *Napoleon's Barber* (US 29)
William Humphrey *Devil-May-Care* (US 29)
Paul Muni *The Valiant* (US 29)
Charles Vanel *Waterloo* (Ger 29)
Severin Mars *L'Agonie des Aigles* (Fr 29)
Manuel Paris *El Barbero de Napoleon* (US 30)
Stefan Jaracz *Pani Walewskiej* (Pol c. 30)
Paul Gunther *Luise Königin von Preussen* (Ger 31)
Gianfranco Giachetti *Cento di questi giorni* (It 33)
Not Tonight, Josephine (US 34)
William Humphrey *Are We Civilized?* (US 34)
Paul Irving *The Count of Monte Cristo* (US 34)
Esme Percy *Invitation to the Waltz* (GB 35)
Corrada Racca *Campo di Maggio* (It 35)
Werner Krauss *Hundert Tage* (Ger 35)
Claude Rains *Hearts Divided* (US 36)
Rollo Lloyd *Anthony Adverse* (US 36)

Emile Drain and Jean-Louis Barrault *Les Perles de la couronne* (Fr 37)
Victor Varconi *L'Heroique embuscade* (Fr 37)
Charles Boyer *Conquest*/UK *Marie Waleska* (US 37)
Curt Goetz *Napoleon ist an allem Schuld* (Ger 38)
Pierre Blanchar *A Royal Divorce* (GB 38)
Emile Drain and Jean-Louis Allibert *Remontons les Champs-Elysées* (Fr 39)
Erich Ponto *Der Feuerteufel* (Ger 40)
Albert Dieudonne *Madame Sans-Gêne* (Fr 41)
Herbert Lom *Young Mr. Pitt* (GB 42)
Hitler's Dream (USSR 42)
Sacha Guitry *Le destin fabuleux de Desirée Clary* (Fr 42)
Lille Napoleon (Swe 43)
Ruggero Ruggeri *Sant' Elena piccola Isola* (It 43)
Sergei Mezhinsky *Kutosov in 1812* (USSR 44)
Charles Sauten *Kolberg* (Ger 45)
Adrián Cúneo (?) *Madame Sans-Gêne* (Arg 45)
Emile Drain *Le Diable Boiteux* (Fr 48)
Pedro Elviro *El Bano de Afrodita* (Mex 49)
Arnold Moss *Reign of Terror* (US 49)
Renato Rascel *Napoleone* (It 51)
Gerard Oury *Sea Devils* (US 52)
Marlon Brando *Desirée* (US 54)
Emile Drain *Versailles m'était conte* (Fr 54)
Daniel Gélin and Raymond Pellegrin *Napoleone Bonaparte* (It/Fr 55)
Napoleon's Return from Elba (US 55)
Robert Cornthwaite *The Purple Mask* (US 55)
Herbert Lom *War and Peace* (US 56)
Dennis Hopper *The Story of Mankind* (US 57)
Rene Deltgen *Königin Luise* (FRG 57)
Pierre Mondy *Napoleon ad Austerlitz* (Fr 60)
Julien Bertheau *Madame Sans-Gêne* (Fr/Sp/It 61)
Mario Corotenuto *Napoleone a Firenze* (It 62)
Raymond Pellegrin *Venere Imperiale* (It 63)
La Malmaison (Fr 64)
Gyula Bodrogi *Hary Janos* (Hun 65)
Janusz Zakrzenski *Popioly* (Pol 65)
Gustav Holoubek *Maria and Napoleon* (Pol 65)
Jock Livingstone *Zero in the Universe* (US/Neth 66)
Vladislav Strzhelchik *War and Peace* (USSR 63–67)
Giani Esposito *The Sea Pirate* (Fr/Sp/It 67)
Harrison Marks *The Naked World of Harrison Marks* (GB 67)
Heinrich Schweiger *Frau Wirtin hat auch einen Grafen* (Aut/FRG/It 68)
Caroline Chérie (FRG 68)
Rod Steiger *Waterloo* (It/USSR 70)
Heinrich Schweiger *Frau Wirtin hat auch êine nichte* (Aut/Hun/FRG/It 70)
Eli Wallach *The Adventures of Gerard* (GB/It/Swz 70)
Napoleon: The Making of a Dictator (US 70)
Napoleon: The End of a Dictator (US 71)
Kenneth Haigh *Eagle in a Cage* (GB 71)
James Tolkan *Love and Death* (US 75)
Aldo Maccione *The Loves and Times of Scaramouche* (It/Yug 76)
Petit manuel d'histoire de France (Fr 79)
Ian Holm *Time Bandits* (GB 81)
Daniel Harris *Stuck on You!* (US 82)
Patrice Chéreau *Adieu, Bonaparte* (Fr/Egy 85).

Pastures (Warner 36) with Rex Ingram; *Stormy Weather* (TCF 43) with Bill Robinson, Lena Horne; *Cabin in the Sky* (MGM 43) with Eddie Anderson, Lena Horne; *Bright Road* (MGM 51) with Dorothy Dandridge; *Carmen Jones* (TCF 54) with Harry Belafonte, Dorothy Dandridge; *Anna Lucasta* (United Artists 58) with Sammy Davis Jr.; *Porgy and Bess* (Goldwyn 59) with Sidney Poitier, Dorothy Dandridge.

No Hollywood films took the subject of contemporary race relations as a main theme until 1949 when three such films came to the screen almost simultaneously, led by *Home of the Brave*, the story of a black veteran undergoing psychiatric treatment following traumatic war experiences. The other two films, *Pinky* and *Lost Boundaries*, dealt with light-skinned blacks passing for white.

The Hays Code ban on miscegenation as a theme was breached by *Island in the Sun* (US 59), which offered twin romances between John Justin and Dorothy Dandridge (who marry in the end) and Harry Belafonte and Joan Fontaine (who part). In Britain the subject had been tackled much earlier in *Pool of London* (GB 50), which depicted the relationship between a Jamaican ship's steward (Earl Cameron) and a white cinema cashier (Susan Shaw).

Production output: A total of 49 all-black silent features are recorded in the US for the period 1917–30; exactly 150 all-black talkies were made in the US 1931–50.

BLACKS IN LEADING ROLES

The fortunes of black leading actors rose in the late 1960s, following the success of the civil rights movement and the cult of 'black consciousness'. A peak was reached in about 1973, when 45 American-made features, 21 of them from major distributors, starred black leading players. By 1982 only eight films had blacks in starring roles, three of which top-lined Richard Pryor. According to the National Association for the

Romance between white and black was treated for the first time in an English-language film in *Pool of London* (GB 50), with Susan Shaw and Earl Cameron (*left*). In America the subject remained too hot to handle until *Island in the Sun* (US 59) offered twin romances between John Justin and Dorothy Dandridge (*centre*) and Harry Belafonte and Joan Fontaine (*right*).

Advancement of Colored People, Hollywood films featuring blacks in 'significant' roles totalled no more than 12 in 1981, 22 in 1982 and 14 in 1983.

The first black film with an all-African cast was the Stoll Co.'s *Nionga* (GB 25), about a young betrothed couple in Central Africa and the tragic ending to their romance, the man being accidentally killed and the bride burned alive in her hut according to local custom. Such films were rare, the only other pre-war examples on record being *Zeliv* (It 28), a story of tribal life enacted entirely by Zulus, *Samba* (Ger 28) and *Stampede* (GB 30). All these films were aimed at white audiences, a fact made abundantly clear in the subtitles to *Nionga*, which referred to its protagonists as 'the savages'.

The first African film drama made by a black African was Ousmane Sembene's *La Noire de . . .* (Sen 67), premièred at the Théâtre Sorano in Dakar on 4 February 1967.

Jewish Films

The first Jewish film with an all-Jewish cast was Stanisław Sebel's screen version of Gordin's *Satan* (Pol 12), produced by Madame Yelizariantz's Sila Co. with a cast drawn from Warsaw's Fishon Theatre. Within a year there were four Polish companies specialising in Jewish films, Sila having been joined by Variag (also run by a woman, Madame Stern), Mintus and Kosmofilm.

US PRESIDENTS

The President of the United States **most often portrayed on film**, as well as **America's most oft portrayed historical character**, is Abraham Lincoln (1809–65). The role has been played in 158 films to date, of which 19 were educational subjects. Those made for commercial release are listed below, together with the other films featuring representations of US presidents. The actor creating the presidential role is given where known, though in some films the actor has been uncredited. The date preceding the presidents' names is the year of inauguration.

1789 GEORGE WASHINGTON (1732–99)
Washington at Valley Forge (US 08)
Barbara Freitchie (US 08)
Benedict Arnold and Major Andre (US 09)
Phillips Smalley *A Heroine of '76* (US 11)
Washington at Valley Forge (US 14)
William Worthington *The Spy* (US 14)
Charles Ogle *Molly, the Drummer Boy* (US 14)
Joseph Kilgour *The Battle Cry of Peace* (US 15)
George MacQuarrie *Betsy Ross* (US 17)
Noah Beery *The Spirit of '76* (US 17)
A Daughter of War (US 17)
George MacQuarrie *The Beautiful Mrs Reynolds* (US 18)
Harold Judson *Deliverence* (US 19)
Schoolmaster Matsumoto (Jap 19)
Arthur Dewey *America* (US 24)
Joseph Kilgour *Janice Meredith* (US 24)
Francis X. Bushman *The Flag* (US 27)
Edward Hern *The Winners of the Wilderness* (US 27)
Alan Mowbray *Alexander Hamilton* (US 31)
Alan Mowbray *The Phantom President* (US 32)
George Houston *The Howards of Virginia* (US 40)
Montague Love *Remarkable Andrew* (US 42)
Alan Mowbray *Where Do We Go From Here?* (US 45)

Douglass Dumbrille *Monsieur Beaucaire* (US 46)
Robert Barrat *The Time of their Lives* (US 46)
Richard Gaines *Unconquered* (US 47)
John Crawford *John Paul Jones* (US 59)
Howard St John *Lafayette* (Fr 62)
Washington at Valley Forge (US 71)
Lorne Green *Washington—The Man* (US c. 75)
Patrick O'Neal *Independence* (US 76)

1797 JOHN ADAMS (1735–1826)
Jack Drumier *The Beautiful Mrs Reynolds* (US 18)
John Paul Jones (US 59)
William Daniels *1776* (US 72)
Pat Hingle *Independence* (US 76)

1801 THOMAS JEFFERSON (1743–1826)
Albert Hart *The Beautiful Mrs Reynolds* (US 18)
P. R. Scammon *My Own United States* (US 18)
Lionel Adams *Janice Meredith* (US 24)
Frank Walsh *America* (US 24)
Albert Hart *The Man Without a Country* (US 25)
The Howards of Virginia (US 40)
Remarkable Andrew (US 42)
Grandon Rhodes *The Magnificent Doll* (US 46)
Ken Howard *1776* (US 72)
Ken Howard *Independence* (US 76)

1809 JAMES MADISON (1751–1836)
Burgess Meredith *The Magnificent Doll* (US 46)

1817 JAMES MONROE (1758–1831)
Charles Brandt *The Beautiful Mrs Reynolds* (US 18)
Emmett King *The Man Without a Country* (US 25)

1825 JOHN QUINCY ADAMS (1767–1848)
No portrayals on screen

1829 ANDREW JACKSON (1767–1845)
F. C. Earle *My Own United States* (US 18)
George Irving *The Eagle of the Sea* (US 26)
Russell Simpson *The Frontiersman* (US 27)
John Barrymore *The Gorgeous Hussy* (US 36)
Hugh Sothern *The Buccaneer* (US 38)
Edward Ellis *Man of Conquest* (US 39)
Brian Donlevy *The Remarkable Andrew* (US 42)
Der unendliche Weg (Ger 43)
Lionel Barrymore *Lone Star* (US 52)
Charlton Heston *The President's Lady* (US 53)
Basil Ruysdael *Davy Crockett, King of the Wild Frontier* (US 55)
Carl Brenton Reid *The First Texan* (US 56)
Charlton Heston *The Buccaneer* (US 58)

1837 MARTIN VAN BUREN (1782–1862)
Charles Trowbridge *The Gorgeous Hussy* (US 36)

1841 WILLIAM HENRY HARRISON (1773–1841)
Douglass Dumbrille *Ten Gentlemen from West Point* (US 42)

1841 JOHN TYLER (1790–1862)
No portrayals on screen

1845 JAMES KNOX POLK (1795–1849)
Addison Richards *The Oregon Trail* (US 59)

1849 ZACHARY TAYLOR (1784–1850)
The Fall of Black Hawk (US 12)
Harry Holden *The Yankee Clipper* (US 27)

1850 MILLARD FILLMORE (1800–74)
No portrayals on screen

1853 FRANKLIN PIERCE (1804–69)
Porter Hall *The Great Moment* (US 44)

1857 JAMES BUCHANAN (1791–1868)
No portrayals on screen

Left
The young Henry Fonda (*left*) as *Young Mr Lincoln* (US 39). The same year John Carradine (*right*), who was actually younger than Fonda, played old Mr Lincoln in *Of Human Hearts* (US 39).

Right
John Fitzgerald Kennedy (*left*) as a young PT boat commander during World War II. Cliff Robertson (*right*) as the future President in *PT 109* (US 63).

1861 ABRAHAM LINCOLN (1809–65)
Uncle Tom's Cabin (US 03)
The Blue and the Grey (US 08)
The Reprieve (US 08)
The Life of Abraham Lincoln (US 08)
The Assassination of Abraham Lincoln (US 09)
Stirring Days in Old Virginia (US 09)
George Stelle *The Sleeping Sentinel* (US 10)
Abraham Lincoln's Clemency (US 11)
The Old Man and Jim (US 11)
The Fortunes of War (US 11)
James Dayton *Lieutenant Grey* (US 11)
Ralph Ince *Under One Flag* (US 11)
A Romance of the '60's (US 11)
Ralph Ince *The Battle Hymn of the Republic* (US 11)
Grant and Lincoln (US 11)
Ralph Ince *The Seventh Son* (US 12)
H. G. Lonsdale *The Fall of Black Hawk* (US 12)
Ralph Ince *Lincoln's Gettysburg Address* (US 12)
Francis Ford *On Secret Service* (US 12)
Francis Ford *When Lincoln Paid* (US 12)
When Lincoln was President (US 12)
Hugh Ford *With Lee in Virginia* (US 13)
From Rail Splitter to President (US 13)
William Clifford *The Toll of War* (US 13)
Lincoln for the Defense (US 13)
Ralph Ince *Songbird of the North* (US 13)
Willard Mack *The Battle of Gettysburg* (US 13)
Ralph Ince *Lincoln the Lover* (US 14)
Ralph Ince *The Man Who Knew Lincoln* (US 14)
Benjamin Chapin *Lincoln's Thanksgiving Story* (US 14) not released
The Sleeping Sentinel (US 14)
Benjamin Chapin *Old Abe* (US 15)
The Magistrate's Story (US 15)
Joseph Henabery *The Birth of a Nation* (US 15)
Francis Ford *The Heart of Lincoln* (US 15)
William Ferguson *The Battle Cry of Peace* (US 15)

Frank McGlynn *The Life of Abraham Lincoln* (US 15)
The Heart of Maryland (US 15)
Samuel Drane *The Crisis* (US 16)
Benjamin Chapin 10 one-reelers collectively known as *The Lincoln Cycle* (US 17)
Ralph Ince *Battle Hymn of the Republic* (US 17)
Gerald Day *My Own United States* (US 18)
Benjamin Chapin *Down the River* (US 18)
Rolf Leslie *Victory and Peace* (GB 18)
Benjamin Chapin *Lincoln's Thanksgiving Story* (US 18)
Benjamin Chapin *Children of Democracy* (US 18)
Benjamin Chapin *Son of Democracy* (US 18)
Meyer F. Stroell *The Copperhead* (US 19)
The Land of Opportunity (US 20)
Ralph Ince *The Highest Law* (US 21)
Ellery Paine *Lincoln's Gettysburg Address* (US 22) talkie
Wild Bill Hickock (US 23)
The Heart of Abraham Lincoln (US 24)
Ellery Paine (?) *An Episode in the Life of Abraham Lincoln* (US 24) talkie
George A. Billings *Barbara Freitchie* (US 24)
George A. Billings *The Dramatic Life of Abraham Lincoln* (US 24)
Charles E. Bull *The Iron Horse* (US 24)
Abraham Lincoln (US 25)
George A. Billings *The Man Without a Country* (US 25)
George A. Billings *Hands Up* (US 26)
Charles E. Bull *The Heart of Maryland* (US 27)
Rev. Lincoln Caswell *Lincoln's Gettysburg Address* (US 27) talkie
Uncle Tom's Cabin (US 27)
The Heart of Lincoln (US 27)
Frank Austin *Court Martial* (US 28)
Walter Houston *Two Americans* (US 29)
George A. Billings *Lincoln's Gettysburg Address* (US 30)
Only the Brave (US 30)

Walter Houston *Abraham Lincoln* (US 30)
Frank McGlynn *Abraham Lincoln, the Pioneer* (US 33)
Frank McGlynn *Abraham Lincoln, the Statesman* (US 33)
Frank McGlynn *The Littlest Rebel* (US 35)
Frank McGlynn *Roaring West* (US 35)
Chic Sale *The Perfect Tribute* (US 35)
Frank McGlynn *The Prisoner of Shark Island* (US 36)
Frank McGlynn *Hearts in Bondage* (US 36)
Segraren vid Hampton Roads (Swe c. 36)
Bud Buster *Cavalry* (US 36)
Frank McGlynn *Western Gold* (US 37)
Frank McGlynn *Wells Fargo* (US 37)
Frank McGlynn *The Man without a Country* (US 37)
Frank McGlynn *The Plainsman* (US 37)
Albert Russell *Courage of the West* (US 37)
Triumph (GB? 37)
Percy Parsons *Victoria the Great* (GB 37)
Frank McGlynn *The Lone Ranger* (US 37)
Frank McGlynn *The Mad Empress* (Mex 39)
A Failure at Fifty (US 39)
Frank McGlynn *Lincoln in the White House* (US 39)
Frank McGlynn and Walter Houston *Land of Liberty* (US 39) compilation film
John Carradine *Of Human Hearts* (US 39)
Henry Fonda *Young Mr Lincoln* (US 39)
Raymond Massey *Abe Lincoln in Illinois* (US 39)
Victor Killain *Virginia City* (US 40)
Charles Middleton *Sante Fe Trail* (US 40)
A Dispatch from Reuters (US 40)
Dreams (US 40)
Not Long Remember (US 41)
Charles Middleton *They Died With Their Boots On* (US 41)
Joel Day *The Days of Buffalo Bill* (US 46)
Jeff Corey *Rock Island Trail* (US 50)
Jeff Corey *Transcontinent Express* (US 50)

G. William Horsley *Lincoln in Illinois* (US 50)
Hans Conreid *New Mexico* (US 51)
Leslie Kimmell *The Tall Target* (US 51)
Thomas Mitchell (?) *The Lincoln-Holmes Incident, a Folktale* (US 52)
Suddenly (US 54)
Stanley Hall *The Prince of Players* (US 55)
The Palmetto Conspiracy (US 55)
Tom Tryon *Springfield Incident* (US 55)
The Abductors (US 57) corpse only
Austin Green *The Story of Mankind* (US 57)
Royal Dano *Lincoln: The Young Years* (US c. 59 TVM)
Lincoln at Gettysburg (US 60)
Raymond Massey *How the West was Won* (US 63)
Dennis Weaver *The Great Man's Whiskers* (US 71)
Charlton Heston *Lincoln's Gettysburg Address* (US 73)
William Deprato *The Faking of the President* (US 76)
John Anderson *The Lincoln Conspiracy* (US 77)
Ford Rainey *Guardian of the Wilderness* (US 77)

1865 ANDREW JOHNSON (1808–75)
Van Heflin *Tennessee Johnson* (US 42)

1869 ULYSSES SIMPSON GRANT (1822–85)
Barbara Freitchie (US 08)
Stirring Days in Old Virginia (US 08)
The Blue and the Gray (US 08)
The Old Soldier's Story (US 09)
The Bugle Call (US 09)
From Wallace to Grant (US 11)
Alvin Wyckoff *Lieutenant Grey of the Confederacy* (US 11)
Grant and Lincoln (US 11)
With Lee in Virginia (US 13)
The Littlest Rebel (US 14)
Paul Scardon *The Battle Cry of Peace* (US 15)
Donald Crisp *The Birth of a Nation* (US 15)

Frank Murray *My Own United States* (US 18)
Wilbur J. Fox *The Warrens of Virginia* (US 24)
Walter Rogers *Abraham Lincoln* (US 24)
Dixie (US 24)
Walter Rogers *Flaming Frontier* (US 26)
Walter Rogers *The Heart of Maryland* (US 27)
Walter Rogers *The Little Shepherd of Kingdom Come* (US 28)
Court-Martial (US 28)
Fred Warren *Abraham Lincoln* (US 30)
Guy Oliver *Only the Brave* (US 30)
Fred Warren *Secret Service* (US 31)
Fred Warren *Operator 13* (US 34)
Joseph Crehan *They Died With Their Boots On* (US 42)
Joseph Crehan *The Adventures of Mark Twain* (US 44)
Joseph Crehan *Silver River* (US 48)
Sunset at Appotomax (US 53)
John Hamilton *Sitting Bull* (US 54)
Hayden Rorke *Drum Beat* (US 54)
Henry Morgan *How the West was Won* (US 63)
Buffalo Bill, l'eroe del Far West (It/Fr/FRG 65)
Antonio Albaisin (?) *Ringo e Gringo contro tutti* (It 66)
Jason Robards *The Legend of the Lone Ranger* (US 81)

1877 RUTHERFORD BIRCHARD HAYES (1822–93)
No portrayals on screen

1881 JAMES ABRAM GARFIELD (1831–81)
Night Raiders (US 39)
Lawrence Wolf *No More Excuses* (US 68)
Van Johnson *Il prezzo del potere* (It/Sp 69)

1881 CHESTER ALAN ARTHUR (1831–86)
Larry Gates *Cattle King* (US 63)

1885 and **1893** STEPHEN GROVER CLEVELAND (1837–1908)
Topack *Lively Political Debate* (US 94)

William B. Davison *Lillian Russell* (US 40)
Pat McCormick *Buffalo Bill and the Indians* (US 76)
Haji Washington (Iran 83)

1889 BENJAMIN HARRISON (1833–1901)
Steele *Lively Political Debate* (US 94)
Roy Gordon *Stars and Stripes Forever* (US 52)

1897 WILLIAM MCKINLEY (1843–1901)
Frank Conroy *This is My Affair* (US 37)

1901 THEODORE ROOSEVELT (1858–1919)
Terrible Teddy, The Grizzly King (US 01)
The 'Teddy' Bears (US 07)
Big Game Hunting in Africa (US 09) reconstruction newsfilm with actor portraying T.R.
Up San Juan Hill (US 09)
T.R. himself in unidentified one-reel comedy starring Matty Roubert (US 14)
T.R. himself in *Womanhood, the Glory of a Nation* (US 17)
W. E. Whittle *General Pershing* (US 19)
The Fighting Roosevelts (US 19)
Jack Ridgway *The Copperhead* (US 19)
E. J. Radcliffe *Sundown* (US 24)
Buck Black *Lights of Old Broadway* (US 25)
Frank Hopper *The Rough Riders* (US 27)
The Man Who Dared (US 33)
Sidney Blackmer *This Is My Affair* (US 37)
Wallis Clark *Yankee Doodle Dandy* (US 42)
Wallis Clark *Jack London* (US 43)
Sidney Blackmer *In Old Oklahoma* (US 43)
Sidney Blackmer *Buffalo Bill* (US 44)
John Alexander *Arsenic and Old Lace* (US 44)
John Morton *I Wonder Who's Kissing Her Now?* (US 47)
Sidney Blackmer *My Girl Tisa* (US 48)
John Alexander *Fancy Pants* (US 50)
Edward Cassidy *The First Travelling Saleslady* (US 56)

Left
Richard Dixon as Richard Nixon in *The Private Files of J. Edgar Hoover* (US 77).

Right
President Reagan has only been portrayed on screen once. He played himself in *It's a Great Feeling* (US 49). (*George Eastman House Stills Collection*)

Karl Swenson *Brighty of the Grand Canyon* (US 66)
Brian Keith *The Wind and the Lion* (US 75)
James Whitmore *Bully* (US 78)

1909 WILLIAM HOWARD TAFT (1857–1930)
The Sculptor's Nightmare (US 08)

1913 THOMAS WOODROW WILSON (1856–1924)
himself in introduction to *The Battle Cry of Peace* (US 15)
himself in *Womanhood, the Glory of a Nation* (US 17)
The Great Victory (US 18)
Orlo Eastman *The Kaiser: The Beast of Berlin* (US 18)
R. A. Faulkner *General Pershing* (US 19)
Alexander Knox *Wilson* (US 44)
Earl Lee *The Story of Will Rogers* (US 52)
L. Kovsakov *The Unforgettable Year 1919* (USSR 52)
Frank Forsyth *Oh! What a Lovely War* (GB 69)
Jerzy Kaliszewski *Polonia Restituta* (Pol/USSR/Hun/Cz/GDR 81)

1921 WARREN GAMALIEL HARDING (1865–1923)
No portrayals on screen

1923 JOHN CALVIN COOLIDGE (1872–1933)
Ian Wolfe *The Court Martial of Billy Mitchell* (US 55)

1929 HERBERT CLARK HOOVER (1874–1964)
Tom Jensen *Fires of Youth* (US 31)

1933 FRANKLIN DELANO ROOSEVELT (1822–1945)
Capt. Jack Young *Yankee Doodle Dandy* (US 42)
Capt. Jack Young *This Is the Army* (US 43)
Herr Roosevelt Plaudert (Ger 43)

Godfrey Tearle *The Beginning or the End* (US 47)
Nikolai Cherkasov *The First Front* (USSR 49)
Secret Mission (USSR 50)
Beau James (US 57)
Ralph Bellamy *Sunrise at Campobello* (US 60)
Richard Nelson *The Pigeon that Took Rome* (US 62)
Stephen Roberts *First to Fight* (US 67)
Stanislav Jaskevik *Liberation* (USSR 70–71)
Edward Herrman *Eleanor and Franklin* (US 76)
Dan O'Herlihy *MacArthur—The Rebel General* (US 77)
Stephen Roberts *Ring of Passion* (US 77, TVM)
Howard Da Silva *The Private Files of J. Edgar Hoover* (US 78)
Teheran '43 (USSR/Fr/Swz 81)
Jason Robards *F.D.R.: The Last Year* (US 81) TVM
Edward Herrmann *Annie* (US 82)

1945 HARRY S. TRUMAN (1884–1972)
Art Baker *The Beginning or the End* (US 47)
Secret Mission (USSR 50)
Call Me Madam (US 53)
uncredited child *Alias Jesse James* (US 59)
James Whitmore *Give 'Em Hell, Harry!* (US 75)
E. G. Marshall *Collision Course* (US 76)
Ed Flanders *MacArthur—The Rebel General* (US 77)

1953 DWIGHT DAVID EISENHOWER (1890–1969)
Harry Carey Jr *The Long Grey Line* (US 55)
Henry Grace *The Longest Day* (US 72)
Robert Beer *The Right Stuff* (US 83)

1961 JOHN FITZGERALD KENNEDY (1917–63)
Kennedy in his True Colours (Chn 62)
Cliff Robertson *PT 109* (US 63)
William Jordan *The Private Files of J. Edgar Hoover* (US 77)

James Franciscus *Jacqueline Bouvier Kennedy* (US 82) TVM
Robert Hogan *Prince Jack* (US 84) TVM

1963 LYNDON BAINES JOHNSON (1908–73)
Ivan Triesault *How to Succeed in Business without Really Trying* (US 67)
Colpo di Stato (It 68)
The Wrecking Crew (US 69)
Andrew Duggan *The Private Files of J. Edgar Hoover* (US 77)
Donald Moffat *The Right Stuff* (US 83)
Kenneth Mars *Prince Jack* (US 84) TVM

1969 RICHARD MILHOUS NIXON (1913–)
Jean-Pierre Biesse *Made in USA* (Fr 67)
The Statue (US 70)
Cold Turkey (US 70)
Million Dollar Duck (US 70)
Jim Dixon *Is There Sex After Death?* (US 71)
Richard Dixon *The Faking of the President 1974* (US 76)
Richard Dixon *The Private Files of J. Edgar Hoover* (US 77)
Anderson Humphreys *The Cayman Triangle* (CayI 77)
Harry Spillman *Born Again* (US 78)
Richard M. Dixon *Hopscotch* (US 80)
Richard M. Dixon *Where the Buffalo Roam* (US 80)
Philip Baker Hall *Secret Honor: The Last Testament of Richard M. Nixon* (US 84) TVM

1974 GERALD RUDOLPH FORD (1913–)
Dick Crockett *The Pink Panther Strikes Again* (GB 76)

1977 JAMES EARL CARTER (1924–)
Ed Beheler *The Cayman Triangle* (CayI 77)
Black Sunday (US 77)

1981 RONALD REAGAN (1911–)
himself in *It's a Great Feeling* (US 49)

The first British example was *The Jewish King Lear* (GB 12), filmed at the Pavilion Theatre and premièred at New King's Hall in the Commercial Road. **America's first Jewish picture** was *A Passover Miracle* (US 14), released by Kalem in two versions, one with English sub-titles, the other with Yiddish.

The first talkie in Yiddish was Sidney M. Goldin's *Style and Class* (US 29), a Judea Films production with Goldie Eisenman and Marty Baratz.

PRODUCTION OUTPUT

According to Rob Edelman's filmography of feature films in Yiddish (*Films in Review* June/July 1978), there were 53 produced in America 1924–61, 17 in Poland pre-1940, 4 in Russia 1925–33 and solitary examples from West Germany in 1948 and Italy in 1949. Mr Edelman believes there may also have been Romanian and Hungarian Yiddish features.

After *Three Daughters* (US 61), production ceased entirely for nearly 20 years. Then in 1980 came Samy Szlingerbaum's *Brussels-Transit* (Bel 80), a story of Polish-born survivors of the holocaust settling in Brussels after World War II. This film, which had a Yiddish commentary and part-Yiddish dialogue, was followed by *The Dybbuk* (Pol 82), a Jewish State Theatre of Poland production from the play by Syymon Szurmiez, and an Israeli offering called *If They Give, Take* (Isr 82). A short directed by David Greenwald, *The Well* (US 84), may herald renewed production of Yiddish films in America.

The revival of interest in Yiddish films was stimulated by the founding of the National Centre for Jewish Film at Brandeis University, Waltham, Mass., established in 1976 with 30 mainly incomplete films from the estate of producer Joseph Seiden. It now houses over 2000 films on Jewish subjects as well as an extensive photo and rare book collection. Despite the lack of any recent product, a Yiddish Film Festival was held in New York in 1978 and the following year a season of Yiddish films ran at Cineplex in Toronto. In Europe, retrospectives of Yiddish cinema were held in Frankfurt by Walter Schobert in 1980, 1982 and 1984. Two feature-length documentaries, *Das Jiddische Kino* (FRG 83) and *Almonds and Raisins* (GB 84), have also been made on the history of Yiddish films. The former introduced a season of Yiddish features on West Germany's ZDF television station in April 1983.

ANTI-SEMITIC FILMS

These have been rare. In 1935, when Joseph Goebbels ordered a search to be made for foreign anti-Semitic films that could be released in Germany, the only example that could be obtained was a primitive Swedish talkie called *Pettersson and Bendel* (Swe 33). Curiously the Nazi-controlled film industry of the Third Reich made no overtly anti-Semitic pictures until just before the war, when Hans Heinz Zerlett directed *Robert und Bertram* (Ger 39), a comedy about two German tramps who get the better of a rascally Jew and save the innkeeper's lovely Aryan daughter from the fate of marrying him. The following year cinematic Jew-baiting began in earnest with *Jud Süss* (Ger 40), *Die Rothschilds* (Ger 40) and *Der ewige Jude* (Ger 40), three films whose virulent hatred was a presage of the vengeance to be wreaked on the race they vilified. Of these *Jud Süss* is undoubtedly the most notorious; it is also the only one to have been released since the war. Dubbed in Arabic, it was distributed in the Arab states in 1955 by the USSR agency Sovexport.

Horror

The character most frequently portrayed in horror films is Count Dracula, the creation of the Irish writer Bram Stoker (1847–1912), whose novel *Dracula* was published in 1897. Representations of the Count or his immediate descendants on screen outnumber those of his closest rival, Frankenstein's monster, by 148 to 96 (see filmography).

Although Count Dracula has been portrayed on screen no less than 148 times, only once has he been depicted as described in Bram Stoker's novel. For the first and only time in movies the Count was correctly adorned with a moustache when Christopher Lee played the role in *El Conde Dracula* (Sp/FRG/It 73).

DRACULA FILMOGRAPHY

The filmography excludes the frequent appearances that Dracula has made in cartoon films. The name of the artiste portraying the vampire is given before the title where this is known.

Drakula (Hun 21)
Max Schreck *Nosferatu, eine Symphonie des Grauens* (Ger 22)
Bela Lugosi *Dracula* (US 31)
Carlos Villarias *Dracula* (US 31) Spanish language
Gloria Holden *Dracula's Daughter* (US 36) Dracula himself seen as corpse only
Lon Chaney Jnr *Son of Dracula* (US 43) despite title, Chaney plays Dracula himself, there is no son in the picture
John Carradine *House of Frankenstein* (US 44)
John Carradine *House of Dracula* (US 45)
Bela Lugosi *Abbott and Costello Meet Frankenstein* (US 48)
Atif Kaptan *Drakula Istanbula* (Tur 53)
El Fantasma de la operatta (Arg 55)
German Robles *El Castillo de los monstruos* (Mex 57)
Jerry Baline *Blood of Dracula* (US 57)
Victor Fabian *Frankenstein Meets Dracula* (US 57)
Victor Fabian *Return of the Wolfman* (US 57)
Victor Fabian *Revenge of Dracula* (US 57)
Curse of Dracula* (US 57)
Francis Lederer *The Return of Dracula* (US 58)
Black Inferno* (US 58)
Christopher Lee *Dracula* (GB 58)
Castle of Dracula* (GB 58)
Dracula* (US 59)
Gene Gronemeyer *The Teenage Frankenstein** (US 59)
Gene Gronemeyer *Slave of the Vampire** (US 59)
Donald Glut (as Dracula's son) *I Was a Teenage Vampire** (US 59)
Richard Christy *Pawns of Satan** (US 59)
Christopher Lee *Tempi duri per i vampiri* (It 59)
Davis Peel *Brides of Dracula* (GB 60)
Chimi Kim *The Bad Flower* (S. Kor 61)
Frankenstein, el vampiro y cia (Mex 61)
Donald Glut (as Dracula's son) *Monster Rumble** (US 61)
Yechoon Lee *Ahkea Khots* (S. Kor 61)
Jeffrey Smithers *House on Bare Mountain* (US 62)
Donald Glut (as Dracula's son) *Dragstrip Dracula** (US 62)
Escala en Hi-Fi (Sp 63)
Kiss Me Quick! (US 64)
Sexy Proibitissimo (It 64)
Jack Smith *Batman Dracula* (US 64)
John Carradine *Billy the Kid versus Dracula* (US 65)
Mga Manugang ni Drakula (Phi 65)
Christopher Lee *Dracula—Prince of Darkness* (GB 65)
Glenn Sherrard *Horror of Dracula** (US 66)
Mitch Evans *Dr Terror's Gallery of Horrors* (US 66)
Pluto Felix *The Worst Crime of All!* (US 66)
Cesar Del Campo (?) *El Imperio de Dracula* (Mex 66)
Chappaqua (US 66)
Cesar Silva *La Sombra del murcielago* (Mex 66)
Dracula's Wedding Day (US 67)
Harrison Marks *Vampire* (GB 67)

Dante Rivero *Batman Fights Dracula* (Phi 67)
Harrison Marks *The Naked World of Harrison Marks* (GB 67)
Bill Rogers (as descendant of Dracula) *A Taste of Blood* (US 67)
John Carradine *Las Vampiras* (Mex 67)
Christopher Lee *Dracula Has Risen from the Grave* (GB 68)
Santo en el tesoro de Dracula (Mex 68)
Dracula Meets the Outer Space Chicks (US 68)
Mondo Keyhole (US(?) 68)
Isabell, A Dream (It 68)
Aldo Monti *El Vampiro y el Sexo* (Mex 68)
Vince Kelly (as descendant of Dracula) *Dracula, the Dirty Old Man* (US 69)
Men of Action Meet Women of Dracula (Phi 69)
Christopher Lee *One More Time* (GB 69)
Alex d'Arcy *The Blood of Dracula's Castle* (US 69)
Paul Naschy *Dracula versus Frankenstein/US: Blood of Frankenstein* (Sp/FRG/It 69)
Tales of Blood and Terror (US/GB 69)
Christopher Lee *The Magic Christian* (GB 69)
Does Dracula Really Suck (US 69) homosexual Dracula
Gabby Paul (?) *Il Risveglio di Dracula* (It 69)
Mad Monster Party (US 69) puppet feature
Ingrid Pitt *Countess Dracula* (GB 70)
Marty Feldman *Every Home Should Have One* (GB 70)
Des Roberts *Guess What Happened to Count Dracula?* (US 70)
Christopher Lee *Nachts, wenn Dracula erwacht* (FRG/Sp/It 70)
Dennis Price *Vampyros Lesbos/Die Erbin des Dracula* (Sp/FRG 70)
Tunnel Under the World (It 70)
Christopher Lee *Taste the Blood of Dracula* (GB 70)
Christopher Lee *The Scars of Dracula* (GB 70)
Eva Renzi (as descendant of Dracula) *Beiss mich Liebling* (FRG 70)
Des Roberts *Dracula's lusterne vampire/Dracula's Vampire Lust* (Swz 70)
Paul Albert Krumm *Jonathan, Vampire sterben nicht* (FRG 70)
Denholm Elliott *Dracula* (GB 71, TVM)
Britt Nichols (as Dracula's daughter) *La Fille de Dracula* (Fr/FRG 71)
Mori Kishida *Chi o Su Me/Lake of Dracula* (Jap 71)
Paul Naschy *Hombre que vino de ummo* (Sp/FRG 71)
Zandor Vorkov *Dracula versus Frankenstein aka Blood of Frankenstein* (US 71)
Howard Vernon *Dracula contra el Dr Frankenstein* (Sp/Fr 71)
Jim Parker *The Mad Lust of a Hot Vampire* (US 71)
The Lust of Dracula (US 71)
Once Upon a Prime Time (Can 71)
Ferdy Mayne *Happening der Vampire* (FRG 71)
Charles McCauley *Blacula* (US 72)
Christopher Lee *Umbracle* (Sp 72)
Dennis Price *Dracula contra Frankenstein* (Sp 72)
Anthony Franciosa *Schloss des Schreckens* (FRG 72)
Dracula, A Family Romance (US 72)
Paul Naschy *La Messe nere della Contessa Dracula* (It 72)
Narcisso Ibañez Menta *La Saga de los Draculas* (Sp 72)

Des Roberts *Dracula Vampire Sexuel* (Swz 72)
Howard Vernon *La Hija de Dracula* (Sp 72)
Christopher Lee *Dracula AD 1972* (GB 72)
David Azivu (?) *Santo y Blue Demon contra Dracula y el Hombre Lobo* (Mex 72)
Christopher Lee *El Conde Dracula/GB: Bram Stoker's Dracula* (Sp/FRG/It 73)
Chabelo y Pepito contra los monstruos (Mex 73)
Paul Naschy *El Gran amor del Conde Dracula* (Sp 73)
Udo Kier *Blood for Dracula* (It/Fr 73)
Christopher Lee *The Satanic Rites of Dracula* (GB 73)
Harry Nillson (as Dracula's son) *Son of Dracula* (GB 73)
The House of Dracula's Daughter (US 73)
Christopher Lee *Tendre Dracula* (Fr 73)
Shadow of Dracula (Can 73)
Jack Palance *Dracula* (GB 74, TVM)
John Forbes-Robertson *Legend of the 7 Golden Vampires* (GB/HK 74)
David Niven *Vampira* (GB 74)
Dracula's Blood (US 74)
Hope Stansbury (as Dracula's daughter) *Blood* (US 74)
Dracula Goes to RP (Phi 74)
Tiempos duros para Drácula (Arg/Sp 75)
Peter Wechsburg (as illegitimate son of Dracula) *Deafula* (US 74)
Dracula is not Dead (GB 75)
Rossano Brazzi (?) *Il cav. constante nicosia demoniaco ovvero Dracula in Brianza* (It 76)
Christopher Lee *Dracula Père et Fils* (Fr 77)
Evelyne Kraft *Lady Dracula* (FRG 77)
Louis Jourdan *Count Dracula* (GB 77, TVM)
Michael Pataki (as Dracula's grandson) *Dracula's Dog* (US 78)
John Carradine *Nocturna* (US 78) 'the first soft-porn-vampire-disco-rock movie'
Christopher Lee *Count Dracula and His Vampire Bride* (GB 78)
Joe Rigoli *Draculin/US: Dracula and Son* (Sp 78)
Fabian Forte *La Dinastia Dracula* (Mex 78)
Enrique Alvarez Felix *Dracula* (Mex 78)
Stefan Sileanu (as the historical Dracula, Vlad the Impaler) *Vlad Tepes/US: The True Life of Dracula* (Rom 79)
George Hamilton *Love at First Bite* (US 79)
Klaus Kinski *Nosferatu: Phantom der Nacht* (FRG 79)
Judd Hirsch *Halloween That Almost Wasn't* (US 79) TVM
Richard Lynch *Vampire* (US 79) TVM
Frank Langella *Dracula* (US 79)
Gianni Garko *Dracula in Oberbayern* (FRG 79)
The Diabolic Loves of Nosferatu (Sp 79)
Peter Lowey *Dracula Bites the Big Apple* (US 79)
Jamie Gillis *Dracula Sucks* (US 80)
Gerald Fielding *Dracula's Last Rites* (US 80)
Andreas Voutsinas *Les Charlots Chez Dracula Junior* (Fr 80)
Louise Fletcher *Mama Dracula* (Fr/Bel 80)
Johnny Harden *Star Virgin* (US 81)
Andres Garcia *El Macho Bionico* (Mex 81)
Dracula Blows his Cool (US 82)
Dracula, Sovereign of the Damned (US? 83)
Kostas Soumas *Dracula Tan Exarchia* (Gre 83)

* amateur productions

Musicals

The first musical with an original score was MGM's *The Broadway Melody* (US 29), with Bessie Love, Anita Page and Charles King, which was premièred at Grauman's Chinese Theatre in Hollywood on 1 February 1929. The songs were: *Give My Regards to Broadway* (George M. Cohan); *The Wedding Day of the Painted Doll, Love Boat, Broadway Melody, Boy Friend, You Were Meant For Me* (Arthur Freed and Herb Brown); and *Truthful Deacon Brown* (Willard Robison).

The first British musical was BIP's *Raise the Roof* (GB 30), directed by Walter Summers with Betty Balfour as an actress bribed by a rich man to ruin his son's touring review.

The first musical in colour was Warner Bros' *On With the Show*, directed by Alan Crosland in two-colour Technicolor with Betty Compson and Joe E. Brown and premièred in New York on 28 May 1929. **The first British** was BIP's *Harmony Heaven* (GB 30) with Polly Ward and Stuart Hall.

The musical with the most song numbers was Madan Theatres' *Indra Sabha* (Ind 32), a Hindi movie with 71 songs.

The Hollywood musical with the most songs was RKO's *The Story of Vernon and Irene Castle* (US 39). In the course of its 93 minutes running time the film proffered, in the words of *Variety*, 'one original song and 40 old pop songs by divers tunesmiths'.

Not many movies attract an audience of blind patrons, but there was a recent exception. In February 1983 the Linda Ronstadt musical *The Pirates of Penzance* (GB 83) opened in Miami and Fort Lauderdale with a braille libretto available on request. Prepared by blind Pittsburgh writer–composer Linda Marcus, the braille text included stage directions and keywords to indicate action and scene changes.

Opera

The first operatic films were of an aria from *Romeo and Juliet* sung by Cossira of the Paris Opéra and Victor Maurel singing the title roles from *Don Juan* and *Falstaff*, premièred at the Phono-Cinéma-Théâtre at the Paris Exposition on 8 June 1900.

The first complete opera to be filmed was Gounod's *Faust* (GB 07), directed by Arthur Gilbert in the Gaumont Chronophone sound-on-disc process. **The first in America** was a three-reel version of *Pagliacci* (US 13), produced in the Vi-T-Phone system by the Vi-T-Ascope Co.

The first sound-on-film operatic production was *Rigoletto Act II* (GB 26), presented by the De Forest Phonofilm process. **The first complete sound-on-film opera** was *La Serva Padrona* (It 32), directed by Giogio Mannini for Lirica Film, with Bruna Dragoni, Enrica Mayer and Carlo Lombardi.

The chorines in the first British musical, *Raise the Roof* (GB 30), were played by the real life Plaza Tiller Girls. *Right*: Betty Balfour, Britain's most popular star of the silent screen, demonstrated her vocal talents in the lead role playing opposite Maurice Evans, who was later lured to Hollywood.

Left
Birth of the musical—*Broadway Melody* (US 29) was all-singin', all-dancin' and starred Bessie Love, a veteran of Hollywood's earliest days who went on performing in movies for over 60 years.

The first feature-length film about interplanetary space travel was Nordisk's *A Trip to Mars* (Den 19). The space vehicle is resolutely 19th century, whereas a decade later science-fiction films were portraying space rockets by no means unlike the real thing. (*Nordisk*)

Science Fiction

The first feature-length science fiction movie was Nordisk's *A Trip to Mars* (Den 19), starring Lily Jacobson and G. S. Tolness. The story was of a space probe to Mars, where the hero finds the inhabitants to be peaceable, high-minded Scandinavian-type people who live on a vegetarian diet and wear 'flimsy, flowing robes'. The daughter of the Martian ruler falls in love with the astronaut and they return to Earth to establish a new order based on ideals of peace and love.

Sex

Sex on screen followed rapidly on the emergence of cinema as a public entertainment. The pioneer producer of sex films was Eugène Pirou, beginning with a three-minute long production titled *Le Coucher de la mariée* (Fr 96), starring blonde and chubby Louise Willy. Based on an act performed by Mlle Willy at the Olympia music-hall in Paris the previous year, the film showed a newly-wed couple preparing for bed. The girl's husband removes her satin slipper and presses it ecstatically to his lips, then she disrobes and puts on her night attire while her husband watches with evident desire. Finally Mlle Willy does a provocative little dance before the couple retire to bed. The film caused a sensation when it was premièred in the basement of the Café de Paris in November 1896 and was soon showing at two other *salles* as well, one in the boulevard Bonne-Nouvelle and the other at 86 rue de Clichy. Pirou followed this success with other sex subjects, such as *Bain de la Parisienne* (Fr 97), *Lever de la Parisienne* (Fr 97) and *La Puce* (Fr 97), most of them based on strip-tease acts playing in the Paris music halls. *La Puce*, for example, showed a maiden afflicted with a flea who removes her garments one by one to locate the offending insect.

Pirou's chief rival in the blue-movie field was Georges Méliès, whose *Les Indiscrets/The Peeping Toms* (Fr 96) came out at the end of 1896. Méliès was the man who brought nudity to the screen in *Après le bal* (Fr 97) and won a wide following with such sensational subjects as *En Cabinet particulier/A Private Dinner* (Fr 97),

L'Indiscret aux Bains de mer/Peeping Tom at the Seaside (Fr 97) and La Modèle irascible/An Irritable Model (Fr 97). In England these films were distributed by the Warwick Trading Co., who described them as 'welcome at any smoking concert or stag party'.

The earliest known American film on a sexual theme is American Mutoscope & Biograph's *The Downward Path* (US 02), a five-scene melodrama about a share-cropper's daughter who follows a downward path to prostitution—in one of the scenes she is encountered soliciting in the streets.

Young ladies who took rides in cars like this in 1910 were in danger of being carried off by a white slaver in spats, according to the sensational Danish sex drama *The White Slave Traffic* (Den 10). (*Nordisk*)

While most of the above films were very much of the 'What the Butler Saw' genre, the longer sex drama designed for general release emerged with Fotorama's *The White Slave Traffic* (Den 10), a two-reel shocker of such drawing power at the box office that within a few months Nordisk had produced a rival version with the same name. It was no less sensational. A publicity still shows a scene of a kidnapped girl being savagely bea-ten. Ole Olsen of Nordisk recalled that at the trade show in Berlin, the German cinema managers all clambered on to their seats for a better view. It was the success of these Danish sexploitation films—other titles included *The Last Victim of the White Slave Traffic* (Den 11) and *Dealer in Girls* (Den 12)—that inspired George Loane Tucker to make the first American feature-length sex picture, *Traffic in Souls* (US 13), starring Jane Gail and Matt Moore. Made clandestinely—not because of the subject, but because Universal did not believe that the American public were ready for feature films—Tucker's $5700 movie garnered record earnings of $450,000.

NUDITY ON SCREEN

Female leads appeared in the nude for the first time in two feature films released in the same week in October 1916. In the Fox production *Daughter of the Gods* (US 16), filmed on location in the lush settings of St Augusta, Jamaica, the nymph-like figure of Australian-born star Annette Kellerman was seen as nature had intended. Miss Kellerman, the Esther Williams of silent movies, was a former professional swimmer who had been the centre of controversy five years earlier when she wore the first one-piece bathing suit. In fact Esther Williams played her in the biopic *Million Dollar Mermaid* (US 52), but by that date the austere provisions of the Hays Code precluded any presentation of the naked human form. The other film with a nude leading lady released the same week was also a Fox feature, *The Ragged Princess* (US 16), a melodrama top-lining winsome 16-year-old blue-eyed blonde newcomer June Caprice. Escaping from an orphanage, where she has been cruelly treated, the ragged waif comes across a woodland lake, strips off her clothes, and runs naked through the trees to plunge into the cooling waters.

The sensation caused in the 1930s by Hedy Lamarr's nude bathing scenes in *Extase* (Cz 33) has given wide currency to the mistaken idea that Miss Lamarr was the first nude actress on screen. She was not even the first nude in Czech movies, a distinction earned by Ira Rina in Gustav Muchaty's *Eroticon* (Cz 29).

Other nude scenes of the pre-*Extase* period were legion. Celio Film's *Idolo Infranto* (It 13) contained a scene set in an artist's studio with a nude model. 'The Naked Truth' was represented by a nude girl in woman director Lois Weber's *The Hypocrites* (US 15). This Paramount release was banned in Ohio and the Mayor of Boston demanded that clothes be painted on to the image of 'Naked Truth', frame by frame. The nude was uncredited, but has been variously claimed as a Miss Margaret Edwards and Lois Weber herself.

D. W. Griffith hired a number of prostitutes to appear naked in the Belshazar's Feast sequence of *Intolerance* (US 16). Joseph Hanabery, Griffith's assis-tant, had been ordered to shoot nude scenes, but decided it was more than he could get away with and had his actresses lightly draped for the orgy. Mean-while Griffith, who was back in New York, did some close shots of nude prostitutes and these were intercut with Hanabery's more discreet scenes. When the film was reissued, in 1942, the New York Censor Board insisted that Griffith's nude inserts be cut.

A nude girl on a crucifix was portrayed in *The Penitentes* (US 16) and a 'Miss Ray' appeared nude in *Le*

Romain Gary shot two versions of *Kill* (US 71), one clothed and the other unclothed. The undraped version, he explained, was for Protestant countries and the other for Catholic countries.

Film du Diable (Bra 17). In *The Tree of Knowledge* (US 20), Yvonne Gardelle appeared naked as Lillith, the temptress who seeks to seduce Adam in the Garden of Eden before the creation of Eve. There were nude bathing scenes in *The Branding Iron* (US 20), *Isle of Love* (US 22)—in the night club scene naked girls threw themselves into a swimming pool as midnight struck—and in Henry Hathaway's *To the Last Man* (US 33), with Esther Ralston as one of the participants. Clara Bow took to nude bathing in *Hula* (US 27).

Sally Rand performed an alfresco dance wearing nothing but a pair of shoes in *Paris at Midnight* (US 26) and a rather more circumspect Elissa Landi played a naked Christian girl bound to the stake in a Roman arena in *The Sign of the Cross* (US 32). Jean Vigo's *A Propos de Nice* (Fr 30) contains a scene of a nude sitting at a cafe table. The 35 mm prints of the film imported into Britain had the scene cut, but the sub-standard gauge prints retained it, since 16 mm film is not subject to censorship in Britain. A full-length nude is observed in the prison scene in *The Yellow Ticket* (US 31), about prostitution in Czarist Russia. The first nude scene in a Russian film, of a widow hysterically mourning in *Earth* (USSR 30), was cut by order of the authorities.

Nude scenes also appeared in *A Man's World* (US 18), *Man, Woman and Marriage* (US 21), *Quo Vadis* (Ger/It 24), *Dante's Inferno* (US 24), *Wege zur Kraft und Schonheit* (Ger 25), *Metropolis* (Ger 26), *Beatrice Cenci* (It 26), *Casanova* (Fr/It 26), *Faust* (Ger 26), *Mandrin* (Fr 28?) and *Secrets of the Orient* (Ger/Fr 28). In most of these films the nakedness was tastefully discrete. Stefan and Franciszka Themerson's *Europa* (Pol 30) had what has been claimed as 'the first full-frontal nude'. The censor demanded that the scene should be cut, but Stefan neglected to do so and the film was released intact.

Following the introduction of the 1934 Hays Code, nudity disappeared from the Hollywood screen for 30 years. The first picture to bypass the ban was Sidney Lumet's *The Pawnbroker* (US 64), in which a woman was shown naked to the waist. The film was passed uncut by the Production Code Administration on the grounds that the scene was an essential element in the narrative. This decision opened the way for artistically valid scenes of nudity and sexual explicitness; it also hastened the end of the Administration itself, since a more liberal attitude towards sex on screen was difficult to accommodate within a code of prohibitions, and a ratings system was adopted instead.

The first film containing nude scenes to be passed by the British Board of Film Censors was *One Summer of Happiness* (Swe 51), in which a young couple were seen embracing in a pool of bullrushes. The decision was based on the fact that, in the words of former BBFC Secretary John Trevelyan, 'it was generally accepted in this country that in Scandinavia people bathed in the nude'. The prohibition of nudity, which had remained absolute since the founding of the Board in 1913 until this breach in 1952, was abandoned for good the following year after a naturist movie called *The Garden of Eden* (US 53) was banned by the BBFC but certified for exhibition by over 180 local authorities including the LCC. Some even gave it a U Certificate. The Board wisely decided that its original decision had been out of keeping with changing social attitudes and modified its policy on nudity. Another 14 years were to pass, however, before the Board felt the public was ready to accept a full frontal nude, and again it was a Swedish film which stimulated the change. *Hugs and Kisses* (Swe 66) was passed by the BBFC in 1967 complete with a scene in which a girl undressed in front of a full-length mirror. This was also the first time that pubic hair was displayed so forthrightly, though there had been some revealing 'flashes' during the scene in *Blow Up* (GB 67) in which David Hemmings wrestles on the floor with Jane Birkin and Gillian Hills.

The cinema of the Eastern world took longer to come to terms with nudity. The same year that *The Pawnbroker* (US 64) was restoring bare bosoms to the American screen, the first Indian films were released in which girls were permitted to be seen in bathing costumes—*April Fool* (Ind 64) and *Sangam* (Ind 64). India still bans nudity and has only recently allowed kissing (q.v.). In Japan, however, nudity had arrived on screen in the fifties, with a scene in *The Princess Yang* (Jap 55) where the heroine enters the bath. Since the heroine was the distinguished dramatic actress Machiko Kyo, it was unthinkable that she should be seen *in person* in the nude, so a stripper was hired from the Ginza to double for her. Foreign films continued to be subject to strict censorship, though not always simply by cutting. In the Japanese release prints of *A Clockwork Orange* (GB 71) the nude scenes went out of focus, while *Woodstock* (US 69) had the emulsion scraped off the footage containing nudes. Nevertheless, Japan has come a long way since a scene of Cary Grant embracing Sylvia Sidney in *Madame Butterfly* (US 32) was cut by the Japanese censor because Miss Sidney's elbow was exposed.

The first full-frontal male nudity to be seen on screen appeared fleetingly in *Dante's Inferno* (It 12). The first explicit scene revealing male genitalia in a commercial feature was the nude wrestling match between Alan Bates and Oliver Reed in Ken Russell's *Women in Love* (GB 69).

The naked form in serious films is usually justified on 'artistic' grounds. Derek Jarman, director of the all-male *Sebastiane* (GB 75), vouchsafed a refreshingly practical explanation for the abundant nudity in this study of religious sexuality in Romano-Britain: 'the budget wouldn't run to authentic costumes'.

The first film made for theatrical release in which the sex act was depicted was *Extase* (Cz 33). The young heroine (Hedwig Kiesler, later known as Hedy Lamarr), who has flown from an impotent husband, runs naked through the woods, bathes, and then has sex with a young engineer in a hut. Curiously *Extase* is celebrated as the first motion picture containing a nude scene, which it was not, rather than the first to show sexual intercourse, which it was.

The first theatrical release to contain a scene of unsimulated sexual intercourse was Jan Lindqvist and Stefan Jarl's *Dom Kallar Oss Mods/They Call Us Misfits* (Swe 67), starring Kenta Gustafsson and Stoffe Svensson.

The earliest known pornographic film which can definitely be dated is *A l'Ecu d'Or ou la bonne auberge* (Fr 08).

There is no doubt that pornographic film-making was well established even by this early date, though for obvious reasons records are sparse. It was in the same year as *A l'Ecu d'Or* was released, 1908, that Russia enacted a law against obscene movies, known

there as 'the Paris Genre'. In Moscow the Mephistopholes Kino decided to test its enforcement by presenting a full programme of such films and was promptly closed down.

The earliest known American pornographic film is *A Free Ride* aka *A Grass Sandwich* (US 15).

Pornography received 'professional recognition' in the USA in 1974, when the Screen Actors Guild relaxed the rule against its members appearing in hardcore movies. Formerly any SAG members performing porno pics did so anonymously.

The first full-length erotic cartoon film was Osamu Tezuka's *A Thousand and One Nights* (Jap 69)—claimed (inaccurately) as 'the first animated film for adults'. David Grant's *Sinderella* (GB 72) was declared obscene by both Bow Street Magistrates' Court and the High Court of Appeal, but later passed by the British Board of Film Censors with cuts amounting to only 26 seconds.

'Soft porn' for theatrical release first started in Japan in 1950 with a wave of teenage sexploitation films with titles like *Teenager's Sex-Manual, Virgin's Clinic, A Virgin's Sex Manual, Bitch* and *Bad Girl*. The title role in the latter was played by the aristocratic Yoshiko Kuga, daughter of a Japanese peer, which gave it an added piquancy for some. The films reflected—and

---

Australia's Annette Kellerman became the first star to appear on screen in the nude in *Daughter of the Gods* (US 16).

different...

THE MIRISCH COMPANY PRESENTS

AUDREY HEPBURN
SHIRLEY MacLAINE
JAMES GARNER

THE CHILDREN'S HOUR

Because of the adult nature of its theme — this motion picture is not recommended for children.

CO-STARRING
MIRIAM HOPKINS FAY BAINTER AND INTRODUCING KAREN BALKIN

PRODUCED AND DIRECTED BY
WILLIAM WYLER SCREENPLAY BY JOHN MICHAEL HAYES

ADAPTATION BY
LILLIAN HELLMAN FROM THE PLAY BY LILLIAN HELLMAN MUSIC BY ALEX NORTH RELEASED THRU UNITED ARTISTS

A
WILLIAM
WYLER PRODUCTION

exploited—the revolution in social values of post-war Japan, where a confused generation of teenagers was apt to identify freedom with license. Remarkably the production of these movies began only three years after the first Japanese screen kiss.

The genesis of the American 'skinflick' is generally attributed to ex-Signal Corps cameraman Russ Meyer, who made his soft-porn debut with *The Immoral Mr Teas* (US 59), a comedy about a man with the unusual ability to undress girls mentally. This modest pioneer effort, shot on a budget of $24,000 in four days, inspired no less than 150 imitations within a year of its release.

Although sexploitation movies are generally profitable in relation to their modest budgets, the first to achieve an outstanding box office success, even by comparison with major studio productions, was *Emmanuelle* (Fr 74). Of the 607 new films released in Paris in 1974 *Emmanuelle* scored the highest number of admissions (1,342,921), ahead of such notable box-office draws as *The Sting* (US 73)—1,154,952 admissions and *The Exorcist* (US 73)—655,092 admissions.

SEX CINEMAS
The showing of pornographic films in public cinemas in the USA began with the wide distribution of *I, a Woman* (Swe 67). In Britain the film had been banned outright.

There are 700 X-rated cinemas in America, playing porno movies exclusively; another 200 cinemas book porno films from time to time (1983 figures). There are 32 cinemas showing exclusively gay movies, of which 14 are in New York.

The highest concentration of porno cinemas in the USA is in the Bible Belt country of North and South Carolina. According to the Chairman of the Adult Film Association, the Carolinas have 75 sex cinemas serving a population of 8·9 million, compared with only 40 in permissive Southern California with its population of over 10 million.

The country with the most profitable pornographic film industry is Italy, where a box office gross of $280 million was reported in 1982. Some $42 million of this went to the government in taxes.
The first film about homosexuality was Richard

Oswald's *Anders als die Andern* (Ger 19), starring Conrad Veidt, which dared to confront the cinema-going public with a subject still proscribed in literature. Following the resumption of censorship, male homosexuality received no further attention until Gustaf Gründgens' *Zwei Welten* (Ger 40). The story by Felix Lutzkendorff was an innocuous romance about two boys and two girls working together on a farm in the summer holidays. Under the direction of Gründgens it became transformed into an idyll between the two boys.

Elsewhere the theme attracted less sympathetic treatment. During the Japanese occupation of Shanghai, the Japanese made a film in China for native consumption called *Chu Hai-tang* (Jap/Chn 43), which attempted to propagate the idea of the Chinese as a decadent race with the story of a Chinese General embroiled with a female impersonator from the Peking Opera.

In Britain the subject remained unbroached on screen until Terence Young's *Serious Charge* (GB 59), about a priest (Anthony Quayle) falsely accused by a youth (Andrew Ray) of making homosexual advances. This made relatively little impact, and it was left to Basil Deardon to make a film sufficiently explicit to actually use the word 'homosexual' in the dialogue. The picture was *Victim* (GB 61), in which Dirk Bogarde portrayed a respected barrister who becomes the victim of blackmail as a result of his relationship with a young vagrant (Peter McEnery). In the meantime American director Joseph Manckiewicz had directed Gore Vidal's screen adaptation of *Suddenly, Last Summer* (GB 59), the story of a homosexual poet whose beautiful cousin (Elizabeth Taylor) lures Italian beach boys for his delectation. Other British films on homosexual themes followed *Victim* in fairly quick succession, including *A Taste of Honey* (GB 61), *The Leather Boys* (GB 63) and *The Servant* (GB 63), but there was little further development of the theme by American film-makers between *Suddenly, Last Summer* and John Huston's *Reflections in a Golden Eye* (US 67), again with Elizabeth Taylor, this time as the wife of an army officer (Marlon Brando) infatuated with a young recruit.

Lesbian love was treated with delicacy and discretion in Leontine Sagan's *Mädchen in Uniform* (Ger 31), a tender study of a girl's infatuation for a teacher in a repressive Prussian boarding school. The first explicitly lesbian film from the USA was *The Children's Hour* (US 62), the second film version of Lillian Hellman's play of the same name. Both pictures were directed by William Wyler, but in the earlier version, titled *These Three* (US 36), the original story of two schoolmistresses having an affair was changed to a heterosexual triangle involving two female teachers and a man. Wyler's remake had Shirley Maclaine and Audrey Hepburn in a sensitively-handled adaptation true to the spirit and the purpose of the play.

Sport

Soccer, the most popular spectator sport in the world, is increasingly the subject of feature movies.

Love is not the only emotion inspired by women on the football field. This lady referee has aroused the hostility of both teams at once in *Women Offside* (Cz 71).

Right
Bill Forsyth's all-Scottish *Gregory's Girl* (GB 81) charmed audiences with its story of first love on the football field. Dee Hepburn played the girl soccer ace, object of inept goalie Gordon Sinclair's attentions.

SOCCER FILMOGRAPHY

The Winning Goal (GB 20)
The Ball of Fortune (GB 26)
Der König der Mittelstürmer (Ger 28)
Die Elf Teufel (Ger 28)
The Great Game (GB 30)
Soccerfans (Cz 31)
Our Football Eleven (Cz 36)
Goal! (Arg 36)
The Goalkeeper (USSR 36)
The Klapzuba Football Eleven (Cz 38)
Alma e Corpo de Uma Raça (Bra 38)
The Great Arsenal Stadium Mystery (GB 39)
Bola ao Centro (Por 47)
Plavi 9 (Yug 50)
The Football Parson (Den 51)
The Merry Duel (Cz 51)
In the Penalty Area (Cz 51)
Women Who Have Run Off-Side (Cz 51)
The Great Game (GB 53)
Small Town Story (GB 53)
11:1 (GDR 55)
A Football Star (Hun 56)
Saeta Rubia (Sp 56)
The Goalkeeper Lives in our Street (Cz 57)
Favourite No 13 (Bul 58)
Gambe d'oro (It 58)
Il Nemico di mia moglie/My Wife's Enemy (It 59)
Our Lads (Rom 59)

Los Economicamente debiles (Sp 60)
Football Fans (Cz 60)
The Last Goal (Hun 61)
Comrade President the Centre-Forward (Yug 62)
Ivana in the Forward Line (Cz 63)
Pelota de cuero (Arg 63)
Third Time (USSR 63)
Allez France (Fr 64)
Fadni odpoledne (Cz 65)
Let's Go Wakadaisho (Jap 67)
Somos los mejores! (Arg 67)
Fish, Football and Girls (Isr 68)
Volver a vivi (Sp 68)
Fight for the Glory (Jap 69)
Aconteceu no Maracanã (Bra 69)
Il Presidente del Borgorosso Football Club (It 70)
Shoot Paragon! (Pol 70)
Sekundomer/Stop Watch (USSR 70)
Women Offside (Cz 71)
The Goalkeeper's Fear of the Penalty (FRG/Aut 71)
Bloomfield (Isr 71)
I Due maghi de pallone (It 71)
Mother Love (S.Kor 72)
Willi wird das Kind schon schaukeln (FRG 72)
Tochka, Tochka, Zapiataia/Dot, Dot, a Comma (USSR 72)
Football of the Good Old Days (Hun 73)
A Goal, Another Goal (USSR 73)
Stubby (Swe 74)

Pandhattam/Play Ball (Ind 74)
Pirveli Mertskhali/The First Swallow (USSR 75)
Furia Española (Sp 76)
The Memorable Day (Bul 76)
Takaya Ona, Igra (USSR 77)
The Boys in Company C (HK 77)
Trener/The Coach (Yug 78)
Striker (Ind 78)
Yesterday's Hero (GB 79)
Everything for Football (Rom 79)
Coup de Tête (Fr 80)
Mundita lito (Uru 81)
The Match (Hun 81)
Gregory's Girl (GB 81)
Escape to Victory (US 81)
At Start of Play (USSR 82)
Pra Frente Brazil (Bra 82)
Eccezzziunale . . . Veramente (It 82)
White Wing (Bra 82)
Referees, Fans and Soccer Players (It 82)
Copa de Ora (Uru 82)
Soccer Attack Centre (It 83)
El Harrif/Street Player (Egy 83)
Was Kostet der Sieg/What Price Victory (Aut 83)
The Champions (HK 83)
Those Glory, Glory Days (GB 83)
Young Giants (US 83)
Excuse Me—Are You Watching Football? (GDR 83)
A Mort L'Arbitre (Fr 84)

Leah Beard and Henry Clive in *As a Man Thirsteth* (US 14). At this date most feature films were still derived from stage melodramas.

Themes

The chart shows the number of feature films produced in the USA and UK respectively on each of the major themes, and the percentage of total production represented by that figure, at each 10-year point from 1914 to 1984 inclusive. Films belonging equally to more than one theme have been credited to each as appropriate, so the percentages do not add up to 100. For example, a backstage crime melodrama set in the 19th century would be counted under Showbusiness, Crime and Historical.

The figures quoted for the USA represent films reviewed in *Variety*, which covers most, though not all, feature-length productions released in North America. The British figures are based on the comprehensive listing of UK output in Denis Gifford's *The British Film Catalogue 1895–1970*, except for the figures for 1974 and 1984, which derive from the reviews in the BFI's *Monthly Film Bulletin*.

THE FILMS OF 1914

This was the year in which the feature-length film took hold in the USA. By far the greater proportion of features were based on stage plays, which is indicative of the fact that the screen was still regarded as a form of 'silent theatre'. In some cases, though by no means all, the story was opened out to take advantage of the opportunity to shoot outdoor scenes and show action which would not have been possible within the confines of a theatre stage. Since the theatre of the day was dominated by melodrama, the stage-derived features also tended towards a mixture of sensation and sentiment, with sex as a distinct, albeit discreet, ingredient. Favourite themes of 1914 were 'the sins of society', heroes or heroines suffering from amnesia, heirs or more often heiresses being abducted by gypsies, and morality stories about the dreadful consequences of drink, drugs and pre-marital sex. The dreadful consequence of the latter was generally syphilis—one 1914 melodrama even included shots of ravaged patients taken in a genuine VD clinic. The other sexual theme presented in terms of a 'warning to the innocent' was white slavery, the Americans following the European lead in exploiting the subject for all it was worth—and it was worth a lot to producers and exhibitors alike. Foreign locales were comparatively few, though there was a sub-genre of films set in Russia (usually shot in New Jersey) about nihilists, Cossacks and noble heroes unjustly consigned to Siberia. This was a time when the Russian immigrant population of New York included many anarchists and other dissidents, including Trotsky, who played bit parts in two such films released in 1914 and 1915.

British feature production of 1914 consisted mainly of crime melodrama, usually centering around titled people in opulent settings.

THE FILMS OF 1924

The most recurring theme in the Hollywood productions of 1924 was physical and/or sexual conflict in the Far North. Variously set in lumber camps or simply the snowy wastes, the locale was sometimes Alaska, sometimes the Yukon, but more often an unidentified region of mountains and forests in which men battled against the elements and each other, and women, few in number but invariably fair of face, battled for the love of a good man. Other popular themes of the year were romance in the South Seas and the thrills of the circus. A particular plot device used unsparingly in the melodramas of 1924 was the effects of bootleg gin—wood alcohol—on those who sought solace from the rigours of prohibition. The victim was invariably the girl friend, led into the paths of unrighteousness by the heavy and struck blind as a result. The remainder of the story was generally to do with how the romantic lead obtained the services of a famed Viennese specialist to restore her sight, and about something

Youth for Sale (US 24) was one of a string of movies of the mid twenties about a girl drinking bootleg gin in prohibition America and going blind as a result. Here the friend who led the stricken girl into dissolute ways is vowing she will look after her until she is cured.

Hardbitten newshounds always wore their hats in the office in the newspaper pix of the thirties. Robert Armstrong with Minna Gombell and Ann Sothern in *The Hell Cat* (US 34).

worse than being struck blind—usually being struck dead—happening to the heavy. Audiences of 1924 were predominately female, which doubtless accounted for the volume of romantic subjects, represented by no less than 120 films or over 28 per cent of the total.

British films of 1924 were still in their 'lost heiress' phase—there had been little progress towards more sophisticated themes since the inception of the feature film.

THE FILMS OF 1934

Hollywood production at this period was dominated by the newspaper story, reflecting how the coming of sound had tended to move the action indoors with a corresponding shift from rural to urban locales. Most were about a newspaperman solving a crime and winning the girl—usually a girl who had been framed or the daughter of an upright citizen who had been framed—in the process. While adultery probably

	1914				1924				1934				1944			
	US		UK		US		UK		US		UK		US		UK	
	No	%	No	%	No	%	No	%	No	%	No	%	No	%	No	%
Action/Adventure	39	16·0	–	–	40	7·1	6	10·3	10	2·3	5	2·9	7	1·9	–	–
Animals	1	–	–	–	7	1·6	1	1·7	7	1·6	1	–	4	1·1	1	2·5
Animated	–	–	–	–	–	–	–	–	–	–	–	–	1	–	–	–
Biopics	1	–	1	3·3	2	–	1	1·7	7	1·6	6	3·5	11	3·0	–	–
Black	–	–	–	–	1	–	–	–	2	–	–	–	1	–	–	–
Comedy	25	10·3	1	3·3	53	12·5	5	8·6	85	19·6	54	31·2	56	15·1	11	27·5
Contemporary issues	6	2·5	–	–	3	–	–	–	4	–	–	–	3	–	–	–
Crime	48	19·8	13	43·3	54	12·7	20	34·4	101	23·3	64	37·0	62	16·8	7	17·5
Documentary	9	3·7	2	6·6	2	–	5	8·6	5	1·2	1	–	7	1·9	3	7·5
Drama	49	20·2	5	16·6	103	24·2	7	12·0	63	14·6	8	4·6	13	3·5	5	12·5
Fantasy[1]	12	4·9	3	10·0	3	–	2	3·4	4	–	2	1·2	21	5·7	5	12·5
Historical[2]	28	11·5	5	16·6	16	3·8	7	12·0	22	5·1	14	8·1	19	5·1	4	10·0
Horror	1	–	–	–	–	–	–	–	2	–	2	1·2	11	3·0	–	–
Literary[3]	12	4·9	6	20·0	6	1·4	3	5·1	13	3·0	3	1·7	6	1·6	–	–
Musicals[4]	–	–	–	–	–	–	–	–	32	7·4	34	19·7	73	19·7	8	20·0
Romance	27	11·1	2	6·6	120	28·2	14	24·1	79	18·2	46	26·6	53	14·3	9	22·5
Science fiction	–	–	–	–	–	–	–	–	–	–	–	–	–	–	–	–
Sex	7	2·9	1	3·3	17	4·0	4	6·8	2	–	–	–	–	–	1	2·5
Show business	10	4·1	1	3·3	21	4·9	–	–	20	4·6	13	7·5	56	15·1	1	2·5
Spies	3	1·2	–	–	3	–	–	–	5	1·2	3	1·2	15	4·1	–	–
Sport	5	2·1	–	–	12	2·8	4	6·8	14	3·2	3	1·7	6	1·6	–	–
War[5]	8	3·3	–	–	1	–	–	–	11	2·5	–	–	32	8·6	3	7·5
Westerns[6]	13	5·3	–	–	59	13·9	–	–	30	6·9	–	–	51	13·8	–	–
Youth[7]	1	–	–	–	7	1·6	–	–	8	1·9	–	–	17	4·6	–	–

[1] Includes ghosts, dreams, time-warps, sorcery and fairy stories, as well as horror of the Frankenstein genre.
[2] Means any period film in which the action is set more than 40 years before it was made.

[3] Denotes films based on famous works of literature.
[4] Includes concert movies.

occupied more footage in both the films of the twenties and thirties than any other single topic, there was a significant change of emphasis after the introduction of the Hays Code. In the 'eternal triangle' films of 1924 it was usually the woman who made the running, often in the guise of a neglected wife or bored daughter 'vamping' a married man. The films of 1934 were much more circumspect in their treatment of infidelity, the man always cast in the role of seducer and the act of adultery scarcely ever reaching consumation.

Apart from the perennial cops and robbers quota quickies, the dominant themes of the early talkies period in Britain were rhythm, romance and Ruritania. No less than 34 musicals were released in 1934, many of them in a Viennese or Balkan setting. The 'I know! We'll put on a show!' type of musical was also to the fore. Statistically comedy was king, with films that ranged from the music-hall humour of George Formby to the sophisticated wit of Noel Coward representing over 31 per cent of the total.

THE FILMS OF 1944

Not surprisingly, wartime movies tended towards escapist fare. Comedies, westerns and musicals were the staple, with most of the musicals set against a showbusiness background—one of the 56 films on this theme was even titled *Show Business*.

With the decline of production in wartime Britain, few discernible trends are apparent, though as in America popular taste demanded lighthearted films.

THE FILMS OF 1954

This was a year so dominated by westerns that even Joan Crawford slipped off her mink to go riding the range in an oater called *Johnny Guitar*. A total of 55 films, more than one in every five features produced, were horse operas. The rest tended mainly in the direction of light romance of the Doris Day type and big budget colour musicals, with only a few distinctive pictures like Hitchcock's *Rear Window* and Elia Kazan's *On the Waterfront* standing out from the general dross.

	1954 US No	%	1954 UK No	%	1964 US No	%	UK No	%	1974 US No	%	UK No	%	1984 US No	%	UK No	%
Action/Adventure	27	10.5	9	7.8	7	4.7	9	12.0	8	3.8	2	2.9	20	7.6	7	16.7
Animals	9	3.5	–	–	6	4.1	1	1.3	8	3.8	–	–	3	1.1	1	2.4
Animated	1	–	–	–	1	–	–	–	2	–	–	–	2	0.8	0	–
Biopics	8	3.1	1	–	3	2.0	1	1.3	11	5.3	3	4.4	8	3.1	1	4.8
Black	1	–	–	–	3	2.0	2	2.6	29	13.9	–	–	4	1.5	0	–
Comedy	25	9.7	29	25.0	44	29.7	12	16.0	31	14.8	13	19.1	71	27.1	16	38.1
Contemporary issues	3	1.2	–	–	2	1.4	1	1.3	8	3.8	–	–	7	2.7	5	11.9
Crime	44	17.1	48	41.4	23	15.6	29	38.7	66	31.6	13	19.1	39	14.9	5	11.9
Documentary	15	5.8	4	3.4	5	3.4	2	2.6	19	9.1	1	1.5	18	6.9	1	2.4
Drama	6	2.3	7	6.0	15	10.1	4	5.3	11	5.3	2	2.9	19	7.3	3	7.1
Fantasy[1]	8	3.1	6	5.2	12	8.1	3	4.0	11	5.3	3	4.4	21	8.0	10	23.8
Historical[2]	30	11.7	14	12.1	9	6.1	11	14.7	15	7.2	9	13.2	13	5.0	9	21.4
Horror	7	2.7	–	–	10	6.8	9	12.0	11	5.3	14	20.1	26	9.9	1	2.4
Literary[3]	5	1.9	4	3.4	4	2.7	1	1.3	4	1.9	4	5.9	2	0.8	3	7.1
Musicals[4]	24	9.3	1	–	16	10.8	7	9.3	11	5.3	3	4.4	10	3.8	3	7.1
Romance	51	19.8	8	6.8	24	16.2	5	6.7	6	2.9	3	4.4	20	7.6	4	9.5
Science fiction	7	2.7	2	1.7	2	1.4	3	4.0	4	1.9	4	5.9	15	5.7	1	2.4
Sex	2	–	1	–	10	6.8	–	–	37	17.7	14	20.1	22	8.4	2	4.8
Show business	13	5.1	4	3.4	6	4.1	3	4.0	4	1.9	1	1.5	7	2.7	2	4.8
Spies	5	1.9	4	3.4	1	–	5	6.7	1	–	4	5.9	5	1.9	0	–
Sport	7	2.7	4	3.4	6	4.1	–	–	9	4.3	1	1.5	8	3.1	3	7.1
War[5]	8	3.1	5	4.3	11	7.4	5	6.7	2	–	1	1.5	5	1.9	1	2.4
Westerns[6]	55	21.4	–	–	15	10.1	–	–	3	1.4	3	4.4	3	1.1	0	–
Youth[7]	2	–	–	–	13	8.8	6	8.0	11	5.3	–	–	37	14.1	3	7.1

[5] Refers to 20th-century wars only.
[6] Not double-counted under 'Historical' unless the film is about actual historical events, nor double-counted under 'Crime'.

[7] Signifies movies for or about teenagers or college students. 'Drama' is a category exclusive of any other category.

No less than 56 of the Hollywood pictures released in 1944 were about showbusiness—including *Show Business* (US 44). From left to right: George Murphy, Constance Moore, Eddie Cantor, Joan Davis.

In Britain the year 1954 saw a return to the predominance of crime films, though the majority were B pictures (soon to disappear). Comedy was in the ascendant, with *Doctor in the House* the top moneymaker of the year and *Hobson's Choice* winner of the BFA's Best British Film award.

THE FILMS OF 1964
Youth pictures became big in the early sixties with a short-lived sub-genre of 'beach movies' that retain a cult following on both sides of the Atlantic even today. Permissiveness and the counter culture were still two or three years away; in the meantime Sandra Dee epitomised teenage USA with wholesome winsomeness. Comedy was enjoying a revival, represented by nearly 30 per cent of all productions compared to less than 10 per cent a decade earlier. Out of fashion was the crime drama, registering only 23 films and 15·6 per cent of production—ten years later, in 1974, there would be nearly three times as many with double the percentage.

Britain was also beginning to discover the charms of youth, symptomatic of the fact that older audiences were staying at home to watch television. Most of the

Joan Crawford in *Johnny Guitar* (US 54), one of 55 westerns released in 1955.

Right
Beach movies were especially popular with drive-in audiences in the sixties. This one was *Bikini Beach* (US 64).

films for this newly affluent teenage market were about pop musicians—Cliff Richard and the Shadows starred in *Wonderful Life*, Gerry and the Pacemakers in *Ferry Across the Mersey* and Freddy and the Dreamers in *Every Day's a Holiday*. Horror had also become a staple of British production, with Hammer riding high.

THE FILMS OF 1974
The year was notable for the virtual extinction of the western, after a 15-year decline, and the paucity of romance. Newspaper films, prolific until the 1950s, had also all but disappeared—the only 1974 movie set in a newspaper office was a remake of *The Front Page* with Walter Matthau and Jack Lemmon. Sex had become a major genre, with pornography making up the greater proportion of the total of 37 sex films reviewed—doubtless there were many more which had failed to attract the attention of *Variety*'s critics. Two new genres just starting to emerge were concert

Sex and sadism predominated in the spate of black exploitation movies which peaked in 1974. A bound and trussed Pam Grier is being menaced by Mr Big in *Foxy Brown* (US 74).

films (mainly rock festivals) and disaster movies. The two examples of the latter released in 1974, *Earthquake* and *The Towering Inferno*, were amongst the most successful of this 1970s phenomenon. Horror, with the accent on blood and gore rather than monsters, was becoming a cult. Typical, and perhaps the most enduring of these violent films, was *The Texas Chainsaw Massacre*. The shortlived spate of black exploitation movies peaked in 1974, most of the 29 films featuring black leading players being of the 'superspade' type and conforming to the modish taste for sex and violence.

It is remarkable that the proportion of crime films made in Britain had always been higher than in the USA, but in 1974 the British percentage of 19·1 fell way below the American percentage of 31·6. Sex, with a nil rating in 1964, had reared its ugly head to score more than 20 per cent in 1974, making it equally as prolific as horror. More surprisingly there were three British-made westerns, exactly the same number as Hollywood's meagre output for the year.

THE FILMS OF 1984
The youth movie had made a comeback in America, though the genre had moved onward from the cheerful romps on the beach of the 1960s, through the rock 'n' roll high-school phase of the seventies, to a strong blend of pubescent sex 'n' violence in the eighties. Sleeper of the year was *Angel*, about a 15-year-old 'honor student by day, Hollywood hooker by night', which matched the adolescent appeal of *Porky's* and the *Lemon Popsicle* movies with the sure-fire attention grabber of a psycho-on-the-loose. Transvestism and Hare Krishna were thrown in for good measure and the kids loved it. Comedy enjoyed a resurgence with hits like *Splash*, continuing a success formula set by earlier eighties films like *Arthur* (US 81) and *Tootsie* (US 82) in which charm took over from sex. Science-fiction and horror continued their upward surge, the com-

paratively small number of films produced in these genres bearing no relation to their enormous box office impact. Fantasy was represented by megabuck blockbusters *Gremlins* and *Ghostbusters*, as well as a string of Santa Claus movies, including one in which the children's favourite was revealed to be a manic axeman.

British films of the eighties ran the gamut from megabuck movies like *Gandhi* (GB 82) and *Greystoke* (GB 84), through medium budget prestige successes like Oscar winning *Chariots of Fire* (GB 81), to low budget Channel 4 backed art movies like *The Draughtsman's Contract* (GB 83). The two pictures of 1984 which probably typify the return to indigenous themes—an enticing combination of the past, privilege and perversion—were *An Englishman Abroad* and *Another Country*, both based on the character of upper class traitor and homosexual Guy Burgess. British cinema appeared by 1984 to be drawing on a rich store of theatrical talent and themes proven on 'the world's least worst television' to consolidate a modest renaissance.

Westerns

The earliest subjects of western interest were *Sioux Indian Ghost Dance*, *Indian War Council* and *Buffalo Dance*, made by the Edison Co. at West Orange, NJ on 24 September 1894. *Bucking Broncho* followed on 16 October and is notable for the first appearance of a cowboy in a film—Lee Martin of Colorado, who is seen riding *Sunfish* in a corral, while his 'pardner' Frank Hammit stands on the rails and discharges the first of many tens of thousands of pistol shots that were to be seen (and later heard) in almost every western that followed. Annie Oakley, immortalised in *Annie Get Your Gun* (US 50), made her film debut a fortnight later on 1 November 1894.

The most violent movie of all time may not belong, as might be expected, to the horror genre. In 1984 America's National Coalition on Television Violence turned its attention to the large screen with a denunciation of the box office hit *Indiana Jones and the Temple of Doom* (US 84), protesting that this cheerful caper contained 215 explicit acts of violence. In a film with a strong juvenile following, the Coalition sternly pronounced, there were no less than 39 attempted murders, 14 killings by the hero, and five acts of terminal mayhem committed by an adorable nine-year-old moppet in the cause of justice. The picture had a PG rating.

A frame enlargement from the first western, *Kit Carson* (US 03). (*Library of Congress*)

The first westerns were copyrighted by the American Mutoscope & Biograph Co. on 21 September 1903. One was titled *Kit Carson* (US 03) and related the story of its hero's capture by Indians and subsequent escape through the agency of a beautiful Indian maiden. There were 11 scenes and the film had a running time of 21 minutes, making it the longest dramatic picture (other than Passion Plays) produced in America at that time. The other film, titled *The Pioneers* (US 03), showed the burning of a settler's homestead by Indians, who kill the homesteader and his wife and carry off his daughter. The picture ends with the dramatic rescue of the child by frontiersmen who have found the bodies of her parents. Running time was approximately 15 minutes. Both pictures were directed by Wallace McCutcheon and filmed on location in the Adirondack Mountains of New York State. *Kit Carson* was made on 8 September 1903 and *The Pioneers* two days later.

Two popular themes of the eighties—fantasy and comedy—came together in the box office hit *Splash* (US 84). Newcomer Daryl Hannah starred.

The more celebrated *The Great Train Robbery* (US 03), generally and erroneously described as the first western and often as the first film to tell a story, was copyrighted by the Edison Co. some six weeks later, on 1 December 1903.

Until 1906 all westerns were shot in the Eastern states, generally in New Jersey. **The first western made in the West** was Biograph's *A California Hold Up* (US 06), shot by O. M. Grove.

The first feature-length western was Lawrence B. McGill's *Arizona* (US 13), an All Star Feature Corporation production with Cyril Scott and Gertrude Shipman. It was released in August 1913, six months before Cecil B. DeMille's *The Squaw Man* (US 14), usually credited as the first feature.

The first western in colour was a British production by a Dutch director, Theo Bouwmeester's *Fate* (GB 11), made in Kinemacolor by the Natural Colour Kinematograph Co. Set in Texas, it was about an Englishman who becomes leader of a tribe of renegade Indians.

The first feature-length colour western was the Famous Players-Lasky production *Wanderer of the Wasteland* (US 24), a Zane Grey horse opera from the novel of the same name. Photographed in two-colour Technicolor by Arthur Ball, it was directed by Irvin Willar, starred Jack Holt, Noah Beery and Billie Dove, and was premièred in Los Angeles on 21 June 1924.

The first western talkie was Fox-Movietone's *In Old Arizona* (US 28), directed by Raoul Walsh and Irving

There has been at least one western in which not a single gunshot is heard. *They Passed This Way* aka *Four Faces West* (US 48) starred Joel McCrea as a bank robber on the run from Charles Bickford's Pat Garrett. Strong characterisation and suspense proved no substitute for the traditional showdown in Main Street as far as the fans were concerned and the film bombed at the box office.

Traditional westerns are necessarily period movies. It was not always so. Edwin S. Porter's *The Great Train Robbery* (US 03) was probably intended to be contemporary. It was filmed only two years after the last hold-up of a train in the USA, an episode graphically recounted in *Butch Cassidy and the Sundance Kid* (US 69).

Cummings and starring Edmund Lowe, Warner Baxter and Dorothy Burgess. It was premièred at the Criterion Theater, Los Angeles, on 25 December 1928.

The first feature-length film with an all-Indian cast was Edward S. Curtis's *The Land of the Head Hunters* (US 14), a story of the son of a tribal chief and his quest for manhood. It was filmed on location on the North-West coast of America.

The first western with Indian dialogue was Universal's talkie serial *The Indians Are Coming* (US 31), in which Chief Thunderbird spoke in his native Sioux. In 1970 Dame Judith Anderson, an Australian, successfully coped with all-Sioux dialogue in her role as Buffalo Cow Head in *A Man Called Horse* (US 70).

The highest earning western was *Butch Cassidy and the Sundance Kid* (US 69), with North American rentals during its initial release of $29·2 million. According to David Pirie's *Anatomy of the Movies* (London, 1981), however, it is beaten into second place if inflation is taken into account. Applying the US cost of living index to the rentals earned during initial release, the real value of the $10 million returned by *Duel in the Sun* (US 47), a David O Selznick production starring Joseph Cotten and Gregory Peck, exceeds the inflation adjusted value of *Butch Cassidy*'s rentals.

The first western star was G. M. 'Broncho Billy' Anderson (1881–1971), who was to have been cast as one of the villains for his western debut in *The Great Train Robbery* (US 03), but proved so inept on a horse that he had to be relegated to extra work. Notwithstanding this inauspicious start to a career dedicated to the relationship of man and horse, Anderson starred in *Life of an American Cowboy* (US 06) and then

went west with a Selig location crew to make one of the earliest westerns shot in the real west—*The Girl from Montana* (US 07). The following year he established a West Coast studio for Essany at Niles, California, and decided to embark on a series of one-reelers based on a central character, reasoning that the weakness of the Edison, Selig and Essany westerns he had played in was that they lacked clearly-defined heroes. His original intention had been to find an actor expert in horsemanship whom he could direct, but actors of any kind being in short supply in California, he eventually decided to cast himself in the role. *Broncho Billy and the Baby* (US 10), a sentimental story of a man-gone-wrong who is reformed by the love of a good woman, was the first

It was a curious convention of the classic B western that more often than not the characters included one called Kincaid; and more often than not he was the villain. The name is by no means a common one, as reference to any telephone directory will testify. The earliest known cast list showing use of the name is for *The Rose of the Rancho* (US 14), a David Belasco–Jesse L. Lasky production in five reels with Dick la Reno as the land-jumper Kincaid.

in a series of nearly 400 Broncho Billy pictures which established Anderson as a major star. A curious feature of the films was their total lack of continuity. If Broncho Billy married in one picture, he would be a bachelor again in the next; he would be reformed inexhaustibly by a succession of good women; and death would only interrupt his career in the saddle until the opening scenes of the next one-reeler. He turned to features in 1918, but competition from his successors, Tom Mix and W. S. Hart, was too strong. After a period of producing Stan Laurel comedies for Metro, he retired in 1923. Nearly half a century after his last silent western role in *The Son of a Gun* (US 18), he made a single excursion into talkies with a guest appearance in *The Bounty Killer* (US 67).

BUFFALO BILL FILMOGRAPHY

Buffalo Bill (Aus 09)
Self *The Life of Buffalo Bill* (US 09)
Self *Buffalo Bill's Far West and Pawnee Bill's Far East* (US 10)
The Five of Hearts, or Buffalo Bill's Love Story (Aus 11)
Self *The Indian Wars* (US 13)
Self *Sitting Bull—The Hostile Sioux Indian Chief* (US 14)
Self *Patsy of the Circus* (US 15)
Duke R. Lee *In the Days of Buffalo Bill* (US 22)
George Waggner *The Iron Horse* (US 24)
John Fox Jnr *The Pony Express* (US 25)
Jack Hoxie *The Last Frontier* (US 26)
Roy Stewart *Buffalo Bill on the UP Trail* (US 26)
Wallace MacDonald *Fighting with Buffalo Bill* (US 26)
Buffalo Bill's Last Fight (US 26) MGM colour short

William Fairbanks *Wyoming* (US 28)
The Indians are Coming (US 30)
Tom Tyler *Battling with Buffalo Bill* (US 31)
Douglas Dumbrille *The World Changes* (US 33)
Earl Dwire *The Miracle Rider* (US 35)
Moroni Olsen *Annie Oakley* (US 35)
James Ellison *The Plainsman* (US 36)
Ted Adams *Custer's Last Stand* (US 36)
Carlyle Moore *Outlaw Express* (US 38)
John Rutherford *Flaming Frontiers* (US 38)
George Reeves *Wild West Days* (US 39)
Roy Rogers *Young Buffalo Bill* (US 40)
Joel McCrea *Buffalo Bill* (US 42)
Bob Baker *Overland Mail* (US 42)
Carlos Munos *El Sobrino de Buffalo Bill* (Mex 44)
Richard Arlen *Buffalo Bill Rides Again* (US 47)
Ugo Sasso (?) *Buffalo Bill a Roma* (It 47)
Monte Hale *Law of the Golden West* (US 49)
Louis Calhern *Annie Get Your Gun* (US 50)

Dickie Moore *Cody of the Pony Express* (US 50)
Tex Cooper *King of the Bullwhip* (US 51)
Charlton Heston *Pony Express* (US 52)
Clayton Moore *Buffalo Bill in Tomahawk Territory* (US 53)
Marshall Reed *Riding with Buffalo Bill* (US 54)
Malcolm Atterbury *Badman's Country* (US 58)
James McMullan *The Raiders* (US 64)
Rick van Nutter *Sette ore di fuoco* (It 64)
Gordon Scott *L'Eroe del Far West* (It/Fr/FRG 65)
Guy Stockwell *The Plainsman* (US 66)
Michel Piccoli *Touche pas la femme blanche* (Fr 74)
Matt Clark *This is the West that Was* (US 74)
Paul Newman *Buffalo Bill and the Indians* (US 76)
Ted Flicher *The Legend of the Lone Ranger* (US 81)

Australian actress Dame Judith Anderson had to master the Sioux language for her role in *A Man Called Horse* (US 70).

The days of the 'real West' overlapped with the movies' version to the extent that there were still authentic western heroes alive—such as 'Buffalo Bill' Cody (d. 1917) and Marshal Wyatt Earp (d. 1929)—when Hollywood was busy creating mythology. One early western, the Selig Co.'s *Custer's Last Stand* (US 08), included among its cast three aged Sioux Indians who had actually participated in the Battle of the Little Big Horn (1876) as young warriors. The producer's hope that he could depend on them as historical advisers came, however, to naught. 'The most we could get out of them', he declared, 'was that the fight was over so quickly that they could remember little about it.'

emerged in the 1920s with the rise of the double-feature programme, were killed off by the voracious appetite of television for them. Theatrical demand for cheap second features rapidly waned after 1950 as TV brought these series films into the living room.

WESTERN OUTPUT
It is estimated that there have been over 3500 multi-reel westerns made since the first two-reeler, the Oklahoma Natural Mutoscene Co.'s *The Bank Robbery* (US 08).

The most popular western star was determined annually with a poll of exhibitors conducted by *Motion Picture Herald* between 1936 and 1954 (when the 'B' western ended). Buck Jones won in 1936, Gene Autry each year from 1937–42, and Roy Rogers from 1943–54 inclusive.

The western hero most often portrayed on screen has been William Frederick Cody (1846–1917), otherwise known as 'Buffalo Bill', a character in 47 dramatic films to date (see filmography). William Bonney (1860–81), alias Billy the Kid, has been portrayed in 44 films; Wild Bill Hickock (1837–76) in 35 films; Jesse James (1847–82) in 35 films; General George Armstrong Custer (1839–76) in 30 films; and Wyatt Earp (1848–1929) in 21 films.

The most prolific western directors were Lesley Selander (1900–79), with at least 107 known feature-length westerns made between 1935 and 1967, and Lambert Hillyer (1893–), with 106 recorded titles between 1917 and 1949.

The only western directed by a woman was Ruth Ann Baldwin's curiously titled Universal production '*49-'17* (US 17).

The last 'B' western was Monogram's *Two Guns and a Badge* (US 54), with Wayne Morris, which was released in September 1954. The 'B' westerns, which

G M ANDERSON (' BRONCHO BILLY "—Essanay)

6 Performers

The first motion picture film to employ the use of actors was a brief costume drama, *The Execution of Mary Queen of Scots* (US 95), which was shot by Alfred Clark of Raff & Gammon, Kinetoscope proprietors, at West Orange, NJ on 28 August 1895. The part of Mary was played by Mr R. L. Thomas, Secretary and Treasurer of the Kinetoscope Co. After approaching the block and laying his head on it, Thomas removed himself, the camera was stopped, and a dummy substituted. The camera was then started again for the decapitation scene. This was **the first use of trick photography or special effect work** in a film.

The first person employed to play a comedy role in a film was M. Clerc, a gardener employed by Mme Lumière at Lyons, France. He was aptly cast in the part of the gardener in the Lumière production *L'Arroseur arrosé* (Fr 95), a film premièred at the Grand Café in Paris on 28 December 1895. Clerc is seen watering flowerbeds with a hose. A mischievous boy, played by a 14-year-old Lumière apprentice called Duval, creeps up behind the gardener and places his foot on the hose to stop the flow of water. As the perplexed gardener holds the nozzle up to his eye to see if there is a blockage, young Duval removes his foot and capers with joy as a burst of water gushes into M. Clerc's face. Clerc and Duval were the first performers to be seen on the screen, as *The Execution of Mary Queen of Scots* had been made for viewing in Edison's 'peep-show' Kinetoscope.

The first professional actors to perform in movies made their screen debuts almost simultaneously on either side of the Atlantic. In America John Rice and May Irwin performed the first screen kiss in *The Widow Jones* aka *May Irwin Kiss* (US 96), which was a scene from the Broadway comedy *The Widow Jones* filmed by Raff and Gammon in April 1896. At about the same time in Britain, Fred Storey played the title role in R. W. Paul's *The Soldier's Courtship* (GB 96), a short comedy made on the roof of the Alhambra Theatre, Leicester Square, and premièred underneath. Storey also got to kiss the heroine, Julie Seale of the Alhambra Ballet. Performers of established reputation rarely appeared in films prior to about 1908 in France and Britain and later elsewhere. There were, however, a few notable exceptions during the primitive period, including Auguste van Biene's role

as the cellist in Esme Collings' *The Broken Melody* (GB 96), from the play of the same name; Joseph Jefferson's performance in American Mutoscope & Biograph's *Rip Van Winkle* (US 96); Beerbohm Tree and Julia Neilson in *King John* (GB 99); Sarah Bernhardt in *Hamlet* (Fr 00); Coquelin in *Cyrano de Bergerac* (Fr 00); Marie Tempest and Hayden Coffin in *San Toy* (GB 00); and Marie Tempest, Ben Webster and H. B. Warner in *English Nell* (GB 00). The only one of these to make a career as a screen actor was H. B. Warner (1876–1958), whose most notable performances were in *King of Kings* (US 27) as Jesus Christ, *Mr Deeds Goes to Town* (US 36), *Lost Horizon* (US 37) and *Victoria the Great* (GB 37).

THE STAR SYSTEM

This emerged in the United States and Europe simultaneously. Previous to 1910 it was the deliberate policy of film-makers not to give their lead players any star billing, lest they should overvalue their services. First to break with this was the American production company Kalem, which in January 1910 began issuing star portraits and posters with the artistes names credited. A few weeks later Carl Laemmle, who had succeeded in luring the still anonymous Florence Lawrence away from Biograph to work for IMP, pulled the kind of outrageous publicity stunt that has enlivened and bedevilled the industry ever since, and in the process created the first real movie star. He began by arranging for a story to break in the St Louis papers that the actress had been killed in a street-car accident. Public interest in the supposed tragedy having been fully aroused, Laemmle placed the following advertisement in the same papers on 10 March 1910: 'The blackest and at the same time the silliest lie yet circulated by the enemies of IMP was the story foisted on the public of St Louis last week to the effect that Miss Lawrence, "The Imp Girl", formerly known as "The Biograph Girl", had been killed by a street car. It was a black lie so cowardly. We now announce our next film *The Broken Path*.' This was followed up with personal appearances by Miss Lawrence and a long interview in the *St Louis Post-Dispatch*; within a year her name was appearing on film posters in larger type than the title.

In Europe the practice of publicising star names

Katsuo Mikoshiba, the Nipponese Chaplin.

began the same year with the outstanding success of two films, one from Denmark, the other from Germany. Asta Nielsen's bravura performance in *The Abyss* (Den 10), one of the first long films to demonstrate a true sense of dramatic construction, brought a hitherto little-known actress almost immediate international recognition and the first of the really prodigious star salaries (c.f. Artiste's earnings, pp. 77–81). Germany's box office success of the year was *Das Liebesglück der Blinden/The Love of the Blind Girl* (Ger 10), starring 'The Messter Girl', a designation that cloaked the identity of Oskar Messter's leading player Henny Porten, who had also scripted the picture. It was received with such acclaim by filmgoers that Messter was persuaded to reveal her name. Once her name was on the credits, Henny proceeded to justify the producers' worst fears by demanding an increase in salary—from the equivalent of $50 a month to $56. Messter refused and she walked straight out of the studio. Having failed to call what he thought was a bluff, the producer sent his assistant, Kurt Stark, to fetch the girl back with a promise that she could have the raise. Henny returned to the studio, married Stark, and went on to become Germany's idol of the silent screen.

NOT CHARLIE CHAPLIN

No actor has been portrayed on screen by *other* actors as often as Charlie Chaplin. It started with Leslie Henson playing Chaplin in a satire by James Barrie called *The Real Thing At Last* (GB 16), which was about an American film producer modernising *Macbeth*. In the same year Fred Evans did a Chaplin role in *Pimple—Himself and Others* (GB 16) and meanwhile Australia's Ern Vockler was doing Chaplin impersonations on stage and appeared as the little tramp in a film titled *Charlie at the Sydney Show* (Aus 16). Essany followed with *Chase Me Charlie* (US 17), in which Graham Douglas impersonated Chaplin (who had left Essany for Mutual) in a compilation of genuine Chaplin extracts

made into a story with linking footage. The Ming Hsing Film Co. of Shanghai made two 'Chaplin films' in the early twenties—*The King of Comedy Visits China* (Chn 22) and *Disturbance at a Peculiar Theatre* (Chn 22)—with British amateur actor Richard Bell taking the part of Charlie. Japan also had a home-grown Chaplin in the person of Katsuo Mikoshiba, who looked almost indistinguishable from the real thing in his baggy pants, bowler and toothbrush moustache, and Germany had her own Charlie Kaplin. The Chaplin impersonation industry seems to have come to a halt with a full-scale biopic, an unauthorised *Life Story of Charles Chaplin* (GB 26) starring Chick Wango in the title role, which was suppressed and never shown. Recently, however, there has been a Chaplin 'comeback'. Chinese comedian Dean Saki played the title role in *Chinese Chaplin and the Kung Fu Kid in Laughing Times* (HK 81), in which the little tramp befriends a poor but beautiful orphan girl obviously inspired by Paulette Goddard's barefoot waif in *Modern Times* (US 36).

ARTISTE'S EARNINGS

Earnings which have now reached as much as $5 million for a single film began at a level commensurate with the penny gaff milieu of early film-making. The earliest known wage rate was the gold Louis ($4·30 or 17s) per day paid in the late 1890s by Star Films of Paris, but not all production companies were so generous. Gene Gauntier was offered $3 to play the lead in Biograph's *The Paymaster* (US 06), the story of a mill-girl in love with the manly young paymaster of the mill. Miss Gauntier was required to be thrown into the millstream by the villain, which she allowed him to do, not liking to mention that she was unable to swim. The producer was so pleased with her pluck that the $3 fee was raised to $5. Alma Lund, who played the female lead in the first film drama made in Norway—*Dangerous Life of a Fisherman* (Nor 07)—was paid the equivalent of $1·50 for her part; the boy who played her son got 75c. R. W. Paul paid Britain's first professional film actor, Johnny Butt, a daily wage of 5s ($1·25) in 1899, which was rather better than the 4s ($1) a day accorded to Chrissie White when she joined the Hepworth Co. at Walton-on-Thames in 1908. 'When I really got on', she recalled, 'I received 8s a day, and when I was a star they paid me 50—shillings, not pounds'. Dave Aylott, who joined Cricks & Martin of Mitcham in 1909, remembered that their terms were 7s 6d a day for principal parts, 5s for minor parts, plus 1s 6d travelling expenses to Mitcham and a bread and cheese lunch with beer. In America at this time the $5 a day received by Mary Pickford when she joined Biograph in 1909 seems to have become standard throughout the industry, nothing extra being paid for 'star' roles.

The escalation in salaries, when it came, was rapid and had to do with two factors: the use of major names from the stage, who had to be paid highly to demean themselves in this way; and the introduction of the 'star' system (c.f. Star system, p. 76) from 1910 onwards. The change began with Film d'Art in Paris, a company established in 1908 to produce prestige films with prestige players. Their leading artistes were paid the equivalent of $40 for each rehearsal and $200 for the actual shoot. Featured players, however, received as little as $2 to $3 a day for services in a major film like *Germinal* (Fr 13), for which the star, Henry Krauss, was paid $700. In England Will Barker paid Sir Herbert Beerbohm Tree a record £1000 to play Wolsey in *Henry*

VIII (GB 11), a two-reeler which was shot in a single day. How far this was from the norm is indicated by the fact that the following year Barker was able to secure the lead player of his *Hamlet* (GB 12), Charles Raymond, for just 10s—which included his services as director of the film!

The first superstar salary was earned not by any of the rising American players, but by Denmark's Asta

Larry Parks as Al Jolson in *The Jolson Story* (US 46) and, *right*, Jolson himself in *The Singing Fool* (US 28). How did they manage to get the hair so wrong?

BIOPICS OF SCREEN STARS

These are relatively rare and have often concentrated on an aspect of the performer's life other than their screen career. The biopics of Diana Barrymore and Lillian Roth were concerned with their subjects' alcoholism, those of Eddie Cantor and Al Jolson dwelt mainly on their singing careers, and Annette Kellerman's on her swimming exploits, while *The George Raft Story* recounted the star's pre-Hollywood days in the gangster milieu of 20s New York. The following performers have had their life stories, in whole or in part, portrayed in feature movies:

DIANA BARRYMORE (1921–60) *Too Much Too Soon* (US 58) with Dorothy Malone in the story, based on Miss Barrymore's memoirs, of how she went to Hollywood to look after her alcoholic father John Barrymore (Errol Flynn) and herself succumbed to drink.

HUMPHREY BOGART (1899–1957) *Bogie* (US 80-TVM) with Kevin O'Connor, based on Joe Hyams' biography of the same title.

EDDIE CANTOR (1892–1964) *The Eddie Cantor Story* (US 53) with Keefe Brasselle in the name role. Cantor himself played a bit part and also sang the songs off-screen.

LON CHANEY (1883–1930) *The Man of a Thousand Faces* (US 57) with James Cagney as the character actor and contortionist extraordinary of the silent screen.

CHARLES CHAPLIN (1889–1977) *The Life Story of Charles Chaplin* (GB 26) with Chick Wango in a British attempt to cash in on the popularity of the cockney lad who had made it in Hollywood. The first biopic of a

screen star, but never released due to a threat of legal action from its subject.

JOAN CRAWFORD (1906–77) *Mommie Dearest* (US 81) was based on Christina Crawford's controversial exposé of her adoptive mother, here portrayed by Faye Dunaway as an insecure but savagely egotistical woman given to beating her children with coathangers.

FRANCES FARMER (1914–70) *Committed* (US 84) was an earnest black-and-white docu–drama with Sheila McLaughlin in an intense performance as the overwrought, alcoholic, leftist and eventually lobotomised Hollywood beauty whose neuroses led to commitment to an asylum. The title is a play on words signifying Farmer's other commitment, to various 'progressive' causes.

Jessica Lange underwent the straightjacketing and lobotomy in a stand-out performance in Graeme Clifford's *Frances* (US 82), a version with less emphasis on politics and more on the relationship with monstrous mother Lillian Farmer, played for hisses by Kim Stanley.

W. C. FIELDS (1879–1946) *W. C. Fields and Me* (US 76) with Rod Steiger in another study of a star disintegrating from drink. The 'Me' of the title was Fields' mistress Carlotta Monti (Valerie Perrine), who nursed the tyrant comic through his alcoholism to the detriment of her own career.

CLARK GABLE (1901–60) *Gable and Lombard* (US 76) with James Brolin struggling bravely in a generally misconceived attempt to portray 'the man rather than the star'.

CORINNE GRIFFITH (1898–1979) *Papa's Delicate Condition* (US 63), based on silent screen heroine Corinne Griffith's own book, is possibly the only biopic about the childhood of a star. Linda Bruhl played the six-year-old Corrie, Jackie Gleason her inebriate father.

JEAN HARLOW (1911–37) *Harlow* (US 65) with Carroll Baker in a travesty of the star's life of which the producer, director and screen-writer should be thoroughly ashamed. *Harlow* (US 65) with Carol Lynley in a rather better attempt at the subject. Originally made for television, it was released to cinemas in an Electronovision version.

AL JOLSON (1886–1950) *The Jolson Story* (US 46) and *Jolson Sings Again* (US 49) with Larry Parks in both highly successful films. Jolson himself did the voice-over for the songs and is also seen in long shot during the 'Swanee' sequence of the first picture.

BUSTER KEATON (1895–1966) *The Buster Keaton Story* (US 57) with Donald O'Connor in what Leslie Halliwell has described as 'a dismal tribute'. Once again the theme is one of drink being the curse of the starring classes.

The Comic (US 69) with Dick Van Dyke as a silent film comedian obviously based on Keaton. Much superior to the above.

ANNETTE KELLERMAN (1888–1978) *Million Dollar Mermaid* (US 53) with Esther Williams playing the Australian girl who invented the one-piece bathing suit and became the first star actress to appear on the screen in the nude (not depicted in the biopic).

Nielsen. For her debut in *The Abyss* (Den 10) she was paid a modest 200kr ($53·60), but the film rocketed her to stardom and by the end of 1912 she was under contract to Berlin producer Paul Davidson with guaranteed annual earnings of $80,000. Compared to Asta Nielsen's salary of over $1500 a week, the highest paid stars in America were Gene Gauntier at $200 a week and Florence Lawrence at $250 a week. At this time Mary Pickford, who was soon to eclipse them all, was trailing at $175 a week at Biograph. The following year, however, Adolph Zukor lured her to Famous Players at $500 a week and this was doubled in 1914 and doubled again in 1915. Already the highest paid woman in the world, on 24 June 1916 she signed a new contract that put her on a par with the highest paid man in the world—Charles Chaplin, who had contracted with Mutual earlier in the year at a salary of $670,000. Miss Pickford's earnings were now half the profits of all her pictures, with a $10,000 p.w. minimum, plus a $300,000 single payment bonus, plus $150,000 p.a. to her mother for 'goodwill', plus $40,000 for examining scenarios prior to signing.

In the meantime Francesca Bertini, Italian 'diva', had become Europe's highest paid star in 1915 at $175,000 p.a., only slightly behind the $200,000 p.a. that Mary Pickford was then earning. European earnings, however, were never to rise above this before World War II, apart from the $450,000 that Alexander Korda paid Marlene Dietrich to star in *Knight Without Armour* (GB

> Samuel Goldwyn on doing business with Mary Pickford: 'It took longer to make one of Mary's contracts than it did to make one of Mary's pictures.'

37). American earnings continued to spiral upward, but with the three highest paid stars—Mary Pickford, Charlie Chaplin and Douglas Fairbanks—combined together as producers under the distribution banner of United Artists from 1919 onwards, it is hard to assess their new earning power. In that same year Roscoe 'Fatty' Arbuckle had become the first star with a guaranteed minimum of $1 million a year, but his contract with Paramount only lasted until scandal destroyed his career in 1922 and he became the first star to be formally banned.

No other star of the silent era matched Arbuckle's salary, but Nazimova was reported to be the highest salaried woman star in 1920 at $13,000 p.w., Tom Mix, the most popular cowboy star of the silents, was earning $17,500 p.w. in 1925 and Harold Lloyd's weekly wage was reported to be $40,000 p.w. in 1926. Salaries in Britain were a sad contrast. Alma Taylor, the most popular female star of the early twenties, was paid £60 p.w. by the Hepworth Co., but they were less generous with their leading male actor, Stewart Rome, who earned only £10 p.w. Ivor Novello, a matinee idol with a strong stage reputation, could command £3000–£4000 per film at his height in the late twenties,

---

BRUCE LEE (1940–73) *The Bruce Lee Story* (US 74) with Hsiao Lung as the Chinese–American actor who achieved international stardom in Hong Kong martial arts movies.

A succession of wholly or semi-fictitious martial arts films followed which purported to portray Bruce Lee: *The Story of the Dragon* (HK 76) with Ho Tsung-tao (Bruce Li); *Bruce Lee—True Story* (HK 76) with Bruce Li; *Bruce Lee and I* (HK 76) with Li Msiu Hsien; *The Dragon Lives* (HK 78) with Bruce Li; *Bruce Lee: the Man, the Myth* (HK 78) with Bruce Li; *Bruce Lee, The Tiger of Manchuria* (HK 78) with Hang Yong Chul; *Young Bruce Lee* (HK 79) with Chuck Norris; *Sexy Isla Meets Bruce Lee in the Devil's Triangle* (Can 7?); *Bruce Lee versus the Gay Power* (Bra 7?). *The Death of Bruce Lee* (HK 76) merely invoked the name, not the character.

CAROLE LOMBARD (1908–42) *Gable and Lombard* (US 76) with Jill Clayburgh as the love of Gable's life, killed tragically in an aeroplane accident at the age of 34. The film failed to illuminate either the romantic myth of the legendary affair or the earthy reality (Lombard commented to a friend 'He's not what you'd call a helluva great lay'). Though even Hollywood could not bring itself to nominate the film for an Oscar, it did succeed in picking up Harvard Lampoon's 1976 Victor Mature Memorial Award for the most embarrassing line of dialogue. The citation read: 'Gable and Lombard, for the screen's greatest insouciant comment following the incendiary demise

of his beloved in a plane crash, as he gazes fondly over the twisted wreckage: "She should have taken the train".'

MARILYN MONROE (1926–62) *Goodbye, Norma Jean* (US/Aus 75) with Misty Rowe, a reasonable look-alike but nothing more, in an exploitation movie that concentrates on Norma Jean Baker's seedy and often degrading existence before her metamorphosis into Marilyn Monroe superstar.

Catherine Hicks essayed the difficult role of legendary sex goddess in *Marilyn the Untold Story* (US 80), a TVM theatrically released in Europe. Based on Norman Mailer's biography, it in fact told little that had not been told before, but then neither did the book. One unusual feature was the portrayal of living and active stars by other actors—Tony Curtis by Bruce Neckels, Jack Lemmon by Brad Blaisdell and Laurence Olivier by Anthony Gordon.

LUBOVA ORLOVA (1902–74) *Lubov Orlova* (USSR 84), straight-life story of Soviet comedienne Lubova Orlova, a much beloved thirties star in the Ginger Rogers mould. The picture was directed by her husband Grigory Alexandrov, who had directed the star in such popular Russian films as *The Circus* (USSR 36), *Volga-Volga* (USSR 38) and *The Bright Path* (USSR 40). Alexandrov, a pioneer who had worked with Eisenstein in the twenties, died during production.

GEORGE RAFT (1895–) *The George Raft Story* (US 61) with Ray Danton as the professional

athlete, gambler, nightclub dancer and intimate of gangsters who turned it all to good account in Hollywood.

BILL 'BOJANGLES' ROBINSON (1878–1949) *Stormy Weather* (US 43) with 'Bojangles' himself in an all-black fictionalised version of his own life story. Also subject of 1979 Broadway musical *Bojangles*.

WILL ROGERS (1879–1935) *The Story of Will Rogers* (US 50) with Will Rogers Jnr playing his father in a bland homage to the celebrated crackerbarrel philosopher and latecomer movie star.

LILLIAN ROTH (1910–) *I'll Cry Tomorrow* (US 55) with Susan Hayward as the Broadway/Hollywood star of the early thirties whose career became another write-off to alcoholism.

RUDOLPH VALENTINO (1895–1926) *Valentino* (US 51) with Anthony Dexter in a flat biopic made at a time when Hollywood's attempts to portray the twenties invariably mixed period cliché with blundering anachronisms.

Valentino (GB 77) with Rudolf Nureyev charismatic in Ken Russell's lush and stimulating evocation of man, myth, place and period.

HANSA WADKAR (1920–71) *Bhumika* (Ind 78) with Smita Patil as the popular Hindi star of the thirties and forties. One of the few foreign-language star biopics.

PEARL WHITE (1889–1938) *The Perils of Pauline* (US 47) with Betty Hutton recreating the career of the silent serial queen in uncompromisingly forties style.

Performers

> The only two actors to appear in Forbes Magazine's annual listing of the 400 richest people in America are ex-cowboy star Gene Autry, reputedly worth $130 million, and Bob Hope, with net assets, 'despite denials', in excess of $200 million.

while the highest sum for a silent film was the £10,000 paid to music hall artiste Sir Harry Lauder for his role as a retired grocer in George Pearson's *Huntingtower* (GB 27).

The coming of sound and the Depression, almost simultaneously, forced most star salaries downward. In 1927 over 40 stars were reputedly earning $5000 or more a week. By 1931 only 23 stars had salaries of $3500 or more. Top earners in that year were Constance Bennett and John Barrymore at $30,000 p.w., a sum soon to be matched by Greta Garbo, who earned $250,000 for *The Painted Veil* (US 34) and the same for *Anna Karenina* (US 35). Highest earnings of 1935 were the $480,833 reported by Mae West to the tax authorities, well in excess of the highest earnings of 1938—Shirley Temple's $307,014, or 1939—James Cagney's $368,333, or even 1946 when Bing Crosby topped both at the box office (rated No. 1 in the Quigley Poll) and at the bank with $325,000. During the forties and fifties top star salaries per film were generally in the $250,000–$400,000 region, with a new peak of $500,000 for a British film—Elizabeth Taylor in *Suddenly Last Summer* (GB 59)—and $750,000 for an American production, earned by both John Wayne and William Holden (plus 20 per cent of the net) on *The Horse Soldiers* (US 59). The 1960s saw the era of the $1 million star salary for single pictures and in the 1970s the multi-million dollar contract. In the mid 1970s Charles Bronson was reported to be earning $20,000–$30,000, plus $2500 living allowance, per day. However, this was far exceeded by Marlon Brando's reputed $3·5 million for 12 days shooting on *Superman* (GB 78), which works out at $290,000 per day. According to a special *Newsweek* report on Hollywood in 1978, the world's highest paid stars were Paul Newman, Robert Redford and Steve McQueen, commanding some $3 million per picture. Each of the three had turned down a $4 million offer to take the starring role in *Superman* (GB 78). Dustin Hoffman accepted precisely that amount for his transvestite role in *Tootsie* (US 82), but an even higher figure of $5 million plus percentage had already been paid to Burt Reynolds for *The Cannonball Run* (US 81). Sean Connery became the highest paid British star when he was lured back into Bond movies with a $5 million bait for *Never Say Never Again* (GB 83). These figures may soon start to look low-rent. According to a report in *Variety*, Sylvester Stallone is receiving no less than $12 million for playing the lead in Golden Globus's aptly titled *Over the Top* (US i.p.).

Record earnings from a single movie were achieved by Marlon Brando in *Superman* (GB 78). He was originally paid nearly $3·5 million for 12 days shooting in his role as Superman's father—a not ungenerous $290,000 a day. In 1982 an out-of-court settlement awarded him a further $15 million, representing 11·3 per cent of the box-office gross, making a total of $18·5 million for his ten minutes of screen time.

The lowest salaries of recent years have seldom fallen below the £1500 that Olivia Hussey claimed she was paid for 11 months work while she was playing the female lead in Zeffirelli's *Romeo and Juliet* (GB 68)—at least in the west. In eastern countries and even Eastern Europe, different standards prevail. Teresa Izewska, star of the award-winning *Kanal* (Pol 57), revealed at the Cannes Film Festival that she earned the equivalent of $12 a month and that the Polish authorities had bought her one dress and one pair of shoes in order to represent them at the Festival. In 1973 *Variety* reported that China's biggest box office star, Shih Chung-chin, drew a salary of $20 a month. She slept in a communal dormitory with other actresses. Things are looking up, however, on the other side of the bamboo curtain. By 1980 a top Chinese star could earn a maximum of 250 yuan ($168) a month, though not all were so generously recompensed. Chen Chong, female lead in box office hit *Xiaohua* (Chn 80), winner of the Hundred Flowers Award, was paid 1000 yuan ($672) for eight months' shooting.

The lowest paid players in American pictures were found in black movies. White director Edgar G. Ulmer recalls paying the 50 chorus girls in *Moon Over Harlem* (US 39) 25c a day each. The shooting schedule was four days and the girls had to pay their car fares from Harlem to the studio in Jersey out of the $1 they earned for a week's work. A record zero budget for an entire cast was achieved by Action Pictures Co. for their all-black feature *Sugar Hill Baby* (US 38). The casting director announced with disarming frankness that there was no money available for salaries, the only inducement offered being the somewhat doubtful 'chance to continue to work in future in productions at good salaries'.

Big names will sometimes appear for very little if they are attracted by the project. Committed feminist Julie Christie agreed to star in *The Gold Diggers* (GB 84) for £30 a day. Another radical lady, Karen Black, received a reported $1038 in total for her starring role in the much lauded *Can She Bake a Cherry Pie?* (US 83).

> The Austral Photoplay Co. financed their comedy *The Laugh on Dad* (Aus 18) by the novel means of charging the actors to perform in it. Anyone buying £10 worth of shares in the company was entitled to free 'motion picture tuition' and a role in the film.

The picture having been made without union approval, Ms Black was disciplined by the Screen Actors Guild. The fine imposed was $1038.

Probably the most recent instance of an established star taking a nil salary (and no per cent) was that of Sylvia Kristel who claims that since the success of *Emmanuelle* (Fr 74) she has been the highest paid actress in Europe. She starred in *Pastorale 1943* (Neth 78) for nothing. It was, she explained, a simple matter of tax avoidance.

At the other end of the scale, the most highly-paid stars have always been susceptible to ingenious attempts by the unscrupulous to benefit from their box office drawing power without the formality of payment. In 1917 a film processor in Chicago created his own Chaplin feature film—at a time when Chaplin was the highest paid star in the world—by matching together shots from his old comedies and then interpolating material from Fox's sensational *The Daughter of the Gods* (US 16), in which Australian star Annette Kellerman appeared in the nude. By clever optical work, he succeeded in creating scenes in which Chaplin and the naked Antipodean beauty appeared to be performing together. The film was released to the underground trade as *Charlie, Son of the Gods*.

Even more audacious was Soviet director Sergei Komarov's deception that secured him the gratuitous services of not one but two superstars, Mary Pickford and Douglas Fairbanks. During the visit of the couple to Moscow in July 1926, Komarov posed as a newsreel cameraman and followed them round with a camera, shooting enough footage to piece together a full-length comedy feature after their departure. Titled *The Kiss of Mary Pickford* (USSR 26), it was an engaging tale of a film extra who is determined to kiss the 'world's sweetheart'—and succeeds! Most remarkable of all was the climactic sequence of the close embrace between Soviet hero

and Hollywood heroine. Although the film has now been shown publicly in the west, no one has been able to offer a convincing explanation of how Komarov managed to contrive this scene.

The first screen artiste to work on percentage was Nellie Stewart, who was paid £1000 plus a per cent of the gross for her role in *Sweet Nell of Old Drury* (Aus 11).

The first American artiste to receive a percentage deal was James O'Neill (father of Eugene), who played the wronged Edmond Dantes in Famous Players' maiden production *The Count of Monte Cristo* (US 13). O'Neill had played the part on stage no less than 4000 times over a period of 30 years and was both too old (65) and too ham for the screen version, but Daniel Frohman knew that his was the name which would draw theatregoers to the cinema and he offered the star 20 per cent of the net profits as an inducement. Returns were undermined by a rival Selig version of *The Count of Monte Cristo*, but the Famous Players version eventually grossed $45,539·32, of which O'Neill received $3813·32.

EXTRAS

The first film with a 'cast of thousands' in a literal sense was Luigi Maggi's Napoleonic epic *Il Granatiere Rolland* (It 10), for which 2000 extras were employed. A similar number participated in Britain's first extravaganza, Charles Weston's feature-length *The Battle of Waterloo* (GB 13).

The largest number of extras employed on a film appeared in the funeral scene of Sir Richard Attenborough's *Gandhi* (GB 82) and comprised a crowd believed to have been in excess of 300,000. Announcements by loudspeaker van, in newspapers and on television and radio summoned over 200,000 volunteer extras to Delhi's ceremonial mall, the Rajpath, where they were supplemented by another 94,560 contracted performers, the majority of whom were paid a fee equivalent to 40p each. The sequence had to be shot in a single morning, that of Saturday 31 January 1981, the 33rd anniversary of Gandhi's funeral. Eleven camera crews shot 20,000 ft of film, more than the total footage of the 188-minute release print of the movie. The edited funeral sequence with its 300,000 performers ran for only 125 seconds of screen time.

The largest number of soldiers used as extras was 187,000 in the last Nazi-made motion picture epic *Kolberg* (Ger 45). For this story about Napoleon's siege of Kolberg, whole army divisions were diverted from the front to play Napoleonic soldiers at a time when Germany was facing the prospect of her defeat. The film was started in 1943 and completed at the end of the following year, with drafts of fresh extras continuously replacing those who had to return to more earnest military duties. Released in January 1945, at a time when few Berlin cinemas were still functioning, *Kolberg* was seen by a considerably smaller total audience than the number which had appeared in it.

Other considerable casts include: 157,000 for monster movie *Wang Ma Gwi/Monster Wang-magwi* (S.Kor 67); 120,000 for *War and Peace* (USSR 67); 80,000 for *The War of Independence* (Rom 12); 68,894 for *Around the World in 80 Days* (US 56); 60,000 for *Intolerance* (US 16)—publicity for the picture claimed 125,000; 60,000 for *Dny Zrady* (Cz 72); 50,000 for *Ben Hur* (US 59), *Exodus* (US 60), *Inchon* (Kor/US 81) and *Khan Asparouch* (Bul 82); 36,000 in *Metropolis* (Ger 26), including 1100 bald men in the Tower of Babel sequence; and 30,000 in *Michael the Brave* (Rom 70). **The year that the largest number of extras were employed in Hollywood** was 1927, when a total of 330,397 days were worked (227,415 by men, 102,892 by women), an average daily call of 1056. Since there were 14,000 extras registered with Central Casting that year, average employment rate was approximately one day in 14.

EXTRAS WHO BECAME STARS

Comparatively few major stars began their film careers as extras, the majority having had stage or, latterly, television experience before entering movies. Those who did do extra work include Theda Bara, Gary Cooper, Marlene Dietrich, Clark Gable, Janet Gaynor, John Gilbert, Paulette Goddard, Stewart Granger, Jean Harlow, Harold Lloyd, Sophia Loren, Marilyn Monroe, David Niven, Ramon Novarro, Merle Oberon, Norma Shearer, Erich von Stroheim, Constance

Above right
Brigitte Bardot as herself in *Dear Brigitte* (US 65), the story of a small boy in Mississippi who writes a love letter to BB and finally gets to meet her when his family take a trip to Paris.

Below right
Not Larry Hagman as J.R., but Larry Hagman as Larry Hagman in a Swedish film called *I Am Blushing* (Swe 81). (*Svenska Filminstitutet*)

Far right
Gloria Swanson as herself in *Airport 75* (US 74). More than half a century earlier she had played herself in *Hollywood* (US 23).

FILM STARS WHO HAVE PLAYED THEMSELVES IN MOVIES

Mary Astor *Hollywood* (US 23)
Anne Bancroft *Silent Movie* (US 76)
Tallulah Bankhead *Stage Door Canteen* (US 43); *Main Street to Broadway* (US 53)
Brigitte Bardot *Dear Brigitte* (US 65)
Ethel Barrymore *Main Street to Broadway* (US 53)
Lionel Barrymore *Free and Easy* (US 30); *Main Street to Broadway* (US 53)
Noah Beery *Hollywood* (US 23)
Dorothy Bellew *The Kinema Girl* (GB 14)
William Bendix *Duffy's Tavern* (US 45); *Variety Girl* (US 47)
Edgar Bergen *Stage Door Canteen* (US 43); *Song of the Open Road* (US 44)
Milton Berle *Let's Make Love* (US 60); *Broadway Danny Rose* (US 84)
Humphrey Bogart *Thank Your Lucky Stars* (US 43); *The Love Lottery* (US 54)
Joe E. Brown *Hollywood Canteen* (US 44)
Coral Browne (as herself in 1958) *An Englishman Abroad* (GB 84)
James Caan *Silent Movie* (US 76)
Eddie Cantor *Thank Your Lucky Stars* (US 43); *Hollywood Canteen* (US 44); *The Story of Will Rogers* (US 52)
Charles Chaplin *Show People* (US 29)
Maurice Chevalier *Pepe* (US 60)
Julie Christie *Nashville* (US 75)
Betty Compson *Hollywood* (US 23); *Hollywood Boulevard* (US 36)
Eddie Constantine *Les Septs pêches capitaux* (Fr/It 62); *Warnung vor einer Heiligen Nutte* (FRG/It 71); *Flight to Berlin* (GB 84)
Jackie Coogan *Free and Easy* (US 30)
Gary Cooper *Variety Girl* (US 47); *It's a Great Feeling* (US 49); *Starlift* (US 51)

Ricardo Cortez *Hollywood* (US 23)
Broderick Crawford *A Little Romance* (US 79)
Joan Crawford *Hollywood Canteen* (US 44); *It's a Great Feeling* (US 49)
Bing Crosby *Star Spangled Rhythm* (US 42); *Duffy's Tavern* (US 45); *Variety Girl* (US 47); *Angels in the Outfield* (US 52); *The Greatest Show on Earth* (US 52); *Let's Make Love* (US 60); *Pepe* (US 60)
Finlay Currie *6·5 Special* (GB 58)
Karl Dane *Free and Easy* (US 30)
Bette Davis *Thank Your Lucky Stars* (US 43); *Hollywood Canteen* (US 44)
Sammy Davis Jnr *Pepe* (US 60)
Doris Day *Starlift* (US 51)
Olivia de Havilland *Thank Your Lucky Stars* (US 43)
Dolores Del Rio *Torero!* (Mex 56)
Marlene Dietrich *Follow the Boys* (US 44); *Jigsaw* (US 49)
Diana Dors *Allez France* (Fr 64)
Jimmy Durante *Pepe* (US 60)
Douglas Fairbanks *Hollywood* (US 23); *The Kiss of Mary Pickford* (USSR 26); *Show People* (US 29)
Marianne Faithful *Made in USA* (Fr 67)
Gracie Fields *Stage Door Canteen* (US 43)
W. C. Fields *Sensations of 1945* (US 44); *Song of the Open Road* (US 44); *Follow the Boys* (US 44)
Barry Fitzgerald *Variety Girl* (US 47)
Rhonda Fleming *The Patsy* (US 64)
Cyril Fletcher *Yellow Canary* (GB 43)
Errol Flynn *It's a Great Feeling* (US 49)
Henry Fonda *Jigsaw* (US 49); *Main Street to Broadway* (US 53); *Fedora* (FRG 78)
Zsa Zsa Gabor *Pepe* (US 60)
Greta Garbo *A Man's Man* (US 29)
Ava Gardner *The Band Wagon* (US 53)

John Garfield *Thank Your Lucky Stars* (US 43); *Hollywood Canteen* (US 44); *Jigsaw* (US 49)
Greer Garson *Pepe* (US 60)
John Gilbert *Married Flirts* (US 24); *A Man's Man* (US 29)
Paulette Goddard *Star Spangled Rhythm* (US 42); *Variety Girl* (US 47)
Elliott Gould *Nashville* (US 75); *The Muppets Take Manhattan* (US 84)
Cary Grant *Without Reservations* (US 46)
Greta Gynt *I'm a Stranger* (GB 52)
Larry Hagman *I am Blushing* (Swe 81)
Creighton Hale *Mary of the Movies* (US 23)
Rex Harrison *Main Street to Broadway* (US 53)
W. S. Hart *Hollywood* (US 23); *Show People* (US 29)
Laurence Harvey *The Magic Christian* (GB 70) as self playing Hamlet
Sessue Hayakawa *Night Life in Hollywood* (US 22)
Sterling Hayden *Variety Girl* (US 47)
Susan Hayward *Star Spangled Rhythm* (US 42)
Katherine Hepburn *Stage Door Canteen* (US 43)
William Holden *Variety Girl* (US 47)
Bob Hope *Duffy's Tavern* (US 45); *Variety Girl* (US 47); *The Greatest Show on Earth* (US 52); *The Oscar* (US 66)
Betty Hutton *Star Spangled Rhythm* (US 42); *Duffy's Tavern* (US 45)
Sidney James *The Beauty Contest* (GB 64)
Al Jolson *Hollywood Cavalcade* (US 39)
Danny Kaye *It's a Great Feeling* (US 49)
Buster Keaton *Hollywood Cavalcade* (US 39); *Sunset Boulevard* (US 50)
Gene Kelly *Love is Better than Ever* (US 52); *Let's Make Love* (US 60)
George Kennedy *The Legend of Lylah Clare* (US 68); *Modern Romance* (US 81)

Alan Ladd *Star Spangled Rhythm* (US 42);
   Duffy's Tavern (US 45); *Variety Girl* (US 47)
Veronica Lake *Star Spangled Rhythm* (US 42);
   Variety Girl (US 47)
Dorothy Lamour *Star Spangled Rhythm*
   (US 42); *Duffy's Tavern* (US 45); *Variety Girl*
   (US 47)
Peter Lawford *Pepe* (US 60)
Janet Leigh *Pepe* (US 60)
Jack Lemmon *Pepe* (US 60)
Peter Lorre *Hollywood Canteen* (US 44)
Bessie Love *Night Life in Hollywood* (US 22);
   Mary of the Movies (US 23)
Linda Lovelace *Linda Lovelace for President*
   (US 75)
Ida Lupino *Thank Your Lucky Stars* (US 43)
Jeanette MacDonald *Follow the Boys* (US 44)
Virginia McKenna *An Elephant called Slowly*
   (GB 69); *The Lion at World's End* (GB 71)
Fred MacMurray *Star Spangled Rhythm*
   (US 42)
Gordon MacRae *Starlift* (US 51)
George Marshall *Variety Girl* (US 47)
Marcello Mastroianni *L'Ingorgo/Bottleneck*
   (It/Fr/Sp/FRG 79)
Harpo Marx *Stage Door Canteen* (US 43)
Virginia Mayo *Starlift* (US 51)
Burgess Meredith *Jigsaw* (US 49)
Ray Milland *Star Spangled Rhythm* (US 42);
   Variety Girl (US 47)
Liza Minnelli *Silent Movie* (US 76); *The
   Muppets Take Manhattan* (US 84)
Bull Montana *Hollywood* (US 23)
Owen Moore *Hollywood* (US 23)
Paul Muni *Stage Door Canteen* (US 43)
Mae Murray *Married Flirts* (US 24); *Show
   People* (US 29)
Nita Naldi *Hollywood* (US 23)
Patricia Neal *It's a Great Feeling* (US 49)
Pola Negri *Hollywood* (US 23)

Paul Newman *Silent Movie* (US 76)
Anna Q. Nillson *Sunset Boulevard* (US 50)
Kim Novak *Pepe* (US 60)
Merle Oberon *Stage Door Canteen* (US 43)
Donald O'Connor *Follow the Boys* (US 44)
Lili Palmer *Main Street to Broadway* (US 53)
Larry Parks *Jolson Sings Again* (US 49)—also
   played Jolson
Mary Pickford *Hollywood* (US 23); *The Kiss of
   Mary Pickford* (USSR 26) made by Sergei
   Komorov without Miss Pickford being
   aware of her own participation
ZaSu Pitts *Mary of the Movies* (US 23)
Eddie Polo *Dangerous Hour* (US 23)
Dick Powell *Star Spangled Rhythm* (US 42)
Jane Powell *Song of the Open Road* (US 44)
Robert Preston *Variety Girl* (US 47)
Dennis Price *Go for a Take* (GB 72)
George Raft *Broadway* (US 42); *Stage Door
   Canteen* (US 43); *The Patsy* (US 64); *Casino
   Royale* (GB 67); *Sextette* (US 78)
Tony Randall *The King of Comedy* (US 83)
Ronald Reagan *It's a Great Feeling* (US 49)
Wallace Reid *Night Life in Hollywood* (US 22)
Michael Rennie *The Body Said No!* (GB 50)
Burt Reynolds *Silent Movie* (US 76)
Debbie Reynolds *Pepe* (US 60)
Ralph Richardson *The Volunteer* (GB 43)
Edward G. Robinson *It's a Great Feeling*
   (US 49)
Patricia Roc *Holiday Camp* (GB 47)
Eddie Rochester *Star Spangled Rhythm* (US 42)
Roy Rogers *Hollywood Canteen* (US 44)
Will Rogers *Hollywood* (US 23)
Sabrina *Just My Luck* (GB 57)
Randolph Scott *Starlift* (US 51)
Larry Semon *Go Straight* (US 25)
Mack Sennett *Abbott and Costello Meet the
   Keystone Kops* (US 54)
Norma Shearer *Married Flirts* (US 24)

Martin Sheen *In the King of Prussia* (US 82)
Brooke Shields *The Muppets Take Manhattan*
   (US 84)
Phil Silvers *Take It or Leave It* (US 44)
Frank Sinatra *Pepe* (US 60); *Cannonball Run II*
   (US 83)
Barbara Stanwyck *Hollywood Canteen* (US 44);
   Variety Girl (US 47)
Tommy Steele *Kill Me Tomorrow* (GB 55); *The
   Tommy Steele Story* (GB 57)
Anita Stewart *Mary of the Movies* (US 23);
   Hollywood (US 23); *Go Straight* (US 25)
Gloria Swanson *Hollywood* (US 23); *Airport 75*
   (US 74)
Blanche Sweet *Souls for Sale* (US 23)
Constance Talmadge *In Hollywood with Potash
   and Perlmutter* (US 24)
Norma Talmadge *In Hollywood with Potash
   and Perlmutter* (US 24); *Show People* (US 29)
Estelle Taylor *Mary of the Movies* (US 23);
   Hollywood (US 23)
Bill Travers *An Elephant called Slowly* (GB 69);
   The Lion at World's End (GB 71)
Ben Turpin *Hollywood* (US 23)
Liv Ullman *Players* (US 79)
Peter Ustinov *Players* (US 79)
H. B. Warner *Sunset Boulevard* (US 50)
Paul Wegener *The Golem and the Dancer* (Ger 14)
Johnny Weissmuller *Stage Door Canteen*
   (US 43)
Orson Welles *Follow the Boys* (US 44)
Cornel Wilde *Main Street to Broadway* (US 53)
Natalie Wood *The Candidate* (US 72); *Willie
   and Phil* (US 81)
Jane Wyman *Hollywood Canteen* (US 44); *It's a
   Great Feeling* (US 49); *Starlift* (US 51)
Ed Wynn *The Patsy* (US 64)
Michael York *Fedora* (FRG 78)
Susannah York *Scruggs* (GB 66)—also played
   heroine; *Long Shot* (GB 78)

In 1913 a production company called the Juvenile Motion Picture Co. was established in Los Angeles with a stock company of child players only—all the artistes were 15 or under.

Talmadge, Rudolph Valentino, Michael Wilding and Loretta Young.

Despite the fact that he was registered at Central Casting as 'Anglo-Saxon type 2008', David Niven's first role was as a Mexican in a blanket in a Hopalong Cassidy oater. He was subsequently an extra in 26 other westerns.

Sadly the reverse process could also apply. Leading players who ended their careers as extras were King Baggot, Mae Busch, Ethel Clayton, Grace Cunard, western star Franklyn Farnum, Flora Finch, Francis Ford (brother of John Ford and a leading man in the late teens), John Ince (brother of early mogul Thomas Ince), Douglas Fairbanks' leading lady Julanne Johnston, Alice Lake, original 'Biograph Girl' Florence Lawrence, western star Kermit Maynard, Marshall Neilan, who had once commanded $125,000 per picture, Florence Turner, who was the first star to be put under contract, and 'country boy' hero Charles Ray. May McAvoy, romantic lead of the twenties who played opposite Al Jolson in *The Jazz Singer* (US 27), retired when talkies took over but later tried to make a comeback as a character actress. She never succeeded in securing a speaking part and ended her career as an extra with MGM in the 1940s.

The dream of stardom via Central Casting occasionally comes true even today. Sixteen-year-old French schoolgirl Sandrine Bonnaire applied for a role as an extra in Maurice Pialat's *A Nos Amours* (Fr 83). She was given the lead instead, winning plaudits from the critics for her performance and sharing in the accolade of a César award, the French Oscar, for 'Best Film' of the year.

BLACK EXTRAS

Demand for black extras in the USA began with the flood of Civil War movies that followed the 50th anniversary in 1911. Tarzan and other jungle movies, together with epics of the ancient world, maintained a steady flow of work and the number of blacks registered with Central Casting peaked at 6816 in 1926. The following year was the best for employment, with

---

NON-ACTORS WHO HAVE PLAYED THEMSELVES IN FILMS
The list excludes the many bandleaders and vocalists appearing in sound movies.

Princess Aicha Abidir *Pierrot-le-Feu* (Fr/It 65)
Dragljub Aleksić, acrobat *Nevinost bez Zastite** (Yug 68)
Queen Alexandra *The Great Love* (US 18); *Women Who Win* (GB 19)
Muhammed Ali, heavyweight boxing champion *The Greatest** (US 77); *Body and Soul* (US 81)
Alfredo Alvarado, exhibition dancer *El Rey del Jorapo** (Ven 80)
Vijay Amritraj, Indian tennis champion *Octopussy* (GB 83)
Mario Andretti, motor-racing driver *Speed Fever* (It 78)
Lady Astor, first woman MP to sit in House of Commons *Royal Cavalcade* (GB 35)
Lt-Commander Auten VC, RNR re-enacted exploit which won him VC in *Q Ships* (GB 28)
Lord Baden-Powell, defender of Mafeking and founder of the Scout movement *Boys of the Otter Patrol* (GB 18); *The Man Who Changed His Mind* (GB 28); *The Woodpigeon Patrol* (GB 30)
Admiral Badger *Victory* (US 13)
Max Baer, boxer *The Prizefighter and the Lady* (US 33)
Bruce Bairnsfather, creator of cartoon character 'Old Bill' *Old Bill Through the Ages* (GB 24)
Joan Bakewell, TV personality *The Touchables* (GB 67)
Adolf Beck, convicted of false murder charge *The Martyrdom of Adolf Beck** (GB 09)
The Duchess of Bedford *The Beauty Contest* (GB 64)
The Duke of Bedford *The Iron Maiden* (GB 62)
Alec Bedser, cricketer *The Final Test* (GB 53)
Saul Bellow, novelist *Zelig* (US 83)

Sonny Berger, Hell's Angels leader *Hell's Angels* (US 69)
Yogi Berra, baseball star *That Touch of Mink* (US 62)
Daniel and Phillip Berrigan, radical Jesuits *In the King of Prussia* (US 82)
Ronald Biggs, train robber *The Great Rock'n' Roll Swindle* (GB 80); *Honeymoon* (FRG 80)
Danny Blanchflower, soccer star *Those Glory Glory Days* (GB 83)
Jasmine Bligh, TV announcer *Band Wagon* (GB 40)
Ada Bodart, assisted Nurse Edith Cavell in establishing her World War I escape organisation *Dawn* (GB 28)
Evangeline Booth, Commandant of US Salvation Army *Fires of Faith* (US 19)
Lord Boothby, politician *Rockets Galore* (GB 58)
Bjorn Borg, tennis champion *Racquet* (US 79)
Horatio Bottomley, politician and financier, three times charged with fraud (convicted 1922) *Was It He?* (GB 14)
The Bowen Family, of Guyra, NSW, victims of psychic phenomena *The Guyra Ghost Mystery* (Aus 21)
Jack Brabham, motor-racing driver *The Green Helmet* (GB 61)
Sir David Brand, premier of Western Australia *Nickel Queen* (Aus 71)
RSM Ronald Brittain, Regimental Sergeant Major of ferocious demeanour *You Lucky People* (GB 55)
Dr Joyce Brothers, sexologist *Stand Up and Be Counted* (US 71); *Embryo* (US 76); *The Lonely Guy* (US 84)
Judge Willis Brown of Salt Lake Juvenile Court *A Boy and the Law* (US 14)
Maurice Buckmaster, spy-master *Odette* (GB 50)
Sir Matt Busby, football manager *Cup Fever* (GB 65)
José Capablanca, chess Grand Master *Chess Fever* (USSR 25)

Andrew Carnegie, multi-millionaire industrialist *Our Mutual Girl* (US 14)
George Washington Carver, distinguished black scientist *George Washington Carver** (US 40)
Dick Cavett, TV chat show presenter *Health* (US 80)
César, sculptor who created the César (French Oscar) *T'es folle ou quoi?* (Fr 82)
Arthur Christiansen, ex-editor of the *Daily Express The Day the Earth Caught Fire* (GB 61)
M. E. Clifton-James, ex-actor who impersonated Montgomery to deceive Nazi Intelligence *I Was Monty's Double** (GB 58)
Ty Cobb, baseball player *Somewhere in Georgia* (US 17)
Sir Alan Cobham, aviator *The Flight Commander* (GB 27)
William Cody, Buffalo Bill *The Life of Buffalo Bill** (US 09); *Buffalo Bill's Far West and Pawnee Bill's Far East* (US 10); *The Indian Wars* (US 13); *Sitting Bull—The Hostile Indian Chief* (US 14); *Patsy of the Circus* (US 15)
Dennis Compton, cricketer *The Final Test* (GB 53)
Michael Curtiz, film director *It's a Great Feeling* (US 49)
Emmett Dalton, youngest of the Dalton brothers, notorious desperadoes *Beyond the Law* (US 18)
Josephus Daniels, US Secretary of the Navy *Victory* (US 13)
Moshe Dayan, Israeli Minister of Defence *Operation Thunderbolt* (Isr 77)
Count de Bauford in unidentified Carl Laemmle film (US 10) about his romance with an American heiress
Cecil B. DeMille, film producer and director *Hollywood* (US 23); *Free and Easy* (US 30); *Star Spangled Rhythm* (US 42); *Variety Girl* (US 47); *Sunset Boulevard* (US 50)
Jack Dempsey, heavyweight boxing champion *Off Limits* (US 53)

some 10,000 black roles cast—the total for the previous three years had been 17,000. There was a decline with the coming of talkies and generally the films of the thirties were more confined in their settings than those of the silent era, requiring smaller crowd scenes. World War II brought an almost complete stop to black casting; despite the million black Americans under arms, Hollywood's doughboy was resolutely white. After the war there was little improvement—in 1948 only 130 black roles were cast in pictures.

CHILD STARS

Adult stars who succeeded in perpetuating screen careers begun in childhood are few: Sir Stanley Baker (debut aged 14); Cyril Cusack (8); Bebe Daniels (7); Judy Garland (14); Betty Grable (13); Glynis Johns (13); Peter Lawford (7); Roger Livesey (14); Hayley Mills (13); Roddy McDowall (8); Donald O'Connor (11); Mickey Rooney (6); Romy Schneider (14); Anne Shirley (4); Jean Simmons (14); Elizabeth Taylor (10); Anna May Wong (12); Natalie Wood (5). Of these, only Garland, McDowall, Mills, Rooney, Shirley (as Dawn O'Day) and Taylor can be regarded as having been child *stars*. The three major child stars of the seventies,

> The *Our Gang* comedies of the early talkie era were made in English, German, French and Spanish. The children were taught to say their foreign language dialogue by rote.

Tatum O'Neal, Jodie Foster and Brooke Shields, have now all experienced their first screen kiss and appear to be successfully negotiating the difficult transition to adult roles.

The first child to earn a million dollars by his own efforts, whether in films or any other business, was Chaplin discovery Jackie Coogan (1914–84), who starred in the former's *The Kid* (US 20) and went on to make a string of silent successes under his own Jackie Coogan Productions banner. By 1924 the ten-year-old superstar had earned some $2 million, a sum which was doubled by his father by shrewd investments. In the meantime he was allowed $6 a week pocket money. On reaching the age of 21, and his father having died in the meantime, his mother cut him off with $5000 and told her that she was keeping

---

Richard Dimbleby, BBC commentator *The Twenty Questions Murder* (GB 50); *John and Julie* (GB 55); *Rockets Galore* (GB 58); *Libel* (GB 59)

Georgi Dimtrov, communist revolutionary tried and acquitted in the 1933 Reichstag Fire trial, Prime Minister of Bulgaria 1946–49 *Kämpfer* (USSR 36)

Walt Disney, creator of Mickey Mouse, etc *Once Upon a Time* (US 44)

Sir Arthur Conan Doyle, novelist and creator of Sherlock Holmes *The $5,000,000 Counterfeiting Plot* (US 14)

Joni Eareckson, paraplegic *Joni** (US 80)

Sgt Arthur Guy Empsey, war hero *Over the Top** (US 18)

Godfrey Evans, cricketer *The Final Test* (GB 53)

Robert Fabian, police detective *Passport to Shame* (GB 59)

Emerson Fittipaldi, motor-racing driver *Speed Fever* (It 79)

Margot Fonteyn, prima ballerina *The Little Ballerina* (GB 51)

Michael Foot, socialist politician *Rockets Galore* (GB 58)

John Ford, director *Big Time* (US 29)

Joe Frazier, boxer *Rocky* (US 77)

Tito Fuentes, baseball player *Solomon King* (US 74)

Samuel Fuller, director *Pierrot-le-Feu* (Fr 65); *Scotch Myths—The Movie* (GB 83)

Dorothy Gibson, Titanic survivor *Saved from the Titanic* (GB 12)

Frank Gifford, American footballer *Paper Lion* (US 68); *Viva Knievel!* (US 77)

Alan Ginsberg, poet *Ciao! Manhattan* (US 72)

Raymond Glendenning, sports commentator *The Galloping Major* (GB 51); *Make Mine a Million* (GB 59); *The Iron Maiden* (GB 62)

Elinor Glyn, pioneer of the sex novel and creator of 'It' *It* (US 27); *Show People* (US 29)

Barbara Goalen, model *Wonderful Things!* (GB 58)

Pancho Gonzalez, tennis coach *Players* (US 79)

John Gorton, Prime Minister of Australia *Don's Party* (Aus 76)

Billy Graham, American evangelist *Souls in Conflict* (GB 55); *Two a Penny* (GB 67)

Sheila Graham, journalist and mistress of F. Scott Fitzgerald (played by Deborah Kerr in biopic *Beloved Infidel* (US 59) *College Confidential* (US 60)

Angèle Grammont, who escaped from old people's home near Lausanne *Angèle** (Swz 68)

Zane Grey, Western novelist *White Death* (Aus 36)

Merv Griffin, TV anchorman *The Lonely Guy* (US 84)

Earl Haig, World War I Commander-in-Chief *Remembrance* (GB 27)

Ernest Haigh, ex-Chief Inspector of Police *Leaves from My Life** (GB 21)

Giscele Halimi, defence counsel in notable 1972 abortion trial *L'Une chante l'autre pas* (Fr/Bel/Cur 76)

David Hamilton, photographer *Tiffany Jones* (GB 73)

General Sir Ian Hamilton, leader of the Gallipoli Expedition *Tell England* (GB 31)

Oscar Hammerstein, composer *Main Street to Broadway* (US 53)

Judge James Hannon, judge who tried Arlo Guthrie for casting litter *Alice's Restaurant* (US 69)

Gilbert Harding, crusty TV personality, famous for rudeness *Simon and Laura* (GB 55); *As Long as They're Happy* (GB 55); *An Alligator Named Daisy* (GB 55); *My Wife's Family* (GB 56); *Left, Right and Centre* (GB 59); *Expresso Bongo* (GB 59)

Norman Hartnell, couturier *The Beauty Contest* (GB 64)

Len Harvey, boxer *The Bermondsey Kid* (GB 33)

Edith Head, Hollywood costume designer *The Oscar* (US 66)

Hugh Hefner, founder of Playboy empire *How Did a Nice Girl Like You Ever Get Into This Business* (FRG 70); Hefner played by Cliff Robertson in *Star 80* (US 83)

Graham Hill, motor-racing driver *The Fast Lady* (GB 62)

Dennis Hills, captive of Idi Amin *The Rise and Fall of Idi Amin* (Ken 81)

David Hockney, artist *A Bigger Splash** (GB 74)

John Hodge MP, Minister of Pensions *Broken in the Wars* (GB 19)

Hedda Hopper, movie gossip columnist *Sunset Boulevard* (US 50); *Pepe* (US 60); *The Patsy* (US 64)

William Morris Hughes, Prime Minister of Australia *Smithy* (Aus 46)

Hubert Humphrey, US Senator *The Candidate* (US 72)

James Hunt, motor-racing driver *Speed Fever* (It 78)

Len Hutton, cricketer *The Final Test* (GB 53)

Father Iliodor, rascally monk, first protégé then opponent of Rasputin *The Fall of the Romanoffs* (US 18)

David Jacobs, broadcaster *Otley* (GB 68)

James J. Jeffries, boxing champion *Pennington's Choice* (US 15)

Admiral Lord Jellicoe *Q Ships* (GB 28)

Al Jennings, convicted bank and train robber *The Bank Robbery* (US 08); *Beating Back** (US 15)

Amy Johnson, aviatrix *Dual Control* (GB 32)

Jack Johnson, boxer *Jack Johnson's Adventures in Paris* (Fr 13); *As the World Rolls on* (US 21)

José José, alcohol and drug addicted popular singer *Gavilán o Paloma** (Mex 85)

Helen Keller, deaf-blind scholar *Deliverance** (US 19)

the rest. By the time a protracted court case had found in his favour, the money was gone.

CONTRACTS, LEGAL AND BINDING . . .

In the days when studios 'owned' stars, the price of security and gigantic salaries was often freedom of behaviour. All big stars had morality clauses in their contracts (first to sign had been Maryon Aye in 1922), but Joan Crawford's with MGM in 1930 even specified the hour by which she had to be in bed. Mary Miles Minter's contract with the Realart Co. in 1919 was dependent upon her remaining unmarried for 3½ years. Others enjoined to remain single were Clara Bow, at Paramount's insistence, and Alice White, whose contract with First National further obliged her to learn two languages during the course of 1930, preferably French and Spanish. Walter Pidgeon, much in demand for musicals before he became a father figure, was forbidden to sing tenor lest he impair his rich baritone voice. Buster Keaton's famous unsmiling face was a contractual obligation. His contract with MGM in the twenties precluded him from smiling on screen, while Charles Butterworth's with Warner Bros prevented him from smiling in public. Similarly, Roscoe Ates' stutter was legally binding in his contract with RKO. First National demanded of Douglas Fairbanks Jnr that he never travel in 'planes. Joe E. Brown was forbidden to grow a moustache. A clause in teetotaller Frank McHugh's contract with First National required that he play drunkards whenever required, while Maurice Chevalier's with Paramount, signed as talkies were coming in, insisted that he remain in character—it was rendered invalid if he ever lost his French accent. In 1931 boxing fan Vivienne Segal was directed by her contract with Warner's not to yell at prize fights in case she strained her voice.

Possibly the most difficult contractual obligation to enforce was the one enjoined on Lois Moran not to grow sophisticated for a year after the release of *Stella Dallas* (US 26). Clara Bow was offered a $500,000 bonus by Paramount in 1926 provided she kept herself free of scandal during its tenure. She failed to collect. All the cast of Cecil B. DeMille's reverential life of Christ, *King of Kings* (US 27), were bound by contract not to accept any roles without De Mille's consent for ten years after the film's release. Dorothy Cummings, who played the Madonna, was further denied the right to divorce, which she promptly did 3 months after the première.

Evel Knievel, motorcycle stuntman *Viva Knievel!* (US 77)
Somchai Koonperm, village chief *Kamnan Poh* (Tha 80)
Jim Laker, cricketer *The Final Test* (GB 53)
Fritz Lang, film director (played by Marcel Hillaire in *Take the Money and Run* (US 69)); *Contempt* (Fr 64)
Nikki Lauda, motor-racing driver *Speed Fever* (It 78)
Ed Koch, Mayor of New York *The Muppets Take Manhattan* (US 84)
Henry Lawson, Australian poet *While the Billy Boils* (Aus 21)
Dr Timothy Leary, guru of LSD *Cheech and Chong's Nice Dreams* (US 81)
Suzanne Lenglen, Wimbledon tennis champion *Things Are Looking Up* (GB 35)
Oscar Levant, pianist *Humoresque* (US 47)
Bernard Levin, journalist *Nothing But the Best* (GB 63)
Prinz Eduard von und zu Liechtenstein, of the Royal House of Liechtenstein *Johann Strauss an der Schönen blauen Donau* (Aut 13)
Sir Thomas Lipton, millionaire grocer and yachtsman *The Lipton Cup* (US 13)
Vincent Lombardi, American footballer *Paper Lion* (US 68)
Chief Lomoiro, Masai tribal leader *Visit to a Chief's Son* (US 74)
Joe Louis, boxer *The Spirit of Youth* (US 37)
Captain James Lovell, astronaut *The Man Who Fell to Earth* (GB 76)
Joan Lowell, yachtswoman *Adventure Girl* (US 34)
Paul and Linda McCartney, ex-Beatle and photographer wife *Give My Regards to Broad Street* (GB 84)
Windsor McCay, cartoonist (*Little Nemo*, etc) and pioneer film animator *The Great White Way* (US 24)
Jem Mace, boxer *There's Life in the Old Dog Yet* (GB 08)

John McEnroe, tennis champion *Players* (US 79)
George McGovern, US Senator *The Candidate* (US 72)
Marshall McLuhan, Canadian academic, expert on media and communications *Annie Hall* (US 77)
George McManus, cartoonist (*Bringing Up Father*, etc) *The Great White Way* (US 24)
Queen Mary *Women Who Win* (GB 19)
Dan Maskell, tennis player *Players* (US 79)
Bob Mathias, twice winner of Olympic decathlon *The Bob Mathias Story* (US 54)
Yehudi Menuhin, violinist *Stage Door Canteen* (US 43)
Cliff Michelmore, TV personality *A Jolly Bad Fellow* (GB 63)
Freddie Mills, boxer *6·5 Special* (GB 58)
Leslie Mitchell, Britain's first TV announcer (1936) and Movietone commentator *Geneviève* (GB 53)
Jim Mollison, aviator who made first east–west crossing of N. Atlantic *Dual Control* (GB 32)
Stirling Moss, motor-racing driver *The Beauty Contest* (GB 64)
James Mossman, broadcaster *Masquerade* (GB 64)
Malcolm Muggeridge, journalist and pundit *I'm All Right Jack* (GB 59); *Heavens Above* (GB 63); *Herostratus* (GB 67); *The Naked Bunyip* (Aus 70)
Audie Murphy, most decorated US Soldier of World War II and subsequently professional actor *To Hell and Back* (US 55)
Pete Murray, disc jockey *6·5 Special* (GB 58)
Ilie Nastase, Romanian tennis champion *Players* (US 79)
Bess Nielsen, Parisian girl given to amorous adventures *On n'est pas serieux quand on a 17 ans* (Fr 74)

Officer Obie, policeman who arrested Arlo Guthrie for casting litter *Alice's Restaurant* (US 69)
Dan O'Brien, San Francisco Chief of Police *Poison* (US 24)
Barney Oldfield, motor-racing driver *Barney Oldfield's Race for Life* (US 16)
Ignace Paderewski, pianist, Prime Minister and later President of Poland *Moonlight Sonata* (GB 37)
Arnold Palmer, golfer *Call Me Bwana* (GB 63)
Huang Pao-Mei, girl spinner in China's Cotton Mill No 17 *Huang Pao-mei* (Chn 58)
Michael Parkinson, TV personality *Madhouse* (GB 74)
Louella Parsons, movie gossip columnist *Stage Door Canteen* (US 43)
Princess Patricia *Women Who Win* (GB 19)
Lieutenant Harold R. Peat *Private Peat* (US 18)
Betty Ting Pei, Bruce Lee's lover *Bruce Lee and I* (HK 76)
Pele, Brazilian soccer player *Young Giants* (US 83)
Pablo Picasso, artist *Le Testament d'Orphée* (Fr 60)
Andre Previn, conductor *Pepe* (US 60)
Luis Procuna, matador *Torero0* (Mex 56)
Yizhak Rabin, Prime Minister of Israel *Operation Thunderbolt* (Isr 77)
Dame Marie Rambert, founder of the Ballet Rambert *The Red Shoes* (GB 48)
Paul Raymond, eroticist *Erotica* (GB 81)
Carlos Reutemann, motor-racing driver *Speed Fever* (It 78)
Robert Ripley, originator of *Believe It or Not* *The Great White Way* (US 24)
Charlie Rivel, circus clown *Scö-ö-ön* (Ger 43)
Jackie Robinson, first black to play major league baseball *The Jackie Robinson Story* (US 50)
Robert Robinson, broadcaster *French Dressing* (GB 64)

In *The Cannonball Run* (US 81), Roger Moore plays not himself, but an English businessman called Seymour Goldfarb who suffers from a delusion that he is Roger Moore.

Occasionally the stars were able to impose unusual conditions on their masters, the studios. At the Warner studios in the early thirties, George Arliss's contract provided that he did not have to remain on set after 4.30 p.m., while John Barrymore's gave him the privilege of not being on set before 10.30 a.m. Moran and Mack, the Two Black Crows, were the only Paramount stars allowed to drive their car within the studio gates. Garbo's desire to be alone was protected by a clause preventing MGM from demands that she make any public appearances. When stage player Margaret Sullavan was persuaded by director John Stahl to accept the lead in *Only Yesterday* (US 33), she was so reluctant to enter films that she had a clause inserted in her contract to the effect that she could quit after ten days if she disliked Hollywood as much as she anticipated. Although she loathed Tinsel Town, she completed the picture and many others. Joe E. Brown's

Picasso as himself in Cocteau's *Testament d'Orphée* (Fr 59).

Sugar Ray Robinson, boxer *Paper Lion* (US 68)

Richard Rodgers, composer *Main Street to Broadway* (US 53)

Theodore Roosevelt, ex-President of the USA *Womanhood, The Glory of a Nation* (US 17)

Lady 'Bubbles' Rothermere, society hostess *The Stud* (GB 78)

Damon Runyon, writer *The Great White Way* (US 24); *O, Baby* (US 26)

Gunther Sachs, millionaire industrialist and playboy *Cardillac* (FRG 69)

Margaret Sanger, birth control pioneer *Birth Control* (US 17)

Ichijo Sayuri, stripper *Ichijo Sayuri: Wet Desire** (Jap 74)

Joe Schmidt, American footballer *Paper Lion* (US 68)

Charles E. Sebastian, ex-Mayor of Los Angeles *The Downfall of a Mayor** (US 17)

Mlle Segree, lover of Landru, murderer of 11 women *Landru* (Ger 23)

Caporal Sellier, bugler who sounded the World War I armistice, re-enacted scene in *The Soul of France* (Fr 28)

Mack Sennet, founder of the Keystone Kops *Hollywood Cavalcade* (US 39)

Ma Sha, reformed pimp and killer *The First Error Step** (Sin 79)

Barry Sheene, world motorcycling champion, and his girlfriend Stephanie McLean *Space Riders* (GB 83)

William Shirer, historian *The Magic Face* (US 51)

Harry Siegenberg, bookmaker *The Stolen Favourite* (SA 19)

O. J. Simpson, football player *The Klansman* (US 74)

George R. Sims, crusading journalist gaoled in celebrated 1885 Maiden Tribute of Modern Babylon case *The Martyrdom of Adolf Beck* (GB 09)

Sir Charles Kingsford Smith, Australian aviator *Splendid Fellows* (Aus 34)

Susan Sontag, writer *Zelig* (US 83)

Mickey Spillane, thriller writer *Ring of Fear* (US 54)

Ringo Starr, ex-Beatle *Give My Regards to Broad Street* (GB 84)

Isobel Lillian Steele, American victim of Gestapo *Captive of Nazi Germany** (US 36)

Preston Sturges, film director *Star Spangled Rhythm* (US 42)

Anne Sullivan, who taught blind deaf-mute Helen Keller to speak and read *Deliverance* (US 19)

Ed Sullivan, TV personality *The Patsy* (US 64)

Hannen Swaffer, journalist *Spellbound* (GB 41)

Crown Princess of Sweden *Women Who Win* (GB 19)

Fuji Takeshi, world junior welterweight boxing champion *Fuji Takeshi Monogatari** (Jap 68)

Yukio Tani, martial arts exponent *Ju-Jitsu to the Rescue* (GB 13)

Alderman C. E. Tatham, Mayor of Blackpool *Sing As We Go* (GB 34)

A. J. P. Taylor, historian *Rockets Galore* (GB 58)

Evelyn Nesbitt Thaw, beauty whose husband murdered her lover, architect Stanford White (played by Joan Collins in *The Girl in the Red Velvet Swing* (US 55) and by Elizabeth McGovern in *Ragtime* (US 81)) *The Great Thaw Trial* (US 07); *Redemption* (US 17)

Wynford Vaughan Thomas, broadcaster *John and Julie* (GB 55)

William 'Big Bill' Thompson, Mayor of Chicago *Is Your Daughter Safe?* (US 27)

W. M. Tilgham, Marshal of Cache, Oklahoma *The Bank Robbery* (US 08)

Mark Twain, humorous writer *A Curious Dream* (US 07)

John van Druten, playwright *Main Street to Broadway* (US 53)

Princess Victoria *Women Who Win* (GB 19)

King Vidor, film director *It's a Great Feeling* (US 49)

Guillermo Vilas, tennis player *Players* (US 79)

The Prince of Wales, later King Edward VIII *The Warrior Strain* (GB 19); *The Power of Right* (GB 19); *Remembrance* (GB 27)

Lech Walesa, founder of Solidarity *Man of Iron* (Pol 81)

Jimmy Walker, Mayor of New York *Glorifying the American Girl* (US 29)

Raoul Walsh, film director *It's a Great Feeling* (US 49)

Cyril Washbrook, cricketer *The Final Test* (GB 53)

Gough Whitlam, Prime Minister of Australia *Barry McKenzie Holds His Own* (Aus 74)

District Attorney Whitman *Our Mutual Girl* (US 14); *Smashing the Vice Trust* (US 14)

Frank Wills, Watergate security guard who discovered break-in *All the President's Men* (US 76)

Peter Wilson, Chairman of Sotheby's *Laughter in the Dark* (GB 69)

Woodrow Wilson, President of the USA *Womanhood, The Glory of a Nation* (US 17)

Walter Winchell, influential American columnist (played by Lew Ayres in *OKay America!* (US 32)) *The Helen Morgan Story* (US 57); *College Confidential* (US 60)

Godfrey Winn, journalist *Billy Liar!* (GB 63)

Maharishi Narish Yogi, guru *Candy Baby* (US 69)

Sam Yorty, Mayor of Los Angeles *The Candidate* (US 72)

Jimmy Young, broadcaster *Otley* (GB 68)

Krzysztof Zanussi, film director *Amator/Camera Buff* (Pol 79)

Florenz Ziegfeld, impresario *Glorifying the American Girl* (US 29)

Adolf Zukor, film producer *Glorifying the American Girl* (US 29)

* Autobiopics

Britain's first black film star—Bermuda-born Ernest Trimmingham in *Jack, Sam and Pete* (GB 19).

contract with Warner's demanded that the studio co-operate with him in running a baseball team. Virginal Evelyn Venable's contract with Paramount in 1933 had a clause inserted by her father preventing her from being kissed on screen. The rather less virginal Clara Bow wrote into her contract with Paramount that none of the workmen or technicians were to use profane language to her or in her presence.

Even today, producers are known to make grudging concessions if the name of the star is big enough. Roger Moore will not sign any contract unless he is guaranteed an unlimited supply of hand-rolled Monte Cristo cigars from Cuba. On one of the Bond movies, the bill for 007's cigars came to £3176·50. Audrey Hepburn also knows how to wipe the thin-lipped smile from producers' faces. Before agreeing to star in *Sidney Sheldon's Bloodline* (US/FRG 83), she imposed a condition that all her costumes were to be designed by Paris couturier Givenchy; and furthermore that, when filming was completed, she would be given the $100,000 wardrobe.

The most married stars in the Hollywood galaxy are Mickey Rooney (b. 1920), whose eight wives have been Ava Gardner (1942), Betty Jane Rase (1944), Martha Vickers (1949), Elaine Mahnken (1952), Barbara Thomason (1958), Margaret Lane (1966), Carolyn Hackett (1969) and Jan Chamberlain (1975); and Lana Turner (b. 1921), whose eight marriages have been to bandleader Artie Shaw (1940), restauranteur Stephen Crane (twice: 1942 and 1943), baseball team owner Bob Topping (1948), Tarzan player Lex Barker (1953), rancher Fred May (1960), writer Robert Eaton (1965) and hypnotist Ronald Dante (1969—divorced same year). Elizabeth Taylor has been married seven times, twice to Richard Burton.

The first black actor to play a leading role in a feature film was Sam Lucas, cast in the title role of *Uncle Tom's Cabin* (US 14).

The first black actor to make a career in films was Noble Johnson, who made his debut in a Lubin western in 1914 playing an Indian chief. After arriving in Hollywood in 1915, he graduated from stunt work and bit parts with the formation of the Lincoln Motion Picture Co., an all-black production company specialising in ghetto films, of which he was president as well as leading player. Johnson starred in three Lincoln productions—*The Realisation of a Negro's Ambition* (US 16), *The Trooper of Company K* (US 17) and *The Law of Nature* (US 18)—before leaving the company to concentrate on the Universal serials he had been making between Lincoln pictures.

Britain's first black screen actor was Bermuda-born Ernest Trimmingham, who made his debut in the British & Colonial production *Her Bachelor Guardian* (GB 12). **The first black actor to play a leading role in a British film** was Paul Robeson as Bosambo in Alexander Korda's *Sanders of the River* (GB 35). He also starred in *Song of Freedom* (GB 37), *Big Fella* (GB 37), *King Solomon's Mines* (GB 37) and *Jericho* (GB 37).

The performer who played in the most movies was Tom London (1883–1963), who was born in Louisville, Ky., and made the first of his over 2000 appearances on screen in *The Great Train Robbery* (US 03). He was given the role of the locomotive driver, which was also his job in real life. By 1919 he was playing starring roles at Universal under his real name, Leonard Clapham, which he changed to Tom London in 1924. When he became too old for lead roles he receded comfortably into character parts, specialising in sheriffs in 'B' westerns. His last picture was Willard Parker's *The Lone Texan* (US 59).

The only British monarch to have acted in films was King Edward VIII when he was Prince of Wales. In March 1919 he performed in two patriotic war dramas—like Indian stars of today he economised on time by playing his scenes for both films at the same time. This was made easier by the fact that he was portraying himself in each and that they had remarkably similar plots. *The Power of Right* (GB 19), directed by F. Martin Thornton for Harma Photoplays, was about a colonel's son who joins the cadets and succeeds in killing an escaped German internee, while *The Warrior Strain* (GB 19) was also about a cadet, this time an Earl's son, who foils a dastardly plot by a German baron to signal the enemy from Brighton. In the latter film the Prince played a scene with Sydney Wood (as the boy's father), and another in which he presents each of the members of the cadet section with a gold watch as a reward for thwarting the wicked baron. Some years later he again played himself in BIP's *Remembrance* (GB 27), a story about disabled war veterans.

NON-ACTORS IN FILMS
Personalities who have played roles other than themselves (see also Personalities playing themselves, pp. 84–5) include:

Horacio Accavallo, world flyweight boxing champion, lead in *Destino para dos* (Arg 67)

Muhammed Ali, world heavyweight boxing champion, as Gideon Jackson, first black US Senator, in TVM *Freedom Road* (US 79)

Viscount Althorp, brother of Princess of Wales, as public schoolboy in *Another Country* (GB 84)

Mrs Morgan Belmont, society leader and member of New York's '400', played the upper crust Diana Tremont in *Way Down East* (US 20)

Peter Benchley, author of *Jaws*, played a reporter in *Jaws* (US 75)

Godfrey Binaisa, President of Uganda, bit parts in *King Solomon's Mines* (US 50) and *The African Queen* (GB 51)

Bricktop, black nightclub proprietor famous in cafe society, as mother figure in *Honeybaby, Honeybaby* (US 74)

RSM Ronald Brittain, Regimental Sergeant Major at Sandhurst Military Academy during 1950s, appeared (usually as a Sergeant Major) in *Carrington VC* (GB 54), *The Missing Note* (GB 61), *The Amorous Prawn* (GB 62), *Joey Boy* (GB 65) and *The Spy with a Cold Nose* (GB 66)

Truman Capote, author, leading role in detective fiction parody *Murder by Death* (US 76)

Primo Carnera, boxer, played Python Macklin in *A Kid for Two Farthings* (GB 55)

Georges Carpentier, boxer, as hero in *Toboggan* (Fr 34)

Viscount Castlerosse, bon viveur, as the man in the bath chair in *Kipps* (GB 41)

Juan Chacon, trade union leader, as Mexican strike leader in *Salt of the Earth* (US 54)

G. K. Chesterton, author, in *Rosy Rapture—The Pride of the Beauty Chorus* (GB 14)

Michael Chow, restauranteur, as underworld boss Fong Wei Tan in *Hammett* (US 82)

Daniel Cohn-Bendit, revolutionary, in Godard's *Vent d'est* (FRG/It 70)

Carmine Coppola, composer, as man in the lift in Francis Coppola's *One from the Heart* (US 82)

James John Corbett, world heavyweight boxing champion, in *The Midnight Man* (US 19)

Quentin Crisp, homosexual liberationist, played Polonius in *Hamlet* (GB 76)

Dionne Quins, world's first surviving quintuplets, in *The Country Doctor* (US 36), *Reunion* (US 36) and *Five of a Kind* (US 38)

Steve Donaghue, champion jockey, as Steve Baxter, hero of *Riding for a King* (GB 26), *Beating the Book* (GB 26), *The Golden Spurs* (GB 26) and *The Stolen Favourite* (GB 26)

Gertrude Ederle, first woman to swim the English Channel, in *Swim, Girl, Swim* (US 28)

David Frost, television commentator, as reporter in *The VIPs* (GB 63)

Athol Fugard, South African playwright, as General Smuts in *Gandhi* (GB 82)

Paul Getty III, grandson of oil tycoon, as film scriptwriter Dennis in *The State of Things* (US/Por 82)

Althea Gibson, black tennis star, as maid in John Ford's *The Horse Soldiers* (US 59)

Robert Graves, poet and novelist, as partygoer in *Deadfall* (GB 68)

Graham Greene, author, as the insurance representative in *Day for Night* (Fr 73)

Germaine Greer, women's liberationist, as Clara Bowden in *Universal Soldier* (GB 71)

Lorenz Hart, of Rodgers and Hart, played the bank teller in *Hallelujah, I'm a Bum* (US 33)

Len Harvey, British boxing champion, played a glass collector turned boxer in *Excuse My Glove* (GB 36)

Hugh Hefner, founder of Playboy empire, as pipe smoking ancient Roman in *History of the World—Part I* (US 81)

Ernest Hemingway, author, uncredited bit part in *The Old Man and the Sea* (US 58)

Xaviera Hollander, prostitute and writer, lead in *My Pleasure is My Business* (Can 74)

Bianca Jagger, jet-setter, leads in *Flesh Colour* (US 79) and *The Great American Success Company* (US 79)

Clive James, Australian pundit, as most drunken of Bazza's mates in *Barry McKenzie Holds His Own* (Aus 77)

Thomas Keneally, Australian novelist, as Father Marshall in *The Devil's Playground* (Aus 76)

Jomo Kenyatta, President of Kenya 1963–78, played an African chief in *Sanders of the River* (GB 35)

Jerzy Kosinsky, controversial Polish-American novelist, as Bolshevik revolutionary Zinoviev in *Reds* (US 81)

Dr Emmanuel Lasker, world chess champion, played Napoleon's chess partner in Lupu Pick's *Napoléon a Sainte-Hélène* (Fr 29)

Tad Lincoln, son of Abraham Lincoln, in *The Highest Law* (US 21); he himself played by Dickie Moore in *Lincoln in the White House* (US 39)

John Lindsay, Mayor of New York, played Senator Donnovan in *Rosebud* (US 75)

Victor Lowndes, chairman of Playboy UK, as Reeve Passmore in *Fledglings* (GB 65)

Compton MacKenzie, author, as Capt Buncher in film of his own novel *Whisky Galore!* (GB 49); as Sir Robert Dysart in *Chance of a Lifetime* (GB 50)

Norman Mailer, writer, as New York architect Stanford White (murdered in celebrated crime of passion) in *Ragtime* (US 81)

Yehudi Menuhin, violinist, in *The Magic Bow* (GB 46)

Freddie Mills, British champion boxer, in *Emergency Call* (GB 52), *Fun at St Fanny's* (GB 56), *Breakaway* (GB 56), *Chain of Events* (GB 58), *Carry on Constable* (GB 60), *Carry on Regardless* (GB 61), *The Comedy Man* (GB 63), *Saturday Night Out* (GB 64)

Jóan Miró, Spanish painter, played the museum curator in *El Umbracle* (Sp 73)

Stirling Moss, motor-racing driver in *Casino Royale* (GB 67)

Beverley Nichols, author, as the Hon. Richard Wells in *Glamour* (GB 31)

Mrs Richard Nixon, wife of ex-President Nixon, walk-on parts in *Becky Sharp* (US 36) and *Small Town Girl* (US 37)

Princess Pearl, daughter of the White Rajah of Sarawak, as Princess Paula in Ruritanian romance *Everything is Rhythm* (GB 36)

Harold Pinter, playwright, as lawyer Saul Abrahams in *Rogue Male* (GB 76)

David Robinson, film critic of *The Times*, in *If* (GB 60), *Fragments of Life* (Hun 79), *Britannia Hospital* (GB 81), and as 1930s drama critic of *The Times* in *Mephisto* (Hun 81)

Babe Ruth, baseball player, subject of *The Babe Ruth Story* (US 48), acted in *Headin' Home* (US 19)

Pierre Salinger, John F. Kennedy's Press Secretary, as poker player in *The Marseilles Connection* (GB/Fr 73)

George Bernard Shaw, playwright, in *Rosy Rapture—The Pride of the Beauty Chorus* (GB 14)

Jean Shrimpton, model, leading lady in *Privilege* (GB 67)

Mickey Spillane, author, played his own creation Mike Hammer in *The Girl Hunters* (US 63)

Jacqueline Susann, novelist, in *Valley of the Dolls* (US 67)

Leslie 'Squizzy' Taylor, Melbourne gangster gunned down in 1927, in race-track drama *Bound to Win* (Aus 19)

Leon Trotsky, revolutionary and founder of the Red Army, played a bit part as a nihilist in Vitagraph's spy drama *My Official Wife* (US 14) and also appeared in *The Battle Cry of Peace* (US 15)

Margaret Trudeau, estranged wife of Premier of Canada, Pierre Trudeau, starred in *The Guardian Angel* (Can 78) and *Kings and Desperate Men* (Can 79)

Gene Tunney, heavyweight boxing champion, in Pathé serial *The Fighting Marine* (US 26)

Hugh Walpole, author, as the vicar in *David Copperfield* (US 35)

Senator John Warner, ex 'Mr Elizabeth Taylor', as a fisherman in *The Mirror Crack'd* (GB 81)

Judge Joseph N. Welch, presiding judge at the McCarthy hearings, played a judge in *Anatomy of a Murder* (US 59)

Bombardier Billy Wells, British boxing champion, starred as the pilot in *The Silver Lining* (GB 19) and played the hangman in *The Beggar's Opera* (GB 53)

White Man-Runs-Him, last survivor of the Battle of the Little Big Horn (at which Gen. Custer's force was massacred in 1876), played in a Ken Maynard western *The Red Raiders* (US 27)

Gough Whitlam, Prime Minister of Australia, as 'man in night club' in *The Broken Melody* (Aus 38); see also under Non-actors who have played themselves

Godfrey Winn, journalist, played an announcer in *The Bargee* (GB 64) and Truelove in *The Great St Trinian's Train Robbery* (GB 65)

Brig.-Gen. Chuck Yeager, first pilot to break sound barrier and US astronaut, as Fred the barman in *The Right Stuff* (US 83). Yeager portrayed in same film by Sam Shepard—one of the rare instances of a name appearing on both sides of the cast list

Yevgeny Yevtushenko, poet, played leading role as Russian space pioneer Konstantin Tsiolkovsky in *Take-Off* (USSR 79)

The performer who has played the most leading roles in feature films is Prem Nazir (1929–), superhero of Malayalam language movies, who was cast in his first starring role in 1952 and had appeared in over 300 movies by the end of the 1970s. The exact tally is hard to verify. Press reports in 1979 that Prem Nazir had completed his 500th starring role were discounted by the star himself. In September 1983 the Indian fan magazine *Filmfare* quoted a total of 580 films with another 30 in the pipeline, but this figure seems improbable. There is a reliable record that he appeared in 27 films in 1983. If this is representative of his output during the 1980s, a total of around 450 is not unlikely. No other star approaches a figure of this magnitude.

The actress who played the most leading roles was the Japanese star Kinuyo Tanaka (1909–77), who made her debut in a featured role in *Genroku Onna/Woman of Genroku Era* (Jap 24) and performed in a total of 241 movies to *Daichi no Komoriuta/Lullaby Song of the Earth* (Jap 76). Nearly all these roles were leads except for a few at the beginning and end of her career. She also directed six films.

The Burmese-born star of Hindi movies, Helen, has led the dance sequences in over 400 Indian musicals since the early 1950s.

The Hollywood star who played the most leading roles in feature films was John Wayne (1907–79), who appeared in 153 movies from *The Drop Kick* (US 27) to *The Shootist* (US 76). In all except 11 of these films he played leading roles. The Duke summed up his simple yet enduring qualities thus: 'I've never had a goddam artistic problem in my life, never, and I've worked with the best of them. John Ford isn't exactly a bum, is he? Yet he never gave me any manure about art.' And: 'I play John Wayne in every part regardless of the character, and I've been doing okay, haven't I?'

Of Hollywood stars still performing, the record for the most screen credits is held by John Carradine (1906–), who has been featured or starred in over 230 movies since his debut in *Tol'able David* (US 30). In addition he has performed in over 180 plays.

The British star with the most screen credits who is still performing in movies is Christopher Lee (1922–), star of English, French, Spanish, German, Italian, American and Australian films. The 150 feature movies and two shorts he played in from *Corridor of Mirrors* (GB 47) to *Safari 3000* (US 84) include 15 in which he recreated his most celebrated role, that of Count Dracula, and one in which he played HRH Prince Philip.

THE MOST POPULAR ACTORS AND ACTRESSES
The earliest recorded popularity poll was conducted by a Russian fan magazine in 1911 and was headed by dapper Frenc comedian Max Linder, followed by Denmark's tragic actress Asta Nielsen, with another

'I play John Wayne in every part regardless of the character . . .'. Here the Duke was playing John Wayne in *The Shootist* (US 76).

Danish star, Valdemar Psilander, in third place. America's first poll was staged by *Motion Picture Story Magazine* in March 1912 and resulted in Maurice Costello being voted most popular male star and the now forgotten Dolores Cassinelli most popular actress. By 1912 Mary Pickford, 12th in the 1912 poll, had displaced her and for the next ten years 'the girl with the golden curls', otherwise known as 'America's sweetheart', topped virtually every popularity poll held throughout the world, including those conduced in Soviet Russia (where her husband Douglas Fairbanks was voted most popular male star in 1925). The most durable star of talkies would appear to be John Wayne, who featured in the annual 'Ten Top Box Office Stars' Quigley Poll 25 times 1949–74 and headed it in 1950, 1951, 1954 and 1971. For the most popular Hollywood stars of the 1970s, see Quigley Poll results.

The first popularity poll confined to British-born stars was conducted by *Pictures and the Picturegoer* in 1915 with the following results: 1 Alma Taylor; 2 Elizabeth Risdon; 3 Charles Chaplin; 4 Stewart Rome; 5 Chrissie White; 6 Fred Evans.

Ten years later the *Daily News* poll showed Alma Taylor and Chrissie White, both of whom had joined the Hepworth Co. as child actresses in 1908, still firmly in the public favour: 1 Betty Balfour; 2 Alma Taylor; 3 Gladys Cooper; 4 Violet Hopson; 5 Matheson Lang; 6 Fay Compton; 7 Chrissie White; 8 Stewart Rome; 9 Owen Nares; 10 Ivor Novello.

During the 1930s America's box office was dominated by children, elderly ladies and gentlemen, and a mouse. Marie Dressler topped the Quigley Poll at age 63 in 1932 and again in 1933; Will Rogers came first aged 55 in 1934; then Shirley Temple rose to the top, aged 7, and remained there for the following three years, until 1939, when Mickey Rooney, 18 years old and playing a high school kid in the *Andy Hardy* series, took the lead and held first place for three years. Mickey Mouse was not eligible for the Quigley Poll, but he beat Emil Jannings by 400,000 votes as No. 1 star in a popularity contest held in Australia in 1931, and knocked Wallace Beery into second place in Japan in 1936.

Bridging this period and the John Wayne era were the Bing Crosby–Betty Grable years of the 1940s. Cumulative Quigley Poll results for the 1960s give the following hierarchy of the biggest box-office draws of the decade: 1 John Wayne; 2 Doris Day; 3 Cary Grant,

A disclaimer before the end credits of *Players* (US 79) insisted that all the characters in the film were wholly fictitious; it was immediately followed by a cast list that included no less than 14 famous tennis personalities, including John McEnroe, playing themselves.

Rock Hudson and Elizabeth Taylor; 4 Jack Lemmon; 5 Julie Andrews; 6 Paul Newman; 7 Sean Connery; 8 Elvis Presley; 9 Sidney Poitier; 10 Lee Marvin. (Of course no such list is definitive. Sophia Loren, who never appeared in the annual Top Ten, was nevertheless voted the most popular star in the world by the US Foreign Press Corps in 1969.) The order for the 1970s: 1 Clint Eastwood; 2 Burt Reynolds; 3 Barbra Streisand; 4 Paul Newman; 5 Robert Redford; 6 Steve McQueen; 7 John Wayne; 8 Woody Allen; 9 Dustin Hoffman; 10 Sylvester Stallone. The early eighties showed little

---

QUIGLEY PUBLICATIONS POLL

The annual Quigley Poll is a poll of exhibitors to determine the top box-office draws. Listed below are the top male and the top female star for each year—the rating of whichever was not No. 1 is given in brackets after the name

Year	Star	Year	Star	Year	Star
1915	Mary Pickford (2)	1936	Shirley Temple	1961	Elizabeth Taylor
	William S. Hart		Clark Gable (2)		Rock Hudson (2)
1916	Mary Pickford (2)	1937	Shirley Temple	1962	Doris Day
	William S. Hart		Clark Gable (2)		Rock Hudson (2)
1917	Anita Stewart (3)	1938	Shirley Temple	1963	Doris Day
	Douglas Fairbanks		Clark Gable (2)		John Wayne (2)
1918	Mary Pickford (2)	1939	Shirley Temple (5)	1964	Doris Day
	Douglas Fairbanks		Mickey Rooney		Jack Lemmon (2)
1919	Mary Pickford (3)	1940	Bette Davis (9)	1965	Doris Day (3)
	Wallace Reid		Mickey Rooney		Sean Connery
1920	Marguerite Clark (2)	1941	Bette Davis (8)	1966	Julie Andrews
	Wallace Reid		Mickey Rooney		Sean Connery (2)
1921	Mary Pickford	1942	Betty Grable (8)	1967	Julie Andrews
	Douglas Fairbanks (2)		Abbott & Costello		Lee Marvin (2)
1922	Mary Pickford	1943	Betty Grable	1968	Julie Andrews (3)
	Douglas Fairbanks (2)		Bob Hope (2)		Sidney Poitier
1923	Norma Talmadge (2)	1944	Betty Grable (4)	1969	Katharine Hepburn (9)
	Thomas Meighan		Bing Crosby		Paul Newman
1924	Norma Talmadge	1945	Greer Garson (3)	1970	Barbra Streisand (9)
	Rudolph Valentino (3)		Bing Crosby		Paul Newman
1925	Norma Talmadge (2)	1946	Ingrid Bergman (2)	1971	Ali MacGraw (8)
	Rudolph Valentino		Bing Crosby		John Wayne
1926	Colleen Moore	1947	Betty Grable (2)	1972	Barbra Streisand (5)
	Tom Mix (2)		Bing Crosby		Clint Eastwood
1927	Colleen Moore (2)	1948	Betty Grable (2)	1973	Barbra Streisand (6)
	Tom Mix		Bing Crosby		Clint Eastwood
1928	Clara Bow	1949	Betty Grable (7)	1974	Barbra Streisand (4)
	Lon Chaney (2)		Bob Hope		Robert Redford
1929	Clara Bow	1950	Betty Grable (4)	1975	Barbra Streisand (2)
	Lon Chaney (2)		John Wayne		Robert Redford
1930	Joan Crawford	1951	Betty Grable (3)	1976	Tatum O'Neal (8)
	William Haines (2)		John Wayne		Robert Redford
1931	Janet Gaynor	1952	Doris Day (7)	1977	Barbra Streisand (2)
	Charles Farrell (2)		Dean Martin and Jerry Lewis		Sylvester Stallone
1932	Marie Dressler	1953	Marilyn Monroe (6)	1978	Diane Keaton (7)
	Charles Farrell (4)		Gary Cooper		Burt Reynolds
1933	Marie Dressler	1954	Marilyn Monroe (5)	1979	Jane Fonda (3)
	Will Rogers (2)		John Wayne		Burt Reynolds
1934	Janet Gaynor (3)	1955	Grace Kelly (2)	1980	Jane Fonda (4)
	Will Rogers		James Stewart		Burt Reynolds
1935	Shirley Temple	1956	Marilyn Monroe (8)	1981	Dolly Parton (4)
	Will Rogers (2)		William Holden		Burt Reynolds
		1957	Kim Novak (11)	1982	Dolly Parton (6)
			Rock Hudson		Burt Reynolds
		1958	Elizabeth Taylor (2)	1983	Meryl Streep (12)
			Glenn Ford		Clint Eastwood
		1959	Doris Day (4)	1984	Sally Field (5)
			Rock Hudson		Clint Eastwood
		1960	Doris Day		
			Rock Hudson (2)		

diminution of Burt Reynolds' megastar popularity, but there is less consistency in the public's choice of favourite actresses, which has tended in recent Quigley Polls to depend on the drawing power of a single film with a strong female leading role.

The largest number of members of one family to have appeared in films is 31 in the case of the Luevas of Los Angeles, Matriarch Augustina Lueva (b. La Refugio, Mexico 1852), 18 of her 21 children and 12 of her grandchildren were reported to be actively employed as film actors in 1928. Six of the children and four of the grandchildren appeared together in an unidentified film of that year.

Other films in which families have appeared together are: *Hearts of the World* (US 18), in which Bobby Harron played the lead, his mother played a French woman, her two daughters Jessie and Mary played her screen daughters, and Bobby's brother Johnny played 'a boy with a barrel'; *Mr Smith Goes to Washington* (US 39) with brothers and sisters Coy,

Right
Above: America's most enduring star, Lillian Gish, making her screen debut in *An Unseen Enemy* (US 12). She crouches in the corner in terror as sister Dorothy Gish takes a close look at the weaponry. *Below*: Britain's most enduring star, Sir John Gielgud, making his screen debut in more relaxed circumstances in *Who Is the Man?* (GB 24). The two screen veterans have been cast together for the first time in Lindsay Anderson's *The Whales of August* (US i.p.).

Below
There were 126 other women with speaking roles in *The Women* (US 39) besides the nine who got the billing.

Vivian, Gloria, Louise, Harry, Billy, Delmar, Garry and Bobs Watson playing the Governor of Montana's children; and *Ein Tag ist Schoener als der Andere* (FRG 70), featuring the seven von Eichborn children, Clarissa, Justina, Evelyn, Jacqueline, Wolfram, Holger and Isabella.

Some film families deliberately avoided working with each other. All six McLaglen brothers were film actors, Victor in America, the others mainly in Britain. When the youngest, Leopold, tried to break into Hollywood pictures in the mid-1930s, eldest brother Victor took out an injunction restraining him. 'There's only room for one McLaglen in Hollywood' asserted Victor.

The most generations of screen actors in a family is four in the case of the Redgraves. Roy Redgrave (1872–1922), father of Sir Michael, made his screen debut in *The Christian* (Aus 11) and continued to appear in Australian movies until 1920. Sir Michael Redgrave (1908–) married actress Rachel Kempson (1910–), and their two daughters Vanessa (1937–)

A number of artistes have portrayed their own parents in films. Marie Lloyd Jnr played 'Queen of the Halls' Marie Lloyd Snr in *Variety Jubilee* (GB 43); Will Rogers Jnr portrayed Will Rogers Snr in *The Story of Will Rogers* (US 52); Dick Powell Jnr was seen as Dick Powell Snr in *The Day of the Locust* (US 74). Marcel Cerdan Jnr played his namesake father in *Edith and Marcel* (Fr 84), the story of Edith Piaf's love affair with middleweight boxing champion Cerdan. In *Adolf Hitler—My Part in His Downfall* (GB 72), Jim Dale plays Spike Milligan, while Milligan takes the role of his own father. The only recorded instance of a character being played by his own brother is in Raj Kapoor's two autobiographical movies *Awara* (Ind 51) and *Shree 420* (Ind 55), with Shashi Kapoor in the roles based on Raj Kapoor.

and Lynn (1943–) and son Corin (1939–) all went into movies. Vanessa's daughters Natasha and Joely made their debut in *The Charge of the Light Brigade* (GB 68) and subsequently appeared in *Dead Cert* (GB 74) and *Joseph Andrews* (GB 77), while Corin's daughter Jemima appeared for the first time in *Joseph Andrews*.

The largest cast of credited performers in a film was 260 in *Dny Zrady/Days of Treason* (Cz 72), the story of the betrayal of Czechoslovakia in 1938, including Gunnar Möller as Hitler, Jaroslav Radimecky as Chamberlain, Alexander Fred as Goebbels, Rudolf Jurda as Goering and Vladamir Stach as Mussolini.

Sacha Guitry's *Napoleon* (Fr 54) had 101 credited roles, but was claimed to have 300 speaking parts. MGM claimed 365 speaking parts (73 credited) for *Ben Hur* (US 59), but this seems impossible for a 217-minute film unless it includes groups of people all speaking at once. As many as 430 speaking parts were claimed for the 188 minute *Gandhi* (GB 83), with 138 credited.

Other films with large casts (credited) include: *Rottenknechte* (GDR 70) with 194; *Baron Muenchhausen* (Ger 45) with 150; *Sweden for the Swedes* (Swe 80) with 142; *Around the World in 80 Days* (US 56) with 138; *A Bridge Too Far* (GB 77) with 137; *Oh! What a Lovely War* (GB 69) with 125; and Karl Ritter's *Pour la Merité* (Ger 38) with 102.

For **the largest cast including extras**, see p. 81.

The largest all-female cast consisted of the 135 speaking roles in MGM's *The Women* (US 39), starring Joan Crawford, Norma Shearer, Rosalind Russell, Paulette Goddard and Joan Fontaine.

The smallest cast in a live-action dramatic feature, excluding movies with an all-animal cast, is none. Kostas Sfikas' *Model* (Gre 74) had no performers, only robots seen in a single set representing a factory yard. The 1 hr 45 min film was intended as a critique of the 'implacable process that transforms mankind into negotiable goods and mere accessories of an industrial machine'.

There have been a number of movies with a cast of one. Olaf Fønns, leading Danish romantic hero of the World War I period, played alone in Fritz Magnussen's *Remorse* (Den 19), made for Dansk Astra Film. The story is of a wealthy man who is ruined and loses his mistress (represented only by a pair of arms), then returns to her in a starving condition, is rejected and kills her. He restores his fortune but, relentlessly pursued by his own accusing shadow, eventually gives himself up. In addition to its solo performance, the film was distinguished by having no inter-titles.

Sunil Dutt's *Yaadein/Recollections* (Ind 64), in which he starred as well as directed and produced, was a single set, solo movie about a husband deserted by his wife. At the end of the film the woman's shadow seen against a wall indicates that she has returned to him. Robert Carlisle's *Sofi* (US 68), an adaptation of Gogol's *Diary of a Madman*, had Tom Troupe as its only performer. Thierry Zeno's *Vase de noces* (Bel 73) starred Dominique Garny, who does not speak throughout the film. It tells the story of a simple man living alone amongst his poultry and pigs who eventually hangs himself. Danilo-Bata Stojković played alone as a man fleeing from imaginary pursuers in Milos Radivojević's *Testament* (Yug 75), which was also without speech. Jean-Pierre Lefebvre's *L'Amour blessé (Confidences de la nuit)* (Can 75) starred Louise Cuerrier as a lonely woman spending a dull evening in her room listening to a talk show, while Britain's only single artiste film had Monica Buferd in the rather more compelling role of *St Joan* (GB 77). Other examples of solo performances are by Anne Flannery in *A State of Siege* (NZ 78), Willeke van Ammelrooy in Frans Zwartje's *It's Me* (Neth 79), and by Alain Cavalier in *Ce repondent ne prend pas de message* (Fr 79).

More recently Julie Harris has played Charlotte Brontë in Delbert Mann's evocation of the author's life and times *Brontë* (US/Ire 83). Interaction with the other members of the Brontë family was conveyed by having Charlotte handle both sides of the conversation. Another powerful portrayal of a real-life character was by Philip Baker Hall as Richard Nixon in Robert Altman's *Secret Honor* (US 84), delivering an 80-min monologue described as 'a fictional meditation'.

The longest screen career is that of Berlin comedian and character actor Curt Bois (b. 1900), who made his film debut in 1909 at the age of nine in *Mutterliebe* (Ger 09). Bois left Germany in 1933 on the accession of the Nazis and made his way to the US via Prague, Vienna, London and Paris. He went to New York to star in a stage play which closed after only one night and thence to Hollywood in 1938. He appeared in such notable films as *Casablanca* (US 42) and Max Ophuls' *Caught* (US 49) before returning to Berlin in the early fifties. Recent films have included *The Boat is Full* (Swz 81) and *Remembrance* (FRG 82), a documentary about his career.

The actress with the longest screen career is Lillian

LONG FILM CAREERS
Considering the lengthy careers of many
stage performers, comparatively few of the
senior generation of film stars have survived
from silent days. In addition to those
mentioned, the following leading players
made their screen debut before 1930 and are
still active in films:
Noah Beery Jnr (b. New York 1913) *The Mark
of Zorro* (US 20)

Bessie Love (b. Midland, Texas 1898) *The
Flying Torpedo* (US 15)
Helen Hayes (b. Washington, DC 1900) *The
Weavers of Life* (US 17)
Cyril Cusack (b. Dublin 1910) *Knocknagow*
(Ire 18)
Sir John Gielgud (b. London 1904) *Who Is the
Man?* (GB 24)
Esmond Knight (b. East Sheen 1906) *The Blue
Peter* (GB 28)

Harry-Krimer (b. France 1897) played
Rouget de Lisle in Gance's *Napoleon* (Fr 27)
Gilbert Roland (b. Chihuahua, Mexico
1905) *The Plastic Age* (US 25)
Mickey Rooney (b. New York 1920) *Mickey
Maguire* short (US 26)
Sylvia Sidney (b. New York 1910) *Thru
Different Eyes* (US 29).

Gish (b. 1893), whose debut was in *An Unseen Enemy* (US 12) and who played the title role of Hillie in *Hambone and Hillie* (US 84).

The largest number of roles played by one actor in a single film is not, as generally believed, the eight members of the d'Ascoyne family portrayed by Alec Guinness in *Kind Hearts and Coronets* (GB 49), but the 27 parts taken by Rolf Leslie in Will Barker's life story of Queen Victoria *Sixty Years a Queen* (GB 13). Others who have equalled or exceeded Sir Alec's eight roles are Lupino Lane, who played all 24 parts in *Only Me* (US 29), Joseph Henabery, cast as Abraham Lincoln and 13 other characters in *The Birth of a Nation* (US 15), Robert Hirsch, seen in 12 roles in *No Questions on Saturday* (US 64), Michael Ripper, with nine in *What a Crazy World* (GB 63), Flavio Migliaccio, who had eight parts in *Como Vai, Vai Bem* (Bra 69) and Rolv Wesenlund, portraying eight characters in the comedy *Norske Byggeklosser* (Nor 71). Perhaps the most economically casted film of recent years was *The Great McGonagall* (GB 74) which had five actors playing 34 parts between them.

DUAL ARTISTE ROLES

The reverse principle to the above, of having more than one performer in a role, is understandably rare except in instances where the character is portrayed as child and adult. Best known example is probably *Saratoga* (US 37), the film that Jean Harlow was starring in when she died. Her stand-in, Mary Dees, played the remaining static scenes in long shot and Geraldine Dvorak assumed the role for the scenes in which the character moved. As neither had a sufficiently Harlowesque twang, the voice was dubbed by radio actress Paula Winslow. Similarly, when George Christians died of a heart attack during the filming of Von Stroheim's *Foolish Wives* (US 22), the role of the American envoy was taken over by Robert Edson.

Louise Brooks and Margaret Livingston both played the girl who gets murdered in *The Canary Murder Case* (US 29). The film was originally shot as a silent, but when Paramount decided to turn it into a talkie, Louise Brooks was unwilling to participate in sound retakes. Miss Livingston was recruited to do the voice-over and the additional scenes necessary, as she had a slight resemblance to Louise Brooks. In *The Last Hunt* (US 56) Anne Bancroft plays the Indian maiden in all the location scenes and Debra Paget took the role

in the studio scenes, an expedient occasioned by the fact that Miss Bancroft had been thrown from a horse and injured just before location shooting was completed.

Eduard von Borsody's *Kautschuk/Green Hell* (Ger 38), a jungle romp set in 19th-century Brazil, had matinee idol René Deltgen and an amateur called Eichorn in the leading role of a young Englishman smuggling rubber seeds in order to establish Britain's Far Eastern rubber plantations. The reason for the dual casting was that UFA had based the jungle scenes on some five reels of location footage that Eichorn had filmed in the Amazon jungle with himself as hero. Deltgen was selected to play in the studio scenes because he resembled Eichorn, whose acting ability did not meet the demands of the story. Also emanating from Brazil was *Macunaima* (Bra 69), a comedy in which Grande Otelo and Paulo Jose shared the title role of a negro who turns white.

Three actresses played Eve in *Resurrection of Eve* (US 73), Nancy Weich in the courtship scenes, Mimi Morgan in the early marriage scenes and Marilyn Chambers in the later marriage scenes. Paddy Madden and Victoria Anoux were twinned in the title role of *The True Story of Eskimo Nell* (Aus 75), one as the beautiful girl of Deadeye Dick's imaginings, the other as the blowsy frump of reality. Other interchangeable heroines were Sheila Finn and Peggy Steffans, who both played Vera in *Hallelujah the Hills* (US 63), alternating according to which of her lovers she was with; and Carole Bouquet and Angela Molina as the servant girl whose virginity is the motivating factor in Louis Bunuel's *That Obscure Object of Desire* (Fr 78).

Twins are very often played by one performer, using double exposure camerawork where necessary, but on at least two occasions twin performers have shared a role. Billy Mauch was credited with the title role of *Anthony Adverse* (US 36) in the boyhood sequence, but in fact several scenes were played by his twin Bobby; and in Celestino Coronado's *Hamlet* (GB 78), Anthony and David Meyer both play the Prince of Denmark.

Equally rare is having both hero and heroine played by the same performer. In *Lanka Dahan/The Burning of Lanka* (Ind 18), A. Salunke was cast as both the lovely Sita, held by a ten-headed monster on the island of Lanka, and her heroic rescuer Rama. At this date respectable Hindu women would not deign to appear on screen. No other example is recorded before 1983, when Anne Carlisle played both the male and female leading roles in Slava Tsukerman's *Liquid Sky* (US 83).

NAMES

The most usual reasons for actors and actresses changing their names are that those they were born with are too long, too difficult to pronounce, or simply unglamorous. It is not hard to understand why Herbert Charles Angelo Kuchacewich ze Schluderpacheru decided to drop it in favour of Herbert Lom, or why Derek Julius Gaspard Ulric Niven van den Bogaerde thought he would go further with a name like Dirk Bogarde. Equally Larushka Mischa Skikne had good reason to change his to Laurence Harvey and nobody complained when Walter Matasschanskayasky chose to call himself Matthau instead (though he was billed as Walter Matasschanskayasky when he played a recurring cameo role as a drunk in *Earthquake* (US 74)).

Briefer names may be just as unacceptable. Sarah Jane Fulks was distasteful to Jane Wyman, as was Alexandra Zuck to Sandra Dee and Diana Fluck to Diana Dors. Olga Kronk preferred Claire Windsor, and not surprisingly Doris Day was as relieved to be free of Doris Kappelhoff as was Cyd Charisse not to have to answer to Tula Finklea. Burl Ivanhoe substituted Ives, while Fabian Forte Bonaparte was satisfied to get along with just his first name. Robert Taylor had rather more appeal for a romantic hero than Spangler Arlington Brugh and Septimus Ryott was undoubtedly correct in thinking that his female fans would prefer him as Stewart Rome. Austrian actor Jake Kratz doubted he would be able to play hot-blooded Latin lovers with a name like that and changed it to Ricardo Cortez. Many performers born with Latin names preferred something Anglo-Saxon: Dino Crocetti opted for Dean Martin, Margarita Carmen Cansino for Rita Hayworth, Luis Antonio Damaso de Alonso for Gilbert Roland and Anna Maria Luisa Italiano for Anne Bancroft. A few reversed the process, and changed Anglo-Saxon names into something more exotic: Bonar Sullivan became Bonar Colleano, Peggy Middleton assumed the more romantic Yvonne de Carlo and Muriel Harding decided that Olga Petrova held a greater air of mystery for a *femme fatale*.

Some actors chose names that others had discarded. Bernard Schwarz chose Tony Curtis, while the real Tony Curtis had become Italy's best loved comedian Toto. American actor Bud Flanagan changed his name to Dennis O'Keefe, while British actor Robert Winthrop altered his to Bud Flanagan. It was fortunate for James Stewart that his British namesake had already decided to change James Stewart into Stewart Granger before the other James Stewart went into movies.

Alternatively an artiste could sometimes get away with adopting a name which already had cachet. Cambodia's leading female star before the communist takeover, Kim Nova, selected her screen name in unabashed imitation of Kim Novak. In 1974 a Cambodian starlet called herself Kim Novy in imitation of the imitation. Charles Chaplin sued a Mexican comedian called Charles Amador who had changed his name to Charles Aplin, but was unable to do anything about a German comedian who appeared on screen as Charlie Kaplin. Currently Hong Kong's Bruce Li is finding fame and fortune treading in the footsteps of the late Bruce Lee.

It was also perfectly possible to have several actors with a legitimate claim to the same name. There were three Robert Lee's working in Hollywood during the 1920s and four Charles Mack's, two of whom styled themselves Charles E. Mack, and additionally a Mrs Charles Mack, who performed under that name.

Some were satisfied simply to change their Christian name: Leslie/Bob Hope; James/David Niven; William/Pat O'Brien; Clarence/Robert Cummings; Hubert/Rudy Vallee; John/Arthur Kennedy; Julius/Groucho Marx; Virginia/Bebe Daniels; Sari/Zsa Zsa Gabor; Marilyn/Kim Novak; Adolf/Anton Walbrook; Julia/Lana Turner; Ruth/Bette Davis.

Joseph Keaton assumed the first name of 'Buster' at

Carole Bouquet and Angela Molina both play the same role in Buñuel's *That Obscure Object of Desire* (Fr 78).

Black character actor Stepin Fetchit named himself after a racehorse which had obliged him by winning. Usually to be found in a tricky situation, this one occurred in *Fox Movietone Follies of 1929* (US 29).

the age of six months when he fell downstairs and Harry Houdini, a family friend, remarked to his father: 'That's some buster your baby took!' Harry Crosby acquired 'Bing' from avid reading of a comic strip called *The Bingville Bugle* when he was at school.

Even simpler was to change a single letter of the name: Conrad Veidt (Weidt); Beulah Bondy (Bondi); George Raft (Ranft); May Robson (Robison); Ronald Squire (Squirl); Gerard Philipe (Philippe); Dorothy Malone (Maloney); Warren Beatty (Beaty); Yul Bryner (Bryner). James Baumgarner was content to drop the 'Baum', Anna Maria Pierangeli split her surname down the middle and eschewed her first names, while Banky Vilma just switched to Vilma Banky.

Choice of a new name is dictated by varied circumstances. Judy Garland (Frances Gumm) took her stage surname from the theatre pages of a Chicago newspaper, whose reviews were written by Robert Garland. It was chosen by George Jessel, to whom the 11-year-old Miss Gumm had appealed for help after being billed as Glumm at the theatre where they were both appearing. Her first name came from a Hoagy Carmichael song *Judy*, of which she was fond. French comedian Fernandel was born Fernand Constandin. His wife called him *Fernand d'elle (her Fernand)*. Luis

Alonso selected his new name of Gilbert Roland as a tribute to the two stars he most admired, John Gilbert and Ruth Roland. Stepin Fetchit, the startled black manservant of twenties and thirties Hollywood movies, named himself after a racehorse which had obliged him by winning. Marilyn Monroe's Christian name was selected for her by Fox talent scout Ben Lyon because of his admiration for Marilyn Miller—the Monroe was her mother's maiden name. Bette (Ruth) Davis took her screen Christian name from Balzac's *Cousin Bette*. Gary (Frank J.) Cooper was named after his agent's hometown, Gary, Indiana. The actor's own hometown would hardly have been appropriate—he came from Helena, Montana. MGM ran a fan contest in 1925 to find a new name for the extravagantly named Lucille Le Sueur. The winner came up with Joan Arden, but as there was already an actress of that name in Hollywood, Miss Le Sueur adopted the name suggested by the runner-up instead—Joan Crawford. Gretchen Young had her first name changed to Loretta by Colleen Moore, who discovered her as a 14-year-old extra in *Her Wild Oat* (US 26). Loretta, said Miss Moore, was the name of 'the most beautiful doll I ever had'. Bela Lugosi, real name Bela Blasko, took his

Right
Could you think of a better name for Lucille Le Sueur, 18-year-old hopeful dreaming of stardom back in 1925? What about something plain and simple like Joan Crawford?

Could You

Use $500?

If So

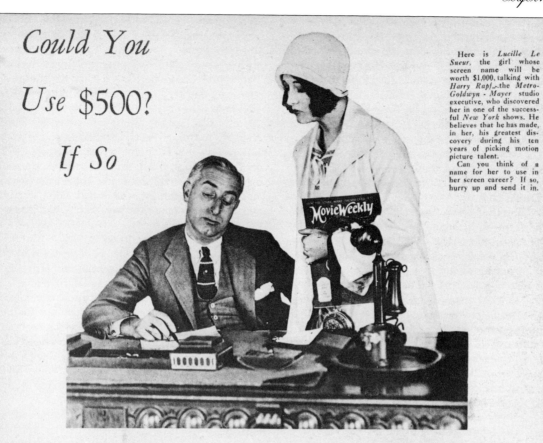

Here is *Lucille Le Sueur*, the girl whose screen name will be worth $1,000, talking with *Harry Rapf*, the *Metro-Goldwyn - Mayer* studio executive, who discovered her in one of the successful *New York* shows. He believes that he has made, in her, his greatest discovery during his ten years of picking motion picture talent.

Can you think of a name for her to use in her screen career? If so, hurry up and send it in.

Hurry Up and Enter

The $1,000 for a Name Contest

NAMES, names, names and more names! The Movie Weekly Contest Editor has been deluged with names. Every mail the postman staggers in under a load of hundreds more. It has seemed like a bombardment of telephone and city directories. Short names, long names, simple names and tongue twisters. First names from Fifi to Prudence and Mary to Hydrodendron. Last names from Smith to de la Montparnasse. Enough of them to name every parlor car that ever will be made.

But among the thousands that have been submitted, we have not selected THE name as yet. You still have a chance to win that $500 prize!

Readers of this magazine are helping us select a suitable screen name for Lucille Le Sueur, newest and one of the prettiest players signed by Metro-Goldwyn-Mayer. She will appear exclusively in films made by that big producing organization.

They have helped us to the extent of very nearly swamping us with suggestions. The response to our appeals, which were accompanied by the incentive of offering

a large cash prize for the name finally selected, has been tremendous. However, the judges will not choose one for the beautiful young actress until the contest has closed. The $500 still is all dressed up and no place to go.

Yes, it's all dressed up except the name after "Pay to the order of ...." Why don't you try to get yours there—by suggesting the winning *nom de screen* for Miss Le Sueur. You still have time. The contest hasn't closed yet. But you'll have to hurry. And we'll hurry with the $500 if you send in THE name.

Contestants may submit as many names as they can originate. Each one must be written on a separate sheet of paper with the senders' name and address on the same side. Read the rules carefully.

The cry for help in giving Miss Le Sueur a screen name that has not finally been answered yet came about this way:

Harry Rapf, Metro-Goldwyn-Mayer studio executive, who "discovered" Miss Le Sueur in one of the successful New York shows, believes he has made his greatest *(Continued on page 31)*

```
─────────────────────────────────────────
            NAME COUPON
(Suggestions must be made on this coupon, a tracing of it
      or a similar one of your own making)

Name Suggested..................................

Your Name.......................................

Your Address....................................
─────────────────────────────────────────
```

MOVIE WEEKLY *Page Sixteen*

screen surname from his hometown of Lugos in Hungary. Richard Burton, formerly Richard Jenkins, assumed the name of his old teacher in Port Talbot. Gig Young (Byron Barr) took the name of the character he played in *The Gay Sisters* (US 42) and former child star Dawn O'Day switched to Anne Shirley to play the heroine of that name in *Anne of Green Gables* (US 34). The story put about by her studio (and still believed in some quarters) that Theda Bara's name was an anagram of 'Arab Death' was so much hokum: the name was selected by director Frank Powell on learning that she had a relative called Barranger. Equally unromantic was Carole Lombard's (Jane Peters) decision to call herself after the Carroll, Lombardi Pharmacy on Lexington and 65th in New York. Greta Garbo might easily have become Greta Gabor. Long before meeting young Greta Gustafsson, her mentor Mauritz Stiller had cherished the dream of discovering and moulding a great star. He asked his manuscript assistant, Arthur Norden, to select a name. Norden, an historian, chose Gábor, after the Hungarian king, Gábor Bethlen. Stiller wanted something less East European, however, and amended it to Garbo. Another monarch was rather more personally involved in naming Lili Damita (Lilliane Carré). Holidaying at Biarritz in 1921 when she was 17, she attracted the attention of the King of Spain, who enquired after the *damita del maillo rojo* (*young lady in a red bathing dress*).

Those who retain their own names may also have cogent reasons for doing so. 'Bradford Dillman', said that actor, 'sounded like a distinguished, phoney, theatrical name—so I kept it.'

The most enduring screen team was that of Indian superstars Prem Nazir and Sheela, who had played opposite each other in 130 movies by 1975.

The Hollywood record pales by comparison. Excluding performers billed together solely in 'series' films, the most enduring screen partners are husband-and-wife team Charles Bronson and Jill Ireland, who have co-starred in 14 films up to and including *Death Wish II* (US 82). Myrna Loy and William Powell played opposite each other in 13 pictures; Ginger Rogers and Fred Astaire, and Judy Garland and Mickey Rooney in ten; Katharine Hepburn and Spencer Tracy in nine; while Jeanette MacDonald and Nelson Eddy, and Greer Garson and Walter Pidgeon were teamed in eight films.

The most extensive screen tests in the history of motion pictures were held for the role of Scarlett O'Hara in *Gone With the Wind* (US 39). MGM shot 149,000 ft of black-and-white test film and another 13,000 ft of colour with 60 actresses, none of whom got the part. Having discarded 27 hours of test film, producer David O Selznick narrowed the choice to three major stars and one unknown—Joan Bennett, Jean Arthur, Paulette Goddard and newcomer Vivien Leigh. The final tests required the four conten-

ders to play the scenes of Scarlett getting into her corset, talking to Ashley in the paddock and drunkenly proposing to Rhett Butler. Miss Leigh's successful test was actually made after shooting of the movie had commenced—perhaps the only instance of a major motion picture going into production before the star role had been cast. Total cost of the 165,000 ft of tests was $105,000—approximately the budget then of an average second feature.

Hollywood's first nude screen tests were held for *Four for Texas* (US 63), which starred Ursula Andress and Anita Ekberg in the *femme* leads. Those actresses who had been unwilling to be tested need not have worried; all nude scenes were cut by the censor.

STARS WHO FAILED SCREEN TESTS
Failing a screen test may not be a passport to stardom, but in some cases it has been no barrier. Bette Davis's first screen test was so appalling that she ran from the Goldwyn projection room screaming. Her next, with Universal, was successful enough for her to be given a job—as a stand-in girl for screen tests of male actors. Clark Gable failed a Warner screen test in 1930 because Jack Warner declared (in Gable's hearing) that he was only 'a big ape'. His next was at MGM, where his prominent ears told against him. Although he failed the test, MGM signed him anyway and he stayed with the studio—contributing significantly to its ascendancy—for 23 years. Another star who failed the rigours of a MGM test was Maurice Chevalier, but he was signed by Paramount in 1928 on the strength of the *same* test.

Shirley Temple, probably the greatest box-office attraction of all time, failed a test for the *Our Gang* series. The screen's most prestigious luminary, Laurence Olivier, was turned down for *Queen Christina* (US 33) after testing opposite Greta Garbo, though it is widely held that Garbo deliberately sabotaged the test in order that the role should go to ex-lover John Gilbert, then in decline.

Brigitte Bardot's puppy fat and spots caused her to fail a screen test with Marc Allégret when she was 16. Jane Russell also failed to pass muster. The report on her 1940 test for Fox read 'unphotogenic'. Warner's comments when she tested for them were 'no energy' and 'no spark'. Another star considered physically unsuitable was Robert Taylor. He failed his test for United Artists in 1933 because Sam Goldwyn thought he was too skinny.

Nothing was found wanting in Ava Gardner's physique. After seeing her test for MGM, Louis B. Mayer expostulated: 'She can't talk. She can't act. She's terrific.'

Less enthusiasm was expressed for Fred Astaire in a studio report on his first screen test, even if the words were much the same: 'Can't act. Can't sing. Can dance a little.'

Not even an established star could afford to be overconfident. According to Hollywood legend, at the height of her screen career Gloria Swanson took a test incognito wearing a blonde wig. She was turned down.

BEAUTY QUEENS

Beauty queens have aspired to screen stardom since Ivy Close won the *Daily Mirror* Beauty Competition in 1909 and was promptly engaged by the Hepworth Stock Co. as a leading player. Within three years she had her own company, Ivy Close Films, starring in such productions as *The Lady of Shallot* (GB 12) and *The Girl from the Sky* (GB 14). (Her hobby, unusually for an Edwardian Miss, was motorcycling.) Other silent stars to graduate from beauty contests were Mary Philbin, who won a contract with Universal on the strength of winning a Chicago contest, Norma Shearer, who won a contest in Montreal in 1918, and Clara Bow, winner of the *Photoplay* beauty contest of 1922 when she was 16.

The talkies attracted the talents of Miss Hungary 1936 in the person of Zsa Zsa Gabor; two Miss Italies of the late 1940s—Lucia Bose and Gina Lollobrigida; Miss Rome 1946—Silvana Mangano; Miss Kansas 1948—Vera Miles; Miss Burbank 1948—Debbie Reynolds; Miss Great Britain 1950—Anne Heywood; Miss Sweden 1951—Anita Ekberg; Miss Deepfreeze 1953—Kim Novak; 'The Most Beautiful Italian Girl in Tunis' 1956—Claudia Cardinale; Miss Viareggio (Italy) 1958—Elke Sommer; Miss Teenage Memphis 1966—Cybil Shepherd; Miss Asia 1971—India's top leading lady Zeenat Aman; Miss Television Europe 1973—Sylvia 'Emmanuelle' Kristel. Stars with long experience of the beauty contest circuit before they broke into movies include Sophia Loren, who was Princess of the Sea 1948, won the Miss Elegance title at the Queen of the Adriatic Sirens contest at Cervia in 1950, and came second in the 1952 Miss Rome contest; and Raquel Welch, who became Miss Photogenic at San Diego, California in 1953 at the age of 13 and subsequently won the titles of Miss La Jolla, The Fairest of the Fair, Miss Contour, Queen of the Southern California Exposition, and Maid of California.

The major contests have produced few film actresses of note. Miss Universe of 1969, Gloria Diaz, attained stardom in her own country, the Philippines, and some five years later another Miss Universe, Amparo Muñoz, embarked on a movie career in Spain. The one Miss America to achieve success on screen was the 1941 winner, Rosemary La Planche Koplan, who became a feature player in RKO movies, while the only Miss Worlds to have appeared in films are the 1964 title holder Ann Sidney, an English girl who subsequently played roles in over 100 American pictures, and the winner of the 1969 contest, Austria's Eva Rueber-Staier.

The shortest adult performer in movies is 2 ft 7 in (0·79 m) tall Tamara de Treaux, an actress and singer from San Francisco. Tamara's most celebrated role to date was E.T., Steven Spielberg's lovable alien from outer space. Although in parts of the film E.T. was an electronic puppet, in others he was played by actors and actresses in costume—besides Tamara, there were 2 ft 10 in (0·86 m) Pat Bilson and legless schoolboy Matthew de Merritt, who played the drunk scene walking on his hands inside the E.T. suit. Tamara's main scene was of E.T. shuffling into the spacecraft for his return home. Her weight—she considers she is too heavy at 2 st 12 lb (18 kg) helped her to perfect what she described as 'a cute Daffy Duck waddle'. Tamara was dwarfed by seven-year-old Drew Barrymore, who towered over her by 17 in.

The shortest actor to play the leading role in a film is Filipino paratrooper and black belt martial arts exponent Weng Weng, who has starred in *Agent 00* (Phi 81) and *For Your Height Only* (Phi 84). Weng Weng measures 2 ft 9 in (0·84 m).

The shortest actor to achieve celebrity in Hollywood and the only dwarf honoured in the Hollywood Walk of Fame is Billy Barty, a 3 ft 9 in (1·14 m) veteran of 150 films and founder of The Little People of America Inc.

All-dwarf casts have been used in two films—a western *The Terror of Tiny Town* (US 38) and Werner Herzog's *Even Dwarfs Started Small* (FRG 70). *The Little Cigars* (US 73) had a cast of five midgets and one full-sized actress, described as 'a busty blonde'. The **largest cast of dwarves and midgets** was 116 in *The Wizard of Oz* (US 39), and an equal number in *Under the Rainbow* (US 81), which was the story of what the original Munchkins got up to on and off the set of *The Wizard of Oz* while they were staying at the Culver Hotel in 1938. (What they got up to was miniature mayhem.)

Hollywood boasts a Media Office of Disability, which promotes the interests of handicapped artistes. In September 1983 the Office reported that in the past year, more than 150 roles for films and television had been cast utilising the services of performers with a physical disability.

The shortest artiste to play major roles, apart from dwarves and midgets, is 4 ft 9 in (1·45 m) Linda Hunt, who made her debut in *Popeye* (US 80) as mother of the giant, Oxblood Oxheart, and won the Academy Award for Best Supporting Actress in 1984 for her role as Billy Kwan, a male Eurasian cameraman in Indonesia, in *The Year of Living Dangerously* (Aus 82). She has since been in the Merchant–Ivory version of Henry James's *The Bostonians* (GB 84) and *Dune* (US 84).

The only leading ladies under 5 ft (1·52 m) were silent-screen heroines Florence Turner and Marguerite Clark, each 4 ft 10 in (1·47 m) tall, and 4 ft 11 in (1·50 m) May McAvoy, who starred opposite Al Jolson in *The Jazz Singer* (US 27). Janet Gaynor and Mary

7 ft 2 in John Aasen became a movie actor in 1928. He could have looked Richard Kiel ('Jaws' of the Bond films) straight in the eye.

Right
The shortest adult actress to play major roles is 4 ft 9 in Linda Hunt, who won the Oscar as Best Supporting Actress for her role as a male cameraman in *The Year of Living Dangerously* (Aus 82).

Pickford were both 5 ft exactly, as was the lesser known Edith Roberts, whose height qualified her to play the title role in *Her Five-Foot Highness* (US 20). **The shortest leading man** was French silent-star Max Linder, the impeccable dandy of the Paris boulevards, who was a mere 5 ft 2 in (1·57 m). Hollywood's shortest male stars are Mickey Rooney and Dudley Moore at 5 ft 3 in (1·60 m). Reports that Alan Ladd was only 5 ft (1·52 m) tall were quite untrue; he was 5 ft 6 in (1·68 m), which made him an inch taller than Dustin Hoffman and the same height as Al Pacino. Nevertheless, Ladd's lack of inches was proverbial in Hollywood. Sophia Loren has confirmed that he had to stand on a box for his love scenes with her in *Boy on a Dolphin* (US 57) and James Mason, when he was invited to co-star with Ladd in

Most mountainous movie star—45-stone Ethel Greer needed some special support in *Hoopla* (US 33).

Botany Bay (US 54), told the producer that he had no intention of standing in a trench for their scenes together.

The tallest screen artiste was Clifford Thompson, claimed to be 8 ft 6 in (2·59 m) and then the tallest man in the world, who played opposite (and above) ZaSu Pitts in Hal Roach's *Seal Skins* (US 32). No other eight-footers are recorded. Artistes of 7 ft (2·13 m) or over include Tex Erikson, 7 ft exactly, who was featured in *Jungle Jim in the Forbidden Land* (US 52); Johan Aasen, a 7 ft 2 in (2·18 m) character actor who entered Hollywood pictures in 1923; Peter Mayhew, 7 ft 2 in ex-hospital porter, who played a mythical monster in *Sinbad and the Eye of the Tiger* (US 77) and the furry wookie Chewbacca in *Star Wars* (US 77); Richard Kiel, 7 ft 2 in without his size 16 shoes, who played the steel-teethed giant villain in Bond movies *The Spy Who Loved Me* (GB 77) and *Moonraker* (GB/Fr 79) and starred in the title role of *The Humanoid* (It 78); John Bloom, 7 ft 4 in (2·24 m), who was Frankenstein's monster in *Dracula v Frankenstein* (US 71); and Jack Tarver, 7 ft 10 in (2·39 m), the giant in Fox's feature-length children's picture *Jack and the Beanstalk* (US 17).

The tallest leading men were 6 ft 7 in (2·01 m) James Arness, who starred in *Them* (US 54) and *The First Travelling Saleslady* (US 56), and Bruce Spence, 6 ft 7 in, in *Stork* (Aus 71), which was scripted by 6 ft 7 in David Williamson, and *Wo die Grunen Ameisen Trauma*

(FRG 84). Christopher Lee is the tallest major star at 6 ft 5 in (1·96 m), an inch taller than Clint Eastwood.

The heaviest screen artiste was Ethel Greer, who weighed 637 lb (45 st 5 lb—289 kg) when she appeared with Clara Bow in *Hoopla* (US 33). Miss Greer's 140 lb (63 kg) husband, visiting the set, remarked of the slender 118 lb (53 kg) Miss Bow: 'I never could see why some fellows go for these skinny girls'.

The most generously proportioned leading lady of all time was Chesty Morgan, the possessor of a 73-in (185 cm) bust, who starred in *Deadly Weapons* (US 75).

STATUES TO STARS

Only a few stars are known to have been honoured with statues to their memory. Rudolph Valentino (1895–1926) was commemorated with a four-foot (1·2 m) high bronze male nude by Roger Burnham representing 'Aspiration', which was unveiled in Hollywood's De Longpre Park on 6 May 1930. *Photoplay* reported that 'not a single great screen figure of Valentino's halcyon days attended'. The statue was generally disliked, both by local residents who objected to nude statuary, and by Valentino fans, who

The Duke stands guard on Wilshire Boulevard in Beverly Hills, California. (*Chris Oberle*)

> The voice on the British Airways P.A. system telling passengers to fasten seat-belts etc. is the voice of Julie Andrews.

were incensed that their idol had not been represented as they chose to remember him. After years of depradations by vandals, one particularly energetic objector succeeded in flattening the figure with a sledge hammer. Reinforced with steel rods it was replaced, but two years later, in 1952, it was wrested from its base again and a despairing parks department removed it to the safekeeping of a distant warehouse. It was restored to its original pedestal in 1976.

A second statue to the Great Latin Lover was unveiled at his birthplace, the small Italian town of Castellaneta, in 1961. This time Valentino himself was represented, a massive eight-foot figure in the flowing robes of the Sheik, sculpted by Luigi Gheno. The robes were in full colour and for some unexplained reason the face was sky blue.

Another star commemorated with two different statues is the beloved crackerbarrel philosopher Will Rogers (1879–1935). At the Will Rogers Memorial at Claremore, Oklahoma, there is an outdoor equestrian statue as well as an indoor bronze figure by Jo Davidson depicting W. R. in typical pose, standing at his ease in a rumpled suit, hands thrust deep into his pockets. A duplicate of the latter stands in the Capitol at Washington, bearing the same epitaph as the one at Claremore: 'I never met a man I didn't like'.

The most popular star of silent westerns, Tom Mix (1880–1940), is commemorated with a statue of a riderless pony at the spot where he was killed in a car crash at Florence, Arizona. In Nagarcoil, South India, there is a statue to one of India's best loved comedians, N. S. Krishnan (1908–57), who was teamed with comedienne T. A. Mathuram in over a hundred pictures before a tragically early death at the height of his career.

A lifesize full-length bronze effigy of Sir Charles Chaplin (1889–1977), the work of sculptor John Doubleday, was erected in London's Leicester Square in 1981. Another Chaplin statue, a 12 ft (3·6 m) high bronze, has been commissioned by the West Bengal government at a cost of $20,000. The most likely location will be in Charlie Chaplin Square, a small Calcutta park behind New Market on Chowringhee Road.

A bronze statue of Bing Crosby (1904–1977) was unveiled at his Alma Mater, Gonzaga University at Spokane, Washington, in 1981. In 1983 Ingrid Bergman's (1915–82) son Roberto Rossellini, together with

his friend Princess Caroline of Monaco, unveiled a statue to the star at her birthplace, the small Swedish hamlet of Fjällbacka. The 1984 Los Angeles Olympics were the occasion of the unveiling of a 21 ft (6·4 m) high bronze equestrian statue of John Wayne (1907–81). Sculpted by western artist Harry Jackson, it stands at La Cienaga and Wilshire in Beverly Hills.

Few statues have been erected to stars in their own lifetime, though the unveiling of the statue to Carl Brisson (1895–1958) in Copenhagen was attended by the star in person. The Prime Minister of Denmark observed in his speech: 'Let us give him the flowers while he is still here.' Another effigy of the living is an 8 ft 6 in (2·6 m) statue of Sylvester Stallone (1946–) as Rocky, originally a prop for *Rocky III* (US 82), which was installed on a permanent site near the Spectrum in Philadelphia in July 1982. Al Jolson's (1886–1950) statue was not erected in his lifetime, but it was paid for in advance by the star as an assurance of his own immortality. Depicting the star on one knee with his arms outstretched in the pose he made famous, the lifesize statue is mounted by his grave in a Los Angeles cemetery overlooking the Pacific Ocean.

The earliest known statue of a star is also of a star still living. Called 'Young Diana', it was sculpted in 1924 by Anna Hyatt Huntingdon and now reposes in the Boston Museum of Fine Arts. The model, who posed in the nude, was the 16-year-old Bette Davis (1908–), making an artistic debut of sorts seven years before her screen debut in *Bad Sister* (US 31). The statue was

Right
John Doubleday's statue of Charlie Chaplin in London's Leicester Square. He has also done a Chaplin statue for Montreux, Switzerland, and an effigy of Sir Laurence Olivier for the National Institute of Film in Peking. (*John Doubleday*)

Left

Young Diana, the bronze statue by Anna Hyatt Huntington claimed to represent the young Bette Davies at the age of 16. (*Museum of Fine Arts, Boston*)

identified in 1982 after Miss Davis had revealed in *Playboy* magazine that she could be seen naked in Boston by anyone so inclined.

The actor who has played the same role the most times in feature films is the Hong Kong actor Kwan Tak-Hing, who portrayed the great South China martial arts hero Huang Fei-Hong (1847–1924) in 77 films out of a series of 85. His first appearance was in *The True Story of Huang Fei-Hong* (HK 49) and his last in *Magnificent Butcher* (HK 80). During the 1970s, when he played in only one Huang Fei-Hong movie, Kwan Tak-Hing continued the role in a television series.

The Hollywood actor to repeat the same role the most times in feature films was William Boyd (1898–1972), a major star of the twenties whose flagging career was revived in the thirties when Paramount chose him as the gentleman cowboy Hopalong Cassidy. Dressed always in black (usually reserved for villains in 'B' westerns), Boyd rode the range as 'Hoppy' in 66 full-length films, starting with *Hop-a-long Cassidy* aka *Hopalong Cassidy Enters* (US 35) and ending with *Strange Gamble* (US 48). The films were among the first American productions aired on television in the forties and Boyd then embarked on a long-running Hopalong Cassidy TV series, having already played the character in a network radio series.

A number of actors established a reputation for playing particular historical characters: Charles Vanel as Napoleon, Frank McGlynn as Abraham Lincoln and Robert Watson as Hitler. Silent player Roy Travers was cast as the Prince Consort eleven times and as Charles Dickens seven times. The most appearances in one historical role was probably by Mikhail Gelovani, who portrayed Stalin in more than 20 Soviet films. The dictator was so gratified by Gelovani's rather wooden projection of him as the wise, all-seeing, noble proletarian that he was never allowed to give the parts any other dimension.

Other actors have found their niche in occupational roles. Arthur Treacher and Charles Coleman seldom played anything but butlers throughout their screen careers, Irish-American actor Tom Dugan played a slow-witted New York cop in over 100 films following his debut in 1926, while Pat O'Brien was cast as a Roman Catholic priest in at least a dozen of his movies. In 1928 Guy Oliver claimed to have been cast as a sheriff in 150 of the 230 westerns he had made and in 1931 Frank Hagney, invariably seen as a boxer, declared ruefully that he had lost the world's heavyweight title no less than 29 times during his career. A number of performers specialised in courtroom dramas, but none with such dedication as Hollywood character actor Richard Tucker, who is known to have played the prosecuting attorney at least 54 times.

Among performers still active in films, the **record for playing the same occupational** role is claimed by veteran Bombay actor Jagdish Raaj. He has been cast as a uniformed police officer in 136 films (as at June 1984) over a period of 30 years.

Some were cast against type. German-born Peter van Eyck, who became Hollywood's stock Nazi beast, only came to California because as an active anti-Nazi he was forced to flee Hitler's Germany. The ability to play a drunk well is a rare one, which enabled Jack Norton and Arthur Housman to specialise in amiable inebriates, seldom playing anything else. Some special talent must also have inspired producers to cast Carmen Nigro as a gorilla in 32 movies, or 33 if his claim to have played the title role in *King Kong* (US 33) can be sustained (it is generally accepted that all the gorilla scenes were

In *Nous étions tous des noms d'arbres/The Writing on the Wall* (Fr/Bel 82), Armand Gatti's story of strife and sectarianism in present-day Northern Ireland, the Protestants are played by Roman Catholics and the Roman Catholics by Protestants.

Jagdish Raaj, the Bombay actor who has played a police officer in 136 films.

acted with models). He last donned his ape suit for *Gorilla at Large* (US 54). 'Cowardly Lion' Bert Lahr was not so lucky. 'After *The Wizard of Oz*', he declared ruefully, 'I was typecast as a lion—and there aren't all that many parts for lions.'

Versatility is harder to quantify. However, it is doubtful whether any performer ever played with a greater variety of accents than Russian-born Hollywood actor Vladimir Sokoloff, who was cast as 35 nationalities during his career ranging from an Italian physicist in *Cloak and Dagger* (US 46) to a blind Chinese beggar in *Macao* (US 52). The only accent Sokoloff never succeeded in mastering was American.

The most delayed come-back: Of the many stars who have retired from films and made a comeback, the one with the longest interregnum was George Burns, who left the screen after *Many Happy Returns* (US 34) and made a happy return 42 years later in *The Sunshine Boys* (US 76) at the age of 80.

The oldest performer to have played a major role in a feature movie is Estelle Winwood, born Lee, Kent, 24 January 1883, who completed her role as Nurse Withers in *Murder by Death* (US 76) on her 93rd birthday. Miss Winwood was the oldest member of the Screen Actors Guild at the time of her death in California aged 101. She made her professional debut at the Theatre Royal, Manchester, in 1898 and claimed to have been the first woman in America to wear lipstick in public.

The oldest star to take the leading part in a feature film was 90-year old Lillian Gish (1893–), who played one of the two title roles in *Hambone and Hillie* (US 84). Miss Gish, who has never been disadvantaged by age nor indeed by anything else since she played her first starring role in 1912, might well have found herself upstaged by Hambone, who happened to be a dog. In the event critical plaudits were divided equally. (Note: most reference books quote Miss Gish's year of birth as either 1896 or 1898. In 1984 the American Film Institute was ungallant enough to make public its discovery of her birth certificate, which conclusively proves a birthdate of 1893—and nonagenarian stardom.)

Other nonagenarian artistes have been A. E. Matthews (1869–1960) in *Inn for Trouble* (GB 60); John Cromwell (1887–1979) in *The Wedding* (US 78); Cathleen Nesbitt (1889–1982) in *The Second Star to the Right* (GB 81); Sam Jaffe (1891–1984)—who played the 200-year-old High Lama in *Lost Horizon* (US 37)—in *Nothing Lasts Forever* (US 82) and *On the Line* aka *Downstream* (US 84), which he completed filming in October 1983 when he was 92 years and 7 months old. Matty, as A. E. Matthews was known, once observed: 'I always wait for *The Times* each morning. I look at the obituary column, and if I'm not in it I go to work.'

At least two centenarians were professional extras. William H. 'Dad' Taylor, born Brownsville, Texas, 9 July 1828, appeared in Edwin Carewe's *Evangeline* (US 29) at the age of 101—a unique instance of a person born during the Georgian era playing in a talkie. The other was Walter 'Cap' Field (1874–1976), who joined the Mexican production company Ammex in 1913 and played his last role in *She's Too Hot to Handle* (US 76) when he was 101. He fondly remembered being 'killed or wounded four or five times' in various small roles in *Gone with the Wind* (US 39). The 'sage' in *The Man Who Would Be King* (US 75) was played by a 102-year-old Moroccan.

The youngest performer in a feature film was Balázs Monori, whose actual birth was shown in *Kilenc Hónap/Nine Months* (Hun 76), the story of a pregnant woman (Lili Monori) torn between two men and striving to improve herself. The director, Márta Meszaros, was reported to be delighted that Balázs's screen debut was so accomplished that no second take was needed.

The youngest performer to receive star billing was Leroy Overacker, known on the screen as Baby Leroy, who was chosen at the age of six months to play the central juvenile role opposite Maurice Chevalier in *Bedtime Story* (US 33). Master Overacker's contract had to be signed by his grandfather, because not only the star but also his 16-year-old mother was under age. The film was about a gay bachelor who becomes encumbered with an abandoned baby whose protruding lower lip matches his

George Burns left the screen after *Many Happy Returns* (US 34) (*left*) and made a happy return 42 years later in *The Sunshine Boys* (US 76) (*above*).

own, a circumstance which leads everyone to believe that Chevalier is the father of the motherless child. All is unscrambled when it is found that the distinctive facial feature of the baby is accounted for by nothing more reprehensible than a button lodged under his lip.

INSURANCE

Insurance of stars' more notable physical accoutrements began when silent screen comedian John Bunny (1863–1915) insured his unlovely face for $100,000.

Faces were most stars' fortunes and it was an enterprising Los Angeles underwriter, Arthur W. Stebbins, who originated the 'scarred face' policy taken out in the early 1920s by Rudolph Valentino, Douglas Fairbanks and Mary Pickford, the latter for $1 million. Some stars, though, owed their success to individual features, not always facial—Chaplin insured his feet for $150,000. Clara Kimball Young (1891–1960), often described as 'the most beautiful woman in films' at the peak of her career, c. 1918, insured her large and luminous eyes for the same amount. Cross-eyed Ben Turpin (1874–1940) insured to the tune of $100,000 against the possibility of his eyes ever becoming normal again—it would undoubtedly have cost him his career. Suave leading man Edmund Lowe (1890–1971) took out a $35,000 policy on his distinguished nose in the mid-1920s and at about the same time Kathleen Key had her lovely neck underwritten at $25,000. A decade later the most famous nose in the

Above
Baby Leroy—a star at six months when he played opposite Maurice Chevalier in *Bedtime Story* (US 33).

Right
The oldest working star—93-year-old Estelle Winwood (*right*) in *Murder by Death* (US 76).

business carried a $100,000 risk for Jimmy Durante (1893–1980).

Alberta Vaughn took out a $25,000 policy in 1925 against the possibility of putting on 20 lb weight by 1 June 1927, while Walter Hiers—literally a Hollywood 'heavy'—insured for an equal sum against losing 45 lb. RKO insured Roscoe Ates' (1892–1962) inimitable nervous stutter in the early thirties. A year or two earlier, when sound arrived, First National had insured Corinne Griffith (1898–1979) against loss of voice. Ironically it was her unsuitability for talkies that finished her career. When Anthony Quinn (1915–) had his head shaved for the role of a Greek magician in *The Magus* (GB 68), he insured heavily against the risk of his hair failing to grow again. Fortunately no claim was necessary.

The first actress to insure her legs was Hollywood extra Cecille Evans, whose appendages were underwritten for $100,000 in 1921. Miss Evans' speciality was 'doubling' her sensational legs for those of stars less well endowed. The 'Girl with the Million Dollar Legs', Betty Grable (1916–73), actually had them insured for more than that—the sum was $1,250,000. The legs may have been incomparable, but the policy did not stand comparison with the record risk of $10 million accepted on Cyd Charisse's (1921–) long and lovely limbs. No actor has ever been described as 'The Man with the Million Dollar Legs', but Fred Astaire (1899–) could have claimed the title—his were insured for just that sum.

It is not only performers who have had parts of their bodies insured. In 1939 the Fleischer Studio took out a $185,000 policy with Lloyd's of London to cover the hands of the 116 animators working on their first full-length cartoon feature *Mr Bug Goes to Town* (US 41).

The first artiste whose life was insured for the duration of a picture was Lillian Gish (1896–), covered for the sum of $1 million during the filming of *Way Down East* (US 20). The insurance company turned down director D. W. Griffith's application for insurance on the other principal players on health grounds. Had they known that Miss Gish was to be exposed on an ice floe in sub-zero temperature wearing only a thin frock every day for three weeks, and that she was to be rescued by the hero just before the floe went over the falls without any trick or stunt work, nor any safety precautions in case the rescue failed, doubtless the application on her behalf would have been refused with even greater promptitude.

When seven-year-old Shirley Temple's life (1928–) was insured with Lloyd's, the contract stipulated that no benefit would be paid if the child met death or injury while drunk.

Siobhan McKenna's insurance policy for *Of Human Bondage* (GB 64) forbade her to drive a car while the

Cyd Charisse and her ten million dollar legs.

Singapore has special rules about 'suggestive prolonged kissing': it is not allowed in Malay films, but is acceptable in others. In Pennsylvania in the 1930s, horizontal screen kisses were banned, vertical allowed.

picture was in production. The first time the Irish actress had taken the wheel she had ended in a ditch, the second time against a wall, the third time up a tree.

The first far eastern country to permit kissing in films was China, the first oriental screen kiss being bestowed on Miss Mamie Lee in *Two Women in the House* (Chn 26). In Japan, where kissing was considered 'unclean, immodest, indecorous, ungraceful and likely to spread disease'—at least by Tokyo's Prefect of Police—some 800,000 ft of kissing scenes were cut from American movies that same year. Indians reacted much the same way, though with less rigour about cuts. According to *The Report of the Indian Cinematograph Committee* (1928), during western films 'when a kissing scene is shown, the ladies turn their heads away'.

Japan's first screen kiss was seen in *Hatachi no Seishun/Twenty-Year-Old Youth* (Jap 46), directed by Yasushi Sasaki. The honour of directing the inaugural kiss should have gone to Yasuki Chiba, who was planning to introduce the daring innovation in his aptly titled *Aru Yo no Seppun/A Certain Night's Kiss* (Jap 46), but he lost his nerve at the last moment and the big clinch between the two lovers was discreetly obscured by an open umbrella. Only four years later the sex act itself was brought to the Japanese screen in *Yuki Fujin Ezu/Picture of Madame Yuki* (Jap 50).

KISSING IN INDIAN FILMS

Kissing was voluntarily renounced by the film producers themselves in the mid-thirties on the grounds that Indians did not kiss in public, and to see them doing so on the screen was pandering to an alien custom. After Independence, when the producers decided that there were sound commercial reasons for a little occidental decadence, they found themselves up against the stern morality of the censors. Some

latitude was permitted, however, if at least one of the partners in the act was a foreigner, or in the case of 'international' versions of films for overseas release only. In one instance two Indians were allowed to be seen kissing each other because the girl was playing the part of a Portuguese. The breakthrough came only in 1977, when for the first time in over 40 years two Indians playing Indians were able to kiss in a major film shown in their own country. The historic embrace took place between Zeenat Aman, a former Miss Asia, and the sub-continent's most romantic leading man, Shashi Kapoor, in Raj Kapoor's *Satyam Shivam Sundaram* (Ind 77), a musical melodrama about a man who falls in love with the compelling voice of an adivasi girl and only learns on their wedding night that half of her face is hideously disfigured by a burn.

The last major film-producing country still banning kissing on screen is Turkey.

The longest screen kiss in a commercial feature movie occupied 3 min 5 sec of Regis Toomey's and Jane Wyman's time in *You're in the Army Now* (US 40). Naomi Levine spent the full duration of Andy Warhol's non-commercial 50 min *Kiss* (US 63) kissing Rufus Collins, Gerald Malanga and Ed Saunders.

The most kisses in a single film were the 127 bestowed by John Barrymore on Mary Astor and Estelle Taylor in *Don Juan* (US 26).

The only Hollywood leading lady who never kissed her leading man on screen was the Chinese–American star Anna May Wong (1907–61). She nearly achieved it in *The Road to Dishonour* (GB 29); indeed her kissing scene with John Longden was shot, but cut by the censor on the grounds that interracial love would be offensive to some patrons. One other heroine of the American screen also faced a kissing ban: Marguerite Clark (1881–1940), at one time Mary Pickford's chief rival as 'America's Sweetheart'. In this case the ban was imposed by her husband, Harry Palmerson-Williams, whom she married in 1918. Although she made another dozen films, her career was severely damaged by the marital edict and she retired in 1921.

In 1980 the woman who had bought the vacant vault next to Marilyn Monroe's in Westwood Memorial Park, Los Angeles, decided to put it up for sale. The prospect of spending eternity next to MM proved irresistible to the gentleman who paid the equivalent of £10,500 for the privilege—over ten times the cost of any similar vault at Westwood.

7 Film Making and Film Makers

Animals

The first animal star to appear regularly in films was 'Hepworth Picture Player Rover', an English collie belonging to pioneer producer Cecil Hepworth who made his debut in his master's outstandingly successful low-budget (£7 13s 9d) box-office hit *Rescued by Rover* (GB 05). A simple melodrama about a dog rescuing a baby who has been kidnapped by gypsies, it was in such demand by exhibitors that the negative wore out and the film had to be made twice. Rover, whose real name was Blair, starred in at least seven other films before his death in February 1914. American historian Kenneth Macgowan dryly observed that Rover was the first screen performer who did not overact.

One of the first animals to achieve something akin to 'superstar' status was Strongheart, an ex-Red Cross dog who had served in the trenches in World War I. Strongheart was a consumate screen actor, but had an aversion to being made to howl. According to Lawrence Trimble, who directed Strongheart in most of his films, he would get so depressed that his work would be below par for several days afterwards. Once he had graduated to canine stardom, however, there was little choice but to indulge these displays of temperament. A double would be brought in to do the howling for him.

The largest cast of living creatures in a film were the 22 million bees employed by Irwin Allen in *The Swarm* (US 78).

The largest number of horses ever assembled for a film was 8000 in the case of King Vidor's *War and Peace* (US 56).

ANIMAL CASTS
There have been three full-length fiction films with all-animal casts. *Bill and Coo* (US 48), produced by comedian Ken Murray, was a comedy feature with a cast of Love Birds in miniature sets. Most of Walt Disney's True Life Fantasies were documentaries about wildlife, but *Perri* (US 57) was based on a novel by Felix Salten about the life of a squirrel. There were no credited human performers in *Jonathan Livingstone Seagull* (US 73), though some fishermen in a boat are seen in the opening sequence. Apart from this, the cast was composed entirely of seagulls. The story, adapted from the novel by Richard Bach (who also wrote the screenplay), is a mystical one of a seagull who acquires grace, is killed doing a noble act, rises from the dead and becomes a bird messiah.

Camera and Camerawork

The largest number of cameras used for a single scene was 48 for the sea battle in *Ben Hur* (US 25). Another 42 cameras were employed on the chariot-race scene. Concealed in statues, in pits in the ground, and behind soldiers' shields, the 42 operators took 53,000 ft of film—equivalent to seven full-length features—in a single day.

The practice of using more than one camera on a scene was introduced by D. W. Griffith, who used three for the big fight between Dorothy West and Mabel Normand in *The Squaw's Love* (US 14). The three cameramen on this occasion were Billy Bitzer, P. Higginson and Bobby Harron. The use of multiple cameras was not confined to special scenes in Hollywood's silent days. Nearly all feature films were shot with twin cameras, one supplying the master negative from which all release prints for the domestic market were struck, the other the negative for all overseas prints.

The largest number of cameras used on one film was 160 in the case of *One Day of War* (USSR 42). A feature-length documentary, the film was shot in a single day by 160 newsreel cameramen at the Russian Front and behind the lines.

The widest aperture lens ever used in production of a feature film was f0·7 by cameraman John Alcott on *Barry Lyndon* (GB 75). Developed for the US space

The hit moppet picture *Benji* (US 74), about a dog who rescues two children from kidnappers, was shot mainly at a height of 18 in (46 cm) from the ground—the camera was showing the action from Benji's viewpoint. In Samuel Fuller's *White Dog* (US 84), the story of a dog trained to attack black people, all shots through the eyes of the dog were in black and white—dogs are colour blind.

programme, the lens was fitted to a specially modified camera and employed in filming an interior scene lit only by candlelight.

The first motorised camera (professional) in series production was the all-metal Bell & Howell of 1912, manufactured in the USA with the motor as an optional fitment.

The first British motorised camera was the Aeroscope, invented by Polish cinematographer Kazimierz Prosznski and manufactured in 1913 by Newman & Sinclair. It was used extensively for newsreel work and also by Cherry Kearton for wildlife cinematography.

The first feature film made with a motorised camera was *A Sainted Devil* (US 24) with Rudolph Valentino, which was photographed at Famous Players' Long Island studio by Harry Fishbeck with an electrically-driven camera of unidentified make. Generally cameramen continued to crank by hand throughout the silent era, due to the fact that it enabled action to be speeded up or slowed down at will. The coming of sound rendered hand-cranking impractical, since variations in film speed would have caused a corresponding and unnatural variation in the delivery of synchronised speech.

The earliest known multi-shot scene (different camera positions being used within a single scene) occurs in G. A. Smith's *The Little Doctors* (GB 01), in which there is a cut from a shot of two children administering medicine to a sick kitten to a close-up of the kitten with the spoon in its mouth.

Prior to the recent rediscovery of this film (see *Sight & Sound*, Summer 1978), the innovation had generally been attributed to D. W. Griffith. In *For the Love of Gold* (US 08), Griffith used a medium shot and a three-quarter shot in a card-game scene where he wanted to register the expressions on the gamblers' faces, and this has been credited as the first use of camera movement within a scene. Another recent discovery of the use of close-up (q.v.) shots within a scene in *The Yale Laundry* (US 07), must cast doubt on whether Griffith was the pioneer of the multi-shot scene even as far as the US industry is concerned.

The first panning shots were used by Max Skladanowski in *Komische Begegnung im Tiergarten zu Stockholm* (Ger 96), a short comedy shot on location in Sweden, and by Lumière representative Eugène Promio in *View of St Mark's Square, Venice* (Fr 96), a panorama of the Square taken from a boat on the Grand Canal.

The earliest known British example of a panning shot appears in a news film of Queen Victoria's Diamond Jubilee Procession shot by R. W. Paul with his 'Kinematograph' camera on 20 June 1897. The camera was mounted on a specially designed tripod with a swivel head. The first in an acted film, a panning shot of Epsom Downs, opens Alfred Collins' *Welshed, a Derby Day Incident* (GB 03).

The first 360° panning shot was made by Edwin S. Porter in *Circular Panorama of the Electric Tower* (US 01), in which the whole of the exhibition grounds of the Pan-American Exposition at Buffalo, NY are seen as the camera slowly revolves. Porter used a geared mounting of his own design for this effect.

The first use of a 360° pan in a full-length dramatic film was by James Whale in *Frankenstein* (US 31), and the following year Rouben Mamoulian employed the technique in *Dr Jekyll and Mr Hyde* (US 32) to give an effect of vertigo during the transformation scene.

No example of a 360° pan is known in any silent feature-film.

Other films with 360° pans are *Rain* (US 32), *La Signora di Tutti* (It 34), *La Strada* (It 54), *Lola Montes* (Fr/FRG 55), *Judgement at Nuremberg* (US 61), *The Manchurian Candidate* (US 62), *Providence* (FR/Swz 77), *Riddles of the Sphinx* (GB 77), *The Swarm* (US 78), *Eagle's Wing* (GB 79) and Mai Zetterling's *Scrubbers* (GB 82). *Laughter in the Dark* (GB 69) had a double 360° pan, while Brian de Palma's *Obsession* (US 76) is notable for both a 360° pan and a 540° pan. The latter shot shows all four walls of a room entered by Genevieve Bujold, then pans on past the door to pick her up on the side opposite.

The first slow-motion film was made in 1898 by Berlin cinematographer Oskar Messter, using a specially constructed high-speed 60 mm camera of his own design. Among the earliest sequences filmed with this camera was one that showed a cat falling off a wall, with a Hipp millisecond watch inset in one corner to indicate the rate of descent. This was shot at 66 frames a second—over four times normal speed—though the camera was capable of filming at speeds of up to 100 frames a second.

The technique has had its widest application in sports and scientific films. The earliest practical application of slow-motion cinematography was for the purpose of gauging the breaking strain of girders, according to Hopwood's *Living Pictures*, published in 1899.

The time lapse technique was pioneered by Oskar Messter of Berlin, who filmed the blooming and wilting of a flower in 1897. The lapse factor was 1500 frames per 24 hours.

The earliest known American example is a 1902 American Mutoscope & Biograph subject of the demolition of New York's Star Theater.

The earliest known wipe appears in G. A. Smith's *Mary Jane's Mishap: or, Don't Fool with the Paraffin* (GB 03), in which Mary Jane does and is blown out of the chimney. A line moving across the screen 'wiped' away the scene of her unfortunate demise and replaced it with one of her forlorn grave. Hitherto the introduction of the wipe has generally been attributed to Georges Méliès in *La Royaume des fées* (Fr 03), but Dr Barry Salt of the Slade School has established that this is a misconception. What looks like a wipe between scenes is in fact no more than the lifting of a backdrop.

The only full-length feature film to have been made without a camera was Barcelona artist José Antonio Sistiaga's remarkable 75-minute animated one-man production in Cinemascope *Ere Ereva Baleibu Icik Subua Arvaren/Scope, Colour, Muda* (Sp 70). Completed in 17 months between October 1968 and February 1970, Sistiaga painted each frame of the film separately and single-handed direct on to the filmstock.

The first close-up was a study of a man called Fred Ott sneezing, copyrighted on 7 January 1894 as *Edison Kinetoscopic Record of a Sneeze* (US 94).

The first close-up in a British film was a 50 ft study of a man enjoying a glass of beer, made by G. A. Smith of Brighton and released under the alternative titles of *Comic Face* and *Man Drinking* in September 1897. The man was played by Tom Green. Both the Edison film and Smith's film consisted of a single shot.

The first known film in which close-ups are interpolated with other shots is *Grandma's Reading Glass* (GB 00). A small boy is seen focusing a magnifying glass on various objects, including a watch, a newspaper, canary, kitten and Grandma's eye. These appear in close-up as seen by the boy, probably the earliest use of the subjective camera technique. The identity of the film-maker who pioneered the interpolated close-up is disputed. The film has generally been attributed to G. A. Smith of Brighton (see above), but Mrs Audrey Wadowska claims that it was made by her father, Arthur Melbourne Cooper of St Albans, and that the roles of Grandma and the small boy were played by Miss Bertha Melbourne Cooper and Master Bert Massey.

The earliest known interpolated close-ups in an American film are contained in American Mutoscope and Biograph's *Grandpa's Reading Glass* (US 02), a film so similar to the Smith/Melbourne Cooper subject above that it was almost certainly a plagiarism—common practice in the early days of filmmaking. The objects viewed by the grandchildren in this film are a bird, a printed page, the eye of a child, the head of an adult woman, the head of an infant, the head of a girl child holding a kitten, and a monkey.

Close-ups of inanimate objects or of hands or feet were not unusual in American films of the early years of the century, particularly in the productions of the American Mutoscope and Biograph Co. (AM & B). Examples include the fire alarm box in Edison's *The Life of an American Fireman* (US 03), a girl's pretty foot in Edison's *The Gay Shoe Clerk* (US 03), the contents of a jewel case in AM & B's *The Great Jewel Mystery* (US 05), gifts in AM & B's *The Silver Wedding* (US 06) and a newspaper article in AM & B's *Trial Marriages* (US 07). Facial close-ups were rarer, though the opening scenes of AM & B's *The Widow and the Only Man* (US 04) introduce the two principal characters with separate close-ups. The persistent claim of D. W. Griffith to have been the only begetter of the close-up—he even went so far as to suggest he could have patented the technique—has now been rejected by most film historians, though many still credit him with having been the first to employ the interpolated facial close-up as a dramatic device to register emotion. Even this had been accomplished a year before Griffith entered the film industry. In the AM & B production *The Yale Laundry* (US 07), a comedy about students at Yale playing a jape on their professors, close-ups are used to show surprise on the faces of the victims. It is precisely this technique of advancing the narrative by means of a close-up shot that Griffith was later to claim as his innovation and his alone. There is a certain irony in the fact that it had been used earlier by an uncredited director of the very company with which Griffith was to establish his reputation. The great director also seems to have overlooked the fact that he himself was the subject of a close-up when he played the part of a clown in *At the French Ball* (US 08), a film made shortly before his directorial debut at Biograph.

Despite the pioneering efforts of the Edison Co., AM & B and 'the Brighton school' (in England), elsewhere the notion that a film should give its audience the same view as a theatre audience received of the stage persisted for many years. As late as 1911 the leading production company in Scandinavia, Nordisk Film, was using a 16 ft long pole attached to the camera as an indication to the actors that they must come no closer. Albert E. Smith recalled that about this period at Vitagraph the actors were always positioned nine yards in front of the camera. Mary Pickford, who claimed that she had been the subject of 'the first close-up' in D. W. Griffith's *Friends* (US 12), said that the 'front office' at Biograph had vigorously protested at the idea on the grounds that audiences were paying to see the whole of the performer, not only the top half.

The closest close-up occurs in *A Farewell to Arms* (US 32). In one shot the camera was 2 in (5 cm) from Helen Hayes's eyes.

The longest close-up is to be seen in *Daaera* (Ind 53) and lasts 6½ minutes.

The first zoom lens was used by cameraman Victor Milner on Rouben Mamoulian's *Love Me Tonight* (US 32). There are two zoom shots in the 'Paris waking' sequence and one in the hunting sequence.

It was many years before zoom lenses became generally available and sometimes considerable ingenuity was exercised to obtain the same effect. Jacques Sigurd wanted the last shot of *Une si jolie petite plage* (Fr 48) to be of the hero and heroine on the beach with the camera tracking away from them until they were merely specks in the distance. He was unable to hire a helicopter and a trolley would have left tracks in the sand. His eventual solution was to have the camera moving forwards, the two performers walking backwards, and the film upside down in the camera.

The earliest recorded use of the telephoto lens (invented in 1891) with a cinematograph camera was by W. K. L. Dickson, the Biograph cameraman covering the Boer War in 1900. Dickson recorded in *The Biograph in Battle* (London 1901) how he had sought to film the Boer positions with a telephoto, an attempt frustrated by poor visibility caused by haze.

The first dissolve from one scene to another was used by Georges Méliès in *Cendrillon* (Fr 99).

The earliest known American example is to be seen in the Edison Co.'s *Life Rescue at Long Beach* (US 01), a 2½-minute drama in five scenes about the rescue of a young lady from drowning. The dissolve effects a transition from the fourth scene, in which the lifeguards are reviving the prostrate maiden, to the climax, in which, fully recovered, she embraces her rescuers. The film is believed to have been directed by Edwin S. Porter, better remembered for *The Life of an American Fireman* (US 03) and *The Great Train Robbery* (US 03).

The first camera dolly was used by British pioneer cinematographer R. W. Paul at the studio he built at New Southgate in 1899. In a lecture he gave before the British Kinematographers' Society in 1936, Paul recalled: 'A trolley mounted on rails carried the camera, which could thus be set at any required distance from the stage, to suit the subject. Sometimes the trolley was run to and from the stage while the picture was being taken, thus giving a gradual enlargement or reduction of the image of the film.' It is not known whether Paul's dolly dates from the opening of the New Southgate studios, but a photograph taken in 1902 shows it in use.

The first use of a camera dolly in a feature film was by Spanish cameraman Segundo de Chomon for Giovanni Pastrone's *Cabiria* (It 14). De Chomon had developed his dolly while working for Pathé in Paris (1906–10) and Pastrone patented it in Italy in 1912.

The dolly arrived in America comparatively late, no examples of its use being known before 1915. Tracking shots were used in two feature films that year, by Alan Dwan on *David Harum* (US 15) to follow the hero as he walks down the street of his small hometown, and by William Bowman in *The Second-in-Command* (US 15). On this film, cameraman William F. Alder employed two dollies, one for forward and backward tracking and the other for sideways movement. This was a notable innovation which did not come to its full fruition until Chinese-born James Wong Howe introduced the 'crab dolly'—a dolly that moves in any direction, including sideways and diagonally—on *The Rough Riders* (US 27).

Britain, having pioneered the dolly, then completely forgot about it until the end of the silent era.

The first use of 'mobile camera' in a feature film was by Graham Cutts on Gainsborough-Piccadilly's *The Triumph of the Rat* (GB 26), with Ivor Novello.

Camera mobility could be achieved without the use of a dolly. F. W. Murnau overcame the problem of how to depict Emil Jannings' drunken view of the wedding feast in *The Last Laugh* (Ger 25) by mounting his cameraman on roller skates. When Sidney Franklin decided to use a hand-held Bell & Howell Eyemo camera on *Quality Street* (US 27), he emulated Murnau's example, but here the scene was not a drunken one and the camera had to be kept steady. The solution was to have an assistant pushing the roller-skated cameraman from behind. James Wong Howe also found roller-skates the answer for the prize fight scene in *Body and Soul* (US 47), but on *He Ran All the Way* (US 51) he needed higher camera angles. A squatting camera operator could not roller-skate, so Howe found another expedient—the cameraman was pushed in a wheelchair.

The hidden camera was pioneered simultaneously in the USSR and USA in 1924. Concealed cameras were used by Russia's master of the newsreel, Dziga Vertov, in making his feature-length documentary about everyday life in the early Soviet state, *Kino-Eye* (USSR 24). Cameraman Mikhail Kaufman filmed open air scenes at Pioneer camps, in markets, at stations, etc., as well as interiors of low life in bars, cafes and thieves kitchens, without his subjects ever being aware of the camera. In America a hidden camera was used by Erich von Stroheim for the scene in *Greed* (US 24) in which Trina rushes out of the junk shop after finding a murdered body. The film was made entirely on location and it was a real street into which ZaSu Pitts dashes distractedly, grabbing the arms of real passers-by as she shrieks her awful news. The reaction of those unwittingly involved was, as von Stroheim hoped, totally believable, as they registered horror and alarm before rushing for help.

These pioneer efforts were followed by a number of other noted uses of hidden camerawork during the twenties. George Webber filmed exterior scenes for *Night Life of New York* (US 25) from a van parked in the streets of the city. Most of *Berlin, Symphony of a Great City* (Ger 27) was filmed in this way by Karl Freund, but where a van was impracticable he concealed the camera in a suitcase, using a special film-stock that he had hypersensitised himself in order to shoot in poor lighting conditions. King Vidor shot most of the New York exteriors for *The Crowd* (US 28) with a hidden camera.

The first British film made with hidden cameras was *Knave of Hearts*/US: *Lovers, Happy Lovers* (GB 54). Director René Clément took the camera out into the streets of London wrapped as a paper bundle, filming at Charing Cross Station in the rush hour and amongst the crowds at Piccadilly Circus.

The first double exposure was accomplished by Georges Méliès in *La Caverne maudite/The Cave of the Demons* (Fr 98), employing the technique of 'spirit photography'. The evil inhabitants of the cave were first filmed against a black backdrop, so that the background was not exposed, then the film was wound back and the cave setting filmed. The effect was of 'ghost' characters superimposed against a solid background.

The more normal use of double exposure was to achieve the effect of two characters played by the same performer appearing on screen simultaneously. This was done by 'duplex cinematography', also pioneered by Georges Méliès and at about the same time as the film above. Méliès adapted a technique already well known to still photographers, by which a small frame enclosing two swing doors was mounted in front of the camera lens. When one door was opened, half the scene was exposed on film. The film was then wound back, one door shut and the other opened, and the rest of the scene shot. If the same performer was filmed each time, he or she would appear to be two characters interacting. Méliès' first attempt at this technique was in *Un Homme de tête/The Four Troublesome Heads* (Fr 98), which shows a magician removing his head three times over and in which he used a combination of both spirit photography and duplex photography.

The first physical contact between two characters played by the same person was accomplished in *Little Lord Fauntleroy* (US 21) when Mary Pickford played both the boy and his mother 'Dearest'. Cameraman Charles Rosher used a 2000 lb camera to achieve absolute steadiness between one take and the next, but the exact details of his extraordinarily advanced technique are still not known. The preparations for each double exposure were amongst the most meticulous and precise in the history of camerawork. It took 15 hours to shoot the scene in which the boy kisses 'Dearest' on the cheek, a take which lasts three seconds on the screen. In another scene they embrace and, in the most spectacular of all, the Little Lord runs and jumps into his mother's arms. The complexity of the operation was enhanced by the fact that Mary Pickford the mother had to be nine inches taller than Mary Pickford the boy. For her adult role in the double exposure scenes she was given platform heels and stood on a concealed ramp, a hazardous operation since she fell off on a number of occasions.

> The attempted suicide of Alex (Malcolm McDowell) in *A Clockwork Orange* (GB 71) was achieved by throwing a Newman Sinclair camera off the top of a building. On the sixth take the camera landed downward as intended. The lens was smashed, but the camera was found to be still in perfect working order.

Mary Pickford greets Mary Pickford in *Little Lord Fauntleroy* (US 21). Note the physical contact.

Double exposure was temporarily abandoned when sound came in, because of the difficulty of post-synching. **The first double exposure with dialogue** was a scene in Fox Movietone's *Masquerade* (US 29) in which Alan Burmingham carried on a conversation with another character also played by Alan Burmingham.

The first triple exposure was achieved by cameraman Al Siegler in Universal's *The Twins' Double* (US 14), in which Grace Cunard played the twin heroines and the villainess, their double—all three characters appearing on the screen at the same time.

The first quadruple exposure was of Dorothy Dalton as four different characters all seen at once in the promo short *Trip to Paramountown* (US 22).

Nowadays multiple exposures tend to be used for naturalistic special effects rather than the trick of showing the same person simultaneously performing more than one role. A **septuple exposure** was used in *Star Trek* (US 79) for the elaborate sequence in which the starship *Enterprise* first approaches the alien invaders. The different exposures, which included shots of the spacecraft, fog, yellow lights, a star-field and cloud effects, were combined in a scene which occupied only 30 seconds of screen time but 48 hours of filming.

Back projection was first employed successfully by director Willis O'Brien for a single scene in *The Lost World* (US 25). It is a technique by which outdoor scenes can be shot in the studio by placing the actors against a rear projected filmed background. The following year back projection was used in the making of *Metropolis* (Ger 26), but it was slow to catch on because of the technical difficulties involved. The breakthrough came with the development of the Teague Back Projector, which was employed for the first time on the Fox production *Just Imagine* (US 30), a science-fiction film set in 1980. Back projection was used to depict a city of the future, with stars Maureen O'Sullivan and John Garrick coasting along in their private aircraft in the foreground.

Back projection in colour was first used by William Wellman on *Nothing Sacred* (US 37).

The first camera crane was used by cameraman William F. Alder for obtaining elevated shots in Metro's *The Second in Command* (US 15), with Francis X. Bushman. At about the same time Allan Dwan devised a more sophisticated elevator on tracks for

use in the Babylonian sequence of D. W. Griffith's *Intolerance* (US 16). The 115 ft (35 m) high structure enabled Griffith to secure a parabolic shot, commencing at the ramparts of the Palace and descending forwards over a sea of extras to ground level and a close shot of the leading players. These early uses of the crane were exceptional. It was not until F. W. Murnau introduced his 20-ton, 200-hp 'Go-Devil' on *The Four Devils* (US 29), and the appearance of an even larger 28-ton apparatus with a 60 ft (18·3 m) elevation on the set of *Broadway* (US 29), that the crane came to be regarded as standard studio equipment.

The first woman cameraman was Rosina Cianelli, who made her camera debut with Paolo Benedetti's *Uma transformista original* (Bra 09), a Méliès-style trick film made at Barbacena, Brazil, with the Lazzari brothers as stars.

The first American camerawoman was Grace Davison, who joined the Astor Film Corp. at its Long Island studios as an actress in 1915 but was taught to handle a camera by veteran Harry Fishbeck. Miss

---

Camera cranes were rare before the advent of the talkies. This 28-ton monster was used by Universal for the filming of *Broadway* (US 29).

Davison photographed *The Honeymooners* (US 15), *Spring Onions* (US 15) and other one-reel comedies.

The first camerawoman to shoot a feature film was Tamara Lobova, who worked on *Suvorov* (USSR 41) together with her husband Anatolij Golovnja. First with a solo camera credit was Galina Pyshkova for *Songs of Abay* (USSR 46).

Chase Sequences

The most destructive chase sequence in a motion picture occurred in H. B. Halicki's *The Junkman* (US 82), in which the mayhem involved the wrecking of over 150 vehicles including two Cadillac Eldorados, two Chrysler Magnums, numerous boats, trucks and motorcycles and two Pitts high-performance aeroplanes.

Costume

The largest number of costumes in any one film was 32,000 for *Quo Vadis* (US 51). *Waterloo* (It/USSR 70) used 29,000 costumes and *Cleopatra* (US 63) 26,000 costumes.

The largest number of costume changes by one performer was by Elizabeth Taylor in *Cleopatra* (US 63). The 65 costumes designed by Irene Sharaff for Miss Taylor cost $130,000. Another 40 costumes and head-dresses designed by Oliver Messel at a cost of $64,800 did not appear in the movie as released.

The largest number of costume changes in a silent movie was 50 by Theda Bara in the course of the eleven reels of *Cleopatra* (US 17).

The most expensive costume ever worn in a movie was the barzucine sable coat that enfolded Constance Bennett in *Madame X* (US 65). It was valued at $50,000.

The most expensive costume designed and made specially for a film was Edith Head's mink and sequins dance costume for Ginger Rogers in *Lady in the Dark* (US 44), which cost Paramount $35,000. By comparison, Elizabeth Taylor's dress of cloth-of-24-carat-gold in which she made her entry into Rome in *Cleopatra* (US 63) cost a modest $6500. However, the total cost of Miss Taylor's wardrobe, which amounted to $194,800, was **the highest sum ever expended on costumes for a single performer in any one film**.

The most expensive single costume of the silent era was made for Mary Pickford to wear in the title role of *Dorothy Vernon of Haddon Hall* (US 24). A sumptuous Elizabethan gown embroidered with real seed pearls, it was designed by Mitchell Leisen at a cost of $32,000.

At the other end of the scale, costumes could cost next to nothing even in Hollywood's most extravagant days; except for the studios' insistence that nothing was worthwhile unless it was expensive. When a rough, workaday costume was needed for Ingrid Bergman in *For Whom the Bell Tolls* (US 43), designer Edith Head selected an old pair of men's trousers and a shirt from the extra's wardrobe. Producer David O Selznick was incensed and demanded that Miss Head should design a new costume. She did so, copying the old garments exactly, then bleaching them and dying them to look as worn as the originals.

The record spent on costumes in relation to budget was the $1 million plus for wardrobe in the $7 million production *Chanel Solitaire* (US 81), a biopic of the legendary French fashion designer Coco Chanel.

The largest costume collection in the world is owned by Western Costume Co. and housed in a six-storey building at 5335 Melrose Avenue, Hollywood, California. The collection consists of approximately one million costumes valued at over $50 million.

Western Costume was established in Los Angeles in 1912. In a curious way its fortune could be said to have been founded on dietary deficiency. Business was slow until a major break came with D. W. Griffith's order for all the Civil War costumes for *The Birth of a Nation* (US 15). Griffith, preoccupied with authenticity, had hoped to use genuine uniforms of the period, but found that progress in nutrition over

Probably the only instance in movie history where the costumes worn by the star were designed by the character she portrayed. Ginger Rogers' dresses in *The Story of Vernon and Irene Castle* (US 39) were specially created for the film by Irene Castle herself.

the intervening 50 years had made the average actor of 1914 too large to fit the average soldier's uniform of the 1860s.

The largest costume collection in Europe is held by Berman and Nathan's of London, who have a stock of over 700,000 costumes.

CHAPLIN'S TRAMP COSTUME

The costume was devised in response to Mack Sennett's request that he 'get into a comedy make-up' for *Kid Auto Races at Venice* (US 14). Chaplin created the costume in a dressing room where Fatty Arbuckle and Chester Conklin were playing pinochle. The moustache was a scrap of crêpe hair borrowed from Mack Swain; the trousers were Fatty Arbuckle's—hence the bagginess—and the Derby came from Minta Durfee's father, Fatty's father-in-law; the cut-away coat belonged to Chester Conklin (or Charlie Avery, according to one account); the size 14 shoes were Ford Sterling's and Chaplin had to wear them on the wrong feet to keep them on. Only the whangee cane belonged to Charlie himself.

Chaplin gave the original costume to his assistant Harry Crocker in 1928 as a central exhibit in the newly-opened Crocker Museum of props and costumes on Sunset Boulevard.

FASHION AND THE MOVIES

Movie costumes began to influence fashion as early as 1912, when it was reported that the natives of Tahiti had become so addicted to westerns that they had taken to wearing stetsons. A rather more far-reaching fashion was initiated by D. W. Griffith when he invented the first pair of false eyelashes in order to give Seena Owen's eyes an abnormally large and lustrous appearance for her role as Princess Beloved in *Intolerance* (US 16). They were made by a wigmaker who wove human hair through the warp of a 24-inch strip of thin gauze. Each day two small pieces were cut from the end of the strip and gummed to Miss Owen's eyelids.

Bessie Barriscale caused a sensation with the backless evening gown she wore in *Josselyn's Wife* (US 19) and soon the middle classes were aping a fashion formerly displayed only by their betters. All classes followed the trend to bobbed hair, which became the style of the twenties after Colleen Moore had created the archetypal flapper role in *Flaming Youth* (US 23). Pola Negri was not only the first to go barelegged and sandalled in summer, but was also the first to paint her toenails. She recalled that when she first did this in about 1923, using a bright red polish, a woman glanced down at her feet and shrieked 'She's bleeding'. Nevertheless, within a few weeks, Miss Negri claimed, women everywhere were lacquering their toenails. Joan Crawford was the first to go barelegged with evening clothes in 1926. She stated that she never wore stockings between then and 1930, when long

dresses returned to fashion. Bare legs for ordinary 'streetwear' were pioneered by blonde starlet Rita Carewe in 1927. To preserve the proprieties, however, Miss Carewe had her legs *polished* to give the impression that she was wearing silk stockings.

Bejeaned teenagers might have made an earlier appearance but for the obduracy of D. W. Griffith. About 1914, 16-year-old Dorothy Gish became the first screen star and one of the first women in America to adopt jeans. She never wore them in films, however, and only once to the studio; a stern message to her mother from Griffith prevented such a solecism from ever being repeated. Another ten years were to pass before a woman wearing trousers as an article of feminine apparel (as opposed to male impersonation costume) appeared on screen in the person of Myrna Loy in *What Price Beauty* (US 24). This seems to have had little impact upon fashion at the time and it was not until Louise Brooks took to wearing silk trousers (indoors only) in 1927 that the practice became accepted amongst the more sophisticated followers of filmdom's fashion decrees. The real breakthrough for emancipated womanhood, though, had to await the release of von Sternberg's *Morocco* (US 30), in which Marlene Dietrich concealed her celebrated legs in slacks. Von Sternberg's purpose was to emphasise the lesbian characterisation of the role, but the innovation was imitated by the women of America to an extent that suggests its implication was wholly lost on them.

Probably the single most influential trendsetter, and the star who made least effort to be one, was Garbo. The enormous fur collars of the twenties owed their genesis to the broad collar designed by Max Ree to conceal her long neck in *The Torrent* (US 26). Garbo's berets, which she wore off-screen, became a universal fashion of the thirties and made a come-back in the sixties after Faye Dunaway had worn one as the thirties woman gangster in *Bonnie and Clyde* (US 67). The diagonally placed Eugénie hat, dipping over one eye, worn by Garbo in *Romance* (US 30), hastened the end of the cloche and introduced the basic configuration that was to dominate hat styles throughout the thirties. Although most fashion design of the period reflected a conscious rejection of the past, Adrian's Eugénie hat was created for a film that was set in the 1850s.

The other major trendsetter of the period was Joan Crawford, whom women fans watched spellbound as she suffered in mink. While her taste in furs was beyond the reach of the majority, the padded-shoulder costume Adrian designed for her to wear in *Today We Live* (US 33) started the vogue for tailored suits that sloped upwards from the neck. Crawford herself was so enamoured with the style that she went on wearing padded shoulders long after they had gone out of general fashion.

By this time the big studios were co-operating with the garment trade—most of the moguls had come

NEW MOODS
of the
MODE

ERMINE proves the perfect link between soft white shoulders and a sweeping black velvet gown that falls to a double "fishtail" train. Ermine tails and a diamond clip give chic to the décolletage. Heather Angel is posed—the lovely Fox film star whose latest picture is "Orient Express." S.21 (Below)

●

Full information about paper patterns for making these six models will be found on page 38.

CHINESE symbols in yellow, red, and silver say inscrutable things on this brown tunic frock with the vivid sash and sleeve linings of yellow crêpe. Adele Thomas, the charming Radio Pictures player, is seriously contemplating the study of Chinese! F.64 (Above)

●

THE daringly low décolletage that has just appeared, to create a revolution in the fashion world. Here it gives an additional thrill to a gown of silver lamé. Note the dramatic belt and bracelets which emphasize Fashion's liking for massive jewellery. The wearer is Carole Lombard, Paramount star. S.20 (Left)

from that industry themselves—so that the costumes designed for the new genre of 'women's pictures' could be in the shops by the time the film was released. It was another Adrian creation for Joan Crawford that began this mass marketing of star costumes, the celebrated *Letty Lynton* dress which she wore in the film of the same name (US 32). Over half a million copies were sold by Macy's of New York alone. The success of the venture encouraged its development. In 1933 a leading department store in Columbus, Ohio called Morehouse Martens 'completed an arrangement by which copies of movie stars' clothes are on sale at the store prior to or coincident with the opening of their pictures'. The initial offerings were a Joan Blondell double-duty dress, a Jean Arthur frock and Claire Dodd pyjamas. The same year Bamberger's of Newark, NJ opened a 'Cinema Shop' devoted exclusively to copies of the clothes worn by stars, and their lead was followed by other major stores from coast to coast, including such noted names as the Hecht Co. of Washington, Goldsmith's of Chicago, Joseph Horne of Pittsburgh ('The Hollywood Shop') and the May Co. of Los Angeles. The desire to look like the stars was no less fervent in Britain, where a magazine devoted to the subject with the title *Film Fashionland* was started in 1934.

Generally, the adoption of a movie fashion brought fortunes either to the designer or to the entrepreneur who succeeded in adapting it to a mass market. The star who launched the style seldom derived any direct benefit, with the notable exception of Shirley Temple. The astute business sense of Mrs Temple ensured that when Fox sold the manufacturing rights to Shirley's party dresses from *Baby Takes a Bow* (US 35), it was Shirley who garnered the lion's share of the profits.

What stars did not wear could sometimes have as much impact on fashion trends as what they did wear. When Clark Gable opened his shirt to reveal a bare and matted torso in *It Happened One Night* (US 34), men's undershirt sales took a 40 per cent dive. Mae West also enjoyed a quite unlooked for effect on fashion, if the Kansas Restaurant Association is to be believed. In 1934 the Association publicly thanked Miss West for stemming the dieting craze stimulated by the sylph-like figures of Dietrich, Crawford and Harlow and for restoring well-rounded curves to healthy US women.

Hollywood also played its part in bringing an exotic touch to American fashion. When Dorothy Lamour wore the first of her celebrated series of sarongs in *Jungle Princess* (US 36), it generated a demand for tropical fabrics that lasted for the next ten years. The Latin-American look that swept the USA in the early forties was instigated by Edith Head's costumes for Barbara Stanwyck in *The Lady Eve* (US 41), and Charles

Anyone could dress like the stars if they were handy with needle and thread. *Film Fashionland* supplied the paper patterns.

LeMaire's designs for Jennifer Jones in *Love is a Many Splendoured Thing* (US 55) began a trend towards oriental fashion.

The decline of the cinema as a cultural force has reduced its fashion impact in the west, but in the orient, where cinema-going continues to increase, it appears to be breaking down traditional prejudices against western modes of dress. Significant of the trend are recent reports that jeans are now being worn by Indian women since Zeenat Aman, number one at the box office, began appearing in them in public.

Directors

The first director—The functions of director and producer were first separated for America's earliest 'spectacle' film *The Passion Play* (US 98). Rich G. Hollaman, the producer, engaged a distinguished stage director, L. J. Vincent of Niblo's Garden Theatre in New York, to direct the picture. Unfortunately, America's first movie director had never seen a movie and nothing could persuade him that the camera was capable of reproducing live action. Convinced that he had been engaged to direct a succession of lantern-slide tableaux, he would rush out on to the set whenever the performance of a scene was progressing favourably and scream 'Hold it!' The film was eventually made by subterfuge. Each afternoon cameraman William Paley would declare that the light was no longer strong enough to continue and as soon as Vincent had departed the actors would reassemble and shoot as much as possible before dark. The two-reel drama was a sensation when it was premièred at the Eden Musée on 30 January 1898, but it is difficult to know whether it would be more accurately described as the first film made by a professional director or the first dramatic film made with no director at all.

The first woman director was Alice Guy (1873–1968), originally secretary to Léon Gaumont, who was given an opportunity to direct after she had complained at the lack of variety in Gaumont productions. She made her debut with *La Fée aux choux*, about a young couple walking in the countryside who encounter a fairy in a cabbage patch and are presented with a child. The film is usually said to date from 1896, but since it is listed No. 370 in the Gaumont catalogue it seems more likely that it was made *c*. 1900. Mlle Guy was Gaumont's sole director of dramatic films until Zecca joined the studios at La Villette in 1905. In 1907 she emigrated to the USA, and founded the Solax Co. on Long Island three years later. Between 1919 and 1922 she directed for Pathé and Metro, then returned to France. Despite her long experience, she was unable to find work as a director in her own country and made a living writing stories based on film scenarios for pulp magazines.

The world's first woman director, Alice Guy, on the set of her first movie *La Fée aux choux* (Fr c. 1900).

The first feature film directed by a woman was the Rex production of *The Merchant of Venice* (US 14), which had Lois Weber as director. Miss Weber was also **the first American woman director**, starting with Gaumont Talking Pictures in New York in 1907, then working for Reliance in 1908, for Rex 1909–13, for the Bosworth Co. 1914–15 and for Universal 1915–19, after which she went independent. Her best known picture was Universal's highly successful *Where Are My Children?* (US 16), a treatise on birth control. As her films became increasingly controversial, she had difficulty in obtaining distribution, and her last picture, *White Heat* (US 34), about miscegenation, was not released.

Sharon Smith, in *Women Who Make Movies* (New York 75), has listed 36 women directors who were active in the United States during the silent era and believes there were others who directed anonymously. The only one to make the transition to sound was Dorothy Arzner, whose *Manhattan Cocktail* (US 28) was **the first talkie directed by a woman**. At the height of her career in the thirties she was listed as one of Hollywood's top ten directors.

The first woman to direct a British production was Jakidawdra Melford, who made her directorial debut with a highwayman picture called *The Inn on the Heath* (GB 14). The first feature by a woman was Dinah Shurey's *Carry On!* (GB 27), a naval war drama, and the first talkie was Elinor Glyn's *Knowing Men* (GB 30).

The first director to direct himself in a full-length feature film was Harold Heath, who played the lead in Anchor Films' detective thriller *£1000 Reward* (GB 13).

The first black American director to direct a film aimed at multi-racial audiences was Melvin van Peebles, former San Francisco cable-car gripman, who made his directorial debut with *La Permission/The Story of a Three Day Pass* (Fr 67). Based on van Peebles' own novel, *The Pass*, it related the story of a black GI on a three-day furlough who has a brief affair with a Parisian shop girl. His first American movie was *The Watermelon Man* (US 70), in which Godfrey Cambridge portrays the white insurance salesman who wakes up one morning to find he has turned black.

The first black American to direct an American film at a major studio was former *Life* photographer Gordon Parks, who directed *The Learning Tree* (US 69) for Warner Bros.

For **the first black director of black films** see p. 49.

The first black African director was Paulin Soumanou Vieyra, born in Dahomey in 1925, who made his directorial debut with *Afrique sur Seine* (Sen 55).

The first director to make a film on percentage was D. W. Griffith, who made *The Birth of a Nation* (US 15) while earning his regular $300 a week with Majestic and was offered $37\frac{1}{2}$ per cent of net profits after the film had been completed.

The first director to earn a million dollars for a single picture was Mike Nichols for *The Graduate* (US 67).

The longest directorial career lasted for 66 years in the case of King Vidor (1894–1982), beginning with a two-reel comedy about auto-racing called *The Tow* (US 14), filmed at Galveston, Texas, where he grew up, and culminating in another short, a documentary about painting called *The Metaphor* (US 80). Vidor's feature-film career had begun with a Christian Science melodrama titled *The Turn of the Road* (US 18), which oddly enough had been financed to the tune of $9000 by a consortium of ten doctors. Between this and his last feature, *Solomon and Sheba* (US 59), came such notable milestones in movie history as *The Big Parade* (US 25)—the most profitable silent film ever made (see p. 36)—his greatest artistic success *The Crowd* (US 28), the first major all-black movie *Hallelujah* (US 29)—see p. 49—a classic tear-jerker *The Champ* (US 31), and a beautifully crafted adaptation of A. J. Cronin's novel *The Citadel* (GB 38) with Robert Donat. Vidor was a romantic, both on and off screen. Looking for a female lead for his first rather primitive comedy *The Tow*, he saw a beautiful girl passing in the back of a car. When he tracked her down, her father refused to let her debase herself in motion pictures. Vidor was determined to secure her services as an actress, but he had also fallen in love with her. They married and she became a major star of the silent screen as Florence Vidor.

The most prolific British director was Darlington-born Maurice Elvey (1887–1967), who directed 149 full-length features from *Her Luck in London* (GB 14) to *Second Fiddle* (GB 57). In addition he directed 41 shorts (mainly two-reelers) from *The Fallen Idol* (GB 13).

The most co-directors on a single film was 16 in the case of *I misteri di Roma* (It 63), an anti-establishment view of 'one day in the life of the city' directed by

---

Below left

Alfred Hitchcock co-directed his first film in 1923 and made his solo directorial debut two years later with *The Pleasure Garden* (GB 25), a searing melodrama set in Africa about a dancer marrying a drunkard who tries to kill her after drowning his native mistress. He made his last film, *The Family Plot* (US 76), 50 years later.

Below right

Hollywood's most prolific director of all time was William Beaudine, begetter of 182 not very distinguished features and a host of shorts. Among them was this curiosity, *The Mad Parade* (US 31), the first full-length feature with an all-female cast, and a war film at that!

Gianni Bisiach, Libero Bozzari, Mario Carbone, Angelo D'Alessandro, Nino del Fra, Luigi di Gianni, Giuseppe Ferrara, Ansano Giannarelli, Guilo Macchi, Lori Mazzetti, Massimo Mida, Enzo Mutti, Piero Nelli, Paolo Nuzzi, Dino Partesano and Giovanni Vento.

Deutschland in Herbst (FRG 78), *Love for Everyone* (Chn 42) and *Paramount on Parade* (US 30) each had eleven directors; *Dreams of Thirteen* (FRG/Neth 74) had ten; *If I Had a Million* (US 32) and *Forever and a Day* (US 43) had seven. All the foregoing were either non-fiction or episodic fiction films. The most directors on a straight fiction film was seven for *Casino Royale* (GB 67), a Bond movie directed by John Huston, Ken Hughes, Val Guest, Robert Parrish, Joe McGrath, Richard Talmadge and Anthony Squire.

The youngest director of a professionally-made feature film was Lev Kuleshov (1899–1970), who was $17\frac{1}{2}$ when he embarked on his four-reel *Proyekt inzhenera Praita/Engineer Prite's Project* (USSR 18) at the Khanzhonkov Studios in Moscow. The only other teenage directors have been Japan's Masahiro Makino, who made his directorial debut in 1927 at the age of 18; George Palmer, $17\frac{1}{2}$, of Melbourne,

DIRECTORS WITH A CAREER SPANNING HALF A CENTURY

ABEL GANCE (1889–1982) 60 years from *La Digue* (Fr 11) to *Bonaparte et la Révolution* (Fr 71).

GRIGORI ALEXANDRANOV (1903–83) 59 years from *The Battleship Potemkin* (USSR 25), co-directed with Sergei Eisenstein, to *Lubov Orlova* (USSR 84).

YULI RAIZMAN (1908?–) 58 years from *A Circle* (USSR 27). Still active.

MANOEL DE OLIVEIRA (1908–) 54 years from *Douru, Faina Fluvial* (Por 31). Still active.

JOHN FORD (1895–1973) 54 years from *Lucille Love—The Girl of Mystery* (US 14) to *Vietnam, Vietnam* (US 68).

ALFRED HITCHCOCK (1899–1980) 53 years from *Always Tell Your Wife* (GB 23) to *The Family Plot* (US 76).

GEORGE MARSHALL (1896–1975) 52 years from Harry Carey westerns and Ruth Roland serials in 1917 to *Hook, Line and Sinker* (US 69).

RAOUL WALSH (1887–1980) 52 years from *The Life of Villa* (US 12) to *A Distant Trumpet* (US 64).

RUDALL HAYWARD (189?–1974) 51 years from *The Bloke from Freeman's Bay* (NZ 20) to *To Love a Maori* (NZ 71).

GEORGE CUKOR (1899–1983) 51 years from *Grumpy* (US 30) to *Rich and Famous* (US 81).

MARK DONSKOI (1901–1981) 51 years from *Life* (USSR 27) to *The Orlovs* (USSR 78).

MICHAEL CURTIZ (1888–1962) 50 years from *Ma Es Holnap* (Hun 12) to *The Comancheros* (US 62).

Apart from Alfred Hitchcock, most of whose work was in America, **the most durable British director** was Maurice Elvey (1887–1967), whose directorial career spanned 44 years from *The Fallen Idol* (GB 13) to *Second Fiddle* (GB 57).

THE MOST PROLIFIC AMERICAN DIRECTORS OF FEATURE FILMS HAVE BEEN:

WILLIAM BEAUDINE (1892–70) 182 features from *Watch Your Step* (US 22) to *Jesse James Meets Frankenstein's Daughter* (US 66), of which 32 were silents and 144 were talkies. In addition he directed over 120 shorts from 1916.

RICHARD THORPE (1896–) 179 features from *Burn 'em Up Barnes* (US 21) to *The Scorpio Letters* (US 67), of which 63 were silents and 116 were talkies.

MICHAEL CURTIZ (1888–1962) 164 features from *Ma Es Holnap* (Hun 12) to *The Comancheros* (US 62), of which 61 were made in Europe before 1926 and the remainder in Hollywood.

SAM NEWFIELD (1900–64) 140 talkies.

ALLAN DWAN (1885–1981) 132 features from *Richelieu* (US 14) to *The Most Dangerous Man Alive* (US 61), plus over 200 shorts from *Brandishing a Bad Man* (US 11). Dwan claimed to have been involved in the making of 1400 films since 1910 as writer, producer or director.

JOHN FORD (1895–1973) 132 features from *The Tornado* (US 17) to *Vietnam, Vietnam* (US 68).

Note: It has been claimed that George Marshall (1896–1975) directed 425 features during his career, but only 88 full-length pictures crediting him as director can be traced for the period 1916–69. Ford Beebe (1888–) is said to have directed over 200 westerns, 'B' pictures and serials from 1916, but only 72 known films give him director credit.

George Cukor (1899–1983) with Candice Bergen and Jacqueline Bisset on the set during the making of *Rich and Famous* (US 81). At 81 he was the oldest director ever signed for a major motion picture.

Vic., who directed the railroad drama *Northbound Ltd* (Aus 26); Yuli Raizman, director of *A Circle* (USSR 27) at the age of 19; Philippe Garrel, whose feature debut *Anemone* (Fr 66), made when he was 19, starred his father Maurice Garrel; Sam Raimi, a 19-year-old who hustled the money for *The Evil Dead* (US 82) on the strength of a 30-min pilot shot on 8 mm; and 18-year-old Laurent Boutonnat, *enfant terrible* responsible for *La Ballade de la Feconductrice* (Fr 80). Boutannat was just old enough to be allowed to see his own film—it won an adults-only rating for its depiction of castration, child slaughter and bestiality.

The oldest director of a major movie was George Cukor (1899–1983), who was 81 when he was signed by MGM in October 1980 to direct Jacqueline Bisset and Candice Bergen in *Rich and Famous* (US 81).

The most versatile film-maker in terms of the most major functions performed on a single movie was Charles Chaplin, who produced, directed, scripted, composed, edited, choreographed, costume-designed and starred in *Limelight* (US 52).

Eric de Guia achieved the seemingly impossible with credits both as star and as cameraman on *Perfumed Nightmare* (Phi 82)—he was also director, producer and editor.

The first woman to take writer–director–star credit on a major feature was Elaine May for *A New Leaf* (US 70).

First with producer–director–writer–star credits was Barbra Streisand for the Jewish musical *Yentl* (US 83).

Editing

The most edited film in terms of total negative discarded was Howard Hughes' *Hell's Angels* (US 30), which consumed 2,254,750 ft of film during the four years it took to make. If all this footage had been shown unedited, it would have run for 560 hr or 23 days non-stop. The cost of the film stock was $225,475. The final release print was 9045 ft (2 hr 15 min running time), a reduction in the ratio of 249:1. A single scene without actors – a brief close-up of the valves of an aeroplane engine – occupied 20,000 ft of film (the length of four full-length features) before Hughes was satisfied.

Other films with extravagant shooting ratios look modest by comparison: Fritz Lang's *Metropolis* (Ger 26) was reduced from 1,960,000 to 13,165 ft, a ratio of 149:1; Charles Chaplin's *City Lights* (US 31) was reduced from 975,000 to 7784 ft, a ratio of 125:1; *Uncle Tom's Cabin* (US 27) was reduced from 900,000 to 13,000 ft, a ratio of 69:1; Charles Chaplin's *The Kid* (US 20) was reduced from 400,000 to 6000 ft, a ratio of 67:1; Leni Riefenstahl's *Olympische Spiele* (Ger 38) was reduced from 1,300,000 to 20,000 ft, a ratio of 65:1; William Wyler's *Ben Hur* (US 59) was reduced from 1,125,000 to 23,838 ft, a ratio of 47:1; Howard Hughes' *The Outlaw* (US 46) was reduced from 470,000 to 10,451 ft, a ratio of 45:1; Erich von Stroheim's *Foolish Wives* (US 21) was reduced from 360,000 to 10,000 ft, a ratio of 36:1; William Wyler's *The Best Years of Our Lives* (US 46) was reduced from 400,000 to 16,000 ft, a ratio of 25:1; Chuck Wein's *Rainbow Bridge* (US 71) was reduced from 252,000 to 10,300 ft, a ratio of 24:1; three with a ratio of 23:1 were D. W. Griffith's *Intolerance* (US 16), reduced from 300,000 to 13,000 ft, Sergei Eisenstein's *October* (USSR 27), also reduced from 300,000 to 13,000 ft, and *Gone With the Wind* (US 39), reduced from 474,538 to 20,300 ft; and *The Longest Day* (US 72), reduced from 360,000 to 17,000 ft, had a ratio of 21:1, or about twice the average.

The most edited single sequence of a movie was the chariot race scene in *Ben Hur* (US 25), for which editor Lloyd Nosler had to compress 200,000 ft of film into a

---

RIGHT–LEFT

In 1928 a Marxist group in Germany called the Popular Association for Film Art presented a compilation film made up entirely of clips from old UFA newsreels, but cut in such a way as to present a revolutionary viewpoint. It brought outraged protests from audiences who had watched the original newsreels without demur and the film was promptly banned. The Marxists claimed that this effectively demonstrated the power of political prejudice; in fact what it most clearly demonstrated was the extraordinary power of a skilled editor to transform a motion picture.

sparse 750 ft, a ratio of 267:1. Historian Kevin Brownlow has commented: 'Those 750 feet are among the most valuable in motion picture history.'

The least edited films include D. W. Griffith's *Broken Blossoms* (US 19), which was made with no retakes of any scene and had only 200 ft trimmed from its original length of 5500 ft; and William Wellman's *The Public Enemy* (US 31), which was reduced by only 360 ft from its original 8760 ft.

Narrative features which were released unedited include *My Hustler* (US 65); Andy Warhol's *Chelsea Girls* (US 66); and Laura Mulvey and Peter Wollen's *Penthesilea: Queen of the Amazons* (GB 74). The ultimate was achieved by *The Lacy Rituals* (GB 73), which was unedited to the extent of including shots of the clapperboard being clapped and even retained the director's cries of 'cut!' on the soundtrack.

NEW FILMS FOR OLD

Skilful editing can create an entirely new film from rearrangement of shots in an earlier one. This was achieved by Fred J. Balshofer, who had made a spy spoof called *An Adventuress* (US 20) in which the then unknown Rudolph Valentino played a bit part, and wanted to cash in on the Latin lover's meteoric rise to stardom. The locale of the new picture, *The Isle of Love* (US 22), was switched from World War I Germany to a desert island by the simple expedient of inserting stock shots of bathing beauties on a palm-fringed beach throughout the film. The problem of expanding Valentino's minor role in the original into the lead for the new picture was overcome in a number of ways. Various shots were repeated several times; long shots were blown up into close-up and intercut with other footage; some scenes were projected on a loop, so that Valentino repeated the same motions several times over; one scene was used as a flashback; and out-takes from the original were inserted into the new film, notably discarded footage of a car ride, which so expanded the scene as to make it seem interminable. Valentino, it is hardly necessary to add, received no recompense for this unauthorised 'star performance'.

Blake Edwards did something of the same kind of reconstruction job with *The Trail of the Pink Panther* (GB 82), the only film ever to have been embarked upon after the death of its star. Peter Sellers (1925–80) was seen once again as the accident-prone Inspector Clouseau in a story knit together from clips and left-over out-takes from five previous Pink Panther films. Linking shots were made with an uncredited look-alike filmed at a distance or heavily disguised, as in one scene where the Inspector sets off for England swathed in bandages from head to foot. When all the usable Sellers footage had been exhausted, the film resorted to flashbacks of a teenage Clouseau played by Daniel Peacock and an 8-year-old Clouseau in the person of Lucca Mezzofanti.

Film Stock

Transparent roll film of a kind suitable for motion picture use (though designed for still photography) **was first manufactured** by the Eastman Dry Plate and Film Co. of Rochester, NY in August 1889. Although Thomas Edison ordered some about this date for experiments in cinematography, it was found unsatisfactory and the first stock used for taking films for the Edison Kinetoscope was supplied by the Merwin Hulbert firm in 50 ft rolls on 18 March 1891. In the meantime, however, Louis Aimé Augustin Le Prince of Leeds, Yorkshire, had succeeded in making experimental cinematograph films on Eastman Kodak stock that he had ordered in the autumn of 1889.

The first commercially-produced films in Britain were made in 1895 by Robert Paul and Birt Acres using stock supplied by the European Blair Camera Co. Ltd of St Mary Cray, Kent. By the end of 1896, film stock specially cut and prepared for motion picture use was being advertised by the Celluloid Co. of New York, Dr J. H. Smith & Co. of Zurich, Switzerland, the Blair Co. of Cambridge, Mass. and London, England, the Eastman Kodak Co. of Rochester, NY and Fitch & Co. of London.

The first perforated film was used by Louis Aimé Augustin Le Prince (1842–90?) in his motion picture experiments conducted at Leeds, Yorkshire, in 1889. The inventor's assistant Longley recalled that 'we had brass eyelets fixed in the band [ie film] similar to the eyelets of boots'. The projector built by Le Prince in 1889 had a wheel with pins 'for gearing into the band of pictures'. Perforated film was not used by Thomas Edison until at least three years later.

Commercially-produced film stock was originally sold unperforated and it was not until 1904 that Eastman Kodak began offering perforation as an optional extra. Even as late as 1922 Richardson's *Handbook of Projection* states 'perforation is usually done by the producer'. Unperforated nitrate stock continued to be available from Eastman Kodak until September 1949.

The first safety film on an acetate base was introduced by Eastman Kodak of Rochester, NY, in the autumn of 1908, but its application was limited due to the fact that it tended to shrink and cockle. The negative safety stock was withdrawn in 1912, though positive safety film continued to be available for use with portable projectors in schools. Little record of production on safety film in the USA survives from this period and the earliest commercially-made movie known to have been released on safety stock, a 345 ft drama titled *La Vendetta del Groom* (It 09), was produced by Cines of Rome.

Sub-standard safety film was produced in 28 mm gauge by Pathé for use with the KOK home movie projector in France in 1912 and in 22 mm gauge by

Kodak for use with the Edison Home Kinetoscope the same year.

Safety film continued to be confined to the sub-standard gauges until 1950, when Eastman Kodak reintroduced 35 mm uninflammable stock, using a triacetate base immune from shrinkage. The revolution in film stock was total and immediate, so that since 1951 virtually no film has been made on the highly inflammable nitrate stock previously in use.

The largest frame format of any film stock was the 2·04 × 2·805 in (65 × 71·25 mm) dimension used in the 70 mm horizontal feed Imax system, developed by Multiscreen Corp. of Canada. The first film produced in this 5·242 sq in format, which is nine times the size of the standard 35 mm frame, was *Tiger Child* (Can/Jap 70), presented at the Fuji Group's pavilion at Japan's Expo 70.

Film Studies

The first course on cinematography was delivered by H. Vodnik at the Slovenija Technical College, Belgrade, Serbia (now Yugoslavia) during the winter semester of 1896–97.

The first in Britain was a course of evening classes commenced under the direction of Robert Mitchell at the Regent Street Polytechnic, London, on 1 October 1913.

The first film school was the State School of Cinematography, Moscow (later the Moscow State Film Institute or VGIK), founded on 1 September 1919 with the support of the Moscow Cinema Committee to train directors, actors, cameramen, lighting experts and art directors. Directors did a three-year course, actors a two-year course, and by government decree all studios were required to reserve a certain number of vacancies for the school's graduates each year. The first Principal was pioneer director Vladamir Gardin (1877–1965), who made the earliest version of *War and Peace* (Rus 15), and notable teachers during the school's formative years were Eistenstein, Pudovkin, Kozintsev, Dovzhenko, Yutkevich and Tisse. During the first year of the school's existence, raw film stock was in such short supply that the students 'shot' imaginary films with no film in the camera.

The first in Britain was the AAT Film School, established at 14 Soho Square under the auspices of Associated Artist Technicians in 1938. The Director of the school was Edward Carrick (1905–) son of the distinguished stage designer Edward Gordon Craig and grandson of Ellen Terry. Classes were offered in scriptwriting, editing, sound, special effects, camerawork and art direction at a fee of 180 guineas for the full two-year course. The school closed down at the outbreak of war.

UNIVERSITY FILM STUDIES

The first course in film studies offered as part of the regular curriculum of a university was instituted at the University of Southern California in 1929. Lecturers included Douglas Fairbanks, Ernst Lubitsch, William de Mille, Clara Beranger and Milton Sills on such topics as 'Photoplay Appreciation', 'Scientific Foundations', 'Growth and Development', 'The Silent Photoplay', 'The Phonophotoplay', 'Principles of Criticism', 'Social Utility of the Photoplay', 'The Actor's Art', etc. By 1932 the university had a fully-fledged Department of Cinematography and offered the first BA degree for students majoring in film studies. Three years later the course was extended to allow a year of graduate study leading to a Master of Arts degree.

In the USA there are over 600 schools and colleges offering nearly 6000 courses in film, of which about 50 award degrees in cinema studies. Full-time film students total 35,000.

Flashback

The first flashback was used in the Lubin production *A Yiddisher Boy* (US 08) and showed the hero involved in a boyhood street-fight 25 years earlier.

The first sound flashback, in which dialogue and sounds from the past are synchronised with an image of the present in order to conjure up a distant memory, was used by Rouben Mamoulian in *City Streets* (US 31). Dialogue heard earlier in the film was repeated over a huge close-up of Sylvia Sidney's tear-stained face as she recalls the past.

The first flashback within a flashback appeared in Jacques Feyder's *L'Atlantide* (Fr 21); thereafter it was bypassed by film-makers as too confusing until Michael Curtiz challenged the audience's comprehension with a flashback within a flashback within a flashback in *Passage to Marseilles* (US 44). The experiment was repeated in John Brahm's *The Locket* (US 46) and then happily relegated to the limbo of great ideas that do not work.

UNCONVENTIONAL FLASHBACKS

These include the multiple flashbacks out of sequence employed by William K. Howard in *The Power and the Glory* (US 33) and Orson Welles in *Citizen Kane* (US 41).

Andre Antoine's *La Coupable* (Fr 16) was told entirely in flashbacks, as was *Saragossa Manuscript* (Pol 74), a Decameron-type fantasy of erotic happenings in the 18th century, which went continuously backwards in time. The original version of Sergio Leone's *Once Upon a Time in America* (US 84) jumped backwards and forwards with such confusing irregularity that *Variety*'s correspondent at Cannes actually logged the sequences: 1933—22 min; 1968—14 min; childhood sequence of indeterminate date—54 min; 1920s—25 min; 1968—7 min; 1920s–30s—61 min; 1968—30 min;

1933—7 min.

Bertolucci's first feature *La Commare secca* (It 62), about the murder of a prostitute in Rome and the subsequent investigation, used the 'against the rules' technique of false flashbacks—deliberately intended to mislead—interspersed with true flashbacks. A charming device was adopted by Keisuke Kinoshita in *Nogiku no gotoku Kimi Nariki/She was like a Wild Chrysanthemum* (Jap 55)—about an old man revisiting his home-town after 60 years and recalling boyhood scenes—when he placed all the flashbacks in an oval-shaped vignette.

Gauges

The standard gauge of 35 mm was adopted by Thomas Alva Edison (1847–1931) of West Orange, NJ, in the spring of 1891 for use with the Kinetoscope peep-show viewing apparatus developed by his assistant W. K. L. Dickson. Edison's choice of four perforations, giving a 4×3 format to the image, was probably dictated by the fact that the film was designed for showing in a viewing machine, not on screen. Had he anticipated that projection would become the normal method of presenting movies, he would doubtless have opted for a wider format, to give an aspect ratio approximating more closely to that of a theatre stage. The Lumière brothers of Lyon, France, who built the first commercially successful projectors, decided to conform to the gauge pioneered by Edison and it was undoubtedly their dominance of the nascent film industry in Europe that established 35 mm as the standard gauge. It was officially recognised as such by international agreement in 1907.

The first use of 70 mm film was by Birt Acres (1854–1918) of Barnet, Herts, for shooting scenes of Henley Regatta on 7–9 July 1896. He soon abandoned use of wide gauge film because of the high cost.

A 70 mm projector was produced by Herman Caster of Canatosta, NY, and introduced into Britain as *The American Biograph* on 17 March 1897 at the Palace Theatre.

The first 70 mm feature film was a special widescreen version of *Fox Movietone Follies of 1929*, premièred in the Grandeur process at the Gaiety Theater, New York, on 17 September 1929.

The smallest gauge ever employed for filming was 3 mm, developed c. 1960 by Eric Berndt and used by NASA in manned space flights in the late 1960s. It had a centre frameline perforation.

The largest gauge ever employed in filming was 75 mm, used by the Lumière Co. of Lyons, France for special large screen presentations at the Paris Exposition of 1900.

DUAL GAUGE

It is not uncommon for sequences of professional feature films to be shot on 16 mm and then blown up (e.g. *Doctor Zhivago* (US 65), *Medium Cool* (US 69), *Easy Rider* (US 69), *Downhill Racer* (US 69)), but only one film has been released in a form which switches from one gauge to another. *Une Sale Histoire* (Fr 77) was a featurette of which the first 28 minutes were in 35 mm and the last 22 minutes in 16 mm.

Lighting

The first film shot by artificial light was a topical of the Berlin Press Club Ball made by Oskar Messter early in 1897. Illumination for filming was provided by four Körting & Matthiessen 50-amp arc lamps on portable stands. Later the same year Georges Méliès of Paris used electric arcs to shoot *Derrière l'omnibus* (Fr 97), a song-film performed by the popular chansonnier Paulus on the stage of the Théâtre Robert-Houdin. (When the film was shown, Paulus would sing from behind the screen.)

GAUGES

3 mm	NASA, USA c. 1968	24 mm	Société d'Explouations Cinématographiques, France 1925	55 mm	Prestwich, GB c. 1902; Cinemascope 55, USA 1956
4 mm	US Air Force 1950s	25 mm	Current Chinese broad gauge	56 mm	Magnafilm, USA 1929
4·75 mm	Pathé-Duplex, GB 1955	25·4 mm	Kinora, GB 1908	60 mm	Demeny Chronophotographe, France 1895; Prestwich, GB 1898
8 mm	Eastman Kodak, USA 1932	26 mm	Société Cinelux, France 1920		
8·75 mm	China 1950s (for use in mobile cinemas)	28 mm	Pathé KOK, France 1912	62 mm	American Mutoscope & Biograph Co., USA 1895
9·5 mm	Pathé, France 1922	30 mm	France 1910 (three 10 mm frames laterally)	63 mm	Veriscope Co., USA 1897
11 mm	Duplex, USA c. 1903			63·5 mm	Spoor-Berggren Natural Vision, USA 1929
13 mm	Prestwich, GB 1899; France c. 1925	32 mm	Vincennes, France 1920 (two 16 mm frames laterally)		
15 mm	Gaumont Pocket-Chrono 1900	35 mm	Edison, USA 1891; Lumière, France 1894; standard from 1907	65 mm	Warner Bros., USA 1930; Joseph Schenck, USA 1930; Todd-AO, USA 1955
16 mm	Eastman Kodak, USA 1923	38 mm	Lee and Turner, GB 1901		
17 mm	Pathé, Spain c. 1920	42 mm	Tri-Ergon sound system, Germany 1929	68 mm	American Mutoscope & Biograph Co., USA c. 1898
17·5 mm	Birtac, GB 1898; Kino d'Ernemann, Germany 1903, etc.	45 mm	Claude-Autant Lara, France 1929 (three 15 mm frames laterally)	70 mm	Birt Acres, GB 1896; Herman Caster, USA 1897; Fox Grandeur, USA 1929, etc.
18 mm	USSR c. 1925	48 mm	Blair Viventoscope, GB 1897		
20 mm	Mirographe, France c. 1920	50 mm	Le Prince, GB 1888; Graphophonoscope, France 1899	73 mm	American Mutoscope & Biograph Co., GB c. 1897
21 mm	Mirographe, France 1900; Edison, USA c. 1905	51 mm	Latham, USA 1895	75 mm	Lumière, France 1900
22 mm	Edison Home Kinetoscope, USA 1912; Cinébloc, France 1921				

The earliest American film made by artificial light was an Edison comedy titled *Willie's First Smoke* (US 99).

The earliest use of lighting effects for their aesthetic value is generally attributed to D. W. Griffith, who employed artificial lighting to obtain a 'fireside glow' in *The Drunkard's Reformation* (US 09), for the 'sunlight effect' in *Pippa Passes* (US 09) and the 'dim, religious light' in *Threads of Destiny* (US 10). Griffith had to overcome the resistance of his cameramen Harry Marvin and Billy Bitzer, who regarded shadows as 'amateurish'.

The first backlighting by reflectors was introduced by D. W. Griffith's cameraman Billy Bitzer on *Enoch Arden* (US 11), which opens with a superbly backlighted shot of the villagers bidding the sailors goodbye. The technique had been discovered by accident. Normally the camera was never faced directly into the sun, but one day Bitzer turned it playfully on to Mary Pickford and Owen Moore as they sat at a shiny-topped table with the sun behind them. Instead of the couple appearing in silhouette, as he expected, Bitzer found that he had obtained a beautifully lit shot with the two artistes' faces bathed in radiance—suitably, since they were in love—the

Above left
Before the advent of artificial lighting—filming *The Heart of a Race Tout* (US 09) at the Selig Polyscape studios in Los Angeles. The move to perpetually sunny California presented early film-makers with a problem—how to shoot interior scenes without the shadows showing. It was soon to drive them indoors. (*Bruce Torrence Historical Collection, c/o Pacific Savings*)

Below left
Shooting by artificial light at the Edison Studios *c.* 1912. These were Aristo carbon lamps.

Above
On the set of *California* (US 27) with the most powerful lighting unit in the history of motion pictures.

effect of the sun's light reflected in the table top. Bitzer devised a system whereby one mirror would reflect the sun into another, which could then be beamed to the back of a performer's head.

The first studio built with a 'dark stage' for filming by artificial light was the Ambrosio Studio at Turin, Italy, where production started in 1907. The illumination installed by chief cameraman Carlo Montuori consisted of street lamps.

The first 'dark stage' in Britain was built in 1914 at the Neptune Studios, Borehamwood to the specification of chief cameraman Alfonso Frenguelli. The lamps were Westminster arcs, some on stands, the others suspended from the roof by pulleys.

The earliest use of incandescent lighting on a feature film has generally been attributed to Erich von Stroheim in *Greed* (US 23). However, Lee Garmes claimed to have used it in a Dorothy Gish movie made in 1919. Garmes did not identify the film, but he made two pictures with Dorothy Gish in that year—*The Hope Chest* (US 19) and *I'll Get Him* (US 19).

The most powerful lighting used on any film was the 58,000 amps that illuminated the set of *The King and I* (US 56). This is equivalent to the illumination of 258 'brute' arc lights.

The most powerful standard lighting unit currently on sale is the 350-amp Titan Molarc, manufactured by the Mole-Richardson Co. of Hollywood.

The most powerful single arc ever used was a giant 13,940 amp, 325 million candlepower lamp used by Colonel Tim McCoy on the western *California* (US 27). The lamp was 40 times the strength of the most powerful arc available today (see above), 54 times as powerful as the most brilliant lighthouse beam, and said to have a beam that would radiate for 90 miles (145 km).

Takes and Retakes

The longest take in a movie comprises the whole of the second reel of Andy Warhol's *Blue Movie* (US 68) and consists of a 35-minute uninterrupted scene of Viva and Louis Waldon making love.

The longest take in a commercially-made feature movie is a 14-minute uninterrupted monologue by Lionel Barrymore in *A Free Soul* (US 31). Since a reel of camera film only lasts ten minutes, the take was achieved by using more than one camera. Alfred Hitchcock's *Rope* (US 48), the story of two homosexual college men who kill a third for the intellectual thrill of it, was shot in eight ten-minute takes (apart from one cut to the housekeeper in the first reel). The effect was of one continuous shot, since the action of the story occupied the same period of time—80 minutes—as the length of the film.

The greatest number of retakes of a single scene was 342 for the episode in Chaplin's *City Lights* (US 31) in which a blind flower girl (Virginia Cherrill) sells the little tramp a flower under the misapprehension he is a rich man. Chaplin kept reshooting the scene because he was unable to find a satisfactory way of making the blind girl think that the tramp was wealthy. Finally he found a simple yet perfect solution. Chaplin is trying to cross a street jammed with traffic. Unable to reach the sidewalk, he sees a limousine parked by the kerb, gets in at one door and out at the other. The girl hears the door close and assumes it is the owner getting out. She hands him the flower, takes his last quarter, and keeps the change.

Difficult dialogue is the most common reason for prodigious numbers of retakes. One scene in *Dr Strangelove* (GB 63) was shot 48 times because Sterling Hayden, playing the mad base commander, fluffed his line 47 times. Marilyn Monroe did 59 takes of a scene in *Some Like It Hot* (US 59) in which her only line of dialogue was 'Where's the Bourbon?'. Hollywood rebel Dennis Hopper had an early run-in with veteran director Henry Hathaway when he was made to repeat a scene in *From Hell to Texas* (US 57) no less than 85 times. 'Kid', Hathaway growled at the moody method actor after the 85th take, 'you'll never work in this town again'. It was in fact some ten years before Hopper was offered another worthwhile role.

The record number of takes of a dialogue sequence is claimed to be the 127 demanded by Stanley Kubrick of a scene with Shelley Duval in *The Shining* (US 80).

ONE-SHOT DIRECTORS

At the other end of the scale, there have been those who earned themselves reputations as 'one-shot' directors, notably G. W. Pabst, Cecil B. DeMille, W. S. 'One-Shot Woody' van Dyke, and D. W. Griffith. According to Lillian Gish, Griffith's masterwork *The Birth of a Nation* (US 15) was made with only one retake of one scene. The single repeat shot was necessitated, much to Mr Griffith's displeasure, by the fact that Mae Marsh forgot to drape herself in the Confederate flag for her suicide scene.

It took 342 takes to get this scene in *City Lights* (US 31). Chaplin spent 534 days making the movie, including 368 days when he shot nothing at all as he sought for a way of showing that the girl, who couldn't see, thought the tramp, who never spoke, was a wealthy tycoon.

Make-up

Little attention was paid to make-up in films before the advent of the close-up (q.v.). **The earliest motion picture in which it is apparent that the actors are wearing make-up** (other than black-face or whiskers) is Edwin S. Porter's *The Whole Dam Family and the Dam Dog* (US 05), in which the cast are made-up to create the illusion of a family resemblance. The pioneer of special make-up techniques for film as opposed to stage performances was D. W. Griffith, who began experiments to achieve a more naturalistic appearance for his performers at Biograph in about 1910. Stage actress Olga Petrova recalled of her film debut in *The Tiger* (US 14): 'I noticed immediately that my co-workers wore a make-up much darker, almost a beige, whereas I wore the usual light Leichner's 1.' There was a good reason for her co-workers' departure from stage practice. The orthochromatic film stock used at this date was insensitive to the red end of the spectrum (scarlet registered as black) and consequently a heavy application of yellow make-up was necessary to create an impression of natural skin tone on screen.

The first studio make-up department was established at First National in 1924 under British-born Perc Westmore (1904–70). Perc later became head of make-up at Warner's, his brother Bud became head of make-up at Universal, and his other brother Wally spent 38 years in make-up at Paramount.

The largest make-up budget was $1 million for *Planet of the Apes* (US 68), which represented nearly 17 per cent of the total production cost. A team of 78 make-up artists worked under the direction of Fox's make-up specialist John Chambers, who won a special Oscar for his remarkable achievement of creating wholly credible ape faces sufficiently mobile to register the full range of human emotions.

The longest make-up job ever performed on a single artiste was the tattooing applied to Rod Steiger in Warner Bros' *The Illustrated Man* (US 69). It took make-up artist Gordon Bau and his team of eight assistants ten hours to complete the torso and another full day was spent on the lower body, hands and legs. Bau's longest job previously had been Charles Laughton's make-up for the title role of *The Hunchback of Notre Dame* (US 39), which he finished in a mere 5½ hours.

Other marathon make-up jobs have included the 4 hours daily spent by Wally Westmore on Fredric March's Hyde in *Dr Jekyll and Mr Hyde* (US 32); 4 hours for Boris Karloff's monster in *Frankenstein* (US 31), and a similar time for Jean Marais' make-up in *La Belle et la Bête* (Fr 45); 4½ hours on Bull Montana's ape-man in *The Lost World* (US 25) and the same for Lon Chaney in *The Hunchback of Notre Dame* (US 23); 5 hours for the principal apes in *Planet of the Apes* (US 68) and also for the 121-year-old character played by Dustin Hoffman in *Little Big Man* (US 70); Klaus Kinski's Dracula make-up for *Nosferatu* (FRG 79) also took 5 hours daily to apply. Boris Karloff's make-up for *The Bride of Frankenstein* (US 35), an elaboration of Jack Pierce's original monster make-up for the 1931 *Frankenstein*, took 7 hours to complete each day. Shooting of scenes involving Karloff—he was in most—had to be delayed until 1 p.m. In the same film Elsa Lanchester's make-up as the female monster was so rigid she had to be fed lunch through a tube. John Hurt was unable to eat at all after the 7-hour ordeal of having his head monstrously deformed for the title role in *The Elephant Man* (GB 80). It was so exhausting that the full make-up could only be applied every second day.

The record for the longest make-up job in a British movie is the 10 hours it took Rick Baker to transform David Naughton into a hairy beast for *An American Werewolf in London* (GB 81).

Producer

The youngest producer to produce a feature-length film for commercial exhibition was 16-year-old George Palmer of Melbourne, Vic., whose thriller *The Mail Robbery* (Aus 25) was released in Victoria and New South Wales. The following year he produced, directed and starred in *Northbound Ltd* (Aus 26), a railroad drama he had written himself. On reaching man's estate Palmer retired from the film business to establish a successful travel agency, but retained an interest in experimental film-making.

Britain's youngest producer was 22-year-old Norman Hope-Bell, who made his professional debut at Cricklewood Studios with an Ernie Lotinga comedy called *Love Up the Pole* (GB 36).

The first woman producer was Alice Guy (see p. 117), who founded the Solax Co. at Flushing, New York, on 7 September 1910. The first of nearly 300 short films produced by her in the next three years was *A Child's Sacrifice* (US 10), starring 'The Solax Kid' (Magda Foy), which was released on 21 October 1910.

The first feature film produced by a woman was Eros Films' *The Definite Object* (GB 20), a gangster movie set in New York produced by Countess Bubna.

One actor who refuses ever to wear make-up is the veteran French star Charles Vanel. Active in movies since 1912, he has worn make-up for only one of his 200 roles to date. That was 60 years ago, and even then Vanel, now France's longest serving screen actor, appeared too old for his role as the romantic lead in Baroncelli's *Le Reveil* (Fr 25). A skilled make-up man made the prematurely middle-aged 32-year-old star look as if he was indeed in his early thirties.

The first talkie produced by a woman was Elinor Glyn's Talkicolor production *Knowing Men* (GB 30), with Carl Brisson and Elissa Landi. She also directed. **The first Hollywood talkie by a woman** was Elsie Janis's *Paramount on Parade* (US 30), which was released in April 1930, two months after Miss Glyn's picture.

The most enduring producer–writer–director partnership is that of Indian producer Ismail Merchant, Polish–German writer Ruth Jhabvala and American director James Ivory, whose 13 films made in collaboration span over 20 years from *The Householder* (Ind/US 63) to *The Bostonians* (GB 84).

The two most successful producer/directors in terms of box office revenue are George Lucas and Steven Spielberg, who between them are responsible for seven out of the nine films which have garnered more than $100 million in North American rentals. Spielberg has to his credit, as both producer and director, the top earner of all time, *E.T. The Extra-Terrestial* (US 82), as well as directing *Jaws* (US 75), which was the first picture to break the $100 million barrier, and the two Indiana Jones blockbusters *Raiders of the Lost Ark* (US 81) and *Indiana Jones and the Temple of Doom* (US 84). Both the latter were produced by George Lucas, who also directed *Star Wars* (US 77) and produced *The Empire Strikes Back* (US 80) and *Return of the Jedi* (US 83). (For rental figures, see Top 25 Earners chart p. 37.)

The most enduring production team—producer Ismail Merchant, director James Ivory and screen-writer Ruth Jhabvala have made 13 films together since 1963. (*Zakiya and associates*)

Schedules

The longest production schedule for a feature movie was the 18 years it took to complete Alvaro Henriques Goncalves' *Presente de Natal* (Bra 71). Goncalves, a lawyer by profession, worked on his full-length animated feature single-handed. This record is shared by Winifred Junge's 4 hr 30 min documentary *Lebenslaeufe/Paths of Life* (GDR 80), which was shot over an 18-year period from 1961 to 1979 and traces the progress of nine members of a primary school class in the East German village of Golzow on the River Oder. Richard Williams' animated feature *The Thief and the Cobbler* (GB i.p.) is reported to be in its 18th year of production (1985).

The longest production schedule for a dramatic film in terms of start date and completion date was 13 years for Leni Riefenstahl's *Tiefland* (FRG 53) and the same length of time for *Dr Bethune* (Chn 77), Chinese tribute to the Canadian chest surgeon who gave his life while serving as a volunteer with the Red Army in 1939. In the case of *Tiefland*, production of what promised to be the most expensive talkie then made was suspended in 1942 after expenditure of 5 million RMs and the complete breakdown of the director's health. At the end of the war Frl. Riefenstahl was banned from working in the film industry, but following her de-Nazification in 1952 she succeeded in reassembling the original cast and completed the film. It recouped its cost but Frl. Riefenstahl, dissatisfied with her work, then withdrew the picture from distribution and it has not been shown since.

Production of *Dr Bethune* started in 1964 but was halted at the outset of the Cultural Revolution on the personal orders of Mao's wife, Jiang Qing, who asserted that the documentary footage of *Dr Bethune* was sufficient to honour his memory. The cameraman who had taken the documentary footage, Wu Yinxian, was also the cameraman on the biopic. Production was resumed with the collapse of the Cultural Revolution.

The longest production schedule for a British film was the 8 years 20 days (6 May 1956–26 May 1964) it took Kevin Brownlow and Andrew Mollo to complete their fantasy of a Nazi-occupied Britain, *It Happened Here* (GB 66). The picture, which occupied a cumulative shooting schedule of ten weeks, started as an amateur production by a group of enthusiastic teenagers and ended as a professional film with a West End release. (Mr Brownlow has asked the editor to point out that in these circumstances he should not be accorded the title of the world's slowest director.)

Other protracted production schedules have included 11 years (1925–36) for Ladislas Starewitch's animated puppet film *Le Roman de Rénard* (Fr 40); 9 years for Léon Delbrove's documentary *Un Jour, Le Genie des Hommes* (Bel 47); 7 years for Harry Hoyt's *The Lost World* (US 25), Michael Kohler's *The Experiencer* (GB 77) and *Flame Top* aka *Down to Earth* (Fin 81),

Casting for *Gandhi* (GB 82), Sir Richard Attenborough chose Candice Bergen to play the role of *Life* photographer Margaret Bourke-White because of her uncanny resemblance to the original. He offered her the part in 1965 when Miss Bergen was still a teenager, an audacious piece of casting for the role of a woman in her late thirties. By the time the film went into production Candice Bergen was 36.

a biopic of the enigmatic Finnish folklorist Maiju Lassila; 5½ years for Edgar Reitz's *Heimat* (FRG 84); 5 years for George Stevens's *The Greatest Story Ever Told* (US 65) and *Eraserhead* (US 77); 4 years for Mel Ferrer's *Vendetta* (US 50), Rudall Hayward's *On the Friendly Road* (NZ 36), Francis Ford Coppola's *Apocalypse Now* (US 79), Joseph L. Mankiewicz's *Cleopatra* (US 63) and Terence Young's Korean War epic *Inchon* (Kor/US 81), starring Laurence Olivier as Gen. MacArthur. Sir Richard Attenborough's monumental biopic of *Gandhi* (GB 82) had a schedule of 20 months from the start of pre-production to delivery of prints, with 26 weeks spent on shooting. The gestation of the movie, however, lasted 17 years from the start of the first of twelve draft screenplays to the pre-production date. Attenborough estimated that during this time he gave up some 40 acting parts and a dozen directorial assignments in order to realise what he described as 'my love affair with this project'.

The shortest shooting schedule for a full-length, commercial feature film made without the use of stock footage was two days in the case of Roger Corman's *The Little Shop of Horrors* (US 60). The story is about a Jewish florist (Jonathan Haze) on New

It Happened Here (GB 66) began as an amateur movie shot by enthusiastic teenagers and was completed eight years later as a professional feature with a West End release. Director Kevin Brownlow is a cinéaste of infinite patience. He spent over 20 years assembling an almost complete version of Abel Gance's lost masterpiece *Napoléon* (Fr 27).

York's Lower East Side who accidentally revives a withering plant of indeterminate species when he waters it with blood from a cut finger. The plant's insatiable and ever-growing appetite for human blood can only be satisfied by feeding it corpses and the florist proceeds to exterminate his neighbours in order to accommodate it. Retribution comes in a not unexpected dénouement when the predator falls victim and is consumed by the object of his adoration.

Also shot in two days (and a couple of hours) was Emile de Antonio's *In the King of Prussia* (US 82), a reconstruction of the attack on the General Electric warhead plant in the mid-west township of King of Prussia by anti-nuclear demonstrators and their subsequent trial. Starring Martin Sheen as himself, and with the defendants, known as the 'Plowshares Eight', as themselves, the film had to be shot in 50 hours to meet the deadline before the defendants had to report for sentencing.

The shortest production schedule for a full-length feature film was for *Twist Around the Clock* (US 61),

Samuel Bronston's massive set for *The Fall of the Roman Empire* (US 64). It was the largest ever built.

released 28 days after Chubby Checker reached No. 1 in the charts and gave Sam Katzman the idea of making a movie to cash in on the new dance craze. Chubby Checker starred.

The shortest time between completion of shooting and the première of a feature film was five hours in the case of Alfred Rolfe's racing drama *The Cup Winner* (Aus 11). The final scenes, consisting of footage of the Melbourne Cup shot by six cameramen, were filmed on 7 November 1911 and the completed drama edited and processed in time for a simultaneous opening at five Melbourne cinemas the same night. It opened in Sydney, 450 miles away, the following day.

AVERAGE SCHEDULES
The only survey of production schedules was conducted by *Sight and Sound* in 1982 in relation to all UK films of the previous year. The 26 dramatic features

surveyed had schedules from start of pre-production to delivery of prints which ranged from five months for *Angel* to two years for *Dark Crystal*, with an average of eleven months. Shooting schedules ranged from three weeks for *Take It or Leave It* to six months for *Gandhi*, with an average of $11\frac{1}{2}$ weeks.

> Cecil B. DeMille's attention to historical accuracy was legendary. It was also expensive. Preparing to make *Cleopatra* (US 34), he dispatched William Cameron Menzies, his art director, to Egypt with instructions to find out the real colour of the pyramids. (The film was in black and white.) Menzies and his aides visited all or most of Egypt's 92 pyramids at a cost of $100,000. His report to DeMille was that the pyramids are in reality the colour that most people suppose them to be—sandy brown.

Set

The largest film set ever built was the 1312 by 754 ft (400×230 m) Roman Forum designed by Veniero Colosanti and John Moore and built on a 55-acre site at Las Matas, outside Madrid, for the last great Hollywood epic of the ancient world, Samuel Bronston's production of *The Fall of the Roman Empire* (US 64). Commencing 10 October 1962, 1100 workmen spent seven months laying the surface of the Forum with 170,000 cement blocks, erecting 22,000 ft (6705 m) of concrete stairways, 601 columns and 350 statues, and constructing 27 full size buildings. The highest point on the set was the Temple of Jupiter, whose bronze equestrian statues surmounting the roof soared 260 ft (79 m) above the paving of the Forum.

The largest indoor set was the UFO landing site built for the climax of Steven Spielberg's *Close Encounters of the Third Kind* (US 77). With a height of 90 ft (27 m), length of 450 ft (137 m) and 250 ft (76 m) breadth, the set was constructed inside a 10 million cubic ft dirigible hangar at Mobile, Alabama, which had six times the capacity of the largest sound stage in Hollywood. The structure included four miles (6·4 km) of scaffolding, 16,900 sq ft (1570 sq m) of fibreglass, 29,500 sq ft (2740 sq m) of nylon canopy and 'enough concrete to make a full-scale replica of the Washington monument'.

The largest single structure ever built as a movie set was the vast 450 ft (137 m) long, 90 ft (27 m) high medieval castle designed by Wilfred Buckland and erected at Pasadena, California, for Douglas Fairbanks' version of *Robin Hood* (US 22). No record survives of its other dimensions, but to be in proportion it must have been at least as big as the *Close Encounters* set (see above), which was exactly the same height and length.

The smallest set used for the entire action of a movie—in terms of confined acting space—was the

One way of creating the illusion of vast settings on a stage of limited size is to create the set in false perspective. This makes the background look a lot more distant than it really is. One problem, though, in using this technique is the size of the performers at the back of the set. In *Maya* (Fr 49), a set representing a street in a red-light district was built in false perspective. The prostitutes seen at the far end of the street were played by little girls of six to eight years old outfitted in the gaudy raiment of harlotry.

lifeboat containing the nine protagonists of Alfred Hitchcock's *Lifeboat* (US 44).

Films which have been made on a single set include the submarine drama *Umini sul fondo* (It 41), the underground railway dramas *Subway Express* (US 31) and *Dutchman* (GB 66) and the Spanish pictures *Historia de una escalera* (Sp 50), set on a staircase, and *Noventa minutos* (Sp 50), which took place in a cellar. Alfred Hitchcock's *Rope* (US 48), the story of an unmotivated murder by two homosexual college men, takes place entirely in the apartment in which the crime was perpetrated and his *Lifeboat* (US 44) was confined to the craft of the title. *La Morte al lavoro* (It 78), *Inserts* (GB 75), *La Droleuse* (Fr 78) and *Yaadein* (Ind 64) were one-room dramas, while Kostas Sfikas' *Model* (Gre 74) took place entirely in a factory yard unpeopled by human beings (there were some robots). Louis Malle's *My Dinner with André* (US 81) was a two-hander consisting of a conversation overheard (by the audience) between a playwright (Wallace Shawn) and an actor (André Gregory) in a smart Manhattan restaurant; while Johnny Legends' spoof of Malle's film, titled *My Breakfast with Blaissie* (US 83) cast Andy Kaufman and Freddie Blaissie in the roles of two enormously egotistical individuals breakfasting at a Los Angeles fast-food emporium. Ettore Scola's *Le Bal* (Fr/It/Alg 84) recounted five decades of social change in France through the medium of dance. Besides having no dialogue, the entire action, covering such diverse episodes of French history as the Popular Front of the thirties, the German Occupation of the forties, the Algerian War of the fifties, and the Paris riots of the sixties, is enacted on a single set representing a typical French ballroom.

Studios

The first film studio in the world was Thomas Edison's *Black Maria*, a frame building covered in black roofing-paper, built at the Edison Laboratories in West Orange, NJ, and completed at a cost of $637·67 on 1 February 1893. Here Edison made short vaudeville-act films for use in his Kinetoscope, a peep-show machine designed for amusement arcades. The building was so constructed that it could be revolved to face the direction of the sun.

The first studio in Europe and **the first in the world in**

The world's largest stage, Pinewood. For *The Spy Who Loved Me* (GB 77), they filled it with 1·2 million gallons of water. (*United Artists*)

which films were made by artificial light was opened by Oskar Messter at 94a Friedrich Strasse, Berlin in November 1896. For illumination Messter used four Körting & Matthiessen 50-amp arc-lamps on portable stands. His earliest productions by artificial light included *From Tears to Laughter* (Ger 96) and *Lightning Artist Zigg* (Ger 96). The first artificially lit studio in the USA, the Biograph Studio at 11 East 14th Street, New York, was not opened until 1903.

The first film studio in Britain was built at the back of the Tivoli Theatre in the Strand in 1897 by the Mutoscope & Biograph Co. Like Edison's *Black Maria*, the studio was mounted on a cup-and-ball fixture that enabled it to be turned in the direction of the sun. It could also be rocked to and fro for 'storm at sea' sequences and similar effects. The glass panels that made up the sides of the studio could be dismantled for 'outdoor' scenes.

The first purpose-built sound stage was Stage Three at Warner Bros Studios, Sunset Boulevard, Hollywood, erected in April 1927. Shooting of *The Jazz Singer* (US 27) commenced on Stage Three the following month.

The largest film studio in the world is Universal City, California, whose 34 sound stages and other buildings cover an area of 420 acres. As many as 6000 staff are employed at times of peak production. Built by Carl Laemmle, the studio was originally opened on a 230-acre lot on 15 March 1915 and had the unique distinction of being a municipality in its own right. Besides the outdoor stages, indoor studio, prop stores, processing labs, zoo and stables, Universal City had its own Town Hall, fire station and police department.

The largest studio stage in the world is the 007 stage at Pinewood Studios, Buckinghamshire, England, which was built in 1976 at a cost of £350,000. It is 336 ft (102 m) long by 139 ft (42 m) wide and 41 ft (12 m) high. Designed by Ken Adam and Michael Brown, the stage was originally built for the James Bond film *The Spy Who Loved Me* (GB 77) and accommodated 1·2 million gallons of water, a full-scale 600,000-ton oil-tanker and three nuclear submarines. The 007 stage is owned by United Artists and Eon Productions and is rented out to other film production companies.

Stunts

The first stuntman was ex-US cavalryman Frank Hanaway, who won himself a part in Edwin S. Porter's *The Great Train Robbery* (US 03) for his ability to fall off a horse without injuring himself.

The first professional stuntwoman was Helen Gibson, who doubled for Helen Holmes in the first 26 episodes of Kalem's serial *The Hazards of Helen* (US 14). Trained as a trick rider and married to cowboy star Hoot Gibson, she was chosen for her ability to do

In *Shooting High* (US 40), Gene Autry played a stuntman doubling for a star played by Robert Lowery. A real stuntman doubled for Autry in the stunt scenes.

stunts on horseback but proved herself adept at other hair-raising exploits, including jumping a speeding motorcycle on to a fast moving locomotive. Unlike most stunt people, she achieved stardom in her own right, replacing Helen Holmes' successor Elsie McCleod as the lead in the long-running *Hazards of Helen*. Generally at this period, actresses were doubled in dangerous scenes by men in drag. Since the introduction of the Sex Equality Act in the USA, it is illegal for stuntmen to double for actresses unless no stuntwoman is willing to take on the assignment.

THE STUNTMAN AS STAR

The claim made by many stars that they performed all their own stunts seldom amounted to anything more than press agents' ballyhoo. Apart from Helen Gibson (see above), the only star who really did all his own stunting was Richard Talmadge (1896–). The reason was twofold—he was an accomplished stuntman himself; and he never became so valuable a star that the studio feared the consequences if he was put out of action. Perhaps the star most often trumpeted as his own stuntman was Douglas Fairbanks; ironically, it was Talmadge who did most of his stunts, including the celebrated slide down the sail in *The Black Pirate* (US 26).

The only stuntman who stands in for children is Bobby Porter, who at 4 ft 9 in (1·45 m) often substitutes for little girls as well as little boys. Among his more spectacular appearances was in the title role of *Annie* (US 82), in which he hung suspended from a 20-storey high drawbridge as stand-in for 9-year-old Aileen Quinn.

The greatest height from which a stuntman has leaped in a free fall was 1170 ft (356·6 m), a stunt performed for *Highpoint* (Can 79) by Los Angeles parachutist Dar Robinson from a ledge at the summit of the CN Tower in Toronto. Robinson opened his 'chute out of shot at a height estimated at 300–350 ft from the ground after six seconds of freefalling, one of reaction time and two for releasing the canopy. The fee, an unconfirmed $150,000, is believed to be a **record payment for a single stunt**.

The longest leap in a car propelled by its own engine was performed by stunt driver Gary Davis in *Smokey*

In 1928 *Photoplay* declared that the oddest job in the movie industry was held by aspiring actor Calvin Austin, who was employed by First National to perambulate the studio with a magnetic cane picking up nails dropped by stage carpenters.

and the Bandit II (US 81). Davis raced a stripped-down Plymouth up a ramp butted up against the back of a double-tiered car-carrier at 80 mph (129 km/h) and described a trajectory of 163 ft (49·7 m) before landing safely on the desert floor.

Swordfights, Shoot-outs and Kung Fu

The earliest known kung-fu movie was *Thief in the Car* (Chn 20), directed by Ren Pengnian for the Shang Wu company of Shanghai and starring Ding Yuanyi and Bao Guiying. **The first kung-fu talkie** was Yang Xiaozhong's *Story of the 'Red Sheep' Hero* (Chn 35) with Wang Huchen and Tong Yuejuan.

The longest swordfight sequence was the 22-minute climax to *Beach of the War Gods* (HK 73), in which Wang Yu as the Chinese superpatriot and swordsman Hsiao Feng destroys large numbers of hated Japanese before dropping dead himself.

Surprisingly the longest clash-of-steel sequence in a Hollywood movie does not exceed 6½ minutes. Stewart Granger was crossing swords with an ignoble marquis (Mel Ferrer) in *Scaramouche* (US 53).

The record for carnage in a shoot-out movie has yet to be positively established, but one critic took the trouble to count the number of deceased persons littering the screen at different times during the course of the sphaghetti western *The Bounty Hunters* (It 70) and came up with a total of 116.

Tank

The largest tank ever built for moviemaking was erected in a disused Zeppelin hangar at Berlin under the direction of art director Max Heilbronner for UFA's *Volga, Volga* (Ger 29), an historical epic about Cossack pirate Stenka Rasin. The tank, which was constructed to represent the Volga river, was 2000 ft (600 m) long.

Underwater Film

The first underwater film was *The Underwater Expedition of the Brothers Williamson* (US 14), made by American cinematographer J. E. Williamson off Watling Island (the site of Columbus's first landfall in the New World) in the Bahamas in March 1914. The filming was done from a four-ton 'photosphere', a spherical chamber designed by Williamson himself which was suspended by a flexible tube from the base vessel lying on the surface. The six-reel documentary feature, which included a scene of a fight between a man and a killer shark (Williamson himself volunteered to fight the shark after the native swimmers hired for the job had deserted), was premièred at the Smithsonian Institution prior to a successful commercial release, running for seven months in Chicago and attracting capacity audiences in London and New York.

The first undersea footage shot for a fiction film was by J. E. Williamson for Universal's *Twenty Thousand Leagues Under the Sea* (US 16).

The first underwater feature in colour was MGM's *The Mysterious Island* (US 29), a Technicolor version of Jules Verne's story of a pioneer submarine journey.

Women

The first film made with an all-female crew was a comedy titled *Sally Sallies Forth* (GB 28), produced with a women-only cast by the lady members of the Amateur Cinema Association. The 'directress' (as she was called) was Frances Lascott, the camerawoman Mrs A. E. Low and the title role—an inexperienced maidservant who disrupts a pompous tea party—played by Sadie Andrews. It was premièred at the Camera Club on 12 December 1928 and *Film Weekly*'s male critic declared it 'a rattling good effort'.

The first professionally-made feature by women was Savithri Ganesh's *Chinnari Pappalu* (Ind 67), produced and scripted in Telegu by Mrs Sarojini Madhusudana Rao, with music by Mrs P. Leela and art direction by Mrs Mohana. **America's first *femme* production** was *The Waiting Room* (US 73), a psychological drama produced and directed by Karen Sperling (grand-daughter of Harry Warner) and Doro Bachrach. The 32-woman crew was selected from 300 applicants attracted from California, Canada, Europe and New York (where the film was made).

Blunders

The most frequent mistakes made in movies are microphone booms visible within the frame, and camera crews reflected in plate-glass windows. Other blunders are legion. Some of the choicest include:

☆ A thrilling horseback chase in the Buster Crabbe western *Gentlemen with Guns* (US 46) culminates in the hero leaping on to the villain and unhorsing him, both crashing to the ground on to a soft mattress inexpertly placed within the frame.

☆ Jungle movies seem especially prone to error. *Lost in the Jungle* (US 11) was set in the Transvaal—several thousand miles from the nearest jungle. *The Adventures of Kathleen* (US 13), a Selig serial, was set in an India populated with lions from the Selig Zoo. As well as African fauna, the Indian 'heavy' was given an

African name, Umballah. Universal's *Call of the Savage* (US 35) had Indian tigers roaring in the African jungle.

☆ Not all inaccuracies are perpetrated through ignorance or accident. *Harlem, USA* (USSR 52) depicted Harlem as a closed black ghetto guarded by brutal white police. According to a review in *Variety*, the film had the 'residents . . . beaten and not permitted to leave the area. Pets are prohibited. White merchants own all the retail establishments and all food sold has been condemned elsewhere.' The domestic product could be just as slanted. The overtly liberal *Hoodlum Priest* (US 61) has a lawyer declaring as a statement of contemporary fact that there were five million people in US prisons—at the time the film was made there were 205,600 prisoners in the USA.

☆ Cliff Edwards was murdered at a subway entrance in Chicago in *Dance Fools, Dance* (US 30). There were no subways in Chicago at that date.

☆ In Edgar Ulmer's *Girls in Chains* (US 43), the night-time murder scene atop the Hoover Dam was intercut with stock footage of the dam filmed in broad daylight.

☆ *In Harm's Way* (US 65), a naval epic about the attack on Pearl Harbor, shows the *Yamato* opening fire on US PT boats and scoring at least one hit. Since the *Yamato*'s 18-in guns are shown at maximum elevation, the shells would in reality have missed the PT boats by at least 18 miles.

☆ As Scarlett leaves the hospital in Atlanta in *Gone with the Wind* (US 39) she runs past a lamp-post lit by electricity.

☆ On the drive home from the airport in *The Parent Trap* (US 61), the gearstick is in neutral.

☆ The heroine of *Adalen 31* (Swe 69), set in 1931, removes her clothes in one scene and reveals bikini marks.

☆ In *The Illustrious Prince* (US 19) the traffic in London drives on the *right* side of the road. The credulity of London audiences was stretched in *A House Divided* (US 20) when a shot of St Thomas's Hospital was identified as the private residence of the family in the story. In *Disraeli* (US 21) a cab approached 'No 10' from the east. Downing Street is a cul-de-sac, the only entry being from the west. Such blunders are not unique to American films. *The Incredible Sarah* (GB 76) perpetrated one of the most inexcusable errors ever to be seen in a British film: a train is seen arriving at what is clearly signed 'London Station'.

☆ Blunders made off-screen include billing Alan Ladd as John Wayne's co-star in *Hell Town*, the title under which *Born to the West* (US 38) was reissued. Ladd was not in the film at all. George Zucco took the main screen credit as star of Monogram's *Return of the Ape Man* (US 44). He was not in the picture either.

☆ A shot of the Persians scaling the walls of Babylon in *Intolerance* (US 16) includes an assistant director in shirt-sleeves and tie.

☆ In *Elvira Madigan* (Swe 67)—set in the mid-19th

century—a car appears briefly at the end of a street. An aeroplane passes overhead during a scene in *Helen of Troy* (US 55).

☆ In one outdoor scene of *The Brothers Karamazov* (US 58) it ceases to snow—on one side of the screen only.

☆ A bookmaker in *The Man Who Could Not Lose* (US 14) needed a packing case to pay off a $10,000 bet. Later in the film he was able to pay a winner $300,000 by handing over a small metal cashbox.

☆ The nostalgia pic *Slumber Party '57* (US 77) succeeded in making two spectacular goofs. A girl is seen reading *Lolita* a year before the novel was published. And a radio commentary of the fourth game of the 1957 World Series is heard to emanate from Yankee Stadium. The game was played in Milwaukee.

☆ In *Hair* (US 79), Treat Williams joins the army in place of John Savage, and goes off to war wearing Savage's dog tags. When he is killed, though, it is the name of the character played by Williams, not the character played by Savage, which appears on his tombstone.

☆ A 1930s news-stand in Wim Wenders' *Hammett* (US 82), set in San Francisco, has an enamel sign which reads 'The News of the World sold here'. Britain's largest-selling Sunday newspaper has never been on news-stand sale in San Francisco or any other part of the USA.

☆ Joan Collins, Kathleen Harrison and Yvonne Mitchell are released from Holloway Gaol in *Turn the Key Softly* (GB 53) and take a tube train bearing a destination board saying 'Uxbridge'. They get off the same train at Piccadilly but the destination board now reads 'Hounslow'.

☆ Stunts are done in a single take whenever possible. Evidently more than one was needed for the scene in *Diamonds are Forever* (GB 71) in which James Bond evades his pursuers by tilting his car to escape down a narrow alley. The car enters the alley tilted on its right wheels and emerges tilted on the left wheels.

☆ The newspaper headline read by the Dead End Kids in *Angels with Dirty Faces* (US 38) has the word 'kidnapper' spelt 'kidnaper'.

☆ TV aerials on the rooftops of Victorian London are conspicuous in *The Wrong Box* (GB 66).

☆ Anachronisms are usually visual or in the dialogue. In *The Draughtsman's Contract* (GB 83) it is a background noise that dispels, at least for ornithologists, the illusion of the film's 17th-century setting. The gentle cooing of a collared dove is not a sound that would have fallen on Jacobean ears. The species was unknown in Britain until 1955.

One of the most inexplicable anachronisms occurs in the version of Nagisa Oshima's *Cruel Story of Youth* (Jap 60) belatedly released in the US in 1984. In a climatic scene towards the end, a huge handprinted poster for *Paris, Texas* (US 84)—in English—looms in the foreground. The scene has obviously been inserted at a later date, but to what purpose?

☆ The first film seen as a child by former BBC Director General Sir Hugh Greene was *Tarzan of the Apes* (US 18). His most distinctive memory of it was the fact that one of the apes wore sneakers.

☆ In *The Taking of Pelham 1, 2, 3* (US 74), Transit Authority offical Walter Matthau tells an overawed visitor that the New York Subway is the most extensive underground system in the world. It isn't. It has 28·2 miles less track than the London Underground.

☆ The deathbed scene of the mother in *Happiness* (US 24) was marred by the fact that the 'corpse' was visibly breathing.

☆ *I'll Tell the World* (US 34) was an unexceptional picture about an American newspaperman's adventures in a Ruritanian kingdom. At one juncture in the script the hero is congratulated on saving the kingdom for the second time. Nowhere in the preceding scenes had he saved it the first time.

☆ President Lincoln admits California into the Union in 1847 in *Der Kaiser von Kalifornien* (Ger 36). In fact James Polk was President at the time; Lincoln did not become President until 14 years later.

☆ Tacky horror movie *Unhinged* (US 83) twice affords glimpses of the clapperboard.

☆ Jacqueline Bisset takes a flight in a Boeing 747 in a scene in *Rich and Famous* (US 81) set in 1969— somewhat before the plane left the drawing board.

☆ *Seven Days in May* (US 64) is about a plot to overthrow the US Government, the seizure of power to take place on the seventh day, a Sunday. This is to coincide with the running of the Preakness horserace. There is no horseracing in the US on Sundays.

☆ In the Agatha Christie whodunnit *Eye of the Needle* (GB 82), set in 1938, the dollar conversion rate is quoted at its 1981 level.

☆ 'Sime' of *Variety* wrote of the society melodrama *Should a Woman Divorce* (US 15): 'It all depends. If her husband wears one evening dress suit and two black bows through six years and five reels, yes. And if he leaves a room with one of the black bows striped in white, reaching the next room with an all-black bow on, yes, again. Or if the most eminent surgeon in New York receives his patients in the dirty-looking white uniform usually worn by an interne on an ambulance, and which the same surgeon had on six years before in Vall, Iowa, still yes. And if a Packard car can leave a depot with the top up, in clear weather, reaching the farm house with the top down, then going to Chicago (from Vall) and again to New York, seemingly on fast passenger trains (along with the principals), divorce the husband or the car by all means.'

☆ *Scarface* (US 83), set in Miami in 1980, shows *USA Today* magazine being sold on the street. *USA Today* was founded in 1982.

☆ The car chase in *Among the Missing* (US 34) is visibly through the streets of Los Angeles, though the setting of the story is New York.

☆ *Gas* (Can 81) is set in what is supposed to be an average town in middle-America. Unfortunately all the cars in the town have Canadian licence plates.

8 Colour, Sound and Scope

Colour

The first commercially successful natural colour process was two-colour Kinemacolor, developed by George Albert Smith of Brighton for the Urban Trading Co., London. Smith made his first colour film by this process outside his house at Southwick, Brighton, in July 1906. It showed his two children playing on the lawn, the boy dressed in blue and waving a Union Jack, the girl in white with a pink sash.

The first commercially produced film in natural colour was G. A. Smith's *A Visit to the Seaside* (GB 08), an eight-minute short featuring the White Coons pierrot troupe and the Band of the Cameron Highlanders which was trade shown in September 1908. Taken at Brighton, it showed children paddling and eating ice cream, a pretty girl falling out of a boat, and men peeping at the Bathing Belles changing in their bathing machines. The first public presentation of Kinemacolor before a paying audience took place at the Palace Theatre, Shaftesbury Avenue, on 26 February 1909 and consisted of 21 short films, including scenes taken at Aldershot, sailing at Southwick, the Water Carnival at Villefranche and the Children's Battle of Flowers at Nice.

The first dramatic film in natural colour was the Kinemacolor production *Checkmated* (GB 10), directed by Theo Bouwmeester, who has also played the lead role of Napoleon. **The first American dramatic film in natural colour** was Eclair's Kinemacolor production *La Tosca* (US 12), with Lillian Russell. A total of 54 dramatic films were produced in Kinemacolor in Britain from 1910–12. In the USA there were only three dramatic productions in Kinemacolor besides *La Tosca*. These were *Mission Bells* (US 13), *The Rivals* (US 13) and *The Scarlet Letter* (US 13), the latter starring D. W. Griffith's wife Linda Arvidson.

The first full-length feature film in colour was a five-reel melodrama, *The World, the Flesh and the Devil* (GB 14), produced by the Union Jack Co. in Kinemacolor from the play by Laurence Cowen. Starring Frank Esmond and Stella St Audrie, it opened at the Holborn Empire on 9 April 1914 billed as 'A £10,000 Picture Play in Actual Colours' in 'four parts and 120 scenes'. Like most of the Kinemacolor dramas, the acting and direction (F. Martin Thornton) were execrable, the colour impressive.

Kinemacolor was an additive process in which both filming and projection were done through red and green filters. The drawbacks were the cost of the special projector used and the wear on the film, which passed through the projector at twice normal speed. Nevertheless, it was installed at some 300 cinemas in Britain and achieved success overseas as well, notably in the United States and Japan. On the production side Kinemacolor was limited in its application because it could not be used for indoor work. There was also a virtue to this, since it encouraged location shooting at a time when black-and-white productions were becoming progressively more studio-bound. One enterprising Kinemacolor venture was **the first colour western**, Theo Bouwmeester's *Fate* (GB 11), set in Texas but filmed in Sussex!

The first all-colour feature film, 1914.

Kinemacolor was particularly well suited for films of pageantry, two of the most successful releases being a newsreel of King Edward VII's funeral in May 1910—at which no less than nine kings were present—and a spectacular two-hour presentation of the 1912 Delhi Durbar. Others included the Coronation of King George V, the Naval Review of June 1911 and the Investiture of the Prince of Wales at Caernarvon. Production came to a halt when Charles Urban, the guiding spirit behind Kinemacolor, left for the US in 1914 to propagate the British war effort through films.

The first colour talkie was Frans Lundberg Films' *Vals ur Solstrålen* (Swe 11), directed by Ernst Dittmer and starring Rosa Grünberg, which was premièred at the Stora Biografteatern in Malmö, Sweden, on 1 May 1911. The 215 ft short was made by the Biophon synchronised disc sound process. The colour process is not recorded, but it was probably stencilled.

The first feature-length sound film in colour was MGM's two-colour Technicolor production *The Viking* (US 28), directed by R. William Neill with Donald Crisp as Leif Ericsson, the legendary discoverer of America, and Pauline Starke as the lovely Helga. It was premièred on 2 November 1928 with synchronised score and sound effects.

The first all-colour talkie feature was Warner Bros' two-colour Technicolor musical *On With the Show* (US 29), directed by Alan Crosland with Betty Compson and Joe E. Brown, which was premièred at the Winter Garden, New York, on 28 May 1929.

The first British talking feature in colour was Talkicolor's *Knowing Men* (GB 30), produced, directed and scripted by Elinor Glyn from her own novel in French and English versions with Danish star Carl Brisson playing opposite Austrian actress Elissa Landi. Although made in colour, the film was released in black-and-white. The first to be released in colour was BIP's *A Romance of Seville* (GB 29), which was originally shown as a silent in 1929 but had sound added in July 1930. Colour process unknown. The first film made as a talkie to be released in colour was BIP's *Harmony Heaven* (GB 30), a musical about a composer (Stuart Hall) who wins fame and the hand of his girl (Polly Ward) despite the attentions of a flirtatious socialite (Trilby Clark).

The first Technicolor film was *The Gulf Between* (US 17), a five-reeler starring Grace Darmond and Niles Welch, produced by the Technicolor Motion Picture Corporation in a two-colour additive process and

Kodak's Eastman Color SP print film, the stock used for most colour features from the mid-fifties onwards, had a life of seven to ten years before the colour faded. A new film stock, Eastman Color Print Film 5384, introduced as standard for professional colour work in 1982, has a life of 90 to 100 years.

The colour values of Van Gogh's celebrated painting of a cornfield are not true to nature, according to director Vincente Minnelli. When he made *Lust for Life* (US 56), there was a scene in which Van Gogh is seen painting the picture (the original was used in the film), followed by a dissolve to an actual cornfield. In order to make the real corn match the colours rendered in the painting, Minnelli was obliged to spray the entire field with golden dye.

premièred at the Aeolian Hall, New York, on 21 September 1917. It was **the first full-length colour feature produced in the USA** and the third in the world.

The first feature in subtractive Technicolor was Chester Franklin's *The Toll of the Sea* (US 22), starring Anna May Wong, which was premièred at the Rialto Theater, New York, on 26 November 1922. **The first Technicolor interior shots** were taken for a colour sequence in *Cytherea* (US 24).

The Technicolor Motion Picture Corporation had been founded by Dr Herbert Kalmus of the Massachusetts Institute of Technology in 1915. The earliest Technicolor process was not unlike Kinemacolor and depended on the use of filters on both camera and projector. Following his development of a reasonably successful two-colour subtractive process, Dr Kalmus took Technicolor to Hollywood in 1923. The main problem was that the double-coated film was given to cupping and scratched more easily than monochrome. To most producers the cost at 27¢ a foot was prohibitive, compared with 8¢ a foot for monochrome stock, but with the coming of talkies the feverish search for novelty by the major studios encouraged its use and 33 all-colour Technicolor features were made in the three years 1929–31.

The first film in three-colour Technicolor was Walt Disney's Silly Symphony cartoon *Flowers and Trees* (US 32), premièred 17 July 1932 at Grauman's Chinese Theater, Hollywood. The first dramatic subject was *La Cucaracha* (US 34), released at the RKO-Hill Street Theater, Los Angeles, on 15 November 1934 and the first three-colour Technicolor sequence in a feature was in MGM's *The Cat and the Fiddle* (US 34).

The first feature made entirely in three-colour Technicolor was Rouben Mamoulian's *Becky Sharp* (US 35) with Cedric Hardwicke and Miriam Hopkins. Not everyone appreciated the innovation. A critic for *Liberty* magazine wrote that the performers looked like 'boiled salmon dipped in mayonnaise'. **The first in Britain** was *Wings of the Morning* (GB 37), a race-track drama starring Henry Fonda and French actress Annabella, which opened at the Gaumont, Haymarket, in May 1937.

The first three-colour film stock which could be used in any standard 35 mm camera was Technicolor Monopack, which was used for the first time on the exterior shots of *Lassie Come Home* (US 42). Formerly special cameras had to be rented for colour work.

The best Technicolor film: Natalie Kalmus, head of the Technicolor colour consultants seconded to all productions in Technicolor, nominated as the best Technicolor film of all time *The Red Shoes* (GB 48).

The most widely used colour process: Technicolor held almost a monopoly of the three-colour field from 1932 until 1952, when *Royal Journey* (Can 52) was released in Kodak's new Eastman Color process. Within three years Technicolor had fallen into second place, with 112 films being produced in Eastman Color in 1955 against 90 in Technicolor. Eastman Color is now used for virtually all colour films produced in the West. Metrocolor, Warnercolor and De Luxe are all processes using Eastman Color stock and films credited 'Color by Technicolor' are generally made with Eastman Color negative but printed by Technicolor laboratories.

The shortest colour sequence consisted of two frames of Alfred Hitchcock's *Spellbound* (US 45). Towards the end of the film, a split-second scene of a gun blast was presented in vivid red Technicolor.

DECLINE OF BLACK-AND-WHITE FILMS

Not surprisingly the USA was the first country to produce more films in colour than black-and-white, the 50–50 stage being reached c. 1955. Elsewhere colour was not considered appropriate to naturalistic, 'social realism' films or to subjects of serious concern. It was only in the 1960s, when colour television and the increasing use of colour in magazines made anything in monochrome unacceptable, that colour movies became omnipresent. In Britain colour became predominant in 1965, when 46 colour films were produced against only 34 monochrome. Only three years later monochrome production was down to a single picture, with 72 colour releases. 1969 was the first year in which British production was 100 per cent colour. France, long the bastion of grainy monochrome effects, had succumbed by 1967, when only four out of 120 films were shot in black-and-white. Japan had reached a 50–50 stage by 1965, but within three years the proportion of monochrome features had dropped to 25 per cent. Italy maintained some black-and-white feature productions up to 1968, when seven out of 153 films were shot in monochrome, but very few after that.

In the Far East the changeover was generally slower. Out of the total of 763 films produced in India in 1982, 43 were black-and-white. All Burmese films were black-and-white before 1983, the year a colour laboratory was established in Rangoon processing Fuji Colour.

Colour and black-and-white production in Great Britain 1937–69					
	C	B/W		C	B/W
1937	2	174	1954	32	78
1938	3	131	1955	33	62
1939	3	81	1956	35	56
1940	1	49	1957	31	84
1941	0	46	1958	23	88
1942	1	38	1959	24	75
1943	1	46	1960	20	90
1944	1	34	1961	32	77
1945	2	37	1962	25	101
1946	6	35	1963	31	76
1947	3	55	1964	34	41
1948	7	67	1965	46	34
1949	6	95	1966	58	11
1950	5	76	1967*	84	6
1951	7	68	1968	72	1
1952	14	87	1969	86	0
1953	14	88			

Since 1970 nearly all production has been in colour.

* Colour television introduced in Britain

Sound

The first presentation of sound films before a paying audience was made by Oskar Messter at 21 Unter den Linden, Berlin, in September 1896. The sound system employed synchronised Berliner discs, but there is no record of the titles of the films or the performers in them. **The first artistes known to have performed in a sound film** were Giampetro and Fritzi Massary, who appeared in a scene from an operetta filmed by Max Skladanowski, probably before the end of 1896.

The earliest known talking films were presented by Clément Maurice of the Gaumont Co. at the Phono-Cinéma-Théâtre of the Paris Exposition on 8 June 1900. They included: Sarah Bernhardt and Pierre Magnier in the duel scene from *Hamlet*, playing Hamlet and Laertes respectively; Coquelin in Rostrand's *Cyrano de Bergerac*; Coquelin and Mesdames Esquilar and Kervich in Molière's *Les Précieuses Ridicules*; Felicia Mallet, Mme Reichenberg and Gabrielle Réjane of the Comédie Française in scenes from *Madame Sans-Gêne* and *Ma Cousine*. In addition there were synchronised opera films (q.v.) and ballet films (q.v.).

The earliest known talking film with original dialogue was *Lolotte* (Fr 00), a comedy written and directed by Henri Joly and premièred at the Théâtre de la Grande Roue at the Paris Exposition. The scene takes place in a hotel bedroom and is played by three characters, a newly-married couple and the patron of the hotel, the latter performed by Joly himself. The dialogue script survives.

Above left
Making a Tri-Ergon sound-on-film talkie in Berlin in 1923.
(*Backnumbers*)

Below left
A soundproof camera booth at Warner's in the early
Vitaphone days.

Right
Enterprising cinema managers with an Allefex machine could
achieve almost any sound effect back in 1912 from rattling
chains to a Force 9 gale.

The first sound films produced in Britain were a
series of song subjects made by Walter Gibbons in
the autumn of 1900 under the name of Phono-Bio-
Tableaux Films. They included Vesta Tilley singing
The Midnight Son, Algy the Piccadilly Johnny and
Louisiana Lou and G. H. Chirgwin giving a soulful
rendering of *The Blind Boy*. There was also an actuality with sound effects titled *Turn Out the Fire Brigade*.
The earliest British talking film was Hepworth's
Vivaphone version of *Cinderella* (GB 13) with Gertie
Potter.
The first sound-on-film process was patented by
French-born Eugene Lauste of Stockwell, London,
on 11 August 1906. It was not until 1910, however,
that Lauste succeeded in recording and reproducing
speech on film, employing an electromagnetic re-
corder and string galvanometer. He used a French

gramophone record, selected at random, for the
initial trial, and by coincidence the first words to be
heard in the playback were 'J'entends très bien main-
tenant' ('I hear very well now'). A colleague in the
film business, L. G. Egrot, recalled visiting Lauste at
his home in Benedict Road about this time: 'He had
already started building his camera to take pictures
and sound together, the front part of the camera
allowing to test the different systems he was experimenting with for sound recording . . . Very often on
a Sunday, a bandmaster friend of his, Mr Norris,
would come along with his band and play in the
garden of the house where, in 1911, Mr Lauste had
had a wooden building erected as an experimenting
studio. The machine was taken out, with all leads,
some pictures would be made and some sound
recorded.'
    Lauste completed his sound-on-film projector and
reproducing apparatus in 1913, and was about to
embark on the commercial exploitation of the process
when war broke out. In 1916 he went to the USA with
the idea of obtaining financial backing, but the entry
of America into the war the following year put an end
to his hopes.
**The first sound-on-film productions to be presented
in public** were shown at the Alhambra Kino in Berlin
on 17 September 1922 before an invited audience of
1000 people. The films were made by the Tri-Ergon
process developed by Joseph Engl, Joseph Massolle

and Hans Vogt and included **the first sound-on-film dramatic talkie**. Titled *Der Brandstifter/The Arsonist* (Ger 22), and adapted from Von Heyermann's play of the same name, it had a cast of three with Erwin Baron playing seven of the nine parts. The other films were mainly orchestral with vocal accompaniment. Press reaction was mixed, criticism being levelled not so much against the level of technical achievement, but at the notion of talking films, which it was said would destroy the essential art of the motion picture—mime—and detract from the cinema's international appeal.

The first American sound-on-film motion picture was *Lincoln's Gettysburg Address* (US 22), a monologue delivered by Ellery Paine, made by Polish-born Prof. Joseph Tykocinski-Tykociner, research professor of electrical engineering at the University of Illinois, and presented in the Physics Building on 9 June 1922. The film was not released commercially.

The first presentation of sound-on-film productions before a paying audience took place at the Rialto Theater, New York, on 15 April 1923, when Lee De Forest showed a number of singing and musical shorts made by the Phonofilm process. The sound films formed a supporting programme to the main (silent) feature, *Bella Donna* (US 23) with Pola Negri. During the following 12 months, 34 cinemas in the eastern United States were wired for Phonofilm sound. The films made at the De Forest Studios between 1923 and 1927 included monologue numbers by Eddie Cantor, George Jessel and Chic Sale; dialogues between Gloria Swanson and Thomas Meighan and between Weber and Fields; Folkina's *Swan Dance*; playlets with Raymond Hitchcock; and orchestral subjects featuring Ben Bernie, Paul Sprecht and Otto Wolf Kahn.

The year 1924 saw three notable sound-on-film 'firsts' from Phonofilm. President Coolidge was filmed delivering a campaign speech on the White House lawn, **the first time that a President of the USA had spoken from the screen; the first Technicolor film with a sound-track was made**, the subject being Balieff's *Chauve Souris* danced in the open air; and **the first dramatic talkie film to be released commercially**, *Love's Old Sweet Song*, a two-reeler directed by J. Searle Dawley with Mary Mayo and Una Merkel in the leading roles. Although the first to exploit sound-on-film commercially, De Forest failed to establish talking pictures as a major entertainment medium and the Phonofilm patents were eventually

When primitive sound-on-disc 'talkies' were introduced during the Edwardian era, volume was sometimes considered rather more important than quality. William Haggar, proprietor of a cinema in Aberdare, Wales, advertised that his films 'can be heard two miles away'.

One of the effects of the introduction of talkies in the USA was to kill off the theatrical stock companies. In 1929 there were still 200 companies playing stock; by 1939 there were five.

taken over by William Fox together with those of the Tri-Ergon system.

The first public demonstration of sound-on-film in Britain took place at the Finsbury Park Cinema on 14 June 1923, when a programme of Phonofilm shorts was trade shown. The *Bioscope* reported: 'Several pictures were projected, including a vocalist rendering a song from *Carmen*, a dancer imitative of Pavlova with dying swan musical effects, and others. The synchronisation was as near perfect as possible, but the articulation sounded to me somewhat throaty.'

The first sound-on-film production shown before a paying audience in Britain was the Technicolor dance subject *Chauve Souris* (US 24), which was shown with musical sound-track at the Tivoli in London in the summer of 1925. **The first talking film seen by a paying audience** introduced a programme of Phonofilm singing and orchestral shorts premièred at the Empire, Plumstead on 4 October 1926 and consisted of Sidney L. (now Lord) Bernstein explaining how Phonofilm worked.

The first sound-on-film talkie produced in Britain was De Forest Phonofilms' *The Gentleman* (GB 25), a comedy short directed and scripted by William J. Elliott. The following year four short dramas were produced at the Clapham Studios by the De Forest Phonofilm Co. of Great Britain and in 1927 there were films of Edith Sitwell reading her own poems and Sybil Thorndike in a scene from Shaw's *Saint Joan*.

The first full-length feature film with sound (in part) was D. W. Griffith's *Dream Street* (US 21), a United Artists release. Described by one cinema historian as 'a dreadful hodgepodge of allegory and symbolism', it was a total failure when originally presented as an all-silent picture at the Central Theater, New York, in April 1921. After it had closed, Griffith was persuaded by Wendell McMahill of Kellum Talking Pictures to add a sound sequence. On 27 April the star, Ralph Graves, was brought to the Kellum Studios on West 40th Street to record a love song on synchronised disc, and this was included when the film reopened at the Town Hall Civic Centre on 1 May. A fortnight later a second sound sequence was added, consisting of the shouts and whoops of Porter Strong shooting craps together with other background noises, and this version opened in Brooklyn on 29 May 1921.

The only other feature movie with vocal sound prior to *The Jazz Singer* (see below) was José A. Ferreya's *La Muchacha del Arrabal* (Arg 22), starring Lidia Lis.

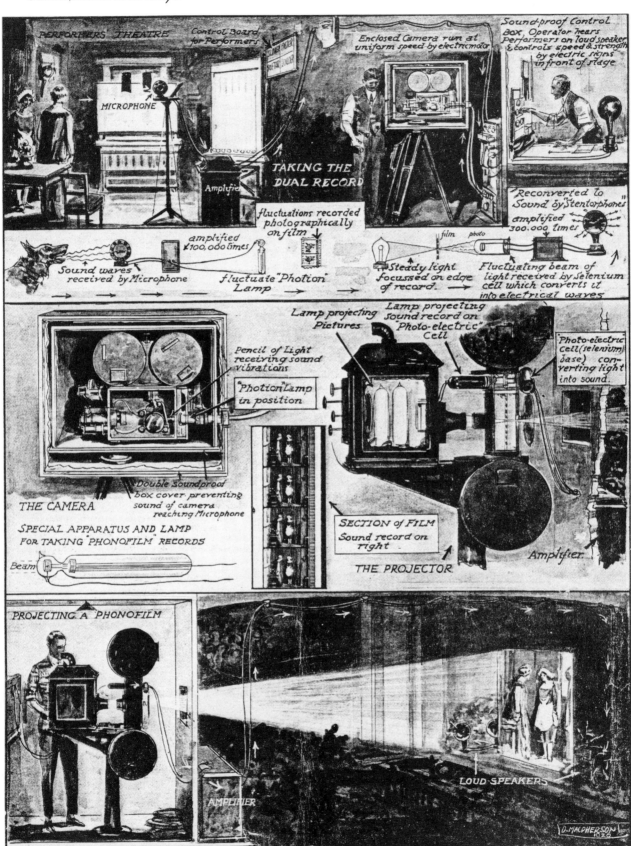

> When the talkies came to the island of Malta in 1930 with the Valetta première of *Broadway Melody* (US 29), the manager of the Royal Opera House asked all his patrons to wear tennis shoes to lessen the noise of late arrivals. Such precautions were not sufficient to make the innovation the success it had been in other parts of the world. The sound-on-disc system got out of sync, so that the men talked in women's voices and vice versa. Come the half-way interval, the show had to be abandoned because a man was found dead in the stalls.

Early sound cameras were confined to soundproof camera booths, so there was little camera movement in the first talkies. The answer to camera noise was the soundproof casing known as a 'blimp', used for the first time with a mobile camera mounted on a dolly for the shooting of *Birds of Prey* (US 31). (*Backnumbers*)

The first talking feature film (in part) was Warner Bros' Vitaphone (sound-on-disc) production *The Jazz Singer* (US 27), directed by Alan Crosland and starring Al Jolson, which opened at the Warner Theatre on Broadway on 6 October 1927. The initial, historic talking sequence takes place in Coffee Dan's, where Jack Robin (Al Jolson) has been singing *Dirty Hands, Dirty Face*. Amidst the applause, Jolson holds up his hands and urges: 'Wait a minute. Wait a minute. You ain't heard nothin' yet! Wait a minute, I tell you. You ain't heard nothin'. You wanna hear *Toot-toot-tootsie*? All right. Hold on.' Turning to the band, Jolson says: 'Now listen: you play *Toot-toot-tootsie*. Three choruses, you understand, and in the third chorus I whistle. Now give it to 'em hard and heavy. Go right ahead . . .'

The second and only other talking sequence was longer and involved a conversation between Jack Robin and his mother (Eugenie Besserer). In view of the many conflicting claims concerning the amount of dialogue in *The Jazz Singer*, it is worth recording that exactly 354 words are spoken in the two talking sequences, 60 in the first and 294 in the second. Jolson speaks 340, Eugenie Besserer 13 and Warner Oland (as the father) one—'Stop!' The dialogue sequences were unscripted, because Warner Bros had only intended to make a film with synchronised music and singing, not a talkie. Jolson, however, ad libbed—the famous line 'You ain't heard nothin' yet' was in fact a catchphrase he used in his stage performances—and studio head Sam Warner liked the snatches of talk enough to keep them in.

The first all-talking feature was Warner Bros' *Lights of New York* (US 28), which was premièred at the Strand Theater, New York, on 6 July 1928. Starring Helene Costello, the picture was so determinedly all-talking that the dialogue continued non-stop from opening credits to end title. Warner's billed it as '100% Talking!'; *Variety* commented '100% Crude'.

The first sound-on-film feature was Fox's *The Air Circus* (US 28), with Louise Dresser and David Rollins, which opened at New York's Gaiety on 1 September 1928. The dialogue sequence lasted 15 minutes. **The first all-talking sound-on-film feature** was Raoul Walsh and Irving Cummins' Fox western *In Old Arizona* (US 28), with Edmund Lowe and Warner Baxter, which was also **the first talkie shot outdoors**. It opened 26 December 1928 at the Criterion, Los Angeles.

The first British talking feature was Marshall Neilan's *Black Waters* (GB 29), a melodrama about a mad captain posing as a clergyman to murder people aboard a fog-bound ship. Starring John Loder and Mary Brian, the picture was produced in the USA by Herbert Wilcox for British & Dominions Sono Art World Wide.

The first talkie made in Britain was Alfred Hitchcock's *Blackmail* (GB 29), produced by British International Pictures at Elstree with Anny Ondra and John Longden and premièred at the Regal, Marble Arch, on 21 June 1929. The first reel had incidental

> The two basic systems for recording sound in the pioneer days—synchronised disc and sound-on-film—was briefly joined by a third in 1925 when Douglas Shearer, brother of Norma, conducted a once-only experiment in matching a film with a radio broadcast. He persuaded Pete Smith, MGM press agent, to make a trailer for *Slave of Fashion* (US 25) in which the two stars of the film, Norma Shearer and Lew Cody, exchanged dialogue. The short was shown simultaneously in a number of Los Angeles cinemas while Cody and Norma Shearer delivered their lines via radio station KFI. Receivers in the cinemas relayed the broadcast through horn amplifiers placed behind the screens. Synchronisation was far from perfect at some of the cinemas, Norma's lines appearing to come from Cody's lips and vice versa, and the experiment was not repeated.

Talkies were shown to a paying public for the first time in Britain in October 1926. *The Graphic* explained how they worked.

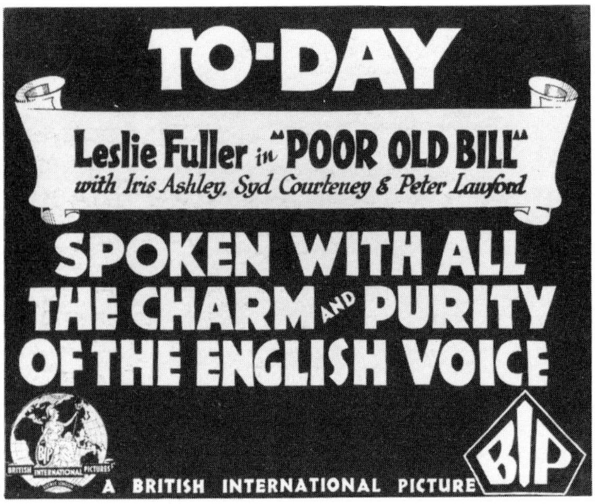

Many English people had never heard an American accent before the advent of the talkies. British producers were quick to exploit insular prejudice.

sound and music only, but the characters began to speak in the second as the plot unfolded. It was billed as '99 per cent talking', a pardonable exaggeration. The posters also carried the slogan 'See and Hear It—Our Mother Tongue As It Should Be Spoken'—a sideswipe at the American–English that had dominated the screen hitherto.

Britain's first all-talking feature was *The Clue of the New Pin* (GB 29) adapted from the Edgar Wallace novel of the same name and produced by British Lion in association with British Photophone. The film was directed by Arthur Maude, starred Donald Calthrop and Benita Hume, and was released on 16 December 1929. An undistinguished production, the film is chiefly memorable for the fact that a rising young stage performer called John Gielgud played a bit part in it.

The first dubbed film was Lee De Forest's Phonofilm production *Love's Old Sweet Song* (US 24). The film contains one exterior scene, in which Una Merkel is strolling down a street when she hears the title song being sung by Mary Mayo from indoors. Since the exterior footage had to be shot silent, the song was dubbed in afterwards.

The first occasion on which another actor's voice was substituted for that of a member of the cast was in *The Patriot* (US 28). The performer concerned, Emil Jannings, threatened legal proceedings if the new sound-track was not erased, and the dubbed voice was removed. The first film released with a substitute voice was *The Wolf of Wall Street* (US 29), in which the heavily accented Hungarian actor Paul Lukas played a partner in a firm of stockbrokers. His dialogue was dubbed by Lawford Davidson. Happily Lukas's accent did not hinder the development of his career—he continued to play major roles in Hollywood pictures for another 40 years.

The first British film to be dubbed was Alfred Hitchcock's *Blackmail* (GB 29). The female lead, Czech actress Anny Ondra, spoke almost no English and her voice was dubbed by Joan Barry (later the mother of heiress Henrietta Tiarks). This was done by the novel method of having Miss Barry read Miss Ondra's lines into a microphone while the latter was performing.

The first use of post-synchronisation with the same actors was in a feature film by Ernst Lubitsch for *The Love Parade* (US 29), as a means of freeing the camera from the constraints of the immobile sound-proof booth used in early talkies. By using a silent camera, he was able to counter the static camera positions that marred most of the pioneer sound projections and dub in the dialogue afterwards.

A new motion picture technique, borrowed from television, is para-dubbing. It was used for Richard Attenborough's and other English roles in Satyajit

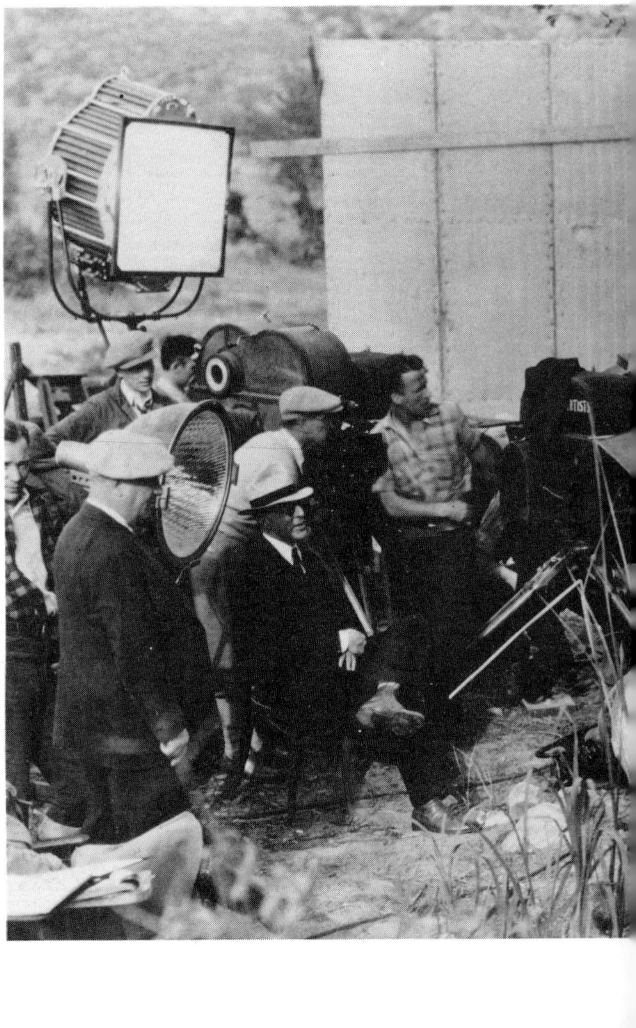

Immobile and highly conspicuous microphones like this one, seen on the set of *Abraham Lincoln* (US 30), put a severe constraint on the actors in early talkies. A step or two away from the mike or even a movement of the head could mean loss of sound.

Ray's *Shatranj ke Khilari/The Chess Players* (Ind 78). Since Attenborough dubbed in Hindi by the normal dubbing system would have sounded absurd, a voice speaking Hindi was dubbed *over* the English voice, which was specially moderated. The effect was the same as in TV interviews where an interpreter does a voice-over translation.

The first film with stereophonic sound was the re-edited version of Abel Gance's *Napoleon Bonaparte* (Fr 27), which was presented with added dialogue and sound effects at the Paramount Cinema, Paris, in 1935. The stereophonic process used had been patented by Gance and André Debrie three years earlier.

The first American productions with stereophonic sound were the Warner Bros' productions *Santa Fe Trail* (US 40) and *Four Wives* (US 40), presented in Vitasound. The first successful system of stereophonic musical accompaniment was Fantasound, developed by Walt Disney Studios in association with RCA and first employed for the sound-track of Disney's feature-length cartoon *Fantasia* (US 41), with music by the Philadelphia Orchestra under the direction of Leopold Stokowski.

By the end of 1929, no less than 234 competing sound systems had been installed in the 9000 cinemas in the USA wired for sound. This Cinephone projector could show both sound-on-film and synchronised disc movies. The disc turntable was soon to become redundant. (*Backnumbers*)

The first use of Sensurround was for the 'quake effects in Universal's *Earthquake* (US 74). A more sophisticated version with Sensurround music was used for *Rollercoaster* (US 77) and this was also the first time that sound effects had been recorded in the process live. Previously, both in *Earthquake* and in *Midway* (US 76), the Sensurround effects were dubbed in at the post-production stage.

The first use of overlapping dialogue—The talking picture borrowed the stage convention, far removed from reality, whereby no more than one character speaks at once. Credit for introducing overlapping dialogue in the interests of naturalism is usually given to Orson Welles for *Citizen Kane* (US 41), but in fact the technique had been used a year earlier in Howard Hawks' wild and witty *His Girl Friday* (US 40), with Cary Grant and Rosalind Russell.

Film stock with magnetic sound track was first produced experimentally by Du Pont for RCA in 1947. It was adopted by Warner Bros in 1949 and Paramount in 1950, but at this stage was used for recording only, the sound being transferred to optical tracks for projection.

The first commercially released film with magnetic track was *This is Cinerama* (US 52).

The first use of radio microphones—'neck mikes'—

Pistol shots could not be recorded by the Vitaphone sound-on-disc system used for making *The Jazz Singer* (US 27) and other early Warner Bros talkies, since the intensity of the sound would have caused the stylus to jump the groove. A drummer simulated the noise instead.

by performers on set was in *My Fair Lady* (US 64). The use of concealed microphones worn on the person enables a vocalist who is moving about the set to perform a whole number in one take.

DOLBY SOUND

A noise reduction system designed to eliminate hiss from recorded sound—as its originator has expressed it, 'real high fidelity means reproducing the silence as accurately as the sound'. It was developed by American-born Ray Dolby in an old dressmaking factory in Fulham, where Dolby Laboratories were established in May 1965 with four employees and a refusal of credit from the bank. The first practical application was by Decca for disc recording, the units being known as the S/N Stretcher because they were for stretching the signal-to-noise ratio. After Ray Dolby had heard some engineers at Pye referring to his equipment as 'a Dolby', he decided to change the name to his own. **The first film with Dolby sound** was Stanley Kubrick's *A Clockwork Orange* (GB 71). This used Dolby noise reduction on all pre-mixes and masters, though the release prints had a conventional optical sound-track. The first film with a Dolby encoded mono sound-track was *Callan* (GB 74) and the first with a Dolby encoded stereo optical sound-track was Ken Russell's *Lisztomania* (GB 75). Some 600 films have been released with Dolby sound to date and worldwide there are over 6000 Dolby-equipped cinemas, including 160 in Britain.

The last wholly silent film (ie without a sound-track) **produced in America** for general distribution was George Melford's *The Poor Millionaire* (US 30), with Richard Talmadge (who played both the hero and the villain) and Constance Howard. It was released by Biltmore Pictures on 7 April 1930, just 30 months and a day after the presentation of the first talkie feature. Only four other silents had been issued in 1930, all of them low budget westerns. The following year there were no silents but four films with synchronised music and sound effects only, including Chaplin's *City Lights* and F. W. Murnau's *Tabu*. Silent produc-

tion in America, however, was not finished for good. In 1950 Georges Sadoul reported that silent features in colour were being produced in San Francisco for the Chinese population of the United States.

The last British silent feature was Argyle Art Pictures' *Paradise Alley* (GB 31), starring John Argyle and Margaret Delone, the story of a miner who takes the blame when his brother shoots a man during a robbery. It was released in March 1931.

European production had made virtually a complete change-over to sound by the end of 1931. Elsewhere, the last silent feature from Soviet Russia—Alexander Medvekin's *Schastye/Happiness*—was released in 1935 and the last seven Indian silents were issued the same year. Japan took longer to make the change. In 1937, 209 out of 524 movies were without dialogue—50 with sound effects and music, 159 silent. The following year saw the virtual demise of the silent, with 16 'sound effects only' films and 15 wholly silent. As late as 1952 in Burma, where only two of the 22 production companies were equipped to make sound films, production totalled 40 silents and 6 talkies.

The last silent feature films for commercial distribution were produced in Thailand at the end of the 1960s. Although talkies had been produced in the 1930s, World War II totally disrupted both the Thai economy and its film industry and subsequently all films were shot silent on 16 mm stock until 1965. Dialogue was supplied by actors and actresses 'live dubbing' in cinemas from a cubicle next to the projection booth. After 1965 the popularity of Indian-style musicals stimulated producers to shoot sound song-and-dance sequences on 35 mm stock for interpolation with otherwise silent 16 mm footage. According to the Thai Motion Picture Producers' Association 'by 1970 all Thai films were shot on 35 mm with sound'.

POST-SOUND SILENTS

A small number of non-dialogue dramatic films (usually with synchronised music and sound effects) have been produced since the last war. The following list excludes ballet films and similar mime productions and also the Burmese, Thai and Chinese–American silents referred to above.

Russel Rouse's atomic spy thriller *The Thief* (US 52) with Ray Milland; Kaneto Shindo's *The Island* (Jap 60), about a family living on a tiny island, which won the One World Prize at Melbourne in 1962 for 'the feature film which can be most universally understood'; the Bengali production *Ingeet* (Ind 61); Luiz Rosemberg Filho's 2¼-hour *Imagens* (Bra 72), which had no music or sound effects; Yoichi Takabayashi's *Gaki Zoshi* (Jap 72); Andrej Brzozowski's *Obszar Zamkniety/The Closed Area* (Pol 72); *Bez/A Film without Words* (Yug 73); Terry Bourke's spinechilling horror meller *Night of Fear* (Aus 73), about a woman who is terrorised by a crazed hermit after her car crashes on a lonely road; the cast-of-one *Vase de noces* (Bel 73); the cast-of-none *Model* (Gre 74), directed by Kostas Sfikas; Morton Hellig's *Once* (US 74) with Christopher Mitchum; Milos Radivojević's *Testament* (Yug 75); *Robinson Columbus* (Den 75); Jérôme Savetry's *La Fille du garde barrière/The Gatekeeper's Daughter* (Fr 75); James Scott's *Coilin and Platonida* (GB 76); V. Miroshnichenko's *Lone Wolf* (USSR 77), from the Turgenev story about a giant woodsman endeavouring to bring up two motherless children as well as care for the estate; Gérard Myriam Benhamou's *Adom ou le sang d'Abel* (Fr 77), about Cain and Abel; *Pentimento* (Neth 78); Pim de la Parra's *Dirty Picture* (Neth 80); *Le Dernier Combat* (Fr 83), about an apocalypse in which the world has been left with only a handful of men and a single woman survivor; Jos Stelling's *De Illusionist* (Neth 83); *Rebelote* (Fr 84), made by youthful French director Jacques Richard as a tribute to the silent days and with a score by Pierre Jansen for performance by a live orchestra—the picture was billed, less than accurately, as 'The first truly silent film since the advent of sound in 1927' (a claim that ignored the large output of silents between 1927 and 1931, as well as the films listed here); and the only full-length cartoon feature without dialogue, Donyo Donev's *We Called Them Montagues and Capulets* (Bul 84), a social comedy loosely based on *Romeo and Juliet*. Mel Brooks' *Silent Movie* (US 76) nearly qualifies for this list, but there was one word of dialogue.

Languages

Hollywood's foreign language output was confined principally to the early talkie period, the largest proportion being in Spanish for the Latin American market. Beginning with a dubbed version of RKO's *Rio Rita* (US 29), a total of 96 Spanish language movies were produced in the USA during the ensuing six years, the majority by Fox, and another 17 were made by Paramount at their Joinville studios in France 1930–33. **The first foreign language feature made in America with live dialogue** was *Sombras de Gloria/Blaze of Glory* (US 30). It was a Sono Art-World production.

During the period 1930–35 a total of 63 French language pictures were produced by MGM, First National, Paramount, Warner Bros, RKO, Universal, Fox, Columbia and Twentieth Century. The Paramount productions were made at Joinville, outside Paris, where they also produced in Spanish, German, Italian, Swedish, Portuguese, Romanian, Polish, Czech and Dutch.

The first foreign language talkie to be subtitled in English was *Two Hearts in Waltz Time* (Ger 29). The titles were written by Herman Weinberg (an Ameri-

In order to simulate the language of the mutants in *Island of Lost Souls* (US 32), Paramount's director of recording Loren L. Ryder recorded a track consisting of a combination of animal sounds and foreign languages played backwards. He then alternately speeded up the loop and slowed it down, producing cadences that were strange and horrifying. Audience reaction was even more dramatic than had been anticipated; the vibratory effect on the eardrums induced instant nausea.

can), who sub-titled a record number of over 400 films during the ensuing 40 years.

The first talkie produced in different language versions was British International Pictures' trilingual *Atlantic* (GB 29), which was released with separate English, French and German sound-tracks. Besides its overseas release, the German version was shown at the Alhambra, Leicester Square, to cater for the large German population living in London prior to World War II.

Multilingual films in which foreign characters speak in their own language were comparatively rare before *The Longest Day* (US 72) broke with former Hollywood practice by having the Germans speaking German and the French speaking French. There had been occasional examples, however, from the earliest days of sound, starting with G. W. Pabst's *Westfront 1918* (Ger 30), with dialogue in French and German. Others included Pabst's *Kameradschaft* (Ger 31), about a mining disaster involving French and German miners; Luis Trenker's *Der verlorene Sohn/The Prodigal Son* (Ger 34), in German and English; Jean Renoir's *La Grande Illusion* (Fr 37), in French, English and German; Nyrki Tapiovaara's *Stolen Death* (Fin 38), a thriller in Finnish, Swedish and Russian; *Carl Peters* (Ger 41), in German and English; *Die Letze Chance* (Swz 45), in German and French; Guy Hamilton's *The Colditz Story* (GB 54), in English and German; *La Chatte* (Fr 58), in French and German; and Jean-Luc Godard's quadrilingual *Le Mépris/Contempt* (Fr/It 63), in which Michel Piccoli spoke Italian, Brigitte Bardot spoke French, Jack Palance spoke American and Fritz Lang spoke German, the need for sub-titles being effectively reduced by Giogia Moll's role as the interpreter.

Even silent films could be multilingual. Rex Ingram stated in *Motion Picture Directing* (New York 1922) that when making films with foreign settings, he made his principals speak the language of the country. Explaining that 'it helps them materially in keeping to the required atmosphere', he admitted ruefully 'few of them like to go to this trouble . . .'

The most multilingual film producing country is India, which has produced films in the following 43 languages since 1931: Angami Naga, Arabic, Assamese, Avadhi, Badaga, Bengali, Brijbhasha, Burmese, Chhattisgadhi, Coorgi, Dogri, English, German, Gorkhali, Gujarati, Haryanavi, Hindi, Kannada, Kashmiri, Khasi, Konkani, Magadhi, Maithili, Malay, Malayalam, Manipuri, Marathi, Marwari, Nepalese, Oriya, Persian, Punjabi, Pushtu, Rajasthani, Sanskrit, Sindi, Sinhalese, Swahili, Tamil, Telegu, Thai, Tulu, Urdu.

The only film made in Latin was Derek Jarman's *Sebastiane* (GB 76), a homophile interpretation of the legend of St Sebastian. The translator, Jack Welch, used ingenious shifts to put Roman barrack-room language of the third century AD into comprehensible Latin, but in one instance had to resort to a Greek word, rendering the epithet *Motherfucker* as *Oedipus*. *Sebastiane* enjoys the unique distinction of being the only English film ever to have been released in Britain with English sub-titles. The only other film in a classical or 'dead' language has been the Sanskrit production *Sankaracharya* (Ind 82).

The first talking film made in dialect was *Mieke* (Bel 30), a comedy made in Antwerp by Felix Bell (Gaston Schoukens) in the Anversois patois.

The only feature film made in Esperanto was *Incubus* (US 65), whose star William Shatner is familiar to TV viewers as Capt Kirk of *Star Trek*. The avowed purpose of using Esperanto dialogue was to give the movie an air of the supernatural. It is one of the few American films to have been released with English sub-titles.

The first Hindi film produced in Britain was the Cabana Film Co.'s comedy-thriller *Bhaag Re Bhaag* (GB 78), which had its world première at Leytonstone State Cinema on 4 February 1978. Produced and directed by M. A. Qayyum, it was a cops and robbers caper set in London and Epping Forest, starring Saghir Rahi and an overweight young English lady credited only as Patsy.

The first feature film in Irish was Bob Quinn's *Poitin/ Poteen* (Eire 78), with Cyril Cusack as a poteen maker attempting to evade the attentions of the Garda in Connemara.

The first feature film in Welsh was Tom Haydon's documentary reconstruction *The Last Tasmanian* (Aus/GB/Fr 79). The curious circumstance of a film set in Tasmania being filmed in Welsh (there were also English and French language versions) is explained by the fact that Haydon's partner in the enterprise was the Welsh anthropologist Rhys Jones.

The first feature film in Gaelic was Barney Platts-Mills' *Hero* (GB 82), a medieval fable about sorcery and magic in a remote corner of the Scottish highlands.

The only full-length feature film made in pidgin English was *Wokabout Bilong Tonten* (Aus 73), filmed in New Guinea with Anton Sil and Taruk Wabei in the lead roles.

Wide Screen

The first wide screen process used for a feature film was Panoramico Alberini, devised by Filoteo Alberini in 1914, which was employed by Enrico Guazzoni for a sequence of *Il Sacco di Roma* (It 23).

The first wide screen system to employ the use of an anamorphic lens—a lens that squeezes a wide image on to standard gauge film as in Cinemascope (see below)—was Henri Chrétien's Hypergonar, used by Claude Autant-Lara in making *Construire un feu* (Fr 27).

The first feature film in wide screen throughout to be released was *Happy Days* (US 30), made in the 70 mm Fox Grandeur process. A wide screen version of *Fox Movietone Follies of 1929* (US 29), was made earlier, but it was released in a conventional frame format.

The first wide screen system to incorporate both wide gauge film and the anamorphic lens was Camera 65, later renamed Ultra-Panavision, which was originally employed on *Raintree County* (US 57).

CINEMASCOPE

This was developed by the French inventor Henri Chrétien from his original anamorphic Hypergonar system of 1927. Fox bought the patent rights in 1952 and **the first Cinemascope feature film**, *The Robe* (US 53), was premièred at Grauman's Chinese Theater in Hollywood on 24 September 1953. **Britain's first Cinemascope production** was also her first wide screen feature: MGM's *Knights of the Round Table* (GB 54), with Robert Taylor and Ava Gardner.

Wide screen is almost as old as the movies. This wrestling match was filmed by the Lamda Co. in 1895 for showing on the Eidoloscope projector.

The first feature made in a wide screen process throughout—*Happy Days* (US 30).

The 70 mm panoramic film introduced by Alberini in 1914. (*Grant Lobban Collection*)

CINEMARA

This was developed by self-taught inventor Frederick Waller of Huntington, New York, who had originated the idea as early as 1939 for an oil exhibit at the New York World's Fair. His intention had been to project moving pictures all over the interior surface of the oil exhibit building, but technical difficulties persuaded him to compromise with a half-dome, using eleven 16 mm projectors to cover the vast area of screen. After the war he resumed work on the process, reducing the number of projectors to three and adopting a wide screen ratio of almost 3:1. The first production in the perfected process was *This is Cinerama* (US 52), which opened in New York on 30 September 1952 and ran for 122 weeks. **The first full-length Cinerama feature** was MGM's *The Wonderful World of the Brothers Grimm* (US 62).

The widest wide screen system ever was Raoul Grimoin-Sanson's Cinéorama, presented at the Paris Exposition of 1900. Ten synchronised projectors threw a 360° image on to a screen 330 ft (100 metres) in circumference. The audience sat on the roof of the projection booth, which was designed to simulate the basket of a giant balloon. The hand-coloured film took the audience on an aerial voyage of discovery, looking down on the great capitals of Europe. Unfortunately, the show had to be terminated after three performances, since the heat of the ten projectors constituted a fire risk. The concept of 'cinema-in-the-round' was not revived until Walt Disney introduced Circarama at the Brussels World Fair in 1958, though on a screen of more modest circumference.

Smellies

The first attempt at combining an appropriate odour with a film was made by S. L. Rothapfel—the celebrated showman 'Roxy'—at the Family Theater, Forest City, Pa., in 1906. Roxy dipped cotton wool in a rose essence and strung it in front of a powerful electric fan during the showing of a news film of the Pasadena Rose Bowl Game. Similar experiments were made in 1929, when Albert E. Fowler, manager of the Fenway Theater, Boston, used a pint of lilac scent tipped into the ventilating system to accompany the credits of *Lilac Time* (US 29). Synthetic orange blossom perfume was sprayed from the ceiling when *Broadway Melody* (US 29) opened on Broadway.

The first film made as a 'smellie' was a wide-screen travelogue about China, *Behind the Great Wall* (US 59), filmed in Totalscope, DeLuxe Color, stereophonic sound and the new wonder of Aromarama. Premièred at the DeMille Theater, New York, on 2 December 1959, the film was accompanied by a range of 72 smells that included incense, smoke, burning pitch, oranges, spices and a barnyard of geese. The process, devised by Charles Weiss, involved circulating the scents through the ventilating system. Unlike most novelty films, *Behind the Great Wall* had the smell of success even without the gimmicks. It won two awards when it was shown at the Brussels Film Exposition unaccompanied by Aromarama.

The first feature 'smellie' was Michael Todd Jnr's *Scent of Mystery* (US 60), a 70 mm Technicolor thriller made in Smell-O-Vision and premièred at the Cinestage, Chicago, on 12 January 1960. The scents used—ocean ozone, pipe tobacco, garlic, oil paint, wine, wood shavings, boot polish, etc.—were piped to each individual cinema seat on cue from the 'smell-track' of the film.

A less sophisticated technique was used to waft the scents of Odorama to spectators of the 'sickie smellie' *Polyester* (US 82), which starred the outsize transvestite Divine playing an all-American housewife whose

The old adage that the inventor is the last man to make money from his invention may often be true, but Milton L. Gunzburg stole a march on the entrepreneurs ready to reap the richest pickings from his enterprise. Inventor of the Natural Vision 3-D process used for *Bwana Devil* (US 52) etc., he secured the sole distribution rights for the Polaroid glasses necessary for viewing three-dimensional movies. Purchasing the glasses from the Polaroid Land Co. at 6c each, he sold them to theatres at 10c each. For a halcyon six months Gunzburg was distributing six million pairs a week till his contract ran out in July 1953. His $6,240,000 profit represented a better return than the box-office gross on any of the shortlived 3-D movies.

3-D OUTPUT

During the 3-D boom that began with the low budget *Bwana Devil* (US 52), over 5000 cinemas in the USA were equipped to show 3-D movies, but the fad was shortlived. 3-D production figures were: 1952—1; 1953—27; 1954—16; 1955—1. In addition there were 3-D movies produced in Japan, Britain, Mexico, Germany and Hong Kong, but many of these (as well as some of the US productions) were released flat.

Sporadic production resumed in 1960 and since the release of the much-hyped *Comin' at Ya!* (US 81) there has been a hesitant revival. The roster to date:

September Storm (US 60)—the first Cinemascope movie in 3-D
The Mask (Can 61)
Wondrous Adventures of a Magician (Chn 62)
The Bubble aka *Fantastic Invasion of Planet Earth* (US 66)
La Marca del Hombre Lobo (Sp 69)
The Stewardesses (US 70)

The Four Dimensions of Greta (GB 72)—first British 3-D feature released as such
The Flesh and Blood Show (GB 72)
Domo Arrigato (Jap 72)
Flesh for Frankenstein (Fr/It 73)
Prison Girls (US 73)
Willie Nelson's Second Annual Fourth of July Picnic (US 74)
SOS over the Tayga (USSR 75)
Tiger Man (HK 76)
The Lollipop Girls in Hard Candy (US 76)
Ape (S. Kor 76)
Dynasty (Tai 77)
Thirteen Nuns (Tai 77)
The Porno Hostess in 3-D (It 79)
Remi (Jap 79)
The Surfer Girls (US 80)
The Capitol Hill Girls (US 80)
Love in 3-D (FRG 80)
What the Swedish Butler Saw (Swe 80)
The Magnificent Bodyguards (HK 81)
Rottweiler aka *Dogs of Hell* (US 81)
Comin' at Ya! (US 81)
Menage à Trois (Fr 82)

Parasite (US 82)
The Spooky Movie Show (US 82)
Friday the 13th Part 3 (US 82)
Treasure of the Four Crowns (Sp 82)
Spacehunter: Adventures in the Forbidden Zone (US 83)
Laughing Laughing (Chn 83)
The Man Who Wasn't There (US 83)
Jaws 3-D (US 83)
Metalstorm (US 83)
Amityville 3-D (US 83)
Venus (Fr? 83)
Scoring! (US 84)
Blonde Emanuelle (Fr? 84)
Emmanuelle 4 (Fr 84)
Hyperspace (US 84)
Chain Gang (US 84)
Tales of the Third Dimension (US 84)
Hit the Road Running (US 84)
Kuftichathan (Ind 84)—Malalayam
Silent Madness aka *Omega Factor* aka *Night Killer* (US 84)
Starchaser: The Legend of Orin (US 85)

---

life stinks. Each member of the audience was given a card numbered from one to ten. When a number was flashed up on screen, the spectator scratched the card with a coin, releasing a revolting odour appropriate to whatever disgusting activity was taking place before his eyes.

Three-dimensional Films

The first presentation of 3-D films before a paying audience took place at the Astor Theater, New York, on 10 June 1915. The programme consisted of three one-reelers, the first of rural scenes in the USA, the second a selection of scenes from Famous Players' *Jim, the Penman* (US 15), with John Mason and Maria Doro, and the third a travelogue of Niagara Falls. The anaglyphic process used, developed by Edwin S. Porter and W. E. Waddell, involved the use of red and green spectacles to create a single image from twin motion picture images photographed $2\frac{1}{2}$ in apart. The experiment was not a success, for much the same reason that 3-D failed 40 years later. Lynde Denig wrote in *Moving Picture World*: 'Images shimmered like reflections on a lake and in its present form the method couldn't be commercial because it detracts from the plot'.

The first 3-D film in colour was *Rêve d'Opium* (Fr 21), produced by the Société Azur in the System César Parolini.

The first 3-D feature film was Nat Deverich's 5-reel melodrama *Power of Love* (US 22), starring Terry O'Neil and Barbara Bedford, premièred at the Ambassador Hotel Theater, Los Angeles, on 27 September 1922. Produced by Perfect Pictures in an anaglyphic process developed by Harry K. Fairall, it related the adventures of a young sea captain in California in the 1840s. The only other American

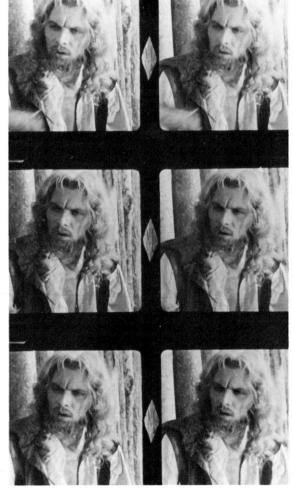

The Russian process used for *Robinson Crusoe* (USSR 47), the first feature-length colour talkie in 3-D, gave stereoscopic relief without the audience having to wear special glasses.

feature in 3-D prior to *Bwana Devil* (US 52) was R. William Neill's *Mars* aka *Radio Mania* (US 22), with Grant Mitchell as an inventor who succeeds in making contact with Mars via television. It was produced in Laurens Hammond's Teleview process.

The first 3-D talkie was a De Forest Phonofilm comedy short titled *Lunacy* (US 24), which opened at the Rivoli and Rialto Theaters in New York as part of the supporting programme on 22 September 1924. The 3-D process was called Plastigram.

The first feature-length talkie in 3-D was Sante Bonaldo's *Nozze vagabonde* (It 36), starring Leda Gloria and Ermes Zacconi, which was produced by the Società Italiana Stéréocinématografica at the Cines-Caesar studios. The 3-D cameraman was Anchise Brizzi.

The first 3-D talkie in colour was an UFA short titled *Zum Greifen Nah/You Can Nearly Touch It* (Ger 37), premièred at the UFA Palast in Berlin on 27 May 1937.

The first feature-length talkie in colour and 3-D was Alexander Andreyevsky's Soyuzdetfilm production *Robinson Crusoe* (USSR 47), starring Pavel Kadochnikov as Crusoe and Y. Lyubimov as Friday. The process used, Stereokino, was the first to successfully dispense with anaglyphic spectacles. Developed by S. P. Ivanov, it employed what were known as 'radial raster stereoscreens'—a corrugated metal screen with 'raster' grooves designed to reflect the twin images separately to the left and right eye. The most difficult technical problem encountered during the production of *Robinson Crusoe* was persuading a wild cat to walk along a thin branch towards the camera. After five nights occupied with this one scene, the cameraman succeeded in getting a satisfactory shot. The effect, according to accounts, was riveting, the animal seeming to walk over the heads of the audience and disappear at the far end of the cinema.

The first British 3-D films were five Stereo-Techniques' shorts directed by Raymond Spottiswoode and presented in the Tele-Cinema at the Festival of Britain in 1951: *A Solid Explanation*; *Royal River*; *The Black Swan* (ballet with Alicia Markova); *Now is the Time*; and *Round is Around* (animated).

The first British feature in 3-D was Montgomery Tully's *The Diamond*/US: *The Diamond Wizard* (GB 54), a thriller with Dennis O'Keefe and Margaret Sheridan. It was released 'flat'.

The first 3-D feature with stereophonic sound was Warner Bros' *House of Wax* (US 53). When it was premièred at the Paramount Theater, New York, with 25 speakers, the *Christian Science Monitor* was moved to deplore the 'cacophony of sound hurtling relentlessly at one from all directions'. André de Toth, director of the movie, may have been able to hear the cacophony, but was unable to see the 3-D effect, as he only had one eye.

Holography

The first successful demonstration of holographic film was given before the Twelfth Congress of the International Union of Technical Association Cinematographers in Moscow in 1977. The system was developed by Prof. Victor Komar of the Cinema and Photo Research Institute and gives an illusion of three-dimensional substance without the use of anaglyphic spectacles. Komar's method involved the deployment of laser beams to create a representation of objects in depth based on wave interference. If a spectator moved from one vantage position to another, he would see the object represented from a different angle, as in natural vision. The first film made in holography was a 30-second experimental subject showing a beautiful girl putting jewellery into a glass case. It could be viewed by a maximum of four spectators at a time.

9 Music

Cinema music is almost as old as cinema. Felicien Trewey's presentation of films at the Regent Street Polytechnic in February 1896, the first before a paying audience in Britain, had a piano accompaniment described in a contemporary newspaper report as 'a trifle meagre'. It was not long before presenters began to recognise the virtue of appropriate music, though whether the quartet of saxophones engaged by the Cinématographe Lumière when it opened in the Boulevard Saint-Denis, Paris, in March 1897 was able to produce something apposite for every item on the programme is not recorded. In America, Albert E. Smith of Vitagraph recalled that the first of their productions to be shown with musical accompaniment was a news film of the burial of the victims of the sinking of the *USN Maine*, premièred at a disused opera house on Lexington Avenue, New York, in March 1898 with an orchestra playing a funeral dirge. Similarly, Henry Hopwood recorded in his book *Living Pictures* (1899) that a news film of the Albion launch disaster, screened only 30 hours after the event, was accompanied by an orchestra playing *Rocked in the Cradle of the Deep*.

The resident cinema orchestra is recorded as early as 1901, when Britain's first picture house, Mohawk's Hall, in Islington, appointed the 16-piece Fonobian Orchestra under the direction of Mr W. Neale. This remained rare, though, until the advent of the super-cinemas after 1914, which generally employed large orchestras under competent if not distinguished conductors. At the smaller houses, a single pianist would do the job, sometimes far from competent, but occasionally brilliant—Shostakovich supported himself while writing his first symphony in 1924 by playing the piano in an 'old, draughty and smelly' backstreet cinema in Leningrad. (He lost the job a year later because he stopped playing during an American comedy to roar with laughter.) Less brilliant at the keyboard, but later to achieve celebrity in another walk of life, was the pianist at the Market Street Cinema in Manchester, about the same time. She was Violet Carson, the hairnetted Ena Sharples of television's *Coronation Street*.

Picture houses that could not afford even the meagre wages of a pianist might fall back on the humble phonograph, which was adequate only if there was no intention that the music should relate to the mood of the film being shown. The manager of the first cinema in Leicester, opened in 1906, recalled that he installed a gramophone (later replaced by a mechanical organ) operated by the girl in the pay-box, but that the choice of records bore no relation to the action on the screen, their only purpose being to drown the noise of the projector.

Inappropriate music could easily destroy the enjoyment of an otherwise meritorious picture, and in the USA the usual practice was for production companies to issue 'cue sheets' of suitable mood music with screen cues, an idea inaugurated by the Edison Co. in 1910 and copied by Vitagraph the following year. The consequence of leaving the choice of music to individual accompanists could be disastrous. Paul McCartney's father Jim McCartney recalls leading a small orchestra providing the music for *The Queen of Sheba* (US 21) when it was presented in Liverpool. For the chariot race sequence they played *Thanks for the Buggy Ride* and for the tragic culmination of the picture, the death of the Queen, they chose *Horsey Keep Your Tail Up*.

The first purpose-built cinema organ (i.e. a unit organ) was designed by Robert Hope-Jones, a Liverpudlian who joined the Wurlitzer Co. of North Tonawanda, New York, in 1910 and killed himself four years later after his employers, exasperated at the expense incurred by his constant improvements in design, had locked him out of the factory on full salary. The first Wurlitzer cinema organs were installed in theatres in 1911.

The first unit organ in Britain was a Compton 3/14 (14 units on three manuals) installed at the Surrey County Cinema, Sutton in 1921.

Britain's first Mighty Wurlitzer was a Model D Unit Orchestra Organ, with six units on two manuals, installed at the Picture House, Walsall, Staffs, in January 1925. Although removed in 1955, the organ is still in use at the Congregational Church at Beer, South Devon.

The largest cinema organ in the world was the Wurlitzer installed at Radio City Music Hall, New York, in 1932. Still in use, it has 58 ranks of pipes controlled from either or both of the twin four-manual consoles.

The largest organ ever installed in a cinema in Britain

was a Christie 4/30 (30 units on four manuals), installed at the Regal (now Odeon), Marble Arch and first played by Quentin Maclean in 1928. It incorporated a piano and a carillon, the latter feature being unique.

The largest British Wurlitzer, a £15,000, 15-ton, 4/21 Wizard, was also inaugurated by Mr Maclean at the Trocadero, Elephant and Castle, in 1930. Removed when the cinema closed in 1961, it now belongs to the Cinema Organ Society and is sited at the South Bank Polytechnic, London.

The only Mighty Wurlitzer still operational in a cinema is the 4/15 at the Gaumont State, Kilburn.

The first film music to be specially composed for the screen was by Romolo Bacchini for the Cines productions *Malia dell'Oro* (It 06) and *Pierrot Innamorato* (It 06).

Italy was the first country whose major films were regularly supplied with an original score, a practice that did not become widespread elsewhere until the 1920s. Notable early examples were *Lo Schiavo di Cartagine* (It 10), with music by Osvaldo Brunetti, *La Legenda della Passiflora* (It 11), for which Mazzuchi composed the music, and rival scores by Walter Graziani and Colombio Aron for the two simultaneous productions of *The Last Days of Pompeii* (It 13). Pizetti's *Fire Symphony* was written to accompany the sequence in *Cabiria* (It 13) in which the young maidens are sacrificed to the fire god Moloch. Mario Costa wrote a distinctive score for *Storia del Pierrot* (It 13) and Tosti lent prestige to *A marechiare ce sta 'na fenesta* (It 15).

The first composition for a French film was Wormser's score for Michel Carré's six-reel production of *L'Enfant prodigue* (Fr 07), the longest film made anywhere in the world at that date. It preceded by a year the score which is usually said to have been the world's first specially composed film music, written by Camille Saint-Saëns for Film d'Art's inaugural production *L'Assassinat du Duc de Guise* (Fr 08). This was an arrangement for piano, two violins, viola, cello, bass violin and harmonium. Other pioneer film composers were: Mikhail Ippolitov-Ivanov, who composed scores for *Stenka Razin* (Rus 08), Russia's first dramatic film, and for Vasili Goncharov's *Song About the Merchant Kalashnikov* (Rus 08); R. N. McAnally, whose composition, originally thought to be for the Salvation Army's *Soldiers of the Cross* (Aus 00), is now believed to have been for their similarly titled religious feature *Heroes of the Cross* (Aus 09); the

Brazilian Costa Junior, composer of a score for *Paz e Amor* (Bra 10), a two-reel 'talkie' with dialogue spoken by actors behind the screen; and V. Strizhevsky, who wrote the music for *Zaporozhskaya Syetch* (Rus 11),

America and Britain trailed behind the countries mentioned above. **The first original score to accompany an American production** was composed by Walter Cleveland Simon for Sidney Olcott's *Arrah-Na-Pough* (US 11), while **the first for a full-length American feature production** was by Victor Schertzinger for *Civilization* (US 15). The same year Joseph Carl Breil became **the first American composer to receive screen credit**, for his score to accompany D. W. Griffith's *The Birth of a Nation* (US 15), but this was not a wholly original work. The 151-page score comprised excerpts from the works of a dozen famous composers, including Beethoven, Schubert, Schumann, Weber and Wagner, together with some original themes by Breil himself, notably the *Love Strain* reflecting the final love scene of the Little Colonel (Henry B. Walthall) and Elsie Stoneman (Lillian Gish).

The first composer to write music for a British film was Sir Edward German, who was paid 50 gns by W. G. Barker for 16 bars of music to accompany the Coronation scene in *Henry VIII* (GB 11). It was reported at the time that Barker 'personally supervised rehearsals of special music which he thinks important in adding to the effectiveness of the subject', which suggests that there may have been a rather more complete score than the single theme by German.

The first film music composed for a sound film was commissioned by Erich Pommer, Gaumont manager for Central and Eastern Europe, for *Les Heures* (Fr 13) aka *Die Stunden*, a 55-minute non-acted 'visual impression' of a day—morning, noon and night. The score was recorded on disc and synchronised with the film. The name of the composer is not known.

The first sound-on-film score was Hugo Riesenfeld's music for Fritz Lang's *Siegfried* (Ger 22), recorded on Phonofilm for its presentation at the Century Theater, New York, in 1925. This was a year earlier than the sound-on-disc Vitaphone accompaniment to Warner Bros' *Don Juan* (US 26), usually claimed as the first synchronised sound feature film.

The first British feature film with synchronised music was Lupu Pick's *A Knight in London* (GB 29), starring Lilian Harvey.

The first film in which the music was dubbed (ie post-recorded) was *Innocents of Paris* (US 29), a Maurice Chevalier confection whose success was mainly due to the theme song *Louise*.

The first song specially composed for a motion picture was *Mother I Still Have You*, written by Louis Silvers and sung by Al Jolson in *The Jazz Singer* (US 27).

> The majority of cinema organs which have survived are now in the hands of collectors or preservation societies. Some, though, have been put to practical use. One of the less probable last resting places of a cinema organ is the Chapel of St Francis in Wormwood Scrubs Prison, where the prisoners are uplifted by the strains of the Ealing ABC's Compton.

The world's most bankable film composer. Four-times Oscar winner John T. Williams has scored six of the seven biggest box-office successes on record.

The first hit-song from a movie was 'Sonny Boy', also an Al Jolson number, from *The Singing Fool* (US 28), composed by Buddy De Sylva, Lew Brown and Ray Henderson. Within nine months of the film's release, the sales of 'Sonny Boy' records had reached 2 million and sheet music 1¼ million.

The first record of a song from a movie was *Mother o' Mine* from *The Jazz Singer* (US 27), sung by Al Jolson and released on the Brunswick label on 6 October 1927 concurrently with the film's première.

The first golden disc awarded for a record selling one million copies was presented to bandleader Glenn Miller on 10 February 1942 for *Chattanooga Choo Choo*, the hit song he and his orchestra had performed in the Fox musical *Sun Valley Serenade* (US 41).

The first sound film with a full symphonic score was RKO's *The Bird of Paradise* (US 32), with music by Viennese composer Max Steiner. It was also the **first complete film score to be issued on disc**, released by RCA Victor as an album of 78s. Formerly producers had been unwilling to have music coming from an unidentified source, on the premise that audiences would be confused by hearing music where there was no visible orchestra. Hence, early sound films tended to confine the musical accompaniment to the front and end credits or to passages of the action where it could be clearly seen to emanate from a radio or gramophone. There is no evidence that audiences were confused, for once Steiner had established the symphonic score as integral to certain types of movie the source was never questioned. Steiner scored no less than 290 films during his seven years with RKO and 30 years with Warner Bros, including *King Kong* (US 33), *Gone with the Wind* (US 39), and his two Oscar-winning movies *New Voyager* (US 42) and *Since You Went Away* (US 44). The symphonic score fell into disfavour in the 1960s with the rise of pop and jazz accompaniments, but after a slow climb back in the 1970s reached its apogee with John Williams' Oscar-winning music for *Star Wars* (US 77).

The only time an orchestra composed entirely of strings has been used to record the musical accompaniment to a movie was for *Psycho* (US 60). Hitchcock wanted music that would help to terrify the audience and composer Bernard Herrman responded with what he described as a black-and-white sound to complement a black-and-white film of a black-and-white story. The shrieking violin strings played a significant part in making *Psycho* the film that many people remember as the most frightening they have ever seen.

The first feature-length rock concert film was Lee Robinson's *Rock 'n Roll* (Aus 59), an all-star performance from Sydney Stadium.

The first woman film composer was Jadan Bai, founder of the Sangeet Film Co. and mother of India's superstar Nargis, who made her musical debut with the score of *Talash-e-Huq* (Ind 35).

The first woman composer to write a complete score for a Hollywood feature was Elizabeth Firestone, daughter of tyre magnate Harvey S. F. Firestone, who scored the Robert Montgomery comedy *Once More, My Darling* (US 47).

The first woman to compose for a British feature was Elizabeth Lutyens, whose score accompanied the Christopher Lee–Diana Dors low-budget thriller *Penny and the Pownall Case* (GB 48).

The most successful film composer of all time—in terms of scoring the music for box-office hits—is Boston Pops resident conductor John T. Williams (1932–) who has composed the scores of six of the seven highest earning films in history: *E.T.* (US 82), *Star Wars* (US 77), *The Empire Strikes Back* (US 80), *Jaws* (US 75) and *Raiders of the Lost Ark* (US 81). He also has the *Superman* movies and *Indiana Jones* to his credit and has won four Oscars.

MUSIC ON SET

Providing music on set to create 'mood' for the performers, a common practice during the production of silent dramas, is usually said to have originated with D. W. Griffith's *Judith of Bethulia* (US 14), though the star of the film, Blanche Sweet, says she has no recollection of it. In fact the idea had originated in Europe at an earlier date, pioneer woman director Alice Guy playing a gramophone on set to assist the actors in emoting during the production of *La Vie du Christ* (Fr 06).

On occasions the practice got out of hand. Garbo was not satisfied with unadorned orchestral music and insisted on being sung to on set, it was reported in 1927. A soloist would join the studio orchestra and serenade her through a megaphone. Another demanding star caused an even greater onslaught of melody, though not entirely of her own volition. During an epic feud between Pola Negri and Gloria

The Philharmonia Orchestra recording Sir William Walton's score for *Hamlet* (GB 48) at Denham.

Swanson, whose respective egos were too great to be accommodated together in one studio, Swanson's director Allan Dwan hired a 70-strong brass band to drown the noise being made on Negri's adjacent set and persuade his opposite number to control the temperamental Polish star. In another instance the practice was itself instrumental in inflating a performer's ego to the point of affecting his career. Erich von Stroheim had commanded that whenever Anton Wawerka, who played the Emperor Franz Josef in *The Merry-Go-Round* (US 22) and in *The Wedding March* (US 28) appeared on set, the orchestra should strike up the Austrian national anthem. The custom even prevailed off set, all the Hollywood restaurants honouring Wawerka with the anthem whenever he entered their doors. The actor became so accustomed to this regal treatment that he suffered a breakdown when *The Wedding March* was completed and his imperial privileges withdrawn.

THE STAR AS COMPOSER

Charles Chaplin composed the score for all his films from *City Lights* (US 31) onwards. Noel Coward produced, directed, scripted and starred in *In Which We Serve* (GB 42) as well as composing the music. Less well known instances are: Robert Mitchum's composition of the music for the songs *The Ballad of Thunder Road* and *Whipporwill* in *Thunder Road* (US 58); the use of a portion of Lionel Barrymore's symphony *Tableau Russe* in *Dr Kildare's Wedding Day* (US 41); David McCallum's theme song for *Three Bites of the Apple* (US 67); and Brazilian soccer star Pele's score for his auto-biopic *Pele* (Mex 78).

10 Titles and Credits

Titles

THE TWELVE LONGEST FILM TITLES

☆ Lina Wertmüller's *Un Fatto di sangue nel commune di Siculiana fra due uomini per causa di una vedova si sospettano moventi politici. Amore·Morte·Shimmy. Lugano belle. Tarantelle. Tarallucci é vino.* (It 79). The English language title was *Revenge*.

☆ *The Persecution and Assassination of Jean-Paul Marat as Performed by the Inmates of the Asylum of Charenton under the Direction of the Marquis de Sade* (GB 66).

☆ *Les yeux ne veulent pas en tout temps se fermer ou peut-être qu'un jour Rome se permettre de choisir à son tour* (Fr/FRG 70).

☆ *Why Do I Believe You When You Tell Me That You Love Me, When I Know You've Been a Liar All Your Life* (GB 83).

☆ *La' il cielo é la terra si univano, la' le quattro stagioni si ricongiungevano la' il vento é la pioggia si incontravano* (It 72).

☆ *Mais que' es-ce que J'ai fait au Bon Dieu pour avoir une femme qui boir dans les cafés avec les hommes?* (Fr 80).

☆ *Those Magnificent Men in Their Flying Machines; or, How I Flew from London to Paris in 25 Hours and 11 Minutes* (GB 65).

☆ *Film d'amore é d'anarchia, ovvero stamattina alle 10, in via dei Fiori, nella nota casa di tolleranza* (It 72).

☆ *Izrada i otkrivanje spomenika velikom srpskom satiričaru Radoju Domanoviću kao i druge manifestacije povodom 100-godišnjice njegovog rodenja* (Yug 75).

☆ *Cafeteria or How Are You Going to Keep Her Down on the Farm after She's Seen Paris Twice* (US 73). Described as 'the short and sweet story of a girl and her 26 cows', this, the longest titled American fiction film, runs precisely one minute.

☆ *F.F.S.S. Cioé: 'Che mi hai portato a fare sopra a posillipo se non mi vuoi pui' bene?'* (It 83).

☆ *The Saga of the Viking Women and their Voyage to the Waters of the Great Sea Serpent* (US? 57)

ODD TITLES

Writing in *Films and Filming*, David McGillivray nominated *Betta, Betta in the Wall, Who's the Fattest Fish of All* (US 69) and *She Ee Clit Soak* (US 71) as 'the most preposterous movie titles ever conceived'. Other unusual titles include *Ojojoj* (Swe 66); *RoGoPaG* (It 63); *I-Ro-Ha-Ni-Ho-He-Yo* (Jap 60); *Ha, Ha, Hee Hee, Hoo Hoo* (Ind 55); *Sssssss* (US 73); *Phffft* (US 54). Rather

Few passages of literature have yielded so many film titles as these brief verses of *The Song of Songs* in the Bible: '...the time of the singing of the birds is come, and the voice of the turtle is heard in our land... Arise, my love, my fair one, and come away... Take us the foxes, the little foxes, that spoil the vines... for our vines have tender grapes...'. From them is derived: *The Voice of the Turtle* (US 48); *Arise My Love* (US 40); *The Little Foxes* (US 41); *Our Vines Have Tender Grapes* (US 45).

more comprehensible curiosities are *Telephone Girl, Typist Girl or Why I Became a Christian* (Ind 25); *After the Balled-Up Ball* (US 17); *In My Time Boys Didn't Use Hair Cream* (Arg 37); *The Film That Rises to the Surface of Clarified Butter* (US 68), but some explanation might be needed for *Egg! Egg?* (Swe 75) and *Cash? Cash!* (Bel 69). *Yes* (Hun 64) was followed by *No* (Hun 65) and the situation remained equally unclear with *Yes No Maybe Maybenot* (GB 75). *I Go Oh No* (Tai 84) is also somewhat enigmatic and the response to *I Know that You Know I Know* (It 82) might be *Okay Okay* (It 83). No answers were vouchsafed to the questions *Who Created the Yoyo? Who Created the Moon Buggy?* (Phi c. 80), though another unspoken question met with the response *No Thanks, Coffee Makes Me Nervous* (It c. 81). Some odd titles make more sense than first appears. *P'Tang Yang Kipperbang* (GB 83) is a recurring phrase in the film's dialogue, representing part of the codes and rituals of teenagers at school in the 1940s. A sci-fi comedy called *Recharge Grandmothers Exactly!* (Cz 84) was about robot grandmothers who take over the running of households. *Nocaut* (Mex 84) is not an unfamiliar word in Spanish, but simply the phonetic spelling of 'Knockout'—the picture is about boxing. Another recent Latin American film has the somewhat unexpected title of *J. S. Brown* (Bra 84) while an oddity called *duBEAT-e-o* (US 84) is also a name title—Ray Sharkey plays the eponymous character with this strange yet unexplained moniker. Wordless titles include Warhol's well-known **** (US 67); ... (Arg 71)—the English language title was *Dot Dot Dot*; and Michael Snow's ⟷ (Can 69). *Film without Title* (FRG 47) was the title of a Rudolph Jugert movie, but it was not apparent whether Vincenzo Ferrari's *Untitled* (It 73) had one or not. The makers of *Don't Worry, We'll Think of a Title* (US 65) evidently had trouble in doing so.

> **The longest single word in a movie title**, and undoubtedly the most unpronounceable, occurs in *Schwarzhuhnbraunhuhnschwarzhuhnweisshuhnrothuhnweiss oder Put-Putt* (FRG 67).

TITLE CHANGES

☆ *Livingstone* (GB 25), was reissued in America in 1933 as *Stanley*. (Livingstone was British; Stanley an American.) Numerous British films have needed title changes for the USA—*Carleton Browne of the F.O.*/US: *Man in a Cocked Hat* (GB 59) and *Never Take Sweets from a Stranger*/US: *Never Take Candy from a Stranger* (GB 60) are two obvious examples, but there is only one recorded instance of a simultaneous title change *within* Britain. *This England* (GB 41), a wartime flagwaver with Emlyn Williams and Constance Cummings, was retitled *Our Heritage* for release in Scotland.

☆ In China *Great Expectations* (GB 46) was released as *Bleeding Tears of Lonely Star*, *Nicholas Nickleby* (GB 46) as *Hell on Earth*, and *Oliver Twist* (GB 48) as *Lost Child in Foggy City*. Olivier's *Hamlet* (GB 48) became *The Prince's Revenge*.

☆ *Peyton Place* (US 57) played in Paris as *The Pleasures of Hell*, in Munich as *Glowing Fire Under the Ashes* and in Hong Kong as *The Cold and Warmth in the Human World*.

Guys and Dolls (US 55) was *Heavy Youths and Light Girls* in Germany, Indonesia changed *I'll Cry Tomorrow* (US 55) to *To Relieve Yourself From the Grief of Your Passions*, while Hong Kong looked for something catchier than *Not as a Stranger* (US 55) and came up with *The Heart of a Lady as Pure as a Full Moon Over the Place of Medical Salvation*.

☆ *Chicago, Chicago* was not the mid-west release title of *New York, New York*, but the Spanish title of Norman Jewison's *Gaily, Gaily* (US 69).

☆ *Dracula 72* (GB 72) did not reach France until a year after its release in Britain. When it did, the title had become *Dracula 73*. Similarly *Airport '79* (US 78) became *Airport '80* on its belated arrival in the UK.

☆ The working title of *Foxes* (US 80) was *Twentieth Century Foxes* until another film company intervened.

☆ The Spanish word for *Grease* (US 78) is *grasa*, but this translates literally as 'fat'. In Spain the movie was released as *Brillantina/Brillantine* and in Venezuela as *Vaselina/Vaseline*.

THE SHORTEST TITLES				DATE TITLES	
These have all had one letter or digit:	3 (US 56)	*111* (Hun 19)	5+1 (Bul 80)	*1514* (Hun 62)	English language title
	3 (US *c*. 80)	*113* (Sp 35)	5+5 (Isr 80)	*1740* (Can 77)	*1918* (US 85)
	3, 2, 1, 0 (Bel 6?)	*117* (Yug 78)	6×6 Jap 62)	*1776* (US 06)	*1919* (Sp 83)
A (Fr 64)	5, 5 (Isr 80)	*298* (Swz 65)	8×8 (US 57)	*1776* (US 72)	*1919* (GB 85)
A (It 69)	007 (Ind 75)	*322* (Cz 69)	8½×11 (US 74)	*1778* (Fr 78)	*1922* (Gre 79)
B (It 69)	7–9–13 (Den 34)	*329* (US 15)	11×14 (US 77)	*1789* (Fr 73)	*1925* (Bul 76)
C (It 70)	8½ (It 63)	*413* (US 14)	12+1 (Fr/It 70)	*1810* (Arg 60)	*1929* (Cz 74)—
D (It 70)	08/15 (FRG 54)	*491* (Swz 64)	16+1 (Jap 74)	*1812* (Rus 12)	English language title
E (Can 82)*	9.25 (Pol 29)	*625* (FRG 67)		*1812* (Ger 23)	
F (US 80)	10 (US 79)	*666* (US 81)	**WORD NUMBER TITLES**	*1812* (USSR 44)	*1929* (Fin 79)
G (US 72)	10.32 (Neth 65)	*813* (US 21)	*Zero* (GB 28)	*1812* (GB 65)	*1931* (GB 32)
G (GB/FRG 74)*	11:1 (GDR 59)	*813* (Jap 23)	*One* (US 80)	*1812* (Hun 73)	*1933* (Can/US 67)
G (Swe 83)*	12–10 (GB 19)	*911* (US 70)	*One, Two, Two* (Fr 78)	*1814* (Fr 11)	*1936* (It 81)
H (US 60)	13–13 (Sp 43)	*1501½* (US 70)	*One, Two, Three* (Ind 64)	*1848* (Rom 80)	*1941* (US 41)
I (Rom 66)	14–18 (Fr 63)	*5000* (US 70)	*One, Two, Three* (Pol 67)	*1860* (It 32)	*1941* (US 79)
I (Swe 66)*	21–87 (Can 63)	*7254* (US 71)	*Two* (USSR 65)	*1861* (US 11)	*1945* (Ger 45)
M (Ger 31)*	23–28 (US ? ?)	*7362* (US 67)	*Two* (Den 64)	*1866* (It 33)—English language title	*1948* (Fr 48)
M (US 51)*	25 (Moz 76)	*13,000* (Sp 41)	*Two* (US 64)	*1880* (Fr 63)	*1958* (Nor 80)
M (Cz 64)	27A (Aus 73)	*33,333* (Swe 24)	*Two* (Ind 65)	*1884* (GB 83)	*1967* (US 67)
O (GB 32)	30 (US 59)	*33,333* (Swe 33)	*Two* (US 74)	*1900* (US 72)	*1968* (US 68)
O (Jap 75)	30 (GB 83)	*77,297* (Cz 63)	*Two* (Sp 79)	*1900* (It/Fr/FRG 77)	*1970* (US 70)
P (Neth 64)	33 (USSR 67)	*750,000* (Gre *c*. 68)	*Two* (US 82)	*1905* (USSR 52)	*1971* (Ven 71)
Q (Fr/It/Bel 74)*	33 (GB 7?)	*300,000,000* (Neth 75).	*Three* (Yug 65)	*1907* (Rom 76)	*1972* (FRG 73)
Q (US 83)*	36–26–36 (US 67)		*Three* (GB 69)	*1913* (Bul 85)	*1983* (GB 83)
V (It 68)	42 (Ind 48)		*Three* (US 74)	*1914* (GB 15)	*1984* (GB 56)
W (US 73)*	42:6 (Swz 69)	**ARITHMETICAL TITLES**	*Five* (US 51)	*1914* (Ger 31)	*1984* (GB 84)
X (Swe 57)	44 (Mor 83)	*1+1* aka *Sympathy for the Devil* (GB 69)	*Seven* (US 79)	*1917* (GB 70)	*1985* (US *c*. 70)
X (US 62)	'49–'17 (US 17)	*1+1* (Can 61)	*Ten* (Jap 71)	*1918* (Fin 55)	*2010* (US 84)
Z (Fr/It 68)*	50–50 (US 23)	*1+1=1* (Yug 64)	*Thirteen* (Cz 83)	*1918* (USSR 58)—	*2084* (Aus 85).
$ (US 72)*	50–50 (Nor 82)	*1+1=2* (Neth 72)	*Fifteen* (Swz 68)		
3 (US 56)	50–50 (US 81)	*1+1=3* (Ger 29)	*Sixteen* (Arg 83)		
3 (US *c*. 80).	58/2b (Fr 57)	*1+1=3* (FRG 79)	*Sixteen* (It 73)	**FULL DATE TITLES**	
	66 (US 66)	*1=2?* (Fr 75)	*Seventeen* (US 16)	These include:	
	66 (US 68)	*2+1* (US 68)	*Seventeen* (US 40)	*22nd June 1897* (Ind 80)	
NUMBER TITLES	69 (US 68)	*2+2=5* (Tun 70)	*Seventeen* (Den 66)	*The 30th January 1945* (FRG *c*. 65)	
1 ... 2 ... 3 (US 52)	69 (US 69)	*2+2=69* (US 68)	*Seventeen* (US 83)	—documentary about Nazi epic *Kolberg*, the date being that of the première	
1, 2, 3 (Hun 62)	69 (Fin 69)	*2×2* (Hun 44)	*Twenty One* (GB 15)	*9/30/55* (US 77)—refers to the date James Dean was killed	
1, 2, 3, 4 (GB 78)	'70 (US 70)	*2×2×2* (=2) (It 68)	*Twenty-One* (US 18)	*1 April 2000* (Aut 53)—signified the original date for the ending of the Allied occupation of Austria.	
2½ (Can 75)	96 (USSR 19)	*3×1=1* (Ger 13)	*Twenty-One* (US 24)		
	97.217 (GB 75)	*4×4* (Phi 84)	*Twenty-Nine* (GB 69)		
* Features	99 (Hun 18)				
	99 (US 20)				

The only film with the main title at the end instead of the beginning was Henry King's *Who Pays?* (US 16). The picture, King's first, was about a girl who has an illegitimate baby and marries another man after the father has been erroneously reported killed. The father eventually reappears. King decided it would be more appropriate to pose the question when the audience knew why it was being asked.

MEANINGLESS OR MISLEADING TITLES

☆ *The Bible* (It 13) was not a biblical epic as its title suggested, but a 6-reel melodrama which included a riot in a theatre, a revolver fight on stage, a car chase, a motorcycle blowing up, and people falling out of trains, fighting to the death in rivers, and kidnapping children. Somewhere amongst all this activity a bible was worked into the plot. Warner's *Tracked by the Police* (US 27) was a Rin Tin Tin vehicle whose title was decided before the script was written. The completed film was certainly about tracking, but the tracker was Rin Tin Tin with never a policeman in sight from first reel to last. Edgar Ulmer's *The Black Cat* (US 34) had nothing to do with the Poe story of the same name (despite a credit to Poe) and nothing to do with a black cat other than the fact that a cat crept in and out of a few scenes, irrelevantly, to justify the title.

☆ *The Axe* (US 77) was released in Britain as *California Axe Massacre*, though it was set nowhere near California. *Big Hand for a Little Lady* (US 66) had its title changed in Britain to *Big Deal at Dodge City*. Whoever thought this one up had not seen the picture. It was set in Laredo.

☆ In the early 1930s, piracy of ideas was rife in the Indian film industry and director Dhiren Ganguly was wont to evade questions about the title of his next film with a courteous 'Excuse me, Sir' before hastily switching to another topic. After a while people began asking him when *Excuse Me, Sir* was due to be released, so he decided to call his current project by that title. *Excuse Me, Sir* (Ind 31), released in Hindi and Bengali versions, was one of the most successful pre-war Indian comedies.

☆ Equally meaningless, and for not dissimilar reasons, was the title of a Warner movie starring Errol Flynn. During the thirties there was a Hollywood convention of using the wholly fictitious title of *Another Dawn* for films purportedly showing at any cinema in a film story. When Warner's ran out of ideas for some-

A number of films have been named after towns (*Dodge City*, *The Philadelphia Story*, *New York, New York*, etc), but there is only one instance on record of a town named after a film. When Hool/Joseph Production chose the small Mexican town of Barra de Navidad for shooting *Cabo Blanco* (US 79), the municipality decided to change the name of the coastal resort to Cabo Blanco.

MGM's Louis B. Mayer, like many Hollywood moguls, had a deep distrust of literature. Silent star John Gilbert, an erudite man with a strong story sense, had a pet project for making a film based on John Masefield's poem *The Widow in the Bye Street*. Mayer rejected the proposal with derision. With the connivance of director Monta Bell, Gilbert got his way. Bell changed the title to *Man, Woman and Sin* (US 27) and Mayer enthusiastically endorsed the script without realising it was the same story.

thing catchy to title the somewhat slender story scheduled for Flynn's next exhibition of sexual bravado, they tagged it *Another Dawn* (US 38).

☆ Universal executives admitted that they had no idea what relevance *You Can't Cheat an Honest Man* (US 39) had on the subject matter, nor what writer–star W. C. Fields meant by this scarcely tenable aphorism.

☆ In *Her Twelve Men* (US 54), Greer Garson played a teacher in charge of a class of 13 boy pupils. The original story by Louise Baker, on which the film was based, was called *Miss Baker's Dozen*, which aptly and accurately tallied the 13 young men.

☆ Boris Karloff barely appeared in *Abbott and Costello Meet the Killer, Boris Karloff* (US 48) and somebody else turned out to be the killer. In *Abbott and Costello Go to Mars* (US 53) they don't; their destination is Venus. *Jesse James vs the Daltons* (US 54) features plenty of Daltons, but no Jesse James.

☆ Warner's *The Return of Dr X* (US 39), in which Bogart played a vampire, was not, as the title suggested, a sequel to their earlier horror pic *Dr X* (US 32), which was about a quite different kind of monster, a murderer with no arms. *Beyond the Valley of the Dolls* (US 70) was equally deceptive; it had no connection with Jacqueline Susann's *Valley of the Dolls* (US 67). Similarly *Piranha II* (It/US 81) had no connection at all with *Piranha* (US 78), nor was *Surf II* (US 84) a follow-up to *Surf*. There never was a film called *Surf*.

☆ *The Amorous Prawn* (GB 62) was about a general's wife who opens their official home in the Highlands to American paying guests. In America the title was changed to *The Playgirl and the War Minister*, despite the fact that there was no playgirl and no War Minister in the film—the date explains the choice, since 1962 was the height of the Profumo Affair. Similarly *Marilyn and the Senator* (US 75) had nothing to do with Marilyn Monroe and Senator Kennedy, despite its promotors' obvious intention to mislead, and the girl entangled with a senator is not even called Marilyn.

☆ *The Seagull* (Ban 79) was indeed a film based on a classic work of literature. It was not, however, a movie version of Chekhov's celebrated play but of Jack London's famous novel *The Sea Wolf*.

☆ Many people who saw and enjoyed Hitchcock's fast-moving thriller *North by Northwest* (US 59) left the cinema wondering what the title had to do with the story. Those of a literary bent may have divined that it was a reference to the character played by Cary Grant, who feigns madness. The words in the title are slightly misquoted from *Hamlet:* 'I am but mad north-northwest; when the wind is southerly, I know a hawk from a handsaw.'

☆ *Waterloo* (Aus 81) is not a reconstruction of the battle, but an Australian documentary on urban planning. On the other hand *Ran-xerox* (Fr 84), which might be taken to be an industrial film about photo-copying, is in fact an erotic feature based on a lascivious French comic strip.

☆ *The Trygon Factor* (GB 66) was about bogus nuns pulling a million pound bank raid. The words of the title were never mentioned nor explained. The title of *I'll Never Forget Whatshisname* (GB 67) had no discernable bearing on the story, nor did *Olly, Olly Oxen Free* (US 78) or *A Clockwork Orange* (GB 71). Woody Allen gave a succinct explanation of the title of *Bananas* (US 71): 'Because there are no bananas in it'.

THE LEAST COMPELLING TITLE

The editor would like to nominate *Chairman Mao Reviews the Mighty Contingent of the Cultural Revolution for the Fifth and Sixth Times* (Ch 67).

Inter-titles and Subtitles

The earliest known use of inter-titles was by R. W. Paul in *Our General Servant* (GB 98), at 320 ft the longest story film then produced in Britain. Presented in four scenes, with linking inter-titles, it related how a new maid was compromised by the master of the house. **The earliest known European example** is Georges Méliès' *L'Affaire Dreyfus* (Fr 99) and **the earliest American example**, Edwin S. Porter's *Uncle Tom's Cabin* (US 03). **The earliest known use of dialogue in inter-titles** occurs in Edwin S. Porter's *The Ex-Convict* (US 04).

Subtitles superimposed over action—as in foreign language films today—**were first used** in a Lubin serial *Road o' Strife* (US 15) in order to avoid interrupting the fast-paced narrative. The only other silent picture examples known are another serial, *Judex* (Fr 17), the monumental *Ben Hur* (US 25) and *Walking Back* (US 28). The reason it was not done more often appears to be the problem presented with foreign-language versions.

The silent film with the most inter-titles in relation to

> The Italian religious epic *The Old Testament* (It 22) was released in America in three versions with different inter-titles—one for Protestants, one for Roman Catholics and one for Jews. The titles were approved by the ecclesiastical committees of each denomination to 'accord with their several doctrines'.

> Demagogic movie mogul Harry Cohn's legendary ruthlessness extended even to the credits on Columbia's releases. Ken Hall's *Smithy* (Aus/US 46), a biopic of the great Australian aviator Sir Charles Kingsford Smith, was made under contract to Columbia by the Australian production company Cinesound with an all-Australian cast and crew. The sole interest of the Hollywood studio was to use up dollar assets frozen in Australia. When Cohn saw the finished product, he ordered fictitious credits substituted for the real ones to disguise its Australian origin. Cohn was nothing if not thorough; even the acknowledgements to the Sydney Symphony Orchestra and the Royal Australian Air Force ended up on the cutting-room floor.

its length was *Every Woman's Problem* (US 25), starring Dorothy Davenport. Nat Levine, then sales manager with a Kansas City film exchange, bought the 2300 ft negative, with no titles, for a bargain basement $10,000. By adding 2600 ft of inter-titles he increased it to acceptable feature length and, by choosing an enticing main title, did well enough at the box office to gross four times his investment. Levine used his profit to go into production on his own account, founding the famous Poverty Row studio of Mascot Pictures. *Every Woman's Problem* was probably the only film in which the titles occupied more time than the action.

Silent films with no inter-titles—Murnau's *The Last Laugh* (Ger 25) has often been described as the first feature-length silent movie to rely solely on the action for the development of the narrative, to the exclusion of explanatory titles. Those that preceded it were: Max Reinhardt's *Eine Venzianische Nacht* (Ger 14); Alexander Tairov's *Le Mort* (Rus 15); *A Page from Life* (It 16); *Remorse* (Den 20); *The Rail* (Ger 21); *The Old Swimming Hole* (US 21); *Warning Shadows* (Ger 22); Karl Grune's *The Street* (Ger 23); Lupu Pick's *Sylvester* (Ger 23); *Lily of the Alley* (GB 23); *The Audacious Mr Squire* (GB 23).

Credits

The first screen credits went to André Heuzé for the films he wrote for the French production company Pathé Frères from 1906.

The first person to receive screen credits in the USA was G. M. Anderson, as the leading man of the Broncho Billy westerns in 1908. As producer and author of the films, and part-owner of the Essany studio, Anderson was in a strong position to promote his own name. Generally performers in American films did not receive screen credit until 1911, when the Edison Co. and Vitagraph Co. led the way.

The first British film known to have included screen credits was the Gaumont Co.'s *Lady Letmere's Jewellery* (GB 08), with Maisie Ellis in the title role. The credits were pictorial, each leading character being portrayed next to a card bearing his or her name and role. It is possible that Gaumont had adopted the practice of screen credits earlier the same year when they released a film version of the Lyceum Theatre production of *Romeo and Juliet* (US 08), with Godfrey Tearle and Mary Malone. In this case the cast had been billed in the advertising for the film.

The film-maker with most screen credits was Cedric Gibbons (1893–1960), whose name appeared as art director on over 1500 films between 1917 and 1955. The feat was achieved by Gibbons' insistence on a clause in his 1924 contract with MGM to the effect that every film produced by the studio in the USA would credit him as art director. In practice the art direction for the majority of these films was in the hands of his subordinates.

Never credited—if they were it would destroy the illusion—are the actors and actresses who do the voice-overs for other performers with unsuitable voices. Dave Prowse, the giant actor who played the sinister Darth Vadar in *Star Wars* (US 77) has a West-Country accent, so he was dubbed by black American actor James Earl Jones. Several of the Bond girls—Ursula Andress, Shirley Eaton, Eunice Gayson and Claudine Auger—had difficulty matching an alluring voice to their undoubted physical attributes. In each case they were dubbed by aspirant actress Nikki van der Zyl, now practicing as a barrister. On *Doctor No* (GB 62) she did every female voice except Miss Moneypenny and a Chinese girl, an assignment that earned her a modest £150. Miss van der Zyl also dubbed Raquel Welch's voice in *One Million Years BC* (GB 66). Although only required to grunt in the picture, Miss Welch's middle-western accent sounded insufficiently prehistoric and Miss van der Zyl was called in to grunt the straight Neanderthal way.

The first pre-credit sequence was in Ben Hecht and Charles MacArthur's *Crime Without Passion* (US 34), which opens with an extreme close-up of the barrel of a gun. The gun fires and blood drips on to the floor. The three Furies of Greek mythology ascend from the puddle of blood in flowing robes and fly over a modern metropolis inciting various crimes of passion. One of the Furies sweeps her arm over the face of a skyscraper, shattering the window glass, which showers down until it forms the words *Crime Without Passion*.

The longest pre-credit sequence lasts for a full half-hour before the opening title of Dennis Hopper's *The Last Movie* (US 71).

The longest credit sequence lasted for 12 minutes in Sergio Leone's *Once Upon a Time in the West* (It/US 68).

The largest number of names credited was 457 for *Superman the Movie* (GB 78).

UNUSUAL CREDITS

In *The Terror* (US 28), the novelty of sound inspired Warner's to have the credits spoken by a caped and masked Conrad Nagel. Other films in which the credits have been spoken rather than written include Orson Welles' *The Magnificent Ambersons* (US 42), Truffaut's *Fahrenheit 451* (GB 66), Tony Richardson's *Hamlet* (GB 69) and Robert Altman's *M*A*S*H* (US 70). The last named had a recurring theme of the front line field hospital's nightly film show being announced over the Tannoy. The last film to be so announced is *M*A*S*H* itself, with full credits. A film

Magnificently primeval as Raquel Welch looked in *One Million Years BC* (GB 66), she failed to master the art of grunting the straight Neanderthal way.

called *Episode* (Aut 35) was released with conventional credits at home, but with spoken credits in Nazi Germany. In this case the reason was more sinister than a mere desire for novelty. The director of the picture, Walter Reisch, was Jewish. The credits were spoken against a musical background and when Reisch's name was reached, the music swelled to make it inaudible.

The only recorded example of sung credits features in *Por que te engana tu marido/Why Does Your Husband Deceive You* (Sp 69). The vocalists are a priest and his choirboys.

Slim Carter (US 57) had novelty credits whereby the cast signed their own names on the screen.

When Broadway was a Trail (US 14) was an early feature film about star-crossed lovers in Dutch colonial New York, then New Amsterdam. The performers were introduced in period costume on the roof of a skyscraper in modern (1914) Manhattan. The end title showed them in modern dress silhouetted against a background of Broadway at Times Square.

Although performer credits have often been superimposed over the image of each performer named, only once have production credits been treated in this way. In the Douglas Fairbanks movie *When the Clouds Roll By* (US 20), the director's credit pictures him wielding his microphone, the cameraman's credit shows him grinding the camera, the scriptwriter's credit has him hunched over the typewriter and so on.

The credits for *Gettin' Back* (US 74) list five different cameramen, one designated simply as 'Paul'. The mystery lenser, per *Variety*, 'split before telling anybody his last name'. *Hells Angels Forever* (US 83), a documentary ten years in the making, credited the various directors and producers of the film with the dates of their participation.

In Mike Snow's curiously titled ⟷ (Can 69), the credits appear in the middle of the film.

Notorious credits include two for authors. *The Taming of the Shrew* (US 28) bore the attribution 'by William Shakespeare, with additional dialogue by Sam Taylor'; while *The Black Cat* (US 34) was credited to Edgar *Allen* Poe, a misspelling of his middle name.

> **LOCAL GIRL NEARLY MADE GOOD**
> During the early thirties supporting player Dorothy Jordan was always given the star billing when her films were shown in her home town of Clarksville, Tennessee, however minor the role.

> Credits unlikely to inspire confidence in a film's audience appeal include the production credit on *Battle of Tagrift* (Lby 81): 'The Administrative Committee for Revolutionary Information and Moral Guidance Branch of the Cinema Department of the Socialist People's Libyan Arab Jarriahiriya'.

(The fact that the film had absolutely nothing to do with Poe's story did not seem to trouble anyone.)

Fritz Lang's *Hangmen Also Die* (US 43) is probably the only film with credits distinguishing the scriptwriter who wrote the script that was used (Fritz Lang) from the scriptwriter who wrote the script that was not (Bertold Brecht). Incensed that Lang had departed so far from his intended ideas, Brecht won a court decision that allowed him a credit disassociating his script from the shooting script.

The perpetual problem of who gets top billing was neatly solved in *On the Run* (Aus 84) by placing lead players Paul Winfield and Rod Taylor's names on screen in the form of a cross. The producers of *Skip Tracer* (Can 78) were more concerned about the other end of the bill—they gave all the extras individual credits.

Some of the odder individual credits are for 'First Aid' in Clint Eastwood's mayhem chase film *Gauntlet* (US 77); 'Technical Consultant on Vampire Bats' in *Chosen Survivors* (US 74); 'Ant Consultant' in *Empire of the Ants* (US 77); for the perfume worn by the leading players in *Marjorie Morningstar* (US 58); for the shoe polish brightening the cast's shoes in *Scent of Mystery* (US 60); for 'Spiritual Counsel' in *Hallelujah the Hills* (US 63); for 'The Assistant to the Assistant to the Unit Publicist' in *The Greek Tycoon* (US 78); and to Federico Fellini, who was not on the picture, 'for encouragement at the right time' in *The World's Greatest Lover* (US 77). *The Killing Fields* (GB 84) displayed the enigmatic credit 'Assistant Footsteps Editor', while Gary Graver's low-budget horror pic *Trick or Treats* (US 82) credits Orson Welles as 'Magical Consultant'. 'Fangs by Dr Ludwig von Krankheit' in Polanski's *Dance of the Vampires* (GB 67) should probably be taken with a pinch of garlic salt.

11 Censorship

The first film known to have been suppressed was taken by Lumière cameraman Francis Doublier in Moscow in the summer of 1896 and showed Prince Napoléon dancing with the 'lady of his affections', a professional dancer. The film was seized by the Russian police and destroyed.

Later the same year *Delorita's Passion Dance* (US 96) became **the first film to be banned in the USA** when it was prohibited from exhibition in Atlantic City, NJ, by order of the Mayor.

The world's first regulated film censorship was introduced under a Chicago City Council Ordinance of 4 November 1907 'prohibiting the exhibition of obscene and immoral pictures'. Effective 19 November 1907, the Ordinance required that every film be shown to the Chief of Police before it was exhibited publicly and an exhibition permit obtained. Penalty for violation was a fine of $50–100 (£10–20), each day of exhibition without a permit to be regarded as a separate offence. One of the first films to fall foul of the censorship in Chicago was a Vitagraph production of Shakespeare's *Macbeth* (US 08), banned by a zealous police lieutenant on the grounds that 'Shakespeare is art, but it's not adapted altogether for the five cent style of art'. He explained: 'The stabbing scene in the play is not predominant. But in the picture show it is the feature.'

The first country to establish a State Censorship Board was Sweden. The Statens Biografbyrå was founded on 4 September 1911 and all films released in Sweden after 1 December 1911 were required to be certified by the Board.

CENSORSHIP USA

The USA is one of four countries where the film industry has a self-regulatory censorship independent of government (the others are Britain, Germany and Japan). The following is a brief chronology of American censorship as regulated by the Motion Picture Producers of America (MPPA).

1922 The Motion Picture Producers and Distributors of America founded March under the presidency of former Postmaster General Will H. Hays in an attempt to regulate the industry from within and combat growing demands for government intervention. At this date there were already eight State Censorship Boards (Maryland, New York, Florida, Ohio, Pennsylvania, Virginia, Kansas, Massachusetts) plus 90 municipal boards of varying degrees of severity.

Roscoe 'Fatty' Arbuckle, the world's highest paid entertainer, became **the first screen star to be banned**. The announcement was made by Will H. Hays of the MPPDA on 18 April, six days after Arbuckle had been acquitted of the manslaughter of 'good time girl' Virginia Rappe. Shortly afterwards Hays drew up a list of 200 people considered morally dangerous whom it was intended to bar from the industry. Heading the list was Wallace Reid, probably the most popular male star in America prior to Fairbanks' ascendancy, whose drug habit was to finish his career before the MPPDA was able to finish it for him.

1924 The 'Hays Formula' introduced—members agreed to submit scripts in advance for comment and guidance. Few did so unless the script was known to be innocuous.

The 'Index' of forbidden books and plays was introduced.

1927 Hays' list of 'Dont's and Be Carefuls' adopted 8 June. Eleven 'Dont's' included 'any licentious or suggestive nudity', 'miscegenation', 'ridicule of the clergy', 'any inference of sex perversion' and 'the illegal traffic of drugs'. 'Be Carefuls' included 'brutality and possible gruesomeness' and 'the sale of women, or of a woman selling her virtue'. Largely ineffective.

1930 First Production Code—known as 'The Hays Code'—drawn up by Martin Quigley, publisher of *Motion Picture Herald*, and Fr Daniel A. Lord of St Louis University. Introduced 31 March. No penalties for evasion.

1931 Prior submission of scripts made binding on members.

1934 Production Code Administration Office established in June. 'Resolution for Uniform Interpretation' required producers to abide by Code. Penalties for evasion introduced.

First Seal of Approval granted by Hays Office to Fox's *The World Moves On* 11 July.

Right Cinecolor was the most widely used two-colour process. First used in 1932—the date of the early colour talkie shown—it was also the last two-colour process to remain in use, the final releases being in 1953. (*Grant Lobban Collection*)

Below Cinerama used three projectors to project three juxtaposed images. If it was done well, you could hardly see the joins. (See p. 147.) (*Grant Lobban Collection*)

The largest frame format—a 5¼ sq in Imax frame (*left*) reproduced actual size . . . and, *below*, how it reproduces on the giant Imax screen. (See p. 122.)

The world's most famous mouse—star of screen and stamps. Mickey made his debut in 1928 and became such a worldwide celebrity that by 1934 he was receiving more fan mail than any mortal star. Disney retired him in 1953, because he felt the world had grown too harsh for such a symbol of innocence, but the mouse made a triumphant comeback 30 years later in *Mickey's Christmas Carol* (US 83). (See p. 209.)

Right PHILATELY HONOURS FILM MAKERS
1 and 2 Charlie Chaplin (1889–1977); 3 and 18 Auguste Lumière (1862–1954), Louis Lumière (1864–1948); 4 Georges Méliès (1861–1938); 5 Dadasaheb Phalke (1870–1944); 6 Stan Laurel (1890–1965), Oliver Hardy (1892–1957); 7 Gerard Philipe (1920–59); 8 Raimu (1883–1946); 9 Alexander Dovzhenko (1894–1956); 10, 12 and 15 Will Rogers (1870–1935); 11 W. C. Fields (1879–1946); 13 Otto Preminger (1906–); 14 D. W. Griffith (1875–1948); 16 Walt Disney (1901–66); 17 Douglas Fairbanks (1883–1939); 19 Marilyn Monroe (1926–62); 20 Martine Carol (1920–67); 21 Eric von Stroheim (1885–1957); 22 Serghei Eisenstein (1898–1948).

CHARLIE CHAPLIN
1889-1977

25
INDIA

1

ČESKOSLOVENSKO
1·40 kčs

Charlie Chaplin
ČESKOSLOVENSKÁ KOMISE UNESCO

2

RÉPUBLIQUE · FRANÇAISE
30f
AUGUSTE · LOUIS · LUMIÈRE
CINÉMA FRANÇAIS
1895-1935
POSTES

3

GEORGES MÉLIÈS
1861-1938
0.50
RÉPUBLIQUE FRANÇAISE

4

DADASAHEB PHALKE
1870-1944
INDIA 20

5

FUJEIRA 10 Ris
الفجيرة ١٠ ريال

6

GÉRARD
PHILIPE
LE CID
POSTES 0.50
RÉPUBLIQUE FRANÇAISE

7

RAIMU
CÉSAR
POSTES 0.50
RÉPUBLIQUE FRANÇAISE

8

А.П. ДОВЖЕНКО
1894-1956
ПОЧТА СССР
4 к
1964

9

WILL ROGERS
Performing Arts USA 15c

10

W.C.FIELDS
Performing Arts USA 15c

11

NICARAGUA A WILL ROGERS
HOMENAJE
1981
5 CENTAVOS 5
1981 MANAGUA ARDIENDO

12

PREMINGER BY KUTSCH
AIR MAIL
50 DIRHAMS
AJMAN

13

MOVIEMAKER US 10c
D.W. GRIFFITH

14

3 CENTS
"I NEVER MET A MAN I DIDN'T LIKE" WILL ROGERS
UNITED STATES POSTAGE

15

WALT DISNEY
UNITED STATES
6c

16

DOUGLAS FAIRBANKS
Performing Arts USA 20c

17

REPUBLIQUE DU MALI
AUGUSTE ET LOUIS LUMIÈRE
POSTE AÉRIENNE
250f
JEAN HARLOW
MARILYN MONROE JUNIOR
DELRIEU

18

RÉPUBLIQUE POPULAIRE DU CONGO
1926~1962
POSTE AÉRIENNE 1971
MARILYN MONROE
RETROSPECTIVE DU CINÉMA 100f

19

RÉPUBLIQUE POPULAIRE DU CONGO
1920~1967
POSTE AÉRIENNE 1971
MARTINE CAROL
RETROSPECTIVE DU CINÉMA 150f

20

RÉPUBLIQUE POPULAIRE DU CONGO
1885~1957
POSTE AÉRIENNE 1971
ERIC VON STROHEIM
RETROSPECTIVE DU CINÉMA 200f

21

RÉPUBLIQUE POPULAIRE DU CONGO
1898~1948
POSTE AÉRIENNE 1971
SERGHEI EISENSTEIN
RETROSPECTIVE DU CINÉMA 250f

22

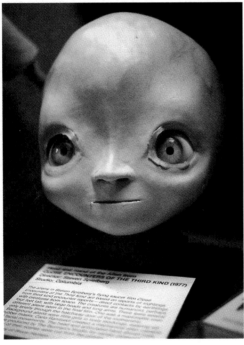

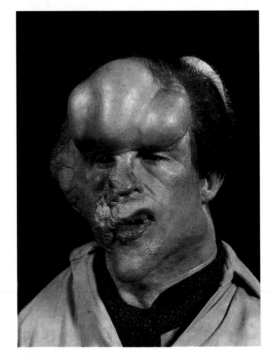

Above left Becky Sharp (US 35) was the first feature-length film in three-colour Technicolor. A reviewer for *Liberty* magazine wrote that the performers looked like 'boiled salmon dipped in mayonnaise'. (See p. 136.)

Above right Like most of the royal family King George VI was an ardent film fan—his favourite star was reported to be Nancy Carroll.

Below left Until 1984 there was no film museum in the movie capital of the world. Now the Hollywood Museum has opened at 7051 Hollywood Boulevard, with an array of exhibits which include the Alien from *Close Encounters of the Third Kind* (US 77). For a list of the world's other movie museums see p. 27. (*Hollywood Museum*)

Below right It took seven hours daily for make-up artist Christopher Tucker to transform John Hurt into the grotesquely deformed Elephant Man. (See p. 126.) (*Christopher Tucker*)

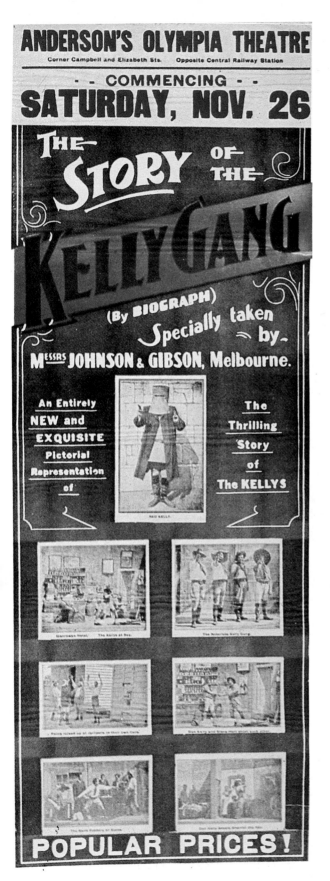

Chrissie White (1896–) and another Hepworth player, Alma Taylor (1895–1974), were the first film actresses to attain stardom in Britain. Having joined the Hepworth Co. as a 4s a week child player in 1908, she had moved on to adult leads by the time she made *Blood and Bosh* (GB 13) and was enjoying not only star billing but a stellar salary of £2 10s a week! (See p. 79.) (*National Film Archive*)

The world's first feature film—*The Story of the Kelly Gang* (Aus 06). Australia was the world's leading producer of feature films until Hungary outnumbered her in 1912. (See pp. 12 and 17.)

Above left Some scenes will always evoke the memory of a song. This shot of Paul Newman and Katherine Ross from *Butch Cassidy and the Sundance Kid* (US 69) declares that 'Raindrops Keep Fallin' on My Head'. Burt Bacharach pulled off the double by winning the Oscar for Best Song (together with Hal David) and Best Score.

Below left Alice in Wonderland is one of a select company of novels which have been filmed a dozen times or more. *Alice* (GB/Pol/Bel 81) was a modern musical version with Sophie Barjac in the name part and Jean-Pierre Cassel as the White Rabbit. The songs were dubbed by Lulu.

Above The cinema in art. *The Cinema* by William Roberts. Painted in 1920. It depicts a long defunct fleapit in London's Warren Street. (*Tate Gallery*)

Above left In Britain and America the first fan magazines started in 1911. This British example of 1919 was shortlived, despite its arresting cover designs. Ivy Duke's career survived *The Shadow Stage* but not the onslaught of the talkies ten years later. (See p. 196.)

Above right Top screen actress of all time? Shirley Temple was 10 when this cover picture appeared in 1938, but she had topped the Quigley Poll of box-office draws since she was seven. She lost the top place to Mickey Rooney in 1939, but held on to her position as most popular actress. Her fan mail was the highest ever received by a human star (Mickey Mouse was Numero Uno)—with 60,000 letters a month during 1936. (See pp. 91 and 184.)

Above Thirties film posters are in vogue—five of the top ten bestselling poster reproductions hail from that decade, including *King Kong* (US 33). Record price for an original film poster is $5400. It advertised an early Disney which had cost less than that to make. (See p. 28.)

1943 Howard Hughes caused the first serious breach of the Code when he exhibited *The Outlaw* (US 43) without a Seal of Approval. Billy the Kid, a criminal and moral transgressor, and his girl Rio, a moral transgressor only, were able to ride off into the sunset without reaping any of the just deserts demanded by the Code. (Or by history—in reality Billy the Kid was shot.)

1954 Code seriously breached when Preminger distributed *The Moon is Blue*, a comedy about virginity, without a Seal of Approval.

1955 *The Man with the Golden Arm* awarded Seal despite explicit treatment of drug addiction.

1956 Revised Code introduced. Nudity, profanity and obscenity remained forbidden in all circumstances. Most other former prohibitions modified.

1961 *The Children's Hour* granted Seal despite theme of sexual deviation—in this case lesbianism.

1964 Sidney Lumet's *The Pawnbroker* was passed uncut with a scene showing a woman naked to the waist. This was the first time nudity had been allowed on screen since the setting up of the Production Code Administration Office 30 years earlier.

1966 The 'blue language' barrier finally crashed by *Who's Afraid of Virginia Woolf*, the Production Code Administration agreeing to give it a Seal (with audiences restricted to over 18's) because it reflected 'the tragic realism of life'.

Code revised again, with no positive prohibitions remaining. Approved films were now divided into 'general audience' and 'mature audience'.

1968 Production Code Administration defied when they refused to approve two British films which contained scenes of oral sex: Michael Winner's *I'll Never Forget Whatshisname* (GB 67) and Albert Finney's *Charlie Bubbles* (GB 68). They were released through subsidiary companies of the intending distributors which were not members of the Association. This device enabled any major distributor to circumvent the Administration and hastened its end.

Code replaced by ratings system under the Motion Picture Association of America Ratings Board, effective 1 November. Four classifications: G = General audience; M = Mature audience; R = Restricted (over

18); X = Over 21 only. M was replaced by GP (General patronage) in 1970, as 'mature' was being misinterpreted as meaning 'X+'. By 1975 R had changed to allow accompanied children under 17, the X restriction had been lowered to over 17, and GP had become PG (Parental guidance). The X rating can be self applied to obviate any requests for cuts.

1981 The last State Censorship Board—Maryland—dissolved after 65 years of activity. During its last full year of operation, the Maryland Censor Board viewed 559 movies and banned eight.

1984 A new PG-13 rating introduced 27 June to designate films which require 'special guidance' from parents for children under 13.

CENSORSHIP GB

The British Board of Film Censors (BBFC) was inaugurated by the Kinematograph Manufacturers' Association in October 1912 with powers effective from 1 January 1913. The moving spirit behind the venture was the film producer Will Barker, who was concerned at the increase in the number of films being produced 'for the smoking room', which he considered would bring the whole industry into disrepute. Together with Col A. C. Bromhead and Cecil Hepworth, two leading pioneer film-makers, he persuaded the Kinematograph Manufacturers' Association that it was up to the trade to put its own house in order, and with the approval of the Home Secretary the Board was established under the Presidency of G. A. Redford, formerly a playreader for the Lord Chamberlain.

The original classification was into 'U' (Universal) and 'A' (Adult). **The first U Certificate** was granted to the Barker production *Mary of Briarwood Dell* (GB 13) and **the first A Certificate** to the Clarendon picture *A Strong Man's Love* (GB 13), both on 1 January 1913. The A Certificate was originally advisory only. It was not until 1923 that the London County Council prohibited unaccompanied children under 16 from attending A films. Most other local authorities in England and Wales followed suit by the end of the decade, though in Scotland the A Certificate always remained advisory only.

The BBFC began its life with only two firm prohibitive rules: no film depicting the living figure of Jesus Christ and no film which contained scenes of nudity would be granted a Certificate. During the first year of operation, the Board examined 7510 films (6861 'U'; 627 'A'), of which only 22 were rejected outright. Reasons included 'indelicate or suggestive sexual situations', 'holding up a Minister of Religion to ridicule', 'excessive drunkenness' and the portrayal of 'native customs in British lands abhorrent to British ideas'. In 1917 the new Chairman, T. P. O'Connor, declared that he would not grant a Certificate to any film in which crime was the dominant feature and warned producers that no criminal was to be portrayed as a victim of social deprivation. By 1925 the following were also

---

During the first 15 years of the US ratings system (1968–83), the proportion of films rated in the various categories were as follows:

G 14%   M and R 43%   GP and PG 38%   X 5%

The X-rated film has all but disappeared in the USA. In 1981–82 no film was rated X and in 1983–84 there was only one. A correspondingly greater number of films are being rated R, up from 23% in the first year, 1968–69, to 58% in 1983–84.

among the 'Dont's': 'Women fighting with knives'; 'Animals gnawing men, women and children'; 'Insistence upon the inferiority of coloured races'; and 'Salacious wit'.

An 'H' Certificate (advisory only) was introduced in 1933 to designate horror films, and 'X' for 'Adult Only' in 1951. A revised rating system took effect in 1970 with the A Certificate reverting to advisory status, a new AA classification signifying a minimum admission age of 14, and a raising of the admission age from 16 to 18 for X films. It was found that few people understood the status of A and AA films and by the end of the seventies Britain was one of the only countries still using X for respectable adult films, often of artistic merit; elsewhere it was being used solely as a label for pornography. The current ratings system, introduced in December 1982, retained the U for Universal, but replaced A with PG (Parental Guidance) and AA and X with a simple numerical classification of 15 and 18 respectively to denote the minimum age for admission. It also added an 18R category to classify porno and violent films only for showing in specially licensed cinemas.

The Board's function and powers have remained fundamentally unchanged since its inception, despite modification of its criteria for certification in line with changing social and moral standards. An *aide-mémoire* states: 'The power of censorship is in the hands of Local Authorities. The BBFC exists to act as an intermediary between Local Authorities and the film industry. Its success or failure can be measured simply in terms of the acceptability of its judgements to the majority of Local Authorities in Britain.'

Local Authorities have the power to alter the Certificate issued by the BBFC or to permit the showing of an uncertified film. They also remain the only agency with the power to refuse the right of exhibition.

The first film to receive an X-rating (adults only) under the British Board of Film Censors system of classification was *La Vie commence demain/Life Begins Tomorrow* (Fr 50), which opened in London on 9 January 1951. The reason for the X Certificate was a sequence dealing with artificial insemination. Previously the film would have had to have been either banned or cut. By the end of the permissive 1960s the number of X films had surpassed the number of A and U films combined.

The first film to receive an X-rating under the Motion Picture Association of America system of classification was Brian de Palma's anti-establishment *Greetings* (US 68) with Robert de Niro, which opened in New York on 15 December 1968.

The largest number of cuts known to have been ordered by a censor to one film is 103 in respect of Faria de Almeida's *Catembe* (Por 64), a critical film by a Mozambique director about the then Portuguese Colony. The most cuts to a Hollywood film was 60 in

the case of D. W. Griffith's *Way Down East* (US 20), a heart-rending Victorian melodrama which had been reducing stage audiences to tears for the previous 30 years without apparently undermining their morals. The pivot of the story concerns the waif-like heroine's (Lillian Gish) illegitimate baby and it was this to which the Pennsylvania State Censorship Board took grave exception. Scenes ordered to be cut in their entirety included the mock marriage (the heroine having been deceived), the mock honeymoon, the heroine announcing that she was with child, and all sequences relating to its birth. Indeed the baby made its first, unheralded appearance in the cut version only shortly before it expired, much to the bewilderment of Pennsylvania audiences. (The Board also insisted, for reasons undisclosed, that the title 'I can never be any man's wife' be changed to 'I can never marry any man'.)

The Japanese censor board insisted on more than 450 'blurs' before permitting the release of Bob Guccione's notorious production of *Caligula* (US 79).

The most banned film is open to dispute, but a recent contender is *Make Them Die Slowly* (US 83), billed as 'The Most Violent Ever'. Publicity for the picture proudly proclaimed that it had been banned in 31 countries.

The country to have imposed the most outright bans, apart from Saudi Arabia, which bans all films, is Abu Dubai with a cumulative total of some 2400. Most of the films affected were declared obscene, anti-Islamic or favourable to Jews.

The first country to abolish censorship of films was Russia under the Kerensky government in March 1917. It was formally reimposed in 1922, though in practice there had been a strong measure of control since the accession of the Bolsheviks to power. In the Stalinist era the Soviet censorship became the most rigorous in the world, to the point of nearly extinguishing the film industry in the 1950s. It probably remains so.

The brief flowering of liberty in the revolutionary Russia of 1917 had resulted in nothing more stimulating than a spate of anti-Tsarist films, most of them centering on the depraved monk Rasputin as the architect of decay. When Germany abolished censorship in December 1918, the worst fears of its upholders were confirmed by the rash of sex films that followed. Their titles in no way belied their content: *Frauen, die der Abgrund verschlingt/Women Engulfed by the Abyss* (Ger 18), *Verlorene Töchter/Lost Daughters*

RIPE FOR CENSORSHIP

The first demand for censorship in Britain came from the cheese industry in 1898, when Charles Urban released one of his scientific films taken through a microscope which revealed the bacterial activity in a piece of Stilton.

The deletion of 'unpersons' from Soviet encyclopaedias and the retouching of historical photographs to eliminate 'enemies of the state' like Trotsky are familiar practices in the Soviet Union. Evidence has now reached the West that a similar revision of history is being undertaken with classic films. Writing in *Sight and Sound* (Winter 1983), Alexander Sesonske reports how he showed Mikhail Romm's distinguished *Lenin in October* (USSR 37) to a class of film students in the spring of 1983. The original film, as Sesonske knew, had attributed to Stalin a leading role in the October Revolution second only to that of Lenin himself; and in nearly every scene depicting Lenin, the tyrant was shown at his right hand, dispensing wise advice and supporting him loyally in committee against Trotsky and other revisionists. The print shown to the students had not a single image of Stalin; he had been eliminated from the film entirely. Some shots had been simply deleted, others cut at the point that Stalin should have appeared. The majority, however, had been skilfully doctored by back projecting the film, then rephotographing the images after placing a large foreground figure, usually a Baltic sailor, to block out Stalin from view. Ironically the revised version of *Lenin in October* is far closer to historical truth than Romm's original.

(Ger 19), *Die Prostitution* (Ger 19), *Hyänen der Lust/Hyenas of Lust* (Ger 19), etc. Homosexuality (q.v.) was also treated on the screen for the first time. It is doubtful whether anything so explicitly sexual was encountered again in films until the 1960s. Censorship was restored by the National Assembly in May 1920.

No other country abolished censorship for adult audiences until 1969, when Denmark took a lead which was to be followed in the 1970s by Austria, Uruguay, Portugal and Upper Volta and in the 1980s by Panama and Argentina. Belgium is unique in never having exercised any censorship of films for adults.

THE UNKINDEST CUTS

The vagaries of censorship have taken many forms. Here are some of them.

☆ The State of Illinois demanded excision of the scene in *The Kid* (US 20) in which Jackie Coogan smashes windows. For similar reasons the censorship board of Ohio tried to ban *Treasure Island* (US 20) altogether lest it should encourage children to piracy.

☆ *The Muppet Movie* (US 79) was cut by the New Zealand censor on grounds of gratuitous violence. The offending scene showed Fozzie Bear being menaced by a drunken sailor with a broken bottle. Sweden banned *E.T.* (US 82) for children under 11 because it was claimed the film showed parents being hostile to their offspring.

☆ 20th Century Fox was obliged to cut a shot of a Botticelli nude from its art documentary *Birth of Venus* (US 52) at the insistence of the Hays Office.

☆ The films of Libertad Lamarque, one of Argentina's major stars of the thirties, were banned in Argentina when Perón came to power in 1945. The reason was that Senorita Lamarque had slapped the face of Péron's mistress Eva Duarte—Evita—on the set of *Circus Cavalcade* (Arg 43) because the aspiring actress had sat in the star's personal chair. When Eva Duarte became the nation's First Lady as Eva Perón, Libertad Lamarque had to flee into exile.

☆ *Bloody Cry* (Chn 34) was banned by the Kuomintang censors because the villain bore a certain physical resemblance to Chiang Kai-shek. Things did not improve after the revolution. By order of Mao in 1949, no Chinese government leaders were allowed to be portrayed on screen, however favourably.

☆ *Sea Dogs of Australia* (Aus 14) was a victim of historical circumstance. Premièred a week after war broke out in August 1914, it was promptly banned by order of the Australian defence authorities because scenes shot aboard HMAS *Australia* were thought to be a security risk.

☆ When the script of *Zaza* (US 39) was returned from the Hays Office, a line in which the heroine screams at the villain 'Pig! Pig! Pig! Pig! Pig!' had noted in the margin against it: 'Delete two pigs'. The Hays Office

Sex may have been rampant in the film version of Somerset Maugham's novel *Rain*, but why did the censors insist that the title should be changed to the name of the woman of easy virtue played by Gloria Swanson—*Sadie Thompson* (US 28)?

permitted the saloon queen Frenchie (Marlene Dietrich) to push money down her cleavage in *Destry Rides Again* (US 39), but insisted on the deletion of the accompanying line 'There's gold in them thar hills!'

☆ The Syrian Ministry of Information banned *Kadr* (Syr 81) on grounds that 'it is badly directed and filled with vulgar scenes which are neither edifying nor interesting, that it is cheaply sensational and lacks a coherent plot'.

☆ *La Coquille et la Clergyman* (Fr 28), the surrealist fantasy directed by Germaine Dulac, was banned by the British Board of Film Censors with the comment: 'This film is so cryptic as to be almost meaningless. If there is a meaning, it is doubtless objectionable.'

☆ *Limelight* (US 52) was banned in the USA for 20 years after its release because director–star Charles Chaplin was politically *persona non grata*. When it was eventually shown in America in 1972, it won an Oscar for the best original dramatic score—a uniquely belated Academy Award.

☆ Karate films were banned in Iraq in 1979.

☆ In 1964 the Peking Cinema Institute banned, along with *Hamlet* (GB 48), *Othello* (US/Fr 51) and *The Three Musketeers* (US 48), an educational film titled *Elementary Safety in Swimming in Rivers, Lakes and Seas*. The safety element was considered a bourgeois tendency likely to undermine revolutionary daring.

☆ No films depicting two-piece bathing suits were allowed on Malta's screens before 1964; a similar ban on bikinis applied to Malta's beaches. In that year an English tourist was charged with indecent exposure for having revealed her midriff while sunbathing, but was found not guilty. The court ruling had an immediate effect on film censorship. A large number of banned youth movies, including the whole Elvis Presley repertoire, were given the censor's seal of approval.

☆ *The Wicked Lady* (GB 45), in which Margaret Lockwood played a high-born lady highwayman, had to be almost entirely reshot for the USA due to the depth of Miss Lockwood's *décolletage*.

☆ Joseph Strick's *Ulysses* (GB 67), from the long banned novel by James Joyce, was only passed by the British Board of Film Censors with the deletion of the more outrageously obscene dialogue from the soundtrack. Strick then took the film to the GLC, who as the licensing body for London could ignore the Board's decision. The GLC passed the film without a single cut. It was later revealed that the sound reproduction in the GLC projection room was so faulty that none of the censors had heard a word of the dialogue.

☆ In contrast to the above, Louis Malle's sexually explicit *Les Amants* (Fr 59) passed the British Board of Film Censors only to fall foul of London Transport. The poster, which showed Rodin's beautiful sculpture of a couple in tender embrace, *Le Baiser*, was banned from buses and the Underground.

☆ *The Grapes of Wrath* (US 40) was allowed to be shown in the USSR, because the authorities considered it painted a sufficiently unattractive picture of the life of the American proletariat during the depression. It was later banned when they found that audiences were immensely impressed by the fact that the itinerant family of the story, intended to represent America's dispossessed, owned an automobile.

☆ After 1942 no photos of Gandhi were allowed on the screen in Indian films, even as incidental props. Prior to World War II many Indian producers and directors had demonstrated their support of the outlawed Indian National Congress by using the Gandhian symbol—the spinning wheel—as decoration, or by having pictures of Gandhi and Nehru on the walls, or by introducing a few bars of a Congress anthem into the sound-track.

The Soviet authorities allowed *The Grapes of Wrath* (US 40) to be released in Russia because they thought it painted a sufficiently harrowing picture of Depression-hit America. But they banned it when they found that their toiling masses were envious of jobless Americans who owned automobiles like this one.

☆ Hatred has been a regrettably potent factor in censorship. All German films were banned in Britain after World War I (a ban imposed by the exhibitors themselves) and until recent years no German film was admitted into Israel. *All Quiet on the Western Front* (US 30), generally acknowledged as one of the greatest pacifist films, was banned in France until 1962 because of its moderate stance towards the Germans. When it was finally released it was booed by Paris audiences. Local censorship boards in the southern states of America between the wars customarily demanded cuts in films that depicted blacks in any role other than a menial one. Even after World War II the Memphis censor cut Lena Horne sequences from MGM musicals and a scene from *The Sailor Takes a Wife* (US 46) in which a white character tips his hat to a black.

☆ On the outbreak of World War II, the neutral Republic of Ireland banned war scenes from newsreels.

☆ Films have sometimes been banned by different censors for diametrically opposite reasons. *Die Reiter von Deutsche Ost-Afrika/The Riders of German East Africa* (Ger 34) was banned by the Nazi government in 1939 as pacifist and by the Allied authorities in Germany in 1945 as militarist.

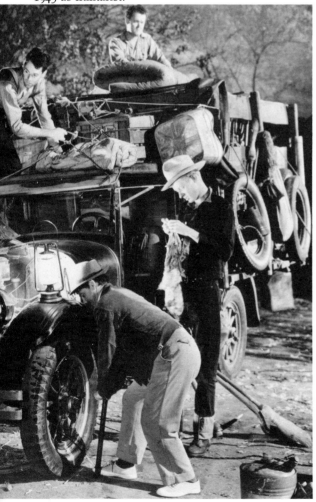

☆ The British are peculiarly sensitive about the treatment of animals in films. Two Australian films fell foul of the British Board of Film Censors the same year. They banned *Orphan of the Wilderness* (Aus 36), a much-loved children's film about a boxing kangaroo, on the grounds that it had involved cruelty to animals. The Board was undeterred by the fact that the Australian RSPCA and the NSW Department of Education had both endorsed the picture. The BBFC was equally adamant about *Thoroughbred* (Aus 36), objecting to a scene of a stable fire. In vain the producers protested that the scene had been shot with rear projection to simulate the flames and that the horses had never been exposed to them. Animal scenes remain contentious not only in Britain but also in former outposts of the Empire. A supernatural thriller called *Calamity of Snakes* (Tai 82), in which the snakes have a bad time, was banned outright in British Columbia.

☆ *The Cow* (Iran 69) was produced under the auspices of the Iranian Ministry of Culture and Arts. On completion it was promptly banned—by the same Ministry of Culture and Arts.

☆ In 1918 the burghers of Villefranche-sur-Rhône banned *Othello* (It 14) from local exhibition because they objected to Desdemona being killed in it.

☆ There was a unique instance in American censorship of a ban on a particular individual being portrayed on the screen. It applied to gangster John Dillinger, whose heroic stature in the mass consciousness had considerably unnerved the American authorities by the time he was gunned down in 1934. For ten years the Hays Office would consider no scripts featuring the gangster, though eight Dillinger movies have been made since 1945.

☆ In 1967 the manager of Center Theater at High Point, NC, USA, was arrested for showing a Julie Andrews picture declared to be obscene. The film, *Hawaii* (US 67), contained scenes of chaste but bare-bosomed native girls. Under a local ordnance, in force since the mid-19th century, any depiction of unclad breasts was an indictable offence.

☆ Probably the most liberal censorship of sexual content during the thirties was that of Nazi Germany. It is doubtful whether such erotic comedies as *Der Ammenkönig* (Ger 35) or Carl Froelich's *Wenn wir alle Engel wären/If We were All Angels* (Ger 36) would have passed any foreign censor. This may well have been because of Josef Goebbels' own sexual predilections and he was the Chief Censor not only in name but in practice. During the twelve years of the Third Reich he personally viewed every one of the 1363 films produced, as well as all newsreels, cartoons, documentaries and other shorts, before they were passed for public showing. There was one exception to the generally permissive tone. Hitler himself had personally ordered that any woman character in a film who broke up a marriage must die before the end.

☆ There is at least one attested case of a film being

refused certification unless the title was changed. *Pure Shit* became *Pure S* (Aus 73).

☆ One local police chief in Sweden about the time of World War I censored all films in which china was smashed—presumably to prevent housemaids from getting the idea that the practice had the endorsement of moviemakers.

☆ In August 1913 Russia banned films showing strikes, 'the life of indentured peasants' and 'difficult forms of labour'. Mexico banned imported films that depicted Mexicans as villains in 1926. The ban was ignored by Hollywood, but the effect on exports south of the border was sufficiently serious for the Hays Office to order no more Mexican heavies in 1930. As a quid pro quo, the censors let it be tacitly understood that it would be quite acceptable for the stock foreign undesirable to be portrayed as Russian, in retaliation for Soviet restrictions on Hollywood imports. France in the twenties had an instruction written into its code 'No displeasing Mexicans, Chinese or Niggers', while Poland at this time banned 'films tending to provoke emigration agitation'. India, meanwhile, had accumulated a list of 50 prohibited subjects, including 'representation of nude statues', 'references to race suicide', 'unnecessary exhibition of female underclothing', 'bathing scenes passing the limits of propriety', 'indecorous dancing', 'vulgar accessories', 'references to controversial politics', 'unpleasant details of medical operations', and 'scenes . . . bringing into disrepute British prestige in the Empire'. The latter piece of chauvinism was matched by Mussolini in 1928. He banned all foreign war films from Italian screens because they gave insufficient credit to Italy's contribution in World War I.

☆ In 1984 Syria banned *Sophie's Choice* (US 82) because it was 'anti-Arab and aroused sympathy with Jews'; *The Birth of the Beatles* (GB 79) because the distributor dealt with Israel; and *Giant* (US 56) because it toplined Elizabeth Taylor, a supporter of the Israeli cause.

☆ Indian pictures have been banned in Pakistan for over 20 years. In June 1981 it was reported from New Delhi that Pakistani customs officials had made a bonfire of 1375 Indian films which had been smuggled into the country. They are also banned in Bangladesh, with the result that plagiarists reproduce popular Indian hits shot-by-shot, line-by-line and costume-for-costume with their own casts. Two big-budget films, *Laila Manju* (Ban 79) and *Bashar Ghar* (Ban 79) were banned by the Bangladesh government in 1979 in an attempt to halt the practice.

☆ A sequence in the iconoclastic *Inter Nos* (Ice 82) in which the Icelandic national anthem is presented in a rock version, escaped censorship but resulted in a special Act of Parliament making it illegal to tamper with the tune.

☆ John Huston's documentary masterpiece *Let There Be Light* (US 45), an account of the psychiatric treatment of shellshocked soldiers in an army hospital, was suppressed by the US Government as 'unsuitable' for public viewing. When Huston himself tried to show a copy to friends at the Museum of Modern Art in New York, the print was seized by Military Police. The film was finally shown, despite the fact that the ban was still officially in force, at the Los Angeles County Museum of Art in November 1980.

☆ The Australian government banned the distinguished explorer–photographer Frank Hurley from shooting a feature film called *Jungle Woman* (Aus 26) in Papua New Guinea on the grounds that 'it would be harmful to show whites and blacks together'. The film was shot in Dutch New Guinea instead and released in Australia, where it is doubtful whether audiences drew any distinction between showing 'whites and blacks together' in Australian controlled or Dutch controlled New Guinea. *Everyone's* described the decision of the authorities as 'Bumbledom gone riot'.

12 Audiences and Exhibitors

Cinemas

The first cinema was the Cinématographe Lumière at the Salon Indien, a former billiard hall in the Grand Café, 14 boulevard des Capucines, Paris, opened under the management of Clément Maurice on 28 December 1895. The proprietors of the show were Auguste and Louis Lumière, the pioneer cinematographers whose films made up the programme. The opening performance included *Le Mur*, *L'Arrivée d'un train en gare*, *La sortie des Usines Lumière*, *Le goûter de Bébé*, *La pêche des poissons rouges*, *Soldats au manège*, *M. Lumière et le jongleur Trewey jouant aux cartes*, *La rue de la République à Lyon*, *En mer par gros temps*, *L'arroseur arrosé* and *La destruction des mauvaises herbes*. Returns from the box office on the day of opening were disappointingly low, as only 35 people had ventured a franc to see the new form of entertainment. This barely covered the rent of 30 francs a day, and the owner of the Grand Café, M. Borgo, doubtless congratulated himself that he had refused Maurice's offer of 20 per cent of the receipts in lieu of rent. Later he was to come to regret his decision, when the Cinématographe Lumière became the sensation of Paris and box office receipts rose to 2500 francs a day. Most historians have assumed that the Cinématographe Lumière at the Grand Café was simply a temporary show and consequently it has usually been claimed as the first presentation of films before a paying audience (which it was not) instead of the first cinema. Although the exact date of its closure is not known, there is contemporary evidence that it was still functioning as late as 1901. The fact that it operated continuously for at least 5 years should be sufficient to justify any claim based on permanence.

The first cinema in the United States was Vitascope Hall, opened at the corner of Canal Street and Exchange Place, New Orleans on 26 June 1896. The proprietor of the 400-seat theatre was William T. Rock and his projectionist was William Reed. Most of the programme was made up of short scenic items, including the first British film to be released in America, Robert Paul's *Waves off Dover* (GB 95), but there was sometimes more compelling fare, such as *The Irish Way of Discussing Politics* (US 96) or *The Lynching Scene* (US 96). A major attraction was the movie *May Irwin Kiss* (US 96), which may be said to

Permanent cinemas were preceded by fairground booths. This glorious wood and canvas castle was photographed at a temporary resting place on the outskirts of Manchester in 1899.

Britain's first thousand-seat cinema—the 1908 Gem at Great Yarmouth. Its renaissance splendour by day was enhanced by 1500 light bulbs at night. Men and women were not allowed to sit together, by council decree.

have introduced sex to the American screen. Admission to Vitascope Hall was 10¢ and for another 10¢ patrons were allowed to peep through the door of the projection room and see the Edison Vitascope projector. Those possessed of a liberal supply of dimes could also purchase a single frame of discarded film for the same price.

The first cinema in Britain: The earliest attempt at establishing a cinema in Britain was made by Birt Acres, whose Kineopticon opened at 2 Piccadilly Mansions at the junction of Piccadilly Circus and Shaftesbury Avenue on 21 March 1896. The manager was Mr T. C. Hayward. The opening programme (admission 6d) consisted of *Arrest of a Pickpocket, A Carpenter's Shop, A Visit to the Zoo, The Derby, Rough Seas at Dover* (original title of *Waves off Dover* mentioned above), *The Boxing Kangaroo* and *The German Emperor Reviewing his Troops*. After only a few weeks operation, Acres' cinema was gutted by fire.

The first cinema in Britain of any permanence was Mohawks' Hall, Upper Street, Islington, opened by the Royal Animated & Singing Picture Co. on 5 August 1901. The manager was Henry N. Phillips. Principal attractions of the inaugural programme were *The Rajah's Dream or The Enchanted Forest* (Fr 00),

USA and UK cinemas from 1945					
	USA	UK		USA	UK
1945	20457	4723	1965	14000	1971
1946	19019	–	1966	14350	1847
1947	18607	–	1967	13000	1736
1948	18395	4706	1968	13190	1631
1949	18570	4800	1969	13480	1581
1950	19016	4584	1970	13750	1529
1951	18980	4581	1971	14070	1482
1952	18623	4568	1972	14370	1450
1953	17965	4542	1973	14650	1530
1954	19101	4509	1974	15384	1535
1955	19200	4483	1975	15969	1530
1956	19003	4391	1976	15976	1525
1957	19003	4194	1977	16554	1547
1958	16000	3996	1978	16755	1563
1959	16103	3414	1979	16965	1604
1960	16999	3034	1980	17372	1590
1961	–	2711	1981	18144	1562
1962	–	2421	1982	18295	1439
1963	12800	2181	1983	18772	1327
1964	13750	2057	1984	19589	–

billed as 'the finest mysterious picture ever placed before the public', and a number of primitive 'talkies' featuring vocalists Lil Hawthorne, Vesta Tilley and Alec Hurley. There were also war films from South Africa and China, scenes of rush hour at the Angel, a 'graphic representation of the sensational sporting spectacle *Tally Ho* taken at the London Hippodrome', a newsreel of King Edward VII presenting medals to the South African war heroes, and scenes of a motor car explosion, Count Zeppelin's airship and 'a visit to a spiritualist'. The show was nightly at 8 p.m., with matinees on Thursdays and Saturdays, and prices of admission were 6d, 1s, 2s and 3s—considerably more than the average of 3d or 6d that most cinemas charged at the time of World War I. The Mohawk, though, was an ambitious enterprise, for while later cinemas were content to offer a piano accompaniment to the films, the Royal Animated & Singing Picture Co. engaged the 16-piece Fonobian Orchestra under the direction of Mr W. Neale. Within a few days of opening, the Mohawk advertised that it was 'besieged at every performance'. Evidently the cinema-going public was fickle, for within a few months the Mohawk had been forced to close its doors. After a period as a music hall, it was reopened as a cinema in 1908 as the Palace, changed hands ten years later to become the Blue Hall Cinema, and finally became a Gaumont before closing in 1962. The building still stands, an empty and derelict shell.

FIRST CINEMAS WORLDWIDE

The cinemas listed below were the first to be established permanently (or intended to be permanent) in their respective countries.

ARGENTINA (1901) 467 Calle Maipu, Buenos Aires
AUSTRALIA (Dec 1896) Salon Cinématographe, 237 Pitt Street, Sydney
AUSTRIA (1903) Münstedt-Kino, the Prater, Vienna
BELGIUM (1897) Théâtre de Cinématographie, boulevard du Nord, Brussels
BRAZIL (31 Jul 1897) Salão de Novidades, 141 Rua do Ouvidor, Rio de Janeiro
BULGARIA (1908) The Modern Theatre, Sofia
CANADA (Oct 1907) The Electric Theatre, Vancouver
CHINA (1903) estab. Shanghai by Antonio Ramos
CUBA (c. 1904) Florodora, Palatiano, Havana
CZECHOSLOVAKIA (1907) Blue Pike, Prague
DENMARK (7 Sept 1904) Kosmorama, Copenhagen
EGYPT (1904) Pathé Cinema, Cairo
FINLAND (1901) Kinematograph International, Helsinki
FRANCE (28 Dec 1895) Cinématographe Lumière, 14 boulevard des Capucines, Paris
GERMANY (Jul 1896) 21 Unter den Linden
GREECE (1907) Constitution Square, Athens
ICELAND (1906) Biógraftheater, Reykjavik
INDIA (1907) Elphinstone Cinema, Calcutta
IRAN (1905) Avenue Cherâq Gaz, Teheran
IRELAND (EIRE) (1909) Volta Cinema, Dublin (manager: James Joyce)
ITALY (c. 1898) Cinema Silenzioso, 21 Corso Vittorio Emanuele, Milan
JAPAN (Oct 1903) Denkikan, Asakusa
LEBANON (1909) Zahret Sourya, Beirut
MAURITIUS (1912) Luna Park, Port Louis

The cartoon weekly *Punch* has always been something of a social barometer. When *Punch* publishes a cartoon about a new trend, it is probably here to stay. Note the middle-class audience in this 1912 drawing (see p. 172).

THE CINEMA AS AN EDUCATIVE FORCE.
Tommy (a regular attender at cinematograph shows, during the performance of a society drama). "IS THAT THE TRUSTING HUSBAND OR THE AMOROUS LOVER?"

Left
An afternoon at the pictures, c. 1921. Sixpence would buy an afternoon of escape from the cares of the workaday world.

MEXICO (1901) Salon Pathé, 5 Calle de la Profesa, Mexico City
NEW ZEALAND (1910) King's Theatre, Auckland
NORWAY (1 Nov 1904) Kinematograf-Teatret, 12 Storthingsgd, Oslo
PORTUGAL (1904) Salão Ideal, Lisbon
ROMANIA (May 1909) Volta, Bucharest
SOUTH AFRICA (19 Dec 1908) New Apollo Theatre, 39 Pritchard Street, Johannesburg
SPAIN (c. 1897) Salón Maravillas, Glorieta de Bilbaô, Madrid
SWEDEN (27 Jul 1902) Arkaden Kino, Gothenburg
SWITZERLAND (11 May 1906) Grand Cinématographe Suisse, 17 Croix d'Or, Geneva
SYRIA (1916) Janak Kala'a, Damascus
THAILAND (1907) The Bioscope, Bangkok
TUNISIA (16 Oct 1908) Omnia Pathé, Tunis
TURKEY (1908) Pathé, Istanbul
UNITED KINGDOM (5 Aug 1901) Mohawk's Hall, Upper Street, Islington
UNITED STATES (26 Jun 1896) Vitascope Hall, Canal Street, New Orleans
USSR (RUSSIA) (1903) The Electric Theatre, Moscow
YUGOSLAVIA (CROATIA) (1900) Znasstveno Umjetničko Kajilšte, Zagreb

It is apparent from this list that the oft repeated claim that the first cinema in the world was the Nickelodeon opened by Harry Davis in Pittsburgh, Pa. in June 1905 is wholly without foundation.

The first purpose-built cinema was the Cinéma Omnia Pathé, on the boulevard Montmartre, Paris, which opened with *Le Pendu* (Fr 06) and supporting programme on 1 December 1906. The world's first luxury cinema, and the first with a raked floor so that everyone could see above the heads in front, it was decorated in classical style with columns and Grecian friezes. The screen, measuring 20 ft by 13 ft, was one of the largest ever installed in a cinema at that time. Admission for the two-hour show ranged from 50c to 3fr—prices at other cinemas were generally in the range of 25c to 2fr.

The first purpose-built cinema in Britain was established by Joshua Duckworth of the Premier Picture Co., a former magic-lantern showman and kinetoscope proprietor, whose Central Hall, Colne, Lancs, was erected at a cost of £2000 and opened on 22 February 1907. At first Duckworth presented both films and variety, but abandoned the latter when he

CINEMAS WORLDWIDE

AFGHANISTAN
1939-1; 1952-9; 1972-20; 1977-45
ALBANIA
1935-10; 1939-18; 1950-14; 1960-176; 1970-189; 1979-450 (includes mobile)
ALGERIA
1935-130; 1939-165; 1950-200; 1972-550; 1979-304
ARGENTINA
1923-800; 1930-1608; 1939-1021; 1950-1855; 1960-1739; 1970-1767; 1979-1794
AUSTRALIA
1919-760; 1925-1216; 1930-1250; 1935-1090; 1939-1371; 1945-1600; 1950-1674; 1960-1800; 1970-1349; 1978-900; 1984-813
AUSTRIA
1921-516; 1925-580; 1930-736; 1935-850; 1949-957; 1956-1210; 1964-1248; 1970-820; 1977-533; 1983-536
BANGLADESH
1976-230; 1984-420
BELGIUM
1920-811; 1930-700; 1939-1100; 1950-1550; 1960-1550; 1972-1081; 1979-545; 1983-652
BOLIVIA
1925-16; 1935-23; 1947-60; 1954-60; 1976-41; 1984-160
BRAZIL
1930-1431; 1939-1450; 1947-1514; 1958-3113; 1968-3234; 1978-3200; 1983-1736
BULGARIA
1920-93; 1925-48; 1935-128; 1939-111; 1947-240; 1957-1400; 1967-2957; 1979-3529
BURMA
1939-131; 1950-150; 1960-380; 1983-400
CAMBODIA
1933-4; 1951-15; 1975-50; 1979-0
CANADA
1922-1087; 1937-1121; 1947-1493; 1955-2085; 1960-1756; 1968-1142; 1977-1392; 1984-2004
CHILE
1930-215; 1939-243; 1947-268; 1960-450; 1972-336; 1979-160; 1984-195
CHINA
1925-120; 1930-185; 1935-276; 1939-275; 1949-596; 1953-770; 1958-1386; 1965-2000; 1982-2670

COLOMBIA
1930-207; 1939-276; 1947-435; 1972-819; 1980-1000; 1984-700
COSTA RICA
1930-21; 1939-40; 1947-52; 1950-77; 1972-136; 1984-40
CUBA
1939-375; 1947-450; 1950-515; 1972-444; 1976-453
CYPRUS
1985-74
CZECHOSLOVAKIA
1919-490; 1925-680; 1930-1200; 1939-1254; 1945-1656; 1951-1928; 1955-2268; 1966-3584; 1972-3469; 1978-3248; 1984-2847
DENMARK
1930-270; 1935-340; 1939-370; 1947-430; 1955-458; 1960-500; 1970-382; 1978-442; 1984-457
DOMINICAN REP.
1984-150
ECUADOR
1930-25; 1935-29; 1939-37; 1950-75; 1960-260; 1977-330; 1983-500
EGYPT
1908-11; 1925-40; 1930-60; 1935-89; 1939-118; 1946-285; 1950-226; 1960-389; 1972-384; 1979-215; 1983-161
EIRE
1945-212; 1950-345; 1955-327; 1960-290; 1970-300; 1975-230; 1980-131; 1984-155
EL SALVADOR
1984-100
ETHIOPIA
1939-33; 1950-11; 1974-31
FINLAND
1911-80; 1922-120; 1927-245; 1932-195; 1937-274; 1942-421; 1947-460; 1952-523; 1957-613; 1962-581; 1970-330; 1979-314; 1983-368
FRANCE
1920-1525; 1925-2947; 1930-3113; 1935-4000; 1939-4600; 1950-5300; 1955-5732; 1960-5821; 1965-5454; 1970-4381; 1975-4328; 1984-5031
GERMANY
1912-1500; 1918-2299; 1920-3731; 1925-3878; 1930-5266; 1935-5100; 1940-6900; 1945-11 150. FRG: 1950-5930; 1955-5100; 1960-6950; 1965-5209; 1970-3634; 1975-3094; 1979-3110; 1984-3687. GDR: 1960-1550; 1968-1300; 1975-880; 1980-839.

GHANA
1984-80
GREECE
1915-147; 1925-138; 1930-224; 1935-122; 1939-170; 1947-300; 1955-450; 1960-1000; 1970-1034; 1979-1504; 1983-1200
GUATEMALA
1930-25; 1939-34; 1950-42; 1975-106
HONDURAS
1925-6; 1930-27; 1950-28; 1972-60; 1984-105
HONG KONG
1920-6; 1950-27; 1954-62; 1972-99; 1978-73; 1981-82; 1985-94
HUNGARY
1907-127; 1912-270; 1921-362; 1930-495; 1939-524; 1945-972; 1951-586; 1960-1200; 1972-981; 1979-1045. (NB: Figs refer to 35 mm cinemas only.)
ICELAND
1912-2; 1930-3; 1984-52
INDIA
1910-5; 1920-148; 1924-171; 1930-309; 1936-910; 1941-1136; 1946-1700; 1950-1950; 1960-3200; 1970-4500; 1975-5363; 1979-6232; 1984-7428. (NB: Excluding mobile cinemas.)
INDONESIA
1930-196; 1939-170; 1950-260; 1960-750; 1972-675; 1977-406; 1985-1560
IRAN
1925-4; 1930-10; 1939-35; 1945-78; 1950-80; 1972-520; 1976-438; 1984-256
IRAQ
1935-7; 1939-20; 1950-71; 1972-137; 1979-87
ISRAEL
1947-216; 1960-226; 1970-257; 1975-227; 1980-230; 1984-156
ITALY
1907-500; 1922-2019; 1930-2405; 1935-3794; 1939-4049; 1955-9543; 1960-10 500; 1970-9680; 1979-7495
IVORY COAST
1980-60
JAMAICA
1930-19; 1939-17; 1950-28; 1972-54
JAPAN
1920-600; 1925-1050; 1930-1120; 1935-1600; 1939-1749; 1947-1477; 1950-2157; 1955-7400; 1960-8477; 1963-6164; 1966-4119; 1970-3246; 1973-2974; 1975-2443; 1977-2453; 1979-2392; 1983-2239

found that pictures alone were a sufficient attraction. In his two-hour programme, he always liked to 'include an educational or travel subject; this I find gives dignity to the show. Good drama and pathetic subjects are always appreciated. The greatest difficulty is experienced in satisfying an audience to which you are playing week after week, with humorous and comic subjects—breaking crockery, tumbling over furniture, or running against the banana cart fails to draw a smile if not positive disapproval.' (*Kinematograph Weekly* 2.7.08). The building continued in operation as a cinema until 1924, then became a spiritualist chapel; in recent years its only use has been as an engineering training workshop.

The large purpose-built cinema followed soon after. First to seat over a thousand people was the 1200 Gem in Great Yarmouth, which opened for business on 4 July 1908 under the management of C. B. Cochran—later to become famous as a West End impresario. The Gem was an impressively ornate building in the Renaissance style with twin cupolas surmounting towers on either side of the entrance. At night it was lit by 1500 powerful electric bulbs—with that engaging disregard for the literal truth which has always characterised cinema publicity, the management dubbed it 'The Palace of 5000 Lights'. One of the odder characteristics of this pioneer venture in bringing mass entertainment to mass audiences was a condition of the license granted to Cochran by the local authority. Men and women were not allowed to sit together, presumably for fear of what they might get up to in the dark. The Gem had another curious distinction, being one of the very few purpose-built cinemas ever to have been converted into a theatre. It still operates as the Windmill Theatre, mainly for summer shows and amateur productions. There is even the occasional film show, usually cartoons for the younger holidaymakers.

JORDAN
1950-17; 1972-34; 1985-15
KENYA
1935-8; 1950-44; 1972-28; 1979-35; 1985-50
KOREA
1935-45; 1939-60; 1950-116. South Korea: 1960-273; 1970-658; 1977-752; 1981-443
KUWAIT
1962-4; 1979-10; 1985—11
LEBANON
1949-48; 1960-82; 1972-170
LIBYA
1951-12; 1962—35; 1972-60; 1977-52
LUXEMBOURG
1933-26; 1939-30; 1950-39; 1955-41; 1972-52; 1975-36; 1979-17; 1985-10
MADAGASCAR
1925-5; 1933-14; 1950-24; 1974-31
MALAYSIA
1925-10; 1935-58; 1939-97; 1950-100; 1960-220; 1972-430; 1977-425
MALTA
1915-30; 1950-26; 1960-49; 1972-39; 1979-35; 1982-34
MAURITIUS
1985-36
MEXICO
1930-615; 1935-701; 1939-823; 1946-1369; 1950-1726; 1960-2232; 1972-1850; 1981-3020
MONACO
1985-3
MOROCCO
1933-51; 1939-62; 1950-90; 1972-155; 1977-276; 1985-c. 300
NETHERLANDS
1925-264; 1930-236; 1935-308; 1939-333; 1950-461; 1955-573; 1960-565; 1966-490; 1970-435; 1975-387; 1980-507; 1984-546
NEW ZEALAND
1925-350; 1930-443; 1935-366; 1939-576; 1945-568; 1950-570; 1960-581; 1970-260; 1975-228; 1979-200; 1984-154
NICARAGUA
1925-11; 1939-24; 1950-47; 1972-85
NIGER
1983-10
NIGERIA
1939-11; 1950-25; 1973-112; 1979-131
NORWAY
1925-252; 1930-212; 1935-241; 1939-247; 1947-291; 1951-452; 1955-508; 1960-668; 1971-442; 1975-464; 1979-455; 1984-467

OMAN
1985-20
OUTER MONGOLIA
1952-50; 1977-60; 1982-59
PAKISTAN
1947-250; 1957-360; 1960-419; 1970-527; 1975-623; 1979-725; 1984-750
PANAMA
1984-50
PARAGUAY
1930-9; 1939-15; 1950-40; 1972-30; 1984-100
PERU
1925-60; 1930-70; 1935-110; 1939-205; 1950-235; 1960-400; 1972-363; 1977-400; 1984-400
PHILIPPINES
1935-273; 1950-450; 1960-634; 1972-704; 1977-900; 1980-1200; 1984-946
POLAND
1925-383; 1935-728; 1939-769; 1950-574; 1967-3694; 1977-3232; 1984-2112. (NB: 1967, 1977 and 1984 figs inc. 16 mm cinemas.)
PORTUGAL
1925-127; 1939-215; 1950-301; 1967-336; 1975-410; 1984-397
PUERTO RICO
1984-150
ROMANIA
1925-304; 1930-357; 1935-380; 1939-372; 1948-383; 1955-350; 1968-573; 1972-462; 1977-578; 1984-635
SAINT HELENA
1985-1
SENEGAL
1975-87; 1979-75
SINGAPORE
1984-70
SOUTH AFRICA
1925-380; 1935-350; 1945-465; 1950-470; 1970-521; 1979-700; 1985-507
SPAIN
1914-900; 1921-570; 1925-1500; 1930-2074; 1935-3252; 1939-3500; 1948-3251; 1955-7325; 1960-6459; 1970-6627; 1974-5178; 1978-4430; 1981-4096; 1984-3663
SRI LANKA
1930-24; 1939-19; 1950-82; 1960-206; 1970-315; 1975-365; 1984-320
SWAZILAND
1985-6
SWEDEN
1920-600; 1930-1182; 1935-843; 1939-1907;

1947-2493; 1955-2494; 1966-1733; 1975-1192; 1979-1210; 1984-1220
SWITZERLAND
1920-178; 1930-302; 1941-351; 1950-410; 1960-615; 1972-539; 1977-494; 1984-460
SYRIA
1925-14; 1935-26; 1950-50; 1960-70; 1972-90; 1977-70; 1983-70
TAIWAN
1960-542; 1972-668; 1983-455
THAILAND
1915-3; 1925-42; 1935-68; 1939-80; 1950-118; 1960-238; 1970-340; 1977-415; 1983-651
TONGA
1985-10
TRINIDAD
1985-26
TUNISIA
1933-61; 1950-50; 1972-65; 1979-76; 1984-85
TURKEY
1925-40; 1930-104; 1939-120; 1950-275; 1960-700; 1970-790; 1979-3000 (claimed)
UK
1914-3170; 1928-3760; 1934-4305; 1939-4901. For 1945-1984 see p. 168.
URUGUAY
1925-101; 1930-122; 1935-137; 1945-175; 1950-177; 1972-223; 1979-94; 1984-79
USA
1910-9480; 1913-15 700; 1923-15 000; 1929-23 344; 1935-15 273; 1940-19 042. For 1945-1984 see p. 168.
USSR
1977-14 700[1]
YEMEN
1985-20
YUGOSLAVIA
1921-231; 1930-397; 1939-383; 1950-736; 1960-1585; 1967-1765; 1977-1385; 1983-1278
VENEZUELA
1930-121; 1939-147; 1950-350; 1954-575; 1964-741; 1975-650; 1984-450
VIETNAM
1912-10, 1925-29; 1930-34; 1939-110; 1950-80; 1960 (S. Vietnam only)-189; 1970 (S. Vietnam only)-102; 1977-199
[1](NB: At the time of the revolution in 1917 the number of Russian cinemas was 1045. No reliable figures are available for the interim years because the USSR counts projection points, not cinemas proper.)

The Fox Theater, Detroit—the world's largest cinema. (*Alfred J. Buttler*)

The first British cinema with a sloping floor was the Picture Palace at St Albans, Hertfordshire, opened by Arthur Melbourne-Cooper of the Alpha Trading Co. in 1908. It was also the first to depart from standard theatre practice by charging more to sit at the back of the stalls than the front. The *Bioscope* reported: 'This arrangement was somewhat resented at first by patrons of the higher-priced seats, but when they found the specially raised floor gave them a better view than could be got from the front, they appreciated the innovation'. The idea was suggested to Melbourne-Cooper by his usherette, whom he later had the good sense to marry.

The first cinema to erect a neon sign was the West End Cinema in Coventry Street, London in 1913. It was also the first building of any kind in Britain to be emblazoned with neon and remained the only one for another ten years.

SOCIAL ACCEPTANCE OF THE CINEMA
Although the cinema was primarily a proletarian form of entertainment in the USA and UK prior to World War I, elsewhere it achieved social acceptance at an earlier date. The first countries in which this was manifest were Russia and Japan, a phenomenon partly accounted for by high admission charges. In Japan seat prices of the earliest cinemas (c. 1903) were generally in a range equivalent to 6d (12c)–3s 9d (90c), well out of

the reach of peasants or artisans. The respectability of the cinema in Russia was attested by the fact that the exclusive Hotel Metropole in Moscow saw fit to open its own cinema in 1906. The interest of the Tsar and Tsarina in films—the court photographer was kept constantly employed filming the Royal Family at leisure—did much to make movies fashionable. An American wrote to a US trade publication in 1913 that the audiences he saw in Russia were of a far better class—and the seats more expensive—than elsewhere in Europe. Cinemas were attended, he said, even by 'very high officials in uniform'.

In France the stage-bound but much admired productions of Film d'Art, with casts drawn from the illustrious Comédie-Française, catered from 1908 for the kind of audiences who looked to film as a silent record of great theatre drama. Around 1910, at a time when even minor American players would only deign to appear in films under the strictest cloak of anonymity, the fact that the leading stars of the Budapest National Theatre were prepared to be seen on screen gave the Hungarian cinema its artistic imprimatur. In Germany *Der Andere* (Ger 12), directed by Max Mack with the distinguished stage actor Albert Basserman in the lead, was the first film to receive serious critical attention in the press and consequent patronage from a new type of cinema audience. The emergence of Denmark's Asta Nielsen as the first star specialising in tragic roles had a profound influence on the cinema in Scandinavia and Central Europe from 1910 onwards, demonstrating the drawing power of original screen drama and 'name' stars to middle-class audiences. As the artistic quality of motion pictures improved, new luxury cinemas opened designed to accommodate the kind of audiences at which these films were aimed. Foremost was the giant Gaumont-Palace in Paris (1911), with a seating capacity of 5000; others included Berlin's 2000-seat Alhambra Platz (1911), the Panellinion in Athens (1911), also with 2000 seats, and Copenhagen's majestic 3000-seat Palads-Teatret (1912).

In America the era of the 'super cinema' began a little later, dating from the opening of the Regent on 116th Street and 7th Avenue in February 1913 and the Vitagraph Theater and the Strand on Broadway in 1914. There has been a tendency to oversimplify American film history by suggesting that the cinema remained a primitive entertainment controlled by unlettered immigrants and largely aimed at immigrant audiences until the advent of D. W. Griffith, whereupon, it is said, the movies became an art form. In fact the influence of Griffith in making the cinema socially acceptable is probably less significant than the emergence of the feature-length film in the United States in 1912–13, a development that took place later than it did in Europe. While the simple one-reeler remained standard, the primitive nickelodeon was an appropriate showplace. The rise of the full-length drama, which was contemporary with the creation of the 'star system', broadened the appeal of the movies and stimulated the erection of theatres adequate to their presentation in an atmosphere of 'comfort and refinement'.

In Britain the feature film was also late in supplanting the modest one-reel melodramas and comedies of predominantly backstreet picture houses. Significantly the humour weekly *Punch*, generally alert to social trends, did not publish its first cartoon about cinema-going until 1912. By that date artist Charles Pears was able to show what was clearly intended to represent a sophisticated, middle-class audience. Few of the 4000 cinemas estimated to be operating in Britain by 1912, however, would have aspired to such a level of patronage unless they were of the standard of London's first luxury cinema, Cinema House in Oxford Street (1910), with its oak-panelled auditorium, adjoining restaurant, and seats upholstered in a 'delicate shade of Rose du Barri velvet'. Generally speaking, middle-class cinema-going in Britain came in with World War I and was due to a combination of circumstances: the relaxation of chaperonage, the provision of better appointed and more luxurious cinemas, the feverish desire for entertainment by officers home on leave, and not least, the vastly improved standard of film-making after 1914.

The largest cinema in the world is the 5041-seat Fox Theater in Detroit. Originally opened in 1928, the Fox is now principally a live entertainment theatre but still shows movies on an occasional basis. After a downward career as the site of Motown reviews in the 1960s, a Kung Fu film palace in the 1970s and a rock 'n' roll emporium in the 1980s, the magnificent Fox, its fading Taj Mahal interior still partially intact, was bought by retired Ford employee Chuck Forbes for $1 million in 1984 and is currently undergoing an $8 million restoration.

The largest cinema ever built was the Roxy, built in New York at a cost of $12 million and opened under

USA and UK weekly cinema attendance (millions)					
	USA	UK		USA	UK
1922	40	–	1954	49	24·5
1923	43	–	1955	46	22·7
1924	46	–	1956	47	21·2
1925	46	–	1957	45	17·6
1926	50	–	1958	40	14·5
1927	57	–	1959	42	11·2
1928	65	25·2	1960	40	9·6
1929	95	–	1961	42	8·6
1930	90	–	1962	43	7·6
1931	75	–	1963	44	6·9
1932	60	–	1964	–	6·6
1933	60	–	1965	44	6·3
1934	70	18·3	1966	38	5·6
1935	75	–	1967	17·8	5·1
1936	88	–	1968	18·8	4·6
1937	85	–	1969	17·5	4·1
1938	85	–	1970	17·7	3·7
1939	85	–	1971	15·8	3·9
1940	80	–	1972	18	3·0
1941	85	25·2	1973	16·6	2·6
1942	85	28·7	1974	19·4	2·7
1943	85	29·6	1975	19·9	2·2
1944	85	30·3	1976	18·4	2·0
1945	90	30·5	1977	20·2	2·1
1946	90	31·4	1978	21·7	2·4
1947	90	28·1	1979	22·1	2·5
1948	90	29·1	1980	19·8	2·0
1949	87·5	27·5	1981	20·5	1·6
1950	60	26·8	1982	22·4	1·2
1951	54	26·2	1983	23·0	1·3
1952	51	25·2	1984	22·9	0·8 (est.)
1953	46	24·7			

Between the wars every big cinema had its own restaurant. This one, opened in 1918, was at the Stoll Picture Theatre in Newcastle upon Tyne. During the 1930s, cafés like this served a four-course luncheon with a roll and butter and coffee for as little as 1s 6d. The last cinema café, at the Odeon in Southampton, closed in May 1982.

the management of Samuel Rothapfel (after whom it was named) on 11 March 1927. With an original seating capacity of 6214, the Roxy employed a total of 300 staff, including 16 projectionists and 110 musicians. The Roxy closed on 29 March 1960.

Europe's largest-ever cinema was the Gaumont Palace, opened in Paris with a 6000 seat auditorium in 1931.

The largest cinema in Britain is the Odeon Theatre, Hammersmith, with 3485 seats.

The smallest cinema in the world to operate as a regular commercial venture was the Miramar at Colon, Cuba, which was reported in 1926 to have 25 seats.

The smallest cinema in the USA was the Silver Star Theater in Silver Star, Montana, which had a seating capacity of 26 in 1925. Silver Star, population 75, boasted two cinemas, with a total seating capacity (126) exceeding the number of citizens. Only eleven of the 15,000 cinemas operating in the US at that date had under 100 seats, of which five were in the State of Montana.

The smallest auditorium in a multiple cinema is in the six-screen Biohoellin at Reykjavik, Iceland, which seats 17.

The highest cinema attendance in the world is in China, with 29,000 million admissions in 1983 (about 79·5 million daily). Not all these are paid admissions, however, as cinema shows in public parks and in rural areas are often free.

Elsewhere in the world, paid admissions totalled the following in 1983: India—4420 million; USSR—4300 million (1982 figure); USA—1173 million; France—197 million; Japan—170 million; Italy—162 million; West Germany—127 million; UK—65 million.

The all-time record figure for any country was 4940 million seats sold in the USA in 1929. The European record is 819 million in Italy in 1955.

The country with the highest per capita cinema attendance in the world is China (pop. 1000 million), with an average 29 visits annually per head of population (1982–83 figures).

The country with the largest number of cinemas in relation to population is San Marino, with one cinema for every 3190 inhabitants (a total of 7). In comparison the USA has one cinema for every 13,750 inhabitants, the USSR has one cinema for every 14,250 inhabitants and the UK, television dominated, is content with one cinema for every 40,000 inhabitants.

Perth, Western Australia, c. 1929. The Prince of Wales cinema offered the special amenity of a refrigerator in the foyer so that shoppers could leave their perishable groceries while watching the show. (*Battye Library of West Australian History*)

At the other end of the scale comes Saudi Arabia (pop. 8 million) with no cinemas, the public presentation of films being illegal as contrary to strict Islamic belief.

The highest number of admissions for a film per capita of population was achieved by the historical epic *Khan Asparoukh* (Bul 82), of which the first of three parts was seen by 6·5 million of Bulgaria's 8·5 million population, equal to 76·5 per cent. Total admissions for the first run of all three parts (shown separately) were 12 million.

SPECIAL AMENITIES FOR CINEMA PATRONS

These were offered by some exhibitors from an early date. A correspondent of the *Kinematograph Weekly* reported in 1907 that it was customary for Italian cinemas to be furnished with a reading-room stocked with the current newspapers and illustrated journals for the benefit of patrons waiting for their friends.

Berlin's first super-cinema, the 2000 seat Alhambra Platz of 1911, served beer during the performance. Each seat had a tip-up tray on the back, similar to those on airliner seats, for the person behind to rest his tankard on. The first air-conditioned cinema was opened in America in 1922, but in hot countries efforts had been made to keep the patrons cool before that date. China Theatres Ltd, which operated a chain of cinemas in the Chinese Treaty Ports, provided cold towels for the audience's comfort. *Moving Picture World* (14 August 1920) recorded: 'The picture is stopped about every reel for an interval to permit him (the chinaman) to whizz his towel across to the attendant in the aisle, who immediately wets it in icy water and whizzes it back.'

Many American cinemas have provided a crèche where mothers could leave their babies, the earliest recorded being at the Alhambra, Milwaukee in 1913. The Strand, opened in New York in April 1914, would take telephone calls for patrons, who were asked to notify the Captain of Ushers, in advance, where they were sitting. In the thirties, London's Cameo cinema allowed patrons to telephone out for nothing, besides giving them free cups of tea and free pre-stamped postcards.

A New York cinema which opened in 1925, the Knickerbocker, had a separate 'Carriage Entrance' for the kind of wealthy clientele the movies were beginning to attract. A resident chiropodist ministered to patrons of the Capitol, NY in the 1920s. Club-like amenities existed at New York's Little Carnegie Theater, which opened in 1928 with a ping-pong room, a bridge salon and a dance floor. The Fox, San Francisco, contained an art gallery with paintings personally selected in Europe by Mrs Fox.

Nothing could compare with the 6000-seat Roxy in New York, with its permanent choir of 100 voices, 50-strong ballet troupe, lavishly appointed drawing room, its own broadcasting station and a fully-equipped hospital with separate male and female wards. No less than 12,900 cases were treated in the Roxy's first year (1929–30) and it was claimed that eight lives were saved. There was also the Bilmarjac Seat Indicator System, which consisted of aisle boxes with a row of discs corresponding to the seats. When a seat was vacated, the disc lit up.

After the Roxy, anything offered elsewhere seemed tame by comparison. However, a Paramount representative who visited Australia in the 1940s was particularly impressed with the 'Crying Rooms', in which mothers nursing infants could watch the film from behind a soundproof glass screen. In addition, there would often be a similar room with glass screen for the use of private parties, a facility that the Paramount representative thought highly desirable as Australians visiting the cinema in a group were often drunk.

A novel device that failed to catch on elsewhere was the automatic ticket dispenser installed at Loew's 175th Street Theater, New York, about 1960. It would take either coins or notes and give change; if the change was paper money it came in the form of a bill rolled like a cigarette and hygienically wrapped in tissue.

In 1979 the Edmonds Theater, Seattle, made a determined pitch for the teenage market by ripping out 40 seats and installing a dance floor. Live bands played for dancing after each performance, the $3 admission covering both the picture and the rock session.

Open-air cinemas are common in Mediterranean countries, but until recently the Oriente cinema in Barcelona enjoyed the special seasonal amenity of a sliding roof which enabled audiences to sit beneath a star-studded sky in summer—and, less romantically, enabled urchins to lob dead cats over the walls.

The first cinema to present a double bill of feature films was the Glacarium in Melbourne, Australia, on 15 May 1911. The programme for the week was *The Lost Chord* (Aus 11) and *The Fall of Troy* (It 10).

During the 1950s small cinemas in Japanese villages would show up to six features on a single programme. This invariably arose from competition between two rival cinemas, one advertising a triple feature, the other outbidding with a quadruple, and so on.

The longest non-stop show took place at the Variety Arts Center in Hollywood on 29–31 May 1983, when 37 low-budget classics were shown in continuous sequence during a 50-hour 'B Movie Marathon'. Tickets cost $15 for the entire show, patrons bringing their own sleeping bags, food and drink, and what *Variety* described as 'assorted life support systems to get them through the gruelling early morning hours'.

The oldest cinema in Britain is the Classic Royal, Charing Cross Road, which opened as the Cinema de Paris on 12 February 1910. In the interim the cinema became the Cameo (1926), the Cameo Revudenews (1936), the Cameo-Royal (1956), the Classic Royal (1972), the Royal (1977) and the Classic Leicester Square (1979). It acquired its present name in 1983.

The oldest British cinema to retain its original fabric is the Electric Cinema Theatre, Notting Hill Gate, opened in February 1911. Among its claims to fame is the fact that mass-murderer John Christie worked there as a projectionist in the 1940s.

The oldest building ever converted to use as a cinema was the Music Hall Cinema, Chester, which was in service as a 'common hall' as early as 1280 and as a place of entertainment by 1616. The building was converted into a legitimate theatre in 1773 and a music hall in 1855. Films were first exhibited there in 1910, but only in 1921 was it reconstructed as a permanent cinema. It closed in 1962 to undergo yet another conversion, this time an ignominious transformation into a supermarket.

The first municipal cinema was the Notodden in Oslo, Norway, established in 1915 under an Act of Parliament of the previous year which allowed municipalities to build and operate cinemas. From 1918 the opening of privately-run cinemas was banned in Oslo and in 1926 the prohibition was extended to the rest of the country, a measure designed to ensure a market for Norwegian films.

The first municipal cinema in Britain was The Anvil, Sheffield, a three-screen multiple opened on 31 March 1983.

The largest cinema chain in the world is GCC Theatres Inc. of Chestnut Hill, Mass., a subsidiary of General Cinema Corporation, which controls 1075 screens at 330 locations throughout the USA. This represents approximately 6 per cent of the total number of American cinemas. The USA has 68 cinema chains each controlling more than a dozen screens.

The oldest cinema chain is the 62-screen Wehrenberg Corp. of St Louis, Missouri, which was established in 1906.

The largest cinema chain in Britain is controlled by EMI/ABC with 296 screens, 21 per cent of the total in the country. Odeon/Rank follows with 202 screens (14·5 per cent), while the Classic Cinemas chain numbers 122 screens (1983–84 figures).

The largest UK cinema chain of all time was Rank's Odeon circuit, with 596 cinemas in 1950.

The highest box office gross for a cinema in any one week was the $468,173 receipts for *Crossed Swords*/UK: *The Prince and the Pauper* (US 78) at New York's Radio City Music Hall during the week commencing 2 April 1978.

Not a notable box-office success elsewhere, the film's remarkable drawing power on this occasion may not have been entirely unconnected with the fact that the closure of Radio City Music Hall had been announced for the following week.

Before the advent of the trailer, cinemas used slides like this one for *The Gorilla* (US 27) to advertise forthcoming attractions. So when did the trailer emerge and who originated it? It was sometime in the twenties, but nobody seems to know exactly when or who.

The last silent cinema in Britain was the Electra at Royton, Lancs, run by the Progress Film Co. In contrast to their name the proprietors refused to countenance anything so new-fangled as talkies and only closed down in 1935 when the renters were unable to maintain a supply of silent films.

Elsewhere the silent cinema survived longer. According to US statistics, there were 36 silent picture houses remaining in 1937, though it is possible that some of these were buildings still licensed to show films, but which had ceased to operate. Finland is said to have had some silent houses running during World War II and as late as 1952 only 50 out of the 150 cinemas in Burma were wired for sound. Thailand continued to produce silent films until the mid-1960s (see Silent Film, p. 144).

The longest continuous run of any film was of Jean Cocteau's surrealist fantasy *Le Sang d'un Poète* (Fr 30), which was on show at the same arts cinema in New York from 1938 until 1953.

The longest running film currently on exhibition is *Emmanuelle* (Fr 74), which is still showing at the Paramount City cinema on the Champs Elysées in Paris where it opened on 26 June 1974. The film topped three million admissions in January 1982.

The longest continuous run of a film in Britain is that of *Midnight Express* (GB 78), which opened at the Odeon, Haymarket on 10 August 1978 and has been on show without a break at five other West End cinemas successively up to the time of this book going to press.

The shortest run of any film with a general release was that of *The Super Fight* (US 70), a feature-length movie of a mock championship fight between the then two undefeated heavyweight champions of history, Rocky Marciano and Muhammad Ali, which was released globally on 20 January 1970. In accord-

FAMOUS NAME CINEMAS

Many famous people have been honoured by having streets or squares named after them; to have a cinema named after you is a rarer distinction. Those so commemorated have included:

Bleriot (Bucharest)
Booker Washington (St Louis, Mo)
King Tut (Rising Star, Texas)
Mozart (Kansas City)
Giuseppe Verdi (Fabbrico, Italy)
Betsy Ross (New York)
Flora McDonald (Red Springs, NC)
Benito Mussolini (Forli', Italy)
Biddle Johnson (Charlotte, NC)
Lord Byron (Paris)
Bonapart (sic) (Stony Point, NC)
Queen Anne (Seattle, Washington)
Garibaldi (Milan)

William Penn (Pittsburgh)
Pius X (Frascati, Italy)
Pershing (Chicago)
Lafayette (Thebes, Illinois)
Mary Anderson (Lexington, Indiana)
Jeanne d'Arc (Bondy, France)
Martha Washington (Detroit)
Volta (Rome)
Paderewski (Browerville, Minnesota)
Pocahontas (Savonburg, Kansas)
Nehru (Chittur Cochin, India)
Laurier (Hull, Quebec)
Cartier (Hull, Quebec)
Montcalm (Hull, Quebec)
Dante (Milan)
Sherlock Holmes (London)
Marconi (Bologna)
Euclid (Bardstown, Kentucky)
Galileo (Florence)
Gandhi (Peddapalli, India)

Duse (La Spezia, Italy)
Victor-Hugo (Paris)
Kennedy Theatre (Coimbatore, India)
Vespucci (Florence)
Puccini (Udine)
Homer (Hibbing, Minnesota)
Shelley (Lerici, Italy)
Johann Strauss (Vienna)
Henry Clay (Lookout, Kentucky)
Winston (Slathwaite, Yorks—renamed in 1943 in honour of Britain's wartime PM)
Napoleon (New Orleans)
Drake (Plymouth, Devon)
O'Higgins (San Pablo, Chile—after Chilean–Irish admiral)
Mount Batten Talkies (Port Blair, Andaman and Nicobar Islands)
Robin Hood (Nottingham)
The Black Prince (Derby).

ance with conditions laid down by the distributor, bonded guards collected all prints after a single showing and took them to be incinerated.

The longest name ever given to a cinema was conferred on a mobile picture show operated by Spanish showman José Fessi Fernandez in the Bordeaux region of France in 1902. It was called the Lenti-electroplastiscromomimocoliserpentographe. **The longest name of a cinema currently in operation** is the comparatively terse Cinema-I-Anjuman-I-Khairiya-I-Niswan, a 200-seat picture house in Kabul, Afghanistan. **The longest single word name** is borne by the Kannikaparameswari in Turyvegere, India.

The shortest name ever given to a cinema was borne by the K in Mattoon, Ill. in 1925.

UNUSUAL CINEMA NAMES

These have abounded since the Cabbage opened in Liverpool in 1914 and the Decadence in Harbin, China, the same year. A Bradford clergyman, the Rev. S. Thomas, opened The World's Window about this date and while Brussels offered High Life, Moscow promised Magic Dreams. Brno, Czechoslovakia made an honest declaration with The Illusion, while Estonia's Bi-Ba-Bo may have meant anything at all, even in Estonian. A name which definitely cloaked a secret was the 555 at Brown's Bay, New Zealand, owned by Mrs Olga Brown—it was 'a private family joke, believed to concern cards'. The first cinema in Peking to show talkies was inappropriately called the Peace and Quiet. The Yank Theatre was located far from any indigenous Yanks, in the Grand Duchy of Luxembourg, and it was unnecessary to travel to Milan to attend La Scala when there was one in the Irish village of Letterkenny, Co. Donegal. Greenland Theatre was nowhere near Greenland, but in Palacode, India. The image of suburban gentility conjured up by Bristol's Kosy Korner Kinema was matched by Mon Repos, only the latter was located in the untamed frontier atmosphere of Russia's Baku oil-

field in 1916. In India many cinemas are still called 'Talkies', such as Swastika Talkies in Bihar, Tip Top Talkies at Gopichettipalayam, Jolly Talkies in Muttom and Molly Talkies in Nedunganpara, or Baby Talkies, Thiruvarar. English Talkies in Ahmedabad shows movies in Gujarati, not English. The Roxy, now no more than a fading memory to New Yorkers, lives on in Motihari, Champaran, Bohar, and Bombay. The White Elephant and the Black Cat both belonged to WWI Glasgow, as did a Cinerama long before today's widescreen spectacle was ever thought of. The Buffalo in Ashington, Northumberland, opened about 1912, was so named because it specialised in westerns.

The oddest names are undoubtedly those found in the United States: Amusu (Lincolntown, Ga.); Hobo (Shawneetown, Ill.); The No Name (Moreauville, La.); Tootles (St Joseph, Mo.); U-No-Us (Rensselaer Falls, NY); Muse-Us (Dayton, Ohio); Tar Heel (Plumtree, NC); Dazzleland (Philadelphia); Glory B (Miami, Okla.); C-It (Ashtabula Harbor, Ohio); The Vamp (Barnwell, SC); Fo To Sho (Ballinger, Texas); Ha Ha (Minneapolis); Hoo Hoo (Doucette, Texas); The Herring (Winton, NC); Cinderella (Detroit); OK (Simpson, Ill.); My (Indianapolis); Your (Detroit); Our (Sparta, Mich.); Why Not (Greenfield, Ind.); It (Huntingdon, W. Va.); Try-It (Buffalo, NY); Hi-Art (Lockport, NY); Good Luck (Seattle, Wash.); Sour Wine (Brazil, Ind.); Oh Gee (Edwardsville, Ill.); Happy Jack (Abilene, Texas); Uses Pictures (Butlerville, Ind.); No Home (Dalton City, Ill.); Pa and Ma's (Cobsden, Ill.); Red Apple (Omak, Wash.); Fattie's (Winchester, Texas); Silent Prayers (Sprigg, W. Va.); Za Za (Plainfield, Ind.); Zim Zim (Cumberland, W. Va.). The Norka in Akron and the Idol in Lodi were simply the town name spelt backwards. In Thibodaux, La., there were two cinemas before the war. The larger was the Grand. Its smaller rival was the Baby Grand.

The largest number of cinemas in one city was 986 in New York in 1913.

The post-war record was held by Tokyo, which had

over 600 cinemas in 1958, two and a half times as many as New York.

The largest number of cinemas showing the same film in the same city at the same time was 246 in New York when the sensational sex film *Traffic in Souls* (US 13) was first released.

The first multiple cinema in Britain was the Regal Twins, Manchester, opened in 1930. It is now known as Studios 1 and 2. The present nationwide movement into multiples began with the twinning of the Odeon, Nottingham in July 1965. **The first triple** was the ABC Lothian Road in Edinburgh, opened on 29 November 1969.

A choice of films at the same cinema was not unknown even before the advent of the multiple. In 1926 the Spanish correspondent of the German film journal *Lichtbildbuehne* reported that he had visited a cinema in Cairo with twin screens in one auditorium showing two different films at the same time.

The largest multiple cinema in the world is Cineplex, a complex of 21 auditoria under one roof, which opened at Eaton Centre, Toronto, Canada, on 19 April 1979. The individual cinemas have a seating capacity of 60–130, with an aggregate of 1700. Cineplex specialises in foreign and minority interest pictures, including undubbed Italian films aimed at Toronto's 400,000 strong Italian community.

Europe's largest multiple cinema is the Palads in Copenhagen, Denmark, with 17 cinemas under one roof. One of Europe's oldest picture houses, it was converted into a multiple by A/S Nordisk Film on 1 September 1978.

The Dekascoop in Ghent, Belgium, is a ten-screen multiple in which ten films are presented simultaneously from a single projection booth.

The northernmost cinema in the world is the 329-seat North Cape Municipal Kino at Honningsvåg (pop. 5000), Norway, which lies on latitude 71° 1', 300 miles north of the Arctic Circle.

The southernmost cinema in the world is the Cine San Martín in Ushuaia (pop. 2200), Tierra del Fuego, Argentina, which lies just north of latitude 55°.

UNUSUAL CINEMAS

Cinemas have been located in odd places ever since someone thought of putting one on top of Mt Portofino, Genoa, in 1907. Motion pictures entered the Arabian harem the same year when one Mehdi Russi Khan persuaded Shah Mohammed Ali to allow him to relieve the boredom of the many royal wives with a 'ladies only' cinema showing Pathé films imported from France. Meanwhile in the less exotic atmosphere of one of London's ancient churches, St Mary Axe, the Rev. Wilson Carlisle was relieving the ennui of his parishioners by introducing elevating and instructive movies into his Sunday services. Some years later, in the early 1920s, the Crawford Memorial Methodist Church at 218th Street, New York, began doubling as a

cinema. The Rev. Lincoln Caswell was worried about dwindling congregations and started up Saturday night cinema performances with full-length features plus a supporting programme of comedies and a newsreel, borrowing the films for nothing from an obliging neighbourhood theatre. The following night he would preach on the moral pointed by the 'big picture'. As a further inducement the stars themselves were invited along, one notable patron being Lillian Gish.

There have been occasional misguided attempts to establish open-air cinemas in Britain, among them the Garden Cinema at Hull, which opened for business on a balmy summer's night in July 1912. Patrons sat on deck chairs in an open-sided marquee. Not surprisingly the cinema was forced to close with the onset of winter and never reopened again. Another attempt was made in 1915, when a roof-top cinema seating 150

A number of churches have doubled as cinemas. This one was the West London Methodist Mission in 1937. Admission was 1d for Sunday School scholars, 3d for others. Sunday School enrolment reached record heights.

was established by Pathé Frères on a building in Wardour Street, London. Two years later an open-air cinema was inaugurated in the middle of Trafalgar Square for the benefit of soldiers and sailors on leave.

In 1913 Secretary of State William Jennings Bryan established a cinema inside the State Department, Washington, for the leisure-time entertainment of the staff.

There is no record of cinemas in prisoner of war camps, but Allied civilians interned at Ruhleben Internment Camp during World War I enjoyed the benefit of a well-appointed picture house.

One Nazi concentration camp is known to have had a cinema. In November 1944 a barracks at Dora, a concentration camp adjacent to Buchenwald, was converted into a cinema as a special privilege for the slave labourers engaged on the assembly of Hitler's V1 and V2 rockets.

In England during World War II, Chislehurst Caves were converted into shelters at the height of the blitz, special trains being run nightly from London. Some people even moved in with their own furniture and a cave cinema was operated to keep the temporary refugees amused during the long winter evenings.

A number of cinemas have been devoted to the films of a single star. The Crystal Hall on 14th Street, New York, showed only Chaplin movies for nine years, 1914–23, with the exception of one week when they decided to vary the programme. Business was so bad they reverted to Chaplin. In Moscow in 1925 there was a cinema devoted entirely to old Clara Kimball Young movies, despite the fact that Miss Young's career was already over by this date. (She had refused to diet when the fashion for slim figures overtook America. In Russia the rotund look never went out.) There are two cinemas which show only Bond movies—the Camera cinema in Berlin and the Kolosseum Kino in Vienna. The 007 pictures are shown strictly in rotation, each one for a week four times a year. In Madras there is a cinema which shows only Sivaji Ganesan movies.

In May 1931 the Grand Cinema in Auckland, New Zealand, changed its name to the London and initiated a policy of showing only Brtish films 'for the first time in the whole Empire'. It was also the last time. Modern-day Helsinki has a Soviet government-owned cinema, The Cosmos, which shows exclusively Soviet films. It runs at a prodigious loss—total box-office take in 1981 was only $83,000.

Cinemas catering to minorities have included one for lepers opened in Trinidad in 1921 and Britain's first and only cinema for negroes, established in Cardiff in 1935. A cinema for children called Smile is run by the pupils of a boarding school at Almetievsk in the Tatar Republic of the USSR. The Harmonic cinema in Frankfurt has women-only performances once a fortnight—the films shown are either made by women or specifically about women. Another cinema with a female bias is the Kineca Omori in Tokyo, which is run by and located in a supermarket. It specialises in European films and silent classics: the people most attracted by such fare in Japan are female and over 25, so supermarket shoppers are prime target audience.

The first cinema in a train was established on the Trans-Siberian Railway by a French company in 1913. Admission was 50 kopeks (12½c or 1s). In Britain cinema coaches on trains were introduced by the LNER on the *Flying Scotsman* between Kings Cross and York in March 1924. The premier presentation was *Ashes of Vengeance* (US 23) with Norma Talmadge. 'Talkie Trains' were inaugurated by the LNER in May 1935 and continued in service till outbreak of war.

A floating cinema was instituted in the USA on the Erie Canal between Troy and Newark, NY in 1907. Called the *Star Floating Palace*, it was a converted canal boat with a 'wainscoted inside' which plied the canal towns giving shows at each. In later years the idea was borrowed by Soviet Russia. When the 'agit-steamboat' *Red Star* was dispatched on a propaganda tour down the Kama and Volga Rivers in 1919, Molotov and Lenin's wife Krupskya, who were in charge, arranged for the construction of a 800-seat cinema on a barge, which was towed behind the *Red Star*.

A cinema called the Fly-In was opened at Asbury Park, NJ, in 1948 with space for 500 cars and 50 aeroplanes.

There is nothing unusual about watching movies in the air, but cinemas are curiously rare at airports. The only one in Europe is at Prague, where it is greatly appreciated by those subjected to the haphazard scheduling of East European airlines. It shows full-length features, mainly Italian westerns with Czech sub-titles, and admission is free to bona fide passengers.

A conventional cinema run in an unconventional way was the Picture House in the little Yorkshire village of Denholme, established as a co-operative venture in 1935 and operated entirely by voluntary labour. A hundred villagers contributed the £200 capital needed and the management of the cinema was in the hands of a committee elected annually. Old Age Pensioners were admitted free, others paid 3d–9d.

A village cinema of the present-day offers the amenity of a pint of ale with the film and supper in the interval. The locale is the Bear Inn, a 16th-century timbered building in the Shropshire village of Hodnet, where a large upstairs room has been converted into a cosy 60-seater cinema with performances on two evenings a week.

The Globe Cinema, a 300-seat picture house in Norwich, was built in 1934 by 14-year-old Alfred Warminger on a £1500 loan from his father. Alfred himself was manager and projectionist, while his two sisters acted as usherettes, with a boy to sell chocolates. There were two shows a night, the cost of admission to the 5 o'clock performance being a penny and to the 7 o'clock performance twopence.

The first children's Saturday matinees were inaugurated by Sidney Bernstein (now Lord Bernstein) of the Bernstein Group of Theatres (later Granada Theatres) with a performance at the Empire, Willesden, on 23 March 1928. Two thousand children paid 3d each to attend a programme which included *Robinson Crusoe* (GB 27), a *Topical Budget* and two shorts.

The first cinema club for children in Britain was the Mickey Mouse Club, the earliest recorded branch being established at the Arcade Cinema, Darlington, in 1933. There were 200 Mickey Mouse Clubs by May 1937. Gaumont–British cinema clubs were in being by 1936 and the Granadiers, organised by the Granada circuit, were founded in 1937.

The first gaol to institute film shows for prisoners was Goulburn Gaol, Sydney, New South Wales, commencing on 3 January 1911 with a programme presented by the Methodist chaplain, the Rev. J. H. Lewin. The *Melbourne Argus* reported: 'Some of the long-sentence prisoners had never previously seen moving pictures and they more especially enjoyed the entertainment. The pictures were of course of an elevating character, including *Waterways of Holland*, *Dogs of Various Countries*, and *The Visit of the American Fleet*.'

In Britain the first regular film shows for gaol inmates were instituted on a weekly basis at Maidstone Prison in November 1937. The inaugural programme was rather dauntingly described as 'three hours of educational and cultural films, specially selected for reformative treatment of prisoners'. The shows were held in the 100-seat prison chapel, admission according to a three-weekly rota (Maidstone held 350 prisoners) being permitted to inmates who had earned a certain number of good conduct marks. The projector was operated by 'lifers'.

The first drive-in cinema was the Camden Automobile Theater, opened by Richard Hollingshead on a 10-acre site off Wilson Boulevard, Camden, NJ, on 6 June 1933 with a presentation of *Wife Beware* (US 33), with Adolphe Menjou. The screen measured 40 ft (12 m) by 30 ft (9 m) and there was accommodation for 400 cars. The sound came from high-volume screen speakers provided by RCA–Victor.

The 'In-Car' speaker was introduced by RCA–Victor in 1941. The screen speakers of the pioneer drive-ins had been replaced in the meantime by multiple-site speakers providing sound for two cars side by side.

The expansion of drive-ins began very slowly; twelve years after the opening of the Camden there were still only 60 in the whole of the United States. The growth years were the same as for television, for no clear reason. In 1949 there were 1000 drive-ins and the peak was reached in 1958 with 4063 against 12,291 hard-tops.

Britain's only drive-in cinema was opened at Maidstone, Kent on 21 April 1984. Remote-control sound boxes are used, obviating the need for power points next to each parking space. This enables the drive-in to double as a garden-centre parking lot during the day.

The first news theatre was the Embassy, Broadway and 46th Street, New York, which opened on 2 November 1929. It ceased showing newsreels and sports films in November 1949 owing to the competition from television—probably the first cinema to close for this reason.

Britain's first news theatre was the Pavilion, Shaftesbury Avenue, opened in 1930.

News theatres were seldom devoted exclusively to newsreels. In 1934 *Kinematograph Weekly* reported that on average only a third of the programme would be news, the rest consisting of general interest shorts, one-reel comedies, cartoons and serials. By the outbreak of World War II there were 22 news theatres in Britain, 16 of which were in London, and the only one showing solely newsreels was the GB Movietone in the West End. **The first all-cartoon cinema**, the Cameo-Royal in Charing Cross Road, had been opened in 1937. With the decline of newsreels in the late fifties and early sixties, most of the surviving news theatres evolved into cartoon theatres. **The last surviving cinema devoted to short films** in Britain was the Cartoon Cinema by the side of platform 19 at Victoria

Birth of the in-flight movie—Imperial Airways, April 1925.

ECONOMY AT THE CINEMA DE LUXE.

Mrs. Jones (completing her fourth hour). "I USED TO STAY ONLY TWO HOURS; BUT ONE 'AS TO MAKE THREEPENCE GO FURTHER THESE DAYS."

By 1916, when this cartoon appeared in *Punch*, cinema was already a mass entertainment. Two hours of entertainment for 3d was within reach of all but the destitute.

Station. Originally a news theatre, it closed down on 27 August 1981 after 47 years in operation. It enjoyed the curious distinction of being the only cinema in Britain without a lavatory. Fidgety patrons had to make a dash for the BR convenience on platform 15.

The first sex cinema in Britain was the 185-seat Compton Cinema Club, London, opened by Tony Tenser in November 1960. The first film shown was *Private Property* (US 60). The cinema's club status enabled it to show films which would not have been eligible for a censor's certificate. Membership was 10s a year.

The first in-flight movie was First National's production of Conan Doyle's *The Lost World* (US 25), shown during a scheduled Imperial Airways flight from London to the Continent in April 1925.

America's first in-flight presentation was a more modest affair consisting of a *Universal Newsreel* and a couple of cartoon shorts shown aboard a transcontinental Air Transport Inc. Ford transport aircraft on 8 October 1929.

The first airline to introduce regular in-flight movies was TWA, commencing with the presentation of *By Love Possessed* (US 61), with Lana Turner and Efrem Zimbalist Jnr, in the first-class section during a scheduled New York–Los Angeles flight on 19 July 1961.

The world's airlines are estimated to spend about $45 to $50 million per annum on acquiring rights to films. A major airline like Australia's QANTAS pays in the region of $30,000 per picture, with a minimum of about 350 showings. The average age of the in-flight audience is about 20 years older than theatrical audiences, hence films that do well at the box office do not necessarily meet the same response a mile up in the air. Conversely a film like *Raise the Titanic* (US 80), which bombed at the box office, won plaudits from air passengers.

Tickets

The highest seat price (excluding charity performances) was for Kevin Brownlow's reconstruction of Abel Gance's silent classic *Napoleon* (Fr 27) when it was shown in Tokyo in October 1981. Top price was 12,000 yen or $44. Both showings were a sell-out. The same picture carried a price tag of £17 top when it was shown at the Empire Leicester Square the previous March.

Average cinema seat prices						
	USA	UK		USA	UK	
1933	23c	10d	1957	50c	2s	4d
1934	23c	10d	1958	65c	2s	4d
1935	24c	10d	1959	66c	2s	4d
1936	25c	10d	1960	69c	2s	6d
1937	23c	10d	1961	69c	2s	8d
1938	23c	10d	1962	70c	2s	10d
1939	23c	10d	1963	74c	3s	1d
1940	24c	11d	1964	76c	3s	4d
1941	25c	1s 0d	1965	85c	3s	8d
1942	27c	1s 2d	1966	87c	4s	1d
1943	29c	1s 4d	1967	$1·19c	4s	5d
1944	27c	1s 5d	1968	$1·31c	4s	10d
1945	29c	1s 5d	1969	$1·42c	5s	5d
1946	33c	1s 5d	1970	$1·55c	6s	1d
1947	33c	1s 5d	1971	$1·65c	34p	
1948	34c	1s 5d	1972	$1·70c	38p	
1949	38c	1s 5d	1973	$1·76c	43p	
1950	44c	1s 6d	1974	$1·88c	50p	
1951	44c	1s 7d	1975	$2·05c	61p	
1952	50c	1s 8d	1976	$2·12c	73p	
1953	50c	1s 8d	1977	$2·23c	83p	
1954	45c	1s 9d	1978	$2·34c	94p	
1955	50c	1s 10d	1979	$2·52c	£1·14p	
1956	50c	1s 11d	1980	$2·74c	£1·42p	
			1981	$2·78c	£1·62p	
			1982	$2·96c	£1·77p	
			1983	$3·15c	£1·90p	
			1984	$3·40	–	

The largest per cent American increase was 36·8 per cent from 1966 to 1967; the largest British was 25 per cent from 1979 to 1980.

The lowest seat price recorded was a farthing by a cinema in London's Whitechapel Road in 1909, though the concessionary admission applied only to four children purchasing tickets together. The regular price for children at the Star Kinema in Newcastle upon Tyne about the time of World War I was ½d, but admission could be obtained by presenting a clean glass jam jar instead. In 1925, during a temporary slump in moviegoing, a desperate cinema manager in Covington, La., admitted patrons in exchange for empty beer bottles. He took $23 and 1812 empties. The cheapest seats noted in the Report of the Indian Cinematograph Committee (1928) were priced at one anna—slightly over one penny. These were 'seats' in a figurative sense, since the lowly price meant only a lowly place on the ground. In the late 1930s some cinemas in Karachi were wont to give free shows, consisting of shorts and long trailers, when their rivals were showing a blockbuster. A cinema opened in Cardiff in 1935 for 'coloured people' only charged a flat rate admission of 1d. Even cheaper was a picture house on Sixth Avenue, New York, which advertised *c.* 1912 a movie of a negro lynching for 1c. On at least one occasion any price for a seat has been accepted. In Victoria, BC, a patriotic cinema manager running *The Luck of Ginger Coffey* (Can 64) allowed patrons to pay whatever they thought the film was worth on their way out.

Currently the lowest admission charges are in China, where the average seat price is reported to be the equivalent of 16c. In the country areas admission is often free.

Probably the cheapest cinema in the USA is Akron's Civic Theatre, whose weekend seat prices are 50c for main floor and back balcony seats and 65c for *loge* seats—exactly the same admission as when it first opened in 1929.

The highest tax on cinema admission prices is levied by the state government of the Punjab in Pakistan, where it was raised to 150 per cent on 1 July 1978.

Robert Jacobsen will never buy a cinema ticket again. The internationally renowned sculptor designed the Danish Film Academy's Oscar, called the Alta, which was first presented in 1984. Instead of a fee, he opted for a free pass for life to every cinema in Denmark.

Audiences

The largest audience ever to view a film simultaneously in the same locale was 110,000 on the occasion of the screening of D. W. Griffith's *Boots* (US 19) at the Methodist Centenary celebration held at the Oval Amphitheater, Columbus, Ohio, on 4 July 1919. Fifty thousand of the audience were accommodated in the stands, the remainder in the arena. The film was projected on a giant screen, with a picture size of 100×75 ft.

The highest number of times a patron has seen the same film is 940 by Mrs Myra Franklin of Cardiff, Wales, whose favourite picture can only be *The Sound of Music* (US 65).

FAN MAIL

Mail began to be sent to the uncredited performers of the early silents even before the advent of named stars. Mary Pickford recalled an occasion at the Biograph Studios in about 1912 when she enquired about a letter she was expecting, and was told that it had probably been thrown away together with the hundreds of other letters addressed simply to 'the Girl with the Curls' or 'the Biograph Girl'. She was amazed to learn that people she had never met should feel impelled to write to someone who had no more substance for them than a mute shadow on a silver screen. Biograph's high-handed method of disposing of unsolicited correspondence did not long survive the onslaught of the fan magazines, which soon took to publishing the stars' studio addresses in response to eager enquiries from the fans. Producers came to realise that a mail count was one method of assessing a rising star's popularity and consequently his or her box office potential, while the stars themselves knew that it was in their own interest to maintain a devoted fan following, even at the cost of the $250 a week it was estimated in the twenties that a major star would need to spend on photographs and postage.

The largest fan mail of the immediate post World War I period was received by 'America's Sweetheart' Mary Pickford, with an average of 18,000 letters a month. It was maintained that Miss Pickford employed a fleet of 18 secretaries to answer them.

Mary Pickford's popularity began to decline in the 'flapper era' and in 1927 it was reported that Colleen Moore was leading the fan mail league table with 15,000 letters a month. Miss Moore was obliged to dispatch an average of 12,000 photographs of herself monthly at a cost of 12c each, including postage. A year later she had been overtaken by Clara Bow, whose count for the month of April 1928 was no less than 33,727 items of mail. The cost of replying was $2550 including $450 for three full-time secretaries. The most popular male star at that time was, somewhat surprisingly, Charles 'Buddy' Rogers, with 19,618 letters. Douglas Fairbanks, generally thought of as the most consistently popular male star of the twenties, rated only 8000 letters, which gave him equal place in the league table with a dog, Rin Tin Tin. Chaplin, who had once created a fan mail record with 73,000 letters in the first three days of his return home to London in 1921, could muster no more than 5000.

The coming of sound virtually ended the screen careers of Colleen Moore and Clara Bow, but ushered in a host of new stars, one of whom was to create a fan

This 1928 cartoon was not too much of an exaggeration. Clara Bow really did have three full-time secretaries answering 30,000 fan letters a month.

mail record which has never been broken. Mickey Mouse, reported Walt Disney at the end of 1933, had received 800,000 letters that year, an average of 66,000 a month. He stressed that all these communications had been addressed to Mickey personally, and not to his creator.

In that heady period of Hollywood history known as 'the era of the Great Stars', neither Gable nor Garbo could compete with a mouse, a child and a singing cowboy. By 1936 seven-year-old Shirley Temple was receiving just over 60,000 letters a month, an all-time record for a mere human being. As age crept up on the golden-curled moppet, the fickleness of film fans once again asserted itself. By the time she had reached the mature age of ten, Miss Temple was no longer at the top. Her place had been taken by the guitar-strumming cowboy Gene Autry, though it may have been some consolation that his peak of 40,000 letters a month came nowhere near her best.

World War II brought a new element into star appeal with the advent of the pin-up picture, and it is probable that a high proportion of the dogfaces who wrote from far-away places to the new record holder, the fighting forces' own Betty Grable, had never seen any of her films. The attraction of her million dollar legs, however, was attested by the average of 30,000 letters a month they inspired.

A number of factors contributed to the decline of fan mail after World War II, chief amongst them the parallel decline in the star system, the rise of other cult heroes such as pop singers and sportsmen, and dwindling audiences in the wake of television. Even in recent years, however, it has been possible for stars held high in public esteem to inspire prodigious quantities of mail at times when they are the focus of news attention, as evidenced by the 150,000 letters received by John Wayne from loyal fans during the two months following his heart operation in June 1978.

The nature of the fan letter writer has seldom been examined, but in April 1927 *Variety* published the results of a survey in which they reported that 10 per cent of all fan mail sent from within the USA came from Poles (or people with Polish names), while up to 8 per cent of the 32,250,000 letters received annually from fans worldwide by Hollywood studios originated from South American countries. The greater proportion of requests for photographs, said *Variety*, came from people who never went to the movies—'they are of the poor kind who cannot afford it and simply pick up coupons or read names on billboards of the various stars...'. An analysis made the following year at Paramount, the studio which received the most fan mail, revealed that 75 per cent of the correspondents were women, despite the fact that female stars received more letters than men.

Fan mail being traditionally associated with film stars, it is worthy of note that no actor or actress has received in the course of a career the number of letters

delivered to Charles Lindbergh following his trans-atlantic flight—a total of 3,500,000.

Space precludes more than the briefest selection of the last 60 years of fan mail:

☆ To Kathlyn Williams 1916: 'Dear Miss Williams, You are my favourite moving picture actress. I would appreciate it so much if you would give me one of your old automobiles, any one, I wouldn't care how small.'

☆ To Enid Bennett 1920: 'I am making a collection of pictures of the most notorious actresses. Please send me yours.'

☆ To Emil Jannings (whose looks were certainly sub-ordinate to his artistry) 1928: 'Dear Miss Jannings, You are my favourite actress. I go to see all your pictures because I like the way you wear your clothes. To me you are the best-dressed actress on the screen, as well as the most beautiful. I try to imitate your clothes and your stylish way of wearing your hair.'

☆ To Una Merkel (following a request for a signed photo) 1933: 'Do not send picture. Am moving and decided I don't want it.' Miss Merkel to fan: 'Picture is sent. You'll take it and like it.'

☆ To Glenn Ford 1946: 'I am 22, pretty, but I never saved my money. You did. That is the real reason I would like to marry you. Please let me know soon, as I have also written to Dick Powell and Larry Parks.'

☆ To Virginia Mayo from Arab Sheik 1948: 'You are the surest proof to me of the existence of God.'

☆ To Frank Sinatra, from girl fan proposing marriage 1956: 'We've never met, but I'm a singer and I feel I can do so much for your career.'

FILM FANS, FAMOUS AND INFAMOUS
Royalty have been among the most fervent supporters of the cinema since its earliest days. At a time when 'animated pictures' had scarcely moved out of the fairground, Queen Victoria was enjoying frequent film shows at Windsor Castle. An ardent film fan, the Queen had a special predilection for movies about children and her favourite was said to be a Riley Bros production called *The Pillow Fight* (GB 98), in which four mischievous schoolgirls bombarded each other with pillows in their bedroom.

The first royalty with private cinema theatres in their palaces were the Crown Prince of Siam and Tsar Nicolas II, both in about 1913. When war broke out and the Tsar took command of his forces in the field, he missed his cinema at the Tsarkoye Selo palace so much that he had another one installed at the Stavka, head-quarters of the Russian Army. The Tsar's favourite film was *The Exploits of Elaine* (US 14), a cliff-hanger type serial which he watched weekly at Stavka throughout the second half of 1916. The deposed Emperor of China, Henry P'u Yi, had a cinema built at the Palace of Established Happiness about 1920, where a steady flow of Charlie Chaplin and Fatty Arbuckle films were maintained, until the emergence of Harold Lloyd, who displaced them as Imperial Favourite. The

Berlin 1931 and the impact of the talkies. Photographs of audience reaction like this are extremely rare. (*Backnumbers*)

Emperor's owlish horn-rimmed glasses were said to have been acquired in tribute to the American comedian.

Queen Alexandra's favourite film was *True Heart Susie* (US 19), in which Lillian Gish played the kind of simple, joyful country girl the Queen sometimes wished she could have been. A private print of the film was kept at Buckingham Palace. Queen Mary's taste, on the other hand, ran to rather more robust fare, her favourite star being the romantic and extremely athletic hero of Hollywood adventure movies Eddie Polo. (Reputedly Queen Mary was the only member of the Royal Family who was not a Charlie Chaplin fan—the reason, according to one fan magazine writer, being the fact that she was not endowed with a very developed sense of humour.) The Queen was said to

Under a local decree of 1984 in the Maharashtra town of Nandurbar, Muslim women are forbidden to visit the cinema. The penalty for violation is the equivalent of $10. Any man reporting a woman in the audience receives a reward of $5.

be the Royal Family's most enthusiastic filmgoer and during World War II, when living at Badminton, she gave a weekly film show for servicemen. However, her youngest son, the Duke of Kent, seems to have rivalled her in his passion for the pictures. When he married Princess Marina in 1934, the Earl of Dudley had a squash court converted into a cinema at his seat, Himley Hall, where the Royal Couple were to spend their honeymoon. During the twelve days of their stay, the Duke and Duchess watched 18 feature films, nine comedies, an unspecified number of documentaries, five newsreels and a specially made life-story of His Royal Highness. Every night of the honeymoon was spent at the movies reported an ecstatic Gaumont–British, who had supplied the 202 reels of film shown.

Both the Duke's brothers shared his delight in the cinema. The Duke of York, later King George VI, was reported in America to have a particular weakness for the films of Nancy Carroll. A greater sensation, though, was the revelation in *Photoplay* in 1931 that the Prince of Wales (later Edward VIII) was in the habit of making incognito visits to one of London's less exclusive suburban cinemas, the Grand in Edgware Road, at least once or twice a week. The Prince always attended with the same girl, it was alleged, she taking her seat at 8.45 p.m. and he slipping into his at precisely 9 p.m., after the house lights had gone down.

No recent information is available about H.M. The Queen's taste in films, the Palace being prepared to say only that 'she most often asks to see those of which she has read favourable reviews'. According to a newspaper report of the late 1950s, however, her favourite stars were then Gary Cooper, Laurence Olivier and Dirk Bogarde. Curiously Her Majesty does not have a private cinema. At Sandringham the shows are held in the Ballroom, at Balmoral in the Large Drawing Room and at Windsor Castle in the Waterloo Room. Films are not shown at Buckingham Palace. Royal film shows are the responsibility of the Equerry in Waiting, who selects the films unless the Queen has made a particular request.

World leaders have also been in the forefront of the world's film fans. Both Stalin and Churchill named *Lady Hamilton* (GB 41) as their favourite film, the British Prime Minister seeing it four times. Churchill's passion for films was not shared by all his wartime colleagues, a number of whom have testified to their displeasure at the PM's habit of breaking off the evening's work to watch the ritual movie and then expecting them to match his alertness and vigour as top-level

discussions continued until three in the morning. At Kremlin film shows, according to Khruschev, Stalin 'used to select the movies himself. The films were usually what you might call captured trophies: we got them from the West. Many of them were American pictures. He liked cowboy movies especially. He used to curse them and give them their proper ideological evaluation but then immediately order new ones.'

Hitler's favourite movie at the time he became Chancellor of Germany was *The Blue Angel* (Ger 30), of which he had a private print. Trenker's *The Rebel* (US 33), was said to be his favourite American film. *The Blue Angel* was later displaced in his affections by Willi Forst's *Mazurka* (Ger 35), which he watched as often as two or three times a week in the small hours of the morning when he was suffering from insomnia. Such was the Führer's devotion to the film, a rumour spread that its star, the bewitching Pola Negri, was under his special protection. In fact Miss Negri had never met Hitler, but found that whenever she went to Nazi Germany she was treated with the kind of privileged deference accorded only to intimates of the Reichs Chancellor. (She later won a libel action against the French cinema magazine *Pour Vous*, which alleged she was Hitler's mistress.)

The Führer is said to have indulged in film shows of a less conventional kind. Pauline Kohler, who served on the staff at Berchtesgaden, claimed that Hitler had a special film made of a prominent German star stripping and exhibiting 'various exercises' which 'threw a terrible light on the perversity of Hitler's sexual desires'. This was shown in the Führer's private cinema at Berchtesgaden, where a selected group of staff were invited to view it on Christmas Day 1937.

Arturo Alessandri, President of Chile in the 1930s, was besotted with the infant Shirley Temple. He had each of her films shown at his official residence in Santiago as soon as it was released and prevailed upon the Chilean Navy to adopt her as their official mascot.

President Anwar Sadat of Egypt watched a movie every day. President Tito of Yugoslavia saw an average of 200 a year—one virtually every night he was in Belgrade. His favourite was the Humphrey Bogart – Bette Davis movie *The Petrified Forest* (US 36), about a group of travellers at a way-station in Arizona who are held up by gangsters.

With the passing of Presidents Sadat and Tito, the most devoted film fan among current heads of state is President Bongo of Gabon. He is reported to watch 'several films every night' at the Presidential Palace, mainly karate movies from Hong Kong and Hindu

Cinemagoing, traditionally a boy-girl activity in most countries, is a predominantly male form of relaxation in West Germany. Despite a population inbalance with women outnumbering men by 54 to 46 per cent, no less than 60 per cent of German filmgoers are male.

melodramas. He has personally financed the making of three feature films, two of them scripted by his wife Joséphine and the third, *Demain un jour nouveau* (Gab 78), based on his own autobiography.

American Presidents have been enjoying films at the White House since June 1914, when Giovanni Pastrone's epic *Cabiria* (It 14) was screened before President Wilson and his Cabinet. The President's favourite star was the statuesque Katharine MacDonald, known as 'The American Beauty'. It is not recorded whether President Truman was obliged to sit through *The Scarlet Pimpernel* (GB 34) the 16 times his daughter Margaret—a devotee of Leslie Howard—had it screened at the White House. Eisenhower's favourite films while President were *Angels in the Outfield* (US 52)—described by Leslie Halliwell as 'unamusing, saccharine whimsy'—*Springfield Rifle* (US 52), *To Catch a Thief* (US 55), and *Rear Window* (US 54). The latter two starred his favourite actress, Grace Kelly. President Kennedy left the selection of films to aide Arthur Schlesinger, who arranged a show every Sunday evening at the White House. *Patton* (US 69) was President Nixon's favourite, while President Carter though unwilling to name a favourite film, was enrolled as an honorary member of Britain's Errol Flynn Fan Club. It behoves the present incumbent of the White House to be discreet about his preferences. The President and Mrs Reagan see films at weekends at Camp David and the White House, making their choices, per the White House Director of Media Relations, 'from movies recommended by friends and staff members, and they enjoy watching some of the old classics . . .'. In answer to the obvious question, the Director of Media Relations reveals that the President 'has viewed one of his own films at the request of his staff'.

KILL OR CURE—THE CINEMA AND YOUR HEALTH

From the earliest years of the cinema there were arguments about whether it was good or bad for you. Some people thought the eyes to be particularly at risk: a Dublin doctor writing to the *Lancet* in 1906 described a patient suffering from post-film blindness which he called 'retinal kinematocution' and he advised that film shows should last no longer than a minute with spectators wearing dark glasses. Others disagreed and in 1914 a French magazine, *Nos Loisirs*, pronounced that nothing was so good for the eyes as two hours of watching films each day.

The following year the cinema showed that it could affect more than the sight. A deaf-mute called Robert Beck was invited to go and see a comedy film; at one point in the action a policeman was suspended in a jet of water and Beck suddenly heard his own laughter. His hearing was totally restored! But laughter can kill as well as cure. When New Yorker Mrs Nellie Ruprecht saw the Wallace Reid film *Clarence* (US 23), she started laughing in the first scene and only stopped

when her hilarity brought on apoplexy. She was pronounced dead on arrival at hospital.

Films can have a strong psychological effect and as early as 1910 at the Elgin State Mental Hospital in Illinois they were showing inmates movies twice a week in the belief that 'they will take the minds of patients from their misfortunes, and stimulate their weakened brains'. But such stimulation could have unfortunate results as was shown eleven years later: an asylum at Ivry near Paris decided to send an apparently cured patient (accompanied by his nurse) to see a film. Unfortunately, it happened to be a sensational drama in which a man has his throat cut, and at this point in the action the audience suddenly heard the nurse scream and saw her struggling with the patient. Apparently he had become mesmerised by the violent affray on screen, had pulled out a knife, and following each movement of the actors, ended up plunging the knife into his own throat.

In 1953 there was a report in the *Daily Express* about an equally unwelcome spectator; a man who, due to the effect of flicker on the screen, developed an irresistible impulse to strangle the nearest person. 'Several times while sitting in cinemas', ran the report, 'he has suddenly found himself with his hands round his neighbour's throat'.

There is at least one attested case of someone being literally 'frightened to death' by a film. In 1956 a small boy in Oak Park, Illinois, died of what the coroner described as 'a heart collapse after extraordinary tension while watching a movie'. The film was *The Creeping Unknown* (GB 55) and the scene that precipitated his death was the explosion of a space rocket.

Happily the cinema has also been responsible for saving life. In 1922 in Atlantic City seven-year-old Katherine Hartwell was in hospital, considered to have only a few hours to live. To take her mind off her suffering, the hospital staff decided to show her a comic picture. At first she watched listlessly, but gradually she became captivated, and that night her condition improved dramatically. The next day she could move for the first time in weeks and the astonished doctors forecast a full recovery.

Premières

The largest audience to attend a world première were the 23,930 persons who paid $2·50 to $50 each to see Robert Altman's *Brewster McCloud* (US 70), starring Bud Cort and Sally Kellerman, at the Houston Astrodome on 5 December 1970. A special 70 mm print was made exclusively for the première at a cost of $12,000, since a standard gauge film would have given insufficient definition on the 156 × 60 ft 'astroscreen'. The *Houston Chronicle* reported in inimitable Texan style: 'The reaction was what you might call mixed. The audience was mostly your younger

> *Goodbye Cruel World* (US 83) was released with an
> audience participation device called 'Choice-A-Rama'
> which allowed patrons a choice of scenes at various
> intervals during the picture. Preliminary showings in a
> number of small towns in Massachusetts
> demonstrated, according to the distributor, the
> audiences' preference for 'violence over peace, bad
> taste over good, and sex over culture'.

hip crowd, but the low intelligibility and the film's
weirdness in general caused things to be a bit sub-
dued. Miss Kellerman runs around nekkid a lot and
there are what you might call bad words. . . .'

The largest number of simultaneous openings was by
Paramount's *Star Trek III: The Search for Spok* (US 84),
which opened at 1966 North American sites on 1 June
1984. Coming only a week after the previous record
for a simultaneous preem, *Indiana Jones and the Temple
of Doom* (US 84) at 1685 sites, the Spok opening meant
that the two films were showing at nearly 20 per cent
of the total outlets in the country.

UNUSUAL PREMIÈRES

Not all premières take place in glittering and star-
studded surroundings. *Oliver Twist* (US 22) had its
British Première at London's historic Foundling Hospital, presumably in tribute to the protagonist's
orphan origins; while the world première of MGM's
Agatha Christie whodunnit *Murder at the Gallop* (GB
63) took place in a tent at a church garden party in rural
Cheshire.

There was only one place to hold the world première
of *Dodge City* (US 40). The last of the real razzmatazz
preems before the austerities of war, the celebration
began with a special train bringing 150 Warner Bros
executives and stars, including the movie's topliners
Errol Flynn and Olivia de Havilland, which was
escorted into Dodge City by an aerial fleet of 50 private
aircraft. Overnight the little Kansan town underwent a
temporary population explosion from 10,000 to
150,000.

There was no problem in accommodating everyone
who wanted to come to the world première of *King of
the Coral Sea* (Aus 54), an adventure story about pear-
lers in the South Seas. It took place on the tiny Pacific
atoll of Thursday Island. With a population of less than
a thousand, everyone was invited.

The première of *The Incredible Mr Limpet* (US 64) was
held underwater. The oddball story of a man who
turned into a fish, the picture was preemed by Warner
Bros on the ocean floor with a submerged screen at
Weeki Wachi, Fla. The invited audience of 250 sat in a
glass tank 20 ft below the surface.

Far-flung simultaneous opening are not so rare, but
when Stanley Kramer decided to hold the world première of *On the Beach* (US 59) on both sides of the Iron
Curtain at the same time there was certainly no prece-

dent. Based on Nevil Shute's novel about the doomed
survivors of a nuclear holocaust, the film opened in 17
cities on 17 December 1959, including New York, Moscow and the city in which the story was set, Melbourne.

If Kramer's intent was to stimulate unity against war
among nations, very different sentiments must have
actuated the Nazis' decision to première Veit Harlan's
epic *Kolberg* (Ger 45) in the besieged fortress of La
Rochelle. *Kolberg* was about the fortitude of the inhabitants of the Baltic town of that name during the
Napoleonic Wars; the staging of its première in such
unpropitious circumstances a symbolic act. Since the
print could not be brought through the lines of the
besieging army, it was dropped into the town by para-
chute.

The most belated première of a feature film took
place at the Cinémathèque Française in Paris in April
1984, when the completed version of André Antoine's
64-year-old *L'Hirondelle et la Mésange* (Bel 20) was
presented for the first time. Six hours of unedited
rushes had been discovered in the State Film Archive
and edited by Henri Colpi as he perceived Antoine had
intended. The reason the unedited film had been
shelved in 1920 was that distributor Charles Pathé was
so disconcerted by the rushes, which revealed a story
of canal life shot in cinéma verité style, that he refused
to release it. The audience at the première, by contrast,
were captivated by the film's lyrical beauty as well as
its understated realism.

Royalty

**The first occasion on which a ruling monarch
attended a public film performance** was on 11 June
1896, when King Christian IX of Denmark (reigned
1863–1906) visited Vilhelm Pacht's exhibition of
Lumière films at his Kinoptikon in Copenhagen's
Raadhuspladsen.

**The first member of the British Royal Family to visit a
public cinema** was Queen Alexandra (1844–1925),
daughter of King Christian IX of Denmark (see
above), who attended a performance at the
Kinomatograph Theatre, Christiania (Oslo), in September 1907 accompanied by the Dowager Empress
of Russia.

**The first British monarch to attend a public cinema
performance** was King George V (reigned 1910–36)
who, accompanied by Queen Mary, saw a matinee
showing of *Quo Vadis?* (It 13) at the Albert Hall on 5
May 1913. The visit was described as 'strictly private',
meaning it was not a Command Performance.

The first Royal Command Film Performance was held
at Marlborough House on 21 July 1896 before 40 royal
guests who had assembled for the marriage of Princess Maud the following day. The show was
occasioned by a request from pioneer cinematog-

rapher Birt Acres of New Barnet, Herts, to be allowed to exhibit publicly a film he had taken the previous month of the Prince and Princess of Wales attending the Cardiff Exhibition (see News Film, p. 214). Before giving his permission, the Prince of Wales commanded Acres to bring the film to Marlborough House for inspection. It was screened in a specially erected marquee together with 20 other short films, including Tom Merry the Lightning Artist drawing Mr Gladstone and Lord Salisbury, the Derby races of 1895 and 1896, Henley Regatta, and scenes showing a boxing kangaroo, a Great Northern Railway express train, and the pursuit of a pickpocket. The royal film was shown twice by popular demand.

The first Royal Command Performance before the Sovereign was held in the Red Drawing Room at Windsor Castle on 23 November 1896, when HM Queen Victoria (reigned 1837–1901) saw a film of the Royal Family taken by W. Downey at Balmoral the previous month (see News Film: Monarch to be Filmed, p. 214). The Queen brought her opera glasses with her to ensure that she missed none of the action. This was the first of many such performances before the aged Queen, who became something of a cinema addict in the closing years of her long life.

The first feature film presented by Royal Command was Cecil Hepworth's production of *Comin' Through the Rye* (GB 16), starring Alma Taylor, which was shown before Queen Alexandra (1844–1925) in the State Dining Room of Marlborough House on 4 August 1916. Hepworth was no stranger to Command Performances, having been present at the very first one when he had acted as assistant to Birt Acres.

The first feature film to be presented by Command of the Sovereign was *Tom Brown's Schooldays* (GB 17), which Lew Warren exhibited before King George V (reigned 1910–35) and Queen Mary at Buckingham Palace on 25 February 1917.

The first Royal Command Performance at a public cinema and the first of the present series of annual Command Performances took place at the Empire, Leicester Square, on 1 November 1946, when King George VI (reigned 1936–52) and Queen Elizabeth, accompanied by Princess Elizabeth and Princess Margaret, saw David Niven and Marius Goring in *A Matter of Life and Death* (GB 46). The novelty of seeing the King 'going to the pictures' caused crowds to gather ten hours before his arrival.

ROYAL COMMAND PERFORMANCE FILMS
1946 *A Matter of Life and Death* (GB)
1947 *The Bishop's Wife* (US)
1948 *Scott of the Antarctic* (GB)
1949 *The Forsyte Saga* (US)
1950 *The Mudlark* (GB)
1951 *Where No Vultures Fly* (GB)
1952 *Because You're Mine* (US)
1953 *Rob Roy the Highland Rogue* (GB)
1954 *Beau Brummel* (GB)
1955 *To Catch a Thief* (US)
1956 *The Battle of the River Plate* (GB)
1957 *Les Girls* (US)

1958 No Performance
1959 *The Horse's Mouth* (GB)
1960 *The Last Angry Man* (US)
1961 *The Facts of Life* (US)
1962 *West Side Story* (US)
1963 *Sammy Going South* (GB)
1964 *Move Over Darling* (US)
1965 *Lord Jim* (GB)
1966 *Born Free* (GB)
1967 *The Taming of the Shrew* (It/US)
1968 *Romeo and Juliet* (GB)
1969 *The Prime of Miss Jean Brodie* (GB)—first X film
1970 *Anne of the Thousand Days* (GB)
1971 *Love Story* (US)
1972 *Mary Queen of Scots* (GB)
1973 *Lost Horizon* (US)
1974 *The Three Musketeers* (Panama)
1975 *Funny Lady* (US)
1976 *The Slipper and the Rose* (GB)
1977 *Silver Streak* (US)
1978 *Close Encounters of the Third Kind* (US)
1979 *California Suite* (US)
1980 *Kramer vs Kramer* (US)
1981 *Chariots of Fire* (GB)
1982 *Evil Under the Sun* (GB)
1983 *Table for Five* (US)
1984 *The Dresser* (GB)
1985 *A Passage to India* (GB)

Projectors

The first projector manufactured for sale was the Lumière Cinématographe, produced under licence by Jules Carpentier of Paris, early in 1896.

The first British projector manufactured for sale was the Theatrograph, produced by R. W. Paul at his Saffron Hill factory, of which the first model to be sold was purchased by conjurer David Devant for £100 and installed at the Egyptian Hall, Piccadilly, on 19 March 1896. It was at just about this time that Paul Cingqueralli arrived in London to offer the Edison Vitascope, which had yet to make its American debut, to prospective purchasers at $25,000 each. Not surprisingly the margin between £100 ($500) and $25,000 effectively dissuaded anyone from purchasing what was later said to be an inferior projector.

Rigg's motorised Kinematograph of 1896. (*Barnes Museum of Photography*)

The giant screen used by the Lumière brothers at the Paris Exposition of 1900. Note the two figures in the foreground.

The first motorised projector was the Kinematograph designed and manufactured by J. H. Rigg of Skinner Lane, Leeds, and demonstrated publicly at the Royal Aquarium, London, on 6 April 1896. Powered by a four-volt electric motor, it was available for sale by the end of the year through the Anglo-Continental Phonograph Co. of London and Rigg's American agent in Philadelphia.

The most powerful projector ever built was the Canadian developed IMAX, made by the Multiscreen Corporation for use at Japan's *Expo '70*, where the Fuji Group used it to show the specially produced multi-image film *Tiger Child* (Can/Jap 70). The projector's ten-element Canon 150 mm F/20 high-precision lens and 25,000 watt Xenon short arc lamp were capable of reproducing a high-fidelity image nine storeys tall. The illumination was four times as great as the most powerful lamp hitherto available. Although the size of the Fuji Co.'s pavilion at *Expo '70* limited the screen size to 60 × 40 ft, the projector was theoretically capable of rendering a sharp image on a screen measuring 126 × 88 ft.

Film Reel

The largest film reel holds 20,200 ft (6157 m) of film, against the 1000 ft (305 m) capacity of a standard 35 mm reel. Produced by the Imax Systems Corporation of Toronto, Canada, for use with Imax projectors, the reel is 4 ft (1·2 m) in diameter.

Screen

The largest screen image ever achieved with a single projector under demonstration conditions was 79 ft 2 in × 99 ft (24·1 × 30 m)—the height of a six-storey building—at the Galérie des Machines on the Paris Exposition site in 1898. The picture throw was 650 ft (198 m) and the screen was kept wet to increase its reflection of light, a task undertaken by the Paris Fire Brigade, who trained their hoses on the mammoth sheet before the show began. The purpose of the demonstration, which was given by Louis Lumière, was to prove to the General Secretary of the Paris Exposition that large screen movies were feasible. Having proved that they were, Lumière was invited to exhibit such films at the Exposition in 1900. Unfortunately, a decision was taken to partition the Galérie des Machines, reducing the seating capacity to 25,000 and halving the picture throw, with the result that the Lumière films had to be presented on a smaller screen allowing only an image of 52 ft 8 in × 69 ft 3 in (16 × 21·1 m).

The largest screen in the world today belongs to the Imax theatre at the Taman Mini Park in Jakarta, Indonesia and measures 96 ft × 70 ft 6 in (28·3 × 21·5 m).

The largest screens in the USA are two identical 70 ft 6 in × 96 ft (21·5 × 29·3 m) screens at Marriott's Great America Parks at Santa Clara, California and Gurnee, Illinois. They were manufactured by Harkness Screens of Boreham Wood, Herts, England, and are used in conjunction with Canadian Imax projection systems.

The largest screen in Britain measures 62 ft × 45 ft and is used with the Imax projection system at the National Museum of Photography, Film and Television at Bradford. The screen is the height of a five-storey building.

The widest screen ever used for projecting motion pictures was erected at the Palais d'Electricité et de la Lumière at the Paris Exposition of 1937 for showing Henri Chrétien's *hypergonar* films, the precursor of Cinerama. The concave screen had a breadth of 195 ft (59·5 m) and was 32 ft 6 in (9·9 m) high. By compari-son the Cinerama screen size was 90 × 26 ft (27·4 × 7·9 m).

The widest screen in use today was installed at the Mercury Cinema, Paris, in 1981 and measures 133 ft (40 m) in breadth.

360° screens, with the audience wholly surrounded by the projected image, exist at the China Pavilion of Walt Disney's EPCOT Center in Florida, where the system is called 'Circle Vision'; and at the L'Espace Gaité cinema in Paris, which presents the 'Panrama' system on a 350 square metre screen.

13 Press and Print

The first book on cinematography was *The History of the Kinetograph, Kinetoscope and Kineto-Phonograph*, by W. K. L. and Antonia Dickson, New York, 1895. Dickson was Thomas Edison's assistant and the inventor of the Kinetoscope 'peep show' motion picture apparatus and Kinetograph camera patented in his employer's name. The book was published in Britain in October of the same year by the Continental Commerce Co. of New York as a give-away to publicise their Oxford Street Kinetoscope parlour.

The first British work on the subject of cinematography was *Animated Photography, or the ABC of the Cinematograph* by Cecil Hepworth, published by Hazell, Watson & Viney Ltd of London in 1897.

The first poem to mention the cinema was in the British journal *Truth* on 30 July 1896. Titled 'The St Stephens Music Hall', it was about the various attractions to be found at this mythical establishment, including the new-fangled films:

Then, of course, of 'Living Pictures' there are
* some at which to laugh,*
And repeated presentations of 'The Animatographe'.

The first work on the aesthetics of the cinema was an essay entitled *The Cinematograph* by a certain O. Winter in *The New Review* of May 1896. Written, astonishingly, only two months after the first-ever public film show in Britain, Winter's essay is scornful of the adulation the early films were receiving. He believed that their apparent realism was a delusion because they reproduced nature without selection and for this reason films would have no artistic future.

The first book on the aesthetics of cinema was Vachel Lindsay's *The Art of the Moving Picture*, published in the USA in 1915.

The first short story about the cinema was 'Our Detective Story' from the *Referee*, a London newspaper, of 24 January 1897. Written by G. R. Sims under the pseudonym 'Dagonet', it centres around a husband whose suspicions are aroused when his wife temporarily disappears in Spain. He has almost forgotten the incident when, some time later, he and she are watching a series of actuality films of Spain at a music hall. Suddenly a lady and gentleman appear on screen arm in arm. It is the wife with the husband's partner: 'The woman was looking up into the man's face . . . His arm stole round her waist—she put up her face—he stooped and kissed her. The audience yelled with laughter.' The husband is outraged and a divorce follows, the films being produced as evidence in court.

The first play to mention the cinema was *Hans Huckebein* by Oskar Blumethal and Gustav Kadelburg, premièred at the Lessing Theatre, Berlin on 16 October 1897. It is a farce about a man, Martin, married to the suspicious Hildegard. She goes to a filmshow and sees a scene shot on a beach, with Martin about to kiss a girl. Hildegard is angry with Martin and things look bleak for him until the end of the play when the girl turns up and reveals that she was hired by the film producer to kiss men on the beach to spice up the films. The piece was successful enough to be staged in London and New York before the end of the year.

The earliest allusion to the cinema in a novel appears in Frank Norris's *McTeague*, published in February 1899. The plot has McTeague taking his girlfriend Trina and her family to see the Kinetoscope. They are all very impressed except Trina's mother who announces 'I'm too old to be fooled . . . dot's nothun but a drick'. The novel was later made into a famous film directed by Erich von Stroheim, called *Greed* (US 23).

Britain's first allusion to cinema in a novel dates from the same year as *McTeague*. In E. F. Benson's *Mammon and Co* (London 1899) an elderly lady called Mrs Murchison, much given to malopropisms, visits the Palace Theatre to 'see the Biography'. She reports that 'Most interesting it was, and the one from the front of the train made me feel quite sick and giddy—most pleasant.'

Researching the early fiction of the cinema, film historian Stephen Bottomore has identified some 15 short stories published before 1912 which deal with films. Of these, strangely enough, all but two or three deal with a similar theme to 'Dagonet's', i.e. the revelation of some hitherto hidden facts through the showing of a film. The facts in question are usually to do with marital infidelity, but sometimes reveal the perpetrator of a more serious crime.

This constant theme in the fiction of early cinema

The first novelisation of a movie. Harold MacGrath had written the scenario of the successful 1913 Selig serial on which the novel was based. Published in 1914, it was illustrated with stills from the film.

may have had some basis in reality. As early as January 1897 the well-known British detective Henry Slater was advertising that he would employ the 'Animatographe' for surveillance 'in all cases and . . . produce the pictures in Court in evidence. Consultations free.' In subsequent years there were persistent reports of husbands or wives seeing their spouses two-timing them in newsreel pictures.

The first book-of-the-film was a special illustrated 'photoplay edition' of Ralph Ince's Vitagraph three-reeler *The Mills of the Gods* (US 12), published by Grosset and Dunlap of New York at 50c in 1912.

The first original work of literature based on a film was Stuart Edward White's *Oil on Troubled Waters*, published in the *Saturday Evening Post* in 1913. Director Alan Dwan had written the film scenario and approached White, a distinguished novelist, with the idea of paying him simply for the use of his name as the supposed author. White was so impressed with the plot, however, that he decided to turn it into a genuine short story for publication. One of the most notable examples of literature derived from a

motion picture is Budd Schulberg's novel *On the Waterfront*, adapted from the screenplay of his 1954 film. Novels had been written from screenplays before, but as with cheap paperback adaptations today this was simply a means of publicising a film at the same time as producing a book with high readership potential. Schulberg's 'book-of-the-film' was probably the first to be conceived as a serious work of literature exploring themes beyond the capacity of the movie camera.

Economically, the book-of-the-film is seldom more than a subsidiary merchandising operation. In what is believed to be a unique case, however, respecting the Faye Dunaway starrer *The Eyes of Laura Mars* (US 78), the highly-successful paperback is reputed to have made a larger profit than the lacklustre movie.

Another book born of a film was *The Jazz Singer*. In this case a newspaper serial was adapted from the novel (by Arline De Haas), which was based on the film script (by Alfred A. Cohn) of the 1927 talkie, which in turn was a rendering of the Broadway show (by Samson Raphaelson), which had been dramatised from a short story called *The Day of Atonement* (also by Samson Raphaelson).

Similarly, the 1972 TV series *Anna and the King* was a spin-off of the film musical *The King and I* (US 56), an adaptation of the stage musical of the same name, derived from the straight movie version of the story, *Anna and the King of Siam* (US 46), taken from Margaret Landon's fictionalised biography which was based on the autobiography of Anna Leonowens.

Not even Shakespeare is immune. Huddersfield Theatre Royal advertised *Hamlet* in April 1952 as 'The Play of the Famous Film'.

The first university thesis written on the subject of the cinema was sociology major Ray LeRoy Short's *A Social Study of the Motion Picture*, which earned its author an MA degree from the University of Iowa in 1916.

The first film script to be published in book form was Henri Ette's *The North Pole*, described as 'A 100% Tone and Speaking Picture with Songs, Choruses and Dances', issued by Ette Publications, Faroe Isles, 1931.

The first script of an American movie issued in book form was *The Mighty Barnum* by Gene Fowler and Bess Meredith, published by Covici-Friede, New York, 1934.

Overleaf
Britain's longest running fan magazine, *The Picturegoer*, survived from 1913 until the early 1960s. Younger fans were catered for by *Film Fun* from 1920 until 1962. The first character portrayed on the front page was Harold Lloyd, who for some curious reason was billed in England as 'Winkle'. Last to be immortalised in this way was Bruce Forsyth—significantly a TV personality, not a film star. (*Backnumbers*)

THE
PICTUREGOER

EVERY SATURDAY
1^D

"THE STOLEN MODELS."
The artist discovers his Ideal subject and
proceeds to sketch her.

Edison Film.

DRAMA

COMEDY

HISTORICAL

TRAVEL

TOPICAL

EDUCATIONAL

The PICTURE THEATRE WEEKLY MAGAZINE.

WHO'S YOUR FAVOURITE?

See page 2 of cover

Twenty Big Pages and a Plate of "FATTY" ARBUCKLE. | C. |

Film Fun. 1d 1/2

No. 1. Vol. 1.　　　　　　　　　　January 17, 1920.

THE ADVENTURES of ☆ WINKLE ☆ ☆ ☆
THE PATHÉ MIRTH WIZARD

WINKLE GETS A "PUNCH" INTO THINGS FOR A START.

1. Allow us, ladies and gentlemen, to introduce the wonderful Winkle! Doubtless you have seen him on the films; but here you have him in an entirely new series of stunts. Here you see him at the fair, reading a billy-doo from the lovely Lucy. Let us stroll into the next picture.

2. "Ha!" he says. "I've got it! I'll splash one of my last tanners at the old rifle-range—pop in seven consecutive bullseyes, and so snaffle sufficient cigars and nuts to enable me to carry on through the evening! A nutty notion!" But, alas! his luck was out. No bullseyes! Nix!

3. But our earnest old student wasn't done with yet. Oh dear, no! Seeing a punching-machine which provided cigars and nuts for prizes, also a hefty-looking sportsman studying the "Punchers' Gazette," close by, Winkle applied his best foot to the merchant's shepherd's plaid trouserings.

4. "Ho!" says the hearty one. "That was you, was it? All right, my lad! Now you're going to go through it!" And he sheds his sports-coat and prepares to do deeds. Note the posish of Winkle, with his dome against the punchery and hat held out. (Continued on page 20.)

The first ever cartoon about the cinema—in this case home movies. *Le Charivari* 19 April 1896. (*Stephen Bottomore*)

The first script of a British movie issued in book form was *The Private Life of Henry VIII*, story and dialogue by Lajos Biro, edited by Ernest Betts, and published by Methuen at 3s 6d in 1934.

Only one script has ever been published by a studio: *In Old Chicago*, by Lamar Trotti and Sonya Levien, Twentieth Century Fox Film Corp., Beverly Hills, 1937.

The first autobiography of a star was Pearl White's *Just Me*, published by Doran of New York in 1916. It is a lively and wholly unreliable account of her rise as the Queen of the Silent Serials.

The star with the largest number of biographies is Charles Spencer Chaplin (1889–1977), whose life and art have been expounded in 259 book-length works.

The most biographied female star is Marilyn Monroe (1926–62), with 36 life stories, followed by Greta Garbo (1905–) with 24.

The first film journal was *Le Bulletin Phonographique et Cinématographique*, established in Paris as a fortnightly during the summer of 1899.

The first film journal in Britain was *The Optical Lantern and Cinematograph Journal*, monthly, price 3d, which commenced publication in November 1904. The opening number included an interview with pioneer producer Charles Urban, in which he deplored films 'depicting crime, immorality, foolhardiness, drunkenness and other vices'; reviews of *Lady Plumpton's Motor* (GB 04), *The Jonah Man* (GB 04) and a rather daring Gaumont offering (of which Mr Urban was doubtless disapproving)

called *Mixed Bathing* (GB 04); and such items of trade intelligence as 'The National Sunday League have introduced animated pictures into their Sunday programmes' and 'Look out for a new style of home cinematograph projector, at two guineas'.

The first American film journal was *Views and Film Index* in 1906.

The first fan magazines were Italy's *Il Cinematagrafo* and Spain's *El Cinematagrafo*, both established in 1907.

America's first fan magazine was *Motion Picture Story Magazine*, founded by J. Stuart Blackton of Vitagraph as a monthly in February 1911.

The first fan magazine in Britain was *Pictures*, weekly 1d, founded on 21 October 1911. It consisted mainly of fiction based on film scenarios, illustrated with stills from the films summarised, but a regular feature called 'Picture Notes from All Parts' retailed such interesting snippets of information as the fact that four million people went to the pictures daily (1911), that Florence Lawrence was making 300 films a year and was America's highest paid star at £50 a week, that newsreel producers had paid £200 for special positions on the Coronation route, and that Leyton Public Library was blaming local cinemas for a decline in the number of books issued.

The most extensive cinema press in the world belongs to India, which had 630 film magazines of all kinds at

Farmer, Ruggles (at the Eldorado Palace): "Here, I want to see this Annie Mattygraph. What time does she come on?"

The earliest known painting of a British cinema interior: *In the Cinema* by Malcom Drummond, 1912–13. (*Ferens Art Gallery, Hull*)

the latest count. During the silent period, Japan had the most prolific film press, with 104 fan magazines existing in 1926, including one of the only journals ever devoted solely to a single star—*Kurishima Notebook*, for fans of the Japanese 'Queen of the Silents' Sumiko Kurishima.

The first cartoon about the cinema was published in France in the satirical newspaper *Le Charivari* on 19 April 1896. It shows a man giving a cinematograph camera to a couple of newlyweds and advising them cynically: 'In 45 years time you'll be able to see again the only agreeable moment of your marriage.' No less than three other cartoons about the cinema followed in *Le Charivari* in May and several others over the next year, some of which used the movies as a vehicle for political satire.

The first cartoon concerning films to be published in a newspaper was also a vehicle for political satire. This was in the *Cape Register* (South Africa) of 19 September 1896 and showed the Edison Vitascope in a political lampoon about excessive customs charges.

Britain's first cartoon about the cinema was in the comic paper *Scraps* for 16 January 1897. It was a simple joke with a country bumpkin, Farmer Ruggles, seeing a poster for the Animatograph and thinking that it was a performer, 'Annie Mattygraph'.

America published its first cartoon on cinema in the comic journal *Judge* on 20 February 1897. It shows Cyrus Jayson walking home along the railway track, somewhat the worse for drink. A train approaches but he thinks it's just a film because he's 'seen them kinettyscope pictures before'.

The first painting on a cinematic theme is an oil of 1907 by American artist John Sloan (1871–1951) titled *Movies, five cents*. It shows a nickelodeon audience watching a film of a couple kissing and is in a private collection in New York.

The first British work of art about the cinema is Malcolm Drummond's *In the Cinema* of 1912–13.

Britain's first cartoon about the cinema. *Scraps* 16 January 1897. (*Stephen Bottomore*)

The first regular film column in a newspaper began appearing in the *New York Morning Journal* in 1909.

The first regular film column in a newspaper in Britain was a weekly feature titled 'Around the Cinema Palaces' written by W. G. Faulkner for the *Evening News*, commencing 17 January 1912. It was to be many years, though, before editors were to regard screen journalism as having any connection with the arts. In 1921 the editor of a leading London newspaper remarked that their film page was intended solely for East End readers, the only film news worthy of attention outside slumdom being the activities of Mary Pickford or Charlie Chaplin.

FILM CRITICISM

This was born with a brief review of *May Irwin Kiss* (US 96) in the *Chap Book* for 15 June 1896: '. . . absolutely disgusting'.

In the early days of screen journalism the trade journals used to carry plot outlines, but there was little attempt to assess the merits of the new films.

> Few critics have been prepared to nominate any one film as either the best or the worst in history, but Alan Brien had no reservations when he summed up Irwin Allen's *The Swarm* (US 78) in a review for the *Sunday Times*: '. . . simply the worst film ever made'.

The first regular film critic was Frank Woods, who began reviewing for the *New York Dramatic Mirror*

> A review of *Luffar-Petter/Peter the Tramp* (Swe 22) in the Swedish magazine *Swing* commented of one of the supporting players: 'Since Miss Gustafsson has so far had only the dubious pleasure of having to play a "bathing beauty" for Mr Erik Perschler in his fire department film, we have received no impression whatever of her capacity. It pleases us, though, to have the opportunity of noting a new name in Swedish films, and we hope we have a chance to mention it again.'
>
> It was mentioned again, but by then the name had changed to Garbo.

with the issue of 1 May 1909. Woods used the penname 'Spectator'. His salary was $20 a week.

None of the performers were identified in early reviews. *Variety* seems to have been the first to discard this anonymity, the issue for 21 January 1911 referring to Mary Pickford's 'cute ways and girlish manner' in *The Italian Barber* (US 11).

The first newspaper to carry film reviews was *Vilag* (*World*), a Budapest daily, which engaged Sándor Kellner as its critic in August 1912. Kellner's sojourn with the paper was brief, since he was determined to get into the production side of the movie business, which he did with spectacular success as (Sir) Alexander Korda.

The first American newspaper to employ a regular film critic was the *Chicago Tribune* with the appointment of John Lawson in 1914. Lawson was killed in an accident soon after and his place was taken by Miss Audrie Alspaugh, who wrote under the by-line 'Kitty Kelly'. Movie historian Terry Ramsaye recalled: 'Kitty Kelly could make or break a picture in the Middle West . . . Her column was a large success, and she became the best disliked name in the world of the film studios'.

Contrast in style. Sex appeal as the British liked it (*left*). Sex appeal as the Americans preferred it (*right*).

14 Awards and Festivals

The first film awards were made in respect of a festival which opened in Monte Carlo on New Year's Day 1898. The competition was open to professionals and amateurs alike but subjects had to be taken in Monaco. The first prize was worth £80, and there were two others worth £40 and £20. The following year the competition was expanded. Prize money was increased to a total of £1200 (30,000 francs) plus a number of honourable mentions and this time it was purely for amateurs. It was organised by the Societé des Bains de Mer who stipulated that each competitor must send in three films of any place or subject which should never previously have been exhibited. The jury was to be composed of 'artists and amateurs' and films were judged on 'originality, artistic merit and photographic quality', according to the *British Journal of Photography*. The prizes were awarded in February 1900 by the Prince of Monaco and the winning entries were shown at the Palais des Beaux Arts. The titles of the winning films are not recorded.

> The only annual festival of silent films is held at Pordenone, Italy. The first festival devoted exclusively to film music was held at Angers, France in 1980 and the first confined to film trailers, the Yokuku Concours, took place in Japan in 1982. The only festival which plays bad movies—correction, deliberately plays bad movies—is the Viennale, which has a section designated 'Cinema Nobody Likes'. Among the most reviled entries at the 1984 Viennale was *Why the UFOs Steal Our Lettuce* (FRG 79), which starred an uneasy looking Curt Jurgens as a Martian.

The first award winning film known by name was Giovanni Vitrotti's *Il Cane riconescente* (It 07), an Ambrosio production which won a gold plaque awarded by the Lumière brothers at an international contest held in Italy in 1907.

The first award made to a feature film was also won by Ambrosio. At the Grand Prix of 25,000 francs at the International Exhibition at Turin in 1912 the prize went to *After Fifty Years* (It 12), an historical drama set in the Austro–Italian War of 1859.

Esther Ralston starred in Dorothy Arzner's *Fashions for Women* (US 27), the first film to win a British award and the first award-winning film anywhere in the world directed by a woman.

Britain's first film festival was the International Festival of Women's Films, held in London in 1928. The first prize went to Dorothy Arzner's *Fashions For Women* (US 27). The only other pre-war festival on record was a non-competitive event held at Malvern in 1931, notable chiefly for the pre-release presentation of the first Bernard Shaw talkie, *How He Lied to Her Husband* (GB 31) with Edmund Gwenn.

The longest continuously held festival is the American International Film Festival, a showcase for non-theatrical movies which has been held annually since 1930. The oldest major festival is the Venice Film Festival, which originated as part of the Venice Biennale in 1932 as a means of reviving the Depression-hit tourist trade. It was competitive from 1934, when *Man of Aran* (GB 34) took the top prize.

Academy Awards

These were instituted by the Academy of Motion Picture Arts and Sciences and first presented on 16 May 1929. The awards that year were to dignify the efforts of film-makers during the 12 months August 1927 to July 1928—and at the same time to dignify, the Academy hoped, the somewhat tarnished reputation the film industry had earned itself in the 'roaring twenties'.

> From 1929 through 1984, a total of 273 men were nominated for Best Director and one woman. The sole femme helmer was Lina Wertmuller for *Seven Beauties* (It 75).

Oscar, the Academy Award trophy, is the figure of a man with a crusader's sword standing on a reel of film. Until 1931 it was known simply as 'The Statuette', but in that year Academy librarian Margaret Herrick chanced to remark 'He looks like my Uncle Oscar' and the name stuck. Plated in 10 carat gold, Oscar has always stood 13½ inches tall, except in war time when the trophy consisted of a gold-plated plaster plaque with the Oscar figure in relief. The value of an Oscar is about $150. Recipients pledge never to sell their statuette except back to the Academy, who will pay $10 for it. Between 1936 and 1939 the members of the Board of the Academy had to pay for the Oscar statuettes out of their own pockets as the Academy was so short of funds. Double Oscar winning scriptwriter Frances Marion says that she sees the statuette as 'a perfect symbol of the picture business: a powerful

> Victor Young, composer, was nominated 19 times but won only one Oscar—for Best Scoring of a Dramatic or Comedy Picture on *Around the World in Eighty Days* (US 56). Sadly it was awarded posthumously—Victor Young had died four months earlier.

The longest time an Oscar remained unclaimed was 40 years in the case of the first Academy award for a documentary, won by *Krakatoa* (US 32). The producer, Joe Rock, was away in London when the 1933 Academy awards were presented and no one came forward to claim the Oscar for him. On his return he found he was unable to prove his entitlement to it as there was no producer credit on the film. It was not until 1973 that documents were found proving that *Krakatoa* was his film and he was able to pick up the statuette that had lain so long in the offices of the Motion Picture Academy. (*Ralph Harding Collection*)

athletic body clutching a gleaming sword, with half of his head, that part which held his brains, completely sliced off'.

The most awards in any category have been won by Walt Disney (1901–66), who was honoured with 26 regular and six special trophies.

The most awards for individual creative achievement are the eight won by costume designer Edith Head (1907–81).

The most awards won by any one film went to *Ben Hur* (US 59) and numbered eleven: Best Picture; Best Director; Best Actor; Best Supporting Actor; Cinematography; Art Direction; Sound; Music Score; Film Editing; Special Effects; Costume.

The most awards won by a British film went to *Gandhi* (GB 83) and numbered eight: Best Picture; Best Actor; Best Director; Best Original Screenplay; Cinematography; Film Editing; Art Direction; Costume Design.

The most nominations for awards were made in respect of *All About Eve* (US 50) with 14. It won six.

Only two films have won 'The Big Five' major awards—Best Picture; Best Director; Best Actor; Best

Katharine Hepburn holds the record for the most Oscars in the performing categories. Her four Best Actress awards were won for *Morning Glory* (US 33) (*above left*), *Guess Who's Coming to Dinner* (US 67) (*above right*), *The Lion in Winter* (GB 68) (*below left*) and *On Golden Pond* (US 81) (*below right*).

Actress; Best Screenplay. They are: *It Happened One Night* (US 34)—Frank Capra; Clark Gable; Claudette Colbert; Robert Riskin; and *One Flew Over the Cuckoo's Nest* (US 75)—Milos Forman; Jack Nicholson; Louise Fletcher; Lawrence Hauben and Bo Goldman.

The most Best Director awards have been made to John Ford, who won four times: *The Informer* (US 35); *The Grapes of Wrath* (US 40); *How Green was my Valley* (US 41); *The Quiet Man* (US 52).

The most Best Actor awards have been won by four actors, each with two Oscars: Spencer Tracy for *Captains Courageous* (US 37) and *Boys Town* (US 38);

Fredric March for *Dr Jekyll and Mr Hyde* (US 32) and *The Best Years of our Lives* (US 46); Gary Cooper for *Sergeant York* (US 41) and *High Noon* (US 52); and Marlon Brando for *On the Waterfront* (US 54) and *The Godfather* (US 72). Tracy, though, received nine nominations during his career, against seven for Brando and five each for March and Cooper. Sir Laurence Olivier has equalled Tracy's nominations, but won only a single Best Actor award for *Hamlet* (GB 48). Perhaps Tracy should also take first place by virtue of the fact that Katharine Hepburn is on record as saying that one of her Academy Awards was doubtless intended for both of them.

The most Best Actress awards have been won by Katharine Hepburn, whose four Oscars were awarded for *Morning Glory* (US 33), *Guess Who's Coming to Dinner* (US 67), *The Lion in Winter* (GB 68) and *On Golden Pond* (US 81). Miss Hepburn also

Despite the fact that crime has been the single most predominant theme in Hollywood movies over the last 50 years, the only film in this category to have won Best Picture was a comedy crime caper, *The Sting* (US 73). Curiously though, period movies, which Hollywood has always regarded with extreme caution, have carried off no less than 23 Best Picture awards—over 40 per cent of the total.

Hattie McDaniel became the first black performer to win an Oscar when she was voted Best Supporting Actress for her role in *Gone With the Wind* (US 39).

enjoys the distinction of having received the most nominations of any performer (13), and of having the longest award-winning career, spanning 48 years.

The first co-stars to win Best Actor and Best Actress award in the same year were Clark Gable and Claudette Colbert, for *It Happened One Night* (US 34). Miss Colbert was so sceptical of her chances of winning the Oscar that she decided not to postpone a trip to New York on a train scheduled to leave on the evening of the ceremony. She was just stepping into the carriage when officials of the Academy arrived to tell her she had won. A motorcycle escort rushed her to the Biltmore Bowl to receive the award, still dressed in her travelling clothes.

Other co-stars who won in the same year have been: Jack Nicholson and Louise Fletcher: *One Flew Over the Cuckoo's Nest* (US 75); Peter Finch and Faye Dunaway: *Network* (US 76); Jon Voigt and Jane Fonda: *Coming Home* (US 78); Dustin Hoffman and Meryl Streep: *Kramer vs Kramer* (US 79); Henry Fonda and Katharine Hepburn: *On Golden Pond* (US 81).

The only tie for Best Actor was between Wallace Beery in *The Champ* (US 31) and Fredric March in *Dr Jekyll and Mr Hyde* (US 31).

The only tie for Best Actress was between Barbra Streisand in *Funny Girl* (US 68) and Katharine Hepburn in *The Lion in Winter* (GB 68).

The following members of the same family have won Oscars in the same year: brother and sister Douglas and Norma Shearer, he for Sound Recording on *The Big House* (US 30), she as Best Actress in *The Divorcee* (US 30); father and son Walter and John Huston, both for *The Treasure of the Sierra Madre* (US 47), as Best Supporting Actor and Best Director, respectively; brothers Richard M. and Robert B. Sherman for Best Song, 'Chim-Chim Cher-ee' in *Mary Poppins* (US 63); and father and son Carmine and Francis Coppola, both for *The Godfather Part II* (US 74), as composer of Best Original Dramatic Score and Best Director respectively.

The shortest performance to win an Oscar was Anthony Quinn's eight-minute *tour de force* as Gauguin in *Lust for Life* (US 56), which won him the 1956 Best Supporting Actor award.

The first Oscar winning debut performance was by Mercedes McCambridge in *All the King's Men* (US 49), for which she won the Best Supporting Actress award.

The youngest Oscar winner was Shirley Temple, who won a Special Award at the age of six for 'her outstanding contribution to screen entertainment during the year 1934'.

The youngest person to receive a regular Academy Award was 9-year-old Tatum O'Neal, who won the Oscar for Best Supporting Actress for her role in *Paper Moon* (US 73).

The oldest Oscar winner was George Burns, who was 80 when he collected his Best Supporting Actor award for *The Sunshine Boys* (US 75).

The first black Oscar winner was Hattie McDaniel, who was awarded Best Supporting Actress for her role as Mammy in *Gone with the Wind* (US 39). Twenty-four years elapsed before another black performer won a regular Oscar: Sidney Poitier was awarded Best Actor for *Lilies of the Field* (US 63).

The only western to win Best Film was *Cimarron* (US 31).

The only sequel to win Best Film was *The Godfather Part II* (US 74). *The Godfather* (US 72) also won.

The first Award winner to refuse an Oscar was Dudley Nichols, voted Best Writer (Screenplay) for *The Informer* (US 35). Nichols gave as his reason loyalty to the Writers Guild, which together with other unions was trying to force a boycott of the Academy Awards in their fight for recognition by the studios.

The first performer to refuse an Oscar was George C. Scott, winner of Best Actor for *Patton* (US 70). His example was followed by Marlon Brando, who refused Best Actor award for *The Godfather* (US 72).

The longest acceptance speech was made by Greer Garson on receiving the Best Actress award for *Mrs Miniver* (US 42)—it lasted over an hour.

THE ACADEMY AWARD FOR THE BEST FILM
Dates given are year award was made
1929 *Wings* (US)
1930 *Broadway Melody* (US)
1931 *All Quiet on the Western Front* (US)
1932 *Cimarron* (US)
1933 *Grand Hotel* (US)
1934 *Cavalcade* (US)
1935 *It Happened One Night* (US)
1936 *Mutiny on the Bounty* (US)
1937 *The Great Ziegfeld* (US)
1938 *The Life of Emile Zola* (US)
1939 *You Can't Take It With You* (US)
1940 *Gone with the Wind* (US)
1941 *Rebecca* (US)
1942 *How Green was my Valley* (US)
1943 *Mrs Miniver* (US)
1944 *Casablanca* (US)
1945 *Going my Way* (US)
1946 *The Lost Weekend* (US)
1947 *The Best Years of Our Lives* (US)
1948 *Gentlemen's Agreement* (US)
1949 *Hamlet* (US)
1950 *All the King's Men* (US)
1951 *All About Eve* (US)
1952 *An American in Paris* (US)
1953 *The Greatest Show on Earth* (US)
1954 *From Here to Eternity* (US)
1955 *On the Waterfront* (US)
1956 *Marty* (US)
1957 *Around the World in 80 Days* (US)
1958 *The Bridge on the River Kwai* (GB)
1959 *Gigi* (US)
1960 *Ben Hur* (US)
1961 *The Apartment* (US)
1962 *West Side Story* (US)
1963 *Lawrence of Arabia* (GB)
1964 *Tom Jones* (GB)
1965 *My Fair Lady* (US)
1966 *The Sound of Music* (US)
1967 *A Man for All Seasons* (GB)
1968 *In the Heat of the Night* (US)
1969 *Oliver!* (GB)
1970 *Midnight Cowboy* (US)
1971 *Patton* (US)
1972 *The French Connection* (US)
1973 *The Godfather* (US)
1974 *The Sting* (US)
1975 *The Godfather, Part Two* (US)
1976 *One Flew Over the Cuckoo's Nest* (US)
1977 *Rocky* (US)
1978 *Annie Hall* (US)
1979 *The Deer Hunter* (US)
1980 *Kramer vs Kramer* (US)
1981 *Ordinary People* (US)
1982 *Chariots of Fire* (GB)
1983 *Gandhi* (GB)
1984 *Terms of Endearment* (US)

THE BERLIN FILM FESTIVAL AWARD FOR BEST FILM
The Berlin Film Festival was established in 1951. There was no overall Best Film award in the first year and from 1952–55 the films were voted for by the audience. The Golden Bear award for Best Picture was inaugurated 1956.
1952 *She Danced for the Summer* (Swe)
1953 *The Wages of Fear* (Fr)
1954 *Hobson's Choice* (GB)
1955 *The Rats* (FRG)
1956 *Invitation to the Dance* (GB)
1957 *Twelve Angry Men* (US)
1958 *The End of the Day* (Swe)
1959 *The Cousins* (Fr)
1960 *Lazarillo de Tormes* (Sp)
1961 *La Notte* (It)
1962 *A Kind of Loving* (GB)
1963 *Oath of Obedience* (FRG); *The Devil* (It)
1964 *Dry Summer* (Tur)
1965 *Alphaville* (Fr)
1966 *Cul de Sac* (GB)
1967 *Le Depart* (Bel)
1968 *Ole Dole Doff* (Swe)
1969 *Early Years* (Yug)
1970 No award
1971 *The Garden of the Finzi-Continis* (It)
1972 *The Canterbury Tales* (It)
1973 *Distant Thunder* (It)
1974 *The Apprenticeship of Duddy Kravitz* (Can)
1975 *Orkobefogadas* (Hun)
1976 *Buffalo Bill and the Indians* (US)—award declined
1977 *The Ascent* (USSR)
1978 *The Trouts* (Sp); *The Words of Max* (Sp)
1979 *David* (FRG)
1980 *Heartland* (US); *Palermo Oder Wolfsburg* (FRG)
1981 *Di Presa Di Presa* (Sp)
1982 *Die Schnsucht der Veronica Voss* (FRG)
1983 *Ascendancy* (GB); *The Beehive* (Sp)
1984 *Love Streams* (US 84)
1985 *Wecherby* (GB); *Die Frau und der Fremde* (FRG)

BRITISH FILM ACADEMY—BEST BRITISH FILM AWARD—BEST FILM AWARD
The award is for the best film of the previous year
1948 *Odd Man Out*
1949 *The Fallen Idol*
1950 *The Third Man*
1951 *The Blue Lamp*
1952 *The Lavender Hill Mob*
1953 *The Sound Barrier*
1954 *Genevieve*
1955 *Hobson's Choice*
1956 *Richard III*
1957 *Reach for the Sky*
1958 *The Bridge on the River Kwai*
1959 *Room at the Top*
1960 *Sapphire*
1961 *Saturday Night and Sunday Morning*
1962 *A Taste of Honey*
1963 *Lawrence of Arabia*
1964 *Tom Jones*
1965 *Dr Strangelove*
1966 *The Ipcress File*
1967 *The Spy who Came in from the Cold*
1968 *A Man for All Seasons*
In 1969 the 'Best British Film Award' was discontinued and replaced by a 'Best Film Award'
1969 *The Graduate* (US)
1970 *Midnight Cowboy* (US)
1971 *Butch Cassidy and the Sundance Kid* (US)
1972 *Sunday Bloody Sunday* (GB)
1973 *Cabaret* (US)
1974 *La Nuite Americaine/Day for Night* (Fr)
1975 *Lacombe, Lucien* (Fr)
1976 *Alice Doesn't Live Here Anymore* (US)
1977 *One Flew Over the Cuckoo's Nest* (US)
1978 *Annie Hall* (US)
1979 *Julia* (US)
1980 *Manhattan* (US)
1981 *The Elephant Man* (GB)
1982 *Chariots of Fire* (GB)
1983 *Gandhi* (GB)
1984 *Educating Rita* (GB)

CANNES FILM FESTIVAL
Palme d'Or for Best Film
1946 *La Bataille du Rail* (Fr)
1947 *Antoine et Antoinette* (Fr)
1948 No festival
1949 *The Third Man* (GB)
1950 No festival
1951 *Miracle in Milan* (It); *Miss Julie* (Swe)
1952 *Othello* (Mor); *Two Cents Worth of Hope* (It)
1953 *Wages of Fear* (Fr)
1954 *Gate of Hell* (Jap)
1955 *Marty* (US)
1956 *World of Silence* (Fr)
1957 *Friendly Persuasion* (US)
1958 *The Cranes are Flying* (USSR)
1959 *Black Orpheus* (Fr)
1960 *La Dolce Vita* (It)
1961 *Viridiana* (Sp); *Une aussi longue absence* (Fr)
1962 *The Given Word* (Bra)
1963 *The Leopard* (It)
1964 *The Umbrellas of Cherbourg* (Fr)
1965 *The Knack* (GB)
1966 *A Man and a Woman* (Fr); *Signore e Signori* (It)
1967 *Blow-Up* (GB)
1968 Festival disrupted; no awards
1969 *If* (GB)
1970 *M*A*S*H* (US)
1971 *The Go-Between* (GB)
1972 *The Working Class Goes to Paradise* (It); *The Mattei Affair* (It)
1973 *Scarecrow* (US); *The Hireling* (GB)
1974 *The Conversation* (US)
1975 *Chronicle of the Burning Years* (Alg)
1976 *Taxi Driver* (US)
1977 *Padre Padrone* (It)
1978 *L'Albero Degli Zoccoli* (It)
1979 *The Tin Drum* (FRG); *Apocalypse Now* (US)
1980 *All That Jazz* (US); *Kagemusha* (Jap)
1981 *Man of Iron* (Pol)
1982 *Missing* (US); *Yol* (Tur)
1983 *The Ballad of Narayama* (Jap)
1984 *Paris, Texas* (FRG)

VENICE FILM FESTIVAL
Best Foreign Film Award (1934–42)
Best Film Award (1946–68)
1932 No official award
1933 No festival
1934 *Man of Aran* (GB)
1935 *Anna Karenina* (US)
1936 *Der Kaiser von Kalifornien* (Ger)
1937 *Un Carnet de Bal* (Fr)
1938 *Olympia* (Ger)
1939 No award
1940 *Der Postmeister* (Ger)
1941 *Ohm Kruger* (Ger)
1942 *Der grosse König* (Ger)
1943–45 No festival
1946 *The Southerner* (US)
1947 *Sirena* (Cz)
1948 *Hamlet* (GB)
1949 *Manon* (Fr)
1950 *Justice is Done* (Fr)
1951 *Rashomon* (Jap)
1952 *Forbidden Games* (Fr)
1953 No award
1954 *Romeo and Juliet* (It/GB)
1955 *Ordet* (Den)
1956 No award
1957 *Aparajito* (Ind)
1958 *Muhomatsu no Issho* (Jap)
1959 *Il Generale della Rovere* (It)
1960 *Le Passage du Rhine* (Fr)
1961 *Last Year at Marienbad* (Fr)
1962 *Childhood of Ivan* (USSR)
1963 *Le Mani sulla citta* (It)
1964 *Red Desert* (It)
1965 *Of a Thousand Delights* (It)
1966 *Battle of Algiers* (It)
1967 *Belle de Jour* (Fr)
1968 *Die Aristen in der Zirkuskuppel* (FRG)
Jury and award system discontinued 1969–80.
1980 *Gloria* (US); *Atlantic City* (Fr/Can)

1981 *Die Bleierne Zeit* (FRG)
1982 *The State of Things* (FRG)
1983 *Prenom Carmen* (Fr/Swz)
1984 *Year of the Quiet Sun* (Pol)

THE GREATEST AMERICAN FILMS OF ALL TIME (1977)

These were selected in 1977 by means of a ballot of the 35,000 members of the American Film Institute, each of whom was asked to name his or her Top Five. A total of 1100 films were nominated, from which the AFI compiled a list of 50 which had received the most 'votes'. A second ballot was then held, the members being asked to select their Top Five from the list of 50. Considering the effort put into this survey, it is less than reassuring to find that four British productions were included amongst the 50 'Greatest American Films' and that two of these (*2001: A Space Odyssey* and *The African Queen*) emerged in the final Top Ten listing, a permutation based on the results of the second ballot. The titles of the AFI's Top Ten Greatest American Films of All Time are, in order of greatness:

1. *Gone with the Wind* (1939)
2. *Citizen Kane* (1941)
3. *Casablanca* (1942)
4. *The African Queen* (1952)
5. *The Grapes of Wrath* (1940)
6. *One Flew Over the Cuckoo's Nest* (1975)
7. *Singin' in the Rain* (1952)
8. *Star Wars* (1977)
9. *2001: A Space Odyssey* (1968)
10. *The Wizard of Oz* (1939)

CINÉMATHEQUE BELGIQUE BEST FILMS OF ALL TIME

In 1952 the committee of the Festival Mondial du Film et des Beaux Arts Belgique asked 100 film directors to select their individual 'Ten Best Films of All Time'. Permutation of the directors' choices gave the following result:

1 *The Battleship Potemkin* (USSR 25)
2 *The Gold Rush* (US 25)
3 *Bicycle Thieves* (It 49)
=4 *City Lights* (US 31)
    La Grande Illusion (Fr 37); *Le Million* (Fr 31)
7 *Greed* (US 24)
8 *Hallelujah!* (US 29)
=9 *Die Dreigroschenoper/The Threepenny Opera* (Ger 31); *Brief Encounter* (GB 45); *Intolerance* (US 16); *Man of Aran* (GB 34)

Sight and Sound TEN BEST POLLS
In 1952, 1962, 1972 and 1982 the British film quarterly *Sight and Sound* conducted international polls of critics in which they were invited to select 'The Ten Best Films of All Time':

1952
1 *Bicycle Thieves* (It 49)
=2 *City Lights* (US 31); *The Gold Rush* (US 25)
4 *Battleship Potemkin* (USSR 25)
=5 *Louisiana Story* (US 47); *Intolerance* (US 16)
=7 *Greed* (US 24); *Le Jour se lève* (Fr 39); *The Passion of Joan of Arc* (Fr 28)
=10 *Brief Encounter* (GB 45); *Le Million* (Fr 30); *La Règle du Jeu* (Fr 39)

1962
1 *Citizen Kane* (US 41)
2 *L'Avventura* (It 59)
3 *La Règle du Jeu* (Fr 39)
=4 *Greed* (US 24); *Ugetsu Monagatari* (Jap 53)
=6 *Battleship Potemkin* (USSR 25); *Bicycle Thieves* (It 49); *Ivan the Terrible* (USSR 46)
9 *La Terra Trema* (It 48)
10 *L'Atalante* (Fr 33)

1972
1 *Citizen Kane* (US 41)
2 *La Règle du Jeu* (Fr 39)
3 *Battleship Potemkin* (USSR 25)
4 *8½* (It 63)
=5 *L'Avventura* (It 59); *Persona* (Swe 66)
7 *The Passion of Joan of Arc* (Fr 28)
=8 *The General* (US 26); *The Magnificent Ambersons* (US 42)
=10 *Ugetsu Monogatari* (Jap 53); *Wild Strawberries* (Swe 57)

1982
1 *Citizen Kane* (US 41)
2 *La Règle du Jeu* (Fr 39)
=3 *Seven Samurai* (Jap 54); *Singin' in the Rain* (US 52)
5 *8½* (It 63)
6 *Battleship Potemkin* (USSR 25)
=7 *L'Avventura* (It 59); *The Magnificent Ambersons* (US 42); *Vertigo* (US 58)
=9 *The General* (US 26); *The Searchers* (US 56)

BRUSSELS WORLD'S FAIR BEST FILMS OF ALL TIME

On the occasion of the Brussels World's Fair of 1958, the 'Twelve Best Films of All Time' were selected by 117 film historians from 26 countries under the auspices of the Bureau International de la Recherche Historique Cinématographiques. The results, with the number of votes cast for each film, were as follows:

1 *The Battleship Potemkin* (USSR 25) 100 votes
2 *The Gold Rush* (US 25) 85 votes
   Bicycle Thieves (It 49) 85 votes
4 *The Passion of Joan of Arc* (Fr 28) 78 votes
5 *La Grande Illusion* (Fr 37) 72 votes
6 *Greed* (US 24) 71 votes
7 *Intolerance* (US 16) 61 votes
8 *Mother* (USSR 26) 54 votes
9 *Citizen Kane* (US 41) 50 votes
10 *Earth* (USSR 30) 47 votes
11 *The Last Laugh* (Ger 24) 45 votes
12 *The Cabinet of Dr Caligari* (Ger 19) 43 votes

BFI MEMBERS' TOP 30 FILMS

On the occasion of its 50th anniversary, the British Film Institute polled 1200 members on their best 30 films of all time. Over 2000 films were nominated and the top 30 were presented at the National Film Theatre in September 1983. Programme director Ken Wlaschin wrote: 'Analysing the results, the top 30 films range in date from 1935 to 1979 but include no silent pictures (Keaton's *The General* came in at number 31). America won 16 positions, Britain four (*The Third Man* came on top), France seven and Japan, Italy and Germany each one. Three directors had two films selected: Billy Wilder, Jean Renoir and John Ford. Most genres were represented, with a preference for comedies and musicals and only one Western and one SF film.' The results:

1 *Casablanca* (US 42)
2 *Les Enfants du Paradis* (Fr 43–5)
3 *Citizen Kane* (US 41)
4 *Singin' in the Rain* (US 52)
5 *2001: A Space Odyssey* (GB 68)
6 *Some Like It Hot* (US 59)
7 *Seven Samurai* (Jap 54)
8 *Gone with the Wind* (US 39)
9 *The Third Man* (GB 49)
10 *One Flew Over the Cuckoo's Nest* (US 75)
11 *Céline and Julie Go Boating* (Fr 74)
12 *The Graduate* (US 67)
13 *Death in Venice* (It 71)
14 *La Grande Illusion* (Fr 37)
15 *Brief Encounter* (GB 45)

16 *Manhattan* (US 79)
17 *Top Hat* (US 35)
18 *Kind Hearts and Coronets* (GB 49)
19 *Apocalypse Now* (US 79)
20 *The Searchers* (US 56)
21 *Orphée* (Fr 50)
22 *Cabaret* (US 72)
23 *Psycho* (US 60)
24 *Henry V* (GB 44)
25 *Jules et Jim* (Fr 61)
26 *La Règle du Jeu* (Fr 39)
27 *Aguirre, Wrath of the Gods* (FRG 72)
28 *Monsieur Hulot's Holiday* (Fr 53)
29 *The Grapes of Wrath* (US 40)
30 *Double Indemnity* (US 44)

WORST FILM AWARDS

Since 1940 the *Harvard Lampoon* has made annual 'Movie Worsts' awards in a range of categories designed to undermine the pretentiousness and sentimentality that mars much of Hollywood's output. An award for 'The Worst Picture of the Century' was made in 1950 to Victor Fleming's *Joan of Arc* (US 48), with Ingrid Bergman as an Americanised and worldly Joan. The award was repeated in 1958, going to Otto Preminger's *Saint Joan* (US 57), in which Jean Seberg had failed to illuminate the mysticism of the Maid. In 1964 it was won by *Cleopatra* (US 63). The *Harvard Lampoon* has presented its award for 'The Worst Film of the Year' to the following:

1940 *The Rains Came* (US)
1941 *The Howards of Virginia* (US)
1942 *Hudson's Bay* (US)
1943–44 No award
1945 *Kismet* (US)
1946 *Weekend at the Waldorf* (US)
1947 *Night and Day* (US)
1948 No award
1949 *Winter Meeting* (US)
1950 *Joan of Arc* (US)
1951 *Our Very Own* (US)
1952 *Tales of Hoffman* (GB)
1953 *Jumping Jacks* (US)
1954 *The Robe* (US)
1955 *Haaji Baba* (US)
1956 *Not as a Stranger* (US)
1957 *The Ten Commandments* (US)
1958 *Raintree County* (US)
1959 *South Pacific* (US)
1960 *The Best of Everything* (US)
1961 *Butterfield 8* (US)
1962 *King of Kings* (US); *Parrish* (US)
1963 *The Chapman Report* (US)
1964 *Cleopatra* (US)
1965 *The Greatest Story Ever Told* (US); *The Carpetbaggers* (US); *Sylvia* (US); *Cheyenne Autumn* (US); *Station Six Sahara* (GB); *Kiss Me Stupid* (US)
1966 *The Sandpiper* (US)
1967 *Is Paris Burning?* (Fr/US)
1968 *Guess Who's Coming to Dinner* (US)
1969 *The Lion in Winter* (GB)
1970 *Easy Rider* (US)
1971 *Love Story* (US)
1972 *A Clockwork Orange* (GB)
1973 *Last Tango in Paris* (Fr/It/US)
1974 *The Great Gatsby* (US)
1975 *Lenny* (US)
1976 *Barry Lyndon* (GB)
1977 *A Star is Born* (US)
1978 *Looking for Mr Goodbar* (US)
1979 *Sgt. Pepper's Lonely Hearts Club Band* (US)
1980–84 Not available

15 Animation

The first animated film using the stop-motion technique to give the illusion of movement to inanimate objects was Vitagraph's *The Humpty Dumpty Circus* (US 98?). Albert E. Smith, who conceived the idea, borrowed his small daughter's toy circus and succeeded in animating the acrobats and animals by shooting them in barely changed positions one frame at a time—the same principle as that used for animated cartoons.

The earliest known British example of animation is an untitled advertising film made by Arthur Melbourne Cooper of St Albans, Herts, for Messrs Bryant & May. Dating from 1899, it consists of an appeal for funds to supply the troops in South Africa with matches, as it seems this was something the Army authorities had overlooked. The animated 'performers' are match-stick men who climb up a wall and form themselves into the legend: 'Send £1 and enough matches will be sent to supply a regiment of our fighting soldiers'.

Some years later, Melbourne Cooper made two charming films featuring animated toys, *Noah's Ark* (GB 08) and *Dreams of Toyland* (GB 08). Strutting teddy bears were featured in the latter with particularly engaging effect.

Meanwhile, in the United States, J. Stuart Blackton, Albert E. Smith's co-partner at Vitagraph, had produced an unusual novelty with *The Haunted Hotel* (US 07), in which furniture moved about seemingly by its own agency.

The following year Pathé pioneered the animation of paper cut-outs in *Paper Cock-a-Doodle* (Fr 08)—the cut-outs being in the shape of exquisitely wrought birds. The pioneer of animation in Russia was Ladislas Starevitch, who applied the stop-motion technique to bring dead insects 'alive' in *The Grasshopper and the Ant* (Rus 11) and *The Stag Beetles* (Rus 11).

The first cartoon film was J. Stuart Blackton's *Humorous Phases of Funny Faces* (US 06), produced for the Vitagraph Co. of New York. Like nearly all early American film cartoonists, Blackton used the technique of showing an artist drawing a still picture which then magically came alive and moved. Most of the illusions were created by means of cardboard cut-outs, but a few genuinely animated drawings featured at the beginning of the film, showing a man and a woman rolling their eyes and the outline of a gentleman with bowler and umbrella apparently drawing himself.

The first British cartoon film was the Charles Urban production *The Clown and His Donkey* (GB 10), drawn by Charles Armstrong.

The first cartoon film to tell a story was Emile Cohl's *Fantasmagorie* (Fr 08), which was premièred at the Théâtre du Gymnase in Paris on 17 August 1908. Cohl made the film for Léon Gaumont, by whom he was employed as a scenarist. Prior to this, nearly all cartoon films were of the artist-drawing-a-living-picture genre. Robert Desnos has described Cohl as the first to 'cut the umbilical cord which still linked the life of the characters on the screen with the secretions of the fountain pen'. He made about 100 cartoons between 1908 and 1918 and can thus be regarded as **the first professional screen animator.**

The first cartoon series was inaugurated by Emile Cohl with the debut of his character Fantôche, a kind of match-stick man combatting the cruel world, in *Le Cauchemar du Fantôche* (Fr 09). **The first cartoon series in America**, also inaugurated by Cohl, was Eclair's *The Newlyweds*, starting with *When He Wants a Dog, He Wants a Dog* (US 13). Based on George McManus's popular cartoon characters in the *New York World*, this was also **the first cartoon series adapted from a comic strip**. In addition to these innovations, the series also gave a new descriptive term to the vocabulary of film-making. It was an advertisement for *The Newlyweds*, appearing in *Moving Picture World* for 15 February 1913, that contained **the first use of the term 'animated cartoon'.**

The first British cartoon series was *Pip, Squeek and Wilfred*, animated by Lancelot Speed from A. B. Payne's popular children's comic strip in the *Daily Mirror*. The series began in 1921 and ran for 26 instalments.

The first animal cartoon character was Old Doc Yak, a tail-coated billy-goat in striped pants, who was brought to the screen by *Chicago Tribune* cartoonist

The first step towards cartoon animation. In this Edison film of November 1900, *The Enchanted Drawing* (US 00), J. Stuart Blackton drew a humorous face which changed its expression while the artist stood aside. This was done by jump cutting and there was no illusion of movement. It was another six years before Blackton pioneered true animation in *Humorous Phases of Funny Faces* (US 06). (*Library of Congress*)

Sidney Smith in a Selig Polyscope series started in July 1913. It was the much-loved animal cartoon characters who eventually gave animated films a distinct appeal of their own as suitable entertainment for children. This development can best be dated from the advent of Pat Sullivan's Felix the Cat in 1919, an animal who 'kept on walking', and who was the first cartoon character to attain the celebrity of a human star. Felix was also **the first animated cartoon character to be merchandised**, both as an image on packaging and, in 1926, as a phenomenally successful cuddly toy.

The first cartoon talkie was *The Audion* (US 22), an animated physics film on the working of the three-element vacuum tube. Made by E. B. Craft of Western Electric, it was premièred at Woolsey Hall, Yale University, on 27 October 1922. The synchronised disc sound system used later developed into Vitaphone.

The first cartoon talkie for theatrical release was Max Fleischer's Koko Song Kar-Tune *My Old Kentucky Home* (US 25?), in which Bimbo the dog plays a trombone and speaks the words: 'Now let's all follow the bouncing ball and sing along'. It was produced by Inkwell Studio Productions with sound-on-film accompaniment by DeForest Phonofilm.

The first all-talking cartoon was Paul Terry's 'Aesop's Film Fable' *Dinner Time* (US 28), produced by Van Beuren Enterprises in the RCA Photophone sound system and premièred at the Mark Strand Theater in New York on 1 September 1928. Walt Disney dismissed it as 'a lot of racket and nothing else'. His own initial venture in talkies, *Steamboat Willie* (US 28), presented at New York's Colony Theater on 18 November 1928, was more auspicious; it marked the debut of the most successful cartoon character of all time, Mickey Mouse.

The first British cartoon talkie was *The Jazz Stringer* (GB 28), with 'Orace the 'Armonious 'Ound, made at Wembley Studios by Joe Noble and his brother George ('Orace's voice) for British Sound Productions and completed December 1928. It was claimed as 'the first lip synchronised cartoon in the world'.

The first colour cartoon was *The Debut of Thomas Kat* (US 20), a Paramount release produced by the Bray Pictures Corporation of New York in the Brewster natural-colour process. The drawings were made on transparent celluloid and painted on the reverse, then filmed with a two-colour camera. An unfortunate kitten, Thomas Kat, had been taught by his mother to catch mice, but inadvertently mistook a rat for the smaller breed of rodent. There was no follow-up to this remarkable pioneering endeavour until 1925, when *The Flying Elephant* (US 25) was made in the Natural Color Kelly Process.

The first colour cartoon talkie was Ted Esbaugh's *Goofy Goat* (US 31), made in two-colour Multicolor and previewed at Warner's Alhambra Theater, Los Angeles, on 6 July 1931.

The first Disney colour cartoon (often erroneously claimed as 'the world's first colour cartoon'), and the first cartoon made in a three-colour process, was the Silly Symphony *Flowers and Trees* (US 32), made in Technicolor and premièred at Grauman's Chinese Theater on 15 July 1932.

Britain's first cartoon talkie in colour was Reunion Films' *Sam and His Musket* (GB 35), made by Anson Dyer in the Dunning two-colour process with voice-over by Stanley Holloway.

The first feature-length cartoon film was Don Frederico Valle's 60-min *El Apostol* (Arg 17). Based on the book by Alfredo de Lafarrere, the film was a political satire on Argentina's President Irigoyen. The team of five animators was headed by Diogones Tabora, a well-known caricaturist, and between them they produced 50,000 drawings for the completed film.

The first full-length cartoon talkie was also surprisingly produced in Argentina. Made by Quirino Cristiani in 1931, *Peludopolis* was another satire on President Irogoyen and used the Vitaphone sound-on-disc system of synchronised sound. Running time was one hour. These two Argentinian cartoon features, and an Italian production *The Adventures of Pinocchio* (It 36), preceded the film which has generally been hailed as the world's first full-length cartoon feature. In fact Walt Disney's *Snow White and the Seven Dwarfs* (US 37) was only the first American cartoon feature, though the world's first to be made in both sound and colour. (A curiosity with the uninviting title of *Einstein's Theory of Relativity* (US 23), produced by Premier Productions in 7 reels, has sometimes been claimed as America's first cartoon feature. According to recent research by Denis Gifford, it would appear that this lost film was mainly live action, with some animated sequences by Max Fleischer.)

Britain's first feature-length cartoon was *Handling Ships* (GB 46), an instructional film made for the Admiralty by Halas and Batchelor. The first made for commercial release was Halas and Batchelor's *Animal Farm* (GB 54), from George Orwell's savage satire on Soviet repression.

The first 3-D cartoon was Norman McLaren's abstract subject *Around is Around* (GB 51).

The first full-length animated feature in 3-D was the 70 mm sci-fi epic *Star Chaser* (US 85).

The first cartoon to be X-rated in Britain was UPA's *The Tell-Tale Heart* (US 53).

The first cinemascope cartoon was Walt Disney's *Lady and the Tramp* (US 56).

The most expensive cartoon ever made is Walt Disney's *The Fox and the Hound* (US 81) at $10 million.

The highest grossing cartoon film of all time is Walt Disney's *The Jungle Book* (US 67), with worldwide rentals of $90.8 million to the end of 1984.

The longest cartoon ever made was Osamu Tezuka's erotic feature *A Thousand and One Nights* (Jap 69), which had a running time of 2 hr 30 min in the original Japanese version.

The multiplane camera, which registers degrees of depth in animation, **was used for the first time** on Walt Disney's *The Old Mill* (US 37).

FEATURE CARTOON OUTPUT

Up to the end of 1984, a total of 351 all-cartoon feature films had been made worldwide. The most prolific country was Japan with 126 full-length cartoon features, followed by the USA (64), France (23), Italy (16), USSR (12), Australia (12), Belgium (11),Hungary (11), Spain (10), W. Germany (10), Great Britain (9), Czechoslovakia (8), China (7), S. Korea (6), Argentina (5), Denmark (5), Canada (4), Sweden (4), Netherlands (2), Iraq (2), Hong Kong (2), Finland (2), Colombia (2), Bulgaria (2), Brazil (2), Cuba (2), Mexico (2), Poland, Israel, Thailand, Romania and the United Nations each produced one.

Cartoon Debuts

BETTY BOOP

Max Fleischer's boop-boop-a-doop flapper of the thirties debuted in *Dizzy Dishes* (US 30). Betty started life as a small dog with long ears and only became a human girl in 1932. Her baby-talk voice was done by five different actresses, of whom Little Ann Little (who spoke in boop-boop-a-doop language in real life) and Mae Questel were the best known.

BUGS BUNNY
Started as a hare rather than a 'wabbit' in Ben Hardway and Cal Dalton's Looney Tune *Porky's Hare Hunt* (US 38). The character only began to assume his real Brooklyn bunny persona in Tex Avery's *Wild Hare* (US 40).

DAFFY DUCK
Tex Avery's Looney Tune *Porky's Duck Hunt* (US 37).

DONALD DUCK
Walt Disney's *The Wise Little Hen* (US 34). His opening (and only) words were: 'Who—me? Oh no! I got a bellyache!' Clarence Nash, always Donald's voice, recalled: 'I had an ambition to be a doctor and somehow or other I became the biggest quack in the country.' He was still quacking 49 years later in *Mickey's Christmas Carol* (US 83).

DROOPY DOG
Created by Tex Avery in MGM's *Dumb-Hounded* (US 43).

FELIX THE CAT
Inspired by Kipling's *The Cat that Walked by Himself* in the *Just So Stories* (1902); created for Pat Sullivan by animator Otto Messmer. Prototype Felix, as yet unnamed, debuted in Paramount's *Feline Follies* (US 19). First of the anthropomorphic animal characters to attain the kind of celebrity accorded to human stars; also first to be merchandised. Television debut WXB2S New York 1930.

GOOFY
Walt Disney's *Mickey's Revue* (US 32).

MICKEY MOUSE
Born 18 November 1928 with première of *Steamboat Willie*. The artist for the MM cartoons was not Disney but Ub Iwerks, though Walt himself did Mickey's voice. By 1934 the Mouse was receiving more fan mail than any other Hollywood star. There were a total of 119 MM cartoons, of which the majority—87—were made in the thirties. There was a 30-year interval between *The Simple Things* (US 53) and the mouse's triumphant return in *Mickey's Christmas Carol* (US 83). Mickey was voiced in his Dickensian role by Wayne Allwine, who was born the year of the previous Mickey Mouse film.

MR MAGOO
UPA's *Ragtime Bear* (US 49).

PLUTO
Walt Disney's *The Chain Gang* (US 30).

POPEYE
Debuted in Max Fleischer's *Popeye the Sailor* (US 33); head animator Seymour Kneitel. The voice was that of William Costello, better known as Red Pepper Sam, whose experience as a talking gorilla on a radio show was thought to qualify him for the role. Success went to his head and he was fired as too temperamental, so Jack Mercer, an artist at the Fleischer Studio with a bent for imitations, took over. Popeye's friend Wimpy gave his name to a disagreeable type of British hamburger.

PORKY PIG
Warner Looney Tune *Haven't Got a Hat* (US 35).

ROAD RUNNER
Together with the Coyote, created by Chuck Jones and Michael Maltese in *Fast and Furry-ous* (US 48).

SPEEDY GONZALES
The Fastest Mouse in all Mexico debuted in Warner Bros' *Speedy Gonzales* (US 55).

SYLVESTER
Kitty Kornered (US 45). His constant prey Tweety Pie had preceded him on screen (see below).

TOM AND JERRY
Hanna-Barbera's *Puss Gets the Boot* (US 39). The love-hate relationship of the amiable adversaries was condemned in the seventies for its 'mindless violence'.

TWEETY PIE
Birdie and the Beast (US 44). American essayist S. J. Perelman held Tweety Pie personally responsible for what he regarded as a reprehensible British habit of referring to all felines as 'puddy tats'.

WOODY WOODPECKER
Knock Knock (US 40). The distinctive woodpecker voice was that of Grace Stafford, wife of Woody's creator Walter Lanz.

Puppets

The earliest use of puppets and live action together in a full-length feature film was by Segundo de Chomon in *La Guerra e il sogno di Momi* (It 16).

The first all-puppet feature film was Frederico Valle's political satire. *A Full-Dress Night at the Colon Theatre* (Arg 19). The first in Europe was Ladislas Starewitch's *Le Roman de Renard* (Fr 31) in which one three-minute sequence necessitated no less than 273,000 different puppet movements. The characters had as many as 150 heads each to capture the full range of expression. Electronically-controlled puppets were first used in Lou Bunin's *Alice in Wonderland* (GB/Fr 50).

16 Shorts and Documentaries

Advertising Films

The first advertising films were made in France, Britain, and the USA, in 1897. The single surviving American example of that year was copyrighted by the Edison Co. of West Orange, NJ, on 5 August 1897. The Library of Congress Catalogue records: 'The film shows a large, poster-type backdrop with the words "Admiral Cigarettes". Sitting in front of the backdrop are four people in costume: Uncle Sam, a clergyman, an Indian, and a businessman. To the left of the screen is an ash-can size box that breaks apart and a girl, attired in a striking costume, goes across the stage towards the seated men and hands them cigarettes. Then she unfolds a banner that reads, "We all Smoke".'

Advertising films were also made that year by the International Film Co. of New York, who were the first company to specialise in such productions. Their clients included Haig Whisky, Maillard's Chocolate and Pabst's Milwaukee Beer, and the films advertising these products were interspersed with entertainment films, in the manner of modern TV commercials, in a grand open-air free movie show in the centre of New York. The giant screen was set on top of the Pepper Building at 34th Street and Broadway and the films rear projected with a powerful Kuhn & Webster 'Projectorscope'. The projectionist was Edwin S. Porter, later to achieve fame as director of *The Great Train Robbery* (US 03). On this occasion, however, the only celebrity he achieved was in the police court, where he was charged with being a public nuisance and causing an obstruction by encouraging people to block the sidewalk.

Three different advertising films are known to date from 1897 in Britain. Walter D. Welford made a film called *The Writing on the Wall* for John Samuel Smith and Co. of Borough High Street, Southwark, manufacturers of bicycle tyres. This was shot in Tottenham and showed a man painting the words 'Ride Smith Tyres' on a brick wall. Rather more ambitious was a production by Arthur Melbourne Cooper of St Albans, which brought to light a contemporary poster for Bird's Custard. An old man is seen walking down stairs bearing a large tray of eggs. He misses his footing, trips, and the eggs cascade on to the floor. Cook

> The world's only archive devoted exclusively to advertising films was established in 1982 at the Poster Museum in the rue de Paradis, Paris. It contains some 25,000 publicity films and TV commercials dating back to the turn of the century.

has no need to worry, though, because she has a liberal supply of Bird's Custard Powder. The company made an agreement with Melbourne Cooper that he should be paid £1 for every copy of the film distributed. The third example comes from Nestlé and Lever Bros, who joined forces in 1897 to purchase 12 Lumière Cinématographes for a combined promotional exercise. Their initial effort was called *The Sunlight Soap Washing Competition* and was available free to showmen. Besides producing their own advertising films, Lever Bros and Nestlé's also sponsored films with no advertising content. On 7 February 1898 they premièred a film of the recent Test Match in Australia at the Alhambra, Leicester Square. This was so successful that it was followed in March by films of the Cambridge crew in training for the Boat Race and later by the Boat Race itself. Mellin's Baby Food also began giving 'advertising entertainments' with the cinematograph the same year.

The most sophisticated of the pioneer advertising films were made by the great French innovator Georges Méliès, who also made the earliest trick films and the earliest 'blue movies'. Méliès' first advertising film, made at his studio at Montreuil-sous-Bois, was for Bornibus mustard. The scene was a restaurant. Two diners get into an argument which grows so heated that they begin to pelt each other with mustard. The camera then cuts to a black table top on which a jumble of white letters are scattered at random. The letters are seen to form themselves into the slogan *Bornibus, sa moutarde et ses cornichons à la façon de la mère Marianne*—all except the 's' of 'Bornibus', which is unable to find its correct place and keeps bumping into the other letters. Méliès recalled that the erratic 's' was always greeted with gales of laughter.

Subsequent Méliès productions advertised shoe

Two frame enlargements from the earliest surviving advertising film in the world, which dates from 1897. (*Library of Congress*)

polish, flour, Chocolat Ménier, tortoiseshell combs, Moritz Beer, Mystère corsets, Xour Lotion (hair restorer), Delion hats and Dewar's Whisky. In the last named, ancestors step down from family portraits to sample the product. The Delion commercial showed live rabbits being pushed into one end of a Heath Robinson-type machine and emerging as fur hats at the other. An attempt was made to placate the animal lovers in the audience by then reversing the film to show the hats entering the machine and becoming live rabbits again. These films were projected on an open-air screen in the Boulevard des Italiens in Paris by Méliès' young daughter Georgette.

While cinema advertising films have lost much of their appeal to advertisers against the lure of television, a new technique for plugging products from the silver screen has been developed in recent years. New York based Associated Film Productions represents some 70 companies who are willing to pay considerable sums to have their products featured as props in a feature movie. Hence the choice of Cheerios, Budweiser and Quaker State Motor Oil as goods consumed in *Honky Tonk Freeway* (US 81) was by no means fortuitous, any more than the Hormel Chili eaten by Robert Redford in *The Electric Horseman* (US 79)—a story, incidentally, about one man's rejection of commercial sponsorship—or the Anhauser Busch beer commercials watched by Peter Sellers in *Being There* (US 79). Associated plugs 200 different brands and guarantees 'positive visibility' in five films a year for a fee in the region of $100,000—strictly small change compared to the cost of a TV commercial. The rewards can be considerable. Sales of Reese's Pieces, a type of peanut-butter candy, spiralled by 85 per cent after a plug in *E.T. The Extra-Terrestial* (US 82) that not only got noticed on screen but mentioned in many of the reviews as well.

The earliest known advertising film in colour was *Das Wunder/The Wonder* (Ger 25), an animated cartoon coloured directly on to the prints by means of a stencilling process. Directed by Julius Pinschewer, the two-minute film advertised 'World-renowned Kantorwicz Liqueur' and was notable not only for its colour but also its use of expressionism in the animated designs, some of them wholly abstract, of animator Walter Ruttmann.

The first British all-colour advertising film was *It's An Ill Wind* (GB 29), made for Tintex Dyes of London. The film related the drama of an office boy emptying a bottle of ink over the typist heroine's jumper. However, with the aid of Tintex Colour Remover and Tintex Dye, the jumper is made like new in the latest fashionable colour.

The first talkie advertising film was *Die Chinesische Nachtigall/The Chinese Nightingale* (Ger 28), an animated silhouette version of the Hans Andersen fairy tale made by the Tri-Ergon Co. of Berlin to advertise a new process they had developed for disc recording. Although the use of synchronised discs was common to many early sound film systems, the process Tri-Ergon were promoting had no apparent connection with film-making, their advertising talkie being made by the sound-on-film process they had pioneered six years earlier.

Britain's first advertising talkie was *Meet Mr York* (GB 29), a cartoon with animation by John Noble which was directed by Bertram Phillips of British Publicity Talking Pictures for Rowntree & Co. of York.

Between 1914 and 1942 the standard length for advertising films in Britain was five minutes. Generally they

A Victorian 'commercial'—one of the earliest advertising films made by Edwin S. Porter in 1897.

contained some element of narrative and often featured famous stars, such as Jack Hulbert and Cicely Courtneidge in a 1926 comedy made for Rufflette Curtain Tape. Shortage of film stock brought the 'story' advertising film to an end in World War II. In the USA, the use of major stars was rarer, partly due to the contract system but also because most advertising films were made in New York. One notable example, however, was a General Electric advertising film of 1933 which had Dick Powell and Bette Davis cast as a suburban couple extolling the virtues of dishwashers and garden floodlighting. Advertising films could also be an entrée for those who had yet to receive the summons to Hollywood. When the Bergström Department Store of Stockholm allowed a 16-year-old salesgirl to play a small role in *How Not to Wear Clothes* (Swe 21) they were unwittingly launching the screen career of Greta Garbo.

Aerial Film

The first film shot from an aeroplane was taken by L. P. Bonvillain, a Pathé cinematographer, piloted by Wilbur Wright at Camp s'Auvours, France, in September 1908. This was over a year before the first still photograph from an aeroplane was taken at Rheims.

The first aerial film of a topical event (non-aeronautic) was made by the Warwick Trading Co. for its *Bioscope Chronicle* newsreel on 21 April 1913. The film showed the Royal Yacht *Victoria and Albert* bearing King George V across the Channel on a visit to Paris, and the arrival at Calais. The pilot, B. C. Hucks, flew the cameraman straight back to Hendon, where a representative of the film company was waiting to rush the canister back to the laboratories.

The complete film of the King's journey from London to Paris, including the aerial sequences, was shown during the matinée performance at the Coliseum at 5.20 p.m. the same day.

Documentary

The term 'documentary' was first used by L. d'Herbeumont in the January 1924 issue of *Cinéopse* (Paris), referring to sponsored and industrial films. Its earliest use in English was by John Grierson in February 1926 in his review of Robert Flaherty's *Moana* (US 26) for the *New York Sun*. Flaherty is generally acknowledged as the first to have brought form and structure to documentary films, commencing with his study of Eskimo life. *Nanook of the North* (US 22); while Grierson himself is regarded as the father of Britain's between the wars 'documentary movement'.

The first documentary film: The majority of pre-1900 films were actualities, but the first of sufficient length to be considered a legitimate documentary record of its subject was *The Cavalry School at Saumur* (Fr 97), which ran for 1330 ft, about 20 min. At around the

The world's most beautiful woman? Nobody would have said so when this 16-year-old appeared in an advertising short called *How Not to Wear Clothes* (Swe 21), but they did when she conquered Hollywood as Greta Garbo.

same time Joseph Perry of the Salvation Army's Limelight Division at Melbourne, Vic., Australia, began shooting some 2000 ft of film illustrating the social work of the Salvation Army. Melbourne had been the first place in the world where the Salvation Army embarked on an organised programme of social work in addition to its traditional evangelism.

The first British documentary was Robert Paul's one-reel production *Army Life, or How Soldiers are Made* (GB 00), premièred at the Alhambra in London on 18 September 1900.

The first feature-length documentaries were Paul Rainey's eight-reel *African Hunt* (US 12); a dramatised production in five reels called *One Hundred Years of Mormonism* (US 12); and *Akaky Tsereteli's Journey Along the Racha and Lechkhuma* (Rus 12) by the Georgian director Vasily Amashukeli.

The first sound documentary for theatrical release was Tri-Ergon's *Life in a Village* (Ger 23), premièred at the Alhambra Theatre, Berlin in September 1923.

Industrial Films

The first industrial film was taken by the American Mutoscope & Biograph Co. for the American Ball Nozzle Co. of Atlantic City on 18 July 1896. The production was supervised by 'agent Stewart' of the American Ball Nozzle Co. and showed the company's product in use in a States fire-engine discharging its jet at maximum pressure. The demonstration took place on North Carolina Avenue before Chief Whippey, ex-Chief Lackey and other prominent members of the Atlantic City Fire Department. The cameraman was W. K. L. Dickson, inventor of the Edison Co.'s Kinetoscope, and the film was used by agents of the American Ball Nozzle Co. as a sales aid which could be shown in a portable Mutoscope. According to D. W. Griffith's cameraman, Billy Bitzer, who joined the American Mutoscope & Biograph Co. in 1896, the firm made other industrial films of 'loom-weaving materials which the travelling salesmen could use to show merchants what they were buying' and 'very large machines, whose working parts could be demonstrated by this method better than they could by chart'.

The first British industrial film was made by Messrs Lever Bros in 1898 and showed the work carried out in the various departments of their Port Sunlight soap factory. Admission to the showing of this film, which was accompanied by variety acts, was open to those producing a coupon enclosed with packets of Sunlight Soap. Mellin's Food gave similar exhibitions with free samples for the audience.

Other early sponsored films included an 1898 production by the Canadian Pacific Railroad designed to encourage emigration to Manitoba, a sales firm of

agricultural horse-rakes and self-binders in action made by a firm of Toronto agricultural engineers in 1899, and a documentary about the Alaskan Gold Rush of 1898–99 commissioned by the North West Transportation Co. The latter cost $40,000 to shoot, making it the most expensive motion picture production on record at that date. In 1904 the North Borneo Co. commissioned the Urban Trading Co. of London to make a film in Borneo as 'a way of bringing the shareholders into a direct knowledge of the country and usages where their money was invested'. Shareholders of America's Diamond Match Co. also had cause to be grateful for industrial films. In 1903 the Japanese government was negotiating with the company for the purchase of match-making machinery, but the board of the Diamond Match Co. suspected that the Japanese only wanted to see the machines in operation in order to copy them and so were unwilling to show them working. The Japanese insisted on a demonstration before purchase. Having reached stalemate, the Diamond Co. called in the Vitagraph Co. of New York to make a demonstration film showing the process without revealing details of the mechanism. The motives of the Japanese proved honourable; after seeing the film they signed a contract worth a million dollars.

The first industrial talkie was Western Electric's *Hawthorne* (US 24), a sound-on-disc production about the company's plant in the Hawthorne district of Chicago.

The highest budget for an industrial film was the $7·5 million spent by the Sony Corp. and Hollywood audio company Glen Glenn Sound on their 30 min, 70 mm *Digital Dream* (US 84)—equivalent to the cost of a medium-budget Hollywood feature. Made as a demo film to promote the technique of digital recording, the film had a computer-captured sound-track entirely in digital, recorded on the Sony PCM-3324. The film could be played back on any standard analog sound system, giving enhanced reproduction eliminating the 'generation losses' common to the editing of analog recorded sound-tracks.

News Films

The first news film (other than sporting events, q.v.) was made by photographer Birt Acres of High Barnet, Herts, on the occasion of the opening of the Kiel Canal by Kaiser Wilhelm II (1859–1941) on 20 June 1895. Besides the arrival of the Kaiser at Holtenau aboard his yacht *Hohenzollern*, Acres took films of the laying of a memorial stone, and of a number of other events held as part of the celebrations, including scenes of the Kaiser reviewing his troops at Hamburg and leading a procession through the streets of Berlin. He also filmed a charge of Uhlan Lancers at the Tempelhof Feld in Berlin, starting a news cameraman's tradition of taking risks in the cause of film reportage by arranging with their commander that the horsemen should charge direct at the camera. Seized with the desire to run for his life as the troop thundered towards him with drawn lances, he nevertheless continued to grind the handle of his camera and was afterwards congratulated by the CO as 'the pluckiest fellow he had ever met'. The first screening took place before the Royal Photographic Society on 14 January 1896.

The first news film shot in Britain was taken by Birt Acres on 27 June 1896 and showed the arrival of the Prince and Princess of Wales at the Cardiff Exhibition. Acres secured special permission to film the Royal party, on the proviso that he himself was not seen. Accordingly, a small aperture was cut in a canvas screen forming one side of a private walkway along which the Prince and Princess would approach the exhibition entrance. Since there was no corresponding hole for the viewfinder, Acres had to begin shooting on receipt of a signal from an official. He filmed the whole scene without being able to see anything of his subject. The film was premièred at a Command Performance at Marlborough House on 21 July 1896.

The first British monarch to be filmed was Queen Victoria (1819–1901) during her autumn holiday at Balmoral in 1896. She recorded the event in her diary for 3 October: 'At twelve went down to below the terrace, near the ballroom, and we were all photographed by Downey by the new cinematograph process—which makes moving pictures by winding off a reel of film. We were walking up and down, and the children jumping about. Then took a turn in the pony chair, and not far from the garden cottage Nicky and Alicky planted a tree.'

Downey was the Royal Photographer. The children who jumped about included the late Duke of Windsor, who must consequently have had one of the longest records of film appearances (including three acting roles) when he died in 1972. 'Nicky and Alicky' were the Emperor Nicholas II (1868–1918) and the Empress Alexandra Feodorovna (1872–1918) of Russia, who had arrived at Balmoral for an informal visit ten days earlier. The film was 'premièred' in the Red Drawing Room at Windsor Castle on 23 November 1896.

The first American President to be filmed was Grover Cleveland (1837–1908), outgoing President on the occasion of President-designate William McKinley's inauguration at Washington DC on 4 March 1897. The inaugural parade, covered by Edison, Biograph and Lumière cameramen, and by one E. H. Amet, included shots of Cleveland, then in the last hour of his Presidency. McKinley had been filmed by Biograph cameraman Billy Bitzer on 18 September 1896, shortly before the Presidential election.

The first Pope to be filmed was Pope Leo XIII (reigned 1878–1903) by Biograph cameraman W. K. L. Dickson in 1898. The film, which showed the Pope in his carriage, riding in his sedan chair, walking, seated on his favourite bench in the Vatican gardens, and bestowing the Papal blessing on an audience, was premièred at Carnegie Hall in New York on 14 December 1898 in the presence of Archbishop Corrigan.

Newsreels

The first newsreel was *Day by Day*, produced by Will G. Barker and presented at the Empire Theatre, Leicester Square, in 1906. It was issued daily except when fog prevented filming.

The first newsreel produced for general distribution was *Pathé-Faits Divers*, founded in Paris early in 1908 under the direction of Albert Gaveau. The name was soon changed to *Pathé-Journal*. Japan's *Daimai News* is variously claimed to have been founded in 1908 and 1909. This was literally intended as a moving-picture newspaper, having been established by the influential daily *Osaka Mainichi*, *Pathé-Journal* did a reverse operation, founding a weekly illustrated newspaper of the same name in November 1912. The photographic news reportage consisted of stills from the newsreel.

The first general newsreel in Britain was *Pathé's Animated Gazette*, founded in 1910, which survived, as *Pathé News*, until February 1969.

The first newsreel in the United States was *Pathé's Weekly*, of which the first issue came out on 8 August 1911, just ten days before its rival *The Vitagraph Monthly of Current Events*. In 1914 it was replaced by *Pathé Daily News*, but in 1917 it was no longer possible to obtain the safety film stock from France which gave Pathé the advantage over its rivals of being able to distribute daily by mail, and the newsreel reverted to weekly issue as *Pathé News* until its closure in 1956.

LOCAL NEWSREELS

This phenomenon seems to have begun with *Paterson's Pictorial Review*, inaugurated by an enterprising cinema owner in Aberdeen in 1907. Generally they emanated from the larger centres of population, such as Marcus Loew's *New York Weekly* (1914) and the San Francisco newsreel *Golden Gate Weekly* (1914), or they could be statewide, such as *Iowa News Flashes* (c. 1935), or regional, like Britain's *Northern Topical News Gazette* (1915) and the *Scottish Moving Picture News* (1917). A rare example of a local sound newsreel was *The Tatler News Reel*, serving the Merseyside area, which was instituted by Capital & Provincial News Theatres Ltd in October 1936. Smaller centres were also represented: Bradford Playhouse started showing 9·5 mm and 16 mm newsreels made by local amateurs in 1938 and the same year The Rex at Brighton introduced a local newsreel produced by the manager, Mr J. C.

Howe. Probably the smallest town in Britain to support a regular locally produced newsreel was Beverley, Yorks, where the manager of the Picture Playhouse, Mr Ernest Symmons, brought the events of the 10,000 strong community to the screen of his own cinema. America could boast a local newsreel serving an even smaller population. Skilled amateur cinematographer W. H. Miller, proprietor of the two cinemas in Cloquet, Minnesota, captured the doings of his 6000 fellow citizens in *The Cloquet Newsreel* which he founded in 1927.

FAMOUS OUTLAWS
CLYDE BARROW
Terror of the Southwest and his Gun Moll
"BONNIE" PARKER
Modern tigress, fast shooting, cigar smoking, blond Jezebel MEET DEATH AT GIBSLAND, LA.

ACTUAL AUTHENTIC PICTURES
Taken immediately after the death of these murderous lovers at the hands of the law.

See the Texas Cop Killers - Slayers of 10 men
— Extra Feature —
"BEYOND THE RIO GRANDE"
WITH 5 FAMOUS WESTERN STARS--- Featuring Jack Perrin, Buffalo Bill Jr., Pete Morrison, Franklin Farnum, Edmund Cobb and Starlight, the Wonder Horse.
An All-Talking Western for the Whole Family to See and Hear!

It was not often that the newsreel was billed above the feature. In this case though the slaying of Bonnie and Clyde took precedence over any horse opera.

The first regular sound newsreel was *Movietone News*, presented at the Roxy Theater, New York, on 28 October 1928. The subjects covered included Niagara Falls, the Army-Yale football game, 'Romance of the Iron Horse', and Rodeo in New York. Regular weekly issue of *Movietone News* to cinemas throughout the USA commenced 3 December 1928.

The first British sound newsreel was *British Movietone*, commencing with an issue showing the Derby and the Trooping of the Colour which was released on 9 June 1929. It survived as the last remaining newsreel produced in Britain.

The first unscheduled event to be captured by the sound newsreel camera was the assassination attempt on Prince Humbert of Italy on 24 October 1929. Cameraman Jack Connolly of *Movietone* had hidden himself behind the Tomb of the Unknown Warrior in Rome in order to secure forbidden pictures of the Prince and Princess paying tribute to the Italian war dead. He had just been discovered by the police when a shot was fired at the Prince, but fortunately the camera was still running and the sound equipment operating.

The last newsreel in the United States was *Universal Newsreel*, founded as *Universal Animated Weekly* in 1913, of which the final issue was released on 22 December 1967. At its peak it was showing in 3300 cinema theatres, but with the competition of television declined to a circulation of 1100.

The last newsreel in Britain was *Movietone News*, founded as *British Movietone* in 1929 (see above), which suffered a decline from its circulation of over 2000 a week at the peak in World War II to only 200 a week when the final issue was released on 27 May 1979. The sign-off items were the Chelsea Flower Show, 'Our Capital City' (London from the air) and 'Highlights of 50 Years'.

> Early sound newsreels were often shot silent and sound effects added afterwards. According to *Picturegoer* (30 April 1932), 'one firm who owned a specially good crowd track put it on every crowd scene they issued. It was easily recognisable to anyone in the trade because at a certain point a dog barked.'

The major remaining producer of newsreels is China, with over 20 studios devoted to their production.

The most costly newsreel ever made was the *Gaumont British* edition of 24 October 1934, which included scenes of the Centenary Air Race shot at Melbourne, Victoria. The Australian footage was mitted to Britain frame by frame by beam wireless for 68 hours at a cost of some $4000 a foot or $30,264 for the brief sequence of 160 frames. It was shown in 1500 cinemas within 48 hours of transmission.

The only woman news cameraman was Dorothy Dunn, a member of the *Universal Animated Weekly* crew in America during World War I.

SPECIALISED NEWSREELS

These have catered to various minorities and sectional interests since the early twenties. The first all-black newsreel was produced by the Renaissance Co. of New York in 1922 and a sound newsreel for blacks called *All-American News* was established in 1942. The last newsreel to be established anywhere in the western world, Heyns Films' *Topical News*, was founded as recently as 1975 to cater to the black population of South Africa. A number of newsreels for women were produced in America, including *Eve's Film Pictorial* in the early 1920s, the world's first colour newsreel, *McCall Fashion News* (1925), and Fox's *Fashion Forecast*, which ran from 1938 to 1940.

Children were catered to in America by *The Junior Newsreel* (1934). Other newsreels were made by young people themselves. In England the boys of Mill Hill public school started the *Mill Hill School Animated News* in 1920. On the other side of the Atlantic *Dartmouth College News* (1928) was a regular 16 mm newsreel made by the college film club for circulation to alumni, and Culver Military Academy was producing a weekly newsreel in 1929.

A sponsored newsreel, the *Ford Animated Weekly*, was produced by the Ford Motor Co. between 1914 and 1921, succeeded by the *Ford News*, which was for circulation to Detroit theaters only, in 1934. A different type

of sponsored newsreel, *Kinograms*, which had commercials interspersing the news items, was introduced on 28 August 1931. The sound was recorded on disc—the only sound newsreel ever to use the synchronised disc system.

Naked capitalism was matched by a socialist newsreel called *The Workers' Newsreel*, of which 16 issues were produced in the USA (1931–32) by the Film & Photo League, an offshoot of the militant Workers' International Relief.

The William J. Ganz Co. of New York began issuing a monthly *Highlights of the News* for home-movie buffs in 1927. A similar enterprise in Britain was Fox Photos' *Film-at-Home News*, inaugurated in September 1933 at an annual subscription of £25 for a 200 ft reel monthly.

Israel produced a *Monthly Newsreel for Immigrants* between 1966 and 1968.

The only all-cartoon newsreel was *Topical Sketch*, founded in Britain in July 1915. Wallace Carlson's *Canimated Nooz Pictorial*, released weekly by Essany from May 1916 to mid-1917, had photographic heads on pen-and-ink bodies. A regular comedy newsreel, titled *Crazy Newsreel*, was issued by 'Gaumont-Skittish News'—otherwise Gaumont–British—from 1937 to 1939.

Soviet Russia has a satirical newsreel called *Fitil/The Fuse*, which deals chiefly with the shortcomings of the bureaucracy. Established in the days of Khruschev's 'thaw', and allowed to survive as a safety valve against discontent, each ten-minute monthly issue comprises a playlet, a documentary report and a cartoon. The documentary sequence of a recent *Fitil* showed children walking to school in the rain, despite regulations enjoining local authorities to supply transport. When the bureaucracy replied that the situation had now been rectified, another issue of *Fitil* showed the same schoolchildren still walking to school, this time in a snowstorm.

Scientific Films

The first anthropological film was made by F. Reynault in 1895 of an African negress making pottery at the Colonial Exhibition in Paris. An analysis of the technique revealed by the film was published under the title 'Poterie crue et origine du tour' in the *Bulletin Société Anthropologique Paris*. The following year Reynault made film studies of the attitudes adopted by recumbent and sleeping negroes and in 1897 he followed this with a film demonstrating tree climbing methods. In 1900 he secured the adoption of this resolution at the International Ethnographic Congress in Paris: 'All anthropological museums should add suitable film archives to their collections. The mere possession of a potters' wheel, a number of weapons or a primitive loom is not sufficient for a full understanding of their functional use; this can only

In 1940 a decree was published in Nazi Germany forbidding anyone to enter or leave a cinema during the showing of the newsreel. The decree was enforced without difficulty; the doors of cinemas were locked until the newsreel ended. The following year Iran, struggling to maintain neutrality, introduced a statute obliging exhibitors to show both a British and a German newsreel in every programme. Neutral Eire took a different tack—they simply banned all newsreels containing war footage.

be handed down to posterity by means of precise cinematographic records.'

The first anthropological film shot on location was a 3000 ft study of the tribal rites of Australian aborigines, taken by University of Melbourne biologist Baldwin Spencer in 1901 with a Warwick Biograph camera at Charlotte Waters, Northern Territory. The film was accompanied by didgeridoo music, recorded on an Edison wax cylinder as the film was being shot.

The first medical films were made by pioneer Polish cinematographer Boleslaw Matuszewski at hospitals in St Petersburg and Warsaw, beginning in May 1897. The subject matter of his earliest attempts included surgical operations—one of them a leg amputation—difficult births and the behaviour of mental patients. Matuszewski was dissatisfied with the results because his camera was defective, but the following year he purchased one of French make and during April and May 1898 he filmed at the Saint-Antoine and de la Pitié hospitals in Paris under the direction of Drs Ballet, Brissaud and Balinski. The results were shown before an invited audience at Warsaw on 3 September 1898, the most impressive films being one of nervous disorders and another of an operation involving removal of part of the skull.

The first medical films taken in Britain were made by a Dr Parchen of London in the spring of 1898 and showed a case of *locomotor ataxia*, in which the patient was unable to stand with the feet together and eyes closed, another of a patient suffering from partial paralysis, with clear views of the wasting of the muscles, and a third of the effects of hip-joint disease. In June of the same year the eminent Parisian surgeon Dr Doyen commissioned Clement Maurice to film his work. By repeated filming of the same operation, Doyen was able to refine his technique by the elimination of all wasteful and unnecessary movements, thereby reducing the time taken to operate and increasing the patient's chances of survival. Although activated by the highest motives, the distinguished surgeon was not above a little self-advertisement. Some years later Eclipse–Radios–Urban released a film called *The Operations of Dr Doyen* (Fr 08), which showed five amputations in the goriest detail. This was shown as entertainment and

was hugely successful, especially in Russia, where audiences often became hysterical and many fainted.

The first American medical film was *Epileptic Seizures* (US 05), shot at Boston with a Biograph camera by Walter G. Chase.

The first medical talkie was a film about internal urethrectomy made at King's College Hospital, London, by the Kodak Medical Department and premièred before the Royal Society of Medicine on 27 June 1929. The commentary, by Sir John Thomson-Walker FRCS, OBE, Senior Lecturer in Uriology, was on synchronised disc. The first American medical talkie was a film of Dr C. R. Murray setting a broken ankle, made at the College of Physicians and Surgeons, Columbia University in 1930. The commentary was by Dr Murray himself.

Microscopic cinematography was first achieved by American scientist Dr Robert L. Watkins, who filmed the action of bacteria through a microscope in 1897.

X-ray cinematography was pioneered by Dr J. Macintyre of Glasgow, who showed a film of the movements of the knee joint of a frog before the Glasgow Philosophical Society in March 1897. Since X-ray motion picture film did not exist, Macintyre had roentgenograms (X-ray stills) taken in sequence and then recorded them on standard cinematographic film. This technique was the earliest application of animation. Direct kinetoentgenography, using X-ray motion picture film, was first achieved by A. E. Barclay in the USA in 1933.

Serials

The first serial was the 12-episode Edison production *What Happened to Mary* (US 12), starring Mary Fuller as a foundling seeking her lost inheritance, of which the first episode was released on 26 July 1912. It has been claimed that the film was not a true serial, but a *series* of episodes each complete in itself. Although it is true that the cliffhanger element, an essential element of later serials, was missing from *What Happened to Mary*, in fact the denouement was not revealed until the final episode, and the various adventures were all part of a continuing storyline. *The Adventures of Kathlyn* (US 13) added the missing ingredient, leaving audiences in an agony of suspense at the end of each episode until the final triumph of the heroine.

The first British serial was *Boy Scouts Be Prepared* (GB 17), directed by Percy Nash in eight parts for Transatlantic films and featuring Sir Robert Baden-Powell playing himself. The story was of a squire's son and a miner's son who join the Scouts and foil a gipsy spy who is supplying fuel to U-Boats. Only three other serials were produced in Britain prior to World War II: Hepworth's *The Amazing Quest of Mr Ernest Bliss* (GB 20), starring Chrissie White and Gerald Ames;

Torquay & Paignton Photoplays' *The Great London Mystery* (GB 20), starring the celebrated magician David Devant and Lady Doris Stapleton; and a solitary talkie serial, Mutual's *Lloyd of the CID* (GB 31), with Charles Saunders in the title role. Between 1946 and 1969 another 26 serials, all of them designed for children's cinema matinées, were produced in Britain.

Other countries commenced serial production with the following films: *Fantomas* (Fr 13); *Sonka, The Golden Hand* (Rus 14); *Los Misterios* (Sp 15); *Les Habitants de la Lenora* (Arg 17); *Ram Banvas* (Ind 18); *The Man in the Black Cape* (It 18); *La Belgique martyre* (Bel 19); *El Automovil gris* (Mex 19); *Die Herrin der Welt* (Ger 20); *El Genio del mal* (Cuba 20); *Sekai no Jo-jo/Queen of the World* (Jap 25). Besides America, France and Spain were the only countries to make many serials.

The first talkie serial was Mascot Pictures' 10-episode jungle yarn *King of the Kongo* (US 29), starring Jacqueline Logan, Walter Miller and Boris Karloff.

The longest serial was *The Hazards of Helen*, directed in 119 one-reel episodes by J. P. McGowan and James Davis for Kalem, and starring Helen Holmes (episodes 1–26), Elsie McLeod (episodes 27–49) and Helen Gibson (episodes 50–119). The first episode was released on 7 November 1914; the last on 24 February 1917. The complete picture had a running time of over 31 hours.

The last Hollywood serial was Columbia Pictures' unremarkable *Blazing the Overland Trail* (US 56), directed by Spencer Bennet.

SERIAL OUTPUT
During the 44-year life of the episode film, American studios put out an estimated 350 silent serials and 231 talkies.

Sports Films

The first film of a sporting event was taken at the Edison Laboratories, West Orange, NJ, and depicted a six-round boxing match fought between Mike Leonard and Jack Cushing on 14 June 1894. Leonard, the better known fighter, was paid $150 for his services and his opponent $50. The ring was only 12 ft square, in order that all the action might be followed by the immobile camera. Having knocked Cushing out in the last round, Leonard summed up after the fight: 'I hit him when I liked and where I liked. I'd hit him oftener, only Mr Edison treated me right and I didn't want to be too quick for his machine. I generally hit 'im in the face, because I felt sorry for his family and thought I would select the only place that couldn't be disfigured.' The film was premièred at a Kinetoscope parlour at 83 Nassau Street, New York, probably at the beginning of August 1894. From a commercial point of view it was not a complete suc-

cess, as each round was shown in a different Kineto-scope peep-show machine for which a separate charge was made. At 10c a round, it cost 60c to see the whole fight, so most patrons opted to pay a single dime to witness the knock-out round only.

The first British sports film and the first anywhere in the world of a regularly scheduled sporting contest was made by Birt Acres of the Oxford and Cambridge Boat Race on 30 March 1895.

The first motion picture of a horse race was also taken by Acres, of the Epsom Derby on 29 May 1895.

The earliest known film of a football match was made by R. W. Paul at Newcastle upon Tyne, England, in November 1896.

Baseball was the subject of a dramatic movie, Edison's *Casey at the Bat* (US 99), just before the turn of the century.

The earliest known record of a basketball game was filmed by American Mutoscope & Biograph at Missouri Valley College (a girls' school) in 1904.

Travelogue

The first travelogue of sufficient length and variety to warrant the term was R. W. Paul's *Tour in Spain and Portugal* (GB 96), a 600-ft film made by cameraman Henry Short during a five-week tour of the two countries in September 1896. It comprised 14 scenes of Lisbon, Madrid and Seville, including a bullfight, and was premièred at the Alhambra Theatre in London on 22 October 1896. At the end of October, Paul issued a booklet publicising the film, a forerunner of the exhibitors' campaign book.

The term 'travelogue' was coined by Burton Holmes, who presented his first such movie, a 50 ft view of St Peter's, Rome, at Oak Park Presbyterian Church, Chicago, in 1897.

In the days when newsreel reportage was as important a means of communication as television news today, it was not unknown for battles to be delayed pending the arrival of the cameramen. On 3 January 1914 the Mexican bandit general Pancho Villa signed a contract with the Mutual Film Corporation assigning them the rights to all battle coverage and undertaking that, whenever possible, battles would be fought in daylight hours and at such times as were convenient to the Mutual cameramen. Villa was as good as his word. He postponed his attack on the city of Ojinaga until the camera operator, engaged elsewhere, arrived to record the victory. In a more savage theatre of war, the Nazi destruction of Gdynia in Poland in 1939 was delayed to allow time for cameramen to move forward and film the German forces from in front as they attacked.

War Film

The first war to be filmed was the Graeco–Turkish War of 1897. Sole cameraman in the field was British war correspondent and pioneer cinematographer Frederick Villiers (1852–1922), who filmed the Battle of Volo in Thessaly, Greece, in April. He wrote in his memoirs: 'Luckily I was well housed during the fighting in front of Volo, for the British consul insisted on my residing at the consulate. To me it was campaigning in luxury. From the balcony of the residence I could always see of a morning when the Turks opened fire up on Valestino Plateau; then I would drive with my camera outfit to the battlefield, taking my bicycle with me in the carriage. After I had secured a few reels of movies, if the Turks pressed too hard on our lines I would throw my camera into the vehicle and send it out of action, and at nightfall, after the fight, I would trundle back down the hill to dinner.' These first historic war films were destined never to be seen by the public. When he finally arrived back in London, Villiers found to his consternation that Star Films of Paris had already flooded the market with dramatised reconstructions of the campaign and there was no demand for the genuine article. He was equally unlucky the following year when he filmed the Battle of Omdurman from a gunboat on the Nile. As the gunboat's battery opened up, the camera tripod collapsed and Villiers' camera hit the deck, the magazine fell out and the film was exposed to the light.

The earliest surviving news film taken during a military campaign consists of scenes of the 5th Northumberland Fusiliers at Orange River, South Africa, during the Boer War of 1899–1902. Made by John Bennett Stanford on 12 November 1899, it is preserved in the National Film Archive.

Frederick Villiers, the first war cinematographer, on the bicycle he rode during the Graeco–Turkish War of 1897. (*Stephen Bottomore*)

17 Television and the Movies

The first film shown on television was British Sound Film Productions' *The Bride* (GB 29), featuring George Robey, which was transmitted experimentally from the Baird Television Studios in Long Acre, London, on 19 August 1929.

The first television station to show films as part of their regular programme service was the De Forest Radio Corporation's W2XCD Passaic, NJ, commencing 1 March 1931. These were mainly documentary and travel shorts, two of the earliest to be aired being *People Who Live in the Desert* (US 30) and *Lumbering in British Columbia* (Can 30). Five days later the Baird Co. followed suit in Britain, starting with a boxing short and airing a Chaplin comedy with the Keystone Cops on 9 March.

The first full-length feature film shown on television was *Police Patrol* (US 25), transmitted in six daily episodes by W2XCD Passaic, NJ, 6–11 April 1931. Directed by Burton King for Gotham Productions, it related the story of a New York policeman (James Kirkwood) who arrests a girl thief (Edna Murphy) the exact double of his sweetheart (also Edna Murphy).

The first feature films shown on television uninterrupted were Cecil B. DeMille's *This Day and Age* (US 33), with Richard Cromwell, and John Cromwell's *The Texan* (US 30), with Gary Cooper, which were both aired by Don Lee Television of Los Angeles on stations W6XS and W6XAO during September 1933. The TV image had 80-line definition.

The first feature film shown in scheduled service in Britain was *The Student of Prague* (Ger 35), starring Anton Walbrook and Dorothea Wieck, transmitted by the BBC on 14 August 1938.

The first film made for television was a short silent comedy titled *Morgenstude hat Gold im Munde/The Early Bird Catches the Worm* (Ger 30), produced by F. Banneitz of Commerz-Film AG, Berlin, on behalf of the German Reichs-Rundfunkgesellschaft. Intended specially for transmission by low-definition television, the actors' movements were exaggerated for visual emphasis and the costumes were designed for greater tonal contrast than in a normal cinema film.

The first film drama made for high definition television was *Wer fuhr IIA 2992?/Who was Driving Car Number IIA 2992?* (Ger 39), a thriller scripted by Gerhart W. Göbel of the Reichspost and produced by UFA in Berlin. Göbel devised the plot after seeing a police announcement on television appealing for help in a murder case. The scenario centred round a hit-and-run driver, since the Nazi Propaganda Ministry would not allow murder as a theme for films to be shown abroad. The film was first shown during television demonstrations in Bucharest and Sofia in 1940 and was also used after the war when the German Post Office resumed experimental transmissions in 1950.

The first British television film drama and **the first TV film aired in scheduled service** was *A Dinner Date with Death* (GB 50), a pilot for a TV series titled *The Man who Walks by Night*, shot at Marylebone Studios by Vizio Films Ltd, 11–14 July 1949, and transmitted by BBC Television on 28 September 1950. Produced by Roy Plomley of *Desert Island Discs* fame, the film was directed by Eric Fawcett, scripted by Duncan Ross, and starred Patricia Jessel and James Cairncross. Designed for a half-hour programme with a break for commercials, it was also **the first British television drama to be televised on network TV in America.**

The first of the major Hollywood studios to enter television production was Columbia, when Ralph Cohn, nephew of production chief Harry Cohn, asked for $50,000 to start a subsidiary for filming TV product. Cohn Snr complied on condition that the $50,000 should be the first and last demand. It was. On 12 June 1952 Columbia Screen Gems, as the subsidiary was named, announced a contract to produce 39 *Ford Theater* programmes for the Ford Motor Co., who would pay 75 per cent of the cost of the first-run rights. The decision of the majors to join television rather than to fight it was a wise one; ultimately it was to mean the survival of Hollywood.

The first feature-length television film or TVM was *High Tor* (US 56), a whimsical ghost story starring Bing Crosby as an idealist who refuses to sell High Tor, a peak of the Palisades on the Hudson River, to property speculators. The film, networked coast-to-coast on 10 March 1956, was shot in twelve days at a cost of $350,000 and is chiefly notable for the fact that it featured Julie Andrews in her American TV debut. *Films in Review*'s critic commented: 'The commercials were a welcome relief'.

TVM OUTPUT

Since regular production of TVMs began in America in 1964, over 1600 have been produced for the US networks. Average budget is currently $2·2 million.

The first of the major Hollywood studios to sell television rights to its films was RKO in December 1955. The studio's entire pre-1949 film library of 740 features was purchased from Howard Hughes by Thomas F. O'Neil of General Teleradio Inc. for a package deal price variously reported as $15 million and $25 million. First of the RKO package to reach the small screen was *King Kong* (US 33) early in 1956. New York's WOR-TV was so overwhelmed at its good fortune in having a genuine Hollywood release to play—formerly only foreign product had been aired—that they transmitted it twice every day for a week. Once RKO had breached the big studios' agreement to have no truck with the tube, the others followed suit, Warner Bros selling off their pre-1949 library to Associated Artists Productions for $21 million in February 1956.

The first motion picture based on a television play was a Merton Park 'B' picture directed by Michael McCarthy titled *Assassin for Hire* (GB 51), scripted by Rex Rienits from his own 1950 TV production.

The first American film from a TV play was Delbert Mann's *Marty* (US 55), with Ernest Borgnine, from writer Paddy Chayevsky's acclaimed TV production about a shy New York butcher courting an equally shy schoolteacher. The motion picture version, which won Academy Awards for Best Picture, Best Director, Best Actor and Best Screenplay, was very much in the TV genre of simple narratives about simple people in a familiar setting, and at variance with Hollywood's fantasy world of the rich and successful living in a world of opulent but emotionally wrought make-believe.

Courtesy Alan Parker.

The first television series based on a film was the BBC's 20-year long marathon *Dixon of Dock Green* (1955–76), starring Jack Warner in the role of Dixon, who had actually been killed off in *The Blue Lamp* (GB 49). In the USA *Peyton Place* (US 57) gave rise to the 1964–69 TV series of the same name.

The first motion picture based on a TV series was *It's a Great Day* (GB 56), with the original cast of Roland and Michael Pertwee's TV series *The Groves*.

The country with the highest number of televised films is Italy, where over 500 stations transmit more than 2500 films a week. The total of approximately 130,000 movies annually (many of course duplicated) equals the entire world output of feature films for the last 30 years.

TV VERSIONS OF THEATRICAL MOTION PICTURES

Films shown on television are generally cut to fit the available programme time, but occasionally the reverse takes place. The TV versions of *Requiem for a Heavyweight* (US 62), *Earthquake* (US 74), and *Airport 77* (US 77) were all expanded by the inclusion of footage edited out of the theatrical version. The two *Godfather* movies (US 71 and US 74) were combined in 1978 to make one marathon TVM lasting 7½ hours. Titled *Mario Puzo's The Godfather. The Complete Novel for Television*, the new version was not only resequenced, so that the saga was related chronologically, but also set a record for expansion—some 75 minutes of out-takes, equivalent to a short feature by itself, was added to the film. The material added to *Earthquake* actually introduced a new character (played by Debralie Scott) and in the case of Joseph Losey's *Secret Ceremony* (GB 68), the producers shot additional scenes three years later to enable the film to fit a two-hour slot on American television. The additions, according to Losey, 'exactly reversed the meaning and intention of my film'.

According to the Association of Independent Producers, 97 per cent of film watching in Britain is done outside cinemas—mainly on TV and video.

MOVIES ON TV: WHO SHOWS WHAT?

Countries of Origin

A total of 1569 feature-length films were shown on British television in the London region during 1984. (Figures for the other TV regions would differ marginally according to how many films were scheduled on ITV–1.) The channel airing the most movies was BBC–1 with 423, or 27 per cent, but Channel 4 almost equalled this figure with 422.

American product dominates the airwaves, representing 63·3 per cent of the total. There was a wide disparity, however, between the proportion of American films shown by BBC–1 and ITV–1. On BBC–1, 76 per cent of the movies aired were American and only 20 per cent British. ITV–1 had a more equal division, with 49·5 per cent of its films hailing from the US and 47 per cent being domestic product.

Films from other English-speaking countries totalled 39, over half of which were aired on BBC–2. Most were from the Antipodes—19 from Australia and 6 from New Zealand—with 11 Canadian productions, two from Ireland and a single South African entry with the engaging title of *e' Lollipop* (SA 75).

Ninety foreign-language films were shown on British television during 1984. France led with 30, followed by Italy with 18, West Germany with 10, India 9, Japan 3, and Mexico and Sweden 2, while countries represented by a single movie each included USSR, Israel, Senegal, Cameroon, Mauritius and Iran. Channel 4 showed the most foreign language movies, with 42 during 1984, representing 10 per cent of its total.

The Old and the New

ITV–1 shows the most up to date product, nearly 35 per cent of films televised in 1984 having been premièred in the previous ten years, though Channel 4 had a higher proportion of 1980s productions—17·1 per cent against ITV–1's 13·7 per cent. (Generally the minimum period before an English-language film made for theatrical release may be aired is three years—most of the more up to date films shown on television are TVM's or foreign language product.) The channel devoting the most airtime to vintage movies is BBC–2, over half of whose films dated from the 1950s or earlier. These included a dozen silent films, though the oldest full-length feature film of all on TV in 1984, the 70-year-old *Tillie's Punctured Romance* (US 14), was shown by Channel 4.

Films on TV in 1984: countries of origin

	BBC–1		BBC–2		ITV–1 (London)		CHANNEL 4		All channels	All channels %
	Number	%	Number	%	Number	%	Number	%		
US films	321	75·9	261	66·1	163	49·5	248	58·7	993	63·3
British films	85	20·1	81	20·5	154	46·8	127	30·1	447	28·5
Other English-language films	10	2·4	20	5·1	4	1·2	5	1·2	39	2·5
European films	6	1·4	29	7·3	6	1·8	27	6·4	68	4·3
Other (inc. USSR)	1	0·2	4	1·0	2	0·6	15	3·6	22	1·4
Total	423		395		329		422		1569	

The most popular film ever shown on US television was *Gone with the Wind* (US 39), which scored a Nielsen rating of 47·6 (ie 47·6 per cent of all sets monitored were showing the film) and a 65 share (65 per cent of all sets turned on in monitored homes were tuned to the film) when the first part was aired on 7 November 1976. The second part was transmitted the following day, scoring a Nielsen rating of 47·4 and a 64 share.

Bob Hope on televised movies: 'The other night I saw a Road picture so cut to make room for 45 commercials that Bing and I weren't even in it.'

Films on TV in 1984: the old and the new										
	BBC–1	%	BBC–2	%	ITV–1	%	CHANNEL 4	%	TOTAL	
										%
1910–14	–		–		–		1	0·2	1	0·1
1915–19	–		–		–		1	0·2	1	0·1
1920–24	–		3	0·8	–		2	0·5	5	0·3
1925–29	–		9	2·3	–		5	1·2	14	0·9
1930–34	6	1·4	6	1·5	3	0·9	32	7·6	47	3·0
1935–39	22	5·2	14	3·5	10	3·0	54	12·8	100	6·4
1940–44	28	6·6	44	11·1	7	2·1	73	17·3	152	9·7
1945–49	37	8·7	42	10·6	18	5·5	43	10·2	140	8·9
1950–54	25	5·9	36	9·1	19	5·8	27	6·4	107	6·8
1955–59	31	7·3	48	12·2	22	6·7	19	4·5	120	7·6
1960–64	16	3·8	34	8·6	31	9·4	14	3·3	95	6·1
1965–69	51	12·1	30	7·6	41	12·5	13	3·1	135	8·6
1970–74	96	22·7	41	10·3	64	19·5	24	5·7	225	14·3
1975–79	81	19·1	70	17·8	69	21·0	42	10·0	262	16·7
1980–84	30	7·1	18	4·6	45	13·7	72	17·1	165	10·5
Total	423		395		329		422		1569	
BBC=818 (52·1%)					ITV=751 (47·9%)					

The **longest film shown on television** in a single day was the 8 hr 27 min epic *War and Peace* (USSR 67), transmitted by Mexico's Channel II on 28 February 1981. **The longest on British television** was Tony Palmer's *Wagner* (GB 83), with Richard Burton, which ran for 5 hr 15 min (including commercial breaks) on Channel 4 on 6 January 1985.

The first feature film to be premièred on television was *African Journey* (Fr 47), with Victor Francen and Harry Baur, which was transmitted by WNBT New York on 1 January 1948.

The first feature to be premièred on network television in the USA was *The Constant Husband* (GB 55), with Rex Harrison and Kay Kendall, transmitted by NBC on 6 November 1955.

The highest fee paid for television rights to a movie was $35 million by CBS to MGM in April 1978 to televise *Gone with the Wind* (US 39) 20 times over the following 20 years. The value of the TV rights represented about 6½ times the production cost of the film.

The highest fee paid for television rights to a British movie is an unconfirmed $20 million to Goldcrest Films by Embassy Communications for US–Canada TV and cable airing of *Gandhi* (GB/Ind 83).

The highest price paid for British TV rights to a movie was an unconfirmed £2,250,000 by the BBC for *The Sound of Music* (US 65) in 1978.

The only Hollywood film ever shown on Soviet television is the Jane Fonda–Susannah York melodrama *They Shoot Horses, Don't They?* (US 69). A tragedy set against the background of a six-day dance marathon in the Depression era, it gave a sufficiently unflattering view of American society to be reckoned ideologically sound for Soviet viewers.

The lowest fees paid for film rights by any national TV network are by Bermuda, where US product may earn as little as $90. Zambia pays in the region of $100 and Haiti from $100 to $200. The most profitable market outside the US is Great Britain, where the two networks pay within the $60,000–250,000 price range for quality product and more for blockbusters.

In the US home market, new films with star names but only modest box-office potential sell to the networks for figures in the $4–6 million region.

Video Films

The first video films were offered for hire by Sears, Roebuck in the USA at $3–6 each in the spring of 1972. Titles included *Stagecoach* (US 39), *Hamlet* (GB 48), *High Noon* (US 52), *The Bridge on the River Kwai* (GB 57), *Cactus Flower* (US 69) and *The Anderson Tapes* (US 71). They were for showing on the Avco Cartavision video player, which retailed at $1600. The first video films for sale were put on the market by Andre Blay of the small Michigan-based company Magnetic Video, who acquired the rights to 50 Fox productions in 1977. The initial titles, which included *M*A*S*H*, *Hello Dolly* and *Patton*, sold for $50 per cassette.

The first film produced expressly for the video market (excluding pornography) was *Tangier* (GB 82), starring Billie Whitelaw.

The highest sales for a video film was achieved by Paramount's *Raiders of the Lost Ark* (US 81), which topped one million in worldwide cassette sales in November 1984. The wholesale value was $25 million. Rights earnings to producer George Lucas from the US and UK sales alone have amounted to over $2.3 million.

> The highest official price for video recorders is in Iran, where a Sony Betamax sells for $11,000. Home video is the only way Iranians can view American films, since none are shown at cinemas. Most tapes are pirate copies brought in from England by an Indian ring.

The highest fee paid for video rights was $60 million by Warner Bros for the foreign rights to the entire United Artists catalogue in 1983. The US rights were bought by Magnetic Video for $44 million—the second highest fee. World rights for individual Hollywood films range between $50,000 and $1 million.

The highest fee paid for video rights to an individual movie was an estimated $15 million by CBS/Fox Video in 1984 for the George Lucas production *The Empire Strikes Back* (US 80).

The country with the highest sale of video films is the USA, with a total of 9 million in 1983. The UK followed with sales of 5·5 million, compared to 7 million for the whole of the rest of Europe. Japanese sales totalled 3 million.

Worldwide ownership of VCRs is estimated at 57 million (1985). The USA has over 16·5 million, Japan has 13,330,000 sets, the UK over 6 million, West Germany approaching 5 million, France 2·2 million, Australia nearly 2 million, the Scandinavian countries 1·5 million and Spain 1 million.

The biggest penetration of VCRs is in Kuwait, where 92 per cent of homes have sets. Total number is 500,000. Among major countries, Australia and Britain have the highest penetration, each with some 30 per cent of TV households equipped with VCRs at mid-1984. It is expected that both countries will achieve 50 per cent penetration by 1986 or 1987. The number of sets in Britain is estimated at 6·25 million. Their users watched an average of 4·5 video films a month.

> A report that 50 per cent of children between 7 and 16 had seen at least one 'video nasty' caused shock and alarm in Britain. Two Birmingham psychologists decided to test the validity of the survey by visiting the same schools and asking the children if they had seen films with 'made-up' horror titles. They found that 68 per cent of the children claimed to have seen the non-existent films on video.

The country with the highest sales of VCRs is the USA, where 7·3 million units were bought in 1984, bringing the total of sets in operation to 16·5 million. Penetration is estimated at 17 per cent of television homes.

MOST POPULAR FILM VIDEOS
According to research on the British video market conducted by Guild Home Video in 1983, the most popular film genre among people renting for home viewing is thrillers with 24 per cent of the total. Horror follows with 21 per cent, followed by comedy at 17 per cent, sci-fi 13 per cent, pornography 9 per cent, children's films and westerns each 7 per cent and musicals 3 per cent. Video renters seem to watch as many movies as cinema audiences in the halcyon days of the 1940s. According to the same survey, 84 per cent of hirers rent at least one video film a week, 46 per cent between two and five films a week, and 5 per cent more than five films a week.

18 AmateurFilms

The first home-movie outfit was the 35 mm Motor-graph projector-cum-ciné camera offered for sale at 12 gns (£12·60) by W. Watson & Sons of High Holborn and advertised for sale in the *British Journal of Photography Almanac* in November 1896. Like most early amateur projectors, it was designed to be used in conjunction with a magic lantern as light source. The machine itself was tiny, measuring only 6×4×5½ in (15×10×14 cm), and was undoubtedly the first camera small enough to be held in the hand. However, due to the wide arc of the turning handle—the name Motorgraph was a misnomer, as it was not motorised—it would have been unsteady unless mounted on a tripod. Used as a projector, the film ran through the gate into a basket, since there was no take-up spool; for use as a camera, film magazines were fitted to the top and bottom. Watson's also supplied a range of about 100 films available to the home-movie enthusiast.

The first sub-standard gauge home-movie outfit was the Birtac, also a combined camera and projector, which was designed by pioneer film-maker Birt Acres and marketed in Britain in 1898 at a price of 10 gns (£10·50), or 12 gns (£12·60) including a developing and printing outfit. The film used was 17·5 mm gauge, chosen because it could be produced by simply slitting standard 35 mm film down the middle. It was supplied in 20 ft daylight-loading cartridges at 2s 6d (12½p) a roll. For projection illumination an upright Welsbach mantle fed from the domestic gas supply was used, the gas being pressurised in a bag with weights loaded on to it. Picture size was claimed to be up to 3×4 ft (0·9×1·2 m).

The first commercially produced films on sub-standard stock for home use were 25 ft subjects in 17·5 mm gauge offered by the Warwick Trading Co. in April 1899 at 10s (50p) each. They could be shown on the Birtac or the Warwick Trading Co.'s own Biokam projector.

An astonishing range of home movie outfits was available to the Victorian amateur cinematographer. Besides the Motorgraph (1896), the Birtac (1898) and the Biokam (1899), English enthusiasts had the choice of the Cynnagraph projector, marketed at 5 gns (£5·25) in September 1898, the French-made Pocket Chrono of

The world's first home movie outfit. The front part of the 1896 Motorgraph could be detached for use as a cine-camera; in conjunction with the lantern at the rear it was a serviceable projector.

1899 at £7, or the La Petite—British made despite its name—offered for £5 10s (£5·50) in 1900. Across the Channel, Oskar Messter of Berlin listed an Amateur-Kinetograph, plus library of films for home viewing, in his October 1897 catalogue. In the same year Reulos & Goudeau of Paris produced the Mirographe and it was they who were to coin the term 'amateur cinematography' for the hobby in 1900. In 1899 Faller's 'ciné-matographe des familles' was introduced.

The first motorised amateur cine camera, the Gaum-ont Pocket Chrono, was introduced in 1899.

Considering the number of home movie outfits which were available by 1900, it is surprising how little is recorded about the pioneer amateur film-makers themselves. None of their films are known to survive and few of their names have come down to us.

The earliest amateur film that can be positively dated (though no longer extant) was made by Russian enthusiast A. P. Fedetsky, who shot some scenes of Cossack trick riders at Kharkov on 29 September 1896. In Britain, the same year, William George Barker started to make his own films; when he had a sufficient number to make up a programme he began giving free film shows. Barker was the first of many amateurs so smitten with cinematography that he decided to turn professional. In 1901 he founded the Autoscope Co. and became one of Britain's major studio heads of the silent era. The first woman known to have taken up the hobby was a Mrs Main, who received favourable mention in Cecil Hep-

Most of the big Hollywood stars of the twenties and thirties had their own private cinemas in which to indulge the exquisite pleasure of watching themselves on screen. Mexican-born Ramon Novarro (1899–1968) scored extra points for self-advertisement by putting his own name up in lights above the door.

worth's *Animated Photography: The ABC of the Cinematograph* (London 1900) for her 'animated pictures of snow sports in the Alpine regions'—evidence that the holiday home movie was pioneered in the reign of Queen Victoria.

The earliest known home movie of a wedding was made for the Marquis and Marchioness of Bute on the occasion of their marriage at Castle Bellingham, Ireland in 1904.

In Shanghai between the wars it became customary to have a film made of family funerals—provided the funeral was sufficiently opulent to enhance the family's social status.

The first private cinema was installed at Esplanade House, Bombay, by millionaire industrialist Jamshedjee Tata in 1898.

The first royal cinematographer was the Crown Prince of Siam, whose enthusiasm for the hobby was noted in 1914. He also had his own private cinema in the Palace at Bangkok.

The first 16 mm camera and projector was the Ciné-Kodak Model A and the Kodascope Model A, respectively, both marketed by the Eastman Kodak Co. of Rochester, NY, on 5 July 1923. The original intention when development of the new gauge began under J. G. Capstaff in 1920 was to introduce a 17·5 mm safety film, but this was rejected owing to the possibility of unscrupulous dealers splitting 35 mm nitrate stock and selling it to amateurs. The choice of 16 mm was a purely arbitrary one, being close to 17·5 mm but obviating this danger. The immediate success of 16 mm was mainly due to the fact that the orthochromatic safety film supplied by Kodak served as both negative and positive, reducing costs considerably.

The first 8 mm camera and projector was introduced by Eastman Kodak in August 1932. The camera used a special 16 mm film which was run through twice,

Even by the early 1920s, inept home movies had earned a reputation for boring the pants off long-suffering guests, as this *Punch* cartoon demonstrates.

THE FAMILY ALBUM: NEW STYLE.

Hostess. "NOW I MUST JUST RUN THROUGH ONE MORE FOR YOU. THIS IS MY BROTHER ARCHIBALD HAVING BREAKFAST IN THE GARDEN, IN TWO REELS."

once in each direction, then slit down the middle after processing. This almost halved the cost of home-movie making. Super-8 mm was introduced in 1965. The perforations were made smaller to allow a 50 per cent larger frame, and much improved definition.

For other sub-standard gauges, see p. 123.

The first cine-camera with battery-operated motor was the British-made 9·5 mm Midas of 1934.

The first amateur cine club was Cambridge University Kinema Club, founded by Peter Le Neve Foster and friends on 28 November 1923. The club's first production was *The Witches' Fiddle* (GB 24). The first British club open to general membership was the Amateur Cinematographers' Association, established in May 1926 with studios in Upper Charlton Street, London W1.

The world's first amateur cine club open to general membership was the Barcelona Kinema Club, established at the end of 1923 with headquarters in disused studios at Horta.

The first amateur film contest, as well as the first film awards amateur or professional, was held in Monte Carlo in 1898 (see p. 200). The first for sub-standard gauges was sponsored jointly by *Photoplay* magazine and America's Amateur Cinema League and was for

the best 35 mm, 16 mm and 9·5 mm movies submitted by 15 February 1928. Prizes of $500 in each of these divisions went respectively to the Motion Picture Club of the Oranges for their comedy *And How!*, Mr B. V. Covert of Lockport, NY for a film about quail hunting, and Clarence Underwood of St Louis for his film about St Louis Zoo. The producer of *And How!*, refrigerator engineer Russell T. Ervin, was awarded a five-year contract with Fox on the strength of the picture.

The first British contest was organised by the committee of the National Ciné Convention for films submitted by 17 October 1929. There were 14 classes of award, including Best Amateur Film Play, Best Travelogue, Best Topical, Best Colour, Best Trick Photography, Best Cartoon and Best Film Illustrating a Gramophone Record. Entries were judged by two directors, the Hon. Anthony Asquith and the Hon. Ivor Montagu, and Danish star Carl Brisson.

The first home talkie projector was the Baker Kinematograph, produced in Canada in 1904. The images of the film were arranged in a spiral on a disc and shown in synchronisation with accompanying sound discs played on a gramophone. The first to use conventional film was the 16 mm De Vry Ciné-Tone, a synchronised record apparatus working on the same principle as Warner's Vitaphone system. It was marketed in the USA at $250 in the spring of 1929 for use with a library of De Vry Ciné-Tone home talkies.

The first to use sound-on-film was the British-made B.T.H., introduced in 1932, which used double perforated 16 mm film. The first home talkie system using single perforated 16 mm film—the standard used today—was the RCA PG-30, which came on the market in the USA later the same year.

The first amateur talkie was an interview with aviator Sir Alan Cobham made by the 'Audiofilm' process in 1928 by Owlpen Pictures, a film society based in Bowden, Cheshire.

The first amateur dramatic talkie was *The Opera Singer*

The amateur gauges: only 8 mm and 16 mm are used today by amateur film-makers, but 9·5 mm still flourishes among collectors of historic movies. (Date of introduction appears in brackets.) *(Grant Lobban Collection)*

(a) 4·75 mm Pathé Monoplex (1955).
(b) Standard 8 mm (1932).
(c) Super-8 mm (1965).
(d) 9·5 mm (1922)—silent and sound.
(e) 16 mm (1923)—silent and sound.
(f) 17·5 mm Birtac (1898)—the first sub-standard gauge.
(g) 17·5 mm Biokam (1899).
(h) 17·5 mm Duoscope (1912).
(i) 17·5 mm Pathé Rural (1925).
(j) 22 mm Edison Home Kinetoscope (1921).
(k) 28 mm Pathé K.O.K. (1912).

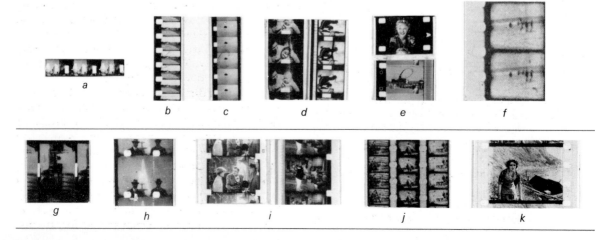

a b c d e f

g h i j k

Eva Braun depicted 'the appalling normality of Hitler's home life' in amateur footage taken at Berchtesgaden.

(GB 29), made on 9·5 mm stock by Apex Motion Pictures of London by a process called 'Cinephone'. Devised by Leslie Wood, the technique used was not divulged. The members of the group asserted categorically that it was not a synchronised disc system and would only admit to having acquired the equipment needed 'from Caledonian Market on Christmas Eve and a suburban lunatic asylum'. The film was completed by the middle of January 1929.

Amateur footage has been used to compelling effect in some documentary features, most notably in Philippe Mora's *Swastika* (GB 73), which contained colour sequences filmed in Agfacolor by Hitler's mistress Eva Braun at Berchtesgaden. The film was only discovered when Lutz Becker, researcher on *Swastika*, happened to meet an ex-Marine at a party in Houston, Texas. The Marine had been a member of a raiding party which had taken Berchtesgaden in 1945 and he had seized some cans of film found in Eva Braun's bedroom. Becker located the badly damaged film in the US Marine Corps archives in Washington and arranged for the best footage to be restored. Sequences used in *Swastika* showed Hitler dancing a jig, drinking tea on the terrace, patting blonde haired children paternally on the head and strolling with Von Ribbentrop against a dying sun. A German lip reader was engaged to deduce what the Fuhrer and his friends were saying to each other, which turned out to be mainly banalities of the 'Let's go for a walk' kind. An actor was coached to speak as Hitler spoke conversationally—as opposed to the ranting style of his speeches—and the voice dubbed on to the sound-track of the home movie footage. Although *Swastika* won critical acclaim and was selected as Britain's official entry at Cannes, it also provoked outraged condemnation from those who considered it dangerous to reveal what one reviewer called 'the appalling normality of Hitler's home life'.

Pioneer video-disc? Charles Urban's Spirograph home movie system, introduced in 1923, used a 10½ in disc bearing 1200 images each measuring 5·6 mm×4·1 mm. Unfortunately it was launched the same year as 16 mm. The rest is history.

The first amateur talkie in the USA was the University of Virginia's *The Highest Degree* (US 29), a three-reel comedy directed by Prof. H. R. Pratt of the School of Dramatics and featuring members of the university dramatic society, The Virginia Players. The 35 mm film was in production in May 1929.

The first colour film for amateur use was Kodacolor, marketed in the USA by Eastman Kodak in July 1928. The two-colour additive process had been developed by French inventor R. Berthon, and Kodak had acquired the rights from the Société du Film en Colours Keller-Dorian in 1925. A special Kodacolor screen was needed ($25), as well as a banded filter for the camera ($15) and another for the projector ($18). The price of Kodacolor film stock was $6 for 50 ft. In Britain, Kodacolor was demonstrated for the first

MAKE YOUR MOVIES IN NATURAL COLOURS...

How much better every shot you take would look in colour. Hitherto you have not been able, either easily or inexpensively, to capture the delight of natural colours for your home cine screen. Now, with DUFAYCOLOR CINE FILM you can take coloured pictures with your 16 mm. cine camera, the only additional apparatus required being a filter supplied free with each spool of film.

And you can show DUFAYCOLOR on your own projector without any alteration or addition; spliced· in with your black-and-white film if necessary. Increased illuminating power is not required.

DUFAYCOLOR 16 mm. Cine Film is sold in 50 ft. and 100 ft. daylight-loading spools—and the price includes processing.

DUFAYCOLOR
16 mm. Safety
CINE FILM

ILFORD LIMITED · ILFORD · LONDON

The first three-colour film stock for amateur use, Dufaycolor, was introduced in 1934. (*Backnumbers*).

time before the Royal Photographic Society on 18 October 1928 and introduced commercially the following year.

The first three-colour film stock for amateur use was 16 mm Dufaycolor, marketed in Britain by Ilford Ltd in 1934. In the USA the first three-colour stock was 16 mm Kodachrome in 1935; 8 mm Kodachrome followed in 1936.

The first film society was the Bungei Katsudo Shashin Kai (Literary Motion-Picture Society), founded in Tokyo, Japan in 1912 with the intention of encouraging the exhibition of foreign films based on works of literary merit.

The first film society in Britain was the Stoll Picture Theatre Club, established on 3 January 1918 with an inaugural programme in which Baroness Orczy presented *The Laughing Cavalier* (GB 17), an adventure movie she had scripted from her own novel. Subscription to the society was one guinea (£1·05) a quarter, which included a season ticket and admission to the club rooms at the Stoll Picture Theatre, Kingsway. Lectures were delivered every month, beginning with popular novelist E. Temple Thurston on 'The Future of the Author for the Film', in which he castigated directors for 'insisting upon constant action to the detriment of the author's idea'. Other early speakers included T. P. O'Connor, Hannen Swaffer, Hillaire Belloc, G. K. Chesterton and St John Ervine, a selection which suggests a pronounced literary bias to the proceedings, though there were occasionally talks of a more general nature, such as 'German Film Propaganda' at the March 1918 meeting.

The first film society in Europe was Le Ciné-Club, founded in June 1920 by Louis Delluc and others at a conference held at La Pépinière cinema in Paris. It had been preceded some ten years earlier in Germany by what might be described as an anti-film society, an institution called the Goethe Society which was established 'to combat the evil influence of the cinema'.

Index

NAMES

Aasen, John 100
Abbott and Costello 91
Acres, Birt 9, 10, 11, 121, 123, 169, 189, 213, 214, 218, 225
Alberini, Filoteo 146, 147
Alexandra, Queen 84, 185, 188, 189
Alexandranov, Grigori 119
Ali, Muhammed 84, 89
Aman, Zeenat 99, 107, 117
Anderson, G. M. 74, 75
Anderson, Dame Judith 74, 75
Andress, Ursula 98, 158
Andrews, Julie 91, 102
Arbuckle, Roscoe 79, 160, 184
Arliss, George 87
Armat, Thomas 10
Armstrong, Charles 206
Arness, James 101
Arzner, Dorothy 118, 200, 201
Astaire, Fred 98, 106
Astor, Mary 82, 107
Attenborough, Sir Richard 128, 142
Autry, Gene 25, 75, 80, 131, 184
Avery, Tex 209

Bai, Jadan 152
Balfour, Betty 58, 90
Bancroft, Anne 82, 94, 95
Bankhead, Tallulah 82
Bara, Theda 82, 98, 114
Bardot, Brigitte 82, 83, 98, 114
Barker, Lex 48
Barker, Will 78, 151, 161, 214, 225
Barry, Iris 22
Barrymore, Diana 78
Barrymore, Ethel 82
Barrymore, John 78, 87, 107
Barrymore, Lionel 45, 82, 125
Bates, Alan 62
Beaudine, William 119
Beery, Noah 82, 94
Beery, Wallace 203
Belafonte, Harry 51
Bellew, Dorothy 82
Benchley, Peter 40
Bendix, William 82
Bennett, Constance 114
Benson, E. F. 192
Bergen, Candice 120, 128
Bergman, Ingmar 38, 40
Bergman, Ingrid 91, 102, 114
Berle, Milton 82
Bernhardt, Sarah 40, 76, 137
Bernstein, Lord 139, 180
Bertini, Francesca 79
Biggs, Ronald 84
Bisset, Jacqueline 120
Bitzer, Billy 108, 124
Black, Karen 80
Blackton, J. Stuart 196, 206, 207
Blatty, William Peter 40
Bogarde, Dirk 37, 65, 95, 186
Bogart, Humphrey 34, 78, 82
Bois, Curt 94
Bonaparte, Napoléon 49, 50
Bonnaire, Sandrine 84
Boutonnat, Laurent 120
Bow, Clara 62, 86, 88, 99, 101, 183, 183
Boyd, William 103
Brando, Marlon 65, 80, 202, 203
Brian, Mary 1
Brisson, Carl 102
Bronson, Charles 80, 98
Bronston, Samuel 129
Brook, Clive 47
Brooks, Louise 94, 115
Brown, Joe E. 82, 86, 87, 136
Brownlow, Kevin 127, 128
Bubna, Countess 126

Burns, George 104, 105, 203

Cagney, James 80
Cameron, Earl 51
Cantor, Eddie 70, 78, 82, 139
Caprice, June 61
Cardinale, Claudia 99
Carradine, John 52, 57, 90
Carrick, Edward 122
Carter, James Earl 122
Chambers, John 126
Chandler, Raymond 45
Chaney, Lon 78, 91, 126
Chaplin, Sir Charles 26, 27, 77, 78, 79, 81, 82, 90, 102, 105, 115, 120, 125, 153, 164, 179, 182, 184, 185, 196, 199
Charisse, Cyd 95, 106
Chekhov, Anton 43
Chevalier, Maurice 82, 86, 98, 105
Chrétien, Henri 146, 191
Christian IX, King 188
Christie, Julie 80, 82
Churchill, Sir Winston 45, 49, 186
Cianelli, Rosina 113
Clark, Marguerite 91, 99, 107
Cleopatra 49
Cleveland, President Grover 54, 139, 214
Close, Ivy 99
Cochran, C. B. 171
Cody, William 74, 75, 84
Cohl, Emile 206
Cohn, Harry 39, 221
Colbert, Claudette 203
Compson, Betty 82, 136
Connery, Sean 80, 91
Coogan, Jackie 82, 85
Coolidge, President 55, 139
Cooper, Arthur Melbourne 110, 172, 206, 210
Cooper, Gary 82, 91, 96, 186, 202, 220
Coppola, Carmine 89, 203
Coppola, Francis 203
Corman, Roger 128
Cortez, Ricardo 82, 95
Coward, Noel 153
Crawford, Joan 69, 70, 78, 82, 86, 91, 92, 93, 96, 97, 115
Cristiani, Quirino 208
Cromwell, John 104
Crosby, Bing 82, 91, 95, 102, 221
Cukor, George 119, 120
Curtis, Tony 79, 95
Curtiz, Michael 84, 119, 122
Cusak, Cyril 94, 146
Cushing, Peter 47, 57
Custer, General 75

Damita, Lil 98
Dandridge, Dorothy 51
D'Annunzio, Gabriele 39
Davis, Bette 82, 91, 95, 96, 98, 102, 103, 212
Davis, Gary 131
Davison, Grace 113
Day, Doris 82, 91
De Carlo, Yvonne 95
Dee, Sandra 95
De Forest, Lee 139, 149, 220
De Havilland, Olivia 82
DeMille, Cecil B. 44, 84, 86, 125, 129
De Mille, William 37, 122
De Oliveira, Manoel 119
De Treaux, Tamara 99
Dickens, Charles 34, 43
Dickson, W. K. L. 7, 8, 22, 111, 192
Dietrich, Marlene 79, 82, 115, 163
Dillinger, John 165
Dillman, Bradford 98
Disney, Walt 28, 136, 184, 201, 207, 208, 209

Dolby, Ray 144
Donskoi, Mark 119
Dors, Diana 82, 95
Dressler, Marie 91
Duarte, Eva 163
Dumas, Alexandre 34, 43
Dunaway, Fay 78, 115, 203
Durante, Jimmy 82, 105
Duval, Shelley 125
Dwan, Allan 119, 153
Dyer, Anson 208

Eastwood, Clint 38, 91, 101
Eddy, Nelson 98
Edison, Thomas 7, 8, 9, 121, 123, 130
Edward VII, King 189, 214
Edward VIII, King 88, 186, 214, 216
Edwards, Blake 121
Eisenhower, President 55, 187
Eistenstein, Sergei 27, 122
Ekberg, Anita 98, 99
Elizabeth I, Queen 49
Elizabeth II, Queen 49, 186
Elvey, Maurice 119

Fairbanks, Douglas 24, 79, 81, 82, 90, 91, 105, 122, 129, 182
Faithful, Marianne 43, 44, 82
Farmer, Frances 78
Farnandel 96
Farrell, Charles 91
Fassbinder, Rainer Werner 26
Fetchit, Stepin 96
Field, Sally 91
Fields, W. C. 78, 82
Finch, Peter 203
Firestone, Elizabeth 152
Flaherty, Robert 212
Fleischer, Max 208, 209
Fleming, Victor 38
Fletcher, Louise 203
Flynn, Errol 82, 187
Fonda, Henry 52, 82, 136, 203
Fonda, Jane 91, 203
Fontaine, Joan 51, 92, 93
Forbes-Robertson, Sir Johnston 43
Ford, Glenn 91, 184
Ford, John 119
Forsyth, Bill 38, 66, 144
Franco, General 45

Gable, Clark 78, 82, 91, 98, 117, 203
Gabor, Zsa Zsa 82, 95, 99
Gance, Abel 119, 143
Garbo, Greta 80, 82, 87, 98, 115, 153, 196, 199, 212, 213
Gardner, Ava 82, 98
Garland, Judy 96, 98
Garson, Greer 82, 98, 203
Gary, Romain 61
Gaynor, Janet 82, 91, 99
Gelovani, Mikhail 103
George V, King 49, 188, 189
George VI, King 186, 189
Gibbons, Cedric 158
Gibson, Helen 131
Gielgud, Sir John 92, 94, 142
Gilbert, John 82, 156
Gish, Dorothy 24, 92, 115, 125
Gish, Lillian 3, 24, 92, 94, 104, 106, 125, 151, 162, 185
Glyn, Elinor 118, 127
Goddard, Paulette 82, 92, 93, 98
Goebbels, Josef 42, 165
Goldwyn, Samuel 30, 79
Goncalves, Alvaro 127
Grable, Betty 91, 106, 184
Granger, Stewart 47, 82, 95, 132
Grant, Cary 82
Greene, Graham 89
Greer, Ethel 101

Grey, Zane 42, 73
Grierson, John 212
Griffith, Corinne 78, 106
Griffith, D. W. 24, 36, 39, 43, 61, 108, 109, 110, 113, 114, 115, 118, 121, 124, 125, 126, 139, 151, 152, 162, 173, 182
Gründgens, Gustaf 65
Guinness, Sir Alec 94
Guy, Alice 117, 118, 126, 153

Hagman, Larry 82, 83
Haines, William 91
Hall, Philip Baker 94
Hanaway, Frank 131
Hannah, Daryl 72
Hardy, Oliver 27
Harlow, Jean 78, 82, 94
Harris, Julie 93
Harron, Bobby 92, 108
Harry-Krimer 94
Hart, William S. 27, 82, 91
Hawks, Howard 143
Hayden, Sterling 82, 125
Hayes, Helen 94
Hays, Will 160
Hayward, Rudall 119
Hayworth, Rita 39, 95
Head, Edith 114, 201
Heath, Harold 118
Hefner, Hugh 25, 89
Hemingway, Ernest 89
Hepburn, Audrey 88
Hepburn, Katherine 91, 98, 202, 203
Hepworth, Cecil 161, 189, 192, 225
Herrman, Bernard 152
Hillyer, Lambert 75
Hitchcock, Alfred 30, 119, 125, 130, 137, 141, 149, 152
Hitler, Adolf 49, 93, 165, 186, 229
Hoffman, Dustin 80, 126, 203
Holden, William 80, 82, 91
Hope, Bob 44, 80, 82, 91, 95, 222
Hope-Bell, Norman 126
Hope-Jones, Robert 150
Hopper, Dennis 125
Howe, James Wong 111
Hudson, Rock 91
Hughes, Howard 28, 120, 161, 221
Hunt, Linda 99, 100
Hurt, John 126
Hussey, Olivia 80
Huston, John 119, 166, 200
Huston, Walter 203
Hutton, Betty 82

Ivory, James 127
Ireland, Jill 98
Ingram, Rex 145

Jaffe, Sam 104
Janis, Elsie 127
Jannings, Emil 142, 184
Jarman, Derek 62, 146
Jenkins, C. Francis 10
Jesus Christ 49
Jhabvala, Ruth 127
Joan of Arc 49
Johnson, Noble 49, 88
Jolson, Al 78, 82, 102, 141, 151, 152
Joly, Henri 137
Jones, Buck 75
Jost, Jon 38
Junge, Winifred 127
Justin, John 51

Kalmus, Dr Herbert 136
Kapoor, Shashi 93, 107
Karloff, Boris 126, 218
Keaton, Buster 27, 78, 82, 86, 95
Keaton, Diane 91
Kellerman, Annette 29, 61, 63, 78, 81
Kelly, Grace 91, 187

Kennedy, President 53, 55
Kiel, Richard 101
Knight, Esmond 94
Komar, Prof Victor 149
Komarov, Sergei 81
Korda, Sir Alexander 79, 199
Krishnan, N. S. 102
Kristel, Sylvia 81, 99
Kubrick, Stanley 125
Kuleshov, Lev 119
Kurosawa, Akira 38

Ladd, Alan 35, 83, 100
Laemmle, Carl 27, 30, 76
Lahr, Bert 104
Lake, Veronica 83
Lamarque, Libertad 163
Lamarr, Hedy 61, 63
Lambert, Christopher 48
Lamour, Dorothy 83, 117
Lange, Jessica 78
Langlois, Henri 22
Larsen, Viggo 39
Lauder, Sir Harry 80
Laurel, Stan 27
Lauste, Eugene 10, 138
Lawrence, Florence 76, 79, 84, 196
Lean, David 26, 27
Lee, Bruce 79
Lee, Christopher 47, 57, 90, 101
Leigh, Vivien 98
Lelouch, Claud 38
Lemmon, Jack 79, 83, 91
Lenin, Vladymir 49
Leo XIII, Pope 214
Leone, Sergio 122, 158
Le Prince, Louis Aimé 7, 121
Leroy, Baby 104, 105
Lewis, Jerry 91
Lincoln, Abraham 53
Lincoln, Elmo 48
Linder, Max 90, 100
Lindgren, Ernest 22
Lindsay, Vachel 193
Lloyd, Harold 27, 79, 82, 184
Lobova, Tamara 114
Lockwood, Margaret 164
Loder, John 1
Lollobrigida, Gina 99
Lom, Herbert 95
Lombard, Carole 79, 98
London, Tom 88
Loren, Sophia 82, 99, 100
Losey, Joseph 221
Love, Bessie 58, 82, 93, 94
Lowe, Edmund 45, 105, 141
Loy, Myrna 98, 115
Lubitsch, Ernst 142
Lucas, George 127
Lukas, Paul 142
Lumiere brothers 8, 9, 10, 27, 123,
    167, 189, 190
Lusiardo, Tito 30
Lutyens, Elizabeth 152

McAvoy, May 84, 99
McCallum, David 153
McCambridge, Mercedes 203
McCartney, Paul 86
McCrea, Joel 73
MacDonald, Jeanette 83, 98
MacGraw, Ali 91
McKenna, Siobhan 106
Mackenzie, Sir Compton 40, 41,
    47, 89
McLaglen, Victor 45, 92
McLaren, Norman 208
McQueen, Steve 35, 80
Mamoulian, Rouben 122, 136
Mao Tse-Tung 49
Marceau, Marcel 44
March, Fredric 202, 203
Marshall, George 119
Martin, Dean 91, 95
Marvin, Lee 91
Marx, Groucho 95
Mason, James 100
Massey, Raymond 47
Matthau, Walter 95
Matthews, A. E. 104
Mauch twins 94

Mayer, Louis B. 156
Mayo, Virginia 83, 184
Meighan, Thomas 91
Melford, Jakidawdra 118
Méliès, Georges 42, 60, 111, 112,
    123, 210, 211
Merchant, Ismail 127
Merkel, Una 142, 184
Messter, Oskar 77, 109, 123, 131,
    137
Meyer, Russ 65
Miller, Glenn 152
Milligan, Spike 93
Mitchum, Robert 153
Mix, Tom 27, 79, 91, 102
Monroe, Marilyn 79, 82, 91, 96,
    107, 125, 196
Moore, Colleen 91, 115, 182
Moore, Dudley 100
Moore, Roger 47, 87, 88
Mussolini, Benito 45

Nash, Clarence 209
Nazimova 79
Nazir, Prem 90, 98
Negri, Pola 83, 115, 153, 186
Nesbitt, Cathleen 104
Newfield, Sam 119
Newman, Paul 83, 91
Niblo, Fred 38
Nicholas II, Tsar 184, 214
Nichols, Dudley 203
Nichols, Mike 118
Nicholson, Jack 203
Nielsen, Asta 27, 40, 77, 79, 90
Niven, David 82, 84, 95
Nixon, Richard 54, 55, 94
Noble, Joe and George 208
Novak, Kim 83, 91, 95, 99
Novarro, Ramon 82, 226
Novello, Ivor 79, 90

Oakley, Annie 72
Oberon, Merle 82, 83
O'Brien, George 28
O'Brien, Pat 95, 103
O'Keeffe, Miles 48
Olivier, Sir Lawrence 79, 98, 102,
    186, 202
Olmi, Ermano 38
O'Neal, Tatum 35, 203
O'Neill, James 81
Orlova, Lubova 79
Owen, Reginald 46, 47

Pabst, G. W. 145
Palmer, George 119, 126
Parks, Gordon 118
Parks, Larry 78, 83
Parton, Dolly 91
Patrick, Lee 34
Paul, R. W. 8, 9, 109, 111, 121, 167,
    189, 212, 218
Pele 153
Picasso, Pablo 87
Pickford, Mary 24, 31, 32, 39, 79,
    81, 83, 90, 91, 105, 110, 112,
    114, 124, 182, 199
Pidgeon, Walter 86, 98
Pirou, Eugene 60
Plomley, Roy 220
Poe, Edgar Allan 43
Poitier, Sidney 91, 203
Polo, Eddie 83, 185
Pommer, Erich 151
Porter, Edwin S. 39, 109, 111, 126,
    148, 210, 212
Powell, Dick 83, 93, 212
Powell, William 98
Preminger, Otto 161
Pryor, Richard 51
Pyshkova, Galina 114

Quinn, Anthony 105, 203

Raft, George 79, 96
Raimi, Sam 120
Raizman, Yuli 16, 119, 120
Ralston, Esther 200
Rasputin, Grigori 49
Rathbone, Basil 47

Ray, Satyajit 142
Reagan, Ronald 55, 83, 187
Redford, Robert 80
Redgrave family 92
Reed, Oliver 62
Reid, Wallace 83, 91, 160
Reynolds, Burt 80, 83, 91
Reynolds, Debbie 83, 99
Richardson, Sir Ralph 83
Richardson, Tony 28
Riefenstahl, Leni 127
Rigg, J. H. 190
Robertson, Cliff 53, 55
Robeson, Paul 88
Robinson, Bill 'Bojangles' 79
Robinson, Dar 131
Rock, Joe 201
Rogers, Charles 182
Rogers, Ginger 98, 114
Rogers, Roy 75, 83
Rogers, Will 27, 79, 83, 91, 93, 102
Roland, Gilbert 94, 96
Rome, Stewart 26, 79, 90, 95
Romm, Mikhail 163
Rooney, Mickey 88, 91, 93, 98
Roosevelt, President F. D. 45, 55
Roosevelt, President
    Theodore 54, 55
Rosher, Charles 112
Roth, Lillian 79
Rothapfel, S. L. 147, 174
Russell, Jane 28
Russell, Ken 62
Russell, Rosalind 92, 93

Sale, Chic 24, 139
Salkind, Alexander 38
Schulberg, Budd 193
Scott, George C. 47, 203
Segal, George 34
Selander, Lesley 75
Sellers, Peter 121
Selznik, David O 38, 74, 114
Sembene, Ousmane 51
Shakespeare, William 34, 40, 42
Shaw, Susan 51
Shearer, Douglas 141, 203
Shearer, Norma 82, 83, 92, 93,
    141, 203
Sheen, Martin 83, 128
Sherman brothers 203
Shields, Brooke 27, 83
Shostakovich, Dmitri 150
Shurey, Dinah 118
Sidney, Sylvia 62, 93, 122
Sims, G. R. 192
Sinatra, Frank 83, 184
Sitwell, Dame Edith 139
Skladanowski brothers 8, 10, 109,
    137
Smith, Albert E. 206
Smith, G. A. 109, 110, 135
Speed, Lancelot 206
Spence, Bruce 101
Spielberg, Steven 127, 129
Spillane, Mickey 40
Stalin, Josef 49, 103, 163, 186
Stallone, Sylvester 80, 91, 102
Stanwyck, Barbara 83
Starewitch, Ladislas 206, 209
Steiger, Rod 126
Steiner, Max 152
Stewart, Anita 83, 91
Stewart, Nellie 81
Streep, Meryl 91, 203
Streisand, Barbra 120, 203
Strick, Joseph 164
Sullavan, Margaret 87
Swanson, Gloria 27, 45, 83, 99,
    139, 153, 163

Tabora, Diogones 208
Talmadge, Constance 83, 84
Talmadge, Norma 83, 91
Talmadge, Richard 131
Tak-Hing, Kwan 103
Tanaka, Kinuyo 90
Taylor, Alma 12, 45, 79, 90, 189
Taylor, Elizabeth 34, 35, 65, 80, 88,
    91, 114
Taylor, Estelle 83, 107

Taylor, Robert 98
Temple, Shirley 80, 91, 98, 106,
    117, 184, 186, 203
Thatcher, Margaret 49
Thorndike, Dame Sybil 139
Thorpe, Richard 119
Tolstoy, Alexander 34, 43
Toomey, Regis 107
Toth, André de 149
Tracy, Spencer 98, 202
Tree, Sir Herbert Beerbohm 76, 78
Trenker, Luis 145, 186
Trewey, Felicien 10, 11, 150
Trimmingham, Ernest 88
Trotsky, Leon 67, 89
Truffaut, Francois 38
Tucker, George Loane 61
Turner, Florence 99
Turner, Lana 88, 95
Turpin, Ben 83, 105

Valentino, Rudolph 28, 30, 79, 82,
    91, 101, 105, 121
Vanel, Charles 126
Van Loon, H. H. 44
Van Peebles, Melvin 118
Veidt, Conrad 64, 65, 96
Victoria, Queen 49, 184, 189, 214
Vidal, Gore 40, 65
Vidor, King 36, 49, 87, 111, 118
Vieyra, Paulin 119
Villa, Pancho 49, 218
Villiers, Frederick 219
Voigt, Jon 203
Von Stroheim, Erich 25, 30, 82,
    111, 153

Wadkar, Hansa 79
Walesa, Lech 87
Wallace, Edgar 42
Waller, Frederick 147
Walsh, Raoul 30, 87, 119, 141
Warhol, Andy 107, 121, 125
Warner, H. B. 76, 83
Washington, President George 52
Wayne, John 80, 90, 91, 101, 102
Weber, Lois 61, 118
Wegener, Paul 83
Weissmuller, Johnny 48, 83
Welch, Raquel 99, 158
Welles, Orson 39, 83, 122, 159
Wertmuller, Lina 154, 201
West, Mae 80, 117
Westmore brothers 126
White, Chrissie 77, 90
White, Pearl 79, 196
Wilcox, Herbert 141
Williams, Esther 61
Williams, John T. 152
Williamson, Nicol 43
Wilson, President Woodrow 55,
    187
Winwood, Estelle 104, 105
Wong, Anna May 107, 136
Wood, Natalie 83
Wotner, Arthur 46, 47
Wu, Butterfly 13
Wyman, Jane 83, 95, 107

Young, Clara Kimball 105, 179
Young, Loretta 82, 96
Young, Victor 201

Zecca, Ferdinand 39
Zukor, Adolph 17, 79, 87

SUBJECT

Academy Awards 201–4
accidents 22
actors, actresses see performers
admission prices 181–2
advertising films 210, 211, 212
aerial films 212
amateur
    cameras 225–6
    cartoons about 196, 227
    club 228
    colour stock 229–30

contest and awards 200, 228
gauges *228*
newsreels 216
projectors 225
royal cinematographer 227
society 230
sub-standard gauges 228
talkies 228–9
trademarks 230
video cassettes 224
animals 108
animated cartoons *see* cartoons
animated films 206–9
anthropological films 216–17
anti-semetic films 56
archives 22, 23, 210
art, the cinema in *197, 199*
audience
    blind 58
    fans 182–7
    health, effect on 187
    highest per capita
        attendance 174
    largest 36, 182
    largest at premiere 187–8
    patron to see film most times 182
authors
    highest paid 40
    most filmed 40, *40–3*
    playing in movies 40, *41*, 89
    remakes 34
    rights 39–40
autobiography, star 196
awards
    Academy 201–4
    amateur 200
    Berlin 204
    British Film Academy 204
    Cannes 204
    first 200
    worst film 205

back projection 112–13
ballet films 47
baseball film, first 218
beauty queens 99
best films of all time 205
Beverly Hills 24
biographies, star 196
biopics
    characters most portrayed 49, 75
    Napoleon 49, 50
    star 78–9
    US Presidents *52–3*
black
    director 118
    extras 80, 84
    films 49, *51*, 68–9, 72
    newsreel 216
    Oscar winner *203*
    performers *51*
blunders 132–4
Bond movies 36, 49, 158, 179
book-of-the-film 193
book on cinema, first 193
boxing film, first 218
box office
    Annual Top Moneymakers 36
    cartoon with highest gross 208
    cinema with highest gross 176
    country with highest gross 37
    film with highest box
        office/budget ratio 38
    film with highest gross 36, 37, 38
    film with highest loss 37
    film with lowest gross 37
    unprofitable films 37
    US earnings 37
    western, highest earning 74
British Board of Film
    Censors 161–3
budget
    average 38
    box office ratio 38
    highest 38
    lowest 38
    rights ratio 38

camera
    amateur 225, 227–8
    first 7–9

hidden 111
mobile 111
most for scene 108
motorised 109
multiplane 208
camera blimp *141*
camera crane *113*
camera dolly 111
camera lens
    anamorphic 146
    telephoto 111
    widest aperture 108
    zoom 110
camerawoman 113–14
camerawork
    back projection 112–13
    close up 110
    dissolve 111
    double exposure 112
    longest take 125
    most retakes 125
    multi-shot scene 109
    panning shot 109
    slow motion 109
    special effect, first 76
    360° pan 109
    time lapse 109
    underwater 132
    wipe 109–10
cartoons, animated
    animal character, first 206–7
    character debuts 208–9
    Cinemascope 208
    colour 208
    erotic 63
    feature 208
    first 206, *207*
    highest grossing 208
    Mickey Mouse 91, *184*, 208, *209*
    newsreel 216
    series 206
    talkie 207–8
    Technicolor 208
    3-D 208
    X-rated 208
cartoons, newspaper *196, 197*
cast
    African 51
    female 92, 93
    largest (extras) 81–2
    largest (featured players) 93
    smallest 93
    typecasting 103–4
censorship 160–6
characters most portrayed in films
    fictional 46–7
    historical 49, 50
    horror 56–7
    President of USA *52–5*
    western 75
children's cinema clubs 180
children's cinema matinees 180
children's newsreel 216
child millionaire 85
child stars 84, 85–6
Cinderella films 30–3
cinema organs 150–1
Cinemascope
    cartoon 208
    first film 146
    three-dimensional 148
cinema theatres
    admission prices *181–2*
    airport 179
    amenities *174, 175*
    attendance 173, 174
    audiences *see* audiences
    cafes 175
    children, cinemas run by 179
    children's cinema club 180
    children's matinees 180
    city with most 177–8
    concentration camp 179
    country with least 174
    country with most 174
    double bill 175
    drive-ins 180
    fairground bioscopes *167*
    first 167–71
    floating 179
    fly-in 179

goal 180
harem 178
highest attendance 174
highest seat price 182
highest tax 182
largest *172, 173–4*
largest chain 176
largest multiple 178
largest screen *190–1*
last silent 176
longest name 177
longest non-stop show 175
longest run 176
lowest seat prices 182
monarch to attend 188
most in city 177–8
multiples 174, 178
municipal 176
music 150–1
names 177
neon sign 172
news theatres 180–1
northernmost 178
oldest 175–6
orchestra 150
outdoor 178
paintings of *197, 199*
private *226, 227*
purpose-built 170–1
royalty to attend 188
screens *190–1*
seat prices *181–2*
sex 65, 181
shortest name 177
shortest run 176
smallest 174
social acceptance of 172–3
southernmost 178
statistics by country 170–1
statistics UK, US 168
train 179
unusual 178–9
video 180
Cinerama 147
close-up 110
club, film making 228
colour
    advertising film 211
    back projection 113
    cartoon 208
    Eastman Color 136, 137
    feature film *135*
    film stock (amateur) 229–30
    first in the world *135*
    most used process 137
    musical 58
    shortest sequence 137
    talkie 136
    Technicolor 136–7
    three-dimensional 148, *149*
    underwater feature 132
    western 73
comedy
    statistics 68, 69
    top moneymakers 36
composers
    film 151–2, *153*
    most successful 152
    stars as 153
    woman 152
concentration camp cinema 179
concern film 152
contracts 86–8
co-productions 23
copyright 39–40
costumes 114–17
cowboy, first in film 72
credits 157–8
crime films 68–9

dialogue
    dialect 146
    dubbed 142
    inter-titles 157
    Latin, Irish, Esperanto etc. *see*
        languages
    most hackneyed line 45
    multilingual 145–6
    none 144–5
    overlapping 143
    script, first 137

director
    Academy Awards 202
    African 118
    black 118
    first 117
    highest paid 118
    longest career 118, 119
    most co-directors on film 119
    most films 119
    most westerns 75
    oldest 120
    on percentage 118
    'one-shot' 125
    woman 75, 117–18, 120
    youngest 119–20
dissolve 111
documentary films 68–9, *201*, 212
Dolby sound 144
double exposure 112
Dracula films 56–7
drive-in cinema theatres 180
dubbing 142, 151, 158

editing 120–1
Esperanto 146
extras 81–2, 84

fan magazines *194, 195*, 196–7,
    198, 199
fan mail 182, *183*, 184
fans, famous 184–7
fashions inspired by stars 115,
    116, 117
feature film *see also* black, cartoon,
    colour, documentary, puppet,
    70 mm, sound, 3-D etc.
    advertising in 211
    first by countries 13–16
    first in Europe 12
    first in UK 12, 13
    first in USA 12, 13
    first in world 12
    least expensive 38
    longest production
        schedule 128–9
    most expensive 38
    shortest production
        schedule 128–9
festivals *see* film festivals
fiction, cinematographic 192
film *see* motion pictures
film company, first 10
film critic 199
film festivals 201, 204
film journals 196–7
film music 151–2
film rights 39–40
film schools 122
film societies 230
film stock
    colour (amateur) 229–30
    first 121
    frame format 122
    gauges 123
    magnetic track 143
    perforated 121
    safety 121–2
flashbacks 122–3
fly-in cinema 179
football films 66, 218
frame, largest 122

gaol film shows 180
gauges
    dual 133
    largest 123
    70 mm 123
    smallest 123
    standard 123
    sub-standard 228
    wide 146, *147*

Hamlet remakes 42
harem film shows 178
Hays Code 160–1
Hollywood
    Beverly Hills 24
    first film 24
    first inhabitant 23
    first studio 24
    first talkie 24
    name 23

Hollywood sign 24–5
holography 149
home movies *see* amateur
homosexual films 64–5
horror films 56–7, 68–9
horse race films, first 218

industrial films 212–13
in-flight movies 181
insurance 105–6

Jewish films 51, 56

kinetoentgenography 217
Kinetoscope 7, 8, 9
kissing 107
Kung-fu 132

language
 classical 146
 Esperanto 146
 Hindi 146
 Irish 146
 Latin 146
 multilingual films 145
 pidgin English 146
 Red Indian 74, 75
 Welsh 146
 Yiddish 56
Latin, film in 146
lens *see* camera lens
lesbianism 64, 65
lighting
 artificial 123–4
 backlighting 124
 dark stage 124
 incandescent 125
 most powerful 124–5
 studio 124
literature on cinema 192
longest films 25–6
Los Angeles
 first film 24
 first studio 24

magazines, fan 194, 195, 196–7, 198, 199
make-up 126
medical films 217
Mickey Mouse 91, 184, 208, 209
microscopic film 217
midgets 99
monarch
 first to attend cinema 188
 first filmed 214
 first portrayed 49
 performer in films 88
monologue, longest 45
motion pictures
 Academy Award winners 201–4
 advertising films 210, 211, 212
 aerial film 212
 amateur 225–30
 Annual Top Moneymakers 36
 anthropological 216–17
 anti Semitic 56
 author's rights 39–40
 award-winning 200–5
 ballet 47
 Best Films of All Time 205
 biopics 49, 78–9
 black 49, 56, 68–9, 72, 80, 88, 118
 blunders 132–4
 budgets 38
 cartoon 206–9
 characters portrayed in *see* characters
 chase sequence 114
 Cinderella remakes 30–3
 Cinemascope 146
 Cinerama 147
 colour *see* colour
 comedy 68–9
 concert film 152
 co-productions 23
 crime 68–9
 directed by woman 117–18
 documentary 68–9
 Dracula films 56–7
 dubbed 142, 151, 158
 exhibition of, first 9–11

feature films *see* feature
fictional character most
 portrayed 46–7
film music 151–2
first by countries 8
first in world 7, 8, 9
flashbacks 122–3
football 66
highest budget 38
highest earnings 36–7
highest loss 37
historical character most
 portrayed 49
Hollywood, made in 24
holographic 149
home movies 225–30
homosexual 64–5
horror films 56–7, 68–9
industrial 212–13
in-flight 181
Jewish 51, 56
Kung-fu 132
largest cast (extras) 81–2
largest cast (featured) 93
largest collection of films 22, 23
least edited 121
literature of 192
longest 25–6
longest close-up 110
longest production
 schedule 127–8
longest run 176
longest screen kiss 107
longest serial film 218
longest series 103
longest sword fight 132
longest take 125
lowest budget 38
lowest earnings 37
made without camera 110
mass destruction of 23
medical 217
microscopic 217
most Academy Awards 201
most admissions 36, 174
most edited 120–1
most kisses 107
most retakes 125
music 151–2
musicals 58–9, 68–9
Napoleon films 49, 50
newsreels 215–17
novel, first filmed 39
nude scene 61–3
oldest American 22
opera 58
pornographic 63, 65
premieres 129
Presidents of US portrayed in
 52–5
produced by woman 120
production *see* production output
puppet films 209
remakes 30–4
retakes 125
rights 39–40
Royal Command
 Performance 189
schedules 127–9
science fiction 60, 68, 69
scientific 216–17
sequels 34–5
serials 217–18
70 mm 123
sex 60–5, 67–70, 181
Shakespeare films 40, 42
Sherlock Holmes films 46–7
shortest run 176–7
shortest shooting
 schedule 128–9
single set films 130
slow motion 109
smallest cast 93–4
smellies 147
soccer 66
sound *see* sound
sponsored 212–13
sports 66, 68–9, 218
stereophonic sound 143, 149
talkies *see* sound
Tarzan films 48

TV movies 221
TV plays (based on) 221
TV rights to 223
TV series (based on) 221
TV versions of 221
themes 67–71
three-dimensional 148–9
travelogue 218
underwater 132
US exports 37
video 224
violence in 73, 132, 162, 163
war 68–9
westerns 68–9, 72–5, 135, 203
wide screen 146–7
women cast 120
Worst Film Awards 205
X-rated 162
X-ray 217
Yiddish 56
youth 69–71
museums of cinema 26–7
music
 cinema 150–1
 composer, most successful 152
 composer, star as 153
 concert film 152
 dubbing 142, 151, 158
 film 151–2
 on set 153
 score issued on disc 152
 stereophonic 143
 symphonic score 152
musicals 58–9, 68–9

Napoleon films 49, 50
news film
 colour 136
 first 213
 monarch filmed 214
 Pope filmed 214
 President filmed 214
 sports 218
 war 219
newspaper
 cartoon on cinema 197
 film column 199
 film reviews 199
 newsreels 214–17
novel
 film rights 39–40
 first allusion to cinema in 192
 first filmed 39
 most filmed 34
 novelist most filmed 42–3
 nudity on screen 61–3, 98

opera films 58
Oscars *see* Academy Awards

painting of cinema interior 197,
 199
panning shots 109
perforated film 121
performer
 Academy Awards 202–3
 African 51
 animals 108
 authors as 40, 41, 89
 autobiography 196
 banned 160
 beauty queens 99
 biogs 196
 biopics of stars 78–9
 black 80, 84, 88
 centenarians 104
 child stars 84, 85–6
 comeback 104, 105
 composers 153
 contracts 81–8
 co-stars 98
 credits 157–8
 dual artiste roles 94–5
 dubbed voice 142
 dwarves 99
 earnings 77–81
 extras 81–2, 84
 families 92–3
 fan mail 182, 183, 184
 first on film 76
 heaviest 101

 highest paid 80
 insurance 105–6
 largest bust 101
 largest cast 81–2, 93
 longest career 92, 94
 longest make-up 126
 lowest paid 80–1
 midgets 99
 million dollar contract 79
 monarch as 88
 most bankable 38
 most biographies 196
 most delayed come-back 104,
  105
 most generations of family 92
 most married 88
 most in one family 92–3
 most roles 88, 90
 multiple roles 94
 names 95–8
 non-actors playing fictional
  roles 89
 non-actors playing selves 84–7
 nonagenarians 104
 nude 61–3
 oldest 104, 105
 on percentage 81
 playing own parent 93
 playing same role most
  times 103–4
 playing selves 82–3
 popularity 90–2
 richest 80
 screen teams 98
 screen tests 98–9
 sex appeal 198, 199
 shortest 99–101
 smallest cast 93–4
 stamps honouring *see* colour
  spread
 stars playing selves 82–3
 star system 76–7
 statues honouring 101–3
 stuntmen 131–2
 tallest 100–1
 typecasting 103–4
 western stars 74
 youngest 104–5
 youngest Oscar winner 203
Pickfair 24
plays, most filmed 34
poem on cinema 192
Pope, filmed 214
popularity polls 90–2
pornographic films 63, 65
posters 11, 28, 184
premieres
 largest audience 187–8
 least delayed 129
 most belated 188
 most simultaneous 188
 siege conditions 188
 television 223
 unusual 188
prequels 35
President (US)
 filmed 214
 portrayed on film 52–5
 taste in films 187
producer
 most successful 127
 producer–writer–director
  partnership 127
 woman 126–7
 youngest 126
production output
 annual by countries 18–21
 annual world 17
 black films 51
 cartoon features 208
 colour 137
 early 13, 17
 foreign language 145
 highest for Hollywood studio 17
 highest UK 17
 highest USA 17
 highest world 17
 lowest UK 17
 lowest USA 17
 multilingual 145
 serials 218

three-dimensional films 148
westerns 75
world 17–21
Yiddish films 56
production schedule
  average 129
  longest 127–8
  shortest 128–9
projector
  amateur 225
  largest reel 190
  manufactured, first 189
  most powerful 190
  motorised 189, 190
publicity
  largest budget 27
  posters 11, 28, 164
  slogans 27–8
  stunts 29–30
puppet films 209

radio microphone 143–4
recordings
  film score 152
  film song 152
reel, largest 190
remakes 30–4
retakes 125
rights 39–40, 221, 224
rock concert film 152
royalty
  amateur cinematographer 227
  appearances in films 88
  film of, first 214
  monarch to attend cinema, first 188
  Royal Command Performances 189
  taste in films 184–6

safety film 121–2
scenario, most improbable 45
science fiction 60, 69
screens 191
screen test 89
script
  censorship 163, 164
  first dialogue 44, 137
  longest monologue 45
  most hackneyed line 45
  obscenities and profanities 44–5
  overlapping dialogue 143
  published 193, 196
  shortest dialogue 44
scriptwriter
  dialogue 44
  first 43
  most co-writers 44
  name in lights 44
  statesmen as 45
seat prices 181–2
sensurround 143
sequels 34–5, 203
serials 217–18
set
  largest 129
  single 130
  smallest 129–30
sex films 60–5, 67–70
Shakespeare on film 40, 42
Sherlock Holmes films 46–7
shoot-out: most carnage 132
shooting schedule, shortest 128
short story on cinema, first 192–3
silent films
  biggest budget 38
  inter-titles 157
  last 144–5
  last cinema to show 176
  most profitable 36
  post-sound 144–5
  sound effects 138
slow motion 109
smallest country with film industry 17
smellies 147
soccer films 66
songs
  composed for film 58
  dubbed 142
  musical with most 58

recorded 152
sound
  advertising film 211
  amateur talkie 228–9
  black talkies 49
  cartoon 207–8
  colour talkie 136
  documentary 212
  Dolby 144
  double exposure 112
  dubbing 142, 151, 158
  effect on legitimate theatre 139
  feature film 141–2
  first talkies 13–16, 137
  flashback 122
  industrial film 213
  magnetic track 143
  medical film 217
  multilingual 145–6
  musical 151–2
  newsreel 215
  overlapping dialogue 143
  post-synchronisation 142
  radio microphones 143–4
  Sensurround 143
  serial 218
  songs 58
  sound-on-film 138–42
  stereophonic 143, 149
  studio 131
  subtitles 157
  talkies—first by countries 13–16
  three-dimensional talkie 149
sponsored films 212–13
sports films 66, 68–9, 218
stamps, film-makers honoured by *see* colour spread
star system 76–7
statesmen
  scriptwriters 45
  taste in films 186–7
statues of stars 101–3
stereophonic sound 143, 149
stills, largest collection 23
studio
  dark stage 124
  first 130–1
  first in Hollywood 24
  largest 131
  largest stage 130, 131
  lighting 124
  sound stage 131
stunts and stuntmen 131–2
subtitles 157
swordfight, longest 132

talkies *see* sound
tank, largest 132
Tarzan films 48
tax on seat prices, highest 182
Technicolor 136–7
television
  films based on TV plays 221
  films based on TV series 221
  films on, age of 222–3
  films on, country of origin 222
  first film made for 220
  first film shown on 220
  most popular film on 222
  rights to movies 223
  TVMs (television movies) 221
theatres *see* cinema theatres
themes 1914–84 67–71
three-dimensional films 147–9, 208
time lapse 109
titles
  censorship of 163, 166
  changed 155
  date 155
  inter-titles 157
  least compelling 157
  longest 154, 155
  main at end 156
  meaningless 156–7
  number 155
  odd 154
  shortest 155
  subtitles 157
trailers 176, 200
trains, film shows on 179

travelogues 218
typecasting 103–4

underwater filming 132

Venice Film Festival 201, 204
video 224
violence 73, 132, 162, 163

war film
  battles delayed for 218
  first 219
  oldest 219
  statistics 68–9
  wedding movie 227
  western films 68–9, 72–5, 135, 203
western stars
  first 74
  most popular 75
wide screen 146–7
woman
  amateur cinematographer 225
  award winner 200, 201
  cameraman 113–14, 215
  composer for films 152
  cast 92, 93
  crew 132
  directors 75, 117–18, 120
  producers 120
  stuntman 131
Wurlitzer 150–1

X films
  cartoons 208
  first 162
  Royal Command Performance 189
X-ray films 56

Zoom lens 110

TITLES

A Nos Amours (Fr 83) 84
Abraham Lincoln (US 30) 142
The Absent-Minded Professor (US 61) 36
The Abyss (Den 10) 77, 79
Adelen 31 (Swe 69) 133
A Dinner Date with Death (GB 50) 220
Adolf Hitler—My Part in His Downfall (GB 72) 93
An Adventuress (US 20) 121
The Adventures of Kathlyn (US 13) 193
African Journey (Fr 47) 223
The African Queen (GB 52) 205
Afrique sur Seine (Sen 55) 118
After Fifty Years (It 12) 200
Aguirre, Wrath of the Gods (FRG 72) 205
The Air Circus (US 28) 141
Airport (US 60) 36
A l'Ecu d'Or (Fr 08) 63
Alice Adams (US 35) 44
Alice in the Jungle (US 25) 28
Alice in Wonderland (GB/Fr 50) 209
All About Eve (US 50) 201, 204
All Quiet on the Western Front (US 30) 164, 204
All the King's Men (US 49) 203, 204
Les Amants (Fr 59) 164
An American in Paris (US 51) 204
An American Werewolf in London (US 81) 126
Among the Missing (US 34) 134
Der Andere (Ger 12) 172
Anders als die Andern (Ger 19) 64, 65
Angel City (US 77) 38
Angels with Dirty Faces (US 38) 133
Animal Farm (GB 54) 208
Anna Karenina (US 35) 80, 204

Anna Pavlova (USSR/GB 84) 23
Anne of the Thousand Days (GB 70) 189
Annie (US 82) 40, 131
Annie Hall (US 77) 204
Another Part of the Forest (US 47) 35
Anthony Adverse (US 36) 94
The Apartment (US 60) 204
Apocalypse Now (US 79) 205
El Apostol (Arg 17) 208
A Propos de Nice (Fr 30) 62
Arizona (US 13) 13, 73
Army Life, or How Soldiers are Made (GB 00) 212
Around is Around (GB 51) 208
Around the World in 80 Days (US 56) 82, 93, 201, 204
Arrah-Na-Pough (US 11) 151
L'Arroseur arrosé (Fr 95) 14, 76
As a Man Thirsteth (US 14) 67
Assassin for Hire (GB 51) 221
L'Assassination du Duc de Guise (Fr 08) 43, 151
L'Atalante (Fr 33) 205
Atlantic (GB 29) 145
L'Atlantide (Fr 21) 122
Atlantis (Den 13) 17
Auntie Mame (US 59) 36
L'Avventura (It 59) 205
Awara (Ind 51) 93

Baby Doll (US 56) 28
Baby Takes a Bow (US 35) 117
La Bal (Fr/It/Alg 84) 130
Bálint Fábián's Encounter with God (Hun 80) 35
The Bank Robbery (US 08) 75
Barry Lyndon (GB 75) 107, 205
Battle of Britain (GB 70) 36
The Battle of the River Plate (GB 56) 189
The Battle of Waterloo (GB 13) 13, 81
The Battleship Potemkin (USSR 25) 119, 205
Beau Brummel (GB 54) 189
Beach of the War Gods (HK 73) 132
Because You're Mine (US 52) 189
Becky Sharp (US 35) 136
Bedtime Story (US 33) 105
Behind the Great Wall (US 59) 147
Being There (US 79) 211
Ben Hur (US 07) 39
Ben Hur (US 25) 22, 27, 38, 40, 108, 120
Ben Hur (US 59) 22, 36, 38, 82, 120, 201, 204
Benji (US 74) 108
Berlin Alexanderplatz (FRG 83) 26
Berlin, Symphony of a Great City (Ger 27) 111
The Best Man (US 64) 40
The Best of Everything (US 59) 205
The Best Years of Our Lives (US 46) 36, 120, 202, 204
Bhaag Re Bhaag (GB 78) 146
Bhumika (Ind 78) 79
Bicycle Thieves (It 49) 205
The Big Parade (US 25) 36
The Big Red One (US 80) 81
Bikini Beach (US 64) 71
Bill and Coo (US 48) 108
The Bird of Paradise (US 32) 152
Birds of Prey (US 31) 141
The Birth of a Nation (US 15) 36, 39, 49, 94, 114, 118, 125, 151
The Birth of New Zealand (NZ 22) 22
The Bishop's Wife (US 47) 189
The Black Bird (US 75) 34
The Black Cat (US 34) 159
Black Joy (GB 77) 49
Black Waters (GB 29) 141
Blackmail (GB 29) 1, 16, 141, 142
Blazing the Overland Trail (US 56) 218
Blessed Event (US 32) 44
Blood Feat (US 63) 27

Bloody Cry (Chn 34) 163
The Blue Angel (Ger 30) 28
The Blue Lagoon (US 80) 27
The Blue Lamp (GB 49) 36, 204, 221
Blue Movie (US 68) 125
Bogie (US 80) 78
Boom! (GB 68) 78
Boots (US 19) 182
Born Free (GB 66) 189
Born Yesterday (US 50) 40
The Bounty Hunters (It 70) 132
Boy Scouts Be Prepared (GB 17) 217
Der Brandstifter (Ger 22) 139
Brewster McCloud (US 70) 187
Bridal Suite (US 39) 28
The Bridge on the River Kwai (GB 57) 36, 204, 224
Brief Encounter (GB 45) 27, 205
Broadway (US 29) 113
Broadway Melody (US 29) 58, 141, 204
Broken Blossoms (US 19) 120
Brontë (US/Ire 83) 93
The Brothers Karamazov (US 58) 133
The Bruce Lee Story (US 74) 79
Brussels-Transit (Bel 80) 56
The Burning of the Red Lotus Temple (Chn 28–31) 25
The Buster Keaton Story (US 57) 78
Butch and Sundance—The Early Days (US 79) 35
Butch Cassidy and the Sundance Kid (US 69) 74, 204
Butterfield 8 (US 60) 205
By Love Possessed (US 61) 181

Cabaret (US 72) 205
The Cabinet of Dr Caligari (Ger 19) 205
Cabiria (It 14) 38, 111, 151, 187
Calamity of Snakes (Tai 82) 165
California (US 27) 124, 125
California Suite (US 79) 189
Caligula (US 79) 162
Callan (GB 74) 144
Il Cane riconescente (It 07) 200
The Cannonball Run (US 81) 87
Can She Bake a Cherry Pie? (US 83) 80
The Care Bears Movie (US 85) 27
Carl Peters (Ger 41) 145
The Carpetbaggers (US 64) 25, 36, 205
Carry On! (GB 27) 118
Carry On Nurse (GB 59) 36
Casablanca (US 42) 28, 204, 205
Casino Royale (GB 67) 119
The Cat and the Fiddle (US 34) 136
Catembe (Por 64) 162
Cavalcade (US 33) 204
The Cavalry School at Saumur (Fr 97) 212
La Caverne maudite (Fr 98) 112
Celine and Julie Go Boating (Fr 74) 205
Cendrillon (Fr 99) 31, 111
Cenerentola (It 49) 32
The Champ (US 31) 203
The Chapman Report (US 62) 205
Chariots of Fire (GB 82) 36, 189, 204
Charlie Bubbles (GB 68) 161
Checkmated (GB 10) 135
Chelsea Girls (US 66) 121
The Chess Players (Ind 78) 143
Cheyenne Autumn (US 64) 205
The Children's Hour (US 62) 64, 65, 161
A Child's Sacrifice (US 10) 126
Chinnari Pappalu (Ind 67) 132
A Chorus Line (US 85) 40
Chu Hai-tang (Jap/Chn 43) 65
Cimarron (US 31) 203
Cinderella films 31
Cinderella (GB 13) 138
Cinderella (US 76) 32

Cinerama Holiday (US 55) 36
Circular Panorama of the Electric Tower (US 01) 109
Citizen Kane (US 41) 122, 205
City Lights (US 31) 120, *125*, 205
City Streets (US 31) 122
Civilization (US 15) 151
Cleopatra (US 13) 13
Cleopatra (US 17) 114
Cleopatra (US 34) 129
Cleopatra (US 63) 25, 36, 38, 114, 128, 129, 205
A Clockwork Orange (GB 72) 62, 112, 144, 205
Close Encounters of the Third Kind (US 77) 37, 129, 189
The Clown and His Donkey (GB 10) 206
The Clue of the New Pin (GB 29) 142
The Colleen Bawn (US 11) 29
The Comic (US 69) 78
Coming Home (US 78) 203
Comin' Through the Rye (GB 16) 189
La Commare secca (It 62) 123
Committed (US 84) 78
El Conde Dracula (Sp/FRG/It 73) 56
Confessions of a Window Cleaner (GB 74) 36
The Constant Husband (GB 55) 223
Construire au feu (Fr 27) 146
Contaminacion (Col 82) 37
Convoy (GB 40) 36, 44
La Coquille et la Clergyman (Fr 28) 164
The Count of Monte Cristo (US 08) 24
The Count of Monte Cristo (US 13) 13, 81
The Courtneys of Curzon Street (GB 47) 36
The Creeping Unknown (GB 55) 187
Crime Without Passion (US 34) 158
Crossed Swords (US 78) 176
The Crowd (US 28) 111
The Cruel Sea (GB 53) 36
Cruel Story of Youth (Jap 60) 133
The Cup Winner (Aus 11) 129
Custer's Last Stand (US 08) 75
Cytherea (US 24) 136

Daaera (Ind 53) 110
The Dam Busters (GB 55) 36
Dance Fools, Dance (US 30) 133
Dance Pretty Lady (GB 32) 47
Dante's Inferno (It 12) 62
A Daughter of the Gods (US 16) 38, 61, *63*, 81
David and Bathsheba (US 51) 36
David Copperfield (GB 13) 13
David Harum (US 15) 111
The Day of the Locust (US 73) 25, 93
Dear Brigitte (US 65) *83*
Death in Venice (It 71) 205
The Debut of Thomas Kat (US 20) 208
Deep Throat (US 71) 38
The Deer Hunter (US 78) 204
The Definite Object (GB 20) 126
Delorita's Passion Dance (US 96) 160
Demain un jour nouveau (Gab 78) 187
Derrière l'omnibus (Fr 97) 123
Destry Rides Again (US 39) 164
The Diamond (GB 54) 149
Diamonds are Forever (GB 72) 36, 133
Digital Dream (US 84) 213
Dinner Time (US 28) 207
The Dirty Dozen (US 67) 36
Dny Zrady (Cz 72) 82, 93
Doctor at Large (GB 57) 36
Doctor in Love (GB 60) 36
Doctor in the House (GB 54) 36, 37

Doctor No (GB 62) 28, 158
Doctor Zhivago (US 66) 36
Dodge City (US 40) 188
Dom Kallar Oss Mods (Swe 67) 63
Don Juan (US 26) 107
Dorothy Vernon of Haddon Hall (US 24) 114
Double Indemnity (US 44) 205
The Downward Path (US 02) 61
Dr Bethune (Chn 77) 127
Dr Kildare's Wedding Day (US 41) 153
Dr Nicola (Den 09) 39
Dr Strangelove (GB 63) 125, 204
Dracula films 56, 57
The Draughtsman's Contract (GB 83) 133
Dream Street (US 21) 139
The Dresser (GB 84) 189
Duck Soup (US 33) 28
Duel in the Sun (US 46) 38, 74
The Dybbuk (Pol 82) 56

The Earth Thirsts (USSR 30) 16, 205
Earthquake (US 74) 143, 221
East Lynne (GB 13) 13
Easy Rider (US 69) 205
The Eddie Cantor Story (US 53) 78
Edison Kinetoscopic Record of a Sneeze (US 94) 110
Edith and Marcel (Fr 84) 93
The Egyptian (US 54) 27
8½ (It 63) 205
The Electric Horseman (US 79) 211
The Elephant Man (GB 80) 126, 204
Elvira Madigan (Swe 67) 133
Emmanuelle (Fr 74) 65, 176
The Empire Strikes Back (US 80) 36, 37, 127, 152
The Enchanted Drawing (US 00) 207
Enoch Arden (US 11) 124
L'Enfant prodigue (Fr 07) 12, 14, 151
Les Enfants du Paradis (Fr 43–5) 205
Episode (Aut 35) 159
E.T. The Extra-Terrestrial (US 82) 36, 37, 99, 152, 163, 211
Europa (Pol 30) 62
Even Dwarfs Started Small (FRG 70) 99
Every Which Way But Loose (US 79) 36
Evil Under the Sun (GB 82) 189
The Execution of Mary Queen of Scots (US 95) 16, 76
Exodus (US 60) 82
The Exorcist (US 73) 37, 40
The Exploits of Elaine (US 14) 184
Extase (Cz 33) 61, *63*
Eye of the Needle (GB 82) 134
The Eyes of Laura Mars (US 78) 193

The Facts of Life (US 61) 189
The Fall of the Roman Empire (US 64) 129
Fanny and Alexander (Swe 83) 26
Fantasia (US 40) 143
Fantasmagorie (Fr 08) 206
A Farewell to Arms (US 32) 110
Fashions for Women (US 27) 200, 201
Fate (GB 11) 135
Faust (GB 07) 58
La Fée au choux (Fr 00) 117, *118*
Feline Follies (US 19) 209
Female Hamlet (Tur 77) 40
The Fighting American (US 24) 28
The First of the Few (GB 42) 36
A Fistful of Dollars (It/FRG/SP 64) 28
Flowers and Trees (US 32) 136, 208
Foolish Wives (US 22) 25, 38, 94, 120

For the Term of His Natural Life (Aus 08) 38
For Whom the Bell Tolls (US 43) 114
For Your Eyes Only (GB 81) 49
Forever and a Day (US 43) 44
The Forsyte Saga (US 49) 189
The Four Devils (US 29) 113
Four for Texas (US 63) 98
The Four Hundred Blows (Fr 59) 38
49th Parallel (GB 41) 36
Four Wives (US 40) 143
Fox Movietone Follies of 1929 (US 29) 96, 123
The Fox and the Hound (US 81) 208
Foxy Brown (US 74) 72
Frances (US 82) 78
Frankenstein (US 31) 109, 126
A Free Soul (US 31) 45, 125
The French Connection (US 71) 204
From Hell to Texas (US 57) 125
From Here to Eternity (US 53) 204
From Russia with Love (GB 63) 36
A Full-Dress Night at the Colon Theatre (Arg 19) 209
Funny Girl (US 68) 203
Funny Lady (US 75) 189

Gable and Lombard (US 76) 78, 79
Gandhi (GB/Ind 82) 81, 93, 128, 201, 204, 223
Gas (Can 81) 134
Das Geheimnis der Lüfte (Aut/Fr 13) 23
The General (US 26) 205
The Gentleman (GB 25) 139
Gentleman's Agreement (US 47) 204
Gentlemen with Guns (US 46) 132
The George Raft Story (US 61) 79
Gettin' Back (US 74) 159
The Getting of Wisdom (Aus 79) 35
Gigi (US 58) 204
Ghostbusters (US 84) 37
The Ghost Goes West (GB 36) 36
The Girl Hunters (US 63) 40
The Godfather (US 72) 36, 37, 203, 204, 221
The Godfather Part II (US 74) 203, 204, 221
The Gold Diggers (GB 84) 80
The Gold Rush (US 24) 27, 205
Goldfinger (GB 64) 36
Going My Way (US 44) 204
Gone with the Wind (US 39) 26, 36, 37, 38, 44, 98, 120, 133, *203*, 204, 205, 222, 223
Goodbye Cruel World (US 83) 188
Goodbye, Norma Jean (US/Aus 75) 79
Good Morning Boys (GB 37) 36
Goofy Goat (US 31) 208
The Gorilla (US 27) *176*
The Graduate (US 67) 36, 118, 125, 204, 205
Il Granatière Roland (It 10) 81
La Grande Illusion (Fr 37) 145, 205
Grand Hotel (US 32) 204
Grandma's Reading Glass (GB 00) 110
The Grapes of Wrath (US 40) 164, 202, 205
Grease (US 78) 36, 37, 155
The Greatest Story Ever Told (US 64) 205
The Great Gatsby (US 73) 205
The Great Train Robbery (US 03) 73, 74, 88, 131
The Great Ziegfeld (US 36) 26, 205
The Greatest Show on Earth (US 52) 36, 204
Greed (US 24) 25, 111, 125, 192, 205
Greetings (US 68) 162
Gregory's Girl (GB 81) *66*, 144
Gremlins (US 84) 37

Greystoke (GB/US 84) *48*
La Guerra e il sogno di Momi (It 16) 209
Guess Who's Coming to Dinner (US 67) 202, 205
The Guinea Pig (GB 49) 44
The Gulf Between (US 17) *136*
The Guns of Navarone (GB 61) 36
Guys and Dolls (US 56) 36

Hair (US 71) 133
Hallelujah! (US 29) 49, 205
Hallelujah the Hills (US 63) 94
Hambone and Hillie (US 84) *94*, 104
Hamlet films 40
Hamlet (Fr 00) 137
Hamlet (GB 13) *13, 43*
Hamlet (GB 48) *153*, 155, 164, 193, 202, 204, 224
Hamlet (GB 69) *43*, 158
Hamlet (USSR 64) 42
Hamlet (GB 77) 38, 94
Hammett (US 82) 133
Handling Ships (GB 46) 208
Hangmen Also Die (US 43) 159
Happy Days (US 30) 146, *147*
Harlem, USA (USSR 52) 133
Harlow (US 65) 78
Harmony Heaven (GB 30) 58, 136
Hawaii (US 67) 165
The Hazards of Helen (US 14) 131, 218
The Heart of a Race Tout (US 09) *124*
Hearts of the World (US 18) 92
Heaven's Gate (US 80) 37, 128
Heimat (FRG 84) 26
Helen of Troy (US 55) 133
The Hell Cat (US 34) *68*
Hell's Angels (US 30) 22, 38, 120
Hell's Angels Forever (US 83) 189
Help! (GB 65) 36
Henry V (GB 44) 205
Henry VIII (GB 11) 151
Hero (GB 82) 146
Les Heures (Fr 13) 151
Highpoint (Can 79) 131
High Tor (US 56) 221
L'Hirondelle et la Mésange (Bel 20) 188
His Girl Friday (US 40) 143
Hobson's Choice (GB 53) 204
Honky Tonk Freeway (US 81) 37, 211
The Horse Soldiers (US 59) 80
The Honor System (US 25) 30
Hoodlum Priest (US 61) 133
Hoopla (US 33) 101
The Horse's Mouth (GB 59) 189
House of Wax (US 53) 149
The Howards of Virginia (US 40) 205
How Green was my Valley (US 41) 202, 204
How He Lied to Her Husband (GB 31) 201
How Not to Wear Clothes (Swe 21) 212, *213*
Hudson's Bay (US 41) 205
The Human Condition (Jap 58–60) 26
Humorous Phases of Funny Faces (US 06) 206
The Humpty Dumpty Circus (US 98) 206
Hungarians (Hun 79) 35
Huntingtower (GB 27) 80
The Hypocrites (US 15) 61

I, a Woman (Swe 67) 65
I'll Cry Tomorrow (US 55) 79
I'll Never Forget Whatshisname (GB 68) 44, 161
I'll Tell the World (US 34) 134
The Illustrated Man (US 68) 126
The Immoral Mr Teas (US 59) 65
Inchon (Kor/US 81) 82, 128
The Incredible Mr Limpet (US 64) 188
The Incredible Sarah (GB 76) 133

Incubus (US 65) 146
In Cold Blood (US 67) 44
The Informer (US 35) 202, 203
In Harm's Way (US 65) 133
In Old Arizona (US 28) 73, 141
In Old California (US 10) 24
In Old Chicago (US 37) 196
In the Heat of the Night (US 68) 204
In the King of Prussia (US 82) 128
In Which We Serve (GB 42) 153
Indian Club Swinger (US 92) 22
Indiana Jones and the Temple of Doom (US 84) 35, 37, 38, 73, 127, 188
The Indians are Coming (US 31) 74
Indra Subha (Ind 32) 58
Innocents of Paris (US 29) 151
Inter Nos (Ice 82) 166
International Velvet (GB 78) 34
Intolerance (US 16) 38, 61, 82, 113, 115, 120, 133, 205
The Iron Horse (US 24) 28
Island in the Sun (US 59) *51*
Island of Lost Souls (US 32) 145
The Isle of Love (US 22) 121
Is Paris Burning? (Fr/US 66) 205
The Italian Barber (US 11) 199
It Happened Here (GB 66) 127, *128*
It Happened One Night (US 34) 117, 202, 203, 204
It's a Great Day (GB 56) 221
It's a Great Feeling (US 49) 55
Ivan the Terrible (USSR 46) 205

Jack, Sam and Pete (GB 19) 88
Jane Shore (GB 11) 81
The Jazz Singer (US 27) 16, 131, 141, 151, 152, 193
The Jazz Stringer (GB 28) 208
Dr Jekyll and Mr Hyde (US 31) 202, 203
Jim the Penman (US 15) 148
Joan of Arc (US 50) 205
Johnny Guitar (US 54) *70*
Jolson Sings Again (US 49) 36
The Jolson Story (US 46) *78*
Jonathan Livingstone Seagull (US 75) 108
Joszek Katus (Neth 67) 38
Le Jour se lève (Fr 39) 205
Journey's End (GB/US 30) 23
Jud Süss (Ger 40) 56
Jules et Jim (Fr 61) 205
Jumping Jacks (US 52) 205
The Jungle Book (US 67) 208
Jungle Woman (Aus 26) 166
The Junkman (US 82) 114
Just Imagine (US 30) 113

Der Kaiser von Kalifornien (Ger 36) 134, 204
Katarin (Malta 77) 15
Kautschuk (Ger 38) 94
Khan Asparouch (Bul 82) 82, 174
The Kid (US 20) 163
The Kill (US 71) 61
The Killing Fields (GB 84) 159, 204
Kind Hearts and Coronets (GB 49) 94, 205
The King and I (US 56) 125, 193
King Kong (US 33) 28, 221
King of Kings (US 27) 28, 86
King of Kings (US 61) 205
King of the Coral Sea (Aus 54) 188
King of the Kongo (US 29) 218
Kino-Eye (USSR 24) 111
Kismet (US 44) 205
Kiss (US 63) 107
Kiss Me Stupid (US 64) 205
The Kiss of Mary Pickford (USSR 26) 81
Kit Carson (US 03) 73
Knave of Hearts (GB 54) 111
A Knight in London (GB 29) 151
Knight Without Armour (GB 37) 79
Knights of the Round Table (GB 54) 146

Knocknagow (Ire 18) 14
Knowing Men (GB 30) 118, 127, 136
Kolberg (Ger 45) 81, 188
Komische Begegnung im Tiergarten zu Stockholm (Ger 96) 109
Krakatoa (US 32) 201
Kramer vs Kramer (US 77) 37, 189, 203, 204

The Lacy Rituals (GB 73) 121
Lady and the Tramp (US 56) 208
The Lady from Shanghai (US 48) 39
Lady Hamilton (GB 42) 45, 186
Lady in the Dark (US 44) 114
Lady Letmere's Jewelery (GB 08) 158
The Land of the Head Hunters (US 14) 74
Lanka Dakan (Ind 18) 94
Lassie Come Home (US 42) 137
The Last Angry Man (US 60) 189
Last Chants for a Slow Dance (US 79) 38
The Last Hunt (US 56) 94
The Last Laugh (Ger 25) 111, 205
The Last Movie (US 71) 158
Last Tango in Paris (Fr/It/US 72) 205
The Last Tasmanian (Aus/GB/Fr 79) 146
The Laughing Cavalier (GB 17) 230
Laughter in Paradise (GB 51) 36
Laughter in the Dark (GB 69) 109
Lawrence of Arabia (GB 62) 26, 204
The Learning Tree (US 69) 118
Lebenslaufe (GDR 81) 127
Lenin in October (USSR 37) 163
Lenny (US 74) 205
Les Girls (US 57) 189
Let There Be Light (US 45) 166
Letty Lynton (US 32) 117
Das Liebesglück der Blinden (Ger 10) 77
Lifeboat (US 44) 130
The Life of Emile Zola (US 37) 204
Life Rescue at Long Beach (US 01) 111
Lights of New York (US 28) 141
Limelight (US 52) 164
Lincoln's Gettysburg Address (US 22) 139
The Lion in Winter (GB 68) 202, 203, 205
Liquid Sky (US 83) 95
Lisztomania (GB 75) 144
The Little Cigars (US 73) 99
The Little Doctors (GB 01) 109
The Little Foxes (US 41) 35, 154
Little Lord Fauntleroy (US 21) *112*
The Little Shop of Horrors (US 60) 128
Live and Let Die (GB 73) 36
Lolotte (Fr 00) 137
Lone Wolf (USSR 77) 145
The Longest Day (US 72) 120, 145
The Longest Most Meaningless Movie in the World (GB 70) 25
Looking for Mr Goodbar (US 77) 205
Lord Jim (GB 65) 189
Lorna Doone (GB 12) 13
Lost Horizon (US 73) 189
The Lost Weekend (US 45) 204
The Lost World (US 25) 112, 126, 127, 181
Louisiana Story (US 47) 205
The Love Bug (US 69) 36
Love Me Stupid (US 64) 205
Love Me Tonight (US 32) 110
The Love Parade (US 29) 142
Love Story (US 70) 36, 189, 205
Love Up the Pole (GB 36) 126
The Loved One (US 65) 28
Love's Old Sweet Song (US 24) 139, 142
Luffar-Petter (Swe 22) 199
Lunacy (US 24) 149

Lust for Life (US 56) 136, 203

Macbeth (US 08) 160
Madame X (US 65) 114
Mädchen in Uniform (Ger 31) 65
Mad Max (Aus 80) 38
The Mad Parade (US 31) *119*
The Magnificent Ambersons (US 42) 158, 205
The Mail Robbery (Aus 25) 126
Make Them Die Slowly (US 83) 162
Malia dell'Oro (It 06) 151
The Maltese Falcon (US 41) *34*
A Man Called Horse (US 70) *74, 75*
A Man for All Seasons (GB 66) 204
Manhattan (US 79) 205
The Man I Killed (US 32) 30
Man of Aran (GB 34) 201, 204, 205
The Man of a Thousand Faces (US 53) 78
The Man who Couldn't Walk (US/Can 66) 28
The Man with the Golden Arm (US 55) 161
Manha Submersa (Por 80) 40
Manhattan Cocktail (US 28) 118
Man, Woman and Sin (US 27) 156
Many Happy Returns (US 34) *105*
Marilyn the Untold Story (US 80) 79
Mars (US 22) 149
Marty (US 55) 204, 221
Mary Jane's Mishap (GB 03) 109
Mary Poppins (US 64) 36, 203
Mary Queen of Scots (GB 72) 189
M*A*S*H (US 70) 158, 204, 224
The Mask of Fu Manchu (US 32) 28
Masquerade (US 29) 112
A Matter of Life and Death (GB 46) 189
Maya (Fr 49) 130
May Irwin Kiss (US 96) 107, 199
Mazurka (Ger 35) 186
Mein Leben für Irland (Ger 41) 22
Melancholy Dame (US 28) 49
Melodie der Welt (FRG 29) 14, 17
Le Mepris (Fr/It 63) 145
The Merchant of Venice (US 14) 118
Metropolis (Ger 26) 82, 113, 120
Michael the Brave (Rom 70) 82
Midnight Cowboy (US 69) 204
Midnight Express (GB 78) 176
Mieke (Bel 30) 189
Mickey's Christmas Carol (US 83) 209
Mickey's Revue (US 32) 209
The Mighty Barnum (US 34) 196
Le Million (Fr 31) 205
Million Dollar Mermaid (US 53) 78
The Million Dollar Mystery (US 14) 29
The Mills of the Gods (US 12) 193
Les Misérables (Fr 09) 12
Les Misérables (Fr 11) 40
Les Misérables (Fr 27) 26
Les Misérables (Fr 33) 26
I misteri di Roma (It 63) 119
Moana (US 26) 212
Model (Gre 74) 93, 130, 145
Mommie Dearest (US 81) 78
Monsieur Hulot's Holiday (Fr 53) 205
Monty Python's Life of Brian (GB 80) 36
The Moon is Blue (US 54) 161
Moonraker (GB 79) 36
Monster Wangnagwi (S. Kor 67) 82
Morgenstude hat Gold im Munde (Ger 30) 220
Morning Glory (US 33) 202
Morocco (US 30) 115
Mother (USSR 26) 205
Mother India (Ind 57) 36
Move Over Darling (US 64) 189

Mr Smith Goes to Washington (US 39) 92
Mrs Miniver (US 42) 203, 204
La Muchacha del Arrabal (Arg 22) 139
The Mudlark (GB 50) 189
The Muppet Movie (US 79) 163
Murder at the Gallop (GB 63) 188
Murder by Death (US 76) 105
Mutiny on the Bounty (US 35) 204
Mutiny on the Bounty (US 62) 38
Mutterliebe (Ger 09) 94
My Breakfast with Blaissie (US 83) 130
My Dinner with Andre (US 81) 130
My Fair Lady (US 64) 144
The Mysterious Island (US 29) 132

Napoleon (US 08) 38
Napoléon (Fr 27) 26, 143
National Lampoon's Animal House (US 78) 37
National Velvet (US 44) 34
Neptune's Daughter (US 14) 29
Network (US 76) 203
Nevada Smith (US 66) 35
The Neverending Story (FRG 84) 38
Never on Sunday (Gre 59) 38
Never Say Never Again (GB 84) 36
A New Leaf (US 70) 120
Night and Day (US 46) 205
The Night of the Living Dead (US 68) 38
1941 (US 79) 25
1900 (It 78) 26
Nionga (GB 25) 51
Noah's Ark (US 28) 22
La Noire de . . . (Sen 67) 51
Northbound Ltd (Aus 26) 126
Not as a Stranger (US 55) 205
Nothing Sacred (US 37) 113
Nous étions tous les noms d'arbres (Fr/Bel 82) 103
Nozze Vagabonde (It 36) 149

Obsession (US 76) 109
Octopussy (GB 83) 36
Of Human Hearts (US 39) 52
The Old Mill (US 37) 208
Oliver! (GB 69) 36, 204
Oliver Twist (GB 12) 12, 13, 16, 39
Oliver Twist (US 22) 188
Olympische Spiele (Ger 38) 120
On Golden Pond (US 81) 37, 202, 203
On the Beach (US 59) 188
On the Buses (GB 72) 36
On the Run (Aus 84) 159
On the Waterfront (US 54) 193, 202, 204
On With the Show (US 29) 58, 136
Once More, My Darling (US 47) 152
Once Upon a Time in America (US 84) 122
Once Upon a Time in the West (It/US 68) 158
One Day of War (USSR 42) 108
One Flew Over the Cuckoo's Nest (US 76) 36, 37, 202, 203, 204, 205
One Million Years BC (GB 66) 158
Ordinary People (US 81) 204
Orphan of the Wilderness (Aus 36) 165
Orphée (Fr 50) 205
Othello (It 14) 165
Othello (Mor/US/Fr 51) 164, 204
Our Very Own (US 50) 205
The Outlaw (US 43) 28, 120, 161
Over the Top (US i.p.) 80

The Painted Veil (US 34) 28
Papa's Delicate Condition (US 63) 78
Paradise Alley (GB 31) 144
Paramount on Parade (US 30) 127

The Parent Trap (US 61) 133
Parrish (US 61) 205
A Passage to India (GB 84) 189
Passage to Marseilles (US 44) 122
The Passion of Joan of Arc (Fr 28) 205
The Passion Play (US 98) 117
Pastorale (Neth 78) 81
The Patriot (US 28) 142
Patton (US 69) 187, 203, 204, 224
The Pawnbroker (US 64) 62, 161
Pele (Mex 78) 153
Peludopolis (Arg 31) 208
Penny and the Pownall Case (GB 48) 152
The Perils of Pauline (US 47) 79
La Permission (Fr 67) 118
Perri (US 57) 108
Persona (Swe 66) 205
The Petrified Forest (US 36) 186
Pettersen and Bendel (Swe 33) 56
Peyton Place (US 57) 36, 221
The Phantom of the Opera (US 25) 29
Pierrot Innamorato (It 06) 151
The Pillow Fight (GB 98) 184
Pink Flamingos (US 72) 38
The Pioneers (US 03) 73
Pip, Squeek and Wilfred (GB 21) 206
The Pirates of Penzance (GB 83) 58
Planet of the Apes (US 68) 126
Players (US 79) 91
The Pleasure Garden (GB 25) 119
Poitin (Eire 78) 146
Polyester (US 82) 147
Pool of London (GB 50) 51
Poor Cow (GB 67) 44
The Poor Millionaire (US 30) 144
The Poseidon Adventure (US 73) 36
Il Posto (It 61) 38
The Power and the Glory (US 33) 122
Power of Love (US 22) 148
Presente de Natal (Bra 71) 127
The President's Mystery (US 36) 45
The Prime of Miss Jean Brodie (GB 69) 189
Prison (Swe 48) 38
The Prisoner of Zenda (US 13) 38
The Private Files of J. Edgar Hoover (US 77) 54
The Private Life of Henry VIII (GB 34) 196
The Prodigal Son (GB 23) 26
Psycho (US 60) 35, 152, 205
Psycho II (US 83) 35
PT 109 (US 63) 53
The Public Enemy (US 31) 121
Pure S (Aus 73) 166
Pygmalion (GB 38) 36, 44

Quality Street (US 27) 111
The Quatermass Experiment (GB 54) 35
Quatermass II (GB 57) 35
Queen Elizabeth (Fr 12) 12, 17, 38
Quella sporca storia del West (It 68) 40
Quiet Days in Clichy (Den 69) 44
The Quiet Man (US 52) 202
Quo Vadis (US 51) 38, 114

The Ragged Princess (US 16) 61
Raiders of the Lost Ark (US 81) 35, 36, 37, 127, 152, 224
The Railroad Porter (US 12) 49
Rainbow Bridge (US 71) 120
The Rains Came (US 40) 205
Raintree Country (US 57) 146, 205
Raise the Roof (GB 30) 59
Raise the Titanic (US 80) 181
Raja Harischandra (Ind 12) 14, 27
The Rajah's Dream (Fr 00) 168
Ramona (US 10) 39
Rashomon (Jap 50) 38, 204

Reach for the Sky (GB 56) 36
Rebecca (US 40) 204
The Rebel (US 33) 186
Rebelote (Fr 84) 145
Rebel without a Cause (US 55) 28
The Red Shoes (GB 48) 137
Reflections on a Golden Eye (US 67)
Reggae (GB 70) 49
Le Règle du Jeu (Fr 39) 205
Die Reiter von Deutsche Ost-Afrika (Ger 34) 165
Remembrance (GB 27) 88
Remorse (Den 19) 93
Renaldo and Clara (US 77) 26
Rescued by Rover (GB 07) 108
Resurrection of Eve (US 73) 94
Return of the Jedi (US 83) 36, 37, 38, 127
The Return of the Pink Panther (GB 76) 36
The Revenge of the Pink Panther (GB 78) 36
Rêve d'Opium (Fr 21) 148
Le Reveil (Fr 25) 126
Rhapsody (US 54) 35
Rich and Famous (US 81) 120, 134
Rio Rita (US 29) 145
The Road to Dishonour (GB 29) 107
The Road to Rio (US 48) 36
Rob Roy the Highland Rogue (GB 53) 189
Robbery Under Arms (Aus 07) 39
Robin Hood (US 22) 129
Robinson Crusoe (USSR 47) 148, 149
Rock 'n Roll (Aus 59) 152
Rocky (US 76) 204
Rocky III (US 82) 37, 102
Rollercoaster (US 77) 143
Le Roman de Rénard (Fr 40) 127, 209
A Romance of Seville (GB 29) 136
Romeo and Juliet (GB 08) 158
Romeo and Juliet (GB 68) 80, 189, 204
Rope (US 48) 125, 130
The Rough Riders (US 27) 111
Royal Journey (Can 52) 137

Sadie Thompson (US 28) 45, 163
The Sailor Takes a Wife (US 46) 165
A Sainted Devil (US 24) 109
Une Sale Histoire (Fr 77) 123
Sally Sallies Forth (GB 28) 132
Sam and His Musket (GB 35) 208
Sammy Going South (GB 63) 189
Samson and Delilah (US 50) 36
Sanders of the River (GB 35) 88
The Sandpiper (US 65) 205
Le Sang d'un Poète (Fr 30) 176
Santa Fe Trail (US 40) 143
Saratoga (US 37) 94
Satan (Pol 12) 51
Saturday Night Fever (US 77) 37
Satyam Shivam Sundaram (Ind 77) 107
Scaramouche (US 53) 132
Scarface (US 83) 134
Scent of Mystery (US 60) 147
Schastye (USSR 35) 144
Scipio Africanus (It 37) 45
Scope, Colour, Muda (Spa 70) 110
Scott of the Antarctic (GB 48) 189
Sea Dogs of Australia (Aus 14) 163
The Searchers (US 56) 205
Sebastiane (GB 73) 62, 146
The Second-in-Command (US 15) 111, 113
Secret Ceremony (GB 68) 221
Secret Honour (US 84) 94
Sgt Pepper's Lonely Hearts Club Band (US 78) 205
Serious Charge (GB 59) 65
Le Serva Padrona (It 32) 58
Seven Beauties (It 75) 201
Seven Days in May (US 64) 134
Seven Samurai (Jap 54) 205

The Seventh Veil (GB 45) 36
The Shattered Illusion (Aus 27) 38
The Shining (US 80) 125
Shooting High (US 40) 131
The Shootist (US 76) 90
Should a Woman Divorce? (US 15) 134
Show Business (US 44) 70
Sidney Sheldon's Bloodline (US/FRG 83) 88
Siegfried (Ger 22) 151
Silent Movie (US 76) 44, 82, 83
Silver Streak (US 77) 189
The Singing Fool (US 28) 78, 152
Singin' in the Rain (US 52) 205
Sixty Years a Queen (GB 13) 94
Skip Tracer (Can 78) 159
Slave of Fashion (US 25) 141
Slim Carter (US 57) 159
The Slipper and the Rose (GB 76) 189
Slumber Party '57 (US 77) 133
Smic, Smac, Snoc (Fr 71) 38
Smokey and the Bandit (US 77) 37
Snow White and the Seven Dwarfs (US 37) 36, 208
Soldati Svobodi (USSR/Bul/Hun/Cz/GDR/Rom/Pol 77) 23, 26
The Soldier's Courtship (GB 96) 16, 76
Sombras de Gloria (US 30) 145
Some Like It Hot (US 59) 28, 125, 205
Someone (US 68) 38
Songs of Abay (USSR 46) 114
Sophie's Choice (US 82) 166
The Sound of Music (US 65) 36, 37, 182, 204, 223
South Pacific (US 59) 205
Spartacus (US 62) 36
Spellbound (US 45) 137
The Spirit of Race (Spa 41) 45
Splash (US 84) 72
Spring in Park Lane (GB 48) 36
The Spy Who Loved Me (GB 77) 36, 130
The Squaw's Love (US 14) 106
A Star is Born (US 76) 205
Star Trek (US 79) 112
Star Trek III: The Search for Spok (US 84) 188
Star Wars (US 77) 36, 37, 127, 152, 158, 205
Station Six Sahara (GB 64) 205
Steamboat Willie (US 28) 207, 209
Stenka Razin (Rus 08) 151
The Sting (US 74) 36, 65, 204
St Joan (GB 77) 93
Stormy Weather (US 43) 79
The Story of the Kelly Gang (Aus 06) 12
Story of the Red Sheep Hero (Chn 35) 132
The Story of Vernon and Irene Castle (US 39) 58, 114
The Story of Will Rogers (US 50) 79, 93
The Student of Prague (Ger 35) 221
Style and Class (US 29) 56
Such Men are Dangerous (US 30) 22
Suddenly, Last Summer (GB 60) 65
The Sunshine Boys (US 76) 105, 203
Sun Valley Serenade (US 41) 152
The Super Fight (US 70) 176
Superman (GB 79) 36, 37, 38, 80, 158
Superman II (GB 81) 36, 37, 38
Suvorov (USSR 41) 114
The Swarm (US 78) 108, 109, 199
Swastika (GB 73) 229
Sweet Nell of Old Drury (Aus 11) 81
The Swiss Family Robinson (GB 61) 36
Sylvia (US 64) 205

Table for Five (US 83) 189
Ein Tag ist Schoener als der
    Andere (FRG 70) 92
The Taking of Pelham 1, 2, 3
    (US 74) 134
Talash-e-Huq (Ind 35) 152
The Tales of Beatrix Potter
    (GB 71) 47
Tales of Hoffman (GB 51) 205
The Taming of the Shrew
    (US 28) 159
The Taming of the Shrew
    (It/US 67) 189
Tangier (GB 82) 224
Tarzan films 48
Tarzan of the Apes (US 18) *48*,
    134
Tarzan the Apeman (US 81) *48*
The Tell-Tale Heart (US 53) 208
The Ten Commandments (US 23)
    38
The Ten Commandments (US 56)
    36, 38, 205
Tenderloin (US 28) 44
Terms of Endearment (US 83) 204
La Terra Trema (It 48) 205
That Obscure Object of Desire
    (Fr 78) *94, 95*
That Sinking Feeling (GB 79) 38
The Terror (US 28) 158
The Terror of Tiny Town (US 38)
    99
Testament d'Orphée (Fr 59) *87*
The Texan (US 30) 220
They Died with their Boots On
    (US 41) 22
They Passed This Way (US 48) *73*
They Shoot Horses, Don't They?
    (US 69) 223
They're Coming to Get Me
    (US 25) 24
The Thief (US 52) 144
Thief in the Car (Chn 20) 132
The Thief of Baghdad (US 24) 38
The Third Man (GB 49) 36, 204,
    205
This Day and Age (US 33) 220
This Happy Breed (GB 44) 36
This is Cinerama (US 52) 143, 147
Thoroughbred (Aus 36) 165
A Thousand and One Nights
    (Jap 69) 63, 208
Three Bites of the Apple (US 67)
    153
The Three Musketeers (Pan 74)
    189

The Threepenny Opera (Ger 31)
    205
Thunderball (GB 66) 36
Thunder Road (US 58) 153
Tiefland (FRG 53) 127
Tiger Child (Can/Jap 70) 122, 190
Tiger Shark (US 32) 30
To Catch a Thief (US 55) 187, 189
Today We Live (US 35) 115
The Toll of the Sea (US 22) 136
Tom Brown's Schooldays
    (GB 17) 189
Tom Jones (GB 63) 204
Too Much Too Soon (US 58) 78
Tootsie (US 82) 37
Top Hat (US 35) 205
The Torrent (US 26) 115
La Tosca (US 12) 135
Traffic Crossing Leeds Bridge
    (GB 88) 9
Traffic in Souls (US 13) 13, 61, 178
The Trail of '98 (US 28) 22
The Trail of the Pink Panther
    (GB 82) 121
Treasure Island (US 20) 163
The Treasure of Sierra Madre
    (US 47) 203
A Trip to Mars (Den 19) *60*
Trip to Paramountown (US 22)
    112
The Triumph of the Rat (GB 26)
    111
Turn the Key Softly (GB 53) 133
Twenty Thousand Leagues Under
    the Sea (US 16) 132
Twilight Zone (US 82) 22
The Twins' Double (US 14) 112
Twist Around the Clock (US 61)
    128
Two Guns and a Badge (US 54) 75
Two Hearts in Waltz Time
    (Ger 29) 145
2001: A Space Odyssey (GB 68)
    205

Ugetsu Monagatari (Jap 53) 205
Ulysses (GB 67) 164
Uma transformista original
    (Bra 09) 113
Uncle Tom's Cabin (US 02) 39
Uncle Tom's Cabin (US 14) 88
Under the Rainbow (US 81) 99
The Underwater Expeditions of
    the Brothers Williamson
    (US 14) 132
Unhinged (US 83) 134

Uni si jolie petite plage (Fr 48) 110
An Unseen Enemy (US 12) 92
Up the Junction (GB 68) 36

Valentino (US 51) 79
Valentino (GB 77) 79
Vals ur Solstrålen (Swe 11) 136
La Vendetta del Groom (It 09) 121
Der Verlorene Schuh (Ger 23) 32
Vertigo (US 58) 205
Victim (GB 61) 65
Les Victimes de l'Alcolisme
    (Fr 02) 39
La Vie commence demain (Fr 50)
    162
The Viking (US 28) 136
The Virgin of Stamboul (US 20)
    29, 44
A Visit to the Seaside (GB 08) 135
Volga Volga (Ger 29) 132

Wagner (GB/Hun/Aut 83) 26, 223
The Waiting Room (US 73) 132
Wanderer of the Wasteland
    (US 24) 73
War and Peace (USSR 63–67) 26,
    82, 223
Waterloo (It/USSR 70) 114
Waves Off Dover (GB 95) 167
The War of Independence
    (Rom 12) 82
Way Down East (US 20) 162
W. C. Fields and Me (US 76) 78
We Called Them Montagues and
    Capulets (Bul 84) 145
The Wedding March (US 28) 153
Weekend at the Waldorf (US 45)
    205
Welshed, a Derby Day Incident
    (GB 03) 109
Wer fuhr IIa 2992? (Ger 39) 220
Westfront 1918 (Ger 30) 145
West Side Story (US 62) 189, 204
What Happened to Mary (US 12)
    217
What Price Beauty? (US 24) 115
What Price Glory (US 26) *45*
When Broadway Was a Trail
    (US 14) 159
When He Wants a Dog, He Wants
    a Dog (US 13) 206
When Knighthood was in Flower
    (US 22) 38
When the Clouds Roll By (US 20)
    159

Where No Vultures Fly (GB 52)
    36, 189
Whisky Galore! (GB 49) 40, 41
White Christmas (US 54) 36
White Dog (US 84) 108
The White Slave Traffic (Den 10)
    61
Who Is the Man? (GB 24) 92
The Whole Dam Family and the
    Dam Dog (US 05) 126
Who's Afraid of Virginia Woolf
    (US 66) 161
Why the UFOs Steal Our Lettuce
    (FRG 79) 200
The Wicked Lady (GB 46) 36, 164
The Widow Jones (US 96) 76
Wild Strawberries (Swe 57) 205
Willie's First Smoke (US 99) 124
Wilson (US 44) 38
Wings (US 27) 204
Wings of the Morning (GB 37) 136
Winter Meeting (US 48) 205
The Wise Little Hen (US 34) 209
The Wizard of Oz (US 39) 99, 205
Wokabout Bilong Tonten (Aus 73)
    146
The Wolf of Wall Street (US 29)
    142
The Women (US 39) 92, 93
Women in Love (GB 69) 62
Women Offside (Cz 71) *66*
The Wonderful World of the
    Brothers Grimm (US 62) 147
The World, the Flesh and the
    Devil (GB 14) 16, 135
The Wrong Box (GB 66) 133

Yaadein (Ind 64) 93
The Yale Laundry (US 07) 109,
    110
A Yank at Oxford (GB 38) 36, 44
The Year of Living Dangerously
    (Aus 82) *100*
Yentl (US 83) 120
A Yiddisher Boy (US 08) 122
You Can't Take It With You
    (US 38) 205
Young Mr Lincoln (US 39) *52*
The Young Ones (GB 62) 36
You Only Live Twice (GB 67) 36
You're in the Army Now (US 40)
    107
Youth for Sale (US 24) 67

Zaza (US 39) 163
Zwei Welten (Ger 40) 65

ACKNOWLEDGEMENTS

The author gratefully acknowledges the help
he has received from the following
individuals and organisations:
Paul Alexander
The American Society of Cinematographers
 Archiva Naţională de Filme, Bucharest
Al Archive al Kawmy Lil-Film, Cairo
The Barnes Museum of Cinematography, St
 Ives
John Baxter
Lord Bernstein
Blackburn District Central Library
British Board of Film Censors
British Film Institute
Brooklyn Public Library
Kevin Brownlow
Bundesstaatliche Haupstelle für Lichtbild und
 Bildungsfilm, Vienna
Canadian National Film Archives
Centre Algerien de la Cinématographie
Centre National de la Cinématographie, Paris
Československy Filmový Archiv
Cheshire Libraries and Museums Department
Cinema Papers (Australia)
The Cinema Organ Society
Cinemateca de Cuba
Cinemateca Nacional Venezuela
Cinemateca Uruguaya
Cinema Theatre Association
Cinema Veterans (1903)
Cineplex Corporation, Toronto
Colne Library & Museum
Columbus Public Library
Compania Cinematografica Nacionale, Chile
Philip C. Craddock
Geoff R. Crambie
Edward Craig ('Edward Carrick')
Det Danske Filmmuseum
Detroit Public Library
Deutsches Institut für Filmkunde
Deutsches Museum, Munich
B. V. Dharap
Steven Dhuey
John M. Hall
Humberto Didonet
Jack Doherty
Brian Dunckley
Eastman Kodak Co.
Monday Ellis
Embrafilme
Patricia Erens
Lennart Eriksson
Michel do Espírito Santo
Filmmuseum Amsterdam
Filmoteca Nacional de España
Filmoteca Polska
Ford Archives, Dearborn
Julian Fox
Fundacao Cinemateca Braileira
Fundacion Cinemateca Argentina
G.C.C. Theatres Inc.
General State Establishment for Cinema &
 Theatre, Iraq
Ghana Film Industry Corporation
Denis Gifford
Gosfilmokond, Moscow
Mulla Gulrajani
Ralph Harding

Harvard Lampoon
Michael Hayes
Riccarla Ann Hayton
Edith Head
Charles E. Herrin
Hungarofilm
Andrew Huxtable
Ilford Ltd
Imax Systems Corporation, Ontario
Instituto Nacional do Cinema, Brazil
Instituto Português de Cinema
Islington Central Library
Japan Film Library Council
Edward Hotspur Johnson
Lionel Jones
Det Kongelige Bibliotek, Copenhagen
Miles Monroe Kreuger
Grant Lobban
E. A. Layzell
Pierre Lebrun
Liam O'Leary Film Archives, Dublin
Locare Motion Picture Research Group
Christopher Lowder
Macau Centro de Informacâo
Magyar Filmtudományi Intézetés
 Filmarchivum
Ian McAuley
Hameeduddin Mahmood
Movietone
Museo Nazionale del Cinema, Turin
National Association of Theatre Owners,
 New York
National Diet Library, Tokyo
National Film Archive, Australia
National Film Development Corporation,
 Pakistan
National Film Library, New Zealand
Nelson District Central Library
Dido Nicholson
Kemp R. Niver
Nordisk Films Kompagni
Norsk Filminstitutt
Øyvind Nustad
Osterreichisches Filmarchiv
Osterreichisches Filmmuseum
Osterreichisches Kulturinstitut, London
Jerry Pam
Araken Campos Pereira Jnr
Betty Phillips
Andrew Pike
Polish Cultural Institute, London
Zakiya Powell
Pusat Perfilman H. Usmar Ismail, Indonesia
Quigley Publications
Jagdish Raaj
Radio City Music Hall
Mrs Eric Reade
Philip Rickman
T. K. H. Robertson
David Robinson
Kevin Rockett
The Royal Film Archive of Belgium
Dr Barry Salt
Cecil Sateriano
Silvana Sammassimo
Caio Scheiby
Kimberly Seabolt
Sinema-TV Enstitüsü, Istanbul
Singapore Board of Film Censors
Société Anonyme Tunisiènne de Production
 et d'Expansion Cinematographique

The Society of Motion Picture & Television
 Engineers
South African National Film Archives
Clive Sowry
Staatliches Filmarchiv der Deutsches
 Demokratischen Republik
Statisches Budesamt, Wiesbaden
Stiftung Deutsche Kinemathek, Berlin
Stratford Shakespearean Festival Foundation
 of Canada
Mark Strotchkov
Sri Lanka State Film Corporation
Suomen Elokuvasäätiö
Svenska Filminstitutet
Technicolor Inc.
Paul Talkington
Thai Motion Picture Producers Association
T. A. Thompson
Bruce T. Torrence
Twentieth Century-Fox International
 Corporation
United Artists
United Methodist Church, Nashville, Te
U.S. Department of Commerce
Universal City Studios
University of Iowa
Variety
Vereniging der Kinemabestuurders van
 Belgie VKBB v.z.w.
Walter N. Vernon
Alex Viany
Dr Hans Vogt
Mrs Audrey Wadowska
Wakaaladda Filimmada Soomaaliyeed
Walt Disney Productions
Herman Weinberg
Western Costume Co., Los Angeles
The White House, Washington
James L. Wilkinson
David Williams
Will Rogers Memorial, Claremore, Okla.
In addition to the acknowledgement above, I
wish to record special thanks to the Librarian
and staff of the British Film Institute
Information Department, who have put both
their resources and their uncommon expertise
at my disposal, and have provided a large
number of illustrations for the book. While
many national archives throughout the world
have been forthcoming with information, I
would like to pay special tribute to two other
film institutes which have particularly
impressed me with their efficiency and
commitment—those of Hungary and
Indonesia.
 Stephen Bottomore, who worked as
researcher on the first edition of the Guinness
Film Facts & Feats, contributed a number of
articles to this edition. These include 'The
Cinema and your Health—Kill or Cure', most
of the 'firsts' in cinema literature and art in the
chapter Press and Print, and the entry on the
earliest film awards in the chapter headed
Awards and Festivals. I am most grateful to him
for allowing me to publish the fruits of his
original research on these topics.
 I would also like to pay tribute to my wife
Karla, who has done much of the updating of
statistics and most of the picture research. I
could not have completed the extensive
revisions to this edition without her
invaluable help.